Tourism: a modern synthesis

Tourism: a modern synthesis

Stephen J Page, Paul Brunt,
Graham Busby and Jo Connell

Australia • Canada • Mexico • Singapore • Spain • United Kingdom • United States

Tourism: a modern synthesis

For more information, contact Thomson Learning, Berkshire House, 168–173 High Holborn, London, WC1V 7AA or visit us on the World Wide Web at:
http: //www.thomsonlearning.co.uk

British Library Cataloguing-in-Publication Data
A catalogue record for this book is available from the British Library

ISBN 1-86152-640-7

First edition 2001 Thomson Learning

Text design by Malcolm Harvey Young, Goudhurst, Kent
Typeset by Saxon Graphics Ltd, Derby

Printed in Italy by G. Canale & C.

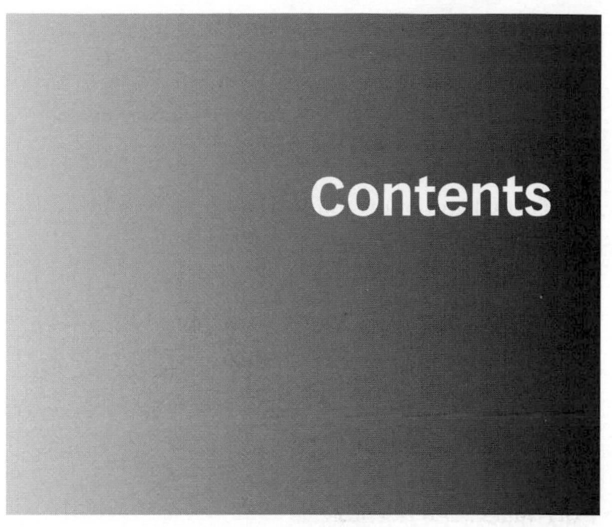

Contents

Authors vii
List of tables ix
List of figures xi
List of plates xiii
Acknowledgements xv
Preface xvii

Section 1: Understanding tourism demand *1*
1 Introduction to tourism: themes, concepts and issues 3
2 The historical development of tourism 33
3 Understanding the tourist: tourism demand 45
4 Understanding the tourist: tourist motivation 59

Section 2: Understanding tourism as a business *71*
5 Tourism supply issues 73
6 Travel and tourism intermediaries 85
7 Transport and tourism 97
8 Tourist attractions 117
9 Tourism accommodation 133

Section 3: Managing tourism operations *151*
10 Human resource management in tourism 153
11 Financing tourism operations 167
12 Tourism and entrepreneurship 183
13 Tourism and information technology 195
14 The role of the public sector in tourism 207

Section 4: Marketing tourism *231*
15 Marketing tourism: concepts and issues 233
16 Marketing tourism: destination management 245

Section 5: The impact of tourist activity *255*
17 Economic impacts 257
18 Social and cultural impacts 275

19 Environmental impacts 293
20 The challenge of sustainability 309

Section 6: Trends and themes in the use of tourist resources *331*
21 Urban tourism 333
22 Rural tourism 349
23 Coastal and resort tourism 367
24 Tourism in the less developed world 385

Section 7: Managing tourist activities *405*
25 The tourist experience 407
26 Managing the tourist experience 417
27 The future of tourism 435

Subject index 460
Author index 469
Place index 473

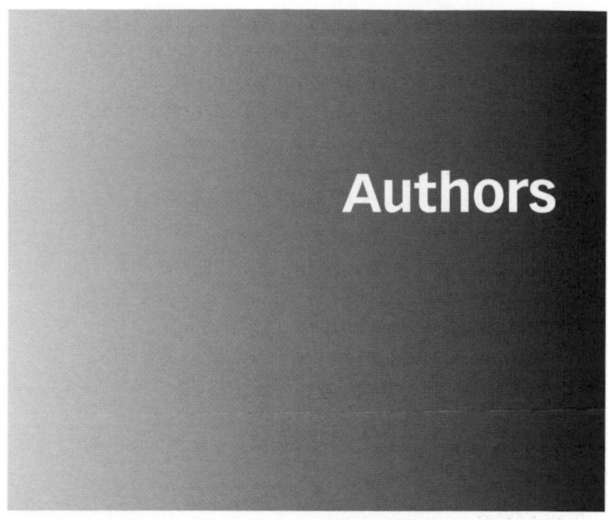

Stephen J. Page is Scottish Enterprise Forth Valley Chair in Tourism, Department of Marketing, at the University of Stirling in Scotland. He was formerly Professor of Tourism Management and Director, Centre for Tourism Research, Massey University, New Zealand. Recently, he has been a Visiting Professor at the University of Plymouth, UK and Edith Cowan University, Perth, Australia and has given seminars at universities in the UK, Singapore, Ireland, France, the Netherlands, Australia and New Zealand. He is the Series Editor for the Thomson Learning, Tourism and Hospitality Management Series and Series Editor of Pearson Education's Themes in Tourism Series. He is also Editor of Elsevier Science's Advances in Tourism Research Series and has been the Associate Editor of the leading tourism journal – *Tourism Management* – since 1996. He has written, co-authored and edited 12 books on tourism, the most recent being *The Geography of Tourism and Recreation: Environment, Place and Space* and *Tourism in South and South East Asia* (both with Michael Hall). He has also advised government agencies and public and private sector bodies as a tourism consultant and maintains a close working relationship with tourism industry agencies particularly in the field of tourist health and safety. He has just completed a funded study of tourist health and safety in the adventure tourism industry in New Zealand and tourism and crime associated with Auckland's hosting of the America's Cup in 1999/2000 in conjunction with two postdoctoral research fellows at Massey University, New Zealand.

Paul Brunt graduated from Bournemouth University in 1986 with an honours degree in Geography and then continued research into tourism decision-making to PhD level. He was appointed to set up the University of Plymouth's tourism degree in 1989 and has since published articles on the socio-cultural impacts of tourism, tourism and crime and a book, *Market Research in Travel and Tourism* (Butterworth-Heinemann).

Graham Busby worked in the travel and tourism industry for several years before joining the staff of Newbury College and, in 1994, the University of Plymouth; he holds degrees from Surrey and the Open University besides a Licentiateship from City & Guilds. He has published articles on tourism education, literary tourism and is currently researching the links between Cornish churches and tourism.

Jo Connell graduated from the University of Plymouth with an honours degree in Rural Resource Management in 1993 and holds a Master's degree in Tourism and Social Responsibility from the University of Exeter. She has published articles on campus-based tourism and social responsibility issues. Her current research focuses on the significance of gardens as a resource for tourism and recreation.

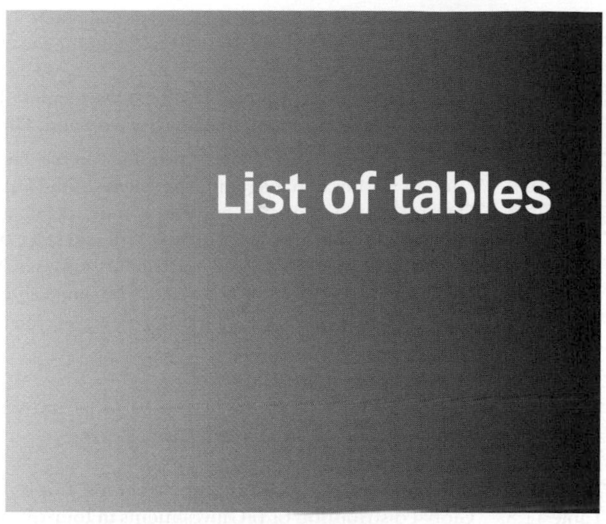

Table 1.1A	Tourist arrivals and markets in ASEAN countries, 1996–98	7
Table 1.1B	Fluctuations in arrivals for select Asian destinations, 1997 and 1998	7
Table 1.2	Disciplines contributing to the study of tourism	9
Table 2.1	Torbay: stages of resort development	36
Table 2.2	Key events in UK tourism, 1945–70	38
Table 2.3	Top ten holiday campsites in England and Wales, 1939 and 1986	40
Table 2.4	UK outbound visits by region, 1990–1998	42
Table 3.1	Factors influencing tourist demand	47
Table 3.2	The population of Chinese residents in New Zealand by birthplace, 1996	51
Table 3.3	Number of overseas visits, January 1997–June 1999	52
Table 3.4	Outbound travel destinations, January 1997–June 1999	53
Table 5.1	Tourism and natural resources	76
Table 5.2	Man-made resources of tourism importance	77
Table 5.3	Changing demographics in western Europe: senior travel, 1990 and 2000	78
Table 5.4	A selection of Las Vegas' mega-hotels	80
Table 5.5	GDP, airline passenger arrivals and car rental volume in Europe, 1994–1997	81
Table 6.1	Examples of integrated tourism companies and their brands	86
Table 6.2	Passengers carried under the largest air travel organizers' licences	89
Table 6.3	Passengers licensed to/or planned by top five groups for the 12 months to September 2000	90
Table 6.4	Types of mass and specialist markets for tours according to price	92
Table 6.5	The largest travel agency groups/consortia/global companies in Canada	92
Table 6.6	Leading corporate travel agency groups in France, 1997	93
Table 7.1	A selection of 'tourist experience' railway journeys	104
Table 7.2	The P&O Stena Line super-ferries	107
Table 7.3	Global airline alliances	111
Table 8.1	Swarbrooke's typology of tourist attractions	118
Table 8.2	Prentice's heritage attraction categories	119
Table 8.3	Visitor statistics for the 'top 20' National Trust properties	121
Table 8.4	Major global amusement/theme park chains, 1999	124
Table 8.5	Financing the Eden Project	127
Table 8.6	Industry-based visitor attractions	129
Table 8.7	Attendance figures for selected events and festivals, 1994–98	129
Table 8.8	Festival visitors in 1998	130

Table 9.1	Millennium and Copthorne Hotels global reach	137
Table 9.2	The accommodation sector in New Zealand, year ending 31 March 1999	139
Table 9.3	Major all-inclusive chains	144
Table 9.4	YHA membership (England & Wales) by category, 1998/99	145
Table 9.5	International Environmental Charter for Youth Hostels	146
Table 10.1	Human resource management problems in the Thai tourism industry	157
Table 10.2	Human resource management problems in the Latin American tourism industry	157
Table 10.3	Organizational structures and entrepreneurial characteristics	160
Table 10.4	Management differences between small and large firms	160
Table 10.5	The primary activity of small tourism businesses in Northland	162
Table 10.6	Recruitment methods used by small tourism businesses	162
Table 11.1	Audited results for SIA, year ending 31 March 1999	168
Table 11.2	Notes to the SIA accounts	169
Table 11.3	SIA segment information	170
Table 11.4	Audited balance sheets for Singapore Airlines Group at 31 March 1999	171
Table 11.5	Multinational tour operator transfer pricing	174
Table 11.6	Payback example	175
Table 11.7	Priority objectives for European Structural Funds	176
Table 11.8	Global distribution of IFC investments in tourism, as at August 1998	177
Table 11.9	Possessions of the National Trust	178
Table 11.10	National Trust: key statistics	178
Table 11.11	National Trust: summary statement of financial activities	179
Table 12.1	Organizational structures and entrepreneurial characteristics	186
Table 13.1	Some of the applications for which Destination Management Systems are used	203
Table 14.1	The funding of National Tourism Organizations in Asia 1995	218
Table 14.2	National tourism organization budgets in Asia: allocation of funds by activity, 1991–95	219
Table 14.3	Promotional budgets of the top 40 National Tourism Organizations in 1994 and 1995	221
Table 14.4	Promotional budgets of Asian national tourism organizations, 1991–95	224
Table 14.5	The top ten target markets for Asian destinations in 1995	225
Table 17.1	Travel account of selected countries, 1993	263
Table 17.2	Asian economic development: percentage rates of GDP growth, 1995–1999	264
Table 17.3	The economic value of whale watching in Vava'u, the Kingdom of Tonga	265
Table 17.4	The multiplier effect in a selection of less developed countries	270
Table 18.1	Contravention of human rights associated with tourism development	287
Table 18.2	Indigenous culture, control and tourism	287
Table 19.1	Summary of environmental impacts in specific habitats	296
Table 20.1	Environmental management at the Hotel Inter-Continental, Nairobi	316
Table 21.1	A general classification of outdoor recreational uses and resources: implications for tourism resource use	335
Table 22.1	Rural services in 1994	353
Table 22.2	Summary of the positive and negative impacts of rural tourism	357
Table 22.3	Principles for tourism in the countryside	364
Table 24.1	Terminology commonly used to describe development status	386
Table 24.2	Selected indices used to construct a human development index for Asian and non-Asian countries	387
Table 24.3	Examples of economic leakage in less developed countries	394
Table 25.1	The much maligned tourist types	409
Table 25.2	Poon's (1993) old and new tourists	410
Table 27.1	International arrivals and visitor forecasts for New Zealand, 1966–2010	439
Table 27.2	Senior population aged 55 or over for main tourism generating countries, 1997	443
Table 27.3	Direct value added resulting from tourism, 1995	445
Table 27.3a	Tourism expenditure in New Zealand, 1995	446
Table 27.4	Airline privatization in Asia–Pacific region, 1985–1995	449
Table 27.5	Overseas visitor accidents in New Zealand using hospital discharge records, 1982–96	454
Table 27.6	The World Tourism Organization's Global Code of Ethics for Tourism	455

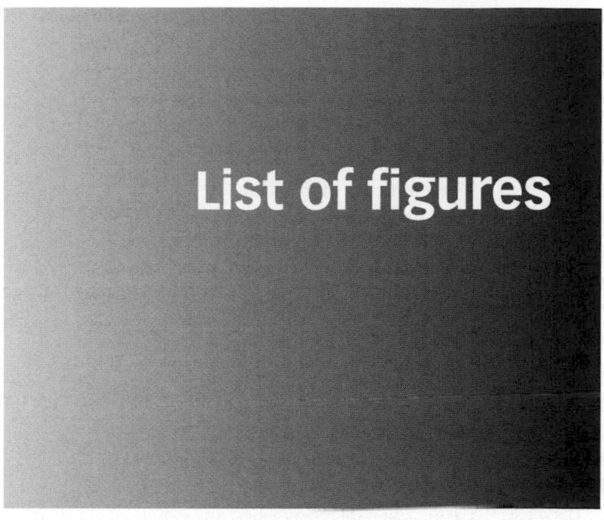

Figure 0.1	Book structure	xix
Figure 1.1	The staircase of tourism qualifications	10
Figure 1.2	Leiper's tourism system	10
Figure 1.3	Chadwick's classification of travellers	15
Figure 2.1	The Butler model of resort development	35
Figure 4.1	Holiday decision-making process	60
Figure 4.2	Maslow's hierarchy of needs	62
Figure 4.3	Plog's tourist types	63
Figure 7.1	The contribution of transport technology to reductions in travel time	98
Figure 7.2	Stagecoach plc operating divisions	100
Figure 7.3	The European cycle route network	102
Figure 7.4	UK short sea ferry crossings	106
Figure 7.5	The Norfolk Broads region	108
Figure 7.6	easyJet costs	109
Figure 7.7	The potential for cost reductions among airlines	110
Figure 9.1	Accommodation types	135
Figure 13.1	The distribution channels in tourism	197
Figure 13.2	Luggage loading and unloading in the airport system	199
Figure 13.3	A typical Destination Management System	203
Figure 14.1	The policy-making process	209
Figure 14.2	Tourist cities in China up to 1991	210
Figure 14.3	The statutory framework for the administration of tourism in the UK	213
Figure 14.4	The structure of national tourism organizations in the UK	213
Figure 14.5	Structure of the Singapore Tourism Board	214
Figure 15.1	The marketing mix	236
Figure 15.2	The buying process	238
Figure 16.1	Location of selected resorts in Mexico	248
Figure 18.1	The dimensions of tourist–host encounters	276
Figure 18.2	The host–guest relationship	278
Figure 18.3	Tourist perception of a scene	281
Figure 18.4	Doxey's Irridex	284

Figure 20.1 A simplified illustration of environmental thinking 310
Figure 20.2 Degrees of sustainability 312
Figure 20.3 Summary of visitor management strategies 323
Figure 20.4 Types of carrying capacity 325

Figure 21.1 The tourist experience of urban tourism 339
Figure 21.2 Functional areas in the tourist city 340
Figure 21.3 The elements of tourism 341
Figure 21.4 How individuals perceive the tourism environment 342

Figure 22.1 Index of rurality 350
Figure 22.2 The context of rural tourism 354
Figure 22.3 The rural tourism spectrum 355
Figure 22.4 Map of Mid-Wales region 360

Figure 23.1 Model of tourist resort development 372
Figure 23.2 The basic morphology of the coastal resort 373
Figure 23.3 Map of Mallorca 375
Figure 23.4 Scenarios of destination development 377
Figure 23.5 Map of Dawlish Warren 380

Figure 24.1 Map of Bhutan 393
Figure 24.2 Map of Solomon Islands 396
Figure 24.3 Map of Zanzibar 398

Figure 25.1 Tourist information search strategy 411
Figure 25.2 The tourist experience 413

Figure 26.1 Managing the tourist experience 421
Figure 26.2 The tourism planning process 422
Figure 26.3 The elements of a tourism plan 424
Figure 26.4 The nature of visitor management 426

Figure 27.1 The future of tourism 441
Figure 27.2 Risk factors for adventure tourism accidents 452

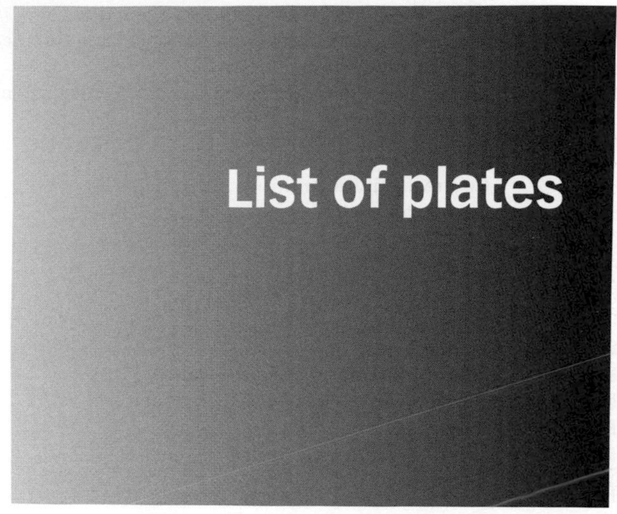

List of plates

Plate 1.1	Tourists in an urban location	4
Plate 1.2	The Sheraton, Denerau Island, Fiji	5
Plate 1.3	Tourist sightseeing train in the Otago region of New Zealand	12
Plate 1.4	Visitor centre in the Waitakere Ranges of Auckland, New Zealand	17
Plate 2.1	Blackpool Pier, UK	34
Plate 2.2	Marine Parade, Dover, UK	36
Plate 4.1	Triton Hotel, Sri Lanka	61
Plate 4.2	Picos de Europa, northern Spain	64
Plate 5.1	Entrance to a Maori meeting house, Northland, New Zealand	78
Plate 5.2	Groningen's red light district, the Netherlands	79
Plate 7.1	A nineteenth-century cable car, San Francisco, USA	100
Plate 7.2	The FEVE narrow-gauge railway, northern Spain	103
Plate 7.3	Dover channel ferry port, UK	105
Plate 7.4	A Singapore Airlines 747-400	109
Plate 7.5	Hong Kong Peak tram	114
Plate 8.1	Auckland's Americas Cup Village, New Zealand	120
Plate 8.2	Covent Garden, London, UK	122
Plate 8.3	Christ Church Gate, Canterbury, UK	124
Plate 8.4	Seated Buddha statue, Polonnaruwa, Sri Lanka	125
Plate 9.1	Timeshare apartments, Malta	134
Plate 9.2	Motel development in New Zealand	136
Plate 9.3	Bandarawela Hotel, Sri Lanka	142
Plate 9.4	Tourist accommodation, Tahiti	146
Plate 16.1	A Brazilian-style band playing in Exeter to promote a new arts and crafts venue	252
Plate 18.1	Looe, Cornwall, UK	279
Plate 18.2	Retail outlet, Cornwall	280
Plate 18.3	Rope-making demonstration	282
Plate 18.4	A guided tour, Bath, UK	285
Plate 18.5	Tamatea marea, Motohi, Northland, New Zealand	288
Plate 18.6	Indigenous craft workshop, western Canada	289
Plate 19.1	Waikiki Beach, Honolulu, Hawaii	298
Plate 19.2	White Rocks Holiday Complex, Malta	298

Plate 19.3	Whale watching, South Pacific	302
Plate 19.4	Hooker Glacier, Mount Cook National Park, New Zealand	302
Plate 19.5	Traffic congestion	303
Plate 19.6	White Cliffs World Heritage Site, Mesa Verde National Park, USA	304
Plate 19.7	Surface erosion	305
Plate 19.8	Lighthouse on Lundy Island, Bristol Channel, UK	306
Plate 20.1	Coverack, Lizard Peninsula, Cornwall, UK	314
Plate 20.2	A fish market	315
Plate 20.3	Promenade enhancement scheme	317
Plate 20.4	Sustainable tourism	318
Plate 20.5	Groningen, the Netherlands	322
Plate 20.6	A Kauri tree	323
Plate 20.7	Guided walks	324
Plate 20.8	A visitor centre, Looe, Cornwall, UK	325
Plate 20.9	Banff, Canada	326
Plate 20.10	Mass tourism	327
Plate 20.11	Tourism off the beaten track	327
Plate 21.1	Crown Casino, Melbourne, Australia	337
Plate 21.2	Waterfront development, Singapore	338
Plate 22.1	Land beyond the urban edge	351
Plate 22.2	A remote rural area	352
Plate 22.3	Ice-cream shop, Cornwall	361
Plate 23.1	A beach in Tahiti	368
Plate 23.2	The coastal environment	370
Plate 23.3	Lundy Island, UK	371
Plate 23.4	Scuba trip to the Great Barrier Reef, Queensland, Australia	373
Plate 23.5	Oponomi, Bay of Island, New Zealand	377
Plate 24.1	Standing Buddha, Aukana, Sri Lanka	391
Plate 24.2	Tourists observing religious temple offering ritual in Bali	392
Plate 24.3	Elephant orphanage, Pinawela, Sri Lanka	399
Plate 24.4	Wood carving by a local craftsman, Polonnaruwa, Sri Lanka	401
Plate 24.5	Opportunities for cultural exchange and purchase of local products, Polonnaruwa, Sri Lanka	401
Plate 25.1	Travellers or tourists?	408
Plate 25.2	What type of tourist would stay here?	410
Plate 26.1	Tour groups, Wellington, New Zealand	419
Plate 26.2	The Acropolis, Greece	420
Plate 26.3	Trail management in Taranaki National Park, New Zealand	422
Plate 26.4	Buchart Gardens, British Columbia	425
Plate 26.5	Taman Mini theme park, Jakarta, Indonesia	426
Plate 26.6	Gasworks Project, Hobart, Tasmania	427
Plate 27.1	A wine tour bus outside a winery in the Yarra Valley, Victoria, Australia	436
Plate 27.2	The hot springs in Rotorua, New Zealand	437
Plate 27.3	Estoril, Portugal	440
Plate 27.4	Chatham Dock waterfront development, Kent, UK	440
Plate 27.5	Market scene, Vanuatu	451

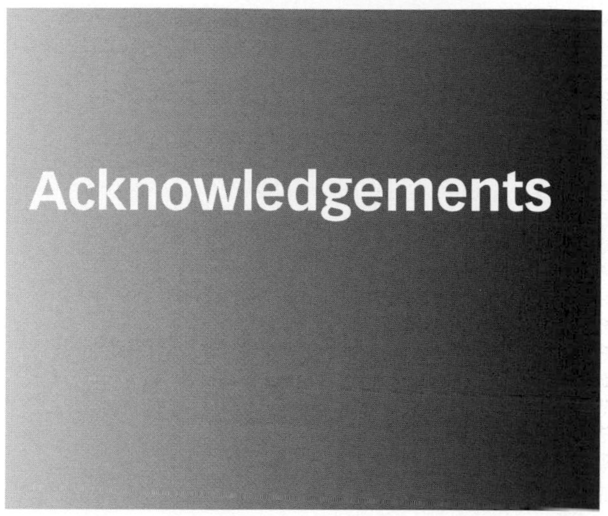

In no particular order: Jason Sorley of Forrester Research Inc., Cambridge, Massachusetts; Frank Considine of the Civil Aviation Authority; James Rothnie, Corporate Affairs Director, easyGroup; Joanna Yellowlees-Bound, Managing Director of Erna Low; Tim Smit, Chief Executive of The Eden Project; Mrs Berni Thompson of Guide Friday; Nicola Pogson of the International Hotel and Restaurant Association; Prue Leith, OBE; Natalie Robinson, P&O Stena Line; Maria José Orozco Rodríguez, Iberia Airways; Pertti Ollila of Finnair; Gaela Hodge, Marketing Executive, ExCeL; Liz Washford, British Energy plc; Linda Hoyle, Sizewell Visitor Centre; Alistair Forbes, Kent & East Sussex Railway; Pat Cade, Public Relations Manager, Chester Zoo; Anna Nicholas, ANA Communications; Tony Potter, MD Copthorne Millennium Hotels; Mark Waugh, YHA; Martin Woods, South Somerset District Council; Janice Roosevelt and Cathy Larkin, Winterthur Museum, Garden and Library, Delaware; Singapore Airlines; Nicole Parker, Days Inns of America Inc.; Naomi Luhde-Thompson, The National Trust; Clare Packer, British Tourist Authority; Tricia Barnett, Tourism Concern, for use of case study material on Burma, Zanzibar and the International Network on Fair Trade; Adama Bah, Gambia Tourism Concern; Dr Hugh Somerville, British Airways Environment Branch; Rosie Austin; Tim Bentley for Figure 27.2; Ajuntament d'Alcúdia for information on tourism initiatives; Allan and Jacqueline Yeoman for Plates 18.6 and 20.9; Mark Orams for Plates 19.3 and 23.4 and for allowing use of his study of whale-watching tourism in Tonga; Ceri Walsh, Teignbridge District Council Warden at Dawlish Warren Nature Reserve. And to Gary, Alison and Frances for their patience and continual support.

The authors are also grateful to John Wiley and Sons for permission to reproduce Figure 1.3 and to Travel and Tourism Intelligence for permission to reproduce Tables 5.3, 5.5, 6.1, 6.2, 6.5, 7.2, 8.4 and 9.3. Also to Singapore Airlines for permission to use Plate 7.5. No mention would be complete without a big thank you to Michael Hall for the provision of a great number of the plates (Plates 1.3, 1.4, 8.3, 18.6, 19.1, 19.6, 20.9, 21.1, 21.2, 23.4, 24.1, 24.2, 25.1, 26.1, 26.2, 26.3, 26.4, 26.5, 27.1, 27.2, 27.3, 27.4 and 27.5) at very short notice. Copyright in these slides rests with Michael and permission for any further reuse of the slides should be directed to Professor C M Hall, Centre for Tourism, University of Otago, PO Box 56, Dunedin, New Zealand. It is also befitting for Stephen Page to acknowledge Massey University for its very formative influence on the career of a tourism academic, particularly the Tourism programme and its staff and their commitment to research and scholarship of which this book is a partial product. If any unwitting use of copyright material has been made in the book, would the owners of the material please contact the authors via the publishers.

Stephen Page would also like to thank his parents for their convivial hospitality while completing the book. Also, Lynn Tunna at Massey University for typing and for helping to compile the on-line testing site/question bank available on the Thomson Learning website.

Tourism is now one of the fastest growing sectors of the economies of many countries as it assumes a dominant role in the service sector. This book is a response to the growing demand for a textbook which serves as both an introductory-level book for students taking an advanced diploma (i.e. an HND in the UK) and undergraduate degree and can equally be used as a general introduction for more specialized courses in tourism. The principal driving force behind this book is the failure of existing texts to strike a delicate balance between being both 'introductory' and yet able to offer some detail and depth to specific issues beyond generalized discussion. There is a growing range of tourism textbooks now on the market in most countries as tourism has naturally become a major growth sector of many tertiary-level institutions offering diplomas, degrees and postgraduate level courses. But surprisingly there are few books that have moved beyond first editions, which is a test of the usability and user-friendly nature of texts which can appeal to both the student and lecturer who seek similar and yet different things from a book.

This book has been developed after extensive experience among the team of authors in teaching, researching and developing tourism curricula over the last decade, and among the author team there is a great international expertise which is reflected in the material presented in this book. No textbook can ever be sufficiently comprehensive and broad so that it appeals to everyone. The material discussed in this book is based on a clear understanding of the nature of tourism curricula in many countries throughout the world and the book is designed to appeal to students as a reference source to use throughout their course. It will certainly be of great use in the first year of their studies but hopefully it will be dipped into at judicious points in their academic studies as a reference source. In this respect, this book is not like many of the other texts on the market. It is different in one respect. It seeks to offer both a knowledge base which students can build upon as they progress through their course but it also offers a wide range of material that accompanies the book in terms of web-based examples, case studies and other related material that existing books do not offer. Many of the existing texts in tourism are now getting dated and have not moved forward to recognize the power of the internet and the value of linking students learning in traditional forms (i.e. the core textbook) with web-based sources and to refer them to interesting and useful internet resources throughout the text.

With any textbook, a number of sacrifices have to be made in terms of what can be included and cannot be included. The editorial pen has been exercised very heavily throughout the book because each contributor has, in most cases, been set a tight word limit so that the book has a high degree of consistency and continuity so that no individual chapters greatly outweigh others. The principle behind the design of the material in each chapter is that it is intended to be the scope and basic principles which an introductory lecture on the topic might want to cover in an up-to-date and discussive way. The book is not a simple compendium of facts and figures. Instead, it is a balance of much-needed concepts associated with the analysis of tourism.

Despite space limitations, the authors have been aware of and have been involved in the recent discussions within the tourism academic community regarding benchmarking statements and levels of attainment. Thus, it is intended that this book will help students to have a thorough understanding of:

- the concepts and characteristics of tourism as an area of academic and applied study;
- the structure of and interactions in the tourism industry;
- the place of tourism in the communities and environments that it affects;
- the nature and characteristics of tourists.

Within this, there will be a wide range of contemporary resource materials and students will gain exposure to some IT systems when accessing the book's website.

One aspect of this book which critics might choose to criticize is the absence of a glossary. Many introductory books on tourism have a set of terms at the end of the book for students to refer to. This book has dispensed with this for a number of reasons. First, in the year 2000 the *Encyclopedia of Tourism* (Jafari 2000) was published by Routledge which will become the basic reference source for all libraries and for students to consult. It comprises entries of varying length on terms and issues in tourism which cannot even begin to be addressed by a scant glossary that a book like this can offer. Second, Thomson Learning (the publisher of this book) will be launching the second edition of its highly acclaimed *International Encyclopedia of Business and Management* (IEBM) (Warner 2001). This will also have a web version and so the need for a simple glossary is obviated by the publication of these two excellent reference sources. There are also a number of other sources such as dictionaries of tourism which can add more depth than a simple couple of sentences in a glossary. Many of the business terms referred to in this book are dealt with in an excellent fashion in the IEBM as well as the smaller pocket versions of the book.

How is this book structured and how can you use it?

The book adopts a fairly straightforward approach to tourism as Figure 0.1 shows. The ways of approaching tourism are dealt with in Chapter 1, which is followed by a discussion of the two discrete areas of tourism: the demand for and the supply of tourism services and products. This distinguishes between the tourists' perspective (demand) and the supply (the industry perspective) and these areas are then integrated to show how the tourism business manages tourism and how supply and demand interacts. Some of the key issues facing the management of tourism businesses are examined in terms of the formation and operation of tourism enterprises. The impact of tourism as a human, social, cultural and environmentally based activity are reviewed in a range of chapters on the impact of tourism. These issues are then placed in the context of the tourism resources which tourists typically (but not exclusively) consume, including a range of environments ranging from urban through to rural, coastal and resort areas to the less developed world. This provides not only the context but a range of real life examples of tourism development and impacts. These impacts and issues then raise the issue of how to manage the tourist experience, whereby management measures (e.g. planning, visitor management and de-marketing tourism in areas which are saturated) are considered. This is discussed in the section on 'managing the tourism experience'. Lastly, the book examines the most difficult area of crystal ball gazing – what will affect the future development of tourism? What issues will create difficulties for tourists and the tourism industry? Are they likely to be any different from those now confronting the tourism industry at the turn of the new millennium? These questions and others are posed and a range of suggested outcomes are examined.

Each chapter commences with a series of Learning Outcomes to outline what the structure and key points are for the reader. This is followed throughout the chapter with illustrations, examples, case studies and bullet points to make the material as digestible and interesting as possible. Difficult concepts are explained where possible with diagrams and plates. For the student seeking to revise and develop their critical understanding of concepts, the website has a large data bank of questions accompanying each chapter which can be used to review progress with the material.

Figure 0.1 **Book structure**

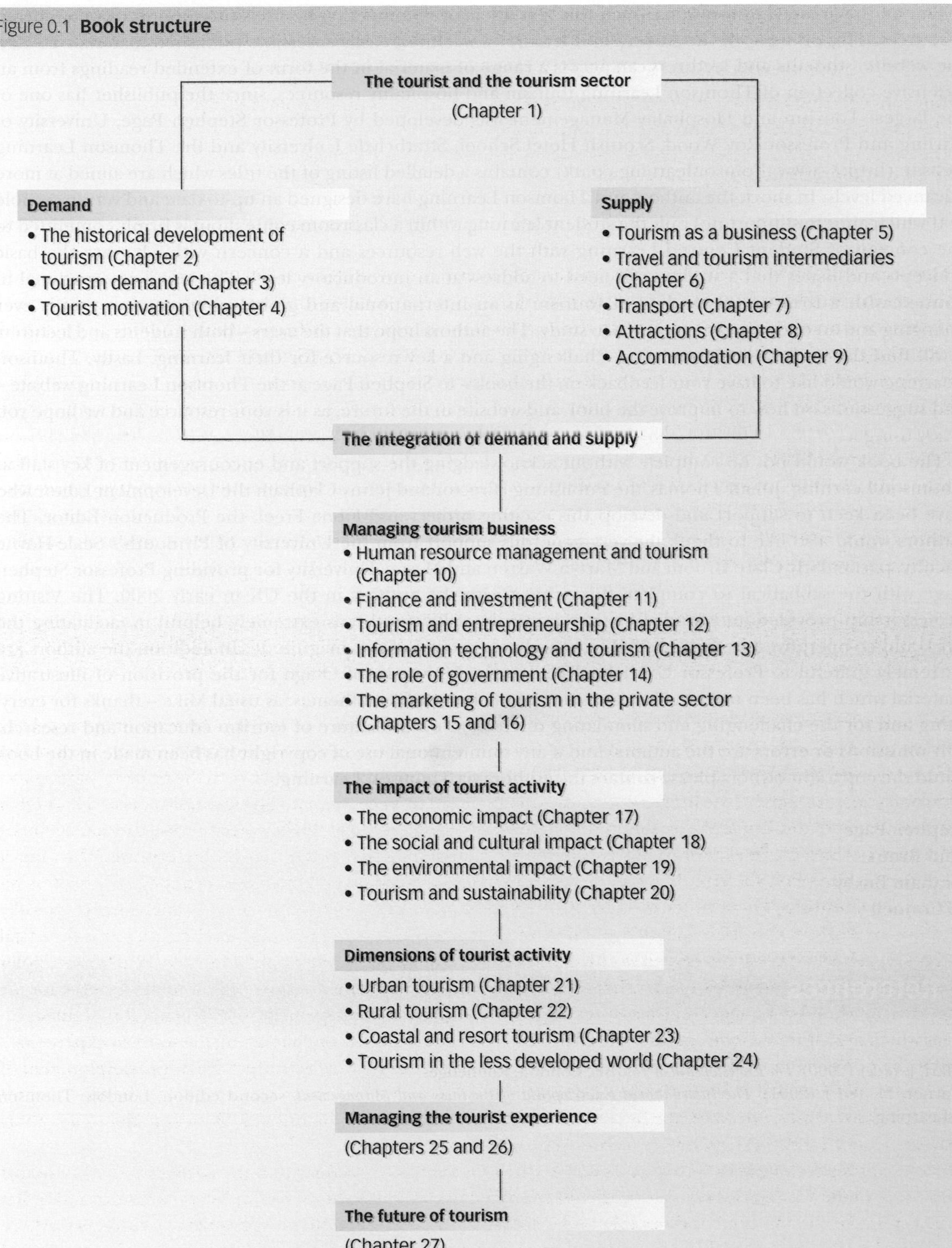

The tourist and the tourism sector
(Chapter 1)
Demand
• The historical development of tourism (Chapter 2)
• Tourism demand (Chapter 3)
• Tourist motivation (Chapter 4)
Supply
• Tourism as a business (Chapter 5)
• Travel and tourism intermediaries (Chapter 6)
• Transport (Chapter 7)
• Attractions (Chapter 8)
• Accommodation (Chapter 9)
The integration of demand and supply
Managing tourism business
• Human resource management and tourism (Chapter 10)
• Finance and investment (Chapter 11)
• Tourism and entrepreneurship (Chapter 12)
• Information technology and tourism (Chapter 13)
• The role of government (Chapter 14)
• The marketing of tourism in the private sector (Chapters 15 and 16)
The impact of tourist activity
• The economic impact (Chapter 17)
• The social and cultural impact (Chapter 18)
• The environmental impact (Chapter 19)
• Tourism and sustainability (Chapter 20)
Dimensions of tourist activity
• Urban tourism (Chapter 21)
• Rural tourism (Chapter 22)
• Coastal and resort tourism (Chapter 23)
• Tourism in the less developed world (Chapter 24)
Managing the tourist experience
(Chapters 25 and 26)
The future of tourism
(Chapter 27)

One of the greatest innovations which this text offers over competing books is the support of web tourism resources. This offers both the student and lecturer a wealth of easily accessible published material. To view the website, students and lecturers can access a range of material in the form of extended readings from an extensive collection of Thomson Learning tourism and hospitality resources, since the publisher has one of the largest Tourism and Hospitality Management lists developed by Professor Stephen Page, University of Stirling and Professor Roy Wood, Scottish Hotel School, Strathclyde University and the Thomson Learning website (http://www.thomsonlearning.co.uk) contains a detailed listing of the titles which are aimed at more advanced levels. In short, the authors and Thomson Learning have designed an up-to-date and very accessible text which aims to support not only the student learning within a classroom context but is firmly committed to the concept of Student Centred Learning with the web resources and a concern with what are the basic concepts and issues that a student will need to address at an introductory level. The text is international in context with a firm understanding of tourism as an international and global phenomenon that is ever changing and an exciting, dynamic area to study. The authors hope that the users – both students and lecturers – will find the book fresh, stimulating, challenging and a key resource for their learning. Lastly, Thomson Learning would like to have your feedback on the book – to Stephen Page at the Thomson Learning website – and suggestions on how to improve the book and website in the future, as it is your resource and we hope you enjoy using it.

The book would not be complete without acknowledging the support and encouragement of key staff at Thomson Learning: Julian Thomas, the Publishing Director and Jenny Clapham the Development Editor who have been keen to support and develop this exciting project and Fiona Freel, the Production Editor. The authors would also like to thank the very generous support from the University of Plymouth's Seale-Hayne Faculty, particularly Clare Broom and Martyn Warren and Massey University for providing Professor Stephen Page with the sabbatical to complete this project with the authors in the UK in early 2000. The Visiting Professorship provided and funded by the University of Plymouth was extremely helpful in facilitating the work and co-operative research needed to complete a project of this magnitude. In addition the authors are extremely grateful to Professor C. Michael Hall at the University of Otago for the provision of illustrative material which has been used to illustrate some of the international themes: as usual Mike – thanks for everything and for the challenging and stimulating discussions on the nature of tourism education and research. Any omissions or errors are the authors' and if any unintentional use of copyright has been made in the book could the copyright owners please contact the authors via Thomson Learning.

Stephen Page
Paul Brunt
Graham Busby
Jo Connell

References

Jafari, J. (ed.) (2000) *The Encyclopedia of Tourism*, London: Routledge.

Warner, M. (ed.) (2001) *The International Encyclopedia of Business and Management*, second edition, London: Thomson Learning.

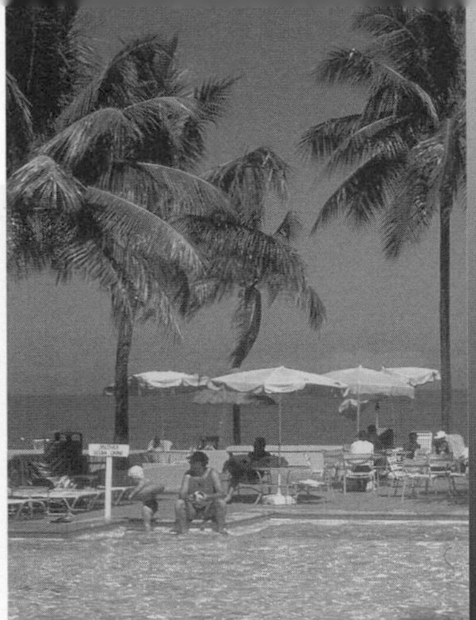

Section 1

Understanding tourism demand

Tourism is a global phenomenon which has experienced rapid growth in the post-war period, particularly in the developed countries of the world. One of the major challenges for understanding what has caused the development of tourism and how we can measure and define tourism is presented in the first three chapters. The first chapter discusses the various problems of defining tourism and the ways in which the demand for tourism (i.e. how many and what types of tourists travel to different places) can be identified to enable us to understand the scale and extent of the growth in tourism globally. This inevitably involves some discussion of tourism statistics and the various measures used by organizations such as the World Tourism Organization in documenting and monitoring the global changes in tourism. The field of study known as 'tourism' is also introduced to the reader to understand how different people from different disciplines study tourism. These issues having been presented, the next chapter expands on the concept of the historical development of tourism, examining some of the factors that have promoted the growth and expansion and decline of tourism in different periods of time. This highlights how dynamic and ever changing tourism activity is, highlighting the time frames over which tourism can grow and subsequently decline when tastes, modes of travel and competing destinations emerge. This is then followed with a more in-depth discussion of how these wider changes in the development of tourism can be affected by the tastes, preferences and factors that shape tourism demand. The focus then shifts to how the individual tourist or group of tourists decide to pursue a tourism experience, focusing on the perennial problem facing tourism researchers and marketers: what motivates a tourist to travel to a specific destination or place? This involves a discussion of the different concepts and theories put forward by researchers to try and explain the range of factors and situations which shape tourist motivation. Therefore, this specific group of chapters begins with a wide-ranging review of the field of tourism and tourism demand. This is followed by an examination of the wider development of places promoted by a growth in tourism demand and then the attention focuses on the tourist as source of demand and the factors which shape specific forms of demand.

1 Introduction to tourism: themes, concepts and issues

Learning outcomes

In this chapter we explore the nature of tourism as a subject area and the problems of defining the terminology of tourism. After studying the chapter, you should be able to understand:

- Why tourism is an important subject to study.
- How different definitions of tourism have been developed and the frameworks used to study tourism.
- The different forms of tourism.
- The difference between domestic and international tourism.
- How to measure tourism.
- Why tourism statistics are important.
- Some of the principal patterns of global tourism.

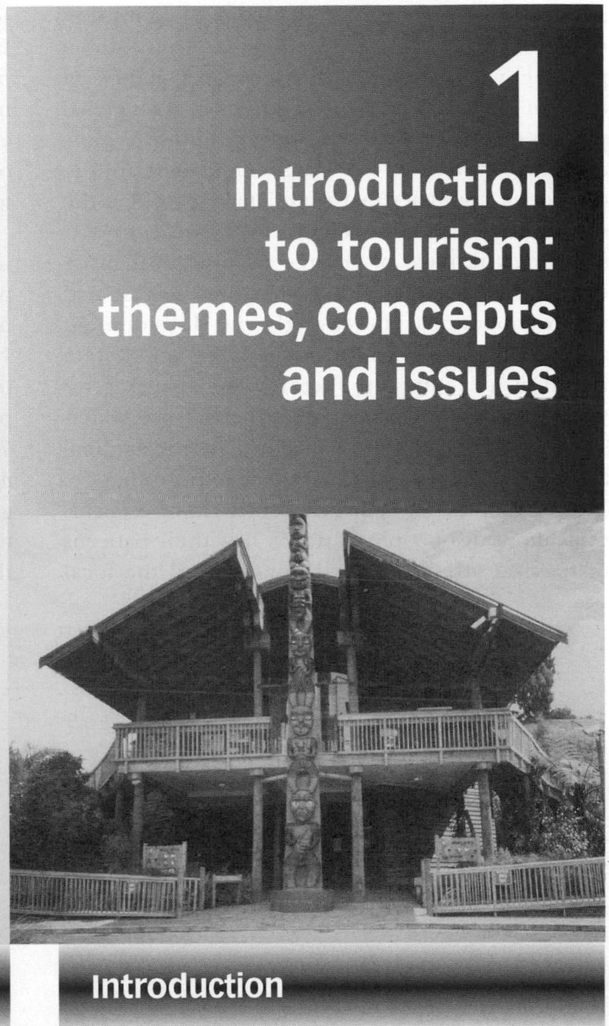

Overview

This chapter presents an introduction to the field of Tourism Studies and the concepts which students need to be acquainted with including the meaning of tourism, what is meant by the term tourist, traveller, visitor and excursionist. The chapter examines the way in which organizations record and measure tourists and the implications for defining tourists. The role of organizations such as the World Tourism Organization is also examined in defining tourism and tourists are also reviewed and many of the leading studies in the growing field of tourism studies are also considered in the chapter.

Introduction

The late twentieth century and the new millennium have witnessed the continued growth of the leisure society where people have continued to value the significance of holidays, travel and the experience of going to see new societies and their cultures. This growth of the consumer society, with its emphasis on discretionary spending on leisure activities in the developed world since the 1950s, reflects the increased availability of disposable income to engage in leisure pursuits and holidays. Although this leisure society was traditionally the remit of the western developed world, during the 1990s trends emerged where there is a greater propensity for the world's population now to travel and engage in holidays in their new-found leisure time; this is reflected in new world regions such as Asia, China and the Indian sub-continent. Most existing tourism textbooks have failed to adopt a truly global perspective to embody the speed of change in tourism on a world scale. Tourism is part of a global process of change and development (known as globalization) which is no longer confined to the developed countries that traditionally provided the demand for world travel. In this respect, understanding the pace of change in tourism is more complex as the processes of change are diverse and not homogenous. Increasingly, the development and change in tourism throughout the world are a function of complex factors that coalesce to generate a process of change that needs to be understood in its local context with a focus on the national and international processes affecting change. Therefore, understanding how these changes occur, what motivates people to travel, how their patterns of tourism affect the environments and the local societies they visit are persuasive questions now facing those organizations, researchers and students of tourism. Increasingly, governments are also recognizing both the value of tourism to their national economies and the problems that tourism development may pose if this activity is pursued as a route to national economic development.

The majority of influential tourism textbooks which have popularized the study of tourism are a product of the 1980s and early 1990s, despite some notable exceptions (e.g. Burkart and Medlik 1974, 1975). The rapid expansion in the number of tourism textbooks and academic journal articles published in top journals such as the *Annals of Tourism Research, Tourism Management* and the *Journal of Travel Research* are one indication of the emergence of the subject as a serious area of study at vocational, degree and postgraduate level throughout the world.[1] The range of available textbooks for

Plate 1.1 Tourists in an urban location: Valetta, Malta
Which of the people in this picture are tourists? It is difficult to identify tourists in an urban location where tourists merge into the background and surveys are used to identify 'who are tourists'.

tourism studies have generally been written from a North American (e.g. Lundberg 1980; Mathieson and Wall 1982; Mill and Morrison 1985; Murphy 1985), European (e.g. Foster 1985; Lavery 1989; Cooper *et al.* 1993, 1998) or Australasian perspective (e.g. Pearce 1987, 1992; Collier 1989; Hall 1991), with few widely available student texts written from an Asian perspective (see Hall and Page 2000 for an exception to this) or an indigenous less developed world perspective. This book aims to address many of the questions and themes which are important in developing an understanding of the process or phenemenon called 'tourism', which is a convenient catch-all term often used without a clear understanding of its meaning, scope and extent. This book assumes no prior knowledge of the subject area conveniently labelled 'Tourism Studies', progressively developing the reader's understanding of the scope, complexity and range of issues which the tourism phenomenon poses for anyone who is serious about the study of the subject. It is easy to underestimate the global significance of tourism as the following statistics suggest.

In 1991 the international tourism industry employed 112 million people world-wide and generated over $2.5 trillion at 1989 prices. In 1996, 593 million tourists travelled abroad (World Tourism Organization 1997). In global terms, the expansion of international tourism continues to generate an insatiable demand for overseas travel. Europe remains the most visited of all regions of the world, where half of all global tourist receipts and almost two thirds of international arrivals occurred in 1996. In 1996, almost 352 million arrivals and US$215.7 billion in receipts were received. Eastern and Central Europe were among the fastest growing areas to benefit from Western European tourism flows. In contrast, the East-Asia Pacific region

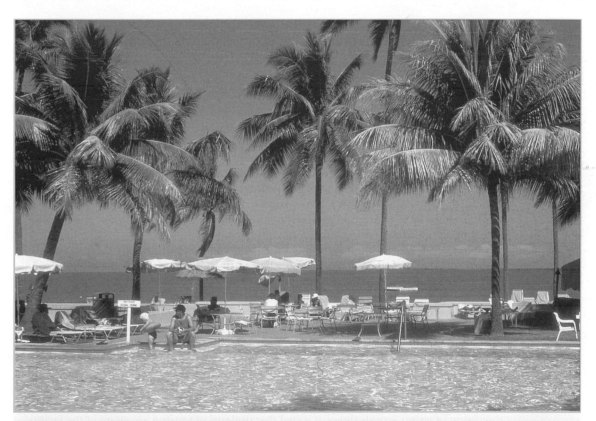

Plate 1.2 The Sheraton, Denerau Island, Fiji
In a resort setting, such as the Sheraton on Denerau Island in Fiji, it is easy to make an assumption that all of the people in the picture are tourists due to their dress and behaviour.

remains the area experiencing the highest growth rates, with total arrivals increasing by 9.3 per cent in 1996 to over 87 million with receipts of US$1 billion. Therefore, it is not surprising that many of the estimates of tourism's significance as a global activity leads many analysts such as the World Travel and Tourism Council to argue that it is the world's largest industry though seeking evidence to substantiate this claim is difficult. Furthermore, there is growing evidence that tourism is a volatile economic activity which can be subject to 'shock waves' such as the Asian economic crisis in 1997–1998 (see Exhibit 1.1) which can rapidly change the economic fortunes of the tourism industry in different countries.

Appendix 1 provides an up-to-date analysis of world tourism trends and it should be consulted throughout this chapter for further detail on the global changes occurring in tourism.

Tourism as an area of academic study

One of the immediate problems that students of tourism face is the fact that one is studying a subject that is associated with people's experiences of travel and their leisure experiences. Prior to the 1980s it was viewed with suspicion and reservation by many academics and analysts as superficial and not really worthy of academic respect in the same way that established disciplines such as history, economics and politics were held in esteem by seats of learning (i.e. academic institutions). This reflects the relative recency with which tourism has been embraced as a subject of serious academic study. Although this situation has now changed with many schools, colleges, polytechnics and

Exhibit 1.1 **The impact of the Asian economic crisis on tourist arrivals in South-east Asia**

C. Michael Hall and Stephen Page

Up until the onset of the Asian financial crisis, South-east Asia was also developing as a major source of outbound tourism. Intraregional travel (i.e. travel within the South-east Asian region) remained significant, though the decline in the region's economies has meant that regionally generated inbound tourism has deflated across the region. Inbound tourism from outside the region has therefore become extremely valuable – and extremely competitive. The decline in the value of the region's currencies in relation to major tourism generating regions of North America and Europe, and even Australia, Japan and New Zealand, has meant that, apart from external perceptions of instability in some cases, the region became an extremely attractive destination in terms of exchange rates.

Tables 1.1A and 1.1B illustrate some of the fluctuations in tourism numbers which have occurred in the region in 1997 and the first half of 1998. Within the region, only Thailand, which has taken a very aggressive stance in attracting tourists, and China have shown substantive tourist growth. Although, in the case of China, it should be noted that growth has occurred because of increased arrivals from Hong Kong, Taiwan and Macau, with arrivals outside these markets actually dropping by 2.2 per cent in the first quarter of 1998.

These dramatic fluctuations, and their wider significance beyond tourism, graphically illustrate the need for a contemporary assessment of tourism in what has been one of the most dynamic regions for the industry over the past two decades. Although, as Qu and Zhang (1997) suggest, it is impossible to take full account of future events with tourism markets within the region being far from mature, unpredictable and in some cases unstable. As the discussion of visitor arrivals shows, it is vital that students of tourism are aware of the factors and issues which are shaping the regions future not only in tourism, but in its wider political, economic, social and environmental context.

Table 1.1A **Tourist arrivals and markets in ASEAN countries, 1996–1998**

Country	1996	1997	1998
Brunei Darussalam	622 354	643 215	964 080
Cambodia*	260 489	218 843	68 783
Indonesia	5 034 472	5 185 243	4 606 416
Laos	403 000	463 200	500 200
Malaysia	7 138 452	6 210 921	5 550 748
Myanmar	–	265 122	273 858
Philippines	2 049 367	2 222 523	2 149 357
Singapore	7 292 521	7 197 963	6 240 984
Thailand	7 192 145	7 221 345	7 842 760
Vietnam	1 607 155	1 715 637	1 520 128

* figures for first quarter 1998. Estimated total for 1998 was 177,500.

(Source: Economic Planning Unit, Ministry of Finance, Ministry of Interior, Cambodia; Directorate General of Tourism, Department of Tourism, Arts and Culture, Indonesia; Ministry of National Planning and Economic Development, Myanmar; National Tourism Authority of Lao PDR, Malaysia Tourism Promotion Board, Department of Tourism, Philippines, Singapore Tourist Promotion Board, Tourism Authority of Thailand, Vietnam National Administration of Tourism)

Table 1.1B **Fluctuations in arrivals for select Asian destinations 1997 and 1998**

Country	1997 arrivals (million)	% change from 1996	1997 tourism earnings US$ billion)	% change from 1996	1998 arrivals (million)	% change from same period in 1997
China	57.6	12.6%	12.0	17.6%	12.4 (Jan–March)	10.6%
Hong Kong	10.4	–11.1%	9.3	–14.7%	4.5 (Jan–June)	–21%
Thailand	7.3	0.7%	7.0	–19.5%	3.8 (Jan–June)	4.8%
Singapore	7.2	–1.3%	6.8	–13.9%	3.0 (Jan–June)	–13.9%
Malaysia	6.2	–13.0%	3.7	–16.3%	n.a.	n.a.
Indonesia	5.2	3.0%	5.3	–15.6%	1.5 (Jan–June)	–15.6%
South Korea	3.9	5.4%	5.1	–5.8%	2.4 (Jan–July)	–5.8%
Philippines	2.1	9.5%	2.8	4.8%	1.1 (Jan–July)	–1.9%

n.a. – not available

universities offering courses in Tourism Studies. Tourism Studies is now more than a practitioner subject taught at craft level: it is offered from certificate level through PhD level (see Figure 1.1) and it is now maturing as a subject area in its own right. But Tourism Studies as a subject area is fraught by a number of problems which any student and researcher needs to be aware of. Some of the principal problems are that:

1 Tourism is not easily recognized as a subject because some analysts view it as an industry, while others view it as a subject or as a process. So there is no universal agreement on how to approach it.
2 Academics argue that tourism is a subject that is conceptually weak, which means that there are no universally agreed sets of laws or principles that all researchers adopt as the starting point for the discussion of tourism. This is made more difficult because tourism is a multidisciplinary subject (see Table 1.2), where different disciplines examine tourism from their own standpoint rather than from a universally agreed tourism perspective. In this respect, the different subject areas which examine tourism use their own concepts and modes of analysis that have been developed in their own disciplines. This means that as a multidisciplinary subject area, tourism lacks integration between the different disciplines studying it which severely limits the intellectual development of the area by the lack of cross-fertilization of ideas across disciplines.
3 There is a wide range of jargon used (e.g. ecotourism, alternative, responsible and sustainability) which refers to many facets of the same issue which makes it perplexing for students and researchers because of the semantic complexity (i.e. the lack of universally agreed definitions of phenomena being studied).
4 The data sources available to tourism researchers are weak compared to other subjects.
5 The different approaches used by researchers from different disciplines and industry backgrounds have led to what Cooper *et al.* (1998) call *reductionism* – that means that tourism is reduced to a series of activities or economic transactions rather than a wider series of concepts and overarching analytical frameworks in which to understand and interpret tourism such the sociologists focus on postmodernism.
6 In academic environments, there is still suspicion about the intellectual rigour with which tourism researchers approach their subject, made more difficult by the tendency for non-specialists to dabble in this area of research as it is perceived as easy to understand and associated with travel and leisure.
7 To date no theoretical constructs or theory which explain the development and internal dynamics as a process of global economic and social change have been developed. Most academics argue that a subject will not advance learning and understanding until theories are developed, which can be tested, modified and rejected or redeveloped. Thus tourism remains theoretically devoid as a subject area. In other words, much of the research in tourism has tended to be descriptive and lacking in contributions to the development of tourism knowledge, using established techniques and methodologies. Although there is evidence that this situation is changing slowly (see Ryan and Page 2000), the absence of theoretically derived research remains a major weakness for students and researchers which is why more insightful studies such as Urry's (1990) *The Tourist Gaze* with its attendant focus on postmodernism and sociological analysis of modern day tourism are the exception rather than the rule in tourism.

As a consequence of these problems, one is forced to look around for a conceptual or organizing framework which helps the student of tourism to understand the holistic nature of tourism and how the main components of tourism can be integrated together which is why the integrated system approach is now examined.

Tourism as an integrated system

One methodology used by researchers to understand the nature of tourism phenomena is a systems approach (Laws 1991). The main purpose of such an approach is to rationalize and simplify the real world complexity of tourism into a number of constructs and components which highlight the inter-related nature of tourism. Since Tourism Studies is a multidisciplinary

Table 1.2 **Disciplines contributing to the study of tourism**

Discipline	Example of contribution to Tourism Studies
Geography	Spatial analysis of where tourism develops and why
Ecology	The impact of tourism on the natural environment
Agricultural Studies	The significance of rural tourism to rural diversification
Parks and Recreation	Recreation management techniques in natural areas such as National Parks used by tourists
Urban and Regional Planning	The planning and development of tourism
Marketing	The marketing of tourism
Law	The legal framework and implications for tourists and tourism operators
Business and Management Science	The management of tourism organizations
Transport Studies	The provision of tourist transport services
Hotel and Restaurant Administration	The provision of hospitality services and accommodation for tourists
Educational Studies	Tourism curriculum design and development
Sociology	Sociological analyses and frameworks to understand tourism as an element of people's leisure time
Economics	The economic impact of tourism
Psychology	Tourist motivation to explain why people travel
Anthropology	The host–guest relationship
Safety Management and Ergonomics	The design and development of environments and activities which are safe for tourists

area of study (Gilbert 1990), a systems approach can accommodate a variety of different perspectives because it does not assume a predetermined view of tourism. Instead, it enables one to understand the broader issues and factors which affect tourism, together with the inter-relationships between different components in the system. According to Leiper (1990), a system can be defined as a set of elements or parts that are connected to each other by at least one distinguishing principle. In this case, tourism is the distinguishing principle which connects the different components in the system around a common theme. Laws (1991:7) developed this idea a stage further by providing a systems model of the tourism industry in which the key components were: the inputs, outputs and external factors conditioning the system (e.g. the

Figure 1.1 **The staircase of tourism qualifications**

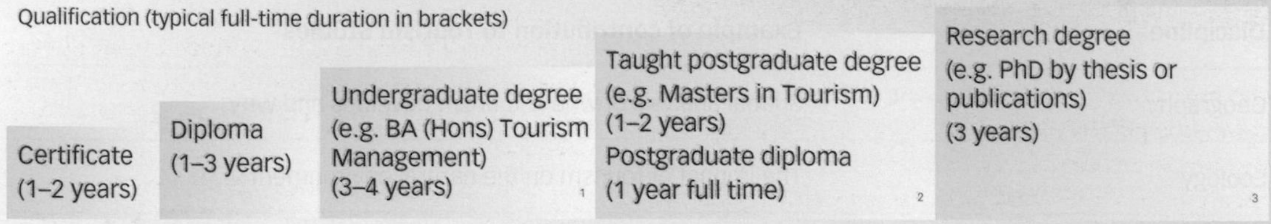

Qualification (typical full-time duration in brackets)

Certificate (1–2 years)	Diploma (1–3 years)	Undergraduate degree (e.g. BA (Hons) Tourism Management) (3–4 years) [1]	Taught postgraduate degree (e.g. Masters in Tourism) (1–2 years) Postgraduate diploma (1 year full time) [2]	Research degree (e.g. PhD by thesis or publications) (3 years) [3]

1 An undergraduate qualification in tourism can also be combined with other course options in universities and non-university institutions, though it is most commonly found as a business/management focused programme.

2 The duration of taught postgraduate programmes at Masters level vary in time from one year full-time in the UK to two years full-time in North-America and Australasia where a thesis is normally undertaken in the second year.

3 Traditionally, the PhD (also known as a doctorate) has been an original contribution to knowledge, written as a thesis based on three years of full-time research. This is normally accompanied by a viva voce examination (an oral examination) where the candidate defends their thesis. In recent years, some universities have allowed the submission of a series of refereed journal articles with a short introduction and conclusion as an alternative form of scholarship to be judged as an original contribution to knowledge for the PhD.

external business environment, consumer preferences, political factors and economic issues). As external factors are important influences upon tourism systems, the system can be termed 'open' which means that it can easily be influenced by factors aside from the main 'inputs'. The links within the system can be examined in terms of 'flows' between components and these flows may highlight the existence of certain types of relationships between different components (see Figure 1.2).

For example:

- What effect does an increase in the cost of travel have on the demand for travel?
- How does this have repercussions for other components in the system?
- Will it reduce the number of tourists travelling?

A systems approach has the advantage of allowing the researcher to consider the effect of such changes to the tourism system to assess the likely impact on other components.

Leiper (1990) identified the following elements of a tourism system: a tourist; a traveller generating region; tourism destination regions; transit routes for tourists travelling between generating destination area and the travel and tourism industry (e.g. accommodation, transport, the firms and organizations supplying services and products to tourists). In this analysis, transport forms an integral part of the tourism system, connecting the tourist generating and destination region which is represented in terms of the volume of travel. Thus, a 'tourism system' is a framework which embodies the entire tourist experience of travelling. The analytical value of such an approach is that it enables one to understand the overall process of tourist travel from both the supplier and purchaser's perspective (known respectively as supply and demand) while identifying the organizations which influence and regulate tourism. This highlights the importance of:

- the tourist
- the integral relationships in the overall tourist experience
- the effect of transportation problems on traveller perception
- the tourists' requirement for safe, reliable and efficient modes of transport and service provision in the destination.

Figure 1.2 **Leiper's tourism system**

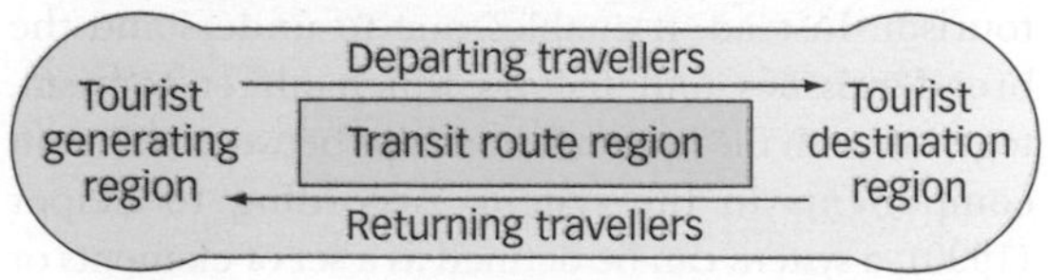

Tourist generating region
Departing travellers
Transit route region
Returning travellers
Tourist destination region

Defining tourism

The terms travel and tourism are often interchanged within the published literature on tourism, though they are normally meant to encompass 'the field of research on human and business activities associated with one or more aspects of the temporary movement of persons away from their immediate home communities and daily work environments for business, pleasure and personal reasons' (Chadwick 1994: 65). These two terms tend to be used in differing contexts to mean similar things, although there is a tendency for the United States to continue to use the term 'travel' when in fact they mean tourism. Despite this inherent problem that may be little more than exercise in semantics (i.e. how to define things), it is widely acknowledged that the two terms are used in isolation or in unison to 'describe' three concepts:

- the movement of people
- a sector of the economy or an industry
- a broad system of interacting relationships of people, their needs [sic] to travel outside their communities and services that attempt to respond to these needs by supplying products (after Chadwick 1994: 65).

From this initial starting point, one can begin to explore some of the complex issues in arriving at a working definition of the terms 'tourism' and 'tourist'.

In a historical context, Burkart and Medlik (1981: 41) identify the historical development of the term 'tourism', noting the distinction between the endeavours of researchers to differentiate between the concept and technical definitions of tourism. The concept of tourism refers to the 'broad notional framework, which identifies the essential characteristics, and which distinguishes tourism from the similar, often related, but different phenomena'. In contrast, technical definitions have evolved through time as researchers modify and develop appropriate measures for statistical, legislative and operational reasons implying that there may be various technical definitions to meet particular purposes. However, the concept of tourism and its identification for research purposes is an important consideration in this instance for tourism statistics so that users are familiar with the context of their derivation.

While most tourism books, articles and monographs now assume either a standard definition or interpretation of the concept of tourism, which is usually influenced by the social scientists' perspective (i.e. a geographical, economic, political, sociological approach or other disciplines) Burkart and Medlik's (1981) approach to the concept of tourism continues to offer a valid assessment of the situation where five main characteristics are associated with the concept.

Furthermore, Burkart and Medlik's (1981) definition of tourism as a concept is invaluable because it rightly recognizes that much tourism is a leisure activity, which involves a discretionary use of time

Exhibit 1.2 **Conceptualizing tourism**

- Tourism arises from the movement of people to, and their stay in, various destinations.
- There are two elements in all tourism: the journey to the destination and the stay including activities at the destination.
- The journey and the stay take place outside the normal place of residence and work, so that tourism gives rise to activities which are distinct from those of the resident and working populations of the places, through which tourists travel and in which they stay.
- The movement to destinations is of a temporary, short-term character, with intention to return within a few days, weeks or months.
- Destinations are visited for purposes other than taking up permanent residence or employment remunerated from within the places visited.

(Source: Burkart and Medlik 1981: 42)

and money, and recreation is often the main purpose for participation in tourism. But this is no reason for restricting the total concept in this way and the essential characteristics of tourism can best be interpreted to embrace a wider concept. All tourism includes some travel but not all travel is tourism, while the temporary and short-term nature of most tourist trips distinguish it from migration. However, there is a growing body of knowledge in tourism which is beginning to look at the relationship between tourism and migration, where migration patterns can influence the nature and scale or tourism patterns especially where it is related to ethnic populations who travel back to family in their native country. Therefore, from the broad interpretation of tourism, it is possible to consider the technical definitions of tourism (also see Leiper 1990, for a further discussion together with Hall 1995 for a concise set of definitions).

Technical definitions of tourism

Technical definitions of tourism are commonly used by organizations seeking to define the population to be measured and there are three principal features which normally have to be defined, as Exhibit 1.3 shows (see BarOn 1984 for a detailed discussion).

Among the most recent attempts to recommend appropriate definitions of tourism was the World Tourism Organization (hereafter WTO) International Conference of Travel and Tourism in Ottawa in 1991 which reviewed, expanded and developed technical definitions where tourism comprises: 'the activities of a person travelling outside his or her usual environment for less than a specified period of time and whose main purpose of travel is other than exercise of an activity remu-

Plate 1.3 Tourist sightseeing train in the Otago region of New Zealand
How would you go about finding out which of the people in this picture are residents and day-trippers and which ones are overseas or domestic visitors? Would you use a survey technique? If so what type?

Exhibit 1.3 **Technical issues in defining tourism: key issues**

- Purpose of travel (e.g. the type of traveller, be it business travel, holiday makers, visits to friends and relatives or for other reasons).
- The time dimension involved in the tourism visit, which requires a minimum and a maximum period of time spent away from the home area and the time spent at the destination. In most cases, this would involve a minimum stay of more than 24 hours away from home and less than a year as a maximum.
- Those situations where tourists may or may not be included as tourists, such as cruise ship passengers, those tourists in-transit at a particular point of embarkation/departure and excursionists who stay less than 24 hours at a destination (e.g. the European duty free cross-channel day trip market).

nerated from the place visited, where "usual environment" is intended to exclude trips within the areas of usual residence and also frequent and regular trips between the domicile and the workplace and other community trips of a routine character where "less than a specified period of time" is intended to exclude long-term migration, and "exercise of an activity remunerated from the place visited" is intended to exclude only migration for temporary work'. The definitions in Exhibit 1.4 were developed by the WTO.

Such definitions can best be thought of as how the 'majority' define these terms. There are, however, different interpretations in some countries where tourism statistics are gathered. Clearly, how the various terms are defined is crucial to the measurement of tourism demand. International comparisons on an equal basis can only be made if like for like is defined, collected and analysed in a similar fashion. Goeldner *et al.* (2000: 17) notes that the National Travel Survey conducted by the Travel Industry Association of America's US Travel Data Center reports on all trips, whatever the purpose, which are in excess of 100 miles and all trips involving an overnight stay whatever the distance. In the UK, the United Kingdom Tourism Survey (UKTS) distinguishes between 'short' holidays (1–3 nights) and 'long' holidays (more than four nights' duration). In order to improve statistical collection and improve understanding of tourism, the United Nations (UN) (1994) and the WTO (1991) also recommended differentiating between visitors, tourists and excursionists. The WTO (1991) recommended that an international tourist be defined as:

> a visitor who travels to a country other than that in which he/she has his/her usual residence for at least one night but not more than one year, and whose main purpose of visit is other than the exercise of an activity remunerated from within the country visited.

Exhibit 1.4 **Definitions of tourism developed by the WTO**

- *International Tourism*: Consists of inbound tourism.
- Visits to a country by non-residents and outbound tourism residents of a country visiting another country.
- *Internal Tourism*: Residents of a country visiting their own country.
- *Domestic Tourism*: Internal tourism plus inbound tourism (the tourism market of accommodation facilities and attractions within a country).
- *National Tourism*: Internal tourism plus outbound tourism (the resident tourism market for travel agents and airlines).

(Source: WTO cited in Chadwick 1994: 66)

and that an international excursionist, e.g. cruise ship visitors, be defined as:

> A visitor residing in a country who travels the same day to a country other than that in which he/she has his/her usual environment for less than 24 hours without spending the night in the country visited and whose main purpose of visit is other than the exercise of an activity remunerated from within the country visited.

Similar definitions were also developed for domestic tourists, with a domestic tourists having a time limit of 'not more than six months' (WTO 1991; UN 1994).

Interestingly, the inclusion of a same-day travel, 'excursionist' category in UN/WTO technical definitions of tourism, makes the division between recreation and tourism even more arbitrary and there is increasing international agreement that 'tourism' refers to all activities of visitors, including both overnight and same-day visitors (UN 1994:5). Given improvements in transport technology, same-day travel is becoming increasingly important to some countries, with the UN (1994:9) observing, 'day visits are important to consumers and to many providers, especially tourist attractions, transport operators and caterers'.

Chadwick (1994) moves the definition of tourists a stage further by offering a typology of travellers (tourists) which highlights the distinction between tourist (travellers) and non-travellers (non-tourists) which is summarized in Figure 1.3. Figure 1.3 is distinctive because it highlights all sections of society which are involved in travel of some kind but also looks at the motivation to travel. It is also useful because it illustrates where technical problems may occur in deciding which groups to include in tourism and those to exclude. From this classification of travellers, the distinction between international and domestic tourism needs to be made. Domestic tourism normally refers to tourist travel from their normal domicile to other areas within a country. In contrast, international tourism normally involves a tourist leaving their country of origin, to cross into another country which involves documentation, administrative formalities and movement to a foreign environment.

The measurement of tourism: tourism statistics

Ritchie (1975, cited in Latham 1989: 55) argued that 'an important part of the maturing process for any science is the development or adaptation of consistent and well-tested measurement techniques and methodologies which are well-suited to the types of problems encountered in practice'. In this context, the measurement of tourists, tourism activity and the effects on the economy and society in different environments is crucial to the development of tourism as an established area of study within the confines of social science. Burkart and Medlik (1981) provide a useful insight into the development of measurements of tourism phenomena by governments during the 1960s and their subsequent development through to the late 1970s. While it is readily acknowledged by most tourism researchers that statistics are a necessary feature to provide data to enable researchers managers, planners, decision-makers and public and private sector bodies to gauge the significance and impact of tourism on destination areas, Burkart and Medlik (1981: 74) identify four principal reasons for statistical measurement in tourism:

- to evaluate the magnitude and significance of tourism to a destination area or region
- to quantify the contribution to the economy or society, especially the effect on the balance of payments
- to assist in the planning and development of tourism infrastructure and the effect of different volumes of tourists with specific needs
- to assist in the evaluation and implementation of marketing and promotion activities where the tourism marketer requires information on the actual and potential markets and their characteristics.

Consequently, tourism statistics are essential to the measurement of the volume, scale, impact and value of tourism at different geographical scales from the global to the country level down to the individual destination. Yet an information gap exists between the types of statistics provided by organizations for

Figure 1.3 **Chadwick's classification of travellers**

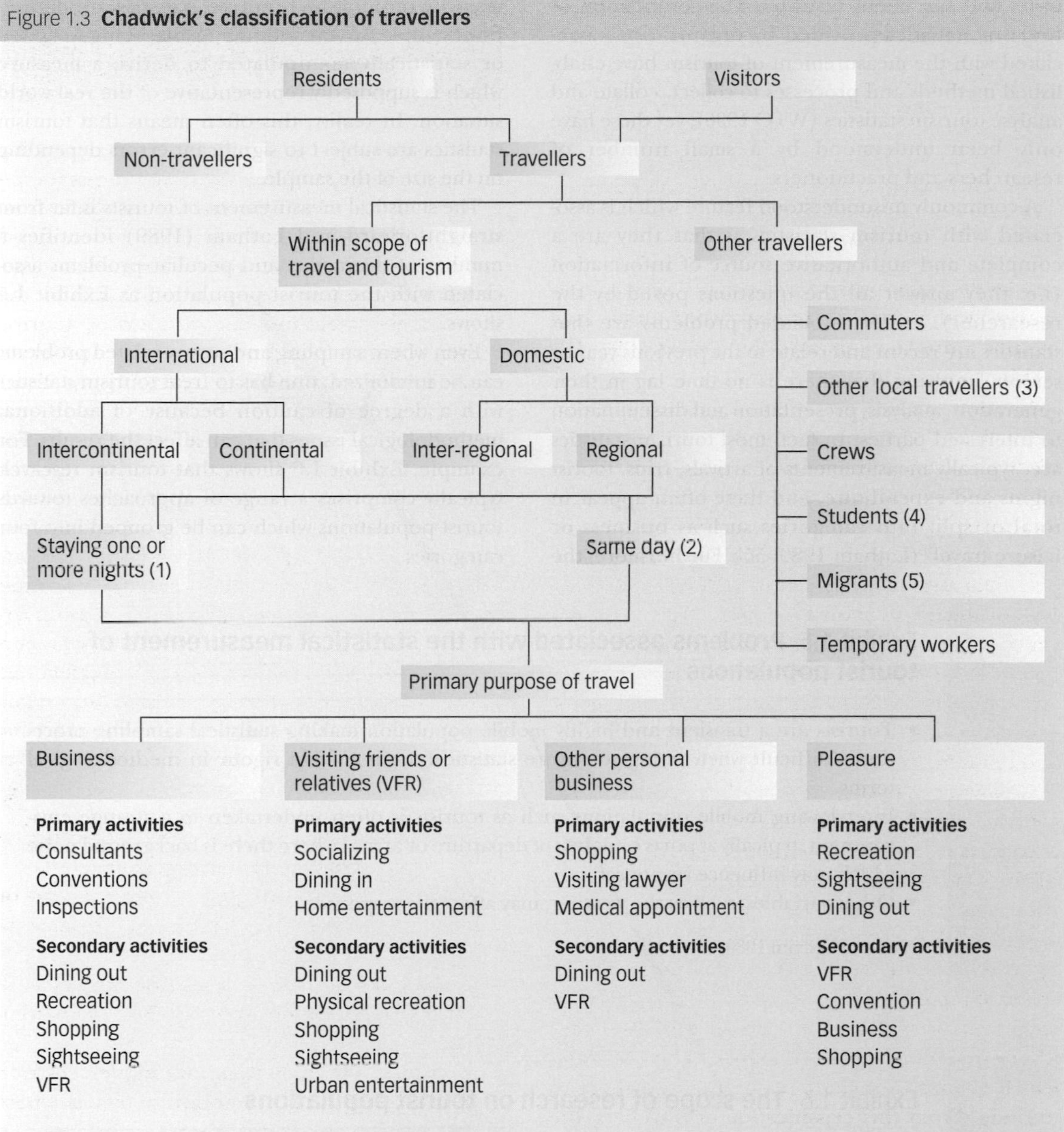

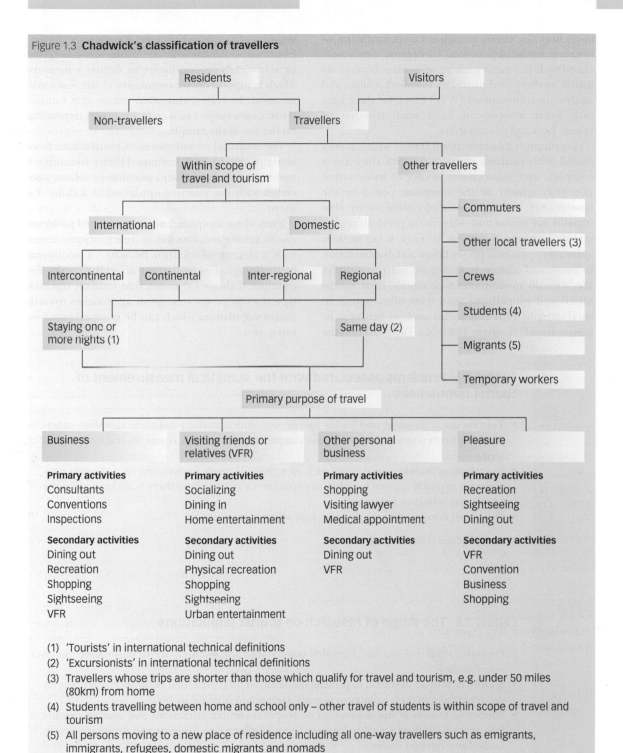

(1) 'Tourists' in international technical definitions
(2) 'Excursionists' in international technical definitions
(3) Travellers whose trips are shorter than those which qualify for travel and tourism, e.g. under 50 miles (80km) from home
(4) Students travelling between home and school only – other travel of students is within scope of travel and tourism
(5) All persons moving to a new place of residence including all one-way travellers such as emigrants, immigrants, refugees, domestic migrants and nomads

(Source: Chadwick 1987)

users and the needs of users. The compilation of tourism statistics provided by organizations associated with the measurement of tourism have established methods and processes to collect, collate and analyse tourism statistics (WTO 1996), yet these have only been understood by a small number of researchers and practitioners.

A commonly misunderstood feature which is associated with tourism statistics is that they are a complete and authoritative source of information (i.e. they answer all the questions posed by the researcher). Other associated problems are that statistics are recent and relate to the previous year or season, implying that there is no time lag in their generation, analysis, presentation and dissemination to interested parties. In fact, most tourism statistics are 'typically measurements of arrivals, trips, tourist nights and expenditure, and these often appear in total or split into categories such as business or leisure travel' (Latham 1989: 55). Furthermore, the majority of published tourism statistics are derived from sample surveys with the results being weighted or statistically manipulated to derive a measure which is supposedly representative of the real world situation. In reality, this often means that tourism statistics are subject to significant errors depending on the size of the sample.

The statistical measurement of tourists is far from straightforward and Latham (1989) identifies a number of distinctive and peculiar problems associated with the tourist population as Exhibit 1.5 shows.

Even where sampling and survey-related problems can be minimized, one has to treat tourism statistics with a degree of caution because of additional methodological issues that can affect the results. For example, Exhibit 1.6 shows that tourism research typically comprises a range of approaches towards tourist populations which can be grouped into four categories.

Exhibit 1.5 **Problems associated with the statistical measurement of tourist populations**

- Tourists are a transient and highly mobile population making statistical sampling procedures difficult when trying to ensure statistical accuracy and rigour in methodological terms.
- Interviewing mobile populations such as tourists is often undertaken in a strange environment, typically at ports or points of departure or arrival where there is background noise which may influence responses.
- Other variables, such as the weather, may affect the responses.

(Source: Latham 1989)

Exhibit 1.6 **The scope of research on tourist populations**

- Pre-travel studies of tourists' intended travel habits and likely choice of destination (*intentional studies*).
- Studies of tourists in-transit to provide information on their actual behaviour and plans for the remainder of their holiday or journey (*actual* and *intended studies*).
- Studies of tourists at the destination or at specific tourist attractions and sites, to provide information on their actual behaviour, levels of satisfaction, impacts and future intentions (*actual* and *intended studies*).
- Post-travel studies of tourists on their return journey from their destination or on-site experience or once they have returned to their place of residence (*post-travel measures*).

Plate 1.4 Visitor centre in the Waitakere Ranges, Auckland, New Zealand
Visitor centres such as this one use a Maori theme to portray local culture and heritage and they collect data on visitor trends related to tourism demand.

In an ideal world, where resource constraints are not a limiting factor on the generation of statistics, each of the aforementioned approaches should be used to provide a broad spectrum of research information on tourism. In reality, organizations and government agencies select a form of research which meets their own particular needs. In practice, most tourism statistics are generated with practical uses in mind and they usually, though not exclusively, can be categorized as follows in Exhibit 1.7.

Exhibit 1.7 Categorizing tourism statistics

- Measurement of tourist volume, enumerating arrivals, departures and the number of visits and stays.
- Expenditure-based surveys which quantify the value of tourist spending at the destination and during the journey.
- The characteristics and features of tourists to construct a profile of the different markets and segments visiting a destination.

National and international tourism data sources

The tourism industry requires reliable statistical data to inform decision-making in the public and private sector organizations alike. Many countries attach a high priority to the collection and analysis of tourism data (Latham 1998). Despite this, national and international tourism data sources are often criticized for lacking consistency and coherence (Hannigan 1994; Lickorish 1997; Smith 1995).

Tourism data are collected by commercial organizations and those requiring the results can subscribe to or purchase reports from them. Organizations which do this sort of work include Mintel, the Economist Intelligence Unit and Eurostat. Moreover, consultants can be commissioned to specifically collect the data required. However, in both cases the expense is such that most turn to national government organizations for tourism data in the main. For international comparisons, however, the World Tourism Organization (WTO) and the Organisation for Economic Co-operation and Development (OECD) collate and publish international travel statistics from member nations.

Data sources

As previously mentioned tourism data can assist in several ways, including the planning and development of tourism, impact assessments or to inform promotional campaigns and market research. In order to assist in these activities tourism statistics crucially provides data on the:

- volume of tourism
- value of tourism.

These are typically measured by:

- frontier arrivals
- accommodation arrivals
- nights spent
- tourist receipts.

However, the effectiveness of the national organizations as providers of related tourism data depend on a variety of factors. These include the scope and frequency of the data collection as well as the methods used in the data collection and analysis. Here, aspects such as sampling techniques and sample size will greatly influence data reliability. Even in large-scale surveys, such as the UK's International Passenger Survey, where some 250,000 plus travellers are interviewed 'sampling error for particular countries varies' (Brunt 1997: 12). Countries with low visitation rates from and to the UK have high sampling errors, whereas popular generating and destination nations have low sampling errors in the survey.

Many commentators in recent years have noted the shortcomings of published tourism statistics (BarOn 1989; Chadwick 1994; Edwards 1991; Latham 1995; Ryan 1995; Smith 1995). Both the World Travel and Tourism Council (WTTC) and the International Monetary Fund (IMF) have recommended that governments effectively collect and analyse tourism data and represent them in the country's national accounts. Sheldon (1993) and Lickorish (1997) suggest that because many countries do not follow such a recommendation, this has resulted in tourism receiving less acclaim as the world's largest industry.

Domestic tourism statistics

Pearce (1995) acknowledges that the scale and volume of domestic tourism world-wide exceeds that of international tourism, though it is often viewed as the poorer partner in the compilation of statistics. For example, most domestic tourism statistics tend to underestimate the scale and volume of flows since certain aspects of domestic tourist movements are sometimes ignored in official sources. The 'visits to friends and relatives, the use of forms of accommodation other than hotels (for example, second homes, camp and caravan sites) and travel by large segments of a population from towns to the countryside are not for the most part included' (Latham 1989: 65). This is supported by the WTO which argues that 'there are relatively few countries that collect domestic travel and tourism statistics. Moreover some countries rely exclusively on the traditional hotel sector, thereby leaving out of the account the many travellers staying in supplementary accommodation establishments or with friends and relatives' (WTO 1984, cited in Latham 1989: 65). Therefore the collection of domestic tourism statistics requires the use of different data sources aside from the more traditional sources such as hotel records which identify the origin and duration of a visitor's stay.

To assist in the identification of who to include as a domestic tourist, WTO (1983) suggests that the following working definition: 'any person, regardless of nationality, resident in a country and who travels to a place in the same country for not more than one year and whose main purpose of visit is other than following an occupation remunerated from within the place visited'.

Such a definition includes domestic tourists where an overnight stay is involved and domestic excursionists who visit an area for less than 24 hours and do not stay overnight. In fact, Latham (1989: 66) points to the variety of definitions which exist aside from those formulated by WTO and the following issues complicate matters:

- *Purpose of visit* – all countries using this concept define a domestic tourist as one who travels for a purpose other than to perform a remunerated activity.
- *The length of trip and/or distance travelled* – certain definitions state that travellers should, for example, be involved in an overnight stay and/ or travel a prescribed minimum distance.
- *Type of accommodation* – for practical reasons, some countries restrict the concept of domestic tourism to cover only those persons using commercial accommodation facilities. (after Latham 1989: 66)

Problems in applying WTO definitions may also reflect an individual country's reasons for generating such statistics, which may not necessarily be to contribute to a better understanding to statistics per se. For example, WTO (1981) identified four uses of domestic tourism statistics as Exhibit 1.8 shows.

Regional and local tourist organizations also make use of such data to develop and market destinations and different businesses within the tourism sector. But how is domestic tourism measured?

Burkart and Medlik (1981) argue that two principal features need to be measured. First, the volume, value and characteristics of tourism among the population of the country. Second, the same data relating to individual destinations within the country.

WTO (1981 cited in Latham 1989) considers the minimum data requirements for the collection of domestic tourism statistics in terms of arrivals and tourist nights in accommodation classified by:

- month
- type of grade of accommodation establishment and
- location of the accommodation establishment and overall expenditure on domestic tourism.

Exhibit 1.8 **Uses of domestic tourism statistics**

- To calculate the contribution of tourism to the country's economy, whereby estimates of tourism's value to the gross domestic product is estimated due to the complexity of identifying the scope of tourism's contribution.
- To assist in the marketing and promotion of tourism, where government-sponsored tourism organizations seek to encourage its population to take domestic holidays rather than to travel overseas (see Hall 1997 for a discussion of this activity among Pacific Rim countries).
- To aid with the regional development policies of governments which harness tourism as a tool for area development where domestic tourists in congested environments are encouraged to travel to less developed areas and to improve the quality of tourism in different environments.
- To achieve social objectives, where socially oriented tourism policies may be developed for the underprivileged which requires a detailed understanding of the holiday-taking habits of a country's nationals.

(Source: WTO 1981)

Latham (1989) argues that it is possible to generate additional data from such variables including length of stay, occupancy rate and average expenditure. Many countries also collate supplementary information beyond the minimum standards identified by WTO, where the socio-economic characteristics of tourists are identified, together with their use of tourist transport, and purpose of visit through the cost of such data collection does mean that the statistical basis of domestic tourism in many less developed countries remains poor.

The methods used to generate domestic tourism statistics are normally based on the estimates of volume, value and scale derived from sample surveys due to the cost of undertaking large-scale surveys of tourist activities. The immediate problem facing the user of such material is the type of errors and degree of accuracy which can be attached to such data. For example Latham (1989) identifies the sample surveys in Exhibit 1.9 which are now used to supplement data derived from hotel records.

International tourism statistics

The two principal organizations which collate data on international tourism are the World Tourism Organization (WTO) and the Organisation for Economic Co-operation and Development (OECD). In addition, international regional tourism organizations such as the Pacific Asia Travel Association and the ASEAN Tourism Working Group also collect international tourism statistics (Hall 1997).

Page (1994) reviews the major publications of the first two organizations in relation to international tourism, noting the detailed contents of each. In the case of WTO, the main source is the *Yearbook of Tourism Statistics*, which contains a summary of the most salient tourism statistics for almost 150 countries and territories. In the case of OECD, their *Tourism Policy and International Tourism*, referred to as the 'Blue Book' is less comprehensive, covering only 25 countries but this does contain most of the main generating and receiving areas. While the main thrust of the publication is government policy and the obstacles to international tourism, it does expand on certain areas not covered in the WTO publication (for a more detailed discussion of data sources see Withyman 1985).

In contrast to domestic tourism, statistics on international tourism are normally collected to assess the impact of tourism on a country's balance of payments. Though as Withyman (1985: 69) argued:

> Outward visitors seem to attract less attention from the pollsters and the enumerators. Of course, one country's outward visitor is another country's

Exhibit 1.9 **Sample surveys used to supplement hotel records**

- *Household surveys,* where the residents of a country are interviewed in their own home to ascertain information of tourist trips for the purpose of pleasure. A useful pan-European study is the EC Omnibus study. Even so, little progress has been made internationally to collate common data on household surveys since OECD's attempt in 1967 to outline the types of data which national travel surveys should collect.
- *Destination surveys,* where high levels of tourist activity occur to a region or resort. Such studies frequently compile statistics on accommodation usage, sample surveys of visitors and may be linked to existing knowledge derived from household surveys.
- *Enroute surveys,* where tourists are surveyed enroute to examine the characteristics and features of tourists. Although it is a convenient way to interview a captive audience depending upon the mode of transport used (see Page 1994), the results may not necessarily be as representative without a complete knowledge of the transport flows for mode of tourist transport being surveyed.

(Source: Latham 1989)

> (perhaps several countries) inward visitor, and a much more welcome sort of visitor, too, being both a source of revenue and an emblem of the destination country's appeal in the international market. This has meant that governments have tended to be generally more keen to measure inward than outward tourism, or at any rate, having done so, to publish the results.

This statement indicates that governments are more concerned with the direct effect of tourism on their balance of payments. Yet such statistics are also utilized by marketing arms of national tourism organizations to base their decisions on who to target in international campaigns. The wider tourism industry also makes use of such data as part of their strategic planning and for more immediate purposes where niche markets exist. Even so, Shackleford (1980) argued that the collection of tourism statistics should be a responsibility of the state to meet international standards for data collection (WTO 1996). However, it is increasingly the case that only when the economic benefits of data collection can be justified will national governments continue to compile tourism statistics. Where resource constraints exist, the collection and compilation of tourism statistics may be impeded. This also raises important methodological issues related to what exactly is being measured. As Withyman (1985: 61) argued:

> In the jungle of international travel and tourism statistics, it behoves the explorer to step warily; on all sides there is luxuriant growth. Not all data sources are what they appear to be – after close scrutiny they show themselves to be inconsistent and often unsuitable for the industry researcher and planner.

The key point Withymann recognizes is the lack of comparability in tourism data in relation to what is measured (i.e. is it visitor days or visitor nights?) and the procedures and methodology used to measure international tourism.

Frechtling (1976) concluded that the approaches taken by national and international agencies associated with international tourism statistics was converging towards common definitions of trip, travel and traveller (see Chadwick 1994 for a fuller discussion). Yet the principal difficulty which confronts tourism researchers is whether business travel should continue to be considered as a discrete part of tourism. Chadwick (1994: 75) notes that 'the consensus of North American opinion seems to be that, despite certain arguments to the contrary business travel should be considered part of travel and tourism'. While BarOn (1984) examines the standard definitions and terminology of international tourism as used by the UN and WTO, research by Ngoh (1985) is useful in that it considers the practical problems posed by such definitions when attempting to measure international tourism and solutions towards the difficulties.

Latham (1989: 59) suggests that the main types of international tourism statistics collated relate to:

- volume of tourists
- expenditure by tourists
- the profile of the tourist and their trip characteristics.

As is true of domestic tourism, estimates form the basis for most statistics on international tourism since the method of data collection does not generate exact data. For example, volume statistics are often generated from counts of tourists at entry/exit points (i.e. gateways such as airports and ports) or at accommodation. But such data relate to numbers of trips rather than individual tourists since one tourist may make more than one trip a year and each trip is counted separately. In the case of expenditure statistics, tourist expenditure normally refers to tourist spending within a country and excludes payments to tourist transport operators. Yet deriving such statistics is often an indirect measure based on foreign currency estimates derived from bank records, from data provided by tourism service providers or more commonly from social surveys undertaken directly with tourists. Research by White and Walker (1982) and Baretje (1982) directly questions the validity and accuracy of such methods of data collection, examining the main causes of bias and error in such studies.

According to Edwards (1991: 68–9), 'expenditure and receipts data apart, tourist statistics are usually collected in one of five ways' (see Exhibit 1.10).

The last area of data collection is *profile statistics,* which examine the characteristics and travel habits of visitors. For example, the UK's International Passenger Survey (IPS) is one survey that incorporates volume, expenditure and profile data on international tourism (see Exhibit 1.11).

Exhibit 1.10 **How international tourism statistics are collected**

- *Counts of all individuals entering or leaving the country* at all recognized frontier crossings, often using arrival/departure cards where high volume arrivals/departures are the norm. Where particularly large volumes of tourist traffic exist, a 10 per cent sampling framework is normally used (i.e. every tenth arrival/departure card). Countries such as New Zealand actually match the arrival/departure cards, or a sample, to examine the length of stay.
- *Interviews* carried out at frontiers with a sample of arriving and/or departing passengers to obtain a more detailed profile of visitors and their activities within the country. This will often require a careful sample design to gain a sufficiently large enough sample with the detail required from visitors on a wide range of tourism data including places visited, expenditure, accommodation usage and related items.
- *Selecting a sample of arrivals* and providing them with a self-completion questionnaire to be handed in or posted. This method is used in Canada but it fails to incorporate those visitors travelling by road via the United States.
- *Sample surveys of the entire population of a country,* including travellers and non-travellers, though the cost of obtaining a representative sample is often prohibitive.
- *Accommodation arrivals and nights spent* are recorded by hoteliers and owners of the accommodation types covered. The difficulty with this type of data collection is that accommodation owners have no incentive to record accurate details, particularly where the tax regime is based on the turnover of bed nights (see Page 1989 for a discussion of this problem in the context of London).

Exhibit 1.11 **The United Kingdom's International Passenger Survey**

As a government-sponsored survey, which began in 1961, the International Passenger Survey now covers all ports of entry/exit to the UK. The International Passenger Survey (IPS) is a survey of people travelling into and out of the UK (Office for National Statistics 1998). A sample of travellers are interviewed using a face-to-face method of data collection. The UK's Office for National Statistics (ONS) commissions the work, together with other government departments, and data collection and survey analysis are performed. The results of the IPS are available in various formats: A 'travel pack' with CDs or disks in dataset form to allow the user to perform their own analysis; MQ6 – Overseas Travel and Tourism is published on a quarterly basis giving the latest information; Overseas Travel and Tourism does the same but on a monthly basis; and Travel Trends is published on an annual basis reporting the results of the IPS. In the 1997 survey, 258,000 respondents were randomly selected for interview, representing approximately 0.2 per cent of all who were eligible. The main questions asked concerned nationality, residence, country of visit (for UK residents travelling abroad), purpose of visit, flight or ferry information, earnings, expenditure and demographic characteristics. The survey had an 83 per cent response rate. A system of stratified random sampling is used, based on the seven principal airports in the UK together with other regional airports, ferry ports and the Channel Tunnel. The IPS provides information on international tourism, outbound and inbound to the UK. Information on the number of visits, length of stay, value are provided as well as other aspects which include method of travel, purpose of visit, age and gender (see Griffith and Elliot 1988 for further details on the sample design features of IPS). According to Latham (1989: 64), IPS' four principal aims are:

1. To collect data for the travel account (which acts to compare expenditure by overseas visitors to the UK with expenditure overseas by visitors from the UK) of the balance of payments.
2. To provide detailed information on foreign visitors to the UK and on outgoing visitors travelling overseas.
3. To provide data on international migration.
4. To provide information on routes used by passengers as an aid to aviation and shipping authorities.

Global patterns of tourism

WTO provides the main source of data for international tourism, collated from a survey of major government agencies responsible for data collection. While most international tourists are expressed as 'frontier arrivals' (i.e. arrivals determined by means of a frontier check), the use of arrival/departure cards (where used) provides additional detail to the profile of international tourists and where they are not used periodic tourism surveys are often used. WTO statistics are mainly confined to all categories of travellers and in some cases geographical disaggregation of the data may be limited by the collecting agencies use of descriptions and categories for aid of simplicity (e.g. rest of the world) rather than listing all categories of arrivals. Appendix 1 provides a range of data which identifies changes in:

- international arrivals and receipts from tourism
- the economic importance of tourism
- changes in regional patterns of tourism by WTO region
- the distribution of hotel capacity world
- changes in the ranking of international tourism destinations.

Patterns of domestic tourism

According to WTO, domestic tourism is estimated to be up to ten times greater in volume than international tourism and yet comparatively little research has been undertaken on this neglected area of tourism activity. Pearce (1995: 67) argues that this may be attributed 'to the less visible nature of much domestic tourism, which is often more informal and less structured than international tourism, and a consequent tendency by many government agencies, researchers and others to regard it as less significant'. This problem of neglect is compounded by a paucity of data, since it is not a straightforward matter of recording arrivals and departures. It requires an analysis of tourism patterns and flows at different spatial scales, to consider spatial interaction of tourists between a multitude of possible origin and destination areas within a country as well as a detailed understanding of inter-regional flows. Where government agencies and other public sector organizations undertake data collection of domestic tourism 'the results are not often directly comparable, limiting the identification of general patterns and trends' (Pearce 1995: 67). For this reason, the

Student exercise

Examine Appendix 1.

- What changes have occurred in the period 1997–98 in visitor arrivals by WTO region?
- Which countries are reporting a deficit in their tourism account (i.e. where receipts are exceeded by expenditure) comparing 1989 and 1997?
- Which WTO regions have reported average annual growth rates in excess of 6 per cent between 1989 and 1998?
- Which regions of the world dominate the world hotel capacity statistics?
- What were the world's top five tourism destinations in 1990, 1995 and 1998?

innovative research undertaken by Pearce (1993) is worthy of attention here since it comprises one of the few systematic analysis of domestic tourism in a country, which in this case is New Zealand.

As Pearce (1995: 67) rightly acknowledges 'there are still few examples of comprehensive inter-regional studies where the analysis is based on a complete matrix of both original and destination regions [since] few appropriate and reliable sets of tourism statistics exist which might be used to construct such a matrix'. Nation-wide surveys are undertaken which are weighted to reflect the population base. One of the few comprehensive studies which yields an origin-destination matrix is the somewhat dated New Zealand Domestic Travel Survey (NZDTS), established in 1983 (New Zealand Tourism Department 1991). Although this study is currently being updated to incorporate the results of a 1996 survey, the only available statistics are those analysed by Pearce (1993) which still outline the basic principles and patterns inherent in this national tourism data set, since the NZDTS has not been updated since 1989/90 although in 2000 work is in progress to update it.

Conclusion

This chapter has introduced the conceptual issues associated with the study of tourism, highlighting the development of the subject area and some of the principal difficulties which students and researchers need to be aware of when attempting to define the subject. It has distinguished between the terms:

- a tourist
- domestic tourism
- international tourism

and

- identified how tourism is measured and why statistical sources are the main data source for students of tourism
- alluded to some of the problems associated with the collection and use of tourism statistics.

It is widely acknowledged that tourism is a multidisciplinary subject rather than a discipline in its own right because other subjects study and contribute to Tourism Studies as it has no core body of knowledge which is distinct and unique to the subject and not modified from other disciplines such as geography, marketing or economics. The lack of any theoretical core of knowledge has also impeded the intellectual development of Tourism Studies from making major leaps forward in understanding the phenomenon called 'tourism'. Intellectually, other disciplines have viewed tourism as a descriptive subject but during the 1980s and 1990s the scale and significance of tourism as a global activity and process with economic implications for governments has elevated the subject's acceptability as an academic area worthy of study. One of the most interesting changes in the status of tourism as a subject area worthy of pursuit is the demand for students and skilled workers who have a grasp of the dynamic and ever-changing nature of tourism and an ability to manage the detrimental impacts of tourism on the population and natural environment. A recent review of tourism research published in *Tourism Management* by Ryan and Page (2000) acknowledged that this was by far one of the major growth areas of research activity in the period 1990 to 1999, as analysts have recognized how all embracing tourism-induced change can be on the natural environment. Although this chapter has addressed a host of technical and semantic issues associated with the measurement and definition of tourists and tourism, which may appear dull and uninteresting, a fundamental understanding of these seemingly tedious issues is fundamental when wider issues of tourism impacts and effects are evaluated: without a baseline or an agreement on what one is observing or measuring, then the results and recommendations will have little meaning if the wrong assumptions or features are measured. One continued problem which tourism researchers consistently make is that they fail to agree clear parameters of what is being observed, measured and evaluated and rarely refer to the technical issues necessary to precisely delimit what they are studying.

What students of tourism need to recognize from this chapter is that tourism is also measured and evaluated by governments and agencies in different and sometimes conflicting ways often making data sources little more than an indication of the order of magnitude of tourism rather than a precise delineation of its scale and volume. Official statistics and data sources have to be treated with caution, as Latham (1989) and other tourism statisticians observe, as problems of accuracy, methodology and consistency confront researchers and students. Furthermore, much of the research which the private sector commissions to examine tourism-related problems is kept confidential from clients even though it sometimes uncritically uses public data sources supplemented with face-to-face interviews with decision-makers where tourism structure plans are being developed for governments. Classifying and enumerating tourists remains a complex problem, not least because the population is highly mobile and they are consuming an experience rather than a tangible product. As a result, any analysis of tourism is highly dependent upon the tools and methods of analysis one employs.

Discussion questions

1. What are the different subjects which contribute to the area known as Tourism Studies?
2. What are the main components of Leiper's 'Tourism system'?
3. What are the problems in trying to calculate the number of tourists which arrive in a country in a given time period?
4. How would you go about locating tourism statistics for a region you are studying?

Notes

1. An academic journal is a means of communication where academics publish the findings of their research. The articles published are normally subject to peer review (i.e. other academics review the work anonymously and judge its suitability for publication). This type of publication is quite detailed and specialized and is one way the subject is judged to make developments in the way people think and examine tourism.

References

Baretje, R. (1982) 'Tourism's external account and the balance of payments', *Annals of Tourism Research*, **9** (1): 57–67.

BarOn, R. (1984) 'Tourism terminology and standard definitions', *Tourist Review*, **39** (1): 2–4.

BarOn, R.R. (1989) *Travel and Tourism Data. A Comprehensive Research Handbook on the World Travel Industry*, London: Euromonitor.

Brunt, P.R. (1997) *Market Research in Travel and Tourism*, Oxford: Butterworth-Heinemann.

Burkart, A. and Medlik, S. (1974) *Tourism, Past, Present and Future*, Oxford: Heinemann.

Burkart, A. and Medlik, R. (1981) *Tourism, Past, Present and Future*, second edition, London: Heinemann.

Burkart, A. and Medlik, R. (eds) (1975) *The Management of Tourism*, Oxford: Heinemann.

Chadwick, R. (1987) 'Concepts, definitions and measures used in travel and tourism research', in J.R. Brent Ritchie and C. Goeldner (eds) *Travel, Tourism and Hospitality Research: A Handbook for Managers and Researchers*, New York: Wiley.

Chadwick, R. (1994) 'Concepts, definitions and measures used in travel and tourism research', in J.R. Brent Ritchie and C. Goeldner (eds) *Travel, Tourism and Hospitality Research: A Handbook for Managers and Researchers*, second edition, New York: Wiley.

Collier, A. (1989) *Principles of Tourism*, Auckland: Longman Paul.

Cooper, C.P., Fletcher, J., Gilbert, D.G. and Wanhill, S. (1993) *Tourism: Principles and Practice*, Harlow: Addison Wesley Longman.

Cooper, C.P., Fletcher, J., Gilbert, D.G. and Wanhill, S. (1998) *Tourism: Principles and Practice*, second edition, London: Pitman.

Internet resources

By going to the weblink at www.thomsonlearning.co.uk students can access the following two studies on the Thomson Learning website. The first is from S. Horner and J. Swarbrooke (1996) *Marketing Tourism, Hospitality and Leisure in Europe* and examines the differences which are made between tourism, leisure and hospitality which is a useful introduction to distinguish between the different terms that are used.

This should be followed by reading Jafar Jafari's (1996) article from the *International Encyclopedia of Business Management* on tourism management that outlines many of the problems of defining tourism and the ways in which it is approached and the issues associated with what is broadly defined as 'tourism management'.

Edwards, E. (1991) 'The reliability of tourism statistics', *EIU Travel and Tourism Analyst*, 1: 62–75.
Foster, D. (1985) *Travel and Tourism Management*, London: Macmillan.
Frechtling, D. (1976) 'Proposed standard definitions and classifications for travel research', Marketing Travel and Tourism, *Seventh Annual Conference Proceedings*, Boca Raton: Travel Research Association: 59–74.
Gilbert, D.C. (1990) 'Conceptual issues in the meaning of tourism', in C.P. Cooper (ed.) *Progress in Tourism, Recreation and Hospitality Management Volume 2*, London: Belhaven: 4–27.
Goeldner, C.R., Ritchie, J.R.B. and McIntosh, R.W. (2000) *Tourism: Principles, Practices and Philosophies*, New York: John Wiley and Sons Inc.
Griffith, D. and Elliot, D. (1988) *Sampling Errors on the IPS*, London: OPCS New Methodology Series.
Hall, C.M. (1991) *Introduction to Tourism in Australia: Impacts, Planning and Development*, Melbourne: Longman Cheshire.
Hall, C.M. (1995) *Tourism in Australia: Impacts, Planning and Development*, second edition, Melbourne: Longman.
Hall, C.M. (1997) *Tourism in the Pacific: Development, Impacts and Markets*, second edition, South Melbourne: Addison Wesley Longman.
Hall, C.M. and Page, S.J. (eds) (2000) *Tourism in South and South East Asia: issues and cases*, Oxford: Butterworth-Heinemann.
Hannigan, K. (1994) Developing European Community tourism statistics, *Annals of Tourism Research*, **21** (2): 415–17.
Inkpen, G. (1998) *Information Technology for Travel and Tourism*, second edition. Harlow: Addison Wesley Longman.
Latham, J. (1989) 'The statistical measurement of tourism', in C.P. Cooper (ed.) *Progress in Tourism, Recreation and Hospitality Management Volume 1*, London: Belhaven: 55–76.
Latham, J. (1995) 'International tourism flows', *Progress in Tourism and Hospitality Research*, **1** (1): 63–71.
Latham, J. (1998) 'Patterns of international tourism', *Progress in Tourism and Hospitality Research*, **4** (1): 45–52.
Lavery, P. (1989) *Travel and Tourism*, first edition, Huntingdon: Elm.
Laws, E. (1991) *Tourism Marketing*, Cheltenham: Stanley Thornes.
Leiper, N. (1990) 'Tourism Systems: An Interdisciplinary Perspective', Palmerston North, New Zealand: Department of Management Systems, Occasional Paper 2, Massey University.
Lickorish, L.J. (1997) 'Travel statistics – the slow move forward', *Tourism Management*, **18** (8): 491–97.
Lundberg, D.E. (1980) *The Tourist Business*, New York: Van Nostrand Reinhold.
Mathieson, A. and Wall, G. (1982) *Tourism: Economic, Physical and Social Impacts*, Harlow: Longman.
Mill, R.C. and Morrison, A.M. (1985) *The Tourism System: An Introductory Text*, New Jersey: Prentice Hall.
Murphy, P.E. (1985) *Tourism: A Community Approach*, London: Routledge.
New Zealand Tourism Department (1991) *New Zealand Domestic Travel Study 1989/90*, Wellington: New Zealand Tourism Department.
Ngoh, T. (1985) 'Guidelines for the harmonisation of international tourism statistics among PATA member countries', in *The Battle for Market Share: Strategies in Research and Marketing*, 16th Annual Conference, Tourism and Travel Research Association, Salt Lake City: Graduate School of Business, University of Utah: 291–306.
Office for National Statistics (1998) *Social Trends 28*, London: Office for National Statistics.
Page, S.J. (1989) 'Tourist development in London Docklands in the 1980s and 1990s', *GeoJournal*, **19** (3): 291–95.
Page, S.J. (1994) *Transport for Tourism*, London: Routledge.
Pearce, D.G. (1987) *Tourism Today: A Geographical Analysis*, Harlow: Longman.
Pearce, D.G. (1992) *Tourism Organizations*, Harlow: Longman.
Pearce, D. (1993) 'Domestic tourist travel patterns in New Zealand', *GeoJournal*, **29** (3): 225–32.
Pearce, D.G. (1995) *Tourism Today: A Geographical Approach*, second edition, Harlow: Longman.
Qu, H. and Zhang, H. (1997) 'The projected inbound market trends of 12 tourist destinations in S.E. Asia and the Pacific 1997–2001', *Journal of Vacation Marketing*, **3** (3): 247–63.
Ryan, C. (1995) *Researching Tourist Satisfaction: Issues, Concepts and Problems*, London: Routledge.
Ryan, C. and Page, S.J. (eds) (2000) *Tourism Management: Towards the New Millennium*, Oxford: Pergamon.
Shackleford, P. (1980) 'Keeping tabs on tourism: a manager's guide to tourism statistics', *International Journal of Tourism Management*, **1** (3): 148–57.
Sheldon, P.J. (1993) 'Forecasting tourism: expenditure versus arrivals', *Journal of Travel Research*, **32** (1): 13–19.
Smith, S.L.J. (1995) *Tourism Analysis: A Handbook*, second edition, Harlow: Longman.
United Nations (UN) (1994) *Recommendations on Tourism Statistics*, New York: United Nations.
Urry, J. (1990) *The Tourist Gaze: Leisure and Travel in Contemporary Societies*, London: Sage.
Walle, A.H. (1996) 'Tourism and the internet: opportunities for direct marketing', *Journal of Travel Research*, **35** (1): 72–78.
White, K. and Walker, M. (1982) 'Trouble in the travel account', *Annals of Tourism Research*, **9** (1): 37–56.
Withyman, W. (1985) 'The ins and outs of international travel and tourism data', *International Tourism Quarterly*, Special Report No. 55.
World Tourism Organization (WTO) (1981) *Guidelines for the Collection and Presentation of Domestic and International Tourism Statistics*, Madrid: World Tourism Organization.
World Tourism Organization (WTO) (1991) *Resolutions of International Conference on Travel and Tourism, Ottawa, Canada*, Madrid: World Tourism Organization.
World Tourism Organization (WTO) (1996) *International Tourism Statistics*, Madrid: World Tourism Organization.
World Tourism Organization (WTO) (1997) *Yearbook of Tourism Statistics*, Vol 1, fiftieth edition. Madrid: WTO.

Further reading

The following are highly recommended as references to follow up on the definition and scope of tourism:

Chadwick, R. (1994) 'Concepts, definitions and measures used in travel and tourism research', in J.R. Brent Ritchie and C. Goeldner (eds) *Travel, Tourism and Hospitality Research: A Handbook for Managers and Researchers*, second edition, New York: Wiley.

Gilbert, D.C. (1990) 'Conceptual issues in the meaning of tourism', in C.P. Cooper (ed.) *Progress in Tourism, Recreation and Hospitality Management Volume 2*, London: Belhaven: 4–27.

Latham, J. (1989) 'The statistical measurement of tourism', in C.P. Cooper (ed.) *Progress in Tourism, Recreation and Hospitality Management Volume 1*, London: Belhaven: 55–76.

Useful web addresses

Australian Tourist Commission (2000)
www.atc.net.au/intell/data (17/1/2000)

Bureau of Tourism Research (2000)
www.btr.gov.au/index.html (17/1/2000)

Tinet – Travel and Tourism Research (2000)
www.tinet.ita.doc.gov/research/programmes (17/1/2000)

World Tourism Organization (2000)
www.world-tourism.org (17/1/2000)

Appendix 1
World tourism statistics

Summary of global tourism in 1998

- In the period 1997–98, world tourism arrivals grew by 2.5 per cent to 635 million, while world tourism receipts (excluding the revenue from international transport) rose to US$439 billion, a 0.3 per cent rise over 1997 reflecting the strong appreciation of the US dollar, the base currency used for comparisons.
- In the period 1992–94, the average increase in international tourism receipts outstripped the world exports in commercial services; in 1997, tourism receipts comprised 8 per cent of total world exports of goods and nearly 35 per cent of the total world export of services.

International tourist arrivals and receipts world-wide 1989–98

	1989	1990	1991	1992	1993	1994	1995	1996	1997	1998
Arrivals (millions)	426	458	464	503	518	553	568	600	620	635
% annual change	8.02	7.45	1.25	8.37	3.09	6.75	2.74	5.48	3.33	2.51
Receipts (US$ billion)	221	268	278	314	323	353	403	438	436	439
% annual change	8.31	21.03	3.66	13.00	3.03	9.13	14.29	8.57	–0.14	0.28

(Source: WTO 1999, World Tourism Highlights, http: //www.world-tourism.org)

International arrivals and tourism receipts 1997 and 1998 by WTO tourism region

	Tourist	Arrivals	% change		Tourism (US$ million)	Receipt	% change	
	1997	1998	98/97	97/96	1997	1998	98/97	97/96
World	619 574	635 134	2.5	3.3	438 165	439 393	0.3	0.1
Africa	23 190	24 679	6.4	5.9	9 018	9 612	6.6	3.3
Americas	118 887	122 682	3.2	1.7	118 855	119 965	0.9	5.7
East Asia Pacific	88 207	86 629	–1.6	–1.1	76 387	68 598	–10.2	–6.8
Europe	369 803	381 076	3.0	4.7	220 494	228 856	3.8	–0.8
Middle East	14 833	15 035	1.4	5.3	9 135	8 022	–12.2	10.8
South Asia	4 834	5 033	4.1	9.0	4 276	4 340	1.5	8.3

(Source: WTO 1999, World Tourism Highlights, http: //www.world-tourism.org)

The tourism balance (receipts–expenditure) by WTO regions 1989 and 1997

Region	1989 US$ million	1997 US$ million
Americas	8 149	35 289
Europe	12 463	14 952
Middle East	780	3 815
Africa	828	2 043
South Asia	849	1 825
East Asia Pacific	–4 300	484

(Source: WTO 1999, World Tourism Highlights, http: //www.world-tourism.org)

Trends of international tourism receipts by WTO region: average annual growth rate 1989–1998				
Region	**Increase 1989–1998 US$ billion**	**Average 1989–93**	**Annual 1994–98**	**Growth rate (%) 1989–98**
Africa	5.1	8.7	8.7	8.8
Americas	59.8	10.9	5.9	8.0
East Asia Pacific	34.4	12.0	2.0	8.0
Europe	113.0	9.0	6.5	7.9
Middle East	3.5	6.1	5.8	6.6
South Asia	2.4	7.9	9.0	9.1
World	218.2	9.9	5.9	7.9

(Source: WTO 1999, World Tourism Highlights, http: //www.world-tourism.org)

Hotel and accommodation capacity: thousands of bed places and market share						
	Bed places (thousands)			**Market share (%)**		
Region	**1980**	**1985**	**1997**	**1980**	**1985**	**1997**
Europe	8 542	8 637	11 731	52.5	47.3	40.0
Americas	6 436	6 933	9 346	39.5	38.0	31.8
East Asia Pacific	763	1 694	6 726	4.7	9.3	22.9
Africa	269	525	835	1.7	2.9	2.8
Middle East	141	254	400	0.9	1.4	1.4
South Asia	126	198	310	0.8	1.1	1.1
Total	16 277	18 241	29 347	100	100	100

(Source: WTO 1999, World Tourism Highlights, http: //www.world-tourism.org)

International tourist arrivals by region 1989–1998

Region	1989	1990	1991	1992	1993	1994	1995	1996	1997	1998
WORLD										
Arrivals (millions)	426.5	458.4	464.0	502.7	518.3	553.4	568.5	599.6	619.5	625.1
% annual change	8.0	7.4	1.2	8.4	3.1	6.7	2.7	5.5	3.3	2.5
AFRICA										
Arrivals (millions)	13.8	15.1	16.2	18.0	18.5	19.1	20.3	21.9	23.2	24.7
% annual change	10.5	9.0	7.6	11.3	2.8	2.9	6.6	7.8	5.9	6.4
AMERICAS										
Arrivals (millions)	87.0	93.6	96.7	103.6	103.6	106.5	110.6	116.9	118.9	112.7
% annual change	4.7	7.6	3.3	7.1	0.0	2.8	3.8	5.7	1.7	3.2
EAST ASIA PACIFIC										
Arrivals (millions)	47.8	54.6	56.4	64.2	71.2	76.8	81.4	89.0	88.0	86.6
% annual change	1.6	14.3	3.4	13.8	10.8	7.9	5.9	9.4	–1.1	–1.6
EUROPE										
Arrivals (millions)	266.3	282.9	283.0	302.4	310.1	334.3	338.5	353.3	369.8	381.1
% annual change	10.5	6.2	0.1	6.9	2.5	7.8	1.3	4.4	4.7	3.0
MIDDLE EAST										
Arrivals (millions)	8.6	9.0	8.4	10.9	11.4	12.8	13.5	14.1	14.8	15.0
% annual change	1.4	4.6	–6.6	30.5	4.4	12.3	5.6	4.3	5.3	1.4
SOUTH ASIA										
Arrivals (millions)	3.0	3.2	3.3	3.6	3.5	3.9	4.2	4.4	4.8	5.0
% annual change	6.5	3.9	3.2	9.9	–2.0	10.1	8.6	5.6	9.0	4.1

(Source: WTO 1999, World Tourism Highlights, http: //www.world-tourism.org)

World's top 20 tourism destinations

Rank 1990	Rank 1995	Rank 1998	Countries	Arrivals (000s) 1998
1	1	1	France	70 000
3	3	2	Spain	47 749
2	2	3	United States	46 395
4	4	4	Italy	34 829
7	5	5	UK	25 750
12	8	6	China	25 073
8	7	7	Mexico	19 810
10	11	8	Canada	18 825
27	9	9	Poland	18 820
6	10	10	Austria	17 352
9	13	11	Germany	16 511
16	12	12	Czech Republic	16 325
17	18	13	Russian Federation	15 810
5	6	14	Hungary	15 000
14	17	15	Portugal	11 200
13	16	16	Greece	11 077
11	14	17	Switzerland	11 025
19	15	18	China, Hong Kong SAR	9 575
20	22	19	Netherlands	9 102
24	20	20	Turkey	8 960

(Source: WTO 1999, World Tourism Highlights, www.world-tourism.org)

2 The historical development of tourism

Learning outcomes

After reading this chapter and answering the questions, you should be able to:

- Understand the principal factors that have influenced the development of tourism in the last 200 years.
- Recognize that an explanation for the development of tourism in a given location or time is often due to a combination of political, economic, social and technological influences.

Overview

Throughout history people have travelled for many different reasons. Travel for pleasure purposes is essentially a more recent phenomenon which has grown rapidly in the last 200 years. From the end of the eighteenth century when only the wealthy few could indulge, tourism has developed into something which many ordinary people consider as a necessity. The development of tourism is bound together with other political, economic, social and technological influences which have a much wider impact. While tourism is now a significant source of income and employment for many nations, it is particularly vulnerable to variations at the macro-level and as such is a volatile industry.

Introduction: tourism before the twentieth century

Domestic travel for pleasure purposes, along lines we could recognize today, began in the eighteenth century. The aristocracy and upper classes made 'Grand' tours of Europe and beyond and within the United Kingdom and northern Europe those who could afford to visited seaside resorts and spa towns. This form of tourism might be more accurately described as 'health tourism', in as much as the drinking of sea water was purported (by a Dr R. Russell in 1750) to contain health-giving properties (Burkart and Medlik 1981; Holloway 1998).

Towards the end of the eighteenth century sea bathing had become popular among the upper classes, with George IV visiting places such as Brighton and Weymouth in the 1780s and the Royal Sea-Bathing Infirmary opened at Margate in 1796 (Burkart and Medlik 1981). According to Walton (1983: 216), referring to the writer William Hutton, who remarked in 1788 that 'Wherever people in the high life take the lead, the next class eagerly follow', this shows how tourism had begun to develop. This theme, where either the 'elite' or 'adventurous' first visit a destination or make an activity fashionable which is subsequently followed by others, is one that was to continue for the next 200 years.

Back in the eighteenth century however, it was 'only the rich and leisured people in society (who) had the free time and money required to travel outside their own immediate area' (Davidson 1993: 5). Another historical theme emerges here; as technological advances take place so does the opportunity for some to earn more and take advantage of greater levels of disposable income and free time for leisure purposes. Certainly, the industrial revolution in northern Europe in the late eighteenth and nineteenth centuries saw 'the value of money increase, and the middle and upper class found they could afford to taste the delights of a week by the briny' (Hern 1967: 151).

The fact that some in society had the financial means to participate in leisure travel is only a partial explanation of the factors that initiated tourism. Time free from work or other responsibilities is also a crucial determinant. In the UK, legislation to create public or 'bank' holidays came in 1871 (four days per year) and as Robinson (1976: 5) states this caused the 'gradual emergence of the week's holiday'.

As well as money and time, the means of travel is another crucial factor in facilitating tourism. In the period from 1900, railways had a significant effect on leisure travel. According to Hern (1967: 8) 'it was the railway that brought an even bigger change in atti-

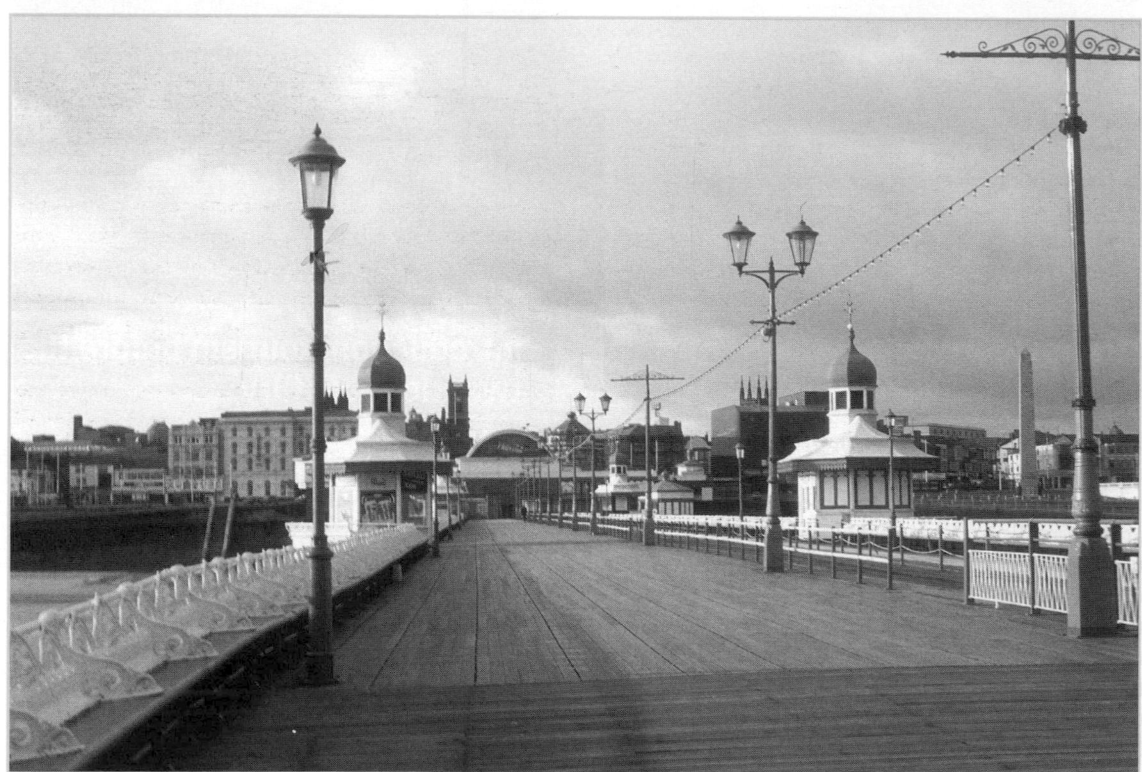

Plate 2.1 Blackpool Pier, UK

A relic of a bygone age, Blackpool Pier is one of three piers built by Victorian developers in the resort which provided an attraction for people to promenade on. The construction of piers in Victorian times in the UK also provided a demonstration of man's power over nature.

tudes, for it changed the class structure of the English Seaside Holiday'. Thomas Cook is widely credited with using railways for leisure travel with guided tours from the early 1840s, through to European and Far East tours by the 1860s. As an example of the level of leisure travel in the mid-Victorian period, there were some 5,000 miles of railway and Brighton received some 132,000 visitors by train in a single day in 1862 (Burkart and Medlik 1981). The coming of the railway enabled people to travel further, faster and at a relatively affordable price.

In line with growing affluence, free time and improved transport systems, seaside resorts developed quickly toward the end of the nineteenth century. 'In England and Wales the number of rail travellers increased twenty fold between 1840 and 1870 and the resorts accounted for their full share of this traffic' (Walton 1983: 24). As more and more people were able to travel so a 'resort hierarchy developed and certain places were seen as embodiments of mass tourism to be despised and ridiculed' (Urry 1990: 16). It is certainly the case that some places consolidated their position as premier seaside resorts (e.g. Brighton and Blackpool), with other locations at an earlier stage in their development.

Butler (1980) developed a model to show how resorts developed over time, moving from the initial stage being 'found' (exploration), through the 'involvement' and 'development' stages to a 'stagnation' stage. Beyond this a number of options are possible from decline to rejuvenation. This is shown in Figure 2.1.

Figure 2.1 **The Butler model of resort development**

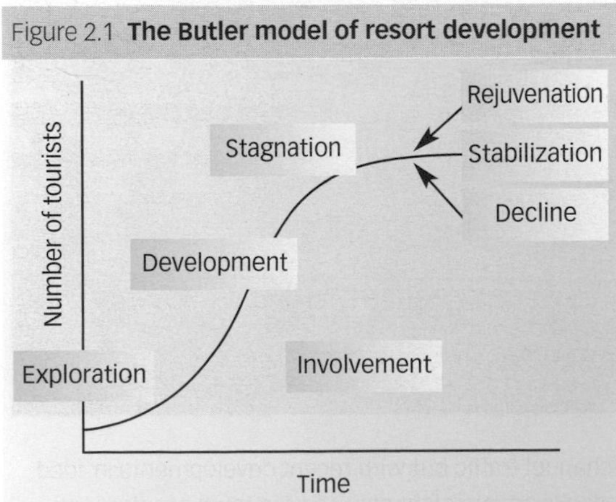

(Source: Modified from Butler 1980)

During the nineteenth century many seaside resorts in the UK were in the involvement or development stages and were not to peak until well into the twentieth century. However, such growth was not uniform. Even locations in close proximity grew at different rates. Agarwal (1997) shows how the Torbay towns of Torquay, Paignton and Brixham in south-west England developed at different rates (see Table 2.1).

In considering the development of tourism before the twentieth century it would be possible to go back to religious pilgrimages of many centuries ago. However, it is fair to argue that in much of the developed world aspects such as increased incomes, availability of free time, the development of railways, concerns over health and an elite class whom others could emulate prompted a growing demand for leisure travel. This began as day trips initially in the late eighteenth century and increasingly throughout the nineteenth century. It was this form of tourism that was to develop further in the twentieth century.

Tourism in the twentieth century: *c.* 1900–1939

The development of tourism in the early part of the twentieth century has numerous themes and exogenous factors. Important are the economic, social and political climate as well as aspects discussed in the previous section, such as affluence, holiday entitlement and technological advances. In the early part of the twentieth century travel was expanding due to growing affluence and continued improvements in transport systems. War, however, was to have a marked effect on many nations and in many ways in 1914 and again in 1939.

Following World War I (1914–18) there was fluctuating prosperity, depression and recovery. Although there was a world-wide economic depression in this period between 1929–31, such efforts were not evenly distributed. Severe unemployment in the UK in some regions (in unskilled occupations) was off-set to some extent by other areas and occupational groups where the economy was making people more wealthy than before (Constantine 1983). In terms of free time, there was a growing recognition of the value of a holiday. Whereas the Bank Holidays Act of 1871 had 'ensured not only crowded trains, but crowded

Table 2.1 **Torbay: stages of resort development**

Stage	Torquay	Paignton	Brixham
Exploration	*c.* 1769–1830	*c.* 1790–1870	*c.* 1880–1920
Involvement	*c.* 1831–1910	*c.* 1871–1918	*c.* 1921–1950
Development	*c.* 1910–1950	*c.* 1919–1950	*c.* 1950–1975

(Source: Agarwal 1997: 69)

beaches' (Briggs 1983: 300), longer holidays were to become more typical. Before the outbreak of World War II the Amulree Report led to the Holidays with Pay Act 1938 (Haywood *et al.* 1989). While this only established voluntary agreements with employers, between 1931 and 1939 the number of workers entitled to paid holidays increased from 1.5 million to 11 million (Constantine 1983). This, coupled with a shorter working week (from 54 hours in 1919 to 48 hours by 1939) (Haywood *et al.* 1989) and a doubling of average weekly wages over the same period (Constantine 1983), all contributed to the development of tourism, particularly in the form of the seaside holiday. It was quite common for factories to close down for a week or fortnight during the summer months thus giving all workers the same holiday entitlement. This 'mass exodus' meant that many workers travelled at the same time to similar

Plate 2.2 Marine Parade, Dover, UK

This Victorian accommodation developed to serve the cross-channel traffic but with recent developments in tourist accommodation, much of the passing trade no longer seeks an overnight stay and the town has declined in terms of the resort life-cycle model.

destinations. Briggs (1983: 300) notes that this was why the resort of Morecambe was nicknamed 'Bradford-by-the-Sea'.

A number of authors (Haywood *et al.* 1989; Lickorish and Jenkins 1997) note that by the 1930s holidays had become an expected part of life by many in employment rather than a luxury preserved for the elite. Improvements elsewhere fuelled the demand for leisure travel. While the 'masses' may have taken a short annual holiday by the sea, wealthier individuals took advantage of technological advances in transportation systems and took more exotic holidays by ocean-liner, aeroplane or motor car. The freedom the car was to offer was quickly recognized. In 1920 there were 200,000 cars on British roads, rising to 1 million by 1930 and 2 million by 1939 (Burton 1995). In addition to private cars, long-distance bus services in the form or 'charabancs' began to challenge the railways for speed, comfort and convenience. Lavery (1989) notes the growing trend towards coach travel during the 1930s, with 37 million passengers being carried on long-distance services and tours in 1939. In continental Europe coach travel for holiday purposes was also widely used in France, Switzerland and Italy.

In an international context, Douglas and Douglas (2000) examined the growth of the P&O steamer routes and their impact on tourist travel from the UK and Europe to the Far East, especially the greater expansion of cruises after the opening of the Suez canal in 1869. P&O's association with the Thomas Cook company ensured that:

> greater numbers of visitors to India, Malaysia and often beyond were in the hands of British travel entrepreneurs. Cook and Sons having rendered most of Europe safe for British travellers undertook their first world tour in 1872–73 (20 days at 1 pound a day), not surprisingly using P&O ships for the main sea travel...By 1886, Cook and P&O were organising trips from Bombay to Jeddah for moslem pilgrims, an activity for which the shipping company later built a special vessel. (Douglas and Douglas 2000: 32–33)

In the case of the South Pacific, similar developments associated with cruising have also been documented by Douglas and Douglas (1996) where they observed the impact of the Canadian–Australian Royal Mail Steamship Line and the New Zealand Union Steamship Line in developing tourism in Fiji with stopover traffic at Suva after 1893. By 1930, monthly services provided by steamships had acted as a catalyst for international tourism and form the precursor of the modern-day luxury liners that called at South Pacific ports. Douglas and Douglas (1996) examined the process in other parts of the South Pacific including Melanesia and Hawaii as well as the emergence of the South Pacific as the playground of European and American tourists. There is also a degree of continuity in the decline and subsequent rebirth of the South Pacific as a cruise ship destination, with vessels calling at many of the ports which had developed in the nineteenth century.

In terms of other forms of long-distance travel, transatlantic crossings between Europe and North America had been possible since 1838 and the following year Samuel Cunard founded the Cunard Line after winning the lucrative North Atlantic mail contract (Briggs 1983). By the 1930s, however, sea travel had expanded considerably and cruising was a popular form of travel among those who could afford to travel this way. Air travel had become a novel form of travel for the elite following, for example, Louis Bleriot flying from France to England in 1909 and the tour operator, Thomas Cook, offering 'Ariel Travel for Business or Pleasure' from 1909. As Coltman (1989) notes, Britain began to subsidize air travel in the 1920s and from this national airlines emerged, while in the USA their growth and development has been linked to the growth of US mail contracts.

In the early twentieth century there were many economic and social changes, particularly during the Edwardian years (1901–1914) in the UK, Europe and North America when these changes impacted upon the recreation and leisure behaviour of the population, with some further expansion of tourism opportunities for the middle and working classes (Clarke and Crichter 1985). Increased leisure time, paid holidays and developments in transport inspired and enabled many to travel, expanding the geographical extent of domestic tourism in many countries dependent upon the transport infrastructure available and its cost. At the same time, following the Edwardian period and aftermath of World War I, a period of economic fragility and austerity, unemployment and financial hardship followed which supressed many of the initial opportunities made available in the Edwardian period. Lower cost forms of domestic tourism, particularly the rise of holiday homes on the fringe of urban areas such as in London's green belt (Hall and Page 1999), provided a substitute for holidays in times of austerity, as did working holidays among the working classes who engaged in traditional activities such as hop picking in Kent when whole families engaged in the activity, living in often cramped conditions. What is apparent is that the development of mass tourism opportunities for the population in specific countries is very much a cyclical process linked to the economy and the availability of disposable income in households. When income is in short supply, cheaper alternatives are often selected.

Tourism in the twentieth century: *c.* 1945–1970

In most developed western countries, there was rapid growth in tourism after World War II. Many aspects, such as holiday entitlements and growing affluence, which affected growth in the previous period continue in the period after 1945, illustrating the continuity as well as change in the way these processes and factors impact upon tourism behaviour. Some of the key events which affected tourism in the post-war period in the UK are summarized in Table 2.2.

Table 2.2 shows that the immediate post-war period was one of continued and rapid growth and recognition of the tourism industry in the UK. The 1950s and 1960s had a great effect not only on tourism throughout the introduction of package holidays by air using charter aircraft, but also in the development of home-centred forms of leisure. Radio and television in the home challenged the cinema as a major form of leisure entertainment. At the same time, growing affluence meant that overseas travel truly came within the grasp of the working classes, having previously been the luxury enjoyed by the upper and middle classes. In contrast to outbound and domestic tourism in the UK, and despite restrictions on overseas currency available for travel, visitors to the UK also became a valuable invisible export for the economy.

One of the major features of tourism in Britain during the inter-war years and through to the

Table 2.2 **Key events in UK tourism, 1945–1970**

Date	Event	Explanation
1945	Holiday camps popular form of domestic tourism	After opening first camp in Skegness in 1937, Butlin had 200 camps accommodating 30,000 guests/week by 1939. Popular as 'all-in' package – one aspect causing shift from traditional resorts
1947	British Tourist and Holiday Board formed Town and Country Planning Act	Stirrings of recognition of public sector involvement in terms of planning for tourism
1948	500,000 overseas visitors to UK	UK now established as holiday destination in overseas markets
1949	National Parks and Access to Countryside Act	National Parks established in England and Wales throughout 1950s – become popular destination for leisure purposes particularly with growth of car ownership
1950	Vladimir Riatz organises first 'mass' air package holiday	300 passengers taken to Corsica as an experiment, soon operating profitably and attracting other operators

Table 2.2 ***continued***

1955	1 million overseas visitors to UK spending £11 million	Visiting friends and relatives market (VFR) becomes important to transport carriers
1958	Boeing 707 – commercially successful jet aircraft introduced	Coupled with rising popularity of air travel and package holidays – enhances growth
1959	M1, UK's first motorway, opened	By 1970 car-borne holidays far exceed railways as a means of transport for holidays
1960	Caravan Sites and Control of Development Act	Further recognition of need for sensitive planning for tourism
1961	Carlton Tower, first skyscraper hotel in London, opened	London well established as focus for overseas visitors to UK
1964	British Travel and Holidays Association (ABTA) becomes British Travel Association	Rationalization and formalization of public sector tourism needed to realize benefits of tourism as eaner of foreign currency
1965	Association of British Travel Agents (ABTA) introduces 'Operation Stabiliser'	Growth of tourism so rapid that some operators go bankrupt leaving tourists stranded/deposits lost. Leads to realization that consumer protection necessary in tourism. ABTA at forefront in anticipation of legislation
1966	Prestige Hotels, first major co-operative marketing group formed	Co-operation to become feature (of horizontal integration in this case) as do other forms of business integration
1968	Countryside Act	Established Countryside Commission (with recreational role) and enables local authorities to set up Countryside Parks
	Transport Act	Provides British Waterways Board with recreation and amenity duties
	Interchange Hotels formed	Second major co-operative marketing group
1969	Development of Tourism Act	Creates statutory tourist boards in England, Wales, Scotland and Northern Ireland and British Tourist Authority. Also introduces hotel development incentives scheme
1970	Trust Houses Merge with Forte	Large hotel chains a feature of accommodation sector

(Source: Modified from Burkart and Medlik 1974; Holloway 1988; Lavery 1989; Lickorish and Jenkins 1997)

1950s and 1960s was the development of the holiday camp. Ward and Hardy (1986) provide a detailed history of the development of holiday camps in the UK, showing that they date back to 1897, with a camp for young men on the Isle of Man. The entrepreneur Billy Butlin is often credited with the concept and development of holiday camps and certainly Butlin's skill was important in its development in the UK. By 1948, it was estimated that 1 in 20 of all holidaymakers in the UK stayed at a Butlin's holiday camp each year (Ward and Hardy 1986: 75). However, from the 1960s the popularity of holiday camps diminished and Table 2.3 shows how, in some locations, the number of camps reduced between 1939 and 1986. Holiday camps as a type of holiday are not restricted to the UK. Exhibit 2.1 shows how Club Méditerranée in Europe grew and continues to offer holidays world-wide (something which Butlin's never did).

Table 2.3 **Top ten holiday campsites in England and Wales, 1939 and 1986**

Location	1939	1986
Skegness	19	1
Towyn	13	0
Ingoldmells	9	0
Rhyl	7	0
Humberston	7	0
Abergele	6	0
Mablethorpe	6	0
Hopton-on-Sea	5	2
Paignton	4	2
New Romney	3	1

Tourism in the twentieth century: post-1970

Tourism in the latter part of the twentieth century shows many features that earlier parts of the century display. The theme of continued expansion remains applicable. By 1997 some 25.5 million overseas visitors came to Britain spending £12 billion (in 1964, 3.3 million overseas visitors came to Britain with a value of £190 million) (BTA 2000). In terms of domestic tourism there were some 134 million trips with a value of £15 billion in 1997 (BTA 2000). The number of domestic trips (UK residents in the UK) has remained relatively constant, though the value has increased. The number of overseas trips by UK resident has increased from 27 million in 1987 to 46 million in 1997 (BTA 2000). The explanation of this present position is similarly due to a range of political, economic, social and technological factors.

Since 1970, the political recognition of tourism as an important part of the British economy has been maintained. While the 1969 Development of Tourism Act laid down a public sector structure, other legislation has also affected the private sector. In 1970, tour operators were required to have an Air Travel Organisers Licence (ATOL) and within the accommodation sector incentives were introduced for the construction of hotels and tourist facilities. Attempts to bring in an accommodation rating scheme failed, resulting in voluntary registration. Following a change of government in 1979 a period of 'economic realism' set in, whereby public sector funding for a variety of services was questioned. This era saw the replacement of former principles of economic management of the national economy based on Keynsian economics (i.e. the use of public expenditure to reflate the economy and pursuit of full employment) with the new monetary economics which sought to replace the state expenditure with a greater role for the private sector to control the money supply and address inflation. In a deflationary environment, public spending on leisure and tourism at national, regional and local state levels was threatened when scarce funds needed to be allocated on a wide range of welfare provision. Consequently, in the 1980s the attitude of the state towards public sector funding for leisure and tourism moved from one of direct financial support

Exhibit 2.1 **Club Méditerranée**

In the late 1930s Billy Butlin's 'super organized' holiday at 'Sunny Skegness', began to be advertised in the UK. Following World War II Butlin's and other holiday camps, such as those from Pontin's, grew rapidly in terms of holiday destinations for domestic holidays within the UK. In Europe, however, it was not until 1950 that Belgian Olympic water polo champion, Gérard Blitz, founded Club Méditerranée (later to become abbreviated to Club Med). Initially, 'le club', was a single village location, Alcudia, on the Balearic island of Mallorca. Blitz, who was later joined by Gilbert Trigano, had the idea for a pre-paid holiday in a hassle-free location where holidaymakers, referred to as 'Gentil Membres' (GMs) could get back to nature and exercise. The concept grew quickly in popularity and in 1954 Club Med opened a ski village in Leysin, Switzerland. Club Med is now a world-wide concern with 105 holiday villages in 33 countries and a cruise ship. Nowadays more flexibility in approach is permitted among the GMs as opposed to the original concept and Club Med aims to attract all types of tourist from single adults, through families to older couples.

(Source: www.clubmed.com)

to passive encouragement and a greater emphasis on user-pay philosophies and leisure as a discretionary rather than a mandatory activity. Previous pump-priming funding for tourism called 'Section 4 Grant Aid' that had been provided under the terms of the 1969 Development of Tourism Act was revoked in England removing the mechanism used to stimulate capital projects. Throughout Europe, legislation for the tourism industry has also been a feature of recent developments which has replaced the state subsidies for tourism with regional incentives for development in areas of decline and high socio-economic deprivation, so that new employment opportunities can be created in 'peripheral regions'. European legislation has also introduced measures to liberalize air and road transport, the harmonization of hotel classifications, the easing of frontier controls and efforts to balance VAT and duty-free regulations in a bid to ease the flow of tourism at a transnational level, so that barriers to tourism are removed.

Politics can influence the tourism industry in other ways too. Disputes can seriously impede travel, especially when conditions escalate. During the 1990s, ethnic conflict in the former Yugoslavia has all but decimated the tourism industry there. Statistics show that arrivals from the UK to Yugoslavia peaked at 656,000 in 1990, after which they fell to 22,000 by 1992 (BTA 2000). In 1991 the Gulf War crisis led to a significant decline in travel from the USA to Europe for several months. In terms of arrivals to the UK, it was 1994 before arrivals reached 1990 levels (BTA 2000). Lickorish and Jenkins (1997) estimate that some 2 million visits and 2 billion dollars worth of traffic to Europe was lost as a result of the conflict. Clearly for the tourism industry such aspects are difficult to foresee, but even relatively short events can have disastrous consequences. The effects of the Gulf War in preventing travel was one of the reasons suggested for the downfall of the International Leisure Group (ILG). At the time ILG was the UK's second largest tour operator (with names such as Intasun, Select and Club 18–30) and airline (Air Europe). While financial difficulties with one of ILGs major shareholders was instrumental, the fact that in the early part of 1991 bookings were seriously down because of people's wariness to travel (in addition to economic factors) played a part in the ultimate bankruptcy of the company.

The explanation of certain events affecting the tourism industry are often due to a combination of factors rather than a single influence. Political issues affecting the industry are difficult to explain without reference to economic factors. In the UK, economic recession in 1980 was the deepest since the 1930s and supressed some aspects of tourism demand. However, in the period since 1970 there has been a rise in affluence of most people in employment within the UK. Between 1971 and 1997 real household disposable income per head nearly doubled, with an equivalent average annual growth rate of 2.6 per cent (ONS 1999). Further recession in the early 1990s, while impacting some parts of the tourism industry, had beneficial effects on others. Economic uncertainty due to high interest rates and fear of redundancy may have caused many consumers to abandon plans for expensive overseas holidays. As a result domestic tourism within the UK grew by 4.5 per cent in 1991 (ONS 1999).

Other exogenous factors affecting society as a whole also influence the tourism industry. As with other developed countries, the UK has seen a declining birth rate and ageing population. Data from the Office for National Statistics (1999) show that births have decreased from 963,000 in 1971 to 745,000 in 1997, while the proportion of people aged over 75 years has increased from 5 per cent to 7 per cent in the same time period. While at one time it may have been possible to consider those who were retired and the elderly as a single group, increasing life expectancy and retirement at a younger age means this is no longer possible. Assuming the financial means are available, early retirement is often now synonymous with a higher propensity to travel. Lickorish and Jenkins (1997) also note that a declining family size may mean that greater family resources are available for holidays. All of these factors point towards an explanation for the increase in the volume of tourism, domestically, in international terms and within the short-break market.

Earlier sections have shown that technological advances had a major bearing on the development of tourism and in the period since 1970 this theme has continued. While the selection of 1970 may be somewhat arbitrary as a category threshold, it was the year that a technological breakthrough in air transport occurred. Lavery (1996) notes that the Boeing 747, the first wide-bodied jet was introduced on a global scale, capable of travelling at 608 mph with 350 passengers. As a result the unit cost per seat fell sharply resulting in an increased supply at cheaper cost. Moreover, by 1980 when Concorde was brought into service, speeds of 1400 mph were possible and transatlantic flights could be made in less than three hours. The introduction of new aircraft such as the Boeing 747–500, which can travel at 620 mph and seat 500 passengers (Lavery 1996), can further reduce the time and cost of travel.

Other technological advances include the opening of the Channel Tunnel transport system, linking France and the UK, in 1994. The system operates with three elements: Eurotunnel, which owns and operates the physical infrastructure; the Shuttle rail service moving passengers, cars and freight between Folkstone and Calais; and Eurostar, a direct passenger service running between London, Paris and Brussels.

By the end of the 1990s, Europe remained the UK's most popular outbound destination, with some 41.5 million visits (BTA 2000). However, as Cope (2000) reports, Europe's popularity had decreased slightly as more UK citizens travelled to the Americas, Africa, Asia and Australia/New Zealand. These trends are shown in Table 2.4. This suggests that in line with other developed countries, outbound travel is becoming more adventurous with long-haul travel to Australasia and Asia-Pacific growing even though North America and Europe remained the dominant destinations in 1998.

Conclusion

This chapter has shown that the development of tourism in the last 200 years has been inextricably linked to political, economic, social and techno-

Table 2.4 **UK outbound visits by region, 1990–1998**

Visits (million)	1990	1995	1998
Europe	26.3	34.7	41.5
Americas	2.4	3.4	4.5
Africa	0.7	1.0	1.2
Middle East	0.2	0.4	0.4
Asia	0.8	1.3	1.6
Australia/New Zealand	0.3	0.4	0.5
Other	0.4	0.5	1.0
Total	31.2	41.9	50.7

(Source: Modified from Cope 2000)

logical influences. While the general theme has been one of growth there are some exceptions and conditions which should be borne in mind. First, tourism is not and never has been a universal activity for all. Throughout history those without the financial means or time available have not been able to participate. While the proportion of those in this category has decreased it has not been eliminated and in recent years the proportion of those not taking a holiday has remained fairly constant. As Crouch (1999) notes, even those in work are finding it increasingly difficult to take time from work and holidays in the future may become more frequent, shorter, spread throughout the year and more intensive.

This leads to a second conclusion, that of the development of the tourism product itself. This chapter has shown that destinations move through a cycle of development which lead to a stage of consolidation (at least) or decline (at worst). Social changes in fashion and a theme of 'been there, done that' means that new types of holiday and activities are needed. A feature of the development of tourism in some locations is the obsolescence of the once popular accommodation stock, now being put to alternative uses or pulled down.

A third feature of the development of tourism that should be considered is the volatility of the market. Again, it is a combination of factors sometimes operating at a macro-level that can have far reaching effects on the industry. Aspects such as political and economic stability in the generating area and destination are crucial. At any time specific changes in tax policies, the value of currency and controls on tourist spending can affect the number of tourists travelling from a country. Similarly, price, competition and the quality or popularity of the product can influence the destination area. History has shown that such aspects can be susceptible to rapid change and greatly alter the tourism industry. When all of these are added to changing consumer tastes and fashion it can be seen why tourism can be seen to be volatile.

Discussion questions

1. Suggest how employment changes have affected tourism.
2. Suggest how economic changes have affected tourism in the last 100 years.
3. Show how changes in fashion have affected the popularity of selected destinations.
4. What different types of tourist go on holiday in the UK and why?

References

Agarwal, S. (1997) 'The resort cycle and seaside tourism: an assessment of its applicability and validity', *Tourism Management,* **18** (2): 65–73.

Briggs, A. (1983) *A Social History of England,* London: BCA.

British Tourist Authority (2000) *Digest of Tourism Statistics No. 23,* London: BTA.

Burkart, A. and Medlik, S. (1981) *Tourism: Past, Present and Future,* second edition, London: Heinemann.

Burton, R. (1995) *Travel Geography,* second edition, London: Pitman.

Butler, R.W. (1980) 'The concept of the tourist area cycle of evolution: implications for management of resources', *Canadian Geographer,* **24** (1): 5–12.

Clarke, J. and Crichter, C. (1985) *The Devil Makes Work: Leisure in Capitalist Britain,* Basingstoke: Macmillan.

Coltman, M. (1989) *Introduction to Travel and Tourism: An International Approach,* New York: Van Nostrand Reinhold.

Constantine, S. (1983) *Social Conditions in Britain 1918–39,* London: Methuen.

Cope, R. (2000) 'UK outbound', *Travel and Tourism Intelligence,* (1): 19–39.

Internet resources

By going to the weblink at www.thomsonlearning.co.uk students can access the following study on the Thomson Learning website. The study is from C. M. Hall and S. J. Page (eds) (1996) *Tourism in the Pacific: Issues and Cases* by N. Douglas and N. Douglas on 'Tourism in the Pacific: historical factors. In it students will be able to examine the issues which can explain how tourism developed in a diverse region such as the South Pacific and the role of western nations and colonialism in the tourism development process.

Crouch, S. (1999) 'Relationship marketing', *Tourism – The Journal of the Tourism Society*, **99**: 13–15.

Davidson, R. (1993) *Tourism*, second edition, London: Longman.

Douglas, N. and Douglas, N. (1996) 'Tourism in the Pacific: historical factors', in C.M. Hall and S.J. Page (eds) (1996) *Tourism in the Pacific: Issues and Cases*, London: Thomson Learning: 19–35.

Douglas, N. and Douglas, N. (2000) 'Tourism in South East and South Asia: historical dimensions', in C.M. Hall and S.J. Page (eds) *Tourism in South and South East Asia: Issues and Cases*, Oxford: Butterworth-Heinemann: 29–44.

Hall, C.M. and Page, S.J. (1999) *The Geography of Tourism and Recreation: Environment, Place and Space*, London: Routledge.

Hern, A. (1967) *The Seaside Holiday: The History of the English Seaside Resort*, London: Crescent Press.

Haywood, L., Kew, F. and Bramham, P. (1989) *Understanding Leisure*, Cheltenham: Stanley Thornes.

Holloway, J.C. (1998) *The Business of Tourism*, fourth edition, Harlow: Longman.

Lavery, P. (1989) *Travel and Tourism*, Huntingdon: Elm.

Lavery, P. (1996) *Travel and Tourism*, third edition, Huntingdon: Elm.

Lickorish, L.J. and Jenkins, C.L. (1997) *An Introduction to Tourism*, Oxford: Butterworth-Heinemann.

Office for National Statistics (ONS) (1999) *Social Trends*, **29**, London: HMSO.

Robinson, H. (1976) *A Geography of Tourism*, Harlow: Longman.

Urry, J. (1990) *The Tourist Gaze: Leisure and Travel in Contemporary Societies*, London: Sage.

Walton, J. (1983) *The English Seaside Resort: A Social History 1750–1914*, Leicester: Leicester University Press.

Ward, C. and Hardy, D. (1986) *Goodnight Campers!: The History of the British Holiday Camp*, London: Mansell.

Further reading

Agarwal, S. (1997) 'The resort cycle and seaside tourism: an assessment of its applicability and validity', *Tourism Management*, **18** (2): 65–73.

Haywood, L., Kew, F. and Bramham, P. (1995) *Understanding Leisure*, second edition, Cheltenham: Stanley Thornes.

Shaw, G. and Williams, A.M. (1994) *Critical Issues in Tourism: A Geographical Perspective*, London: Blackwell.

Ward, C. and Hardy, D. (1986) *Goodnight Campers!: The History of the British Holiday Camp*, London: Mansell.

3 Understanding the tourist: tourism demand

Learning outcomes

After reading this chapter and answering the questions, you should be able to:

- Recognize the different forms of tourism demand.
- Understand the range of factors influencing tourism demand including particular factors at the destination and generating areas.
- Be aware of those influences on tourism demand which the tourism industry can affect from those which are beyond its control.

Overview

Demand for tourism has a number of forms, from tourists who are ready and willing to undertake the activity, through to potential consumers to those who are unwilling to travel. Moreover, there are numerous influences affecting the overall demand for tourism. This chapter discusses the different types of demand and its determinants.

Introduction

According to Hall and Page (1999: 50) 'one of the fundamental questions tourism researchers consistently seek to answer is: why do tourists travel? This seemingly simple proposition remains one of the principal challenges facing tourism research'. Attempting to define demand as a concept is a complex task and it really depends upon the disciplinary perspective which the researcher adopts. For example, the geographer is pre-eminently concerned with 'the total number of persons who travel, or wish to travel, to use tourist facilities and services at places away from their place of work or residence' (Mathieson and Wall 1982: 1). The geographer then examines these issues in a spatial (i.e. geographical) context to assess the impact on domestic and international tourism. In contrast, the economist examines the 'schedule of the amount of any product or service which people are willing to buy at each specific price in a set of possible prices during a specified period of time. Psychologists view demand from the perspective of motivation and behaviour [see Chapter 4 in this book]' (Cooper *et al.* 1993: 15). Attempting to explain what demand means in simple terms is probably expressed most clearly by Pearce (1995) as the relationship between individuals' motivation to travel and their ability to do so. This means that a range of factors influence tourism demand in both the tourist generating and destination areas. However, before examining the factors influencing demand, it is first necessary to consider more closely the different types of demand.

The elements of tourism demand

Aggregate/effective/actual demand

Meaning largely the same, effective or actual demand refers to the precise number of tourists. It is most easily visualized by reference to tourism statistical sources, where the total numbers of people travelling from one country to another or by purpose of visit are shown. Tribe (1995) includes the fact that effective demand refers to more than the desire for a tourist product but that the demand is real and 'backed by cash'. Clearly tourism suppliers require demand for their products, but too much effective demand poses the problem of exceeding the supply of products. As Heape (1997: 8) notes 'the likelihood of demand exceeding supply, for once, has led to a reappraisal of retail discounting. Recently Going Places [a UK travel agency chain] announced that it was ceasing discounting ... partly about a focus on profit but also reflects the wider issue of a possible shortage of holidays'.

Suppressed demand

It is often suggested that suppressed demand can be sub-divided into potential and deferred demand (Cooper *et al.* 1998; Swarbrooke 1999). Both are referring to those who do not travel for some reason, the nature of that reason being the distinguishing factor. With those who might be classified as potential demand, they are more likely to become actual demand in the future when circumstances allow. It may well be that waiting for additional income or holiday entitlement is needed for that suppressed, but potential, demand to become actual or effective. It can be seen that the reason behind potential demand relates more specifically to factors associated directly with the individual. With deferred demand, the reasons for the 'suppression' is down to problems on the supply side. It may be that accommodation shortages, transport difficulties or the weather prevent people from travelling to their chosen destination. Again, though, once such problems are overcome, those in this category move upwards and become effective or actual demand. For the tourism industry it is crucial to ensure that those who could be classified within either of the two suppressed demand categories become effective demand. This is because such individuals represent potential new customers if the stumbling blocks to travel are removed.

No demand

In the previous chapter it was shown that there have always been those who do not participate in tourism. Reasons for this may be a lack of money (which may be resolved later in life) or an unwillingness or inability to find the time necessary. Whether the reasons are through choice or otherwise, those in this category represent 'no demand'. In the context of visitors to tourism attractions, Swarbrooke (1999) questions whether attempts to convert such individuals to visitors are cost effective. It can be seen that demand for tourism has several forms, from those who could be described as a definite 'yes', through 'maybe' to 'no'. What is also suggested is that there is a variety of factors that might influence the demand for tourism products that may affect the individual or the destination.

Factors influencing demand from the tourist generating area

There are numerous factors influencing demand from the tourist generating area and some of the principal factors are illustrated in Table 3.1

From Table 3.1 it can be seen that the range of factors influencing demand from the generating

Table 3.1 **Factors influencing tourist demand**

Economic determinants	**Social–psychological determinants**	**Exogenous determinants**
Personal	Demographic factors	Supply of products
Distribution of incomes	Motivations/preferences	Political/economic stability
Cost of tourism products	Attitudes	Technological advances
Cost of transportation	Amount of leisure time	Access
Value of currency/exchange	Past experiences	Level of tourism development
Government tax policies and controls on tourist spending	Cultural awareness	Barriers to travel e.g. laws

(Source: Modified from Bull 1995; Ioannides and Debbage 1998; Mathieson and Wall 1982; Tribe 1995)

area can be grouped into three broad categories of determinants. Some of the social and psychological determinants are more fully discussed in Chapter 4 and a range of exogenous determinants were discussed in the previous chapter. Here we will concentrate on the economic determinants, with particular reference to income, time, currency and government controls, with a brief discussion of demographic influences.

Personal incomes

The availability of the necessary finance is perhaps the most commonly thought of variable influencing tourism demand. We might all long for an exotic holiday, but the harsh awareness of our bank balance is often an impenetrable barrier. If this is accepted, then increases in personal incomes are likely to influence the demand for tourism. As our income increases, so does our purchasing power and a wider range of tourism products may become available to us. Such aspects are well documented within the tourism literature (Cai 1999; Haywood *et al.* 1995; Ioannides and Debbage 1998; Pearce 1989; Sinclair and Stabler 1997). As was discussed in Chapter 2, incomes in the UK have risen in real terms in the last 30 years and, as such, it is not surprising that a consequential rise in tourism purchases has also occurred (Hall and Page 1999). However, demand for tourism is said to be 'elastic' in that changes or threats to income are likely to influence demand. Certainly during economic recession, it has been shown that spending on tourism products lessens since it is a discretionary rather than an essential item of individual and household expenditure.

Distribution of incomes

Within a tourist generating nation how incomes are distributed is also likely to affect tourism demand. A skewed income distribution, for example where there are relatively few wealthy and many poor, is likely to limit the proportion of people who can afford to travel internationally. In wealthier developed countries, a more equal income distribution may result in a high overall level of tourism demand. Clearly there must also be a willingness to spend on tourism products. According to the Office for National Statistics (1999), in 1995, four in ten households in the UK felt that they could not afford a week's holiday, compared to six in ten in Portugal and one in ten in Germany. This is a point often overlooked by tourism researchers who naturally assume that such barriers do not exist when looking at the tourism generating propensity of the population in individual countries.

What is apparent is that the propensity for holidaymaking, especially multiple departures, is greater among higher occupational and income groups. Those not taking a holiday are more numerous among the lower income groups. Added to this are differences in the patterns of domestic and outbound demand within countries. As with other aspects in society (e.g. unemployment), holidaymaking is not evenly distributed across all social groups, or geographically, within countries. In the UK for example, higher income and socio-economic groups are over-represented as are those living in the more prosperous areas of the South East (Hall and Page 1999).

Holiday entitlements

The growth of leisure time over the last two centuries has greatly increased the amount of time available for tourism, especially in the developed world. According to Gartner (1996) this was a trend which could be observed through the 1980s. Since then the trend has seen some reversal. There are of course variations. In Germany and Italy typical holiday entitlement amounts to 28 days, in addition to 12 or 14 public holidays, whereas ten days is normal in Japan (Gartner 1996). Increases in holiday entitlement are likely to result in increases in tourism demand, as the extra time may allow trips to more distant destinations or longer stays. Conversely, reductions in the time available for leisure is likely to cause a negative effect on the demand for travel.

The patterns of public and school holiday periods give rise to seasonal patterns of tourism demand in developed countries. One aspect which has resulted is the growth of supplemental, shorter holidays in addition to the main holiday, often referred to as short breaks. Low levels of holiday entitlements do act as a real obstacle upon the opportunities for recreational travel, while a high entitlement encourages such travel. Kay and Jackson (1991), in a study of UK adults' recreational constraints, found that 36 per cent of their respondents felt that lack of time was their main limitation to take a holiday.

Value of currency/exchange rates

A destination's exchange rate has a far reaching influence on tourism demand from a generating area. As such, international tourism is highly susceptible to exchange rate fluctuations that can alter the cost of a holiday considerably (Bull 1995; Mathieson and Wall 1982). The potential consequences of changes in exchange rates are immediately acted upon by the tourism industry and travellers alike. Travel to the United Kingdom by US travellers rose and fell in line with exchange rates in the 1980s. Crouch (1994) identified the impact of an unfavourable exchange rate to include: less travel abroad; a reduction in expenditure of length of stay; changes in the method or length of travel time and a reduction in spending by business travellers. While such phenomena are easily comprehended, Sandbach (1999) argues that a movement in exchange rates of at least 10 per cent is necessary before a consequential correlation in visitor movement can be traced and for some destinations (with high international appeal or very strong economies) movements of 20 per cent have been necessary to seriously change tourism demand.

Government tax policies and controls on tourist spending

Approaches taken by governments can greatly influence tourism demand. Examples include exchange control, currency export prohibition, taxation of tourists and residents and visa regulations. Bull (1995) shows that government fiscal and control policies can change tourist flows and specific destinations can gain or lose potential profitability. According to Pearce (1989) more than 100 countries used to have certain restrictions which limited the amount of currency citizens could obtain for foreign travel. It is suggested that the upsurge of Japan as a major tourism generating country is, in part, related to the liberalization of currency exchange regulations and the easing of the procedures for obtaining passports. In much of Eastern Europe, when under communist regimes, overseas travel was strictly controlled. When this was eased, stark changes in the demand for inbound and outbound tourism resulted.

Many governments have used tourism as a source of tax revenue and Bull (1995) notes three specific types:

- taxes on commercial tourism products
- taxes imposed on consumers in the act of being tourists
- user-pays charges.

Some countries impose exit or travel taxes on their residents who wish to travel overseas. To some extent these can be seen as an attempt to deter foreign travel to reverse the detrimental effects of exchange outflows. Generally speaking, such taxes are often too small to significantly prevent tourism consumption. A variety of economic-related factors can be shown to influence tourism demand on the tourism generating area. While over time regulation has reduced and holiday entitlements and incomes have increased, those who are most price or time elastic may be more significantly affected by these economic determinants.

Demographic variables

Although Chapter 4 examines the demographic variables in more detail in terms of tourist motivation to travel, it is evident that a range of demographic variables affect demand. For example, the age of a traveller will often exert an influence on the type of travel product they choose and destination, particularly as research on youth tourism and the backpacker market indicates how influential age is on the selection of this type of experience. The impact of education can also be a major determinant of both employment type and income earning potential and therefore the type of tourism experience one seeks. Similarly, stage in the family life-cycle has a bearing on the availability of time and disposable income available for tourism. Other factors such as home ownership, occupation and ethnic group are increasingly being recognised as major determinants of tourism demand as Exhibit 3.1 suggests.

Factors influencing demand at the tourist destination area

In a similar vein, the level of demand at a tourist destination is influenced by several factors. Dominant among these are the price of the tourism products, the supply of tourism products and services and their overall quality. Moreover, the government of the destination area can affect the trading operations of suppliers or the way tourists purchase goods and services and thereby influence demand.

Price

Tourism suppliers, such as in accommodation and transport sectors may well price their goods or services independently, but a close watch on the reaction of their competitors is clearly necessary (Burkart and

Exhibit 3.1 **Travel patterns of Chinese New Zealanders: tourism, migration and ethnic reunion**

Kathy Feng and Stephen Page

China and its population have emerged as a major contributor to migration in the Asia–Pacific region and as a major exporter of labour, has brought economic benefits to the country of $8 billion in 1994 from remittances (*Migration News* 1997). Furthermore, a significant number of skilled and professional people, students and business investors have emigrated overseas. This has certainly increased since the takeover of Hong Kong. The Chinese migratory wave is part of a world-wide trend of ethnic Chinese people on the move. In turn, this migration of the Chinese is a manifestation of the 'global village' phenomenon, when people of all races world-wide have become much more mobile and move in search of a lifestyle that suits them better. The main unknown relationship is how migration and tourism interact, especially among migration groups with a new outbound travel habit, where the family networks have expanded and evolved into a global network. Ethnicity is also an emerging area of study. Ethnicity is increasingly being recognized as a powerful driver of return visits to relatives and friends in the country of origin of the migrant.

In terms of Chinese immigrants' travel habits and patterns of both domestic and international travel, relatively little is known with a few notable exceptions (e.g. Lew and Wu 1995). In a New Zealand context, local, regional and global processes may be shaping migration, with travel and patterns of tourism that are distinctive and complex. Many forms of migration generate tourism flows, in particular through the geographical extension of friendship and kinship networks. These flows of tourism are very much structured by the life course of migration, with each round of migration creating a new spatial arrangement of friendship and kinship networks, which potentially represent visiting friends and relatives (VFR) tourism flows.

There is a growing interest in the role of ethnic groups as a growing market segment within the literature on consumer behaviour (e.g. Rossiter and Chan 1998) which has implications for tourism marketing in relation to the recognition of niche markets. Research by Thanopoulos and Walle (1998) and Ostrowski (1991) identified the significance of expatriates and the market for outbound and inbound tourism in destinations, a feature explored by King and Gamage (1994) in relation to expatriate travel by Australian immigrants travelling back to Sri Lanka. Ostrowski (1991: 125) outlined the sociological explanations of travel for ethnic reunion where: 'ethnic tourism is foreign travel to an ancestral home without the intention of permanent settlement, emigration or remigration, or undertaking temporary work'. The problem with this type of research area, according to King (1994: 174) is that 'very little attention is paid to travel motivated by ethnic reunion motives'. Research is complicated by the government agencies in origin and destination countries who record VFR on embarkation/disembarkation cards as opposed to reunion motives. As King (1994) argues, national tourism organizations are neglecting a powerful market segment where the visitor profile is poorly understood. In fact King (1994: 174) argues that:

> For ethnic reunion travellers, such motivation commonly derives from a sense of belonging to or identifying with a way of life that has been left behind. The sense of lost 'roots' is a potent influence for travel and affects successive generations of migrants, not only the first. It is a particularly strong influence in the countries of North America and Australasia whose recent history has been built on a history of migration, but is also significant in other parts of the world, such as Africa.

The most frequently cited study of travel for ethnic reunion is that of Greek-Americans in Ohio by Thanopoulos and Walle (1988) which argued that over 1 million Greek residents in the USA were potential travellers to Greece. Ostrowski (1991) also pursued this line of argument with the post-communist changes in Poland, inferring that there were similar opportunities for Poland in nurturing the ethnic reunion market. But why is ethnic reunion so important for tourism?

Once the individual/family emigrates, the conditions in the host country and process of adaptation are taken into account together with the challenge posed by a new culture, expatriate acculturation process, sociological factors (e.g. language ability and family and kinship ties) and the opportunities in the local labour market which also affect the individual/family's perceived assimilation into the host community. In the new country, existing and perceived family networks and links with other new immigrants also combine to establish a sense of belonging to the country of origin. One can also infer from the existing literature on migration and acculturation, that over time, the local conditions prevailing in the host country together with the strength of family and kinship ties will influence the patterns of domestic and international tourism. In the case of domestic tourism, the immigrants will develop a domestic tourism activity pattern whereby the key tourist sites and attractions are visited as a means of establishing a sense of belonging in the country and to understand the nature of their new country, following the itineraries of overseas visitors from similar ethnic groups. It is in the international travel patterns, however, where the pursuit of ethnic reunion has the most powerful influence, tending to dominate the travel patterns of new emigrants when they are able to afford and have opportunities to travel overseas.

The Chinese population in New Zealand

In 1986, the removal of immigration barriers in New Zealand diversified the ethnic base of the population. Immigration has become the main factor in the growth of the Chinese population in New Zealand. This accounted for 83 per cent of growth between 1986 and 1991; and 75 per cent of growth between 1991 to 1996 (New Zealand Official Yearbook 1998). This resulted in the Chinese population increasing to 40,158 people in 1991 and 70,227 in 1996 (Statistics New Zealand Census 1992, 1997). As a result, the Chinese ethnic group constituted the largest minority group of Asian origin in New Zealand in 1996 (see Table 3.2). More than half (44,184 in 1996) of the country's Chinese New Zealanders live in Auckland and more than half of these were newcomers. About 77 per cent Chinese were born overseas, particularly in Asia. These data indicate that the majority of Chinese New Zealanders are first-generation settlers. More than 70 per cent of Chinese migrants came to New Zealand after the new immigration policy commenced, particularly after 1991 when the 'Point System' was introduced.

Table 3.2 **The population of Chinese residents in New Zealand by birthplace, 1996**

	NZ	Australia	Pacific Island	UK and Ireland	Europe and former USSR	North America	Asia
Male	8 085	90	159	102	36	75	24 990
Female	7 578	84	162	87	33	90	27 894
Total	15 663	174	321	192	69	162	52 881

	Other	Total overseas born	Not specified	Total	Total NZ
Male	117	25 569	255	33 909	1 777 461
Female	141	28 488	252	36 318	1 840 839
Total	255	54 057	504	70 227	3 618 303

(Source: Statistics New Zealand 1997)

In a recent study by Feng and Page (2000) of a sample of Chinese New Zealanders in Auckland which considered their travel habits and the significance of ethnic reunion, they identified the main destinations for overseas travel. Table 3.3 indicates that 23 per cent of Chinese New Zealanders travelled overseas once between January 1997 and June 1999 which was a period of two and half years. During the same period, 19 per cent travelled overseas twice, 10 per cent took three trips, 2 per cent travelled four times and nearly 4 per cent travelled five times or more, while 41 per cent did not take any overseas trip. In other words, 59 per cent of Chinese New Zealanders took at least one overseas trip in the past two and half years. Meanwhile, New Zealanders made 1,162,757 overseas trips in the year ended September 1998 (Page 1999a). Given an estimated total population of 3,792,000 for New Zealand (New Zealand Official Yearbook 1998), at most 31 per cent of New Zealanders made a visit overseas.

Table 3.3 **Number of overseas visits, January 1997–June 1999 (sample size N=358)**

Number of overseas visits	Respondents count	Percentage of total
0	148	41.46
1	83	23.25
2	68	19.05
3	37	10.36
4	8	2.24
5 or more	13	3.64
Not specified	1	

(Source: Feng 1999)

Table 3.4 shows that China is a dominant destination for Chinese New Zealanders, as 50 per cent of the respondents who travelled in the given period of time visited China. Among the respondents who travelled to China, more than 91 per cent of them were born in China. The remaining percentage of the respondents originated from Hong Kong, New Zealand and Taiwan. Thus, it is apparent from the survey that those who were born in China are more likely to visit China as one of their outbound travel destinations.

Table 3.4 **Outbound travel destinations, January 1997–June 1999**

Country	Respondents	Percentage (%)
China	104	50.00
Australia	64	30.77
Japan	3	1.44
Singapore	23	11.06
Hong Kong	93	44.71
South Korea	1	0.49
Taiwan	21	10.19
Thailand	7	3.37
USA	19	9.13
Canada	10	4.81
UK	2	0.97
France	3	1.44
Malaysia	15	7.21
Indonesia	2	0.96
Fiji	6	2.88
Other countries	7	3.37

(Source: Feng 1999)

If 'ethnic tourism' is related to immigrants choosing their countries of origin as their outbound travel destination, the results from Feng and Page (2000) reveal a high predisposition towards ethnic tourism among the Chinese immigrants in New Zealand. The New Zealand Chinese ethnic groups in the survey tended to travel back to their countries of birth as their principal choice of outbound destination. This indicates the close linkage between the Chinese immigrants' adopted country (New Zealand) and their countries of birth. In a theoretical context, Cohen (1997) discusses the complex process of globalization (see Chapter 5 for more detail) and the link to global diasporas (migratory movements) and the way that ethnic groups now identify with both their host country and place of origin in a global environment in which many people now operate. This is particularly the case when the majority of the population are recent immigrants as the family ties and ethnic links are still close and there is also an identity and association with the new country they have settled in. The argument is supported by the study of Australian Vietnamese travel patterns (Nguyen and King 1998). That study revealed that most Australian Vietnamese (most of the first generation) expressed a desire to travel back to reaffirm their ethnic links as soon as they had the opportunity to do so.

As a result of the close linkage between their adopted country and their countries of origin, it is suggested that Chinese New Zealanders could have high demand for travelling for ethnic reunion purposes. This, according to King (1994), implies that ethnic reunion has a high level of awareness owing to family connections and shared cultural values. For the tourism industry, considering Chinese New Zealanders' travel frequency and the potential two-way flows of migrants returning to their home country and friends and relatives visiting them in their adopted country offers a market opportunity. Thus, the ethnic group is a potential niche market which is frequently overlooked. Airlines may miss potential business opportunities as there are no direct flights from New Zealand to China. Of course, there are other implications which airlines need to consider before opening new routes. Moreover, King (1994) argued that ethnic tourism, as a form of tourism and in turn, as a form of migration, is an important market segment. This exhibit also highlights the significance of demographic factors such as ethnicity in the determination of patterns of tourism demand.

Medlik 1981). The relationship between price and demand is an inverse one. Higher prices result in lower demand and vice versa. Low prices in Spain and the Balearic Islands caused huge demand from UK tourists in the 1960s, 1970s and 1980s. However, in a volatile market, fashion and environmental damage combined to cause a downturn in the region's popularity. In addition to the price of what might be thought of as the central part of the tourist product (accommodation and transport), the demand for tourism is also influenced by other expenditure associated with the holiday. In this respect, the influence of price is not straightforward. While tourists are sensitive to the cost of a holiday and changes in the price, a reduction may result in the perception of a lower quality product. Bull (1995) notes that because accommodation in Switzerland is high, Switzerland is perceived as an expensive destination. In fact domestic and other items are not so expensive in European terms.

Competition

If the number of suppliers providing goods and services in the destination increases with demand, the level of competition among suppliers also increases. The extent of this form of supply competition will relate to both the number and size of the suppliers involved. Where a single supplier provides the service a condition of 'monopoly' exists, while a market dominated by a few large firms is said to be oligopolistic. Tribe (1995) notes the cross-channel ferry market as an example prior to the opening of the Channel Tunnel. At a global scale, the structures within the tourism industry vary considerably between countries and industry sectors. In some cases where there are numerous suppliers of a particular service 'pure competition' exists. Tribe (1995) argues that a jet carrying 350 passengers could charge 350 different prices, but must battle against other airlines to fill seats at competitive prices although the use of yield management by airlines is addressing this issue (see Page 1999b). In other locations, licences to operate restrict the number of carriers permitted to fly to a destination, such as the agreement which at one time allowed British Airways a monopoly on the London to Bermuda route.

Government controls at the destination

Just as governments in the generating area can influence demand, so can those at destinations.

Regulation can directly limit the number of tourists, through visa restrictions, and a case in point are those in force in Bhutan. Other countries restrict the opportunity for charter flights to enter, again influencing demand, but possibly more as an attempt to promote the national airline. It is possible for countries to control the amount of tourist expenditure (e.g. Egypt) or restrict the amount of currency that can be exchanged. Moreover, governments at tourist destinations can manage capacity through planning regulations and thereby restrict competition. However, it should be noted that some legislation may be necessary to preserve the quality of the environment and present 'over supply' causing degradation of the destination and a downturn in demand.

Other factors influencing tourism demand

While there are some factors which mainly influence tourism demand at the destination or from the generating area there are others which fall between these categories but are nevertheless important determinants. Among these are the promotional efforts of the destination and the time/cost of travel.

Promotional efforts of the destination

While it could be argued that the promotional efforts of a destination are largely due to the destination itself, aspects of imagery and how such efforts are received make this influence distinctive. Brunt (1997) notes that one of the aspects which makes tourism distinctive is that not only must tourists part with money and time, but that holidays cannot be 'test-driven' before purchase. As such promotion is different within tourism than in other industries. When contemplating a visit to a new destination the consumer must use various means to secure information that will enable them to make a decision. Brochures remain dominant in the UK to market overseas holidays, though more recently the use of the internet has quickly proved to be a valuable marketing tool.

Hence, the success of promotional efforts can influence tourism demand and to some suppliers at a destination such efforts are beyond their control. This, to some extent, enhances the argument of a 'volatile market', when media reports of crime or pollution or other distractions can drastically affect demand despite the best efforts of marketers.

Time/cost considerations

A final consideration affecting tourism demand is the cost and time involved in the travel component itself. The time and cost of travel over very long distances may be prohibitive and influence demand. As such, it is likely that the faster people can travel to destinations the more popular the tourism product will be. For example the time saving involved with cross-channel journeys by Eurostar were vital in generating demand for this service. Such aspects were clearly identified in reports at the time: 'a new purpose built high-speed line will open for Eurostar between Lille and Brussels, cutting 3 hours 15 minutes [journey time] by 45 minutes' (Anon 1996: 39). As a result of this time saving 'the service claims to have 40% of the total Paris to Brussels market' (Anon 1996: 39).

Conclusion

The demand for tourism products is clearly crucial to the survival of the tourism industry. Recognition of the barriers to demand leads marketers to price products against the competition and to engage in promotional efforts. In some countries, there are growing moves by employers to recognize that a holiday is essential to the health and well-being of the workforce and leave entitlements have been improved accordingly. In other cases, there are growing concerns in Europe that hours of work are increasing overall in countries like the UK while in other countries they are declining, providing more leisure time. Whatever the situation, this chapter has shown that a complex array of factors affect the demand for tourism. The discussion of ethnic tourism also highlights how new trends may be emerging that the tourism industry has not fully appreciated. The discussion has also shown that there are numerous factors which influence demand which are beyond the control of those within the tourism industry. Exogenous factors such as terrorist acts or economic stability are obvious examples, but attitudes of governments in the generating or destination areas have also been shown to be influential.

Discussion questions

1. Outline the different types of tourism demand.
2. What are the main economic-related determinants influencing tourism demand?
3. To what extent is price important in influencing tourism demand?
4. What are the main factors influencing demand at the tourist destination area?

References

Anon (1996) 'Eurostar to branch into regions', *Travel Trade Gazette UK*, 6 March: 39.

Brunt, P. (1997) *Market Research in Travel and Tourism*, Oxford: Butterworth-Heinemann.

Bull, A. (1995) *The Economics of Travel and Tourism*, second edition, Harlow: Longman.

Burkart, A. and Medlik, S. (1981) *Tourism: Past, Present and Future*, second edition, London: Heinemann.

Cai, L. (1999) 'Relationship of household characteristics and lodging expenditure on leisure trips', *Journal of Hospitality and Leisure Marketing*, **6** (2): 5–17.

Cohen, R. (1997) *Global Diasporas*, London: University College London Press.

Cooper, C.P., Fletcher, J., Gilbert, D. and Wanhill, S. (1993) *Tourism Principles and Practice*, second edition, London: Pitman.

Cooper, C.P., Fletcher, J., Gilbert, D., Wanhill, S. and Shepherd, R. (1998) *Tourism Principles and Practice*, second edition, Harlow: Longman.

Crouch, G. (1994) 'The study of tourism demand: a review of findings', *Journal of Travel Research*, **33** (1): 2–21.

Feng, K. (1999) 'The Nexus Between Tourism and Immigration: A Study of Travel Patterns of Chinese New Zealanders', Thesis presented in partial fulfilment of the requirements of the degree of Master of Business Studies at Massey University, Auckland, New Zealand.

Feng, K. and Page, S.J. (2000) 'An exploratory study of the tourism, migration–immigration nexus: experiences of Chinese residents in New Zealand', *Current Issues in Tourism*, **3** (3): 246–81.

Gartner, W.C. (1996) *Tourism Development*, New York: Van Nostrand Reinhold.

Hall, C.M. and Page, S.J. (1999) *The Geography of Tourism and Recreation: Environment, Place and Space*, London: Routledge.

Haywood, L., Kew, F., Bramham, P. and Spink, J. (1995) *Understanding Leisure*, second edition, Cheltenham: Stanley Thornes.

Heape, R. (1997) 'Demand greater than supply?', *Tourism*, **92** (1): 8.

Ioannides, D. and Debbage, K.G. (eds) (1998) *The Economic Geography of the Tourist Industry*, London: Routledge.

Kay, T. and Jackson, G. (1991) 'Leisure despite constraint: the impact of leisure constraints on leisure participation', *Journal of Leisure Research*, **23**: 301–13.

King, B. (1994). 'What is ethnic tourism? An Australian perspective', *Tourism Management*, **15** (3): 173–76.

King, B. and Gamage, M.A. (1994) 'Measuring the value of the ethnic connection: expatriate travellers from Australia to Sri Lanka', *Journal of Travel Research*, **33** (2): 46–50.

Lew, A. and Wu, L. (eds) (1995) *Tourism in China: Geographic, Economic and Political Perspectives*, Boulder: Westview Press.

Mathieson, A. and Wall, G. (1982) *Tourism: Economic, Physical and Social Impacts*, Harlow: Longman.

Migration News (1997) October, University of California at Davis (accessible at http://migration.ucdavis.edu).

Internet resources

By going to the weblink at www.thomsonlearning.co.uk students can access the following studies on the Thomson Learning website. The first study is a chapter from M. Oppermann and K. Chon (1997) *Tourism in Developing Countries*. This examines many of the issues associated with understanding the demand for tourism in developing countries. It explains the problems of generating data on tourism for the analysis of demand beyond the principal sources such as the World Tourism Organisation.

The second study is a chapter from E. Laws (1997) *Managing Packaged Tourism* and outlines the way in which tour operators harness tourism demand and create a demand for the consumer. This is a useful study that looks at the issue of demand from the tourism industry's perspective.

New Zealand Official Yearbook (1998) *New Zealand Official Yearbook*, Wellington: Department of Statistics.

Nguyen, T.H. and King, B. (1998) 'Migrant homecomings: Viet Kieu attitudes towards travelling back to Viet Nam', *Pacific Tourism Review*, **1**: 349–61.

Office for National Statistics (1999) *Social Trends*, **29**, London: ONS.

Ostrowski, S. (1991) 'Ethnic tourism: focus on Poland', *Tourism Management*, **12** (2): 125–31.

Page, S.J. (1999a) 'New Zealand outbound', *Travel and Tourism Analyst*, **2**: 21–40.

Page, S.J. (1999b) *Transport and Tourism*, Harlow: Addison Wesley Longman.

Pearce, D. (1989) *Tourist Development*, Harlow: Longman.

Pearce, D. (1995) *Tourism Today: A Geographical Analysis*, Harlow: Longman.

Rossiter, J. and Chan, A. (1998) 'Ethnicity in business and consumer behaviour', *Journal of Business Research*, **42** (2): 127–34.

Sandbach, M. (1999) Exchange Rate and the Inbound Market. *Insights: The Tourism Intelligence Service*. July, 1–2.

Sinclair, M.T. and Stabler, M. (1997) *The Economics of Tourism*, London: Routledge.

Statistics New Zealand (1992) *The 1991 Census*, Wellington: Statistics New Zealand.

Statistics New Zealand (1997) *The 1996 Census*, Wellington: Statistics New Zealand.

Swarbrooke, J. (1999) *The Management and Development of Tourist Attractions*, Oxford: Butterworth-Heinemann.

Thanopoulos, J. and Walle, A. (1988) 'Ethnicity and its reference to marketing: the case of tourism', *Journal of Travel Research*, **26** (3): 11–14.

Tribe, J. (1995) *The Economics of Leisure and Tourism*, second edition, Oxford: Butterworth-Heinemann.

Further reading

Crouch, G. (1994) 'The study of tourism demand: a review of findings', *Journal of Travel Research*, **33** (1): 2–21.

Tribe, J. (1995) *The Economics of Leisure and Tourism*, second edition, Oxford: Butterworth-Heinemann.

Uysal, M. (1998) 'The determinants of tourism demand: a theoretical perspective', in D. Ioannides and K. Debbage (eds) *The Economic Geography of the Tourist Industry: A Supply Side Analysis*, Routledge: London: 79–95.

4 Understanding the tourist: tourist motivation

Learning outcomes

After reading this chapter and answering the questions, you should be able to:

- Understand theories and models relevant to the explanation of tourist motivation.
- Recognize the importance of those factors that influence or circumscribe the tourism decision-making process.
- Realize the importance of segmentation as a vital tool in a marketing strategy.

Overview

The question of why people go on holiday is fundamental to the study of tourism. What motivates people to engage in different forms of behaviour concerned researchers and academics long before it was applied to the field of tourism. Nevertheless, how can the patterns of tourism activity evident today be explained? Is it merely an outcome of people's freedom to choose where they go on holiday or are there different factors at work which initiate the desire to travel and then influence which destination is ultimately selected? Added to this is the question of the benefit to the tourism industry of knowledge about how its customers reach their purchasing decisions. This chapter will investigate these issues.

Introduction

Previous chapters have identified the nature of tourism demand, but this does not address the fundamental question of why people go on holiday. A brief glance at the rows of brochures in a travel agency shows a huge diversity of tourism products and visiting an international airport reveals thousands of people travelling that day. How can we explain this diversity of tourism activity? At one level people may choose where they wish to travel to, so the patterns of tourism activity could be explained in terms of individual choice. However, immediately the thought of a holiday occurs there is an awareness of some of the constraints that may face the individual. Is there enough money or holiday entitlement and what about family commitments? Is the individual aware of the tourism opportunities available? Clearly as individuals we do not have limitless choice; our actions are inevitably influenced by a wide variety of opportunities and constraints.

While there are factors influencing individuals, by the nature of their particular circumstances, there are also social divisions in all countries which may also circumscribe choice in tourism. While there may well be a wide diversity of tourism products available social divisions may influence this diversity in terms of inequality of opportunity. Just as there are inequalities in many countries in terms of education, employment, housing, income, so there are inequalities in tourism.

If we were able to sit on a satellite and observe the patterns of tourism activity down on earth, an explanation of what we could observe could not be made solely on a matter of choice. Certainly some people might choose to sit on a beach, while others choose to go sightseeing and others go off the beaten track in remote locations. Choice is an important factor, but in a wider perspective we are rarely 'free' to make those choices – they are constrained and influenced by a variety of factors.

It can be seen, therefore, that an answer to the question of 'why do people go on holiday', is not straightforward. Different writers and researchers have grappled with the explanation of this question and this chapter will review some of their arguments.

Aspects of tourism motivation

Figure 4.1 shows one way in which the decision-making process to go on a holiday could be visualized. It is not suggested that all decisions are made in the same way and that individuals consider carefully each aspect that could influence them. Brunt (1990) noted differences in the ways that researchers approached explanations of decision-making. Some explanations suggest that humans respond to stimuli in a predetermined predictable way rather more akin to how we would respond if we felt too close to a fire.

Such explanations reflect the 'behaviourist' tradition. An alternative, the 'cognitive' approach, acknowledges that individuals may be irrational and unpredictable and that much human behaviour is subjective. Brunt (1990) argued that both schools of thought could be applied to decision-making in tourism. Some people's decisions appear to be more

Figure 4.1 **Holiday decision-making process**

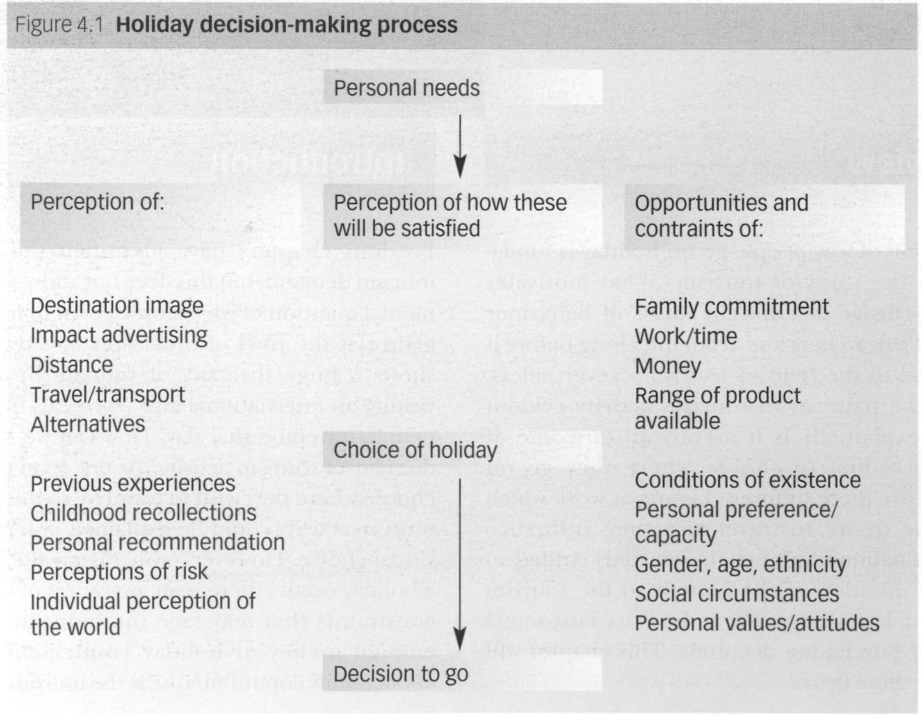

ad hoc reactions to, say, advertising while others, visiting the same destination, have gone through a carefully organized planning procedure. While it is fair to say that how people decide to go on holiday and what influences their decisions are individual, the aspect which initiated the whole process is individual too. This brings us back to motivation (defined as that which makes a person act in a particular way). Everyone has personal and unique needs, which may be unacknowledged, but that exists as an inseparable part of all of us.

Maslow's hierarchy of needs

Maslow (1943) is acknowledged with the best known theory of motivation. Although originally related to the field of clinical psychology his work has been more widely applied. Maslow argues that our individual needs fall into five broad categories, as shown in Figure 4.2. Maslow suggested that that these five categories formed a hierarchy, beginning with lower order physiological needs and moving through to higher order self-actualization needs.

He argued that each of the needs expressed in a category would be satisfied before the individual sought motivation from the next category of need. It can be seen that once the basic human requirements of thirst and hunger have been met the need for these to motivate the behaviour and actions of an individual may no longer apply. At this point the individual may be motivated by higher order classification until that of self-actualization. Several tourism researchers have applied Maslow's model in the context of tourism motivation (for example, Cooper *et al.* 1998; Pearce and Caltabiano 1983). Such work, for instance, recognizes that tourist motivation changes over time and tourists may have several 'motives' to travel. In addition, Pearce (1992) suggested that individuals have a tourism 'career

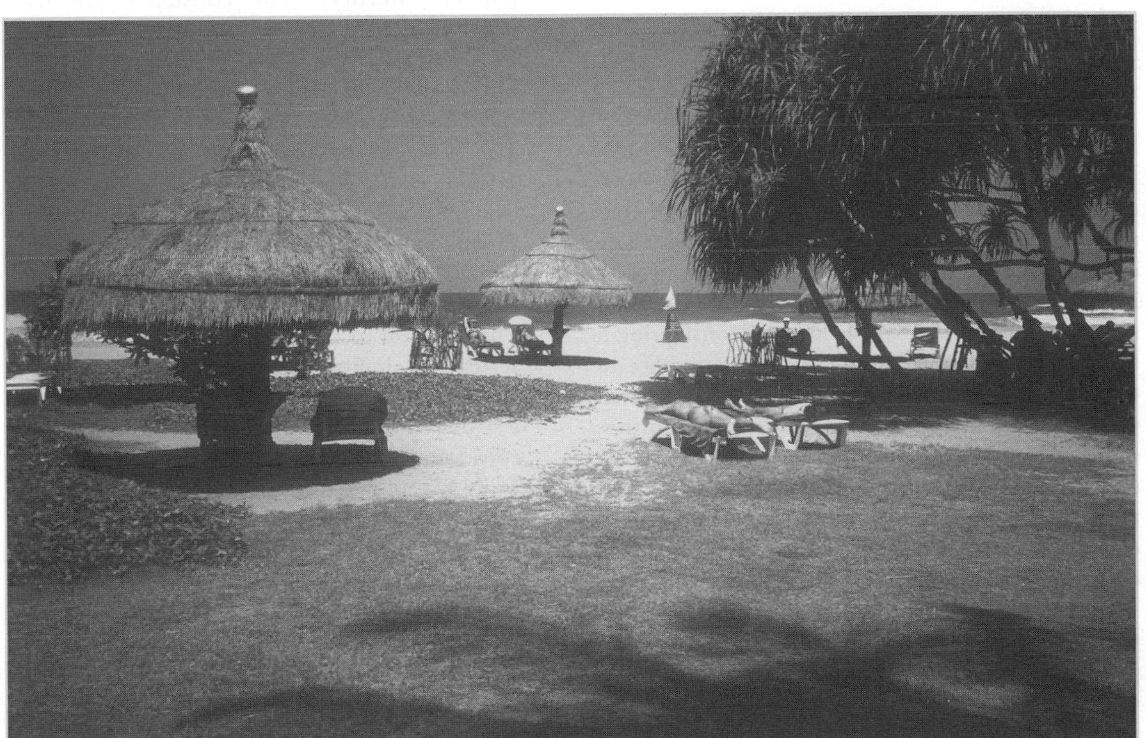

Plate 4.1 Triton Hotel, Sri Lanka
Everyone has personal and unique needs and perceptions of what will satisfy that need will, consequently, vary. Here, at the Triton Hotel in Sri Lanka, visions of such idyllic surroundings may result in future bookings.

Figure 4.2 **Maslow's hierarchy of needs**

1	Physiological needs	Hunger, thirst, rest, sex, activity	Lower
2	Safety needs	Freedom from threat, fear, anxiety. Feeling secure	
3	Belonging and love (social) needs	Receiving and giving affection and love, friendships	
4	Esteem needs	Self-esteem, esteem for others. Self-confidence, reputation, prestige	
5	Self-actualization needs	Personal self-fulfilment	Higher

ladder', in essence, that tourist motivation is an ever changing process and we move up the 'ladder' as we progress through the various life-cycle stages.

Gilbert's tourism consumer decision process

Maslow's hierarchy of needs can be seen to be useful in demonstrating how our initial needs and wants can be explained. The satisfaction of these needs may ultimately, in our context, lead to the purchase of a holiday. Another way of considering this process is in terms of push and pull factors. The desire to satisfy our needs may 'push' us into considering a holiday, but once we begin to consider where to travel a range of 'pull' factors come to bear which will influence, from the range of opportunities, which destination is selected. As Sharpley (1994: 99) states 'the motivation to satisfy needs, combined with personal preferences, pushes the tourist into considering alternative products; the final choice depends on the pull of alternative holidays or destinations'.

Gilbert (1991) acknowledges the push and pull factors influencing the tourism consumer decision process. Here, he suggests that the process has four distinct stages:

1 *Energizers of demand*
These are the various forces, including motivation, which initiate the decision to visit an attraction or go on holiday at the outset.
2 *Effectors of demand*
Information about a destination will have been received by various means (brochures, newspapers, internet). The consumer will have developed their own ideas and perceptions about the destination and this perception may enhance or reduce the likelihood of a visit.
3 *Roles and decision-making*
The role of the tourist as a consumer will influence the final choice of holiday. For example, different members of a family will have a varying impact on the where, when and what the family will do on holiday.
4 *Filterers of demand*
The decision to travel is heavily influenced by a series of demographic and socio-economic constraints and opportunities. While there may be a strong 'push', demand is filtered through such constraining factors.

Dann's perspectives on tourism motivation

To this point our investigation of tourist motivation could, perhaps, be most easily related to what might be termed a 'leisure' holiday. However, as we have seen previously, tourism takes many forms and visiting friends and relatives or business travel may result from different motives or even be more related to the actual purpose of the visit (for example a family reunion) than the needs and wants of the tourist.

Dann (1981) in a study of tourist motivation identified seven perspectives within an overall approach:

1 *Travel as a response to what is lacking yet desired*
The suggestion here is that tourist motivation may result from a desire for something new or different that cannot be provided in the individual's home environment.
2 *Destination pull in response to motivational push*
Here, as previously discussed, Dann acknowledges the distinction between the needs, wants and desires (push factors) of the individual and how these are shaped by perceptions of the destination (pull factors).
3 *Motivation as fantasy*
Tourists may be motivated to travel to engage in forms of behaviour or activities that are not culturally acceptable in their home environment. One context of this is travel to enable deviant behaviour such as gambling, drugs or prostitution (Brunt *et al.* 2000). Here, because such activities may be illegal in the home country but not in others, this creates the desire to travel.
4 *Motivation as classified purpose*
Here, Dann acknowledges that some are motivated to travel or 'caused' to travel by the nature or purpose of the trip. Visiting friends and relatives is one example or the opportunity to undertake specific leisure activities another.
5 *Motivational typologies*
Here, Dann notes that there are different types of tourist (see next section) and such forms may influence the motivation to travel.
6 *Motivation and tourist experiences*
Tourism often involves travel to places not visited previously. As such, some are motivated to travel by what they expect to experience in contrast to their home area and other holiday experiences.
7 *Motivation as auto-definition and meaning*
The ways in which tourists define their situations and respond to them is argued to provide a better understanding of explaining tourist motivation. Such an approach is seen in contrast to simply observing behaviour as a means to explain tourist motivation.

Plog's tourist typologies

One of Dann's perspectives (motivational typologies) suggests that tourist types, or how personality traits enable us to classify tourists, could provide an explanation for why some travel to certain destinations. One of the best known theories in this area was developed by Stanley Plog (1974) based on the US population. Plog identified two opposite types of tourist each at the end of a continuum (see Figure 4.3). Allocentrics are tourists who seek adventure on their holidays and are prepared to take risks. As such, they prefer holidays in more exotic locations and prefer to travel independently. At the other extreme are psychocentrics. Such tourists look rather inwardly and concentrate their thoughts on the small problems in life. On holiday they are not adventurous, but prefer locations that are similar to their home environment. Such tourists may repeatedly return to the same destination where they have experienced a satisfying experience safe in the knowledge of the familiar. In between these two extremes other categories exist, such as near-allocentric, mid-centric and near-psychocentric.

Figure 4.3 **Plog's tourist types**

Type	Characteristics
Allocentric	Enjoy travelling independently, cultural exploration, often in above average income groups, seek adventurous experiences on holiday
Mid-centric	The majority of the population, go to known destinations, but do not go for exploration and adventure. May travel to destinations previously 'found' and made popular by allocentrics
Psychocentric	Tend to be rather unsure and insecure about travel. Go to places similar to their home environment

While Plog's typologies are a simple, easy-to-understand model which can explain, to some extent, aspects of tourist motivation, there are some difficulties in its application. One aspect, for example, is that both tourists and destinations change over time. Young adults may well be allocentric at certain stages in their life-cycle and more mid-centric at other stages, when children are present, for example. Similarly, in the 1950s the Costa del Sol in Spain was considered exotic, but in a short space of time had

Plate 4.2 Picos de Europa, northern Spain
A walker at 9000ft in the Picos de Europa in northern Spain. Is he sufficiently off the beaten track to be classified as an allocentric tourist?

developed into a 'mass' tourism destination, no longer likely to attract allocentric tourists. Other tourism researchers have developed systems for defining tourists. Cohen (1972) for instance notes four categories (Organised Mass Tourist, Individual Mass Tourist, Explorer and Drifter) and Smith (1989) identifies seven types (Explorers, Elite, Off-beat, Unusual, Incipient Mass, Mass and Charter).

It can be seen that there are several ways in which we can explain the 'push' factors in tourism motivation. Once the motivation to embark on a holiday has been determined numerous 'pull' factors effectively influence our choice of destination. Within this, aspects such as the purpose of the holiday and tourist typologies may well be particularly influential. However, the circumstances that affect us as individuals, both personally and wider external influences greatly affect the nature of the holiday and the final selection of a particular destination. These influences on tourist motivation will now be investigated.

Factors influencing tourist motivation

While we have seen that the decision to go on holiday is an outcome of personal motivation, the selection of a destination/type of holiday is set against a series of constraints of which individuals are aware. The choice of the final holiday is limited because some holidays are too expensive, are not suited to the time we have available, are too far away or may even involve activities that are beyond our capabilities. There are numerous ways that such constraints could be organized. Here our discussion will focus on two broad categories:

- *Personal and family influences*, including age, stage in the family life-cycle and gender issues.
- *Social and situational influences*, including the tourism and work relationship, social class and income issues.

Age

An individual's age is an important influence on the nature of tourism participation. Typically young adults are shown in advertising as travelling independently or else attracted to package holidays aimed specifically at their age group (Club 18–30 or 2wenties). To some extent tourism participation could be seen as wage earning symbols of adulthood for young people. Given that as young adults time to experiment, to develop confidence in one's own identity, experience sexuality and relationships, are important at this age, tourism can provide a useful outlet for such needs (Haywood *et al.* 1989). By the time of old age there is an inevitable reduction in an individual's physical and mental facilities and as such a reduction in the more active holiday pursuits. However, it is clearly incorrect to equate retirement with old age. In contemporary society where retirement has come for some in their fifties, such people represent an attractive 'target' for tourism operators. Often free from family commitments which may have limited time, together with an attractive pension, such individuals may approach early retirement as a welcome gift. Opportunities may well expand as the individual enters retirement and only retract when the individual becomes elderly.

Family life-cycle

Closely overlapping with age, the family life-cycle groups people not only by their age but also by aspects of material status and the presence of children. Numerous classification systems exist.

Rapoport and Rapoport (1975)

Stages

1 Adolescence (15–19 years old)
2 Young adult (to late 20s)
3 Family establishment (25–55)
4 Later years (55+).

Youell (1996)

Stages

1 Bachelor stage
2 Newly wed/living together
3 Full nest (couple with child)
4 Empty nest (children left home)
5 Solitary survivor.

Such classifications, while useful, need constant updating. Looking at the two systems it can be seen that little account is made of single parent families, gay people and extended families. Such models imply the stages to be the 'norm' and pay little attention to those choosing not to have children or cultural differences in families by ethnic class. Despite these concerns, it is fair to say that different stages in a life-cycle are characterized by different interest, activities and opinions. These translate to different holiday requirements at each stage and some companies can effectively 'capture' loyalty at an early stage and maintain this throughout the life-cycle (Disney, for example).

Gender

Gender as an influence in tourism decision-making is not widely researched or discussed. Yet one of the primary relations between individuals in any society is based on gender. Thus, gender is a crucial determinant in terms of tourism participation. Clarke and Crichter (1985) argue, in the context of leisure participation, that women have less leisure time than men, undertake fewer leisure activities and spend a higher proportion of their time in and around the home and family. If this is accepted, then there are also clear implications for gender to be an issue in tourism participation and motivation. One illustration may well be that where women have primary responsibility for household organization and childcare, a self-catering holiday might not fully provide a means of escape from the home environment when this is an important motivator.

Tourism and work

Work provides a means for tourism and often work also provides the motivation for tourism. Whatever the balance, leisure, tourism and work are inseparable. However, as Parker (1983) argues, by and large, leisure and work are competitors of our time, a feature also examined by Roberts (1999). If one increases then the other decreases. The nature of work, though, is an important influence on tourism not just in terms of competition for time though. Where an individual's work is boring, arduous or monotonous, tourism may well represent an escape. Opposing this, some are fortunate to find their work exciting, enjoyable and possibly difficult to disassociate from their leisure. Here a holiday may be seen as a means to extend one's work interests. Zuzanek and Mannell (1983) identified four hypotheses in terms of a work/leisure relationship:

1 The Trade-off Hypothesis – work and leisure are competitors for time and an individual chooses between them.
2 The Compensation Hypothesis – leisure and holidays compensate for the boredom and troubles associated with work and everyday life.
3 The Spin-off Hypothesis – where the nature of an individual's work produces a similar pattern of leisure activities.
4 The Neutralist Hypothesis – where there is no discernible relationship between leisure and work.

What can be seen here is that in the vast majority of cases different types of work produce different levels of satisfaction, which in turn influences individual needs and wants and hence leisure and tourism motivations.

Social class and income

Lumsdon (1997: 42) suggests that social class be 'considered to be one of the most important external factors, assessed primarily by occupation and level of income'. Herein lies a problem, though. Social class is an awkward concept in that there are numerous dimensions associated with power, money, prestige, culture and background. Nevertheless, social class is used throughout social research and as a means of segmenting the population (along with gender and age) for the purposes of surveys and opinion polls.

So what is social class and how might it be an influence in terms of tourism motivation? Social class was defined for the UK population census in 1911 to facilitate the analysis by arranging the large number of occupational groups within a small number of categories. Hence individuals were assigned to a social class category where:

Class
I: Professional occupations
II: Intermediate occupations
IIIN: Skilled occupations non-manual
IIIM: Skilled occupations manual
IV: Partly skilled occupations
V: Unskilled occupations
VI: Armed forces and inadequately described.

This initial system took no account of differences between individuals in the same occupation groups (e.g. in terms of remuneration) and over the years other systems have been introduced. For example, in 1951 (amended 1961) the seven social class groups were replaced by 17 socio-economic classes for the UK census. Here the aim was to bring together people with jobs of similar social and economic status. Further, in common use is a system devised by the Market Research Society (*Economist* 1992) where class and occupation are grouped:

Class
A Professional/senior managerial
B Middle managers/executives
C1 Junior managers/non-manual
C2 Skilled manual
D Semi-skilled/unskilled
E Unemployed/state dependants.

The implications for leisure and tourism participation is that from the higher social class categories to the lower there is an increase in television viewing, a decline in membership of library membership and book-reading, a decline in holidaymaking, sports participation and countryside recreation (Haywood *et al.* 1989). The statistical data suggest that higher social class groups enjoy a more active and varied range of leisure activities. Edwards (1987) has shown that for many tourism is price elastic (i.e. small price increases may result in many people seeking cheaper alternatives). As higher incomes are generally synonymous with the higher social class groups then this has an influence on the type of holiday which can be selected.

While it is fair to accept that aspects of social class do influence tourism, such assumptions should be approached with caution. Most class categories do not also relate to life-cycle, hence a young professional worker with four children may be in a higher class, but may have less disposable income than a working couple in the skilled manual class who have no dependants.

It is also pertinent to note that social class has other more subjective dimensions, more associated with class imagery. Here, an individual's accent, style of speech, residence, social network, job, educational background, dress, car, income, race, family background and leisure activities may be more influential. The subjective judgements associated with upper, middle or working class may also affect the nature and type of holiday as well as other aspects of life. For a long time what Cohen (1972) referred to as 'elite' tourists have led the way and made certain destinations 'popular', before moving onto other destinations when they become 'too' popular. Clearly, while social class and income are important determinants of tourism motivations, they are also associated with a complexity of perceptions, tastes and meanings.

Tourist motivation and segmentation

So far this chapter has shown that people are motivated to travel for a variety of reasons. However, understanding the tourist and their motivations is far from easy. For instance, Laws (1991) argued that however convenient it is to categorize travellers not all individuals fall neatly into behavioural models or typological classifications. Moreover, it is not realistic to assume that accurate descriptions of tourists through their reasons for travel, gained at the time of purchase will remain constant throughout the travel experience. Despite such concerns, by identifying types of customers and classifying them into groups or market segments, a process called segmentation, tourism suppliers may be able to deliver their products more effectively. Through segmentation marketers can establish common reasons behind the purchase of tourism products within a market segment. Through an understanding of this common purchasing behaviour by market segment it becomes possible to target market segments with particular products. Clearly different groups of tourist will make varying economic contributions as a result of their activities. Wealthier tourists may be more valuable to destinations than other tourist types, thus efforts may be specifically made to target such groups.

It can be seen, therefore, that understanding tourist motivation to facilitate segmentation can be a valuable tool to tourism suppliers. In short, segmentation can be used to inform differentiated marketing and enable strategies to be designed to attract the most valuable types of tourist. Bull (1991) identifies three methods of segmentation.

Segmentation by purpose of travel

Here, as in many tourism statistical sources, the purpose of a trip is used to divide groups of tourists. Commonly, business travellers are separated from those on a leisure holiday, with those visiting friends and relatives making a third group. Occasionally, the leisure holiday might be further sub-divided into groups reflecting sun, sea and sand or sunlust holidays from a sightseeing or wanderlust tour. Travel for health and for sport may be additional sub-divisions.

Psychographic segmentation

Segmentation based on lifestyle factors, or activities, interests and opinions is known as psychographic segmentation. Behavioural characteristics are identified, such as common purchasing behaviour asking researchers to identify product-specific links. This enables tourism suppliers to target certain types of individuals with their products in the knowledge that such groups may be more receptive than the population at large.

Interactional segmentation

Interactional segmentation concentrates on the effect different types of tourists have. To some extent this subsumes the other methods. If we consider several different types of tourist visiting the same destination, those on a leisure holiday may have a higher expenditure value than those visiting friends but less than incentive travellers where a company is footing the bill for much of their expense. Such tourists will also make different demands on tourism resources.

While there are a wide range of factors influencing the marketing decisions of tourism suppliers, understanding consumer needs comes high on any organization's list of priorities. Segmenting the tourism market on the basis of tourist motivations is a complex process, but can provide a foundation for the development of media and the means to position a product correctly in the marketplace.

Conclusion

This chapter set out with the question of 'why do people go on holiday'. At the outset it has been shown that a variety of 'push' factors may motivate the desire to travel. Such factors may result from the particular relationship an individual has with their work or home environment. Alternatively the motivation to travel may be driven by other forces as in the case of needing to visit relatives or go on a business trip. Other types of tourist may be motivated by higher order psychological needs, such as for self-esteem.

While people are themselves instrumental in their motivation, once a decision to travel has been made a variety of pull factors influence that decision. While in theory we may be free to choose our tourism activities, our choice is inevitably limited by an awareness of constraints which influence and circumscribe the range of opportunities. Understanding what motivates tourists and influences their selection of a destination is complex, but a vital part in the success of any tourism organization's marketing strategy.

Discussion questions

1. What models aid our understanding of tourist motivation?
2. Discuss the extent to which people are free to choose where they go on holiday.
3. How important is social class in understanding tourist motivation?
4. What are the main uses of tourist segmentation?

References

Brunt (1990) 'Tourism trip decision-making at the sub-regional level: with special reference to southern England', unpublished PhD Thesis, Bournemouth University, UK.

Brunt, P., Mawby, R. and Hambly, Z. (2000) 'Tourist victimization and the fear of crime on holiday', *Tourism Management,* **21** (4): 417–24.

Bull, A. (1991) *The Economics of Travel and Tourism,* Melbourne: Pitman.

Clarke, J. and Critcher, C. (1985) *The Devil Makes Work,* Basingstoke: Macmillan.

Cohen, E. (1972) 'Towards a sociology of international tourism', *Social Research,* **39** (1): 64–82.

Cooper, C.P., Fletcher, J., Gilbert, D., Wanhill, S. and Shepherd, R. (1998) *Tourism Principles and Practice,* second edition, London: Longman.

Dann, G.M.S. (1981) 'Tourist motivation: an appraisal', *Annals of Tourism Research,* **6** (4): 408–24.

The Economist (1992) 'The class of 1992', *The Economist,* 12 September: 27–30.

Internet resources

By going to the weblink at www.thomsonlearning.co.uk students can access the two following studies on the Thomson Learning website. The first study is a chapter from C. Ryan (1995) *Researching Tourist Satisfaction: Issues, Concepts, Problems.* This examines how to measure tourist attitudes and the approaches used by researchers in designing methods to measure attitudes. It fits with the general field of understanding tourist motivation from a practical manner when attempting to measure different aspects of tourist behaviour.

The second study is by E. Laws (1997) *Managing Packaged Tourism* and traces the evolution of the package holiday industry in Western Europe, highlighting the tourists' motivation in taking holidays through the packaged route. This is a useful study since it identifies many of the factors associated with the reasons why package holidays, often referred to as 'mass tourism' and the three 'Ss' (sun, sea and sand), have expanded rapidly since 1945 and some of the underlying motivational factors for tourists.

Edwards, A. (1987) *Choosing Holiday Destinations: The Impact of Exchange Rates and Inflation*, Special Report No. 1109, London: Economist Intelligence Unit.

Gilbert, D.C. (1991) 'An examination of the consumer decision process related to tourism', in C.P. Cooper, (ed.) *Progress in Tourism, Recreation and Hospitality Management, vol. III,* London: Belhaven.

Haywood, L., Kew, F. and Bramham, P. (1989) *Understanding Leisure,* Cheltenham: Stanley Thornes.

Laws, E. (1991) *Tourism Marketing, Services and Quality Management Perspectives,* Cheltenham: Stanley Thornes.

Lumsdon, L. (1997) *Tourism Marketing,* London: Thomson Learning.

Maslow, A.H. (1943) 'A theory of human motivation', *Psychological Review,* **50**: 370–96.

Parker, S. (1983) *Leisure and Work,* London: Allen and Unwin.

Pearce, P. (1992) 'Fundamentals of tourist motivation', in D. Pearce and R. Butler (eds) *Tourism Research: Critiques and Challenges,* London: Routledge.

Pearce, P. and Caltabiano, M. (1983) 'Inferring travel motivation from travellers experiences', *Journal of Travel Research,* **22**: 16–20.

Plog, S. (1974) 'Why destination areas rise and fall in popularity', *Cornell Hotel and Restaurant Administration Quarterly,* November: 13–16.

Rapoport, R. and Rapoport, R.N. (1975) *Leisure and the Family Life-cycle,* London: Routledge.

Roberts, K. (1999) *Leisure in Contemporary Society,* Wallingford: CAB International Publishers.

Sharpley, R. (1994) *Tourism, Tourists and Society,* Huntingdon: Elm.

Smith, V. (ed.) (1989) *Hosts and Guests: The Anthropology of Tourism,* second edition, Philadelphia: University of Pennsylvania Press.

Youell, R. (1996) *The Complete A–Z Leisure, Travel and Tourism Handbook,* London: Hodder & Stoughton.

Zuzanek, J and Mannell, R. (1983) 'Work leisure relationships from a sociological and social psychographical perspective', *Leisure Studies,* **2** (3): 327–44.

Further reading

Dann, G.M.S. (1981) 'Tourist motivation: an appraisal', *Annals of Tourism Research,* **6** (4): 408–24.

Lumsden, L. (1997) *Tourism Marketing,* London: Thomson Learning.

Sharpley, R. (1994) *Tourism, Tourists and Society,* Huntingdon: Elm.

Smith, V. (ed.) (1989) *Hosts and Guests: The Anthropology of Tourism,* second edition, Philadelphia: University of Pennsylvania Press.

Section 2

Understanding tourism as a business

In the previous section, the focus was on the demand for tourism services and how the tourist affects the demand through individual factors, tastes and preferences. This recognizes the tourist as a consumer and this raises the question of how the tourism industry fulfils this demand and in some cases how does it generate demand for the services and products it offers? This section addresses these issues by commencing with a review in Chapter 5 of the term 'tourism supply' and what the scope and nature of the tourism sector is. This should not be seen in isolation from tourism demand, but for the ease of explanation, the supply issues are explained separately. Having provided a broad overview of what exactly constitutes tourism supply, attention shifts to a more detailed analysis of each sector in the travel and tourism industry so that the reader can appreciate the wide range of suppliers and sectors which exist and interact to produce the tourism experience. In Chapter 6, the nature of travel and tourism intermediaries, which assemble and distribute tourism products to the consumer through various distribution channels, are reviewed, particularly the changes which have occurred with new technology such as the internet. This illustrates how intermediaries have to work with a wide range of suppliers to deliver the tourism experience and the major suppliers of products and services are then reviewed. The transportation sector is discussed in Chapter 7 to illustrate the wide range of modes of transport which the tourist utilizes, as well as the significance of transport as an integral part of the tourism experience. Major new developments in transport technology are also discussed. This is followed by a discussion of the scope and nature of tourism attractions (Chapter 8) where the emphasis is on the ways in which they can be classified and the issues affecting their development and role in the tourist activities. Lastly, the accommodation sector is reviewed in Chapter 9, emphasizing the significance of processes such as globalization in the world-wide expansion and development of accommodation. The different types of accommodation which the tourist uses are discussed, together with current developments in the accommodation sector.

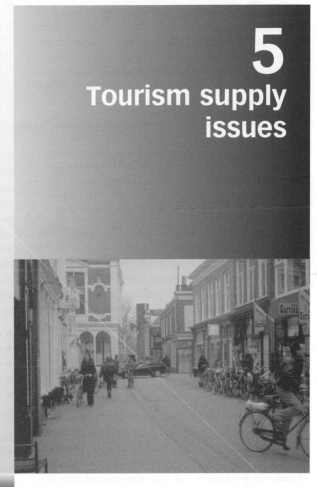

5 Tourism supply issues

Learning outcomes

After studying this chapter, you should:

- Be familiar with the wide range of tourism suppliers.
- Be aware of some issues relating to these suppliers.
- Understand how the public sector is involved in tourism supply.

Overview

The purpose of this chapter is to provide the reader with an appreciation of the many types of tourism supplier, providing examples of the organizations involved and the scale of operations, together with some of the issues facing them.

Introduction

The analysis of the tourism sector by economists has traditionally distinguished between the demand for goods and services and the ways in which the demand is satisfied and how this affects the *consumption* of tourism goods and services. Economists also examine how the supply of tourist services are produced (i.e. the *production* side). In the real world, the tourism industry considers supply in terms of three basic questions: 'what to produce?', 'how to produce it?' and 'when, where and how to produce it?' (see Bull 1991 for more detail). The analysis of tourism supply is 'poorly researched within most conventional texts on tourism, [as] the issue of supply attracts comparatively little attention' (Hall and Page 1999: 92) and consequently it remains a neglected area of study, often based on simplistic descriptions of the tourism industry.

Few studies provide a conceptual framework in which supply issues can be examined although recent research with geographical studies of tourism (e.g. Hall and Page 1999; Shaw and Williams 1994) have argued that the production of tourism services and experiences offer new directions for research. The difficulty is that the tourism industry remains sceptical of tourism researchers and there is a gap between the research needs of industry and the sensitive nature of much of their commercial data and the perspectives of academic researchers who are often inexperienced in the business and managerial aspects of tourism. A number of studies of tourism supply (e.g. Sessa 1983; Sinclair and Stabler 1992) indicate that supply issues can be classified and divided into:

> three main categories: first, descriptions of the industry and its operation, management and marketing; second, the spatial development [the geographical development] and interactions which characterise the industry on a local, national and international scale; and third, the effects which result from the development of the industry. (Sinclair and Stabler 1992: 2)

In contrast, the more incisive analysis by Sessa (1983: 59) considers 'tourism supply is the result of those productive activities that involve the provision of goods and services required to meet tourism demand and which are expressed in tourism consumption'. Although the tourist is a mobile consumer at different geographical scales, much of what can be deemed tourism supply is fixed at specific points in geographical space and time (i.e. spatial fixity) there are growing trends, which other chapters examine (e.g. Chapter 9 on accommodation and hospitality services), that show that the tourism supply by transnational corporations are relocating capital and finance to a wider range of international locations to fulfil the demand for tourism services. Furthermore, tourism supply issues are critical in the analysis of tourism because it helps to understand how the tourism industry is both organized and distributed geographically, particularly if one adopts a holistic perspective using the tourism system and the supply aspects as critical inputs to the system. Tourism supply issues also exist in an environment in which policy, planning, development issues and political factors impinge upon the regulatory framework which influences the extent to which the tourism industry operates in a regulated-through-to-deregulated environment.

Determinants of tourism supply

According to Sinclair and Stabler (1997: 58):

> Tourism supply is a complex phenomenon because of both the nature of the product and the process of delivery. Principally it cannot be stored, cannot be examined prior to purchase, it is necessary to travel to consume it, heavy reliance is placed on both natural and human-made resources and a number of components are required, which may be separately or jointly purchased and which are consumed in sequence. It is a composite product involving transport, accommodation, catering, natural resources, entertainment, and other facilities and services, such as shops and banks, travel agents and tour operators.

What this quotation illustrates is that the scope of tourism supply issues is extremely broad and wide ranging and comprises many disparate suppliers, providing a combination of tangible and intangible products. While a number of useful books examine tourism supply issues (e.g. Bull 1991; Sinclair and Stabler 1992, 1997), for the purposes of this chapter the key aspects of supply which are examined are derived from the work of Inskeep (1994). The main aspects of supply examined here (and in more detail in other chapters) are:

- attractions and activities
- accommodation
- transportation
- institutional elements
- other tourist facilities and services.

(Source: Adapted from Inskeep 1994)

Before one can examine any of these individual aspects of supply, it is also important to recognize that the tourism industry and individual firms are directly influenced by the market conditions which affect the economic/business environment in which tourism and/other economic activities operate. Although there is not space within this chapter to examine these issues in detail (see Sinclair and Stabler 1997 for more detail), four market situations normally prevail in the tourism sector.

Perfect competition

Within economic models of perfect competition, economists make a number of assumptions related to tourism issues. These are that a large number of consumers and firms exist so that neither can affect the price of the undifferentiated product; and that there is free entry into and exit from the market with no barriers to the market. However, in the real world few conditions exist where perfect competition can prevail.

Contestable markets

Contestable markets exist where there are 'insignificant entry and exit costs, so that there are negligible entry and exit barriers. Sunk costs [known more commonly as capital] which a firm incurs in order to produce and which would not be recoupable if the firm left the industry are not significant' (Sinclair and Stabler 1997: 61). What this means is that producers cannot react immediately, despite the onset of information technology and greater market intelligence whereas consumers can react immediately. In other words, businesses compete with each other for the consumer by adopting different pricing strategies so that market segmentation can occur and operators contest the price. Yet firms in contestable markets charge similar prices because it is frequently a mass market and little product differentiation may exist. In economic terms, this means that existing operators cannot charge more than the average cost because more competitors would enter the market to compete. This is due to the low sunk costs and low entry/exit barriers which rivals would have.

Oligopoly

Oligopoly exists where there are a limited number of suppliers who dominate the tourism sector. This is particularly the case where 'tourism has a dualistic industrial structure which is polarised between large numbers of small firms (typically in retailing, accommodation services) and a small number of large companies (for example in air transport)' (Williams 1995: 163). What this means is that in an oligopoly, a firm can control its price and output levels because there are entry and exit barriers. Many of the supply conditions are ultimately dependent upon the suppliers who determine the output and pricing level. Although in an ideal world, oligopolies set prices where profits are maximized and may even collude to establish a monopoly and increase profit levels, in the real world producers may alter prices and output without reference to competitors to gain market advantage. Sinclair and Stabler (1997: 81) argue in the case of the air transport market that:

> Although a domestic monopoly or oligopoly structure has been common, with a single state supported airline or a small number of competing airlines, deregulation has made some markets competitive in the short run. In the international market some routes are competitive, being served by many carriers. Most of the others are served by at least two carriers, indicating an oligopolist market, although a few routes are served by a single carrier which may be tempted to exercise monopoly powers.

Thus, where a large number of small firms operate in the tourism industry, a competitive market exists. However, where a limited number of operators or tourism businesses exist, an oligopoly situation may also verge on the conditions akin to monopoly if the competition is limited.

Monopoly

This is probably easily described as the opposite of perfect competition, since it is where a company or firm can exercise a high degree of control over a product or level of output. This means that businesses can charge a price which is above the average cost of production, indicating that consumers pay a higher price than would be the case in a more competitive market situation. Quite often, monopoly situations exist which are detrimental to the interests of consumers, but in the transport sector, monopolies may exist where the state is the main provider of a service due to the lack of a viable service from the private sector. Even where governments have privatized monopolies on tourism provision (e.g. with air travel), the enterprises can react in a way where the free market leads to oligopolistic or monopolistic behaviour prevailing in specific areas which has been the case in the airline industry in the USA (see Page 1999).

Therefore, in any analysis of tourism supply issues and market conditions, Sinclair and Stabler (1997: 83) argue that a number of factors need to be considered and evaluated which include:

- The number and size of firms.
- Entry and exit barriers to specific tourism businesses.
- The extent to which market concentration exists in a specific tourism sector (i.e. where a small

number of large operators control the majority of the market such as the UK tour operator sector which has a small number of large integrated operators controlling the business).

- Economies and diseconomies of scale.
- The costs of capital and operation.
- The extent to which price discrimination exists and products are differentiated.
- Pricing policies.

This suggests that in any assessment of the market structures which exist in the supply of tourism, there are a wide range of factors that can affect the operation, management and development of the tourism sector. In other words, the products and services that tourism businesses provide are a function of changing market conditions and businesses need to constantly consider the market and adapt their business strategies to remain competitive. Attention now turns to the principal sectors of the tourism industry.

Attractions and activities

Tourism attractions are a vital part of the tourism industry because they provide the focus for tourist activities and yet Lew (1987: 54) recognizes that 'although the importance of tourist attractions is readily recognised, tourism researchers and theorists have yet to fully come to terms with the nature of attractions as phenomena both in the environment and the mind'. Although a number of influential studies now exist on tourism attractions (e.g. Swarbrooke 1995), there is still a debate on their role and effect on the tourist and the supply of tourism services. Attractions are difficult to categorize because they span a wide spectrum of types within both the natural and man-made environments and sometimes a combination of each. As a result, there are a wide range of typologies.

Natural resources as attractions

The identification of attractions based on natural resource is complex since Cloke and Park (1985: 34) believe the term to be 'a culturally-defined and abstract concept. In essence, anything can be regarded as a resource if it offers a means of attaining socially-valued goals'. In other words, individual perception of any given natural resource will vary significantly: the beauty lies in the eye of the beholder. Gunn (1994) has discussed the importance of natural resources as tourist attractions and categorized them according to five natural features as shown in Table 5.1.

A review of these resources shows that many are inter-dependent and rely on management. One example that illustrates the inter-relationships which exist is a National Park. National Parks provide a degree of management, balancing the number of activities with conservation whenever possible. One of the greatest pressures which these resources face as tourist attractions are related to access (Page 1999) and are often compounded by the interaction of both tourist and recreational users who consume the same resource, often with differing impacts.

Table 5.1 **Tourism and natural resources**

Resource	Tourism-related development
Water	Marine and fresh-water resorts, harbours
Topography	Mountain and hill resorts
Vegetation	Spring flower sites, autumn foliage areas, Savannah safari sites
Wildlife	Safari areas, whale-watching areas
Climate	Sites suited to beach use, winter sports, and other climate-reliant activities

(Source: Gunn 1994)

Man-made resources as attractions

In the post-war period, one of the major growth sectors within the global tourism industry has been the evolution and development of man-made environments for tourism, often epitomized by the development of Disneyland and more recently by theme parks (see Chapter 8). The development of man-made attractions reflect the evolution of tourism spending for attractions as visitors are prepared to spend time and money on man-made attractions that fulfill a wide range of needs during their holiday experience. Swarbrooke (1995) lists man-made tourist attractions in Table 5.2.

These attractions will form the basis of Chapter 8 where the different types will be considered in some detail and, therefore, this section will address one of the issues facing managers, that of changing demographics. In western industrialized countries, the proportion of senior citizens is changing dramatically; consideration of Table 5.3 illustrates why managers need to review whether their product has appeal to a wide age range.

Within the 'senior' market there are widespread changes – the real challenge will be providing for the active, large age 70-plus segment; the forecast indicates that there will be particularly significant domestic demand from this group. Whilst the concept of 'edutainment' is appropriate for school and college-age visitors, does this apply to the senior tourist? Access to relevant data is clearly important for managers and this sector 'appears to be more active in marketing research than the literature suggests in as much as the propensity to undertake customer surveys can be used as a tool to assess marketing research activity' (Brunt and Dunster 1999: 7); their survey was based on responses from 316 attractions in England and Wales.

Activities

Inskeep terms activities as an important area of the attraction sector and in this context will be interpreted as comprising special events such as festivals, conferences and sports-related tourism. There is a growing interest in such events as the seminal study

Table 5.2 **Man-made resources of tourism importance**

Man-made and purpose-built to attract tourists	Man-made but not originally designed to attract visitors
Theme parks	Cathedrals and churches
Open air museums	Stately homes
Heritage centres	Archaeological sites
Craft centres	Castles
Safari parks	Historic gardens
Entertainment complexes	Steam railways
Museums and galleries	Reservoirs
Health spas	Factory tours and shops
Casinos	Farms open to the public

(Source: Swarbrooke 1995)

Table 5.3 **Changing demographics in western Europe: senior travel, 1990 and 2000**

Age group	Population (millions) 1990	2000	Change in trips taken (%) 2000/1990 (D)	2000/1990 (I)
55–59	20.2	19.9	+54.3	+58.5
60–64	22.1	20.8	+45.6	+51.3
65–69	17.8	17.5	+47.1	+82.4
70–74	13.8	15.7	+120.9	+100.0
Over 75	16.6	25.8	+198.4	+168.6
All seniors	90.6	99.7	+79.6	+78.3

Note: D = domestic trips; I = International trips

(Source: Adapted from Viant 1993)

Plate 5.1 Entrance to a Maori meeting house, Northland, New Zealand
This is a sacred place for the local community and has a significant cultural meaning which visitors need to respect in terms of the local customs and traditions.

by Getz (1991) and the *Journal of Festival Management and Event Tourism* (now renamed *Event Management*) indicates because localities now recognize both the economic and marketing benefits of events and festivals as generating tourist-related revenue and employment for their area and region, particularly where seasonality is pronounced. Festivals and other events are discussed in Chapter 8.

Accommodation

Accommodation is a fundamental requirement for tourists who stay overnight in a locality and it comprises a significant sector of the tourism industry in many regions simply because of the capital investment and sunk costs in this form of infrastructure to support tourism. Accommodation is reviewed in Chapter 9 and here the emphasis is on one of the more recent trends in the accommodation sector which is the rise of the mega-hotel and its growth in Las Vegas, USA. It was only in 1997 that the destination exceeded the 100,000-room point but, because of the scale of building, there were more than 125,000 hotel rooms in the year 2000. Table 5.4 illustrates the size of some Las Vegas hotels.

It is not just the number of rooms that make these hotels impressive properties; the 43-storey Mandalay Bay is 'set in over 60 acres (and) has an artificial lake set out as a beach-fringed tropical lagoon, a sea of predators – home to crocodiles and sharks – and a 2,000-seat live music venue' (Fockler 1999: 64). Relating to the origin of their name, The Venetian 'includes a Grand Canal with gondolas, a 315-foot campanile, Doges Palace, Bridge of Sighs and St Marks Square' whereas Hilton's Paris features 'a 50 storey half-scale Eiffel Tower'. The Las Vegas Convention and Visitors Authority (LVCVA) projects that for every 1,000 new rooms opened an

Plate 5.2 Groningen's red light district, the Netherlands
Most Dutch cities have a red light district. The one in Sydney, Australia has been described as 'sin city'.

Table 5.4 **A selection of Las Vegas' mega-hotels**

	Number of rooms
MGM Grand Hotel & Casino	5 005
Luxor Hotel Casino	4 427
Excalibur Hotel Casino	4 032
Circus Circus Hotel & Casino	3 808
Mandalay Bay	3 775
Flamingo Hilton	3 642
Las Vegas Hilton	3 174
The Mirage	3 049
The Venetian	3 036
The Bellagio	3 005
Paris Hilton	2 914

(Source: Fockler 1999)

extra 275,000 visitors a year are needed. Given the scale of development, active marketing needs to be complemented by new direct flights since many visitors arrive by air: a total of 30,227,287 passengers deplaned in 1998. Fockler (1999: 65) comments:

> one of the urgent strategic goals for the LVCVA is to increase domestic services into (the) international airport. The LVCVA calculates that a 20% increase in flights is needed if Las Vegas is to reach its target of 6 million more visitors by the end of 2000. Visitor volume in 1999 was predicted to be 32.3 million.

To see further statistics, view the website at www.lasvegas24hours.com.

Transportation

Transport 'is acknowledged as one of the most significant factors to have contributed to the international development of tourism' (Page 1999: 1). Transport provides both the essential link between the tourism origin and destination areas and facilitates the movement of holidaymakers, business travellers, people visiting friends and relatives and those undertaking educational tourism. Not only is it the dynamic element in the tourism supply chain (see Page 1999 for more detail) but it is an also an integral part of the tourism industry. As a supplier of tourism services to move people from home area to their holiday destination or the location they wish to visit, transport is an element of the supply sector that links many of the other elements of the tourism product together. In other words, it links the tourist to the destination, the accommodation, attractions and resources they consume and impact upon during their leisure time when on holiday. For example, at the destination, tourists quite often use rental cars to travel outside of the confines of the tourist resort or region they are staying in. The rental car provides a mechanism by which the tourist can undertake the 'touring' element in a flexible and unstructured manner compared to the use of public transport that determines when and where the tourist can visit. The supply of rental cars can be categorized into the global players (Hertz, Avis, National, Budget and Europcar) and small-scale, local businesses. As Bull (1991: 63) observes the global players have shown 'extreme sensitivity to competitive activity from each other ... (ensuring) very similar product lines and tariff rates' – and, as a result, stability in this particular market. The two key determinants of rental demand are airline passenger arrivals and GDP growth (Russell 1999); the first of these is another illustration of the inter-dependence common between the supply components.

According to Russell (1999) the impact of car rental on GDP growth led to a multiplier effect whereby for every one percentage point rise in GDP, car rental volume increased by 1.06 in Western Europe between 1994 and 1997. The car rental sector is very under-researched and recent data difficult to acquire. Table 5.5 illustrates the linkages between GDP, airport arrivals and car rental.

The issue of partnerships has been mentioned above, in relation to the airlines, and the same imperative to achieve competitive advantage applies to the rental companies; Hertz, for example, has links to the Spanish, Swiss and Canadian railway companies as well as with many airlines and hotels. On the other hand, Europcar is 50 per cent owned

Table 5.5 **GDP, airline passenger arrivals and car rental volume in Europe, 1994–1997**

	1994	1995	1996	1997
GDP, current prices (Euro bn)	6 218	6 465	6 792	7 150
Real EU GDP growth (%)	2.9	2.7	1.7	2.6
Air passengers (mn)	189.4	219.7	233.6	246.5
Car rental days (mn)	144.3	155.4	166.9	177.3

(Source: Russell 1999)

by the French hotel chain Accor and 'special accommodation and rental packages' feature the Accor brands Sofitel, Novotel, Mercure and Ibis (Russell 1999: 10). As with other sectors of the tourism business, the development of the internet will have a significant effect on car rental. Russell (1999: 25) refers to Hertz and Alamo having offered 'discounts of up to 20% on normal rental rates for reservations made on line', the administration costs being lower than through conventional methods. A new entrant to the marketplace in 2000 was easyRentaCar, an offshoot of easyJet, with the ultimate intention of having rental stations at all their destinations. A key feature was the starting price of £9 per day compared to around £20 from the competitors. However, only one model was offered, painted in the easyGroup 'house' orange with the web address displayed on the sides. James Rothnie, Corporate Affairs Director, believes that the car rental business is where the airline industry was five years ago – before the low-cost carriers began to have an impact. For further information see www.easyrentacar.com.

Institutional elements

The term institutional elements refers to the influence of agencies and organizations in the public and private sector which affect, manage and regulate the supply of tourism services and business interests. Within the tourism industry, a number of public sector bodies such as national tourism organizations (see Chapter 14) are charged with managing the public sector role of planning the tourism supply within countries. In England, there are ten regional tourist boards of which South West Tourism covers an area of south-west England based on the Regional Development Agency boundaries. At the local level, most local authorities in Britain provide a tourism marketing service and many finance the operation of tourist information centres (TICs) in their area. An example of marketing at the local level by the public sector is the branding of an area, like Catherine Cookson Country – based on the novelist. The local council has attracted visitors to a part of north-east England which has traditionally been perceived as one associated with a declining industrial sector and this represents a good illustration of place-marketing (see Ashworth and Voogd 1990). In other parts of the UK, partnerships have been developed between the public and private sectors whereby promotion of the area is devolved to hybrid bodies such as the North Devon Marketing Bureau and Norwich Area Tourism. This is not unique to the UK and many other parts of the world have also developed such initiatives.

The growth of partnerships is partly driven by the financial imperative (i.e. when one has no choice due to limited budgets) whereby local authorities cannot provide the range of services they would like to; the same applies to the operation of tourist information centres in the UK which have had to become more commercial. However, 'the ability of TIC personnel to provide a complete service from information provision through to holiday booking is edging closer and new technology can assist in making this function more effective' (Connell and Reynolds 1999: 508). In addition, within the private sector, tourism industry lobby groups exist which represent the specific interests and views through a membership subscription. As tourism has grown so have the number of 'common-interest' associations representing sectoral interests. Some are trade associations in the sense that membership is corporate; in Britain, the Association of British Travel Agents is a misnomer since it represents several hundred tour operators as well as retailers. Other associations represent individual membership; in Britain, the Institute of Travel and Tourism comprises employees drawn predominantly from tour operation, retail, and transport organizations whereas membership of the Tourism Society is drawn largely from the tourist boards, education and consultancy. One of the few truly global bodies, with a very diverse sectoral membership, is Skål International, founded in 1932 and representing approximately 25,000 tourism middle and senior management staff in 80 countries (Busby 1998); more information can be found at the website www.skal.org. One of the areas where both the private sector and private sector interests overlap is in the area of training programmes which also have a major role in the human resource issues affecting the tourism sector (see Chapter 10).

Education and training for tourism

Many tourism companies state that their employees are their principal asset; the tourist experience can be made – or destroyed – by the level of service a visitor receives. A number of issues surround the supply of labour in tourism; in both developed and less developed countries, seasonality of demand (see Ball 1989) can result in temporary employment for large numbers and this, in turn, can lead to a low level of commitment to one employer. Staff turnover generally, even in year-round destinations, can be high; low wages and lack of a clear career structure are usually a key factor. The national culture can also influence staff who may perceive certain service jobs to be low status. The introduction of an English school qualification, the GCSE Travel and Tourism, in the late 1980s, has at least raised awareness of the value of tourism in the UK. Surprisingly, integrated tourism training and education is a relatively new phenomenon in many countries although hotel and catering courses have existed in some European nations for several decades.

In Britain, two examples can be used to illustrate that tourism as a business came of age in the 1980s. First, since pioneering the 'Welcome Host' concept in 1991, the Wales Tourist Board has now awarded nearly 50,000 people with the certificate, paving the way for other tourist boards and further refinement with the International Welcome Host and Welcome Management schemes. Welcome Host is designed for the wide range of personnel who come into contact with visitors, from hotel receptionists to taxi drivers, and is delivered in a single day. At the other end of the training spectrum, in terms of both duration and intellectual requirements, is the development of tourism degrees; the first were offered, in 1986, at what are now the Universities of Northumbria and Bournemouth. From two in 1986, there are now tourism degrees at nearly 70 universities and colleges. What should be noted is that not all courses are vocationally oriented, there is a wide range of disciplinary content; for example, tourism can be studied with subjects such as theology as a joint honours degree (Busby 2001). Degrees identified as Tourism Management do usually feature a salaried, year-long placement in the industry in either the UK or overseas (Busby *et al.* 1997). As an international comparison, dramatic growth in tourism courses at a higher level has been mirrored in New Zealand and Australia – in the latter, it has even become formal government policy (Busby 2001).

Other tourist facilities and services

The public sector usually plays a prominent role in the provision of basic infrastructure which one can also categorize under tourism supply issues. These can comprise health facilities, power, water, sewerage, and roads are needed for residents as much as tourists and it is unlikely that the private sector would invest heavily unless a substantial return on capital could be envisaged. Bull (1991: 203) observes that where 'tourism is sufficiently identifiable and separable as an infrastructure user, it may be possible to avoid "subsidising" tourists by levying user-pays charges ... where tolls are charged on highways, bridges and parking, a free pass may be issued to local residents'. One critical element of tourism infrastructure worth considering in some detail is airport provision, an aspect that Page (1999) believes has largely been overlooked. The world's largest airport operator is BAA. Since being privatized by the British government in 1987, it has made substantial investments in its airports and developed the retailing arm. Just a few of BAA's investments will be considered: the new £400 million terminal at London Stansted opened in 1991 and increased capacity from 2 million to 8 million passengers a year. A £160 million refurbishment and expansion programme at Gatwick and Heathrow began in 1994 to provide more seating, catering and retail outlets. A further improvement to London's infrastructure was opened in 1998 in the form of the £450 million Heathrow Express, linking London Paddington to the airport with four trains an hour each way.

BAA also manage all or some aspects of airports overseas; these include Pittsburgh, Indianapolis, Harrisburg, Newark and, as one partner in a consortium, Melbourne. Using its corporate expertise for a different transport mode, in 1999, a 15-year contract was signed with Eurotunnel 'to operate its retail facilities in its Folkestone and Calais terminals' (website: www.baa.co.uk). Another company to perceive the inherent value in airports is Stagecoach plc which acquired Glasgow Prestwick in April 1998, having developed from its scheduled bus operations into other forms of transportation.

Conclusion

Tourism supply issues illustrate that the tourism sector operates in a dynamic business environment which is subject to constant change in both the tastes and trends which tourists pursue and the regulatory environment in which tourism operates. It is evident that attempts to conceptualize and develop frameworks and models of tourism supply have been limited within established studies of tourism and largely descriptive sector-by-sector studies have prevailed. As a result, the consumption of tourism services and goods are often emphasized to the neglect of the production of tourism goods. What one often overlooks is that although tourism is a dynamic business activity based upon the discretionary spending, within specific tourism businesses, it is the constraints upon production which inhibit a situation of perfect competition. To the contrary, the retailing of tourism goods and services is highly competitive in most countries whereby the construction of tourism products based upon different elements (e.g. accommodation, transport and attractions) is increasingly subject to a greater degree of control by regulatory bodies. At the same time, tourism businesses are being forced to re-examine their traditional methods of production because of reduced profit margins and competition from new entrants using technology such as the internet (see Chapter 13). The increased competition is also manifest in the pressure which multinationals and large national corporations are placing on the existing suppliers of tourism services due to the financial leverage and control which they exert through increased concentration of their activities, particularly through integration in the tourism sector (see Sinclair and Stabler 1997).

Discussion questions

1. What is meant by the term tourism supply?
2. What are the different sectors of the tourism industry which combine to supply tourists with products, services and experiences?

Internet resources

By going to the weblink at www.thomsonlearning.co.uk students can access the following study on the Thomson Learning website. The study is from S.J. Page (1994) *Transport for Tourism* and examines the complex issue of how to conceptualize the supply of services for tourists which in this case focuses on the transport sector. It identifies one fundamental concept – the supply chain which has been widely used in logistics – and helps understand how the supply of services are interlinked and dependent upon a wide range of inputs within a systems framework.

3. How easy is it to identify elements of a tourism industry in terms of tourism supply?
4. What are the different approaches used by economists to examine competition with the supply of tourism services?

References

Ashworth, G.J. and Voogd, H. (1990) *Selling the City*, London: Belhaven.

Ball, R.M. (1989) 'Some aspects of tourism, seasonality and local labour markets', *Area*, **21**: 35–45.

Brunt, P. and Dunster, A. (2000) 'The propensity of visitor attractions to carry out customer surveys', *International Journal of Tourism Research*, **2** (5): in press.

Bull, A. (1991) *The Economics of Travel and Tourism*, Melbourne: Pitman.

Busby, G. (1998) 'Skål International: the development of a tourism interest group', *Journal of Vacation Marketing*, **4** (2): 161–74.

Busby, G. (2001) 'Vocationalism in higher level tourism courses: the British perspective', *Journal of Further and Higher Education*, **25** (1): in press.

Busby, G., Brunt, P. and Baber, S. (1997) 'Tourism sandwich placements: an appraisal', *Tourism Management*, **18** (2): 105–10.

Cloke, P.J. and Park, C.C. (1985) *Rural Resource Management*, London: Croom Helm.

Connell, J. and Reynolds, P. (1999) 'The implications of technological developments on tourist information centres', *Tourism Management*, **20**: 501–509.

Fockler, S. (1999) 'The US gaming business, *Travel & Tourism Analyst*, **1**: 45–69.

Getz, D. (1991) *Festivals, Special Events, and Tourism*, New York: Van Nostrand Reinhold.

Gunn, C.A. (1994) *Tourism Planning*, third edition, Washington: Taylor & Francis.

Hall, C.M. and Page, S.J. (1999) *The Geography of Tourism and Recreation*, London: Routledge.

Inskeep, E./WTO (1994) *National and Regional Tourism Planning*, London: Routledge.

Lew, A. (1987) A framework for tourist attraction research, *Annals of Tourism Research*, **14** (4): 553–75.

Murphy, P. (1985) *Tourism – A Community Approach*, London: Methuen.

Page, S.J. (1999) *Transport and Tourism*, Harlow: Longman.

Russell, P. (1999) 'Car rental in Europe', *Travel and Tourism Analyst*, **1**: 1–28.

Sessa, A. (1983) *Elements of Tourism*, Rome: Cantal.

Shaw, G. and Williams, A. (1994) *Critical Issues in Tourism: A Geographical Perspective*, Oxford: Blackwell.

Sinclair, M.T. and Stabler, M. (eds) (1992) *The Tourism Industry: An International Analysis*, Wallingford: CAB International.

Sinclair, M.T. and Stabler, M. (1997) *The Economics of Tourism*, London: Routledge.

Swarbrooke, J. (1995) *The Development and Management of Visitor Attractions*, Oxford: Butterworth-Heinemann.

Viant, A. (1993) 'Enticing the elderly to travel', *Tourism Management*, **14** (1): 52–60.

Williams, S. (1995) *Recreation in the Urban Environment*, London: Routledge.

Further reading

Hall, C.M. and Page, S.J. (1999) *The Geography of Tourism and Recreation: Environment, Place and Space*, London: Routledge.

Learning outcomes

After studying this chapter, you should:

- Understand the functions of travel and tourism intermediaries.
- Be able to identify some of the major organizations.
- Have an awareness of key issues in travel product distribution.

6 Travel and tourism intermediaries

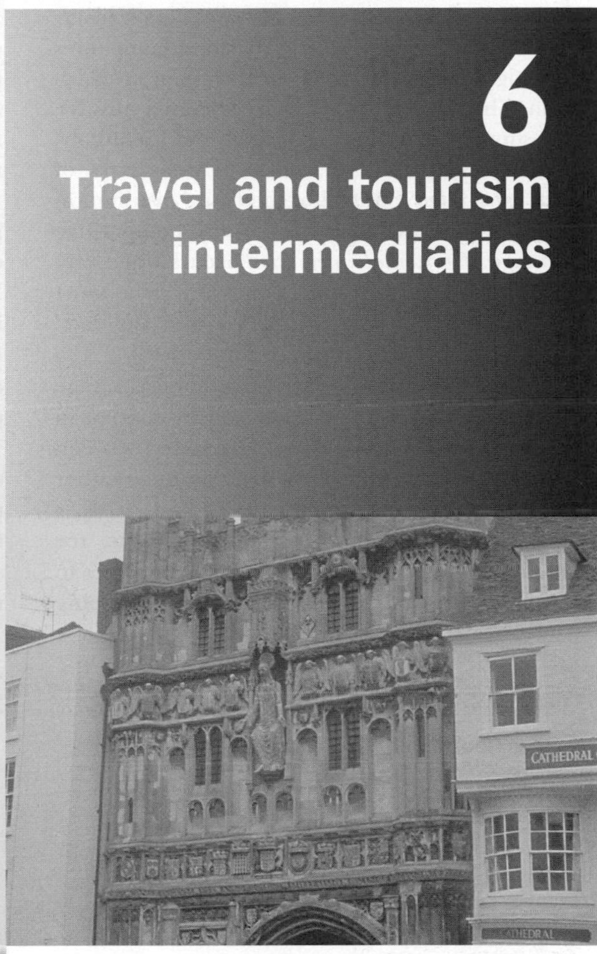

Overview

The travel product, be it an airline seat or hotel room, differs from manufactured goods in that it must be sold or lost; it cannot be stocked indefinitely. This feature has led to the creation of thousands of intermediaries around the world packaging two or more complementary travel elements. This chapter considers the diverse range of intermediaries in the travel and tourism industry by dividing them into those that principally affect the commercial world and those concerning leisure travel.

Introduction

The tourism industry comprises thousands of businesses, ranging across several sectors, from transport and accommodation to visitor attractions. Each of these sectors offers a variety of products but all can be enhanced through improved distribution; this is commonly achieved through intermediaries who 'package' several different sectoral components (e.g. accommodation, transport and ancillary services). One of the largest categories of intermediary is the tour operator; some are truly multinational corporations (MNCs) with operations world-wide. The largest in Europe include Thomson, Airtours, First Choice, TUI and Kuoni. These companies achieve *financial economies of scale* through the bulk purchase of aircraft seats and hotel rooms for a whole season. The customer benefits in two ways: the cost of a *package holiday* is competitively priced compared to the individual arrangement of the components and purchase can be made conveniently through a high street travel agent, by telephone or internet.

Further economies of scale are achieved by companies purchasing or establishing companies operating at different levels in the chain of distribution. Thomson Holidays owns Britannia Airways, at the supplier of aircraft seats level, and Lunn Poly, at the high street retail level; this is an example of *vertical integration*. Control of the entire distribution channel gives the organization a competitive advantage. *Horizontal integration* occurs when one type of intermediary acquires another of the same type – for example, the (British) Airtours Holidays' purchase of the Scandinavian tour operator SAS Leisure, thus providing greater geographic coverage and market share of the package holiday business in Europe. *Complementary integration* is enacted between companies offering complementary products rather than competing ones; in the 1960s and 1970s, a number of airlines acquired hotel chains, for example. *Economies of scope* allow some companies to organize *diagonal integration*; Saga Holidays, by being a direct-sell tour operator, obtains addresses for its customers and this has allowed them to market other products, such as insurance. American Express, as a financial services company, has the scope to sell its foreign exchange and traveller's cheque products through its own retail outlets.

Vertical and horizontal integration, in particular, provide companies with a much greater degree of control in Britain; in the late 1980s, the Monopolies and Mergers Commission (MMC) investigated the proposed takeover of Horizon Holidays by the Thomson Group since the combined group would represent a large proportion of the total inclusive tour market – Thomson was allowed to proceed. Again, in 1997, the MMC investigated tour operators' ownership of travel agency chains and insisted that the links between companies be made transparent. Table 6.1 shows some of the companies and their brands under common ownership.

Table 6.1 **Examples of integrated tourism companies and their brands**

Thomas Cook Group	**Airtours**	**First Choice**	**Thomson**
Airlines	*Airlines*	*Airline*	*Airline*
JMC	Airtours International	Air 2000	Britannia
Flying Colours	Premiair[1]	Leisure International	
Caledonian	Air Belgium		
	Cruise ships	*Cruise ships*	*Cruise ships*
	Airtours: 4 ships	2	3
	Costa Cruises: 7 ships		
	Hotels		
	30 properties		
	2 time-share complexes		

Table 6.1 **cont.**

Tour operations	*Tour operations*	*Tour operations*	*Tour operations*
Thomas Cook	Airtours Holidays	First Choice	Thomson
Neilson	Aspro Holidays	Unijet	Magic Travel Group
Club 18–30	Bridge Group brands	Hayes and Jarvis	Crystal Holidays
Style	Cresta Holidays	Eclipse	Simply Travel
Time Off	Panorama	Rainbow	Blakes Boating
	Direct Holidays	Schools Abroad	Austravel
	Tradewinds	SkiBound	Ausbound
	Euro Sites	Sovereign	Fritidsresor[5]
	Manos	2wenties	Greyhound International
	Sunquest[2]		Headwater
	Alba Tour[2]		Holiday Cottages Group
	Simon Spies[3]		Jetsave
	Ving Group[3]		Portland
	Frosch Touristik[4]		
Retail outlets	*Retail outlets*	*Retail outlets*	*Retail outlets*
Thomas Cook	Going Places	Bakers Dolphin	Lunn Poly
ARTAC Worldchoice Alliance	Advantage Travel Centres	Holiday Hypermarket	Callers-Pegasus
	Travelworld	Holiday Express	Sibbald Travel
		Intatravel	

Notes
1 Premiair is part of the Scandinavian operation.
2 Some of the North American operations.
3 Some of the Scandinavian operations.
4 Germany.
5 Scandinavian.

The brands and subsidiary businesses listed above are not definitive; they are merely intended to illustrate the level of integration.

(Sources: Jewell *et al.* 1999 and individual company websites)

A new category of intermediary

Consumer protection within the European Union has led to the creation of a new category of intermediary: *the travel organizer.* Any individual or company is so defined if they create a package consisting of two or more components from accommodation, transport or other key tourist service as long as it is provided for a duration of 24 hours or overnight. The Directive on Package Travel Regulations, implemented in Britain in 1993, is intended to provide greater financial protection for the consumer and makes the travel organizer contractually liable for the components of the package. Overnight, thousands of businesses became eligible for this definition whereas previously they were not called tour operators; many of these organizers are not 'outbound' operators, merely arranging different elements within the country. In England, it is the role of the Trading Standards Departments to police the regulations. Consensus on interpretation of the regulations has slowly emerged (eg. a school which organizes a residential trip once a year will not need to be financially bonded before being allowed to take money since it meets the criterion of 'occasional' organization).

Disintermediation

In the short time since the category of *travel organizer* appeared, the advent of *disintermediation* has begun to have an impact. Suppliers of travel products can eliminate the need to use an intermediary and sell through the World Wide Web (see Chapter 13). There is nothing radically new in the concept since direct-sell tour operators have always taken telephone bookings instead of using agents; however, what is different at the start of the twenty-first century is the sheer scale of business conducted over the internet.

Disintermediation is affecting both leisure and business (corporate) travel. American Airlines-owned SABRE is a Global Distribution System, featuring data on hundreds of airlines, and is now available to the public through its Travelocity website. The best trading period in 1999, for this operation, was 'three straight weeks with $3 million each week in sales' (Macdonald-Wallace 1999: A-140). Microsoft launched its own web-based travel reservations system, entitled Expedia, in 1997 and a UK operation in 1998; Expedia is categorized as a travel agency as it is acting for a range of suppliers. In the first month of operation in the UK, Expedia booked £360,000 worth of travel (Hodge and Condon 1998). Whilst disintermediation is clearly a threat to traditional travel agencies, the internet has also created opportunities for some small companies; for example, www.where-to-fish.com links thousands of fishing locations with accommodation in the area. For business travellers, disintermediation offers two benefits: the elimination of the traditional agency role (cost savings) and the ability to make their own travel arrangements on the office computer. Alford (1999: 114) reports that 'Texas Instruments expects to save up to $11 million by providing access to the Internet Travel Network for its 400 most frequent travellers'.

Leisure tourism

The tour operator

Tour operators are traditional intermediaries, packaging transport of some form with accommodation and, usually, the services of a representative at the destination. In many countries there are both outbound and inbound tour operators; in Britain, each has a trade association representing their interests, respectively, ABTA (the Association of British Travel Agents) and BITOA (British Incoming Tour Operators Association). There is also a much clearer distinction between tour operators and travel agents in Britain than in many other European countries; the EC Directive term of travel organizer referred to above indicates the lack of agreement Europe-wide. British tour operators using flights for their packages must obtain an Air Travel Organizers' Licence (ATOL) from the Civil Aviation Authority; this protects the consumer in the event of the tour operator ceasing to trade (Laws 1996 details ATOL financing). Tables 6.2 and 6.3 illustrate the scale of operation for the larger British tour operators; approximately 20 belong to an influential body called the Federation of Tour Operators (FTO) whilst at the other end of the spectrum, the Association of Independent Tour Operators (AITO) represents approximately 150 companies with annual carryings of less than 200,000. It is important to remember that these are only the figures for package holidays by air; many operators also offer coach or rail-based arrangements. Exhibit 6.1 illustrates the impact of one tour operator on the leisure tourism market.

The larger tour operators are said to sell to the mass market, whereas many AITO member-companies organize specialist holidays. However, as Curtin and Busby (1999: 142) observe:

> it is becoming more difficult to clearly define a tour operator's market segment ... a pattern is gradually forming between market segments determined by price, volume and price-elasticity of demand. There are mass market clients who pay for a high priced, quality product and other mass market clients who pay the cheapest price possible for a volume-intensive product [see Table 6.4].

The calculation of demand elasticity is discussed in Chapter 17.

The EC Directive further emphasized the role of the tour operator in establishing and monitoring the standards of quality in the overseas resort.

Retail multiples

Multiples are travel agencies so-called because they are found in numerous locations nationally, they are usually owned by a large parent company; Table 6.1 lists the named retail outlets for the four largest British tour operators. Over the last decade, Thomson and Airtours in the UK, have established or acquired many new retail outlets; in mid-1999, Thomson possessed nearly 900 whilst Airtours controlled 707 Going Places branches, 118 Travelworld outlets and 350 Advantage Travel Centre franchises. There is on-going concern about the extent to which vertically integrated agencies can control which tour operators' brochures are displayed. Concentration in the retail travel sector is not unique to Britain. In Canada, between 1997 and 1999, the number of agencies declined from 5,000 to just over 4,000 as 'many smaller players have been swallowed up by larger companies or have become part of a franchise or consortium' (Loverseed 1999: 85). Table 6.5 illustrates the largest agency groups in Canada.

Table 6.2 **Passengers carried under the largest air travel organizers' licences**

Twelve months to September	1999	1998	% change
1 Thomson Holidays	4 254 571	3 732 398	3
2 Airtours	3 040 678	2 913 254	4
3 JMC Holidays	2 618 691	2 635 419	–1
4 First Choice	1 945 883	1 914 222	2
5 Unijet Travel	929 121	933 440	(0)
6 Avro	620 920	596 814	4
7 Trailfinders	563 537	469 538	20
8 Cosmosair	370 400	360 067	3
9 Gold Medal Travel	344 988	269 904	28
10 Virgin Holidays	339 894	233 761	45

Table 6.3 **Passengers licensed to/or planned by top five groups for the 12 months to September 2000**

Groups and licence holders	Passengers planned at: Dec. 1999		Dec.1998	
1 Thomson Group total (Thomson Holidays, Lunn Poly, Crystal Holidays, Port Philip Group, Something Special Holidays, Holiday Cottages Group, Magic Travel Group)			5 079 848	4 440 427
2 Airtours Group total (Airtours, Cresta, Paris Travel Service, Swiss Travel Service, Panorama, Direct Holidays)			4 553 750	3 930 324
3 Thomas Cook Group (Thomas Cook, JMC Holidays, Time Off, Style Holidays)			3 775 653	2 710 924
4 First Choice Group (First Choice, Skibound, Schools Abroad, Unijet, Hayes & Jarvis, Meon Travel, Sunsail)			3 103 423	3 068 410
5 Cosmos Group (Cosmosair, Cosmos Coach Tours, Avro, Distant Dreams)			1 083 828	1 132 439
		% Total		% Total
Total licensed to or planned by the top ten groups	20 149 002	68	17 891 549	64
Total licensed to or planned by the top four groups	16 739 575	57	14 789 506	53
Total for all ATOL holders	29 583 780	100	27 942 133	100

(Source: CAA 1999)

In the 1990s there was also significant growth in the number of call centres for a range of products including travel agency services. Thomas Cook Direct opened its second centre in 1998, in Falkirk, and now employs over 700 staff. Furthermore, the evidence suggests that they are dealing with entirely new business (i.e. it is not at the expense of their own high street retail outlets).

The independent travel agent

The traditional travel agent selling a wide range of products, from rail tickets to package holidays, has been under threat for more than a decade as the influence of the multiples has increased through vertical integration. In Britain, two common interest groupings developed as an outcome of this threat: the National Association of Independent Travel Agents (NAITA) and the Alliance of Retail Travel Agents' Consortia (ARTAC).

NAITA has developed the Advantage Travel Centre name for marketing purposes whilst ARTAC formed a link with the multiple AT Mays, in 1997, and trades under the World Choice banner; it is arguable that being involved with a multiple no longer makes these agents independent. In the late 1990s, yet another organization, operating outside the trade body ABTA came into existence, called the Global Travel Group.

Exhibit 6.1 **Airtours – an example of integration**

The extent of integration is demonstrated by reference to Airtours; their internet 'home page' in February 2000 states that the company and its associates 'carry passengers from 17 countries, with 1613 travel outlets, 17 telesales centres, 42 aircraft, over 40 principal tour operating brands, 46 resort properties, 10 cruise ships and 2 vacation ownership resorts – besides employing over 20,000 people worldwide'. David Crossland, the chairman, commented in a press release on 3 February 2000 that Airtours 'as the world's largest air inclusive tour operator will continue to develop new channels of distribution for our products'. Examples of these new channels of distribution are illustrated by Airtours' February 2000 launch of www.ombro.com in Scandinavia, the company's first internet-only tour operator, which enables clients to tailor-make their own packages.

Rather than incur heavy costs establishing a new 'dot com' in the USA, Airtours purchased TSI for £240 million – also in February 2000; TSI is the world's largest cruise distributor although it has no high street presence. It uses the internet and telephone with about 11 per cent of TSI's cruises being booked online in 1999; the company also sells car rental and hotel accommodation. The company has strategic links with other travel companies; for example, Carnival Corporation, a major American cruise operator, owns 25.8 per cent of Airtours' issued share capital and Carnival jointly with Airtours have acquired the Italian-based Costa Cruises. The latter held 19 per cent of the European-originating cruise market at the time of acquisition. Airtours' business is conducted through a number of divisions. The UK Leisure Group operates the various branded products, such as Airtours Holidays, Cresta and Panorama, besides the 728-branch Going Places retail chain. This group reported a turnover, for the year ended September 1999, of £1,838.3 million.

The Scandinavian Leisure Group is active in Denmark, Norway, Sweden, Finland and Poland with brands such as Spies, Saturn, Globetrotter and Ving, whereas the European Leisure Group sells a range of brands in Belgium, Holland, France and Germany. Currently, Airtours owns 36 per cent of Fti, one of the five principal tour operators in Germany. Fti has itself vertically integrated, and its airline started operations in May 1999 with three Airbus A320 aircraft. The North American Leisure Group sells the holiday brands of Sunquest, Suntrips and Vacation Express in Canada and the USA; total turnover, for the year to September 1999, was £323 million.

Airtours' Accommodation Division comprises cruise ships, hotels and time-share apartments. Currently, there are four cruise ships offering between 790 and 1,432 berths each; in the winter 1999/2000 season, three were based in the Caribbean and one in the Canary Islands. A total of 18 hotels are owned, accommodating over 400,000 customers per year; the properties are world-wide as demonstrated by a 65 per cent stake in Blue Bay Resorts which has properties in Mexico and the Caribbean. Turning to another component of this division, time-share, or vacation ownership as it is also called, is one of the most dynamic parts of the leisure industry; The Beach Club, Grand Canary, provides 158 luxury apartments which sell at between £5,500 and £14,000 per week. In Orlando, Florida, the Oasis Lakes provides 70 apartments. Finally, the Aviation Division looks after Airtours' world-wide aviation interests; brand names include Airtours International, Air Belgium, Fly Fti and Premiair (Scandinavia). Independent research suggests that Airtours International and Premiair operate the highest load factors, world-wide, at above 93 per cent.

In 1999, Airtours attempted to acquire Britain's fourth-largest tour operator, First Choice, but suffered a setback when the European Commission decided to block its £850 million bid. The Commission decided to block the bid on the grounds that the remaining three integrated companies (Thomson, Thomas Cook and Airtours) would have a dominant presence in the market. Airtours lodged an appeal against this decision in December 1999. Financial journalist, Grant Ringshaw (2000: B3), noted in February 2000 that the company was in talks with the Bank of Scotland to start an internet-based bank; this 'would be the first major move by a holiday company into mainstream financial services'. The Bank of Scotland already has experience of operating joint ventures with the likes of supermarket chain Sainsbury's and the Japanese firm Sony. It would mean that the bank would have access to a large customer base with 10.5 million holidays sold each year – which provides an example of diagonal integration.

Table 6.4 **Types of mass and specialist markets for tours according to price**

Market	Price elastic	Price inelastic
Economy mass	High volume	Medium–high price
	Low price	High volume
Luxury mass	Medium volume	Medium volume
	Medium price	High price
Premium mass	Low volume	Lower volume
	High price	Higher price
Specialist	Low volume	Lower volume
	High price	Higher price
Premium specialist	Minimum volume	Minimum volume
	Higher price	Maximum price

(Source: Curtin and Busby 1999)

Table 6.5 **The largest travel agency groups/consortia/global companies in Canada**

	Number of branches/member agencies	
	1996	**1998**
Gem Travel	754	800
Giants Travel	790	756
Thomas Cook	280	300+
Uniglobe	226	230
TravelPlus[a]	210	210
Travel T-COMM	205	205
Consultour	200	200
Carlson Wagonlit	148	200+
CAA	135	141
INTRA	121	135

[a] TravelPlus was due to come under the umbrella of Carlson Wagonlit in 1999.

(Source: Loverseed 1999)

Business tourism

Business tourism is both a large and non-seasonal component of the global industry, accounting in 1990 for 63 million of the 425 million international trips. The expenditure per capita for business tourism is usually greater than that for leisure travel. It comprises several forms: general business travel, conference-related travel, exhibitions/trade fairs, and incentive travel. The major distinguishing feature of business travel is that, unlike leisure travel, the employer usually pays all costs and the destination is dependent on the business to be conducted rather than individual choice and trips can be made at very short notice. This reflects the premium pricing of products for business travellers on airlines and in the accommodation sector. According to O'Brien (1998: 38): 'Europe is now the largest business travel generating region in the world, accounting for close to 47% of the global travel market – as against about 30% for the USA'; the estimated value of the European market was US$186 billion in 1998, although with the gradual expansion of Asia–Pacific business travel will certainly expand in those mega-urban regions and Extended Metropolitan Regions (focused on Japan, South Korea, China, Taiwan, Malaysia, Singapore, Indonesia and a number of other South-east Asian locations (Hall and Page 2000) which have developed as a function of globalization, national governments promoting economic development through an export-oriented strategy funded by foreign direct investment. What this example shows is that much of the world's business travel is oriented towards urban centres where much of the business activity and facilities are located, making it locationally dependent in many cases.

Business travel agents

As with leisure retail travel, there has been concentration in this sector; independent business travel agents in Britain face multiples such as BTI Hogg Robinson, American Express, Portman Travel Group and Carlson Wagonlit. BTI, Business Travel International, is a global alliance of corporate travel agents represented by Hogg Robinson in the UK; in 1997/8, they 'acquired Kuoni's French and Italian business travel operations and bought out its Finnish and Russian agency partners' (O'Brien 1998: 52). BTI Hogg Robinson also purchased a 51 per cent stake in the Rider Travel Group, one of the largest Canadian business travel agency groups. Table 6.6 illustrates the mix of revenue for leading agency groups in France.

Companies with high expenditure on business travel requirements will employ a corporate travel buyer in order to control overall costs; in Britain, the Institute of Travel Management was created in the late 1950s to represent these individuals, whereas agents are represented by the Guild of Business Travel Agents (GBTA). Some companies put out to tender the entire travel management function of their business and receive regular monitoring reports on employee travel trends; the corporate agent may receive a management fee for this rather than commission on sales.

Exhibition and conference providers

Exhibition and conference tourism is a well-developed form of tourism, with many South-east Asian cities competing for this lucrative market and building facilities to attract the largest conventions

Table 6.6 **Leading corporate travel agency groups in France, 1997**

Agency name	Sales volume (Ffrancs bn)	Business travel share (Ffrancs bn)	Number of sales outlets Business	Leisure
Havas Voyages	13.5	8.5[a]	306	326
Carlson Wagonlit	6.8	5.1	151	164
Manor	5.5	4.2	62	166
Selectour	5.5	3.6	100	330
Protravel Internet	1.7	1.3	30	37

[a] for Havas Voyages American Express (HAVE).
(Source: HAVE; TIM cited in O'Brien 1998)

and exhibitions. Other cities in Asia–Pacific, such as Melbourne, compete head on with Singapore whereas cities such as Auckland are still trying to attract investors to make a significant private sector investment to nurture this market. One example which illustrates the scale and features of business venues is ExCeL, a world-class event facility that was due to open in November 2000. It will 'provide Europe's exhibition and events industry with the first totally integrated, state-of-the-art technology and communications infrastructure – the only one of its kind in Europe' according to the operators. It is East London's largest single development since the construction of Canary Wharf in 1988, occupying a 100-acre site in Docklands and offering 90,000 square metres of exhibition, conference and event space and adding a major tourism boost to a region which has had a chequered history of developing tourism infrastructure and markets (Hall and Page 1999; Page 1995). As part of the development, five hotels will provide 1,200 bedrooms, 400 apartments and 20,000 square metres of restaurants and shops – in the first phase. Listed buildings alongside are also being utilized so that a 'total destination atmosphere' is created. In the first year of operation, 120 events are scheduled, estimated to attract over 2 million visitors. For ExCel's facilities, see http://www.ExCeL-London.co.uk.

Incentive, conference and exhibition organizers

The New-York-based Society of Incentive and Travel Executives (SITE) defines Incentive Travel thus:

> Incentive travel is a global management tool that uses an exceptional travel experience to motivate and/or recognize participants for increased levels of performance in support of the organizational goals.

In terms of value, the Society estimates that the North American incentive travel market is worth in excess of $10 billion per annum and world-wide it exceeds $20 billion. The first known incentive travel programme is believed to have been a 'Weekend in New York', organized for NCR Corporation employees by NCR and the Plaza Hotel in 1906. Key targets for incentive travel have been the sales staff of companies simply because it is easy to measure their productivity and the return on the investment can be measured in financial terms. SITE state on their website that what 'distinguishes incentive or motivational travel from traditional travel is the focus on creating an extraordinary experience for the winner, or one that builds morale, communicates the corporate message, or fosters improved communications between employees and/or the company and its customers'. For further information on the Society of Incentive & Travel Executives (SITE) see http://site-intl.org/index.htm.

Conclusion

This chapter has reviewed the concept of travel intermediaries who perform a vital function in the assembling and packaging of individual tourism products for the consumer. Although this may vary in different parts of the world, the basic concept is to provide consumers with a network of distribution to fulfil their needs. One of the greatest challenges for this sector of the tourism business is the impact of technology and the way in which disintermediation has begun, a feature examined in more detail in Chapter 13. A great deal of integration has occurred within the tourism sector, which has reduced the number of major industry providers and one consequence is concentration within the tourism sector, not just at a national level but increasingly at a global level.

Keeping abreast of change and developments in this sector is difficult given the pace of change and scale of competition. At the time of writing, the UK-based Thomson Holiday Group was the focus of a £1 billion offer from a German-based company (Preussag) seeking to develop a major holiday business, which will certainly be of interest to the European Commission. The challenge of change has meant that this sector of the tourism industry has seen smaller operators subject to acquisitions and mergers to gain economies of scale and scope (Sinclair and Stabler 1997). At the same time, the challenge of new technology has further concentrated attention on declining profit margins where many of the larger holiday companies seeking to make profits on volume sales rather than on high-value niche products. In short, the mass packaging of tourism products for certain socio-economic groups still offers the basic revenue for holiday companies although more sophisticated consumers look for other things.

Questions

1. Discuss the impact on consumers of increasing consolidation in the retail travel sector.
2. Identify the benefits for a company using an incentive travel scheme.
3. Explain the advantages to a tour operator of strategic links with overseas-based companies.
4. List the features which distinguish business travel from leisure travel.

References

Alford, P. (1999) 'The impact of technology on tourism marketing, e-commerce and database marketing', in F. Vellas and L. Becherel (eds) *The International Marketing Of Travel And Tourism – A Strategic Approach*, Basingstoke: Macmillan: 111–18.

Civil Aviation Authority (CAA) (1999) *ATOL Business*, Issue 13, January, London: Civil Aviation Authority.

Curtin, S. and Busby, G. (1999) 'Sustainable destination development: the tour operator perspective', *International Journal of Tourism Research*, **1** (2): 135–47.

Hall, C.M. and Page, S.J. (1999) *The Geography of Tourism and Recreation: Environment, Place and Space*, London: Routledge.

Hall, C.M. and Page, S.J. (eds) (2000) *Tourism in South and South East Asia*, Oxford: Butterworth-Heinemann.

Hodge, G. and Condon, C. (1998) Net travel jets into Great Britain, 30 December, Forrester. Company website.

Jewell, G., Williamson, B. and Archer, K. (1999) 'The Airtours Cruise intranet: streamlining the distribution of information, knowledge and money', in D. Buhalis and W. Schertler (eds) *Information and Communication Technologies*, Vienna: Springer-Verlag: 337–46.

Laws. E. (1996) *Managing Packaged Tourism*, London: Thomson Learning.

Loverseed, H. (1999) 'Travel agents in Canada', *Travel and Tourism Analyst*, **1**: 71–86.

Macdonald-Wallace, D. (1999) 'UK tourism and the internet: the slow stumble towards success', *Insights*, March, A139–142.

O'Brien, K. (1998) 'The European business travel market', *Travel and Tourism Analyst*, **4**: 37–54.

Page, S.J. (1995) *Urban Tourism*, London: Routledge.

Ringshaw, G. (2000) 'Airtours plans bank', *The Sunday Telegraph*, 27 February.

Sinclair, M.T. and Stabler, M. (1997) *The Economics of Tourism*, London: Routledge.

Further reading

Bray, R. and Raitz, V. (2000) *Flight to the Sun: The Story of the Holiday Revolution*, London: Continuum.

Laws. E. (1996) *Managing Packaged Tourism*, London: Thomson Learning.

Sinclair, M. T. and Stabler, M. (eds) (1992) *The Tourism Industry: An International Analysis*, Wallingford: CAB International.

Internet resources

By going to the weblink at www.thomsonlearning.co.uk students can access the following study on the Thomson Learning website. The study is from E. Laws (1997) *Managing Packaged Tourism* and outlines the ways in which tour operators distribute their products to the consumer and serves as a useful case study in understanding this vital role that tour operators play in the travel and tourism intermediary sector. It highlights the significance of the complex marketing process which tour operators engage in and the long time frames involved in planning and distributing the products to the final market.

Learning outcomes

After studying this chapter, you should:

- Be able to recognize the principal types of tourist transport.
- Be familiar with the development of tourist transport.
- Understand some of the issues facing transport operators.

7 Transport and tourism

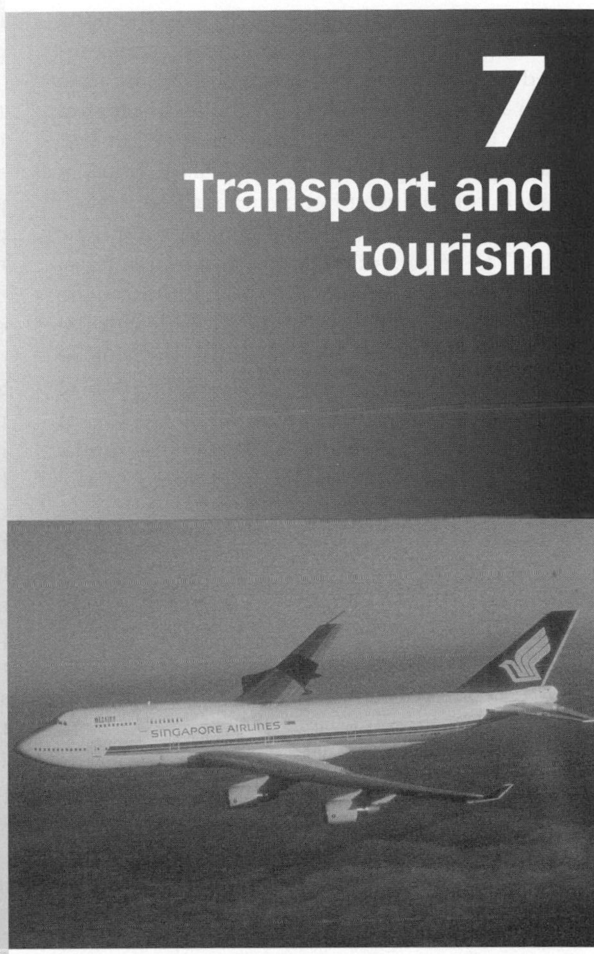

Overview

The purpose of this chapter is twofold: first, to provide facts and features of different tourism transport types and, second, to identify some of the issues facing the industry in the twenty-first century. Given the range of transport types and the number of issues associated with each, this chapter is necessarily selective.

Introduction

Transport is a fundamental component of the tourism industry. Transport is a precondition for travel: it facilitates mobility and the movement of tourists from their place of origin (i.e. their home area) to their destination and back. Transport is frequently neglected in the analysis of tourism, often being relegated to a passive element of the tourist experience. Yet transport remains an essential service element of tourism and in some cases it can form the focus of the tourism experience *per se* (e.g. cruising and scenic train journeys). Various forms of transport have been associated with the development of tourism and technological developments in transport combined with the rise in personal disposable incomes have led to the expansion of both domestic and international tourism. For example, in the nineteenth century, the development of the railway network in the UK led to the creation of numerous seaside resorts and, in cases such as Buxton, the rejuvenation of some spa resorts; it also led to the very first excursion arranged by Thomas Cook – from

Leicester to Loughborough – in 1841. In the twentieth century, improvements in motor transport created opportunitites for holidays by car and mass tourism by coach operators. Major technological advances in aircraft performance since World War II have opened up non-stop, long-haul routes at extremely competitive prices; cheaper flights have, in turn, affected the traditional long-stay domestic holiday. The impact of technology on tourist travel time is illustrated by Figure 7.1 which illustrates the time compression of travel through time with the decline in travel times. To illustrate the role of transport in the development and organization of tourism, discussion will focus on a variety of different forms of transport to illustrate the fundamental linkages with tourism and some of the impacts they may cause.

Land-based transport

The car

The car is widely neglected in tourism studies because it is now such an accepted part of everyday life that the impact and use in tourism is taken for granted and overlooked.

Both the early study by Wall (1971) and Patmore (1983) identify the fundamental changes in mobility in the post-war period in western industrialized society and the rise in car ownership. One of the principal changes to take place in the post-war period in both outdoor recreation and domestic tourism is the major effect of the car on patterns of travel: it has made travel more convenient and less dependent upon public transport. The car offers considerable flexibility in the way people can travel and access tourism resources and sites outside of urban areas. The major change that the car has induced is that tourists and recreationalists are no longer dependent upon the existing forms of transport infrastructure such as the train to fulfil their tourism and recreational needs. What the car has done is transform the tourists ability to organize and develop their own itineraries and activity patterns without being dependent upon existing transport provision. For the resource managers of sites such as National Parks, one outcome has been the need to manage the impact of the car on key sites (e.g. honeypots, which are high-use sites) and popular locations which tourists visit. In some cases (e.g. The Goyt Valley in Derbyshire) the Peak

Figure 7.1 **The contribution of transport technology to reductions in travel time**

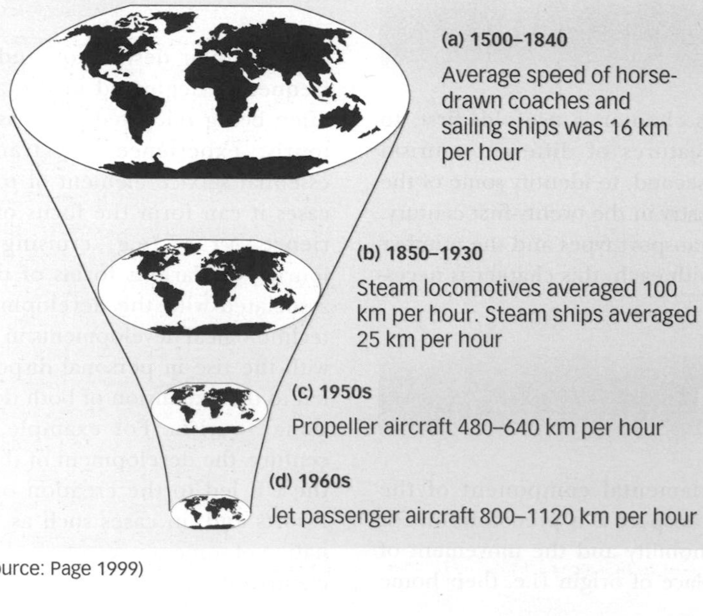

(a) 1500–1840

Average speed of horse-drawn coaches and sailing ships was 16 km per hour

(b) 1850–1930

Steam locomotives averaged 100 km per hour. Steam ships averaged 25 km per hour

(c) 1950s

Propeller aircraft 480–640 km per hour

(d) 1960s

Jet passenger aircraft 800–1120 km per hour

(Source: Page 1999)

District National Park has managed the use of cars by providing alternative forms of transport to key tourism and recreational sites where over-use is a potential threat to the local resource base. In more remote areas such as the coastal zone to the north of Perth in Western Australia, the impact of four-wheel drive vehicles is now an uncontrollable phenomenon which is contributing to the destruction of the sand dune environment and is now the subject of management strategies. It illustrates all too well the difficulty of managing a form of transport which is subject to the whim of the individual in its use in time and space. In urban areas, the car is also a major problem for small historic cities such as Canterbury, York, Chester and Cambridge which have provided out-of-town centre car parking to address the environmental impact of congestion on the town centre environment which is highly used by tourists. In some cities, such as Groningen in Northern Holland, the car is virtually banned from the historic city and cycling is a preferred form of transport together with walking, which has assisted in the preservation of the built heritage, since no major provision has had to be made for car parking.

Coach and bus transport

In the road-based transport sector (excluding the car) a number of different forms of passenger transport serve the needs of tourists. These can be classified into:

- express coach services
- packaged tours on coaches (see Dostal 1999)
- urban and rural bus services to tourist locations (see Page 1999)
- airport taxi and shuttle services (see Page 1999)
- sightseeing tours in urban and rural areas (see Chapter 12 on the development of Guide Friday).

The most important one to consider in this context is the express coach service, given its competition with rail and air transport, its fundamental role in the evolution of domestic holidaymaking in the post-war period (see Chapter 2) and its redevelopment as a budget-priced option for tourist travel in the 1990s. Prior to examining the express coach service sector as a specific tourist-related form of transport, it is useful to consider recent developments in the organization and management of transport services which have altered the ownership structure of such operations. One example is that of Stagecoach plc in the UK which is set to become one of the largest world-wide operators of bus and coach services. The company is also pursuing a strategy of integration within the transport sector by acquiring non-road-based forms of transport such as rail and airports (e.g. Prestwick in Scotland). Stagecoach was established in 1980 by Brian Souter and Ann Gloag (brother and sister) and in April 1993, the company was floated on the Stock Exchange with a market capitalization in excess of £2.5 billion. As Figure 7.2 shows, the company has grown to incorporate a wide range of businesses. For example, Stagecoach has a 49 per cent stake in the Virgin Rail operation which is one of the newly established train operating companies in the UK (see Page 1999 for a case study on tourist rail travel and privatization). Stagecoach also owns South West Trains and the Island Line on the Isle of Wight. In the case of aviation, the acquisition of Prestwick Airport in 1998 was a strategic decision to enter the expanding low-cost aviation market in the UK, with the airport recording 600,000 passenger movements a year. Stagecoach also own one third of Porterbrook, the newly established train rolling stock leasing company. One of the newest ventures by Stagecoach was the acquisition in July 1999 of Coach USA which cost £1.2 billion. Coach USA is the largest provider of coach services in the USA, with a fleet of 6,500 coaches serving 33 states of the USA and Canada.

However, despite the size of the company, it is estimated to have less than 2 per cent of the total market share of $40 billion coach travel market in North America. Coach USA itself was a product of 70 acquisitions since it was established in September 1995, illustrating the dynamic nature of the transport sector in a privatized and highly deregulated environment in both the UK and North America. This is also reflected in the company's aggressive acquisition of assets in Australia and New Zealand, where a number of urban public transport bus operations have been acquired in the 1990s. In Portugal, it operates 135 buses on 60 routes and carries 27 million passengers on regional routes. In Hong Kong, Stagecoach operates 1,200 buses, carrying 200 million passengers a year and has given a vital link in to operations in mainland China. This is reflected in the 25 per cent stake with Kwoon Chung buses in China and this offers many opportunities for the budget long-distance transport market in post-communist China.

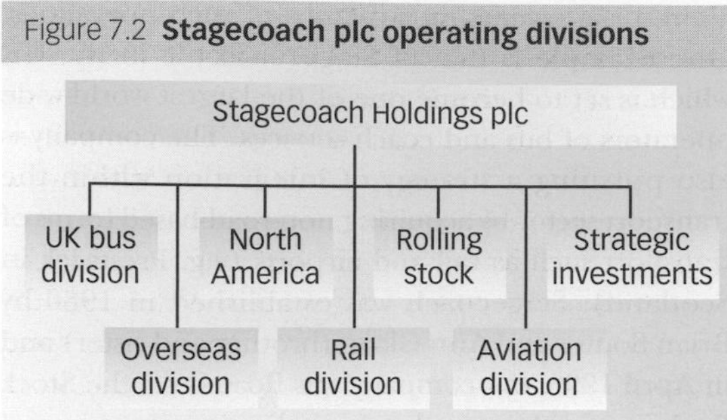

Express coach services

These services are normally operated on a hub-and-spoke principle, using a series of key locations as gateways in major cities with services to outlying districts that are fed into the hubs. In the UK pre-privatized National Express coach network offered a low-cost budget long-distance coach service throughout the UK with government subsidies for operating services to unviable areas. In the post-privatization era, major competition developed on the main trunk routes between rail, air and coach services in a highly deregulated environment and the outcome has been a wider range of operators now competing on the former National Express routes, with National Express (now a privatized company) which is a diversified operator that now has interests in rail and subsidiary transport interests. For the tourist market, express coach services in the 1980s within the UK saw major innovations in the product range (e.g. more comfortable non-stop Rapide services with toilets and on-board service) which segmented the growing market for coach travel (see Dostal 1999; Page 1994b). In the 1990s, these innovations in service for tourists, particularly the introduction of seasonal services to

Plate 7.1 A nineteenth-century cable car, San Francisco, USA
Tourist transport, such as this cable car, can prove to be a popular tourist attraction in its own right.

domestic coastal resorts from key urban centres have also given rise to the growth of the youth travel market for European coach travel, particularly with the opening of Eastern Europe. One result is that with the development of low-cost airlines, youth discounts on European rail travel, the youth market is a fiercely contested market sector for which the operators now compete very aggressively. In most cases, express coach services are the lower end of the tourist market, since they are the cheapest form of travel because of the trade-off with the time taken to travel in a European context. One of the new developments in the 1990s by coach operators in the improvement to hub terminals which now resemble the airline terminal concept, with former non-service philosophies replaced with the airport retailing philosophy that a customer waiting for any form of transport is a potential consumer as reflected in mainline rail and airport terminals in the late 1990s.

Cycling

The cycle is arguably the most sustainable form of tourist transport one can use because it does not require fuel and does not always have a major impact on the built and physical environment, with the exception of mountain biking where it constitutes a recreational activity. Tourist cycling is now a well-established form of tourism in many countries, particularly where provision has been made through the development of cycle routeways. In the case of New Zealand, distinct patterns of cycle tourism exist (e.g. see Ritchie 1998). In the UK, developments in recreational and tourist cycling are exemplified by the work of Sustrans (Sustainable Transport), the civil engineering charity formed in 1979, which is co-ordinating the National Cycle Network in Britain. This will cover 9,000 miles of cycle route by the year 2005 and is supported with £43.5 million of National Lottery finance. The first 5,000 miles of the network officially opened on 21 June 2000 as a result of the partnership with over 400 local councils and other organizations.

Significantly, the national network has been planned with the intention of linking to visitor attractions; to this end, the National Trust and Sustrans have worked on a number of joint initiatives which make journeys for cyclists more enjoyable and are largely traffic free. As Page (1999: 281) notes Sustrans 'has a pan-European perspective on cycle tourism, with its European Cycle Route Network'; one example of these routes is the 5,000-kilometre Atlantis route from Skye, in Scotland, to Cadiz in Spain as reflected in Figure 7.3. The cycle is also a popular pastime for domestic tourists and increasingly many cities are now making provision of cycle paths within the built environment which visitors can enjoy through the hire of cycles. This is even evident in locations such as the Norfolk Broads in the UK where cycle routeways have been developed and managed to encourage low-impact tourism on a fragile environment. This follows good practice which is epitomized by the tourism and recreational activities that are planned and managed in the Netherlands, which makes a major use of cycling as a pastime and sustainable form of day-to-day transport. The nature and profile of cycle users for tourism purposes is now becoming well documented as reflected in the work of Lumsdon (1997).

Rail travel

Train transport for tourism takes two forms: combined leisure and business, which is scheduled, and predominantly leisure-based services 'where train travel becomes the focus of the tourist experience' (Prideaux 1999: 73). An example of the latter is Queensland Rail (QR) which developed *The Queenslander* in 1986 in order to revive the fortunes of its long-distance services; one of the reasons for this decline was the growth in Australian car ownership – one for every 1.87 persons, according to Prideaux (1999). Queensland Rail identified a range of market segments which could be promoted:

1 Long-distance rail passenger services: *The Sunlander, Westlander* and *Inlander*
2 Luxury on wheels: *The Queenslander*
3 Nostalgia
4 Youth/budget market
5 Trains as tourist attractions: *Kuranda Scenic Railway*.

(after Page 1999)

The QR developments illustrate 'a diversity of markets so far neglected by other rail organisations in Australia as well as in other countries' (Prideaux 1999: 85) although in some countries such as Singapore and India, these markets are increasingly being recognized. This illustrates the need for a

Figure 7.3 **The European cycle route network**

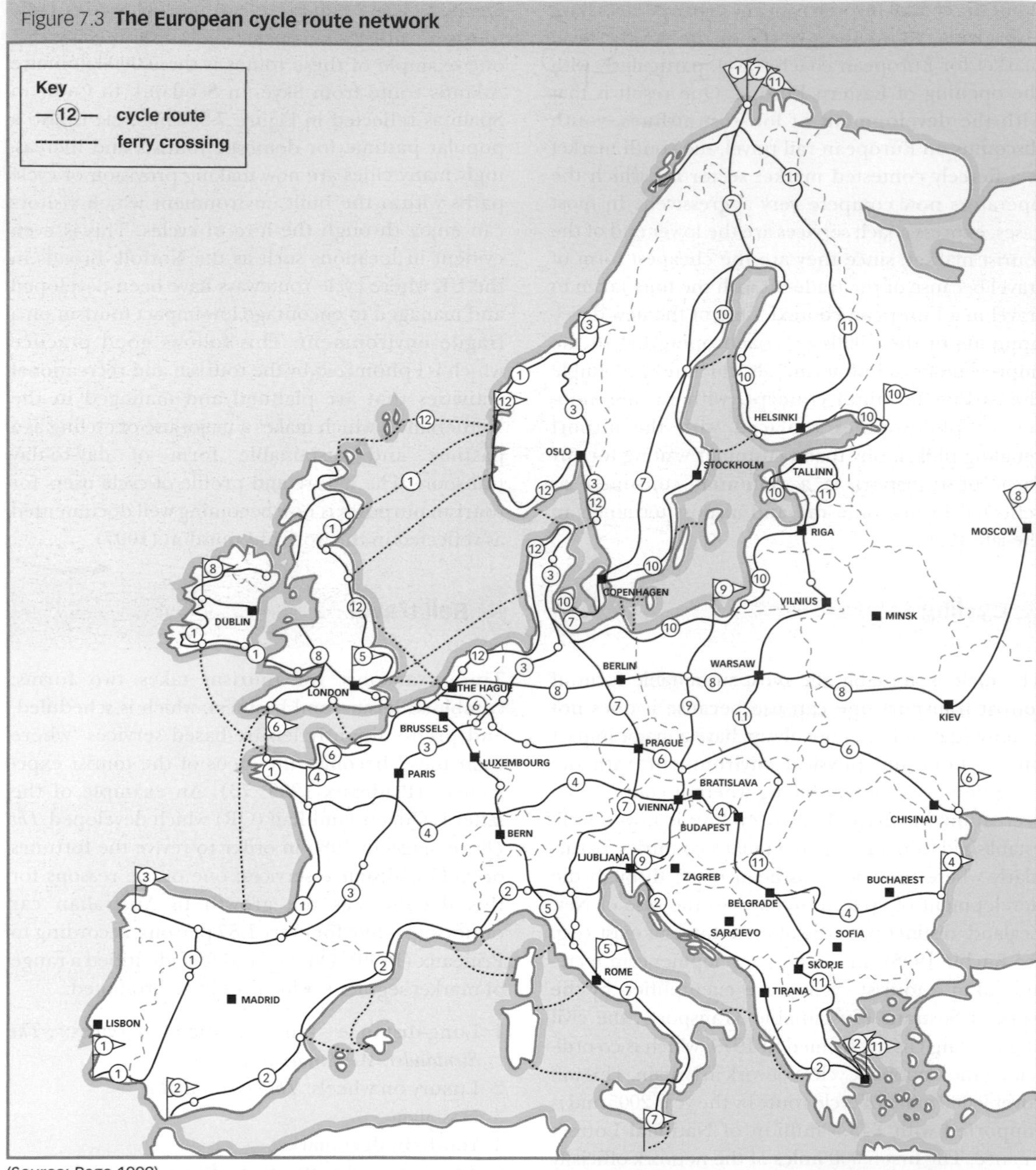

(Source: Page 1999)

recognition of different products to meet different tourist needs and greater positioning of specific rail-tourism products to recognize the complexity of the tourist transport market. FEVE operate a scheduled train service along the northern coast of Spain providing another means of transport for the independent traveller.

An example of a rail operator with a substantial mixture of leisure and business traffic is VIA Rail which operates from the Atlantic to the Pacific coast of Canada on a total of approximately 14,000 kilometres of track. In the Quebec City–Windsor corridor, high-speed trains link the country's largest business centres including Toronto and Montreal.

Plate 7.2 The FEVE narrow-gauge railway, northern Spain
The FEVE narrow-gauge railway runs along the coast of northern Spain and is itself something of a tourist attraction.

To the east, named trains operate through scenic areas to Nova Scotia whilst *The Canadian* runs three times a week between Toronto and Vancouver – one of *National Geographic's* top five 'Great Journeys of the World'. VIA Rail operates 451 trains a week to 450 destinations besides the scenic and high-speed services and its management of the rail business illustrates how it has improved its performance through reducing administration costs by 66 per cent since 1990 as well as operating costs by 22 per cent and in a climate of declining state subsidy. It has followed a similar route to development as many of the train operators in the privatized UK network (see Page 1999 for more detail). Table 7.1 illustrates the geographic diversity of 'tourist experience' trains.

Water-based transport

Water-borne transport is frequently overlooked in many studies of tourism since air travel dominates the world patterns of travel. However, it is certainly the case that the need to cross bodies of water, particularly where tourists use recreational vehicles (e.g. motor homes) and pursue land-based travel means that crossing bodies of water presents transport operators with seasonal markets that can help offset the costs of all-year round operation. Within the water-based transport sector, three main forms of transport can be identified: cruising, ferries and canal boats.

Cruising

The cruise product can take many forms; small-scale, specialist ships exist to take niche market clients to Antarctica and the Galapagos Islands and, at the other end of the spectrum, there are gigantic mass-entertainment ships which are themselves the destination. The product, obviously, comprises both transport and accommodation – and a number of cruises out of Asia go 'nowhere' since they are provided for the

Table 7.1 **A selection of 'tourist experience' railway journeys**

Scheduled	Geographic region	Semi-scheduled	Geographic region
Trans-Siberian	Russia	ROVOS	South Africa
The Blue Train	South Africa	E & OE	Thailand – Malaysia
The Canadian	Canada	China's Orient Express	China
Shinkansen	Japan	Rocky Mountain Railtours	Canada
VSOE	Western Europe		

gambling market. As an activity, cruising has been growing at a dramatic rate: Peisley (1998b: 2) refers to demand in the USA increasing from 3.2 million passengers in 1989 to 5.05 million in 1997. The average annual growth rate over this period was 5.6 per cent. This level of growth is not confined to North America; UK ocean cruise passenger numbers grew from 416,000 in 1996 to 625,000 in 1998 (Peisley 1998a). The size of cruise ships has also dramatically increased over the last decade with the major operators, such as Carnival, Royal Caribbean International and P&O Princess, ordering 100,000-ton-plus ships which bring significant economies of scale. These forms of luxury travel have led to a revival of cruise tourism at a global scale after the decline of the cruise liner in the post-war period when the aircraft offered much lower costs of transatlantic and world travel. In the new millennium, cruising has been relaunched as a luxury activity which is now more accessible to greater numbers of people with the luxury of five-star holiday resorts.

Ferries

One of the busiest waterways in the world is the English Channel which will be used to illustrate the significance of car ferries in tourism; a ferry service has been recorded in history between Dover and Calais since Roman times and evidence in medieval records also confirms the vital strategic and trade route which existed between these two ports. It remained the main crossing point between the UK and mainland Europe for many years. However, it is only since the end of World War II that a truly comprehensive 'product' has become available with the size of ships increasing in order to provide more of an 'experience' for travellers and a major business activity on-board the vessels for the ferry operators. The opening of one of the largest ever European tourist transport infrastructure projects, in the form of the Channel Tunnel, altered services on this route by the end of the 1990s and provided a new form of competition with the sea-based services which were subsequently rationalized, reorganized and repositioned to compete with the new operator.

As Page (1999: 265) notes, 'planners failed to recognize how the cross-Channel ferry industry would respond to the competition' created by the Tunnel's opening. Furthermore, duty-free sales were abolished in June 1999 and a substantial proportion of the ferries' revenue came from this source. It is not surprising then that P&O and Stena Line decided to merge their interests on the Dover–Calais route rather than compete; P&O Stena Line now offers 35 departures a day in each direction. This is a good illustration of a co-operative venture and alliance to compete with a new transport operator in an environment where the two main competitors pre-Channel Tunnel (i.e. P&O and Stena Sealink) were fiercely competitive and unwilling to co-operate until the business realities of a new threat changed their business practices. Figure 7.4 illustrates the extent of ferry crossings on the UK short sea crossing sector.

According to P&O Stena Line, their research indicates that many passengers feel their holiday starts once they board the ship, leading the company to improve facilities as well as standards. Given that

Plate 7.3 Dover channel ferry port, UK
Dover is one of the busiest channel ferry ports in Europe.

there would be a major loss of revenue from the abolition of duty-free sales, P&O Stena implemented their 'Brand World' strategy, working with market leaders such as Sony, Coca-Cola and Kenco to upgrade on-board facilities. This even includes a floating version of the London West End restaurant Langan's Brasserie. Table 7.2 illustrates the size of fleet ships and capacities together with year of construction.

This commitment to improving the quality of the experience has helped the Line to maintain a significant market share; between January and September 1999, P&O Stena held 38 per cent of the passenger market and 31 per cent of the tourist vehicles market on the short channel crossing. The Line carries approximately 12 million passengers a year and employs over 4,000 people. The following industry accolades reflect the investment in quality and facilities: 'Best Short-Sea Cross-Channel Operator 2000' and 'Coach Sea Route of the Year'.

Pleasure craft on inland waterways

Within countries which have an industrial heritage based on canals and inland waterways (e.g. northern European countries, the UK, Eire) a significant vacation market has developed based on pleasure boats designed to use the former canal and waterways that were previously developed to serve the transport needs of a former era. In cities such as Birmingham and Gloucester in the UK, the network of canals is so extensive that they have become the focus of urban regeneration projects where tourist use of pleasure craft is an integral part of the strategy to relaunch the area's appeal to the tourist seeking a heritage product.

To illustrate the scale and significance of this growing market for pleasure craft as part of a holiday experience, the example of the Norfolk Broads in

Figure 7.4 **UK short sea ferry crossings**

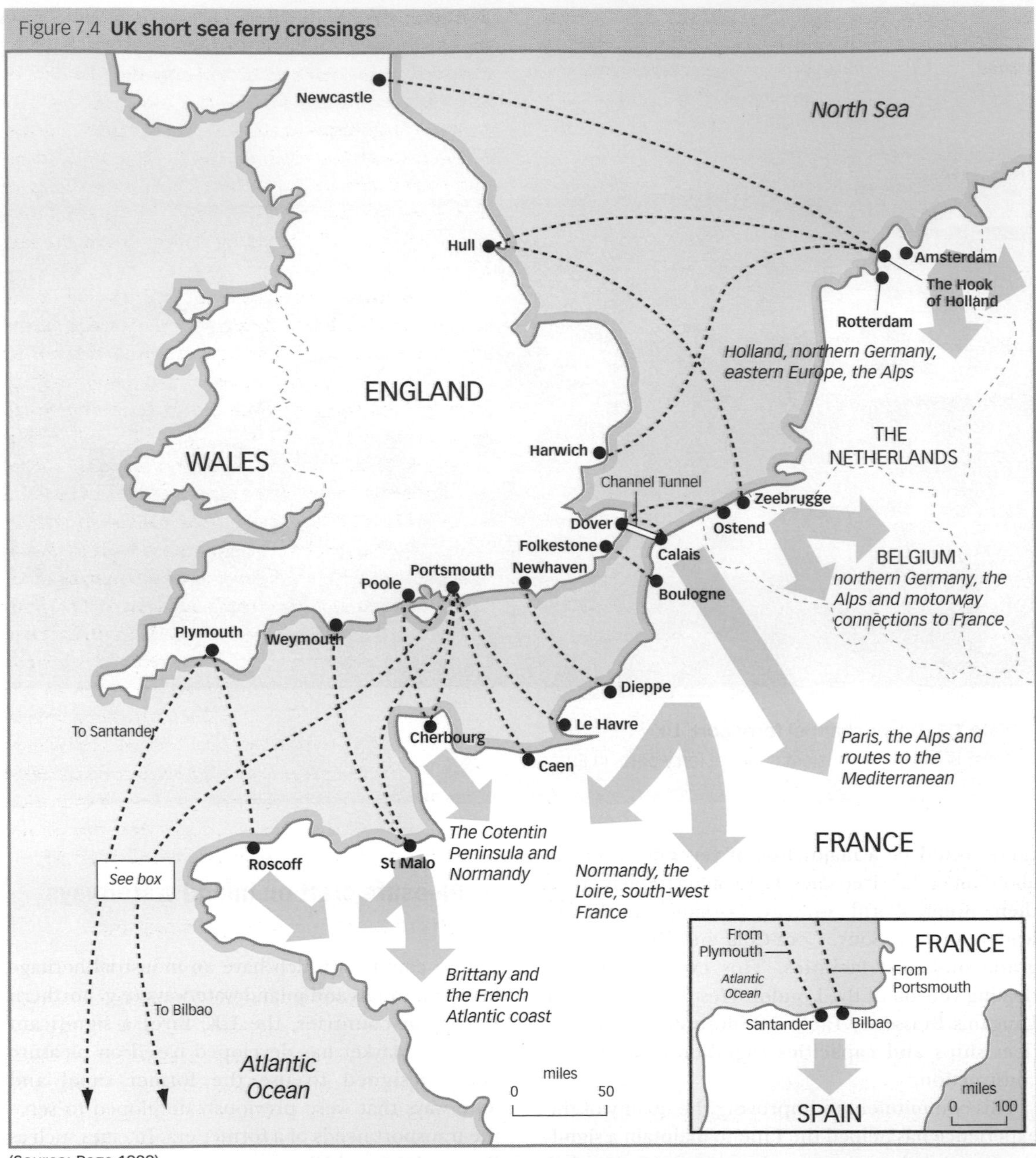

(Source: Page 1999)

the UK (Figure 7.5) suggests that even seemingly sustainable modes of tourist transport such as the canal or pleasure boat are not without environmental impacts. The Norfolk Broads is a wetland region in East Anglia created through the flooding of peat diggings in the medieval period. The region comprises a number of rivers and their tributaries which offer opportunities for recreational and tourism-related boating activities. The hire-boat industry was pioneered by John Loyne in the 1880s and popularized in 1908 by H. Blake and Company which set up purpose-built vessels for hire aimed at the rail-based visitors. In 1995, the boat companies in the region owned 1,481 craft hired to approximately 200,000 visitors a year. The single most important environmental impact of the hire-boat

Table 7.2 **The P&O Stena Line super-ferries**

Name	Built	Gross tonnage	Capacity – tourist vehicles	Capacity – passengers
P&OSL Aquitaine	1991	28 838	600	2 000
P&OSL Provence	1983	28 559	550	2 000
P&OSL Burgundy	1992	28 138	600	1 420
P&OSL Dover	1987	26 433	650	2 290
P&OSL Calais	1987	26 433	650	2 290
P&OSL Canterbury	1980	25 122	600	1 800
P&OSL Kent	1980	20 446	460	1 825

industry has been the damage to the river banks caused by the wash from vessels together with a number of other impacts induced by the visitors' effect on wildlife and the potential conflict with other activities such as angling. Yet the economic impact of boating in the region is estimated to contribute £25 million to the local economy and supports over 1,600 jobs while indirect tourist spending contributes to over 5,000 jobs.

Air transport

Apart from so-called 'air taxis', all civil aviation falls into one of two categories: scheduled and charter traffic. Scheduled airlines are those which operate to a clearly defined, published timetable, irrespective of whether a flight is full or not. Until the 1980s, many schedule airlines were state owned and run for reasons of national prestige; a classic example of privatization occurred in 1987 when the British government sold British Airways. In contrast, chartered aircraft, by definition, are chartered out to a third party; this may be a seat-broker who will sell smaller blocks of seats to small tour operators or it may be a large tour operator who requires the whole aircraft for a summer or winter season's flying. In reality, the large operators such as Airtours, Thomson, First Choice and Cosmos in the UK, possess their own airlines; they are, however, run as separate 'cost centres'. The evolution of air travel is a complex area which is historically determined by international bodies such as the International Civil Aviation Organisation (ICAO) and the International Air Transport Association (IATA). The regulations they established have, combined with bilateral agreements, established the framework for international air travel up until the deregulation era in the late 1970s.

A key feature of international civil aviation in the last 20 years has been 'deregulation'. Starting in the USA, in 1979, the federal government relaxed its control over route allocation and pricing, leading, inevitably, to the establishment of numerous small airlines, many of which no longer exist; although it pre-dates 1979, South West Airlines benefited from the ability to fly on any route and has pursued a policy of issuing boarding cards instead of tickets, serves no meals and operates as many flights a day as possible (see Page 1999 for a detailed analysis of air travel in a climate of deregulation). In 1999, South West was serving 55 cities across the USA. In Europe, a policy of 'liberalization' was adopted whereby member states gradually opened up access to key routes and, since 1997, EU airlines have been able to operate on any route within the Union. The advent of large-scale computerized systems, known as GDSs or Global Distribution Systems, has helped to market the increasing number of routes and operators; GDSs are discussed in more detail in Chapter 13.

The rise of the low-cost carrier

With the 'liberalization' of civil aviation in Europe, so-called 'low-cost' carriers – such as Debonair, Ryanair and easyJet – have been established. Because major airports, such as Heathrow and Gatwick in Britain, have a scarcity of takeoff and landing 'slots', these carriers have had to base themselves at less significant airports, such as Luton and Stansted, although associated costs can also be lower.

Since 1995, easyJet has developed a substantial network which, in 2000, comprised 28 European routes from bases at Luton, Liverpool and Geneva. The airline does not disguise how it can offer low fares; in fact, it positively advertises the reasons (see Figure 7.6). Despite controlling costs carefully, the airline operates relatively young, quiet Boeing

Figure 7.5 **The Norfolk Broads region**

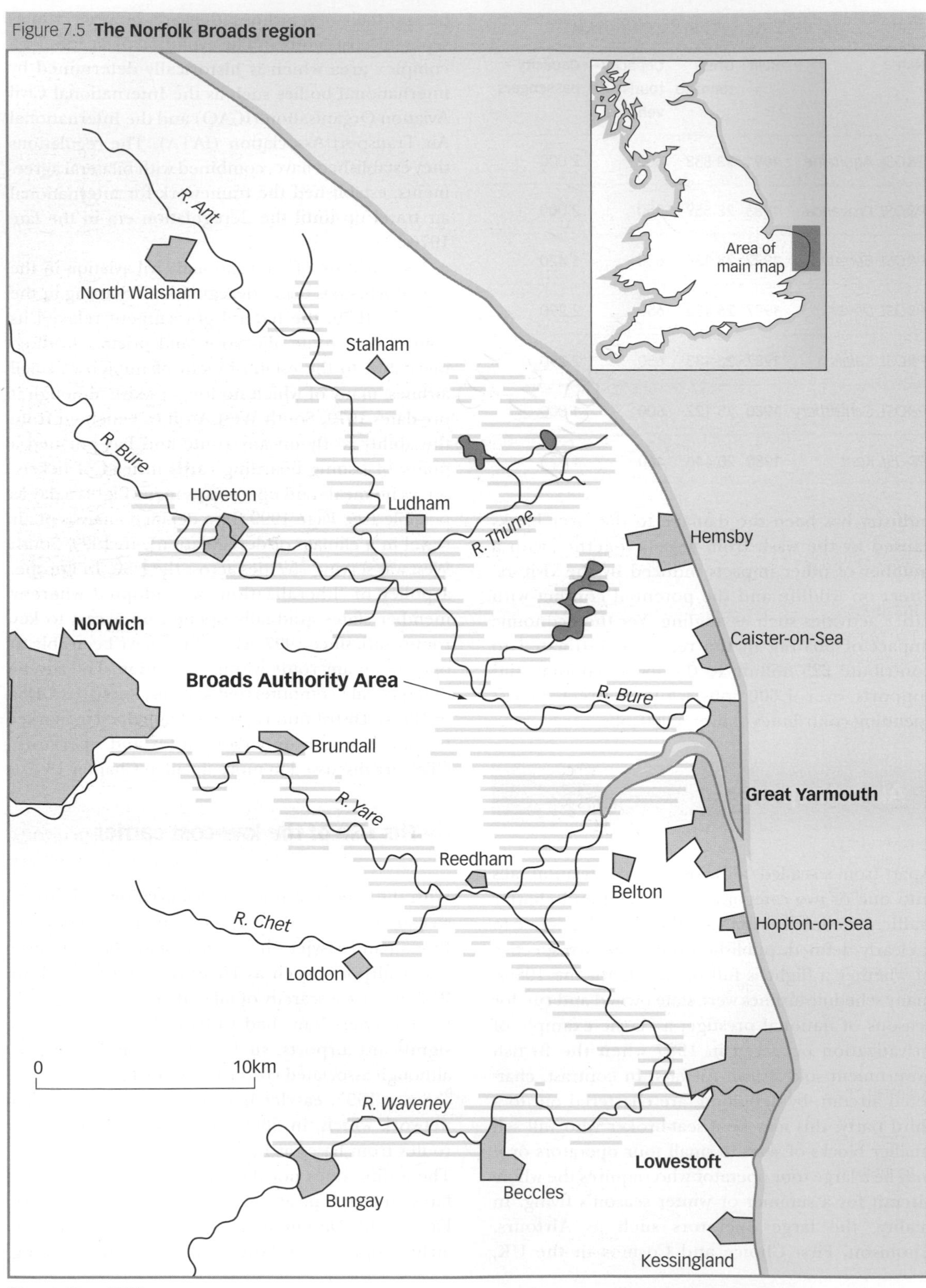

(Source: Page 1999)

Plate 7.4 A Singapore Airlines 747-400
The range of the Boeing 747-400 has affected tourism in the Pacific Islands because of its long-range capability. Melbourne to Los Angeles takes about 13–14 hours non-stop, with no refuelling en route.

Figure 7.6 **easyJet costs**

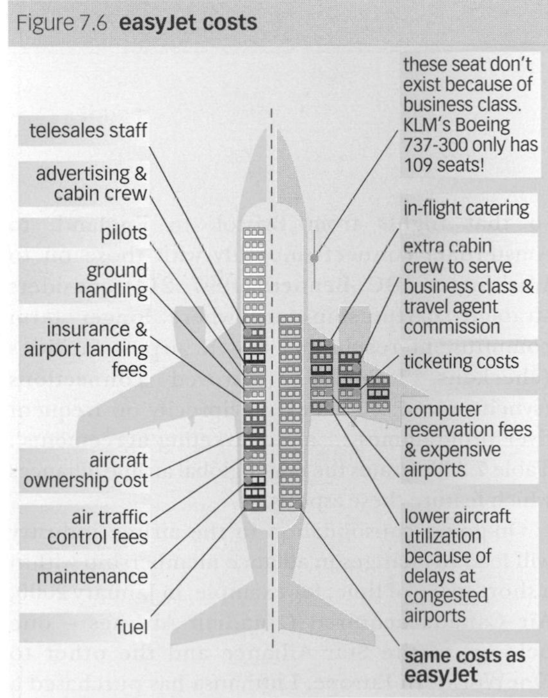

737–300 aircraft and has 15 of the 737–700 on order. easyJet has developed its presence at Luton to such an extent that, in January 2000, it accounted for 80 per cent of the entire airport throughput – even over a 12-month period it accounts for about 60 per cent. The threat of the low-cost carriers has led to British Airways establishing their own, called go based at Stansted. Since being launched in 1998, the carrier has built up a route network featuring 21 destinations, although not all are year-round. Also based at Stansted is Dutch airline KLM's low-cost carrier which has been given the interesting name Buzz. French (1999: 13) believes the ex-UK low fare market will 'grow by between 12% and 15% a year'. Figure 7.7 illustrates the range of variables which can be controlled to improve profitability and indicates where costs savings can be made in airline operations in the fiercely competitive market.

Figure 7.7 **The potential for cost reductions among airlines**

Cost items	Cost drivers		
	Route network	**Fleet composition**	**Company policies**
Aircraft crew costs	XXX	XXX	XXX
Engineering overheads	X	XXX	
Direct engineering costs	X	XXX	X
Marketing	XXX		X
Aircraft standing	XXX	X	
Station and ground services	X		X
Passenger services	X		X
General and administrative costs	X		X
Fuel		X	
Airport and en route costs	X		
Direct passenger service			X

Notes
XXX Significant cost reduction potential
X Some cost implications

(Source: Page 1999, modified from Seristö and Vepsäläinen 1997: 21)

Alliances and the passenger volume conundrum

At the beginning of the twenty-first century, there are a number of airline alliances; these have grown from 'inter-line' agreements into substantial, co-ordinated reservation and marketing agreements for groups of airlines. Bennett (1997) identifies two forms: tactical (informal) and strategic (informal). The tactical partnership provides marketing advantages at low risk to the parties; 'code-sharing' allows one airline to market flights from regional airports to an international one (a so-called 'hub') for onward connection to inter-continental destinations. For example, KLM and North West code-share so that flights from Bristol, in England, to Amsterdam connect smoothly with those on to Washington, DC. Bennett (1997: 214) considers strategic partnerships are where longer term commitment results in 'shared airport facilities (check-ins, lounges), improved connections (synchronized schedules), reciprocity on frequent flyer programmes ... and marketing agreements'. Table 7.3 illustrates the major global airline alliances which feature these aspects.

On-going consolidation in the airline industry will lead to changes in alliance membership within a short space of time; for example, in January 2000, Air Canada acquired Canadian Airlines – one belongs to the Star Alliance and the other to OneWorld. In Europe, Lufthansa has purchased a

Table 7.3 **Global airline alliances**

Star Alliance	**Number of destinations**	**Fleet size**	**Principal hub(s)**
Air Canada	120	244	Toronto, Montreal, Vancouver
Air New Zealand	48	79	Auckland, Los Angeles, Sydney
All Nippon Airways	65	144	Tokyo, Osaka
Ansett Australia	142	126	Melbourne, Sydney
Austrian Airlines	123	88	Vienna, Salzburg
Lufthansa	301	324	Frankfurt, Munich
Mexicana	50	54	Mexico City, Cancun, Los Angeles
SAS	101	185	Copenhagen, Oslo, Stockholm
Singapore Airlines	93	94	Singapore
Thai	73	77	Bangkok, Chiang Mai, Phuket, Hat Yai
United Airlines	259	592	Chicago, Denver, San Francisco, Los Angeles, Washington, DC
Varig	120	87	Rio de Janeiro, São Paulo
Total	760+	1 858	
OneWorld Alliance	**Number of destinations**	**Fleet size**	**Principal hub(s)**
Aer Lingus	34	38	Dublin
American Airlines	237	933	Dallas/Fort Worth, Chicago
British Airways	261	340	London, Manchester
Canadian Airlines	135	131	Toronto/Montreal
Cathay Pacific	47	62	Hong Kong
Finnair	61	58	Helsinki, Stockholm
Iberia	96	215	Madrid, Barcelona, Miami
LanChile	45	47	Santiago
Qantas	116	135	Sydney
Total	666	1 959	

(Sources: Various websites including www.oneworldalliance.com and www.star-alliance.com)

20 per cent stake in British Midland which, in turn, has led to the latter joining the Star Alliance. French (1999: 8) believes that the rationale for alliances in previous years has been based on the hub-and-spoke system 'in that other airlines' route structures could be added into the system', in other words, that 'economic success was to be found in sheer traffic volume'. British Airways is one airline that has now challenged this assumption and has begun to reduce capacity on some routes where there is heavy competition; French (1999) cites a scaling back in services to Jakarta, Central America and the Caribbean with those to Pittsburgh being dropped entirely for the winter of 1999/2000.

Yield management

According to Kimes (1997), yield management (YM) has its origins in the deregulation of civil aviation in the United States; in order to compete with the new airlines offering low fares, established carriers such as United needed to be able to offer some seats at a low fare but retain high fares on most. 'Yield management is a method which can help a firm sell the right inventory unit to the right type of customer, at the right time, and for the right price' (Kimes 1997: 3). The concept has come to have equal validity for the hotel and cruising businesses since any capacity not sold cannot be held onto; for example, an unsold bed night cannot be retained – it is lost revenue and better to achieve some price than none at all. Kimes (1997) identifies a number of conditions that are essential for yield management to work:

- fixed capacity
- high fixed costs
- low variable costs
- time-varied demand
- similarity of inventory units.

Added to these conditions, there are a number of required features of the business, namely:

- market segmentation capability
- historical demand and booking pattern data
- knowledge of competitor pricing
- development of an over-booking policy
- links to the corporate management information system.

Importantly, airline yield management systems enable some seats to be retained for those premium fare passengers who always book late. Page (1999: 23) refers to research which shows 2–5 per cent revenue gains resulting from implementation of such a system, it:

> also indicated that if another competitor implemented a YM system, both saw improvements in revenue ... this suggests that YM is not a zero-sum game and that YM may force passengers to pay fares nearer to what they are prepared to pay rather than lower fares resulting from competitive pressures between the carriers.

One area where airline yields may be improved in the future is in the introduction of new transport technology, particularly the introduction of larger aircraft. For this reason, attention now turns to Exhibit 7.1 which examines the development of the new generation of aircraft to replace the jumbo jet.

Conclusion

The tourist use of transport remains a poorly understood area of tourism studies, with most researchers making the assumption that the tourist experience (see Chapter 25) begins when the tourist arrives at the destination. It does, in fact, begin when the tourist leaves their home environment and boards a form of transport. Therefore, one needs to understand how the role of transport features in the holiday process as well as in domestic tourism and more frequent recreational trips. It is evident that technological changes in transport have led to major innovations in the accessibility of specific tourism resources and the development of resorts and locations for tourism activity. Without the transport mode, access would be very limited and restricted. It is really the post-war period that has seen the greatest revolution in transportation making tourist destinations more accessible to a much greater population as living standards and income has increased per capita. Yet one should also not forget that large sectors of the world's population still do not enjoy high per capita incomes and the disposable income to engage in outbound and domestic tourism. This is certainly the case in many parts of South Asia (see

Exhibit 7.1 **Future changes in air travel**

Many forecasts of changes in global air travel recognize that annual growth rates in excess of 5 per cent per annum may pose a significant challenge for airlines and airports in accommodating the level of expected growth (see Page 1999, 2001 for examples of the likely impacts in the Asia–Pacific region). One solution mooted by carriers is the move towards larger aircraft which are currently under development by the leading aircraft manufacturers (Boeing in the USA and the Airbus Industries consortium in Europe).

The most recently unveiled plan by Airbus Industries for the Airbus A3XX illustrates the potential changes that may occur in air travel over the next decade. The A3XX is a £10 billion project which will produce a jet aircraft capable of seating between 650 and 900 passengers (depending on the configuration used) which compares with the 400–500 seating capacity of Boeing 747 (the 'jumbo jet'). The A3XX will have wingspan of 79.5 metres, be 73 metres long and 24.1 metres high. The predicted fuel savings of 20 per cent over conventional aircraft flying at present could see the price of a transatlantic ticket between the UK and USA fall to £100, almost half the price of current discounted flights. With a top speed of 565 miles per hour (equivalent to the top speed of a Boeing 747) it means that speed has not had to be sacrificed for size, while the range of the aircraft will be 8,800 miles (compared to 8,430 miles for a Boeing 747). In March 2000, the UK government announced that it would provide a loan package to Airbus Industries of £530 million to assist in the implementation of the A3XX project.

One of the major challenges of increased aircraft size is that they will need to fit into the existing infrastructure (e.g. airport aprons and slots), so that the A3XX intends to fit within the 80 × 80 metre horizontal box so that airports can accommodate the new aircraft without massive redevelopment work. Airbus Industries expect that the A3XX will be able to use the existing runways, taxiways and gates although it will place additional pressure on ground handling facilities, with increased numbers of passengers at check-in, gates and in holding areas. The gate handling facilities will certainly need expanding to accommodate the increased numbers at the gates and ground handling facilities (e.g. luggage transfer) will have additional pressures placed upon them. Some airport authorities are also concerned about the complementary infrastructure required to serve the needs of passengers to get to and from terminals, where existing airports are already facing growth problems from additional increases in passenger use.

There are varying forecasts on the likely demand for larger aircraft like the A3XX which will seat over 400 passengers. The Boeing Group's 20-year outlook (Boeing 1999) expects a demand for a further 930 747 or larger aircraft by the year 2018. In contrast, Airbus Industries (1999) expect a demand for 1,208 aircraft by 2018 in the 400-plus-seat category (i.e. 747 and larger category). This optimistic forecast is based on the assumption that in the period 1999–2018, world airports will be able to accommodate a 95 per cent increase in daily departures. In terms of the usage of aircraft, the top 25 airports are expected to absorb 30 per cent of all world air traffic by 2018 and half the aircraft will be used on flights from the top 60 airports which will be located in North America, Europe and Asia–Pacific. In 2018, Airbus Industries forecast that the top 10 airport pair routes will use 193 of the 1,208 very large aircraft (747 or larger). What this indicates is the dominance of the Asia–Pacific region in the demand for large-scale aircraft to move high traffic volumes (see Page 2001 for more detail) and the effect will be that Tokyo Narita, London Heathrow, Los Angeles, Hong Kong and Singapore will be the top five airport hubs using these new large aircraft to gain additional passenger capacity and fuel savings on long-haul routes.

Hall and Page 2000) although in the case of China, it is an outbound and domestic market that is growing exponentially. What is also clear from this chapter is the pace of change and development in the transport sector which provides new opportunities for tourist travel, realizing latent demand (i.e. facilitating travel where demand may not have existed because of the prohibitively high cost of travel for low-income groups). The introduction of budget travel, especially the low-cost carriers remains a major development that has expanded the range of destinations for the budget-conscious traveller. This also leads to change in the marketplace and fierce competition between carriers to gain market share.

The pace of change is certainly fast and the transport sector is one where innovation and new technology will continue to shape the scale of tourist flows and the cost of travel. A thorough understanding of the relationship between transport and tourism is a major prerequisite for any analysis of the factors which facilitate and constrain the development of tourism and any discussion of its role cannot ignore the important role which governments play is shaping policy and infrastructure development to encourage inbound and outbound tourism.

Discussion questions

1. Why is transport important to the study of tourism?
2. Has the development of cruising in the late 1990s become a new product based on the concept of luxury experiences?
3. Identify the impact of low-costs carriers on the European airline market.
4. The interaction between transport and tourism is poorly understood. Why is this the case?

Plate 7.5 Hong Kong Peak tram
The tram to the Peak in Hong Kong is another example of a tourist attraction in its own right.

Internet resources

By going to the weblink at www.thomsonlearning.co.uk students can access the following study on the Thomson Learning website. The study is from S.J. Page (1994) *Transport for Tourism* and examines the way in which the links between transport and tourism need to be understood.

References

Bennett, M. (1997) 'Strategic alliances in the world airline industry', *Progress in Tourism and Hospitality Research*, **3**: 213–23.

Dostal, A. (1999) 'Bus and coach operators', *Travel and Tourism Analyst*, **5**: 1–17.

French, T. (1999) 'British airways and the new airline economics', *Travel and Tourism Analyst*, **6**: 3–16.

Hall, C.M. and Page, S.J. (eds) (2000) *Tourism in South and South East Asia*, Oxford: Butterworth-Heinemann.

Kimes, S. (1997) 'Yield management: an overview', in I. Yeoman and A. Ingold (eds) *Yield Management – Strategies for the Service Industries*, London: Cassell: 3–11.

Lumsdon, L. (1997) 'Recreational cycling: is this the way to stimulate interest in everyday urban cycling?, in R. Tolley (ed.) *The Greening of Urban Transport Planning for Walking and Cycling in Western Cities*, second edition, Chichester: Wiley: 113–27.

Page S.J. (1994a) *Transport for Tourism*, London: Routledge.

Page, S.J. (1994b) 'European bus and coach travel, *Travel and Tourism Analyst*, **1**: 5–30.

Page, S.J. (1999) *Transport and Tourism*, Harlow: Addison Wesley Longman.

Page, S.J. (2001) 'Gateways, hubs and transport interconnections in South East Asia: implications for tourism development in the twenty-first century', in P. Teo, T. Chang and H. Chong (eds) *Interconnected Worlds: Tourism in South East Asia*, Oxford: Pergamon.

Patmore, J.A. (1983) *Recreation and Resources*, Oxford: Blackwell.

Peisley, T. (1998a) 'The cruise market in mainland Europe', *Travel and Tourism Analyst*, **1**: 4–25.

Peisley, T. (1998b) 'The North American cruise market', *Travel and Tourism Analyst*, **4**: 1–22.

Prideaux, B. (1999) 'Tracks to tourism: Queensland Rail joins the tourist industry', *International Journal of Tourism Research*, **1** (2): 73–86.

Ritchie, B.W. (1998) 'Bicycle tourism in the South West of New Zealand: planning and management issues', *Tourism Management*, **19** (6): 567–82.

Seristö, H. and Vepsäläinen, A. (1997) 'Airline cost drivers: cost implications of fleet, routes and personnel policies', *Journal of Air Transport Management*, **3** (1): 11–12.

Wall, G. (1971) 'Car owners and holiday activities', in P. Lavery (ed.) *Recreational Geography*, Newton Abbot: David and Charles.

Further reading

Ingold, A. and Huyton, J. (1997) 'Yield management and the airline industry', in I. Yeoman and A. Ingold (eds) *Yield Management – Strategies for the Service Industries*, Cassell, London.

Mason, G. (2001) 'Marketing low-cost airline services to business travellers', *Journal of Air Transport Management*, **7** (2): 103–9.

Page, S.J. (1999) *Transport and Tourism*, Harlow: Addison Wesley Longman.

Learning outcomes

After studying this chapter, you should:

- Be familiar with some definitions of the term attraction.
- Recognize the importance of attractions to a destination area.
- Be aware of the wide range of attractions.

8 Tourist attractions

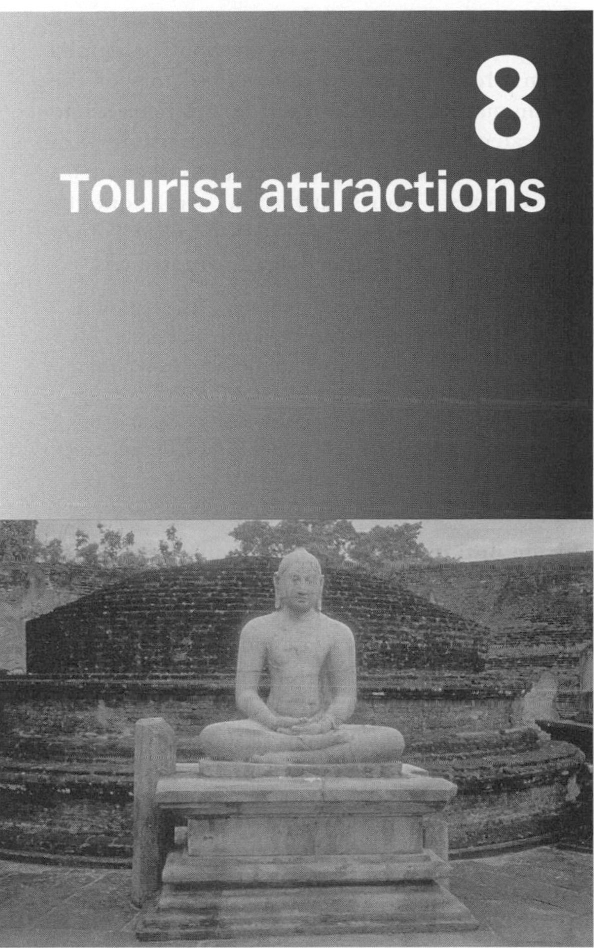

Overview

Tourist attractions comprise a wide range of man-made and natural features appealing to either mass tourism audiences or small sectoral interests; this chapter reviews the various types and uses the English Tourism Council categories to consider them in more detail.

Introduction

For the majority of tourists, the attractions at a destination are the reason for visiting – it is the *raison d'être.* Attractions are often used to market the destination and where they are of international significance, such as the Eiffel Tower in France, they are used as icons to promote the image of the destination to certain tourism markets. In a recent study by Faulkner *et al.* (1999) into destination competitiveness, they identified the core tourism attractions for the diverse region of South Australia, based on content analysis of promotional literature from the tourism industry. They found that the core tourist attractions were:

- heritage tourism
- urban tourism (i.e. Adelaide)
- festivals and events
- big river tourism (i.e. the Murray River)
- nature-oriented tourism
- wine tourism, known as the cradle of the Australian wine industry
- the outback
- coastal South Australia.

This illustrates the wide range of man-made and resource-based attractions in the South Australia region which appeal to different sectors of the tourism market. It also indicates how difficult it is to easily categorize and summarize the attractiveness of a tourism region based on its attractions when such a diversity exist. Tourist attractions are frequently termed 'visitor attractions' and the Scottish Tourist Board (STB) (1991) argued that an attraction is:

> a permanently established excursion destination, a primary purpose of which is to allow public access for entertainment, interest or education, rather than being principally a retail outlet or a venue for sporting, theatrical or film performances. It must be open to the public without prior booking, for published periods each year, and should be capable of attracting tourists or day visitors as well as local residents.

This definition excludes the growing numbers of tourist shopping villages (TSVs – see Getz 2000); these are purpose-built developments of designer outlets, such as those at Clark's in Somerset, Gretna and Bicester (UK), although out-of-town complexes also require consideration. Hall and Page (1999: 112) remark on the difficulty of identifying tourist shopping 'since it is also an activity undertaken by users such as residents'. The scale of some shopping complexes suggests that large numbers of *excursionists*, if not tourists, must be attracted; the West Edmonton Mall in Canada contains 800 retail outlets and leisure facilities as well (Getz 2000). Even individual shops can become tourist attractions *per se*; for example, The Tailor of Gloucester, in Gloucester (UK), based on the children's book by Beatrix Potter. From a different perspective, Virgin's Paris Megastore 'became a landmark and a tourist destination ... (attracting) as many visitors as the Louvre ... It seems that every teenaged Japanese and German tourist makes a pilgrimage' (Branson 1998: 258).

Returning to the STB definition, by requiring the attraction to be 'permanently established', it excludes many sporting and cultural events. Swarbrooke (1995: 7) emphasizes the need to differentiate attractions from destinations since:

> attractions are generally single units, individual sites or very small, easily delimited geographical areas based on a single key feature. Destinations are larger areas that include a number of individual attractions together with the support services required by tourists.

This begs the question whether some attractions are of such a scale, providing substantial serviced accommodation, that they might be a destination according to this definition; for example, Disney World, Orlando. From another viewpoint, accommodation providers such as Center Parcs and Oasis in Europe offer such an all-inclusive concept that, perhaps, they should be classified as attractions. Swarbrooke (1995) does, however, provide a straightforward typology of attractions as shown in Table 8.1.

Swarbrooke's typology includes events and these can be on such a scale as to warrant the term major attraction in their own right. To illustrate the lengths, quite legitimately, that some commentators have gone to in categorizing attractions, Prentice (1993) lists 23 types of heritage attraction as shown in Exhibit 8.1 and Table 8.2.

What undeniably 'turns a tract of land, monument, park, historic house or coastline into a heritage attraction is often the attitude of the public' (Millar 1999: 6). Allied to this aspect is the fact that the public's motivation to visit a site varies over time; Uzzell (1998: 14) refers to the war generation visiting battlefield sites, after 1945, but as those individuals cease 'to be with us, (there is) ... less to do with remembrance and more to do with a day-trip excursion, less of a memorial and more of a tourist attraction'. A further feature to add to any typology is ownership. In Britain, the public and voluntary ('not for profit') sectors are key 'players' besides commercial organizations. In 1995, 84 per cent of country parks were owned by central or local government as were 44 per cent of museums and galleries and 36 per cent of historic properties. The dynamism of this sector is revealed by the fact that 'just under 47% of all attractions in the UK have opened to the public since 1980' (Hanna 1999b: A98) which indicates the rapid growth in tourists attractions, especially with regional development

Table 8.1 **Swarbrooke's typology of tourist attractions**

Natural	Man-made but not originally designed primarily to attract visitors	Man-made and purpose-built to attract tourists	Special events

Exhibit 8.1 **Categorizing tourist attractions**

This categorization is impressive through its very comprehensiveness but as Prentice (1993: 39) recognizes, some attractions are hardly worthy of the label, citing genocide and field sports. The heterogeneity, or diverse nature, of these 23 types must be remarked on and, as Prentice (1993: 40) observes, some aspects of an area are not site specific; seeing roadsigns written in Welsh 'can be a significant part of an area's attractiveness to tourists'.

Table 8.2 **Prentice's heritage attraction categories**
Natural history attractions: nature reserves, nature trails, rare breeds centres, wildlife parks, zoos, butterfly parks, geological sites including caves, cliffs and waterfalls
Science-based attractions: science museums, technology centres, 'hands-on' science centres
Attractions concerned with primary production: agricultural attractions, farms, vineyards, fishing, mining, water impounding reservoirs
Craft centres and craft workshops: water- and windmills, potters, woodcarvers, glass-makers
Attractions concerned with manufacturing industry: the mass production of goods including pottery, porcelain, breweries, distilleries, economic history museums
Transport attractions: including transport museums, preserved railways, canals
Socio-cultural attractions: prehistoric and historic sites and displays including domestic houses, social history museums, costume museums, toy museums
Attractions associated with historic persons: including sites and areas associated with writers and painters
Performing arts attractions: including theatres, street-based performing arts, circuses
Pleasure gardens: including period gardens, arboreta, model villages
Theme parks: including 'historic' adventure parks but excluding amusement parks (where the principal attractions are exciting rides and the like)
Galleries: principally art galleries
Festivals and pageants: including historic fairs and countryside festivals
Fieldsports: fishing, hunting, shooting
Stately and ancestral homes: palaces, manor houses
Religious attractions: cathedrals, churches, mosques, shrines, wells

Table 8.2 ***cont.***
Military attractions: castles, battlefields, naval dockyards, military museums
Genocide monuments: sites associated with the extermination of other races
Towns and townscape: principally historic townscape
Villages and hamlets: principally 'rural' settlements, usually of pre-twentieth-century architecture
Countryside and treasured landscapes: including National Parks
Seaside resorts and 'seascapes': principally seaside towns of past eras and marine 'landscapes'
Regions: including pays lande, counties or other historic areas identified as distinctive by their residents or visitors (for example, Thomas Hardy Country in Wessex)

Plate 8.1 Auckland's Americas Cup Village, New Zealand
This Village was constructed for the 2000–2001 America's Cup in Auckland and was used as a catalyst for a limited redevelopment of a waterfront area. It will be reused in 2003 when Auckland hosts the Americas Cup again.

incentives from the European Union (EU) European Regional Development Fund and the proceeds of the National Lottery as grant in aid. Such incentives, combined with investment in attraction infrastructure has directly impacted upon the density of attractions in regions within the UK and Europe. In simple terms, popular tourism areas have witnessed significant growth in the number of new attractions opening over the last 30 years. The British Tourist Authority (BTA) (1996) measures the density of attractions by the number per 1,000 square kilometres and per 100,000 population in the regions. In 1995, the West Country had the largest number of attractions: 625 compared to 248 in London. However, the West Country had 31.8 attractions per 1,000 square kilometres compared to 157.2 for London. When a per capita measure is used in the UK, the West Country had 16.8 attractions per 100,000 population whereas London possesses 3.6. The English, Northern Ireland, Scottish and Wales Tourist Boards have monitored attraction trends for many years and, for the purposes of this chapter, the categories used by the English Tourist Board (now Council) can be used as a convenient categorization of attractions in an international context. This is now used as a convenient framework with illustrations from the UK and USA to illustrate the scope and nature of attractions (see Hall and McArthur 1996 for a selection of examples from Australia and New Zealand).

Historic houses and monuments

In the UK, the National Trust is an independent charity, established in 1895, which owns and maintains historic houses, castles, monuments, gardens and tracts of land. A number of Acts of Parliament between 1907 and 1971 provide the guidelines under which the Trust is run. Table 8.3 illustrates the popularity of Trust properties.

Prentice's (1993) typology also identified genocide monuments (Foley and Lennon 2000) of which there are now a large number; many have been the recipients of 'hot interpretation'. Uzzell (1989) coined this term to describe those visitor sites which produce emotional reactions; an example is seen at Oradour-sur-Glane in France where Nazi troops, in 1944, barricaded over 640 villagers in the

Table 8.3 **Visitor statistics for the 'top 20' National Trust properties**

	1998/99	1997/98
Wakehurst Place	282 699	305 935
Fountains Abbey & Studley Royal	275 831	286 409
Polesden Lacey	234 540	239 467
Stourhead Garden	213 285	240 174
St Michael's Mount	204 596	201 280
Quarry Bank Mill	186 927	176 723
Sissinghurst Castle Garden	171 885	183 434
Lanhydrock	166 193	180 269
Bodiam Castle	164 063	172 348
Corfe Castle	163 618	174 500
Chartwell	158 976	157 592
Bodnant Garden	150 106	156 591
Waddesdon Manor	141 837	149 472
Sheffield Park Garden	138 385	147 580
Nymans Garden	136 040	160 676
Hidcote Manor Garden	124 532	126 645
Cliveden	123 925	148 321
Kingston Lacy	122 660	122 736
Cragside House and Park	121 482	139 730
Belton House	120 140	118 036

(Source: National Trust 1998/99 Annual Report)

church and set fire to the building. After the war, the French government decided to leave the old village exactly as it was, bar a small museum; Uzzell and Ballantyne (1998: 156) observe that, for many, the village is now a day-trip destination rather than a memorial and, although visitors are not 'spared the horror of what happened, one suspects that the anger and anguish will slowly be muted. The numbers for whom Oradour-sur-Glane provides a cathartic experience are declining'.

Museums and galleries

This category of attraction comprises a very diverse range of properties, some are internationally renowned and attract millions of visitors, others are on a local small scale, run on a low budget and may be run by voluntary labour as trusts. Six out of the top ten museums and galleries in Britain, in 1998, offered free admission and this partly explains why the British Museum in London received over 5.6 million visits (Hanna 1999a); the capital's pre-eminence in tourism terms is confirmed by the locations of the other nine – all are in London except for one in Glasgow and one in Birmingham. In a London context, the sheer volume of tourists visits to musuems has seen the new era of commercialism and managerialism introduced progressively since the 1980s to meet a shortfall in government funding by a greater commercialism, specifically targeted at merchandising and visitor spending on food and beverages.

The issue of measuring visitor numbers has been raised by Davies (1995) who considers the method of calcuating total visits by aggregating the number of visits to individual museums and galleries to be flawed. The British Tourist Authority method of basing their figure of approximately 80 million per annum on regional tourist board returns provides statistics from about 70 per cent of institutions.

Plate 8.2 Covent Garden, London, UK
Since its redevelopment in the 1970s, Covent Garden has become a popular piazza and nucleus for visitor activity in London's cultural district with theatre, opera and ballet venues.

Davies argues that this assumes around 30 per cent of institutions (between 500 and 1,000) are too small to be considered and, second, that there is general unreliability concerning attendance data, especially at free entry museums. Davies believes the market size in Britain to be more like 110 million visits per annum.

The British Museum

Established in 1753, this internationally renowned museum contains six and a half million objects, ranging in size from pottery shards to huge statues. As an innovative institution, the British Museum is committed to modern technology and has introduced COMPASS; the Collections Multimedia Public Access System will allow visitors to see the collections in a new light 'such as visualising the sites from which objects come ... (it) will also demonstrate the possibilities of 3D imaging ... (and) may contribute to the creation of a national standard' (www.british-museum.ac.uk). One of the most important building developments of recent years is the Great Court Scheme; further details are available on their website (www.british-museum.ac.uk).

Winterthur Museum, Garden and Library

An internationally significant museum in North America, which also includes a significant garden, is the Winterthur Museum in Delaware state, USA. The 966-acre estate is the former home of Henry Francis du Pont (1880–1969) whose family built the du Pont chemicals empire, in nearby Wilmington, into a multinational business. The museum, which opened in 1951, features American decorative arts and contains more than 89,000 objects spanning the years 1640–1860 in the nation's history. It has been called the American equivalent of Britain's Victoria and Albert (V&A) Museum.

Besides the main location, the Winterthur Museum also owns five large and five small historic houses at Odessa, 23 miles south of Wilmington, Delaware. The Winterthur is very much a working museum which also houses a research library of over 72,000 books and 500,000 manuscripts, microfilms, periodicals and photographs connected with American arts to 1920, their European antecedents and American history. The museum's name comes from the Swiss town where the du Pont family originated; the donor, Henry du Pont, was born at the property and began collecting American antiques in the 1920s which entailed his children growing up in a 'museum-in-progress' with all the sights and sounds of construction evident. Further details on the property and events can be found at their website: www.winterthur.org.

Cathedrals and churches

These attractions are classic examples of Swarbrooke's (1995) 'man-made attraction' but not designed to attract tourists' classification. In the UK, most cathedrals still provide free admission as do churches when not locked to avoid vandalism. The English Tourist Council data on the top ten in 1998 illustrate the importance of London: Westminster Abbey received an estimated 3 million visits (Hanna 1999a), although the importance to tourism of the great regional cathedrals still 'shines' through with Canterbury Cathedral in Kent achieving almost 2.5 million visits a year prior to introducing a charge for entry. Westminster Abbey is one of Britain's premier attractions, so staff faced the difficult task of balancing the needs of tourists with those of worshippers – on busy days, over 10,000 visitors crowd the place. In 1998, a 'Recovering the Calm' strategy was put in place and the Abbey is now quieter with both daily and Sunday congregations increasing. The visitor experience is also a quality one as the research for the Association of Leading Visitor Attractions (ALVA) shows: over 80 per cent rated their Abbey visit as good or excellent, 89 per cent considered the marshals welcoming and 90 per cent would recommend their friends to visit. (The website address is www.westminster-abbey.org.)

Leisure parks and piers

This category, in Britain, comprises attractions as diverse as Legoland (near Windsor), Eastbourne Pier, Blackpool Pleasure Beach and Alton Towers. The last held the record in 1998 for most admissions of

Plate 8.3 Christ Church Gate, Canterbury, UK
This medieval gate is an architectural attraction in its own right and now acts as a gate to Canterbury Cathedral where visitors are charged an admission fee in order to manage tourists in the urban environment.

'charging attractions': 2,782,000 visitors whereas Blackpool Beach, with free admission, received an estimated 7.1 million (Hanna 1999a). Blackpool Pleasure Beach features the tallest and fastest roller-coaster in the world; the £12 million ride opened in 1994 and is just one of 11 on site. In 1997, Playstation – The Ride opened; this catapults visitors 210 feet into the air, followed by free-fall descent. In the United States, there are now more than 15 theme parks which attract 'more than 2 million visitors ... and 30 attracting one million visitors a year, with particular concentrations in Florida and California' (Yale 1998: 268). As mentioned in Chapter 7, tourism attractions are a vital part of the tourism industry because they provide the focus for tourist activities; this is nowhere so evident with the theme parks of Walt Disney World and Universal Studios in Orlando, Florida. In 1999, Tokyo Disneyland attracted the most visitors for any theme park world-wide, admitting 17.45 million (Stevens 2000). As in other sectors of the tourism industry, in the last few decades there has been the emergence of global theme park chains, illustrated in Table 8.4.

Wildlife attractions

In the last decade, zoos have had to contend with negative media portrayal of penned animals, leading some to amend their names; in Devon, Paignton Zoo has added the term 'Environmental Park' to emphasize an active conservation side. None the less, the most popular attraction in this category, in 1998, was London Zoo with 1,052,886 visits (Hanna 1999a). However, having opened in 1997, the London Aquarium reached third place with 683,000 visits in 1998; this attraction is located in the former County Hall building. Two other major aquaria have opened recently in the UK: Blue Planet at Cheshire Oaks, Ellesmere Port, the largest in the country, and the National Marine Aquarium, in Plymouth. The latter attracted 365,000 visitors in the first season, having opened in 1998. Aesthetic and architectural

Table 8.4 **Major global amusement/theme park chains, 1999**

	Number of parks world-wide	Attendance (million)
Walt Disney Attractions	9	89.20
Premier Parks/Six Flags	35	47.50
Universal Studios	5	20.90
Anheuser Busch	9	19.60
Cedar Fair Ltd	8	13.50

(Source: Stevens 2000)

Plate 8.4 Seated Buddha statue, Polonnaruwa, Sri Lanka
It is not just cathedrals and churches which attract thousands of visitors; the buildings and statues of other religions form an important resource for tourism.

features are important in the design of both of these attractions.

At Britain's largest zoo, Chester, the emphasis – as at Paignton – is on conservation; over 240 species in the collection are now listed as rare or threatened in the wild. The zoo dates from 1930 when George Mottershead realized his childhood vision; he kept the collection going through World War II and by the 1950s 'Always Building' was a slogan as the zoo grew to its present size, becoming a charitable trust along the way. Chester Zoo is the largest in size of all UK zoos, at 110 acres. In the 1980s, continued investment resulted in the Zoofari Monorail, a Chimpanzee islands complex and huge 'Europe on the Edge' aviary. As with other attractions, commercial sponsorship is essential and Chester was lucky to secure $3 million from Jaguar Cars for the Spirit of the Jaguar exhibit. Approximately, 60,000 of the 900,000 plus visitors each year are schoolchildren on organized visits, cementing the aim of education being used to underpin the conservation work. As part of on-going investment, the Zoo opened 'Islands in Danger' – an imaginative habitat for endangered island creatures, including Komodo Dragons and Birds of Paradise – in summer 2000. One of the most successful new additions is the Twilight Zone – Europe's largest free-flight bat cave, housing over 200 fruit bats (Rodriguez Island and Seeba's). The daylight hours are reversed, and visitors walk through the bats' territory, as they fly around. In Singapore, a similar experience was added to their zoo, with a Nightime Safari a popular tourist activity building on the interest in wildlife.

Gardens

Gardens as attractions in their own right comprise three types; they may have originated as scientific collections, such as Kew in London with approximately 1 million visits a year or are complementary to a historic property – Hampton Court Gardens which receive an estimated 1.2 million free admissions (Hanna 1999a). In some situations, the house may not be open to the public or may be of secondary importance to the gardens. Third, the gardens may be the deliberate result of municipal action in providing recreational facilities for residents.

Some gardens have been restored to their former glory; a notable example in Britain being the Lost Gardens of Heligan in Cornwall, restored by entrepreneur Tim Smit. The public's imagination was captured by two well-produced television series (further details are provided in Chapter 12). In the case of Claude Monet (1840–1926), the impressionist painter, his garden at Giverny in western France draws visitors to the scenes he painted on so many occasions (see http://www.giverny.org/gardens/index.htm).

Farms

Farm attractions comprise visitor centres, museums, self-guided trails and what might be described as 'livestock experiences' – principally aimed at children; they can be permanent or event based. Whilst 'there is no doubt that the consumer recognizes the farming environment as part of the overall tourism product' (Busby and Rendle 2000), the issue of authenticity remains in the background; many successful farm attractions are no longer commercial farms although the public may not be aware of this. A new category of 'farm attraction' was introduced for British attraction statistics in 1997 as a result of rapid growth in previous years; in fact, 84 per cent of all these farms have opened since 1980 (Hanna 1999b). In the 1998 figures, Hanna (1999a)

Exhibit 8.2 **The Eden Project**

The Eden Project is the 'brain-child' of Tim Smit, one of the entrepreneurs profiled in Chapter 12; whilst the Lost Gardens of Heligan, as Tim admits, 'was the mother for the idea and the media links were used in the same way to build up an expectation', the attraction is different in that major scientific aims have also been established. This project blends the world of science into an entertainment which is educational as Tim comments; it is 'notable for having communications/media experts at the heart of the institution rather than as peripheral add-ons'. The attraction is based in a 60-metre-deep former china clay pit and covers 15 hectares (34 acres); within this area are two giant 'biomes'. The larger (covering 1.5 hectares) will house plants from the humid tropics and reach to 50 metres; the smaller biome will contain plants from the Mediterranean, southern Africa and south-west USA. Outside the biomes, the grounds will contain temperate climate plants and demonstration areas. As a core concept, Eden has a scientific base which presents the visitor with an understanding of biodiversity.

Eden is an exemplar of tourism development: the attraction is based, as much as possible, on sustainable practices. The primary energy source for heating will use sustainable fuel in the form of 'biomass' provided by willow wood chips; buildings on-site will have earth roofs in order to demonstrate natural insulation; and the rainwater run-off will be used for humidification in the Humid Tropics biome. Instead of using glass panes, the biomes will be covered in a Teflon-coated foil (ETFE) and no two panes will be exactly the same size. ETFE foil has a number of beneficial properties: it provides greater insulation than glass, is recyclable, requires less steelwork to support it than glass, is 'self-cleaning' and strong. Since the original concept team meeting of horticulturalists and architects in 1995, much has been achieved. The financing package is complex and has been assisted by the county of Cornwall gaining EU Objective 1 status which illustrates it relative lagging region status in the EU. The funding details are shown in Table 8.5.

Table 8.5 **Financing the Eden Project**

	£ million
Total project cost	**79.9**
Public sector funding:	
Millennium Commission	37.15
European Regional Development Fund	10.00
Restormel Borough Council	.30
English Partnerships	3.00
Cornwall County Council	.20
Prosper (Devon and Cornwall)	.22
Single Regeneration Budget	.38
China Clay Area LEADER II	.02
European Social Fund	.05
Sub-total	51.32
Debt	
Bank	15.89
Cornwall County Council	3.00
South West Water	1.00
McAlpine Joint Venture	1.50
Sub-total	21.39
Charitable donations	1.00
Commercial sponsorship	1.85
Donations in kind	1.68

Eden is the type of attraction Cornwall needs for the twenty-first century; it complements the wide range of attractions currently available and is on a large enough scale to draw international visitors. In presenting the economic argument, consultants Ernst and Young considered the attraction could receive 750,000 visitors a year, of which 30 per cent would be new to the area. By 2005, Eden could be employing 169 staff with the concomitant multiplier effect on the local economy. There can be no doubt that the Eden Project will have a catalytic effect on tourism to Cornwall and, to some extent, the neighbouring county of Devon. (Further information can be found on the website: www.edenproject.com.)

lists four free admission farms in the Top Ten with Callestock Cider Farm (near Truro in Cornwall) receiving as many as 300,000 visitors. It is also interesting to note that in ninth place, in Britain, was 'Hedgehog Hospital and Farm' in Devon.

Country parks

In Britain, these attractions have the 'highest proportions of local authority ownership (75%) and of free access (91%), excluding car park charges' (Hanna 1999b: A100). One of the principal reasons for this is that, in the late 1960s, 'local authorities were empowered to provide country parks, including facilities for sailing, boating, bathing and fishing'; they were not intended 'for those who are seeking the solitude and grandeur of the mountains, but for the large urban populations' (Cullingworth and Nadin 1994: 180). Thirty years later, there are approximately 300 in Britain (see Hall and Page 1999 for more detail). The Queen Elizabeth Country Park is a typical example of these attractions; it is owned and managed by Hampshire County Council and covers 1,400 acres of the South Downs – in an AONB (Area of Outstanding Natural Beauty). Interpretation of the park is provided at the Visitor Centre which houses an audio-visual theatre and an exhibition space; educational use by schools is encouraged. Conservation is also an important element of the park since 38 species of butterfly and 12 species of wild orchid are found there.

Visitor centres

The range of visitor centres in Britain is very diverse: from Cadbury World, in Birmingham with over 500,000 visitors a year, to Gatwick Skyview, in Sussex, to the Rob Roy Centre, at Callander in Scotland. Many of the 400+ centres in Britain have opened since 1990, with free admission offered at 54 per cent of them, in 1998.

According to Hanna (1999b: A100), 'local authorities have a strong presence, owning 34 per cent of all visitor centres' and that 80 per cent have opened since 1980. Visitor centres are, in many cases, central to the tourist experience and interpretation of the 'site'; for example, in the United States of America, Yale (1998: 7) states that, at Kittyhawk, 'where the Wright Brothers first flew in a heavier-than-air machine in 1903 there would be nothing to draw visitors were it not for the centre'.

Workplaces

In many cases, these attractions are open as part of a coherent public relations strategy and in some cases a deliberate policy designed to capitalize on the growth in industrial tourism – for example, British Energy's Sizewell B nuclear power station on the Suffolk coast. This is the only PWR (pressurized water reactor) in the country and the company, understandably, wish to reassure the public; one of the inquiry outcomes, prior to construction, was that there should be a visitor centre. This duly opened, in 1989, with free admission, and at the peak of construction in 1993–94 was receiving approximately 50,000 visitors a year. Since then, numbers have remained fairly level with 21,175 recorded for 1999; of these, approximately 45 per cent are pre-booked groups of students (primary to tertiary) and 'opinion formers' together with international nuclear industry visitors. The company website also offers 'virtual tours' (see www.british-energy.com).

The British Nuclear Fuels' reprocessing plant at Sellafield, in north-west England, provides another example of trying to improve the public image through greater awareness via 'a nothing to hide day trip tour of the site and an ambitious visitor centre, recording over 130,000 visitors each year' (Lee 1998: 221). Not surprisingly, given that these are working environments, Hanna (1999b: A101) states that 'workplaces had the highest degree of visitor congestion despite the lowest average number of visitors (27,000)'. He goes on to observe that only 29 per cent in the UK charge admission. Whilst Stevens (2000) suggests that in France there are 10 million visits to over 5,000 industrial sites, the British Tourist Authority identified 314 workplaces open to the public in Britain. A new form of 'industrial tourism' is also beginning to develop; Stevens (2000: 74) notes that quite a number of well-known companies have actively invested in 'their attraction product at their main point of production … Guinness will be replacing the Hop Store Visitor Centre with a new

£70 million attracton at the Old Brewery in Dublin'. A selection of these developments is illustrated in Table 8.6.

Steam railways

Although many hundreds of miles of railway line were closed in the UK 1960s, as a result of the Beeching Act, enthusiasts have managed to re-open many stretches across Britain and, invariably, they are significant tourist attractions when steam locomotives are added. One example will be presented here: that of the Kent & East Sussex Railway. The first stage was re-opened in 1974, from Tenterden to Rolvenden, followed three years later by an extension to Wittersham Road. In 1990, Northiam was reached – a total of seven miles from Tenterden. The latest stretch to Bodiam opened on 2 April 2000, just over ten miles from Tenterden. Much of this work has been accomplished by the 500 volunteers; in fact, the development of the Kent & East Sussex Railway has only been possible because of them. This emphasizes the significance of the voluntary sector in maintaining tourist attractions such as these as trusts as they would probably not be viable commercial enterprises if the cost of labour was included in the development and operational costs.

Table 8.6 **Industry-based visitor attractions**

Company name	Country	Industry	Visitors per annum
Hershey	USA	Chocolate	2 000 000
Kellogg's	USA	Food	1 000 000
Swarovski	Austria	Crystal	650 000
Cadbury	England	Chocolate	500 000
Waterford Crystal	Ireland	Glass	400 000
Guinness	Ireland	Beer	400 000

(Source: Stevens 2000)

Special events

Major events

Smith and Jenner (1998: 73) argue that 'to quantify event-based tourism would be just a little more scientific than picking a number for a lottery. Only a relatively small number of events have ever been researched'. The event may be the only reason for the tourist to visit an area or it may be complementary. Perhaps, the single key characteristic of a special event 'is its transience' (Smith and Jenner 1998: 74); the festival or sporting fixture may be held annually or more infrequently and it is this that creates the sense of importance. Table 8.7 illustrates the variety and scale of some international events held between 1994 and 1998. The figures do not allow for the temporal dimension; for example, the Notting Hill Carnival numbers were compressed into one weekend whereas those for the Calgary Stampede were spread over ten days.

Some major events are literally 'one-offs' and the London String of Pearls Millennium Festival is a good example. During the year 2000, 67 public and private buildings were open to the public – some for the first time and some offering special exhibitions. The attractions stretched from Kew in the west of

Table 8.7 **Attendance figures for selected events and festivals, 1994–98**

Event	Attendance
Olympic Games, Atlanta, 1996	9 000 000
Football World Cup, USA, 1994	3 600 000
Notting Hill Carnival, UK, 1997	2 000 000
Calgary Stampede, Canada, 1998	1 100 000
Chicago Blues Festival, 1997	600 000
Rotterdam Film Festival, 1995	167 000
British Formula One Grand Prix, 1997	150 000

(Source: Adapted from Smith and Jenner 1998)

London to Greenwich in the east and were clustered around the River Thames.

Local events as tourist attractions

Contrary to Smith and Jenner's (1998: 89) view that 'the majority of visitors to most events live locally or are tourists who just happen … to be in the right place at the right time', research into the impact of the second annual Daphne du Maurier Festival of Arts and Literature, held in Fowey, Cornwall in 1999, found that a significant number of visitors travelled from outside the region for what was not a well-known event (Busby and Hambly 2000) (see Table 8.8).

The future for tourist attractions

Technology continues to play a major role in the development of attractions and not just in theme parks; museums have had to respond to the burgeoning demand of visitors for interactive displays and the development of the UK's most costly attraction – the London Dome is a case in point. Observing the development of theme parks in Japan, Hall and Page (1999: 108) comment that, from the mid-1990s, 'a greater awareness of the market to sustain these developments is required, particularly the entertainment value – are they a passing phase in the tourism and leisure industry, or likely to be the norm for mass entertainment?'. This is more than a rhetorical question and applies equally to theme parks globally. Alton Towers has maintained its pre-eminent position in Britain through sustained investment by owners the Tussauds Group; recent examples of their product development are Nemesis and, in 1999, Oblivion – the world's first vertical drop ride. This illustrates the capital-intensive nature of tourist attraction development, where the financial backing of large leisure groups such as the Tussauds Group help to ensure a regular investment policy to remain internationally competitive.

The development of themed hotels, such as the Pyramid in Las Vegas, implies that we may be just a short time away from what was portrayed in the movie *Westworld*, based on Michael Crichton's novel, where tourists stay at a themed destination and encounter robot humans acting out their historical role. Companies such as Iwerks, in the United States, have developed virtual reality to a stage where large-scale introduction to the public is now possible.

Conclusion

The attractions sector is characterized by a diversity of attraction types. As Prentice (1993) remarks, the

Table 8.8 **Festival visitors in 1998**

Residence of festival visitor	%	Number of days festival attended	%
Cornwall	44	1 day	26
Other south-west counties	18	2–3 days	31
South-east England	14	4–7 days	26
Midlands	14	8–10 days	17
North, north-west, Yorkshire and Humberside	8		
Overseas	2		

(Source: Busby and Hambly 2000)

extent of heterogeneity is great. Some types of attraction appeal to a wide range of visitor market segments whilst others are very specialist; some attractions form the key reason for visiting that destination, for example, DisneyWorld, Orlando. Attractions are an integral part of the tourism product though they also need to be supported by a wider tourism infrastructure in the destination for the wider benefits to be harnessed for the area. Influencing visitor behaviour to attract tourist spending has become a very sophisticated undertaking in the 1990s and it highlights the significance of on-going investment for the attraction to be viable. It should also be emphasized that attractions also have a market within the local community. This community value has been a frequent argument for the management and maintenance of attractions by the public sector, though there is increasingly a trend towards management by the private sector or a management company to commercialize and profit from tourism. The need for constant investment and innovation is also apparent in order to maintain competitive advantage. Brand leaders, such as Kellogg's and Guinness, believe a high-profile presence in the tourism market will reinforce their 'fast-moving consumer good' sales. Finally, the rapid development of technology is likely to lead to the introduction of new forms of attraction, quite possibly virtual reality parks on a much wider scale.

Discussion questions

1. Identify the key features of a tourist attraction.
2. Discuss which market segments are most likely to be drawn to garden attractions.
3. How will industry tourist attractions develop over the next ten years?
4. Discuss whether virtual reality is likely to lead to a decline in visits to key heritage sites because of what can be made available through technology.

References

Branson, R. (1998) *Losing my Virginity – the Autobiography*, London: Virgin Publishing.

BTA (1996) *Sightseeing in the UK, 1995*, London: BTA.

Busby, G. and Hambly, Z. (2000) 'Literary tourism and the Daphne du Maurier Festival, *Cornish Studies 8*, Exeter: University of Exeter Press.

Busby, G. and Rendle, S. (2000) 'The transition from tourism on farms to farm tourism', *Tourism Management*, **21** (6): 635–42.

Cullingworth, J.B. and Nadin, V. (1994) *Town and Country Planning in Britain*, eleventh edition, London: Routledge.

Davies, S. (1995) 'Attendance records', *Leisure Management*, **15** (2): 40–44.

Faulkner, B., Oppermann, M. and Fredline, E. (1999) 'Destination competitiveness: an exploratory examination of South Australia's core attractions', *Journal of Vacation Marketing*, **5** (2): 125–39.

Foley, M. and Lennon, J. (2000) *Dark Tourism*, London: Continuum.

Getz, D. (2000) 'Tourist shopping villages: development and planning strategies', in C. Ryan and S.J. Page (eds) *Tourism Management: Towards the New Millennium*, Oxford: Pergamon: 211–26.

Hall, C.M. and McArthur, J. (eds) (1996) *Heritage Management in Australia and New Zealand: The Human Dimension*, Melbourne: Oxford University Press.

Hall, C.M. and Page, S.J. (eds) (1999) *The Geography of Tourism and Recreation: Environment, Place and Space*, London: Routledge.

Hanna, M. (1999a) 'Visitor trends at attractions in 1998', *Insights*, July, F9–F12.

Hanna, M. (1999b) 'Sightseeing trends in 1998', *Insights*, November: A93–A102.

Lee, T.R. (1998) 'Evaluating the effectiveness of heritage interpretation', in D. Uzzell and R. Ballantyne (eds) *Contemporary Issues in Heritage and Environmental Interpretation: Problems and Prospects*, London: The Stationery Office, 203–31.

Millar, S. (1999) 'An overview of the sector', in A. Leask and I. Yeoman (eds) *Heritage Visitor Attractions – An Operations Management Perspective*, London: Cassell, 1–21.

Prentice, R. (1993) *Tourism and Heritage Attractions*, London: Routledge.

Internet resources

By going to the weblink at www.thomsonlearning.co.uk students can access the following study on the Thomson Learning website. It is a chapter from S. Horner and J. Swarbrooke (1996) *Marketing Tourism, Hospitality and Leisure in Europe* and examines the role of visitor attractions in Europe and the way in which they have different marketing requirements compared to other sectors of the tourism industry.

Scottish Tourist Board (1991) *Visitor Attractions: A Development Guide,* Edinburgh: Scottish Tourist Board.

Smith, C. and Jenner, P. (1998) 'The impact of festivals and special events on tourism', *Travel and Tourism Analyst,* **4**: 73–91.

Stevens, T. (2000) 'The future of visitor attractions', *Travel and Tourism Analyst,* **1**: 61–85.

Swarbrooke, J. (1995) *The Development and Management of Visitor Attractions,* Oxford: Butterworth-Heinemann.

Uzzell, D.L. (1989) 'The hot interpretation of war and conflict', in D.L. Uzzell (ed.) *Heritage Interpretation: Volume 1: The Natural and Built Environment,* London: Belhaven: 33–47.

Uzzell, D.L. and Ballantyne, R. (eds) (1998) *Contemporary Issues in Heritage and Environmental Interpretation: Problems and Prospects,* London: The Stationery Office.

Yale, P. (1998) *From Tourist Attractions to Heritage Tourism,* second edition, Huntingdon: Elm.

Further reading

Hughes, H. (2000) *Arts, Entertainment and Tourism,* Oxford: Butterworth-Heinemann.

Swarbrooke, J. (1995) *The Development and Management of Visitor Attractions,* Oxford: Butterworth-Heinemann.

9 Tourist accommodation

Learning outcomes

After studying this chapter, you should:

- Be aware of the diverse range of accommodation for tourism.
- Be familiar with key commercial operators.
- Have some understanding of current trends in this sector.

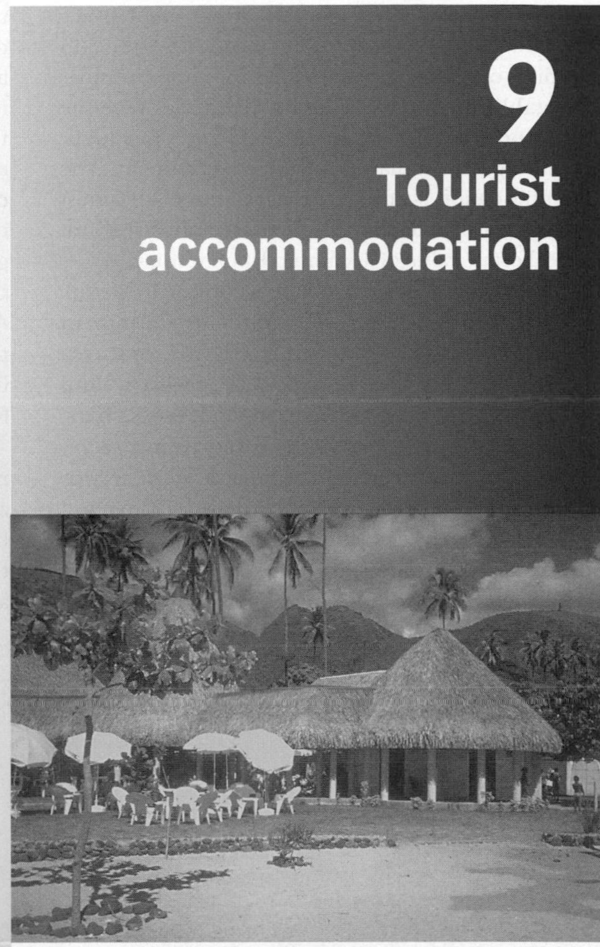

Overview

The purpose of this chapter is to provide the reader with an appreciation of the various types of accommodation and some of the issues for tourism; it describes the range of properties available and trends within this sector.

Introduction

According to Medlik (1989: 4) 'hotels play an important role in most countries in providing facilities for the transaction of business, for meetings and conferences, for recreation and entertainment ... In many areas hotels are important attractions for visitors who bring to them spending power and who tend to spend at a higher rate than when they do when they are at home'. What Medlik's (1989) key study of the hotel sector shows is that for many forms of tourism (excluding visiting friends or visiting relatives), the tourist requires some form of accommodation for an overnight stay or longer. And part of that accommodation consumption often involves discretionary spending which is at a higher rate than their normal leisure spending or household expenditure. In that sense accommodation in the tourism and wider hospitality sector has the potential to realize spending from visitors at different rates, particularly as the diversification of the accommodation sector into a wide variety of niche markets and products based on price has offered a new range of opportunities for the tourist in recent years (e.g. the growth of budget accommodation). One should also not forget that the accommodation sector, like other areas of the tourism industry is a major employer, given the labour-intensive nature of the accommodation sector and spending of visitors gives rise to various opportunities for establishments to generate additional revenue from food and beverage sales and products, depending on the nature of the establishment. The accommodation sector is, perhaps, one of the most capital-intensive areas of the tourism industry given the real estate value of accommodation venues.

The accommodation product, according to Medlik (1989) comprises the *location* of the establishment (i.e. where it is based in terms of a city or rural area and its relative accessibility to tourists and customers), its facilities (i.e. its bedrooms, bars, restaurants, meeting rooms and sports and recreation facilities), its service (i.e. what level of service the provider offers will depend upon its grading and facilities and market niche), its image (i.e. how it is portrayed to customers and the way it is marketed) and its price. In addition, the price will also depend upon the customers being sought since accommodation units appeal to a range of users. These users are typically: holidaymakers, business travellers and, increasingly, the short-break leisure market designed to fill weekend capacity not utilized by business travellers. Tourist accommodation has been developed, over time, to a position where virtually all tastes are catered for; from holiday villages that encourage guests to spend their time on-site to basic bunk-house barns that cater for a single-night stay at very low cost. Another variation is the concept of time-share which provides an investment for one or two weeks per year in a property, with the option of exchanging weeks for locations elsewhere.

Forms of accommodation have been developed to meet the purposes of individual and group travellers as Figure 9.1 illustrates. En route accommodation has evolved with changes in mode of transport such that the railway terminus hotel of the nineteenth and twentieth centuries is today represented by the

Plate 9.1 Time-share apartments, Malta

Figure 9.1 **Accommodation types**

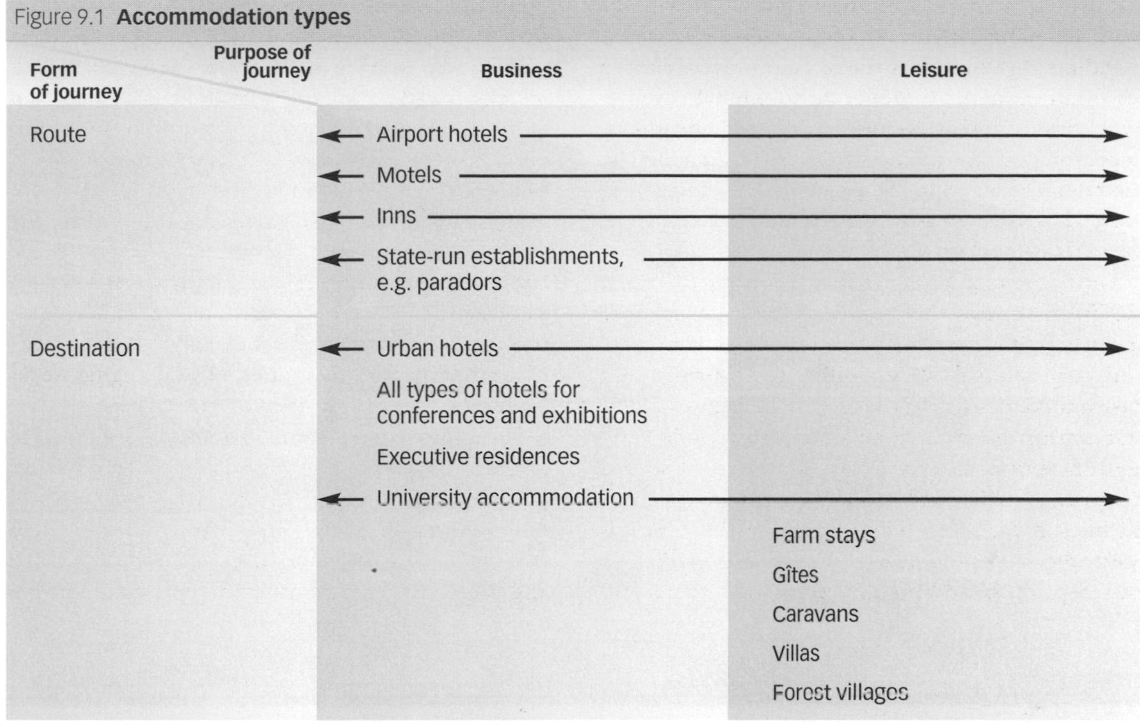

(Source: Adapted from Hall and Page 1999)

airport hotel where accommodation at major gateways now comprise a significant sector of the accommodation stock in many countries. Motels represent the logical extension of the coaching inn, although some companies have restored these older properties to high-standard contemporary business use and in the USA and Australasia they represent a major sector of accommodation supply.

In some countries, the state is directly involved in the operation of accommodation; for example, in Spain there are *paradors* and in Portugal *poussadas* although this trend has declined in recent years with the state and state-related tourism interests withdrawing from accommodation interests due to the costs of operation and high capital requirements for upgrading schemes and an absence of management skills.

The range of accommodation choice at the destination is even greater, as is the scale. For centuries, there have been properties with a handful of letting bedrooms whereas the mega-resort hotel is a phenomenon of the late twentieth century. Another development in the last 40 years is the rise of the hotel chain; Exhibit 9.1 details one example: Millennium and Copthorne Hotels plc.

> These multi-national hotel firms are usually based in Europe, the United States or Japan and this gives them a significant advantage over competitors in the destination country 'because of their favoured access to their domestic markets (and) their knowledge of what these customers want. (Go and Pine 1995: 10)

Globalization and the accommodation sector

The term globalization refers to the process of internationalization which is now associated with the growing world-wide trend towards products and tastes among consumers that are now being recognized and fulfilled by international companies. The global form of a company is one which recognizes the trends towards new tastes and preferences and provides products and services on a global scale to meet these new trends in consumer tastes. Some critics of globalization in the accommodation sector argue that this leading to the McDonaldization of the tourism product line, where the experience of a hotel stay in

Plate 9.2 Motel development in New Zealand
Most models of tourist accommodation locations indicate that motels tend to be located in strips adjacent to major routeways for accessibility and to obtain passing overnight traffic. This example is at Paihai, Bay of Islands, New Zealand.

one country is identical to that in another country. In other words, the experience of products and services is becoming homogenized by the global operators, especially in the accommodation sector where the consumer can be assured of a standard level of service and provision regardless of the country they visit. Research on globalization has identified three levels of internationalized or transnational corporations (as they are often termed). These are: global corporations, multinational corporations and smaller multinationals (see Taylor and Thrift 1986). Research by Gannon and Johnson (1995) rightly acknowledges that definitions of what constitutes an international, transnational or multinational operation are vague. They classify an international hotel company as a firm which has direct investments and other interests (e.g. contractual agreements) in more than one country. What this indicates in the accommodation sector is that there are few global transnational operators who specialize on particular regions. It is the multinational corporation that is probably the most active in this area, with a concern for operations outside of their country of operation. Within the accommodation sector, any company pursuing a global strategy can operate in countries where their head office is not located through a number of approaches. These are: franchising, licensing, non-investment management agreements and through the acquisition and merger with existing operators. One example of this is illustrated in Exhibit 9.1 where the development of a global brand was based on the acquisition and purchase of properties outside of the UK using two different brands to develop two distinctive products in the international hotel market.

The operating performance of the global hotel industry

The major research source for the analysis of the world hotel industry is the Horwath and Horwath (1999) *The Worldwide Hotel Industry Study* (twenty-

Exhibit 9.1 **Millennium and Copthorne Hotels**

This group is currently the largest 'pure' hotel company listed on the London Stock Exchange as a result of spectacular growth since being 'floated' in April 1996. Its foundations, however, go back to the days of British Caledonian Airways when the business was established as a hotel management company – CHM (Caledonian Hotels Management) – to serve the various route destinations. The next stage in the group's development occurred when CHM became Copthorne, with hotels in Britain, France and Germany, having been acquired by Irish airline Aer Lingus; in October 1995, CDL Hotels International paid £219 million for the business and, as stated, it was listed on the Stock Exchange the following year. Table 9.1 illustrates the geographic range of the group's properties in February 2000.

Table 9.1 **Millennium and Copthorne Hotels global reach**

	Hotels	Rooms
Millennium, Regal, Copthorne and Quality brands	74	17 871
Other brands owned or leased in USA	16	3 465
Management contracts in USA	19	3 707
Chain-managed hotels in USA	2	1 469
Chain-managed hotels in Asia	5	3 077
Partner hotel (Orchard Singapore)	1	683
Total	**117**	**30 272**
Total London	5	2 216
Total UK	17	4 073
Total USA	13	5 639
Total France	3	519
Total Germany	2	676
Total Australia	1	390
Total New Zealand (excluding Quality chain)	13	1 892
Total Singapore (inc. Waterfront and partner hotel)	5	2 407
Total Indonesia	1	405

Total Malaysia	1	318
Total Philippines	1	454
Total including partner hotels	57	16 773
Total inc. other owned hotels in Regal purchase	73	20 238
Total inc. US management contracts	92	23 945
Total inc. US chain-managed hotels	94	25 414
Total inc. Asian-owned/leased hotels	99	28 491
Total inc. NZ chain-managed hotels	117	30 272

Millennium as a brand was launched in October 1995 with the New York Millennium Broadway hotel; there are now 13 in seven countries. These are four-star deluxe properties in premier locations in major international gateway cities, serving both business and leisure visitors. Within the properties, there are two categories of room: standard and superior, Millennium Club with the latter offering latest technology, late checkout and other facilities. The Copthorne brand features four-star hotels in major business locations, in regional locations, in the UK, France, Germany, New Zealand, Malaysia and Singapore. Whilst Copthorne Europe hotels focus on business travellers, those in New Zealand extend into resort areas.

Both brands offer meeting facilities, in London, the Millennium Conference Centre offers 1,100 square metres of pillar-free floor space for up to 640 delegates. Also in London, the Britannia boasts the first completely new ballroom in Mayfair for over 20 years; up to 775 guests can be catered for. The group has won a number of industry awards including 'Best Hotel Group UK' (in three different years), 'Best UK Hotel' – for the London Tara – and 'Best Business Hotel Group'.

In December 1999, Millennium and Copthorne Hotels plc acquired the US interests of Regal Hotels International; during 2000, properties in Anchorage, Boulder, Minneapolis, Boston, Los Angeles, Cincinatti, Chicago, Nashville, Scottsdale, St Louis, Durham and New York were rebranded as Millennium.

ninth edition) which is supplemented by individual country studies of national hotel performance and the state of the accommodation sector (see Table 9.2 on the New Zealand accommodation sector). World-wide, the Horwath and Horwath study covered properties with an estimated 720,000 hotel rooms for 1998, with occupancy rates (i.e. the percentage of the room total that is occupied by guests) having dropped slightly from 67.7 per cent in 1996–97 to 66.7 per cent in 1998. Globally, there are an estimated 15 million hotel rooms offering a capacity of 5.5 billion room nights. Within this accommodation stock, around 30 per cent are chain affiliated, with estimates of this rising to 60 per cent by 2050 indicating the rising role of the global hotel chain. The main explanation for this drop is attributed to the decline in visitor arrivals in Asia following the Asian crisis (see Chapter 1, Exhibit 1.1).

Internationally, the average daily room rate in hotels increased to US$90.89 although the revenue per available room was US$62.96, although the best performing hotels recorded a considerably better revenue per available room in 1998 of US$94. The occupancy rates by world region were highest in Australia and New Zealand with a rate of 69.4 per

Table 9.2 **The accommodation sector in New Zealand, year ending 31 March 1999**

Accommodation type	Month											
					1998						**1999**	
Hotels	**Mar**	**April**	**May**	**June**	**July**	**Aug**	**Sept**	**Oct**	**Nov**	**Dec**	**Jan**	**Feb**
Number of establishments	565	560	568	556	551	563	563	564	570	572	574	572
Capacity (stay unit nights) (000)	736	708	728	702	733	735	726	751	739	764	763	695
Guest nights (000)	643	559	451	377	483	491	496	597	670	585	655	716
Occupancy rate (per cent)	55.8	49.2	41.0	36.8	41.8	43.0	43.8	50.1	57.9	45.4	48.8	64.1
Average stay (nights)	1.8	1.8	1.8	1.8	1.9	2.0	1.9	1.8	1.7	1.7	1.8	1.7
Motels												
Number of establishments	1 444	1 442	1 448	1 445	1 440	1 462	1 466	1 469	1 474	1 475	1 485	1 480
Capacity (stay unit nights) (000)	659	637	661	639	665	678	649	670	652	677	680	613
Guest nights (000)	769	741	544	425	603	543	587	716	654	702	932	790
Occupancy rate (per cent)	60.0	55.0	43.1	37.3	44.1	41.5	45.8	51.7	53.2	47.5	58.0	63.7
Average stay (nights)	1.8	1.8	1.8	1.8	1.9	1.9	1.8	1.8	1.7	1.8	1.9	1.7
Hosted												
Number of establishments	410	399	390	381	370	403	427	441	449	455	450	460
Capacity (stay unit nights) (000)	82	78	73	68	70	74	74	79	77	79	78	72
Guest nights (000)	49	37	21	15	25	25	27	39	42	46	58	55
Occupancy rate (per cent)	33.7	26.7	18.1	15.2	19.9	20.2	21.2	27.9	31.9	31.4	37.9	42.8
Average stay (nights)	1.7	1.8	1.8	2.0	2.2	2.2	2.1	2.0	1.8	1.8	1.9	1.8
Backpackers/hostels												
Number of establishments	255	252	253	250	245	256	271	278	274	278	277	279
Capacity (stay unit nights) (000)	364	351	384	372	375	397	398	421	399	427	428	376
Guest nights (000)	216	187	135	107	137	132	140	172	198	233	265	253

Table 9.2 **cont.**

Occupancy rate (per cent)	52.0	45.3	29.6	25.6	31.7	29.3	30.2	35.2	43.2	48.6	55.3	59.5
Average stay (nights)	2.0	2.1	2.2	2.2	2.2	2.3	2.2	2.1	2.0	2.0	2.0	1.9
Total excluding caravan parks/ camping grounds												
Number of establishments	2 674	2 653	2 659	2 632	2 606	2 684	2 727	2 752	2 767	2 780	2 786	2 791
Capacity (stay unit nights) (000)	1 841	1 774	1 846	1 780	1 842	1 883	1 849	1 922	1 867	1 938	1 939	1 756
Guest nights (000)	1 676	1 523	1 151	925	1 247	1 192	1 250	1 524	1 564	1 565	1 910	1 813
Occupancy rate (per cent)	55.6	49.5	38.5	33.8	39.7	38.7	40.6	46.5	52.0	46.2	53.0	62.1
Average stay (nights)	1.8	1.8	1.8	1.9	1.9	2.0	1.9	1.8	1.7	1.8	1.9	1.7
Caravan parks/camping grounds												
Number of establishments	414	407	394	382	366	382	390	407	414	418	414	415
Capacity	1 657	1 581	1 508	1 426	1 432	1 477	1 449	1 641	1 613	1 676	1 666	1 507
Guest nights (000)	426	454	201	140	187	167	224	332	315	760	1 463	530
Occupancy rate (per cent)	12.0	12.2	6.7	5.3	6.1	5.8	7.2	9.1	9.5	17.4	32.1	16.3
Average stay (nights)	2.2	2.3	2.4	2.6	2.4	2.4	2.2	2.2	2.0	2.7	3.3	2.1
TOTAL												
Number of establishments	**3 088**	**3 060**	**3 053**	**3 014**	**2 972**	**3 066**	**3 117**	**3 159**	**3 181**	**3 198**	**3 200**	**3 206**
Capacity (stay unit nights) (000)	**3 499**	**3 355**	**3 354**	**3 206**	**3 274**	**3 360**	**3 297**	**3 563**	**3 480**	**3 614**	**3 605**	**3 263**
Guest nights (000)	**2 102**	**1 978**	**1 352**	**1 064**	**1 434**	**1 359**	**1 473**	**1 856**	**1 879**	**2 325**	**3 373**	**2 344**
Occupancy rate (per cent)	**34.9**	**31.9**	**24.2**	**21.1**	**25.0**	**24.2**	**26.0**	**29.3**	**32.3**	**32.9**	**43.4**	**41.0**
Average stay (nights)	**1.9**	**1.9**	**1.9**	**1.9**	**2.0**	**2.0**	**1.9**	**1.9**	**1.8**	**2.0**	**2.3**	**1.8**

(Source: Department of Statistics)

cent in 1998 with a rate of 68.9 per cent in North America dropping to 60.3 per cent in South America with the lowest occupancy rate.

Within the hotel sector occupancy and operating performance in terms of revenue per room varied by category of hotel, with luxury hotels recording the greatest occupancies at 69.8 per cent and revenue per room of US$146 whereas the economy end of the market recorded an occupancy rate of 63 per cent and revenue per room of US$58.94. Not surprisingly, the airport hotels were among the group of hotels with the highest occupancy rates being adjacent to gateways, with a 74 per cent occupancy rate in 1998. This was followed by serviced apartments with a rate of 72 per cent and Country Inns with a rate of 68.5 per cent. For resorts and bed and breakfasts the rate was below 60 per cent although motels recorded an occupancy rate of 64.7 per cent and city/urban properties recorded a rate of 65.3 per cent.

Those hotels affiliated to chains consistently outperformed the independently operated properties, with the independents generating a greater proportion of their business from the domestic market. The only exception to this is in North America, where the domestic market generates 84 per cent of business for the chains and 79 per cent for the independently operated. The mix of visitors as hotel guests shows that business travellers are a significantly higher proportion of guests in the luxury sector (37 per cent) whereas in the economy end of the market, it is dominated by leisure travellers (35.2 per cent).

Other significant market segments according to Horwath and Horwath's (1999) study are tour groups, conference delegates, airline crew, government officials (e.g. those attending events such as the Commonwealth Heads of Government Conference) and other travellers. Although business guests tend to stay a shorter period of time in hotels than leisure travellers, they consistently spend greater sums per day than the leisure traveller. The balance of domestic to international visitor is 48:52 per cent in chain-affiliated hotels compared to 51:49 per cent in independently run hotels. Although this varies by region, it does indicate the significant role of inbound tourism in many countries and the fact that domestic tourism is often overlooked despite its significance as a business travel market.

Characteristics of the accommodation sector

All types of accommodation are confronted with some common characteristics. *Seasonality* affects those properties where one market – such as 'summer sun' dominates. In these situations, marketing efforts attempt to fill rooms at off-peak times through short breaks which offer the likes of 'three nights for the price of two'. Many accommodation providers work with their regional tourist board to develop local products such as festivals in the spring and autumn.

Related to seasonality is the issue of *occupancy* level; for large hotels this has been assisted with the development of yield management systems which seek to achieve a better fit with the market so that occupancy is spread across the week and month and year to avoid too many peaks and troughs in their business. *Location* can be of paramount importance in the siting of accommodation units; Ashworth (1989) proposed a model of urban hotel location based on one simple principle: distance decay – the prestigious properties locate in the central locations with the greatest accessibility to the market and adjacent to convention centres and other large venues. There is a tendency for hotels to locate in urban areas and to seek out the most accessible locations. In some situations, conversion of former office blocks and redundant warehouses (e.g. the Palace Hotel in Manchester is located in a listed insurance building) are used as prestigious locations for up-market hotels. At the same time, gateways such as airports remain high value locations as the discussion of world-wide hotel trends above suggested while intersections on major routeways (e.g. motorways) are also assuming a significant role for mid-range hotels in the absence of available in-town sites. In rural environments, location is often related to the scenic and aesthetic qualities of the landscape so that visitors can enjoy the rustic image and landscape attraction while in coastal locations, sea views assume a premium price in the location of accommodation.

Grading systems vary from one country to another; some are statutory and others voluntary. In 1999, the UK finally harmonized the tourist board 'crown' scheme with the 'stars' awarded by the two motoring organizations, the RAC and the AA; the result: stars for hotels and diamonds for other serviced accommodation. England does not operate a statutory registration scheme for tourist accommodation; at a major conference organized by the English Tourism Council in 1999, some of the arguments given for the introduction of one were: 'the unacceptable level of customer dissatisfaction ... no formal channel for complaints ... no mechanism for taking action against persistent offenders... (the) enforcement of fire regulations, building controls, environmental health is poorly resourced' (see www.englishtourism.org.uk for more detail).

Opponents of statutory grading schemes argue that further regulations stifle enterprise and that there is no firm evidence that in countries where it has been implemented standards have been raised. Furthermore, the tourist experience includes visits to theatres, restaurants and shops but these are not subject to grading; despite the latter point, there is little doubt that, for many tourists, their accommodation acts as a 'base' whilst on holiday and although they may tolerate low standards in some shops the same cannot be applied to where they sleep.

Classifying the accommodation sector

The accommodation sector is a diverse and complex phenomenon which is in a state of constant change and evolution. As a result, it is impossible to come up with a definitive classification that will embrace all forms of accommodation at any one point in time because of the pace of change in this sector. However, for the purpose of simplifying the nature of the accommodation sector, the first major distinction one can make is between the serviced and non-serviced sectors. The serviced sector is accommodation with services and facilities provided which can be included in the charge for the product. In the non-serviced sector, the product is accommodation only.

Serviced accommodation

Hotels

As mentioned already, the hotel is among the most visible and easily identifiable subsector within the accommodation business (which is referred to as the lodging sector in the USA). Cooper *et al.* (1998) argue that the traditional view of a hotel was premises which had rooms, food and beverage services and catered for short-stay visitors.

Recent developments in the hotel sector include the growth of health resorts (which is one of the fastest growing sectors of the business in Europe) and the introduction of long-stay five-star hotels such as Marriott Executive Residences, including the recently opened property in Budapest and TownePlace Suites which has properties in different American states. According to Cooper *et al.* (1998), hotel businesses world-wide are dominated by small family-owned operations, although they also contradict themselves by stating that this sector has

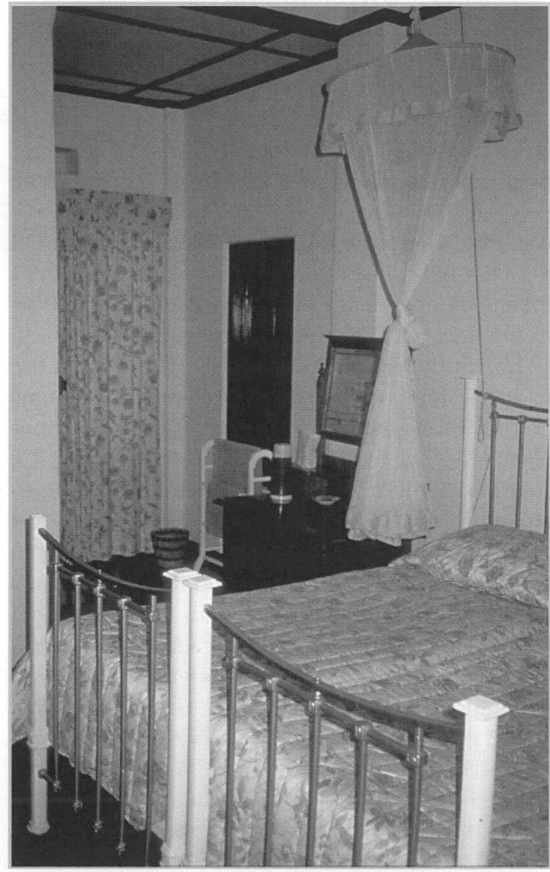

Plate 9.3 Bandarawela Hotel, Sri Lanka
A hotel bedroom, complete with mosquito net.

declined. Yet the recent evidence from the Horwath and Horwath (1999) survey combined with the analyses of small businesses operators in the tourism and hospitality sector indicates that the tourism industry in the new millennium has moved past this point. The rise of the hotel chains and the development of newer more innovative forms of hotel accommodation and the decline of the traditional seaside resorts in many western European locations has seen a shift towards urban and rural properties. This is evident in the evolution of new luxury health resorts and hotels which are moving the hotel sector into new market segments while traditional family-run businesses relying upon domestic tourists are facing increased competition in many countries with the larger hotels and the appeal of cheap package holidays and new products (e.g. cruises and motoring holidays).

In fact, one example of a response to the development of chain hotels has been the formation of independent groupings such as Consortia as illustrated in Exhibit 9.2. What Exhibit 9.2 also illustrates is the way in which the independent family-run hotel is being increasingly marginalized in the distribution channels for a growing range of accommodation products with the advent of GDSs and other marketing groups such as consortia.

In addition to the hotel sector, the serviced sector also comprises a number of other accommodation types which offer serviced accommodation in a small family-style environment, often with fewer than 12 bed spaces. Within an international context, there are a number of key features of this sector including the UK's world-renowned guesthouse sector where fewer regulations and controls apply to the provision of accommodation and it operates as a flexible

Exhibit 9.2 **Consortia in the independent hotel sector**

A number of consortia have developed in recent decades in order to compete with the power of the hotel chains; independent hotels group together to obtain the benefits of national and international marketing and bulk purchasing discounts. Two consortia will be reviewed here: Minotels and Leading Hotels of the World.

Minotel International is a registered non-profit-making association under Swiss law; it was founded in 1983 to 'secure the loyalty of its current customers, to open up new markets and to resist the competition of existing or future hotel chains' (www.minotel.com 2000). Ten years later, Minotel represented 650 hotels in 28 countries and by 1999 this had grown to 750 hotels – all are medium to superior quality hotels. With 95 per cent of Minotel hotels managed by their owners, there is clearly a personal touch to the consortium.

Occupancy levels are boosted by contracts with over 100 tour operators, based across five continents, who print an estimated 20 million brochures a year and sell Minotel hotel vouchers. The advent of the internet has boosted the consortium's position in the market still further and by 2004 Minotel expects to feature 2,500 hotels, of which 500 will be in the USA and Canada.

The Leading Hotels of the World is one of the oldest groupings of independent hotels dating from the 1920s when it was known as the Luxury Hotels of Europe and Egypt and featured 38 legendary hotels – such as the Savoy in London, Negresco in Nice and King David in Jerusalem. A sales office was opened in New York in 1928 and the organization became known as Hotel Representative Inc., eventually shortened to HRI. By the 1960s, HRI represented 70 luxury hotels and 16,000 rooms although a truly global presence was not achieved until 1980 by when the name had changed to the Leading Hotels of the World. By the early 1990s, 235 hotels belonged to the consortium and 21 reservation offices had been opened. At the beginning of the twenty-first century, there are 315 member hotels including such names as The Gleneagles in Scotland, the Ritz in Paris and Madrid and the Peninsula in Hong Kong.

accommodation resource, often picking up seasonal trade and closing during the low season. In countries such as New Zealand, the development of farm accommodation and farm stays fit within this category while in Canada, the development of inns such as the Heritage Inns of Canada fulfil a similar role at a lower cost than luxury hotels. A range of other developments, including the rise of the resort offering a more diverse range of accommodation and services is shown in Exhibit 9.3. The exhibit also indicates that the accommodation sector cannot easily be separated from the tourism sector since it is a key element of the tourism economy and is linked to the image and concept of the destination, although in some cases it can create an enclave where the tourists stay within the resort and have little interaction with the area in which they are staying.

Exhibit 9.3 **The resort and accommodation**

The term resort is here taken to mean the provision of accommodation and substantial other services at one location. Poon (1998: 62) defines all-inclusive resorts as those 'which include virtually everything in the prepaid price – from airport transfers, baggage handling, government taxes, rooms, all meals, snacks, drinks and cigarettes to the use of all facilities, equipment and certified instructors … the result is that the use of cash is eliminated'. The emphasis on everything being included obviously has an impact on local purchasing by tourists and, in many cases, the resort itself; because the 'multiplier effect' was negligible, The Gambia took the decision to abolish 'all-inclusives' from operating in the country. The all-inclusive concept originates from holiday camps and villages such as Butlin's in Britain and the French-based Club Méditerranée. Club Med dominates the league table of all-inclusive chains as Table 9.3 illustrates.

Table 9.3 **Major all-inclusive chains**

Resort	No. of resorts	Total no. of rooms	Headquarters
Club Med	131	74 156[a]	France
Allegro Resorts	26	8 184	Dominican Republic
Robinson Clubs	24	5 737	Germany
Club Valtur	20	3 668	Italy
Super Clubs	12	3 238	Jamaica
Club Aldiana	10	2 635	Germany
Clubs International	12	2 547	USA
Sandals	10	2 032	Jamaica

[a] bed/berths rather than rooms.

(Source: Poon 1998)

Budget accommodation

At the low-cost end of the serviced market are budget forms of accommodation. Some forms have developed as a result of transport improvements; for example, motels, budget hotels and some guesthouses. Branding assists the process of marketing; for example, it informs the customer that a Forte Travelodge at one end of the country is likely to offer the same facilities 300 miles away; there are over 190 of these lodges in the UK, all offering en-suite rooms with satellite television and easy check-in/out.

The Days Inns' concept of 'budget-luxury' is another example of market segmentation. As a result of travelling in New England, Cecil B. Day, the founder of Days Inns, realized that there was a gap in accommodation for the typical American family travelling on a limited budget. Day opened his first motel, which combined budget and luxury features, in Tybee Island, Georgia, in April 1970 on the premise of providing quality lodging at a fair and reasonable price. Since then, Days Inns has grown into one of the largest franchized lodging systems in the world, opening its 1,900th hotel in November 1999. There are now Days Inns in Canada, China, Colombia, Czech Republic, Hungary, India, Mexico, Philippines, South Africa, United Kingdom and Uruguay, in addition to the USA.

At a lower cost, the YHA (Youth Hostels Association) offers 230 locations in England and Wales but also, as a member, the choice of more than 4,500 world-wide. Unlike other forms of budget accommodation, membership is a prerequisite; as the following data (Table 9.4) show, the organization comprises adults as well as younger members and should be compared to a total of 6,439 in the first year of operation, 1931.

The YHA is more than simply an accommodation provider, it is virtually an environmental movement in its own right and has expressed opinions on afforestation in the Lake District and industrial development in the countryside; the Association is represented on 20 official or voluntary bodies connected with the environment. The Association has developed its own seven-point Environmental Charter for youth hostels globally, shown in Table 9.5.

This is a notable development in the accommodation sector, as Cooper *et al.* (1998) indicate, whereby environmental issues have assumed a greater role in the consumers awareness of impacts of their stay on the environment. To summarize, Cooper *et al.* (1998) suggest that the following areas are of concern for the accommodation sector in terms of cost and image which include: water use, energy use, recycling, waste disposal, the impact of the hotel when they are located in a fragile location (Plate 9.4 illustrates tourist accommodation in Tahiti constructed to reflect the vernacular architecture of the village hut).

Table 9.4 **YHA membership (England and Wales) by category, 1998/99**

Category	Members
Under 18	44 185
Adult	182 547
Group	6 853
Annual life	1 335
Full life	43 543
Total	278 463

(Source: YHA 1999 Annual Report)

The non-serviced accommodation sector

In contrast to the serviced sector, a great many innovations have occurred in the non-serviced sector. For example, the growth of self-catering accommodation has been a major change for the post-war accommodation industry in many countries and much of this growth has been at the expense of the traditional guesthouse and small family-run hotel sector. Where the self-catering complexes have provided recreational and entertainment facilities (e.g. Center Parcs in the Netherlands and the UK and Oasis in Cumbria, UK).

Apartments form a central component of the accommodation provided in self-catering units and in the Mediterannean and Australasia this market

Table 9.5 **International Environmental Charter for Youth Hostels**

1	*Consumption* We will reduce our consumption of the world's resources and minimize waste
2	*Recycling* We will use recycled products wherever feasible and recycle waste
3	*Pollution* We will use efficient and environmentally sound methods of waste reduction and disposal
4	*Energy conservation* We will monitor and minimize our consumption of energy, promote energy efficiency and use renewable energy wherever possible
5	*Transport* We will encourage the use of public transport, car sharing and travel between hostels by foot or cycle
6	*Nature* We will consider the environment when caring for hostel grounds and encourage the protection of specially designated conservation and heritage areas in England and Wales
7	*Environmental education* We will create suitable areas for study and information display, with an accent on every individual's ability to bring about changes which contribute to environmental conservation

(Source: YHA)

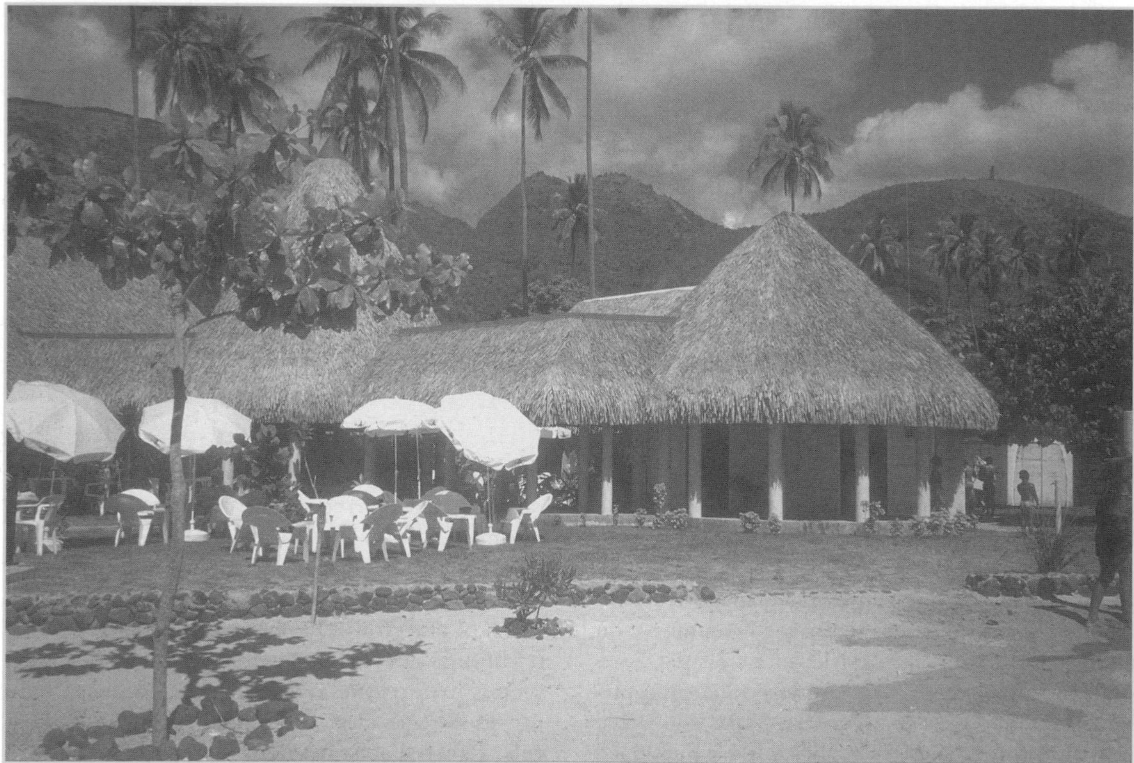

Plate 9.4 Tourist accommodation, Tahiti
An example of tourist accommodation modelled on the vernacular architecture of the local village hut.

Exhibit 9.3 **Center Parcs and Oasis**

A different type of resort accommodation is provided by Center Parcs and Oasis; they are both 'holiday villages' set in a forested environment with an emphasis on 'green' aspects; they are not all-inclusive in the sense that one price covers everything but they are 'resorts' in as much as everything needed is on-site. Both are owned by large parent organizations: Center Parcs by Scottish & Newcastle Breweries and Oasis by the Rank Group which also operates Butlin's, Haven and Warner sites. Center Parcs also has sites in Germany, Belgium, France and the Netherlands from where it first developed as an independent company.

An important feature is the scale of these villages; for example, Oasis offers 750 villas at the Penrith location on the edge of the English Lake District. Oasis and Center Parcs also have a major effect on local employment; the typical number of full-time equivalent (FTE) jobs is 1,000 per location. Gordon (1997: C22) states that the Oasis concept is based on the demand for year-round short breaks and the public's aspiration for a natural environment; each village features a central area contiguous to a large lake, a 'subtropical water-world and health spa ... and constant year round temperature ... (together) with a selection of restaurants' (including the Hard Rock Café) and wide range of sports facilities. There is no reason to leave the site (the Oasis Penrith location covers 400 acres) and, given that the villas are let on a self-catering basis, the clientele are encouraged to buy from the on-site supermarket if the restaurants are not patronized.

The reader is recommended to consult Gordon's (1997) study as it details the development approach adopted by Oasis. Website addresses are: www.centerparcs.com and www.oasishols.co.uk.

has been a popular addition to both coastal and urban locations reflected in the high occupancy rates discussed by the Horwath and Horwath (1999) accommodation survey. This sector also includes developments such as *gîtes* (a French holiday cottage). In some cases self-catering accommodation is also being packaged in the mass markets by specialist operators while new innovations (e.g. house swaps) have also added additional capacity for holiday accommodation to compete with the serviced sector. Further forms of accommodation which are notable are university campus accommodation (see Connell 2000), camping and caravan sites while specialist operators such as Eurocamp have developed sited tents and caravans for the budget-conscious family and small group travellers. One of the least known and understood sectors which is not strictly non-serviced is the visiting relatives category. In some cities such as Auckland in New Zealand, up to 50 per cent of the inbound UK visiting relatives market will stay in the home of a relative or acquaintance and while it makes a major contribution to the local tourism economy, it is poorly understood and not researched. Similarly, the growth of global family networks in an age of increasing travel among certain ethnic groups such as the Chinese may also create a market for visiting relatives that does not use serviced accommodation or non-serviced accommodation but stays with a network of family and friends in different countries (see Exhibit 3.1).

Non-accommodation hospitality services

The hospitality services which are often associated with the accommodation sector are not always provided with this sector. In many locations, these services are also provided outside of accommodation establishments and comprise restaurants, fast-food outlets, cafeterias and public houses, bars, clubs and canteens. Ashworth and Tunbridge (1990) observed that after accommodation, these are the most frequently used services by tourists since in 1990, of £15 billion of tourist expenditure in the UK, £2 billion was spent on eating and drinking. Bull and

Church (1994) argue that this sector has undergone massive change in the UK reflected in employment change in hotel and catering. One of the greatest changes has occurred in the fast-food sector which has grown nationally in the UK while other sectors have expanded through the use of part-time employment. The dominance of transnational corporations such as McDonald's, KFC and Burger King have resulted in the market being dominated by a limited number of brands. For the tourist, this has meant that the fast-food sector has competed directly with other forms of food retailing in city and smaller town locations and is a good illustration of the theme of globalization. However, as Smith (1983) found, tourist use of catering facilities is also determined by what is on offer and where it is located, with accessible city centre locations fiercely contested by the fast-food outlets. In more recent years, the evolution of franchising by Railtrack in the UK has turned mainline railway stations into fast-food locations which now directly compete for the tourist and non-tourist consumer and also compete with the rail operators for discretionary leisure spending.

What is complex when calculating the effect of tourism on any given area is the separation of use by residents from that by visitors; this differs from accommodation expenditure where there will be little local occupancy. This is one of the major difficulties with quantifying the impact of both the accommodation and more complex and diverse hospitality sector. In certain destinations, for example the tourist-historic city, those establishments offering food – and possibly other entertainment – 'have two important locational characteristics ... a distinct tendency to cluster together into particular streets or districts ... and they tend to be associated spatially with other tourism elements including hotels' (Ashworth and Tunbridge 1990: 65). This is demonstrated most clearly in many Dutch cities where entertainment facilities (e.g. sex shops and brothels) locate in a distinct area where other food and hospitality services have developed nearby given the nature of the attraction and visitor appeal of these icons of the built environment. Regional cuisine may be one of the key attractions in tourist decision-making, lending weight to calls for improved standards; on the standards issue, see Prue Leith's reasons for selecting Stafford, England, for her 'food museum' project in Chapter 14. The food of a region can be drawn to the attention of potential tourists through the medium of television; in Cornwall, the seaside town of Padstow has been only slightly jokingly re-named Padstein as a result of the major impact of the local restaurateur's 'Taste of the Sea' series – his businesses are now a key employer in the district.

Conclusion

Within the accommodation and hospitality services sector, the global brand has emerged as one of the most significant developments and is an on-going trend where the process of globalization is evident. The consequence for the built environment and the tourist experience as critics would argue is the growing McDonaldization of the accommodation and hospitality services sector, running contrary to developments in local and regional cuisine and hospitality as reflected in the wine and food festivals and theming of tourism products (see Hall *et al.* 2000). A further illustration of globalization as the Horwath and Horwath (1999) report indicated is the further consolidation of the chain hotel companies in the accommodation sector. For example, in the first nine months of 1997, there were $US4.5 billion of acquisitions and mergers in the accommodation sector with a further $US 20 billion under discussion indicating the growing significance of transnational and multinational corporations in the global accommodation sector.

The market for accommodation is also becoming much more diverse with a product and price range being developed for an increasingly sophisticated tourism market. This is evident as Chapter 13 suggests with the rise of the internet as a search tool to identify a wider range of products to consider in the decision to book accommodation and travel services. Added to this is the rise of the environmental lobby which is reflected in consumer demands for a greater attention to environmental sensitivity (see Stabler and Goodall 1997). This is reflected in the cost savings hotels are now attaching to seizing the environmental advantages of less laundering, savings in water consumption and reduction in the use of consumables. Thus, the accommodation sector cannot be separated from trends in the wider tourism sector because they are in some cases leading the way forward in environmental management where such initiatives are developed and implemented. The accommodation sector is also a key element of the tourists' experience of a destination and is often sold as part of a product and therefore quality standards and satisfactions levels with holiday experiences are intrinsically linked to the accommodation sector.

Discussion questions

1. Identify the advantages and disadvantages of accommodation consortium membership for independent hotels.
2. Discuss the benefits of branding for hotel chains.
3. How has the development of self-catering accommodation impacted upon the serviced sector in European coastal resorts?
4. The rise of budget accommodation in the serviced sector is now driven by the demand for quality at a lower cost. How far does this result from wider developments in the tourism industry?

References

Ashworth, G.J. (1989) 'Urban tourism: an imbalance in attention', in C.P. Cooper (ed.) *Progress in Tourism, Recreation and Hospitality Management, vol. 1*, London: Belhaven: 33–54.

Ashworth, G.J. and Tunbridge, J.E. (1990) *The Tourist-Historic City*, London: Belhaven.

Bull, P.J. and Church, A. (1994) 'The geography of employment change in the hotel and catering industry of Great Britain in the 1980s: a sub-regional perspective', *Regional Studies*, **28**: 13–25.

Connell, J.J. (2000) 'The role of tourism in the socially responsible university', *Current Issues in Tourism*, **3** (1): 1–19.

Cooper, C., Fletcher, J., Gilbert, D., Wanhill, S. and Shepherd, R. (1998) *Tourism – Principles and Practice*, second edition, Harlow: Longman.

Gannon, J. and Johnson, K. (1995) 'The global hotel industry: the emergence of continental hotel companies', *Progress in Tourism and Hospitality Research*, **1**: 31–42.

Internet resources

By going to the weblink at www.thomsonlearning.co.uk students can access the following four studies. There are a significant number of resources listed below because the area of accommodation and hospitality services has been dealt with in only one chapter and there is a growing literature on this area including the study by C. Verginis and R. Wood (1999) *Accommodation Management: Perspectives for the International Hotel Industry*, Thomson Learning: London, which is ideal for advanced study.

From the website, the first resource is a chapter from F. Go and R. Pine (1994) *Globalization Strategy in the Hotel Industry* on globalization which deals with many of the fundamental concepts and issues associated with this process and how it affects the international hotel industry.

The second chapter is also from F. Go and R. Pine (1994) *Globalization Strategy in the Hotel Industry* and focuses on the international hotel industry and how it is organized and operates.

The third study is a glossary of terms which are associated with economics such as globalization and are derived from A. Cooke (1994) *The Economics of Sport* and should be read in conjunction with the later chapter in this book on the economics of tourism.

The fourth study is by Y. Guerrier (1996) and is an article from the *International Encyclopedia of Business and Management* on 'Hospitality management' which is a useful overview of the field of hospitality and how it relates to tourism. It highlights how accommodation and hospitality services are complementary to tourism services and are important guest services in their own right for hotels and other establishments.

This should be read in combination with information from the Confederation of the National Associations of Hotels, Restaurants, Cafes and similar Establishments in the European Union and European Economic Area (HOTREC) on www.hotrec.org.

Go, F. and Pine, R. (1995) *Globalization Strategy in the Hotel Industry*, London: Routledge.

Gordon, C. (1997) 'Oasis Forest Villages – developing with the environment', *Insights*, November: C19–28.

Hall, C.M. and Page, S.J. (1999) *The Geography of Tourism and Recreation: Environment, Place and Space*, London: Routledge.

Hall, C.M., Sharples, L., Cambourne, B. and Macionis, N. (eds) (2000) *Wine Tourism Around the World*, Oxford: Butterworth-Heinemann.

Horwath and Horwath (1999) *The Worldwide Hotel Industry Study*, twenty-ninth edition, New York: Horwarth and Horwarth.

Medlik, S. (1989) *The Business of Hotels*, second edition, Oxford: Heinemann.

Poon, A. (1998) 'All-inclusive resorts', *Travel & Tourism Analyst*, **6**: 62–77.

Smith, S.L.J. (1983) 'Restaurants and dining out: geography of a tourism business', *Annals of Tourism Research*, **10**: 515–49.

Stabler, M.J. and Goodall, B. (1997) 'Environmental awareness, action and performance in the Guernsey hospitality sector', *Tourism Management*, **18** (1): 19–33.

Taylor, M. and Thrift, N. (1986) 'Introduction: new theories of multinational corporations', in M. Taylor and N. Thrift (eds) *Multinationals and the Restructuring of the World Economy*, London: Croom Helm.

Section 3
Managing tourist operations

The previous chapters examined both tourism demand and supply issues and the major challenge which these pose for the tourism sector is the maximization of demand to meet its supply. This management challenge is one which concerns tourism managers and dominates strategic long-term goals, and day-to-day tourism operations, where the tourism sector seeks to fill demand and meet the customers needs through a range of mechanisms. This section of the book focuses on the wider context of tourism operations, by examining the tools and issues which the tourism industry has to deal with on a day-to-day basis as well as those which assume strategic importance. This is reflected in the major issue which most tourism enterprises see as critical to maintaining a competitive business – having appropriate staff for the tasks in hand. This is discussed in Chapter 10 in relation to global issues of human resource management which affect the tourism industry. The nature of human resource management and the particular challenges it poses for the future development of tourism are reviewed. This is followed by a particularly specialized area of tourism activity vital to the development of tourism businesses and operational performance – finance. Finance is largely neglected in many studies of tourism and so Chapter 11 introduces some of the broad concepts and principles which tourism managers need to understand, and explains how different tourism businesses secure funding and the various techniques used to review a business' financial performance. This is very much linked to the next chapter (Chapter 12) which examines the vital area of tourism and entrepreneurship and the characteristics and activities of key individuals who have had a major impact on a specific sector of the tourism industry. The chapter highlights the influence of key individuals who are responsible along with companies they own and operate for the provision of tourism services and experiences. This is then followed by one area which has required businesses to seek capital and expertise to stay competitive – the role of information technology (Chapter 13). The discussion examines not only the role and use of information technology but the impact of new forms of technology such as the internet and World Wide Web. The section concludes with a review of the role of government and public sector tourism organizations in the operation and management of tourism activities (Chapter 14) which often undertake marketing activities and direct the tourism industry in certain localities.

10 Human resource management in tourism

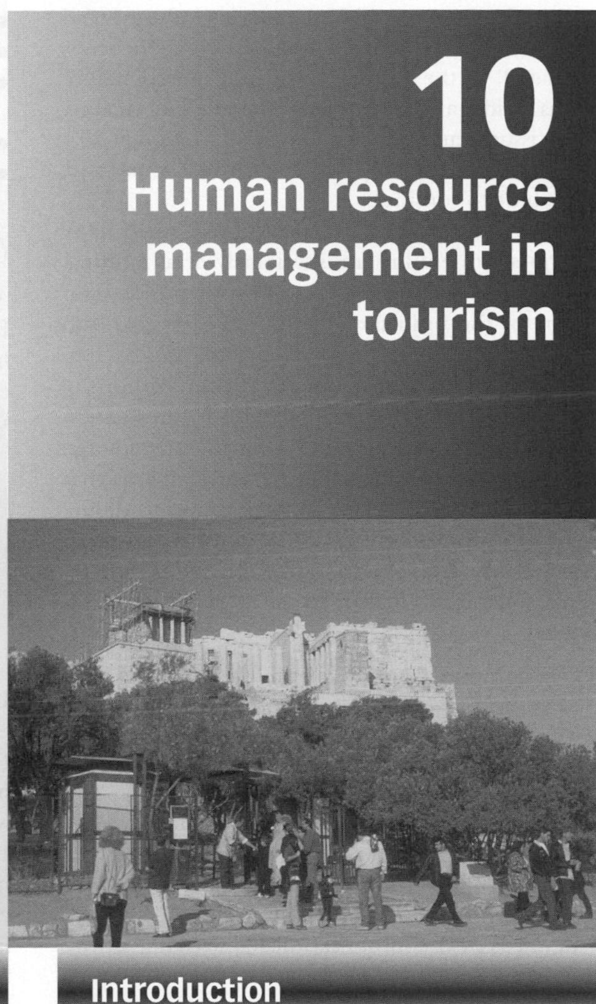

Learning outcomes

This chapter seeks to develop an awareness of critical issues associated with human resource management in tourism. After studying this chapter, you should be able to:

- Gain an understanding of the people dimension in tourism as a fundamental element in the success of tourism enterprises.
- Assess the scope of the human resource manager's job in tourism.
- Consider how agencies are involved in human resource management issues in tourism.
- Examine how future changes in work patterns will affect human resource issues in tourism.
- Assess the role of human resource issues in small tourism businesses.

Overview

This chapter examines the role of human resource management (HRM) in the tourism industry and its growing importance as a factor inhibiting business performance. The chapter considers the significance of HRM in the functioning and operation of tourism businesses and the global problems which many companies face in staff training, development and retention. The chapter also examines a number of examples of good practice in HRM for tourism and the problems which small tourism businesses face in this area. The significance of HRM for tourism managers is also considered.

Introduction

Tourism is a people industry: tourists are people, customers and clients and their activities are subject to the normal vagaries of human behaviour (i.e. decision-making about what to buy and consume) which is both predictable and unpredictable depending on the situation and context. The tourism experience or product is entirely dependent upon people for its delivery – or more simply put it is dependent upon the human factor (Baum 1993) and it frequently involves contact with people from different backgrounds, locations and cultures. Therefore, tourism can be conceptualized as a client purchasing 'the skills, service and commitment of a range of human contributors to the experience that they are about to embark upon' (Baum 1993: 4). For the tourism experience to be successful, managers within the tourism industry need to ensure that the tourism product or experience is 'mediated' to the customer which by its very nature means a wide range of human resource issues emerge. These issues can be best summarized in Exhibit 10.1 which outlines the scope of the activities a manager might have to consider.

Since tourism is a global business, with many enterprises operating transnationally or as multinational enterprises across several continents, certain sectors of the industry (e.g. the hotel sector) also have to adopt an international or global approach to human resource management (HRM). Within the published studies of HRM in tourism, there are a common range of themes that consistently emerge which help to identify a number of elements that need to be considered when attempting to define the nature and scope of HRM in tourism. Baum (1993: 9–10) cites the following 'universal themes' which consistently feature in the analysis of HRM in tourism. These are:

- Demographic issues related to the shrinking pool of potential employees and labour shortages, which surface when the economy is performing well and other career options pay higher rates of pay, a feature which many London hotels were facing in the year 2000.
- The tourism industry's image as an employer.
- Cultural and traditional perceptions of the tourism industry.
- Rewards and compensation for working in the sector.
- Education and training.
- Skill shortages at the senior and technical levels.
- Linking human resource concerns with service and product quality.
- Poor manpower planning.
- A remedial rather than proactive approach to human resource issues.

(Source: Adapted from Baum 1993)

Aside from the scope of HRM issues identified in Exhibit 10.1, it is evident that the tourism sector also has a number of unique problems which need to be considered when attempting to define the scope of HRM in tourism.

So what do we mean by the term 'human resource management'?

In simple terms, HRM can be termed as a form of employment management which Torrington and Hall (1987) identify as focused on the managerial need for human resources to be provided and deployed. In line with the functions of management, the concern within HRM is the planning, monitoring and control of the human resource as a management activity. More complex analyses of HRM identify the concern for the individual human resource system within any organization to be able to realize the strategic objectives of

Exhibit 10.1 **The scope of human resource management issues for a tourism industry manager**

1 A critical awareness of the scope and nature of the labour market.
2 The design of jobs.
3 Recruitment, selection, appointment and retention of staff.
4 Induction, equal opportunities, training and development.
5 Evaluation of staff performance.
6 Salaries and incentives.
7 Employment termination, grievance and dispute procedures.
8 Industrial relations and employment law.
9 Motivation of staff.

(Source: Modified from Baum 1993)

the organization (i.e. the delivery of excellent customer service to tourism consumers). One can also distinguish between 'hard' HRM approaches which are essentially financially driven and concerned with controlling the salary cost and are extremely directive – it is therefore described as utilitarian and managerialist. In contrast, 'soft' approaches to HRM are centred on the principle of the development of the employees and are much more humanist, with employees as assets rather than liabilities (Cornelius 1999). In practice most organizations adopt a pragmatic approach to HRM depending on a wide range of factors including the economic and operating environment, the size of the organization, the extent to which the labour market is supplied with adequate staff and the corporate culture. What should be evident from this brief discussion of HRM is that it is far more than simple personnel management and in its most highly effective state it should adopt a holistic approach to employment management. In a 'people' business such as tourism, this assumes a significant role because of the need to derive quality from the employees and their interaction and exchanges with customers so that it becomes critical that the people with the right skills are in the right jobs. Since tourism is a global business which operates at a wide range of scales, this chapter will examine HRM issues in tourism at the international level and the scale of the individual tourism enterprise to illustrate the issues which students need to be aware when examining the tourism sector. (For a more specific discussion of the detailed nature of HRM functions readers are directed to the Further reading section and introductory texts on HRM.)

Agencies and HRM issues in tourism: international perspectives

Within the existing studies of HRM in tourism, there is a reasonable consistent view on the human problems which face the tourism industry and at the international scale there are a wide range of approaches and responses to the problems. In many of the Tourism Master Plans developed for countries (see Inskeep 1994 for more detail), human resource issues normally assume a significant position. There are also a range of bodies which have an active involvement in HRM issues in tourism and Exhibit 10.2 explains the work of one such organization – the World Travel and Tourism Council.

In some countries, the public sector is actively involved in the provision of organizations and assistance for the tourism sector to assist in human resource development, through policies, planning and the implementation of initiatives. A good example of this is the establishment of CERT in Ireland nearly 40 years ago as a national initiative funded by the state government (Walsh 1993). Even where the state is involved, it may often be the case that a range of bodies have overlapping responsibilities. The organizations which are typically involved are: state education providers; private training and educational providers; national employment or manpower agencies; associated bodies such as trade unions and the national, regional and local level tourism agencies. Co-ordinating and liaising with such a host of bodies can be complex and time consuming. Furthermore, changes in political philosophy, such as in the UK after 1979, saw the state assistance progressively cut back and the emphasis being placed on the private sector. Where national tourism organizations (NTOs) are involved in training, their function can range from direct control of the training system at one extreme through to a limited policy role. The World Tourism Organization collates information from time to time and publishes it in reports, but even those data are partial. More progressive countries such as Singapore with its Singapore 21 Strategy have a key concern for human resource issues in tourism and it reflects the vast investment and significance of tourism to the national economy.

Where tourism and human resource issues assume national significance, as was the case in Ireland between 1987–1992, tourism employment growth was used to assist in reducing adult and youth unemployment. In this context it can become a carefully targeted activity and resourced due to its significant to national economic development. In contrast, other countries such as New Zealand prefer to leave the private sector to determine the agenda for human resource issues for the tourism industry. The scope and extent of human resource issues in countries seeking to develop their tourism industry are evident in Tables 10.1 and 10.2 where the range of problems which the state and private sector need to address through a more co-ordinated approach to HRM in tourism are

Exhibit 10.2 **The role of the World Travel and Tourism Council (WTTC)**

The WTTC is a global business leaders forum for travel and tourism from all sectors of the industry. It has representatives and offices throughout the world and it sponsors a WTTC Human Resource Centre which produces a publication entitled 'Global Good Practices in Travel and Tourism Human Resource Development with the publication sponsored by American Express. It provides case studies of good education and training across the tourism sector with a view to disseminating real world experiences to a world-wide audience of human resource professionals. The article by Pizam (1999) reports the results of a WTTC and American Express-funded study of tourism and human resource issues in Latin America.

In the most recent WTTC *Steps to Success* (Volume 3:1), the scope of articles of good practice comprised: customer service training in Hungary and Australia; institutional frameworks (the role of NTOs) – Scotland; Mexico; intercultural training at Four Seasons Hotel and Resorts; management tools and practices at the Shangri-la Hotel, Hong Kong; peer training in the USA and speciality training in the USA and Australia.

To illustrate the scope of one such article and the value in a human resource context, the example of the Investors in People Initiative at the Scottish Borders Tourist Board is briefly outlined.

The Investors in People Initiative: The case of the Scottish Borders Tourist Board

The Scottish Borders Tourist Board (SBTB) is a statutory tourism authority covering the region bordering England and is one of 14 area tourist boards in Scotland. One of the corporate objectives of SBTB is recognizing that staff training and development are essential for business growth and in the management of change which is essential in the fast-moving field of tourism. In 1994, SBTB began working with the Investors in People (IIP) to improve employee relations and to link staff development more closely to business objectives. IIP is a national standard that sets the level for good practice in improving organizational performance through people. Following a self-evaluation process, SBTB recognized that it had a number of human resource systems in place. IIP was seen as a means of increasing staff motivation and in highlighting the clear benefits of training. After a period of 18 months, the SBTB transformed the way it planned and implemented human resource functions. After self-evaluation and evaluation of SBTB in February 1996, SBTB was the first area tourist board to gain IIP status. This has significantly sharpened the human resource function and led to a more 'people focused' business plan with improved training for its staff. The outcomes for the SBTB are outlined as follows:

- Improved staff morale.
- Enhanced employee skills and knowledge.
- Improved training practices leading to enhanced performance, reflected in more efficient use of resources and positive customer feedback.
- Improved staff awareness of staff training and development.
- Improved SBTB Board management being linked to training and development needs.
- Training and development outputs linked to certifiable standards.
- Improved status as a tourism organization.

For further detail consult: http://www.scotland.holiday.net

Table 10.1 **Human resource management problems in the Thai tourism industry**

1	A shortage of trained personnel, especially at the managerial level
2	A lack of tourism instructors
3	Poor foreign language skills of tourism staff
4	No single agency responsible for human resource development in the tourism industry
5	Lack of co-operation between the public and private sector

(Source: Modified from Esichaikul and Baum 1998)

Table 10.2 **Human resource management problems in the Latin American tourism industry**

1	A lack of effective managerial training
2	Educational institutions have inappropriate provision for the needs of the tourism industry
3	Lack of co-ordination between the educational sector and the tourism industry
4	Limited number of tourism instructors
5	Inadequate investment in training by the private sector
6	Insufficient and inadequately designed in-house training programmes
7	Limited exposure to foreign language training
8	A lack of travel agency training programmes
9	Service delivery and customer relations given inadequate attention together with inadequate levels of education among employees
10	Too few internship opportunities for tourism students
11	Poor regulation of training institutions
12	Inadequate government fiscal incentives to facilitate industry training
13	Limited public sector support for tourism
14	Low wages and salary levels for employees in the tourism industry
15	Negative attitudes towards service occupations

(Source: Modified from Pizam 1999)

apparent. However, focusing on the role of the state and public sector as the sole agent responsible for HRM issues overlooks the fact that individual businesses need to take an active role in such issues and for that reason the discussion now turns to this topic.

Tourism and HRM issues: the response and role of the individual business

For the individual business, there is a need to recognize the macro-economic processes which are at work within the business environment. For example, one of the greatest challenges for the future development of tourism employment is the change to the nature of work (see Exhibit 10.3).

For the medium-sized and large tourism enterprise, human resource issues and the factors affecting their performance are usually highly linked to the staff and workforce and therefore recognizing the role of recruitment and on-going development of the staff resource to achieve strategic goals become

Exhibit 10.3 **The future of work in the UK: implications for HRM in tourism**

The recent research project being funded by the Economic and Social Research Council in the UK (http://www.leeds.ac.uk/esrcthefutureofwork) provides a wide range of perspectives on the changing nature of work which human resource managers need to be aware of. For example, in the period 1981–98, the number of people working from home increased from 345,920 to 680,612. Likewise the number of workers reporting no fixed place to carry out their work tripled from 641,900 in 1981 to 1,824,154 in 1998, with such mobile workers comprising 7 per cent of those in work. For the tourism industry, this is a proportion of potential employees no longer in the market for 'people' based workplace-based jobs which dominate the tourism sector, especially the hospitality sector. Aside from an ageing population which means greater flexibility in the nature of employees companies can recruit, the concept of career mobility and lifelong learning (i.e. one is constantly learning) means a greater contribution to staff turnover as staff aspirations change. Add to this the concept of continued business re-engineering, where companies are in a constant state of flux to adapt their business practices to the marketplace, then downsizing and outsourcing and continued change adds a greater degree of fluidity to staff careers. The growth in part-time employment and employee turnover pose additional challenges for human resource managers. For example, in the period 1991–96, up to 25 per cent of full-time British workers changed job each year (Booth and Francesconi 2000). In an industry sector which frequently complains of staff recruitment and retention problems due to its image and the perception of low pay, such statistics pose a serious challenge for the tourism industry. Combined with the changes in the nature of work, the human resource manager needs to anticipate manpower requirements in a context of changes in leisure time which will impact on the demand for labour. A recent report by the World Tourism Organisation (WTO) (1999) *Changes in Leisure Time* examined 18 countries and how future changes would affect tourism demand and the factors influencing leisure time (e.g. hours of work, paid leave entitlement, retirement trends and consumer behaviour) and their use. Therefore, anticipating future changes in labour may be reflected in the innovative approach of organizations such as British Airways with its 'People Empowered' initiative where people of any race and nationality are employed and they seek to reflect the demographic makeup of the UK workforce (i.e. a workforce in the UK which is 50 per cent female, with 33 per cent of management posts held by women). It encourages initiatives such as job-sharing, part-time work and nursery places for staff to ease the demands of full-time work and childcare. The aim of the initiative according to British Airways is to attract and retain staff who are committed and share in the success of the airline.

essential. A re-investment in the human resource through on-going training and development of the employees skills and ability to create and add value to the organization are inherent qualities for which successful tourism enterprises are recognized throughout the world. The scale of the human resource function will often reflect the size of the organization and specific functions (e.g. training and development) may be allocated to specific individuals whereas in smaller organizations, the commitment to core functions (recruitment and retention) may be all that is possible due to work pressures and constraints on staff time. However, one also has to recognize that in some countries, the large tourism organizations (e.g. airlines and hotel chains) may be major employers but the backbone of the tourism industry is the small business sector.

Human resource management issues in small tourism businesses

Research on tourism and small businesses is comparatively limited and there is no universal definition of the term. According to Morrison (1996: 400):

> a small tourism business is financed by one individual or small group and is directly managed by its owner(s), in a personalised manner and not through the medium of a formalised management structure ... it is perceived as small, in terms of physical facilities, production/service capacity, market share and the number of employees.

The definition of a small tourism business according to employee size varies with each research study. For example, a Deloitte Touche Tomatsu (1994) study of small tourism businesses adopted a cut off of fewer than ten employees. In contrast, Thomas *et al.* (1997) study in the UK acknowledged that in the EU it could range up to 50 employees, with micro-enterprises employing fewer than ten employees. Morrison (1996: 401) has argued that 'traditionally the tourism industry has been dominated by the small business and this still remains true in the 1990s. Currently in Ireland ... firms with less than 15 employees account for around 79% of all Irish tourism businesses'. In New Zealand, it is nearer to 90 per cent. In this sector of the tourism industry, the literature on small businesses indicates that four types of firm can be discerned, which has a bearing on HRM. Table 10.3 highlights the typology. This is also reflected in the different management differences between small and large firms as highlighted in Table 10.4. The short-term time horizon of small businesses and owner-managed structure relies more on personal skills, especially leadership qualities and experience. The implications for HRM in small tourism firms are as follows:

- Small businesses normally have constraints on the resource base and are therefore unable to fund developments in HRM to the same degree as large firms.
- HRM is widely acknowledged as a major component in small businesses becoming more competitive and productive as well as for organizational success.
- HRM is often of marginal interest for family-owners where a family business exists.
- The most important area for small businesses to improve their performance is in the recruitment and selection of personnel.
- Small firms tend to use marginally qualified staff in the tourism sector, especially in the rural environment (Page and Getz 1997).
- Management training is normally limited among owner-managers, with time constraints and a perception of no need for training limiting the development of human resource processes.
- Many managers in small businesses do not apply strict principles of HRM, being unable to delegate, and fail to define lines of authority and responsibility for employees.

To illustrate the problems of HRM issues in small tourism businesses, Exhibit 10.4 on New Zealand tourism small businesses examines the issues from a managerial and supply perspective.

Therefore, what the case study shows is that while small tourism businesses may be the backbone of the tourism sector in many countries, the extent to which HRM practices are developed and implemented in this sector are limited from the experience of surveys undertaken in this area. Probably the greatest challenge for this sector is to communicate the benefits of investing human resources as the example of the SBTB shows where a company decides to invest in its major asset – its staff.

Table 10.3 **Organizational structures and entrepreneurial characteristics**

Category	Entrepreneurial characteristics
Self-employed	Use of family labour, little market stability, low levels of capital investment, tendency towards weakly developed management skills
Small employer	Use of family and non-family labour; less economically marginalized but shares other characteristics of self-employed group
Owner-controllers	Use of non-family labour, higher levels of capital investment, often formal system of management control but no separation of ownership and control
Owner-directors	Separation of ownership and management functions, highest levels of capital investment

(Source: Modified from Goffee and Scase 1983, cited in Shaw and Williams 1994)

Table 10.4 **Management differences between small and large firms**

Small firms	Large firms
Short-term planning horizon	Long-term planning horizon
React to the environment	Develop environmental strategy
Limited knowledge of the environment	Environment assessement
Personalized company objectives	Corporate strategy
Communication informal	Formal and structured communication
Informal control systems	Formalized control systems
Loose and informal task structure	Job descriptions
Wide range of management skills	High specialist/technical skills demanded
Income directly at risk in decision-making	Income derived from a wider performance base
Personal motivations directly affect performance	Broader based company performance

(Source: Carter 1996)

Exhibit 10.4 **HRM issues in small tourism businesses in New Zealand**

New Zealand is a country characterized by small businesses. As Cameron *et al.* (1997) report, small and medium-sized enterprises (SMEs) comprise 99 per cent of all businesses in New Zealand and they employ 60 per cent of the working population and 85 per cent of businesses employ fewer than five people. The Deloitte Touche Tomatsu (1994) study surveyed 232 small tourism businesses with fewer than ten employees and found that over 50 per cent had set up since 1989, the highest number of startups in 1991–92 (26 per cent), reflecting the dynamic nature of this business sector. Over half of the sample provided set up funds from their own sources and 70 per cent had no experience of tourism before starting up. This is particularly worrying when the HRM issues are considered as they may not be sufficiently aware of the HRM issues and related employment issues such as seasonality. This was reflected in the employment composition of the sample, where 146 businesses employed 312 full-time staff at the time of startup and by 1994, they employed 342 full-time staff in 183 firms. The major development was in part-time employment. This poses major HRM issues in terms of recruitment, selection and retention of seasonal staff.

A similar situation prevailed in a later study by Page *et al.* (1999) which surveyed 297 small tourism businesses in the Northland region of New Zealand. The composition of the businesses surveyed is shown in Table 10.5. The dominant mode of business operation was individual owner-operator (34.5 per cent) with others distributed between trust owned and local authority owned (local museums). As Table 10.6 shows, the majority were in the accommodation sector (40 per cent) with a further 22 per cent operating restaurants, cafés and eating establishments. The remaining responses were spread across a wide range of activities. The majority of business owners said they were motivated to own a tourism business (54 per cent) was the enjoyment of that form of work.

In terms of employment, the 297 businesses employed 811 full-time and 741 part-time employees (working less than 30 hours a week). This varied by season with employers reporting 1,150 employees during normal trading which increased to 1,576 in the busy months and 959 in the shoulder season (the off-peak season). How far these patterns are typical of other national examples of tourism and hospitality employment are unclear. For example, in the case of the UK Bull and Church (1994) indicated that 60 per cent of employees in the UK hotel and catering industry in 1989 were females and the industry was made up of 64 per cent of part-time employees. In Northland, the majority of employees were located in urban-based tourism businesses. When examining the recruitment policies of small tourism businesses, Table 10.6 shows which methods were used with the overwhelming response being word of mouth as a means to fill vacancies. This reflects the findings of Curran *et al.* (1993) where the importance of word of mouth was seen as a major recruitment method in the UK among small businesses. The difficulty this raises is the potential for discriminatory recruitment methods be it gender or racially biased.

Table 10.5 **The primary activity of small tourism businesses in Northland**

Activity	**N**	**%**
Hotel	26	9
Motel	68	23
Backpackers	19	6
Farmstay	6	2
Restaurant/café	43	14
Lunchbar	24	8
Souvenir/gift shop	21	7
Adventure tourism operator	29	10
Visitor attraction	15	5
Museum	6	2
Bus/coach operator	10	3
Tour operator	2	0.67
Travel agent	6	2
Other	20	6
No response	2	0.67[1]
Total	297	100

[1] May not sum to 100% due to rounding error

Table 10.6 **Recruitment methods used by small tourism businesses**

	N	**%**
Job centre	21	7.07
Local press	77	25.93
Polytechnics	15	5.05
Word of mouth	203	68.35
New Zealand Employment Service	65	21.89
National press	16	5.39
Others	23	7.74

Managing HRM issues in the tourism sector in the new millennium

The major challenges for the tourism industry in the new millennium are aptly summarized by Cooper *et al.* (1998: 458):

> the challenges facing the tourism industry will only be met successfully by a well-educated, well-trained, bright, energetic, multilingual and entrepreneurial workforce who understand the nature of tourism and have a professional training. A high quality of professional human resources in tourism will allow enterprises to gain a competitive edge and deliver added value with their service.

People really do make a difference in what is undoubtedly a people business. Yet within many of the international research studies of HRM in tourism, there are concerns that there is, and will continue to be, a severe shortage of trained and able staff.

One of the greatest challenges which faces any employee in the tourism sector is the ability to respond and adapt to change, especially at a managerial level. In a high technology sector where knowledge and managerial skills are vital, managing staff and the recruitment and retention of high-calibre staff is vital. The 1980s and early 1990s can best be described as years of unsophisticated and reactive human resource policies in the tourism sector and in the new millennium this needs to change because the new economic climate in which tourism operates combined with the growth of the knowledge economy means that change and competition will continue to intensify. Those businesses which are not adopting progressive human resource policies in line with other sectors of the service sector will be left behind and find it difficult to compete when much of the work is people and skills

Exhibit 10.5 **Human resource management issues for the Wales tourism industry**

The recent Wales Tourist Board (WTB) (1999) *A Tourism Strategy for Wales: Achieving Our Potential* outlines a key objective:

> *To improve professionalism and innovation by raising the profile of the industry, and by enhancing skills, training and motivation within the industry.*

The WTB (1999: 52) recognizes that 'delivering a constant quality experience for visitors is a central theme' of their strategy, since customers are more discerning and this requires investing in people in an industry characterized by low pay, poor career prospects, high turnover of staff with its seasonal demand for labour in Wales. A number of initiatives have been launched to address these problems including:

- *Springboard Wales,* launched in 1998 to attract high-calibre staff and skilled staff into the tourism and hospitality sector aimed at school leavers and adults returning to work.
- *The Education and Training Action Group* (ETAG), which aims to attract unemployed people into the growth industries of tourism and leisure.
- *The New Deal,* a UK-wide initiative to encourage existing businesses to recruit staff who are unemployed and provide training to help them develop the skills need for the job.
- *The Tourism Training Forum for Wales,* was established in 1998 with industry representatives and a wide membership to identify action including greater co-ordination between educational establishments and businesses in human resource issues and training for new employment opportunities in tourism and hospitality.

(Source: Wales Tourist Board 1999)

based. More sophisticated human resource policies need to be developed and implemented in the following areas for the tourism sector to be responsive to add value to its staff and change the sectors' image as an employer:

- induction of staff
- appraisal and staff performance evaluation
- effective staff communication
- rewarding initiative and excellence
- empowering staff
- improved industry–education collaboration.

Some of these objectives and a range of others linked to human resource issues are illustrated in Exhibit 10.5 based on the recent Wales Tourist Board (1999) *A Tourism Strategy for Wales: Achieving Our Potential* which reflects the co-ordinating and lead role an NTO can play. One of the critical areas which remains important is education and training.

Conclusion

World-wide many universities embraced tourism and hospitality education in the 1980s and 1990s to improve provision in the area although critics might argue that the rush to capitalize on this new growth area has led to poor provision among some providers who have seen the growth in student numbers and revenue as more important than the destinations and career opportunities of its graduates. For example, in the UK there are now over 80 sub-degree and degree awarding qualifications in higher education establishments. In New Zealand, almost every university has developed tourism degrees and compete with each other for students, a feature which the new Labour government has been highly critical of. As opposed to investing educational resources in a few centres of excellence with well-funded programmes and industry linkages to ensure careers for its graduates, the resource base is spread thinly and a potential over-supply of graduates is starting to emerge. More importantly, tourism education globally needs to take stock of what manpower requirements are needed in each area, seeking to provide in-depth knowledge for those graduates who want to seek a career in this sector underpinned with appropriate theoretical and practical experiences so that the demands of the industry are aligned with the supply from training establishments. In some developed countries, tourism is just another academic subject in universities which does not have a strong enough vocational element to make the graduates 'industry-ready'. The tourism curriculum on most programmes needs regular updating, industry input and support and more emphasis on the human resource implications of lifelong learning and upskilling once graduates have entered a career in this dynamic sector of economic activity. Without addressing these issues, the tourism sector and interface with education providers will not be bridged to improve HRM for the industry.

Discussion questions

1. What is the purpose of human resource management?
2. What problems do tourism businesses face in relation to human resource issues?
3. How do the human resource problems facing small and large tourism businesses differ?
4. What types of role does a human resource manager play in a large tourism organization?

Internet resources

By going to the weblink at www.thomsonlearning.co.uk students can access the following study on the Thomson Learning website. The study is by A. Goldsmith, D. Nickson, D. Sloan and R. Wood (1996) *Human Resource Management for Hospitality Services* which examines the fundamental question – 'What is human resource management?' and serves as a useful introduction to complement the discussion in this book on human resource management in tourism.

References

Baum, T. (1993) *Human Resource Issues in International Tourism*, Oxford: Butterworth-Heinemann.

Baum, T. (1995) *Managing Human Resources in the European Tourism and Hospitality Industry: A Strategic Approach*, London: Chapman and Hall.

Booth, A. and Francesconi, M. (2000) 'Flexible employment, part-time work and career development in Britain', *Research in Labour Economics*.

Bull, P. and Church, A. (1994) 'The hotel and catering industry of Great Britain during the 1980s: sub-regional employment change, specialisation and dominance' in C. Cooper and A. Lockwood (eds) *Progress in Tourism, Recreation and Hospitality Management Volume 5*, Chichester: John Wiley.

Cameron, A., Massey, C. and Tweed, D. (1997) 'New Zealand small business: a review', *Chartered Accountants Journal of New Zealand*, **76** (9): 4–12.

Carter, S. (1996) 'Small business marketing' in M. Warner (ed.) *International Encyclopedia of Business and Management*, London: Thomson Learning.

Cooper, C., Fletcher, J., Gilbert, D., Wanhill, S. and Shepherd, R. (1998) *Tourism: Principles and Practice*, Harlow: Longman.

Cornelius, N. (1999) *Human Resource Management: A Managerial Perspective*, London: Thomson Learning.

Curran, J., Kitchin, J., Abbott, B. and Mills, V. (1993) *Employment and Employment Relations in the Small Service Sector Enterprise – A Report*, ESRC Centre for Research on Small Service Sector Enterprises, Kingston upon Thames: Kingston University.

Deloitte Touche Tomatsu (1994) *Small Business Survey 1994: New Zealand Tourism Industry*, Christchurch: Deloitte Touche Tomatsu Tourism and Leisure Consulting Group.

Esichaikul, R. and Baum, T. (1998) 'The case for government involvement in human resource development: a study of the Thai hotel industry', *Tourism Management*, **19** (4): 359–70.

Goffee, R. and Scase, R. (1983) 'Class, entrepreneurship and the service sector: towards a conceptual clarification', *Service Industries Journal*, **3**: 146–60.

Inskeep, E. (1994) *National and Regional Tourism Planning*, London: Routledge.

Morrison, A. (1996) 'Marketing the small tourism business', in A. Seaton and M. Bennett (eds) *Marketing Tourism Products: Concepts, Issues and Cases*, London: Thomson Learning.

Page, S.J. and Getz, D. (eds) (1997) *The Business of Rural Tourism: International Perspectives*, London: Thomson Learning.

Page, S.J., Forer, P. and Lawton, G. (1999) 'Tourism and small business development: *Terra incognita?*', *Tourism Management*, **20** (4): 435–59.

Pizam, A. (1999) 'The state of travel and tourism human resources in Latin America', *Tourism Management*, **20** (5): 575–86.

Shaw, G. and Williams, A. (1994) *Critical Issues in Tourism: A Geographical Perspective*, Oxford: Blackwell.

Thomas, R., Friel, M., Jameson, S. and Parsons, D. (1997) *The National Survey of Small Tourism and Hospitality Firms Annual Report 1996–1997*, Leeds: Leeds Metropolitan University.

Torrington, D. and Hall, L. (1987) *Personnel Management: A New Approach*, London: Prentice Hall.

Wales Tourist Board (WTB) (1999) *A Tourism Strategy for Wales: Achieving Our Potential*, Cardiff: Wales Tourist Board.

Walsh, E. (1993) 'Republic of Ireland', in T. Baum (ed.) *Human Resource Issues in International Tourism*, Oxford: Butterworth-Heinemann: 201–16.

World Tourism Organization (WTO) (1999) *Changes in Leisure Time*, Madrid: World Tourism Organization.

Further reading

Baum, T. (1993) *Human Resource Issues in International Tourism*, Oxford: Butterworth-Heinemann.

Baum, T. (1995) *Managing Human Resources in the European Tourism and Hospitality Industry: A Strategic Approach*, London: Chapman and Hall.

Lee-Ross, D. (1999) *Human Resource Management in Tourism and Hospitality*, London: Cassell.

Riley, M. (1997) *Human Resource Management in the Hospitality and Tourism Industry*, Oxford: Butterworth-Heinemann.

Wood, R.C. (1997) *Working in Hotels and Catering*, London: Thomson Learning.

Learning outcomes

After studying this chapter, you should be able to:

- Comprehend some of the features of published company accounts.
- Understand why accounting ratios are used.
- Be aware of sources of funding.

11 Financing tourism operations

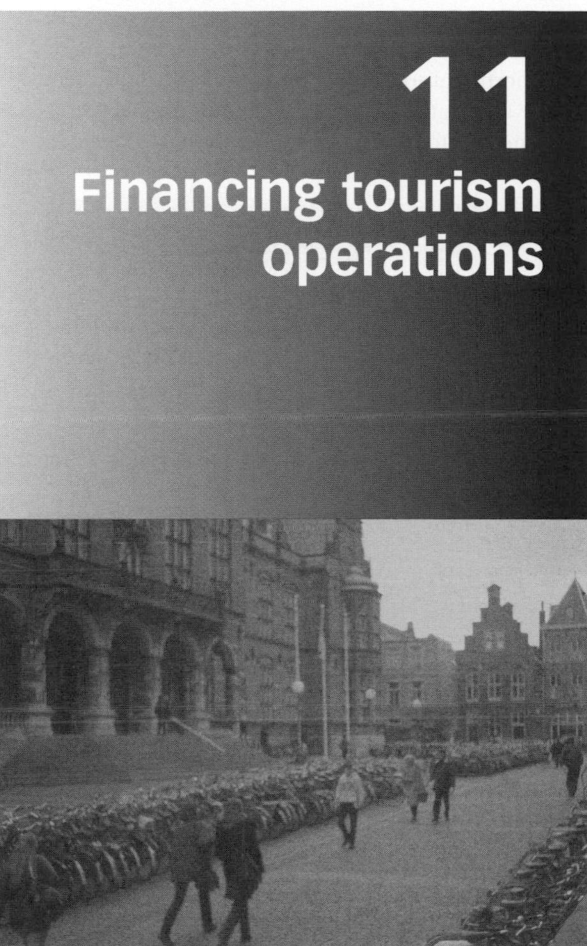

Overview

The purpose of this chapter is to provide the reader with an appreciation of the world of finance as it applies to the tourism industry. It does not attempt to cover many aspects of accountancy as a concept; it merely introduces the reader to the features of published company accounts and provides examples of performance measurements used.

Introduction

The development and management of the tourism industry is dependent upon the accessibility to capital and sources of finance so that businesses can be developed and for existing businesses, to enable them to expand and develop their markets for tourism products and services. Although many tourism businesses are based within the private sector and their access to sources of finance for investment purposes is normally obtained from banks, finance houses and other lending institutions, there are also a number of other public sector agencies which assist the tourism sector with pump-priming funds and product development. The issue of finance and investment is largely neglected in existing studies of tourism, especially in many textbooks with much of the published literature based on finance and accounting texts which are not specifically rooted in tourism and hospitality research. This chapter seeks to adopt a tourism focus in which the various elements of financing tourism operations and their financial performance are examined. Although this chapter is not a comprehensive analysis of tourism finance and investment it does provide a framework for further analysis since it focuses on the three major areas pertinent to tourism businesses which are: the private sector, the voluntary sector and public sector assistance for tourism from supranational agencies.

The private sector

Within the private sector, it is widely recognized that tourism businesses exist to make a profit on the assets and investment they deploy in their business operations. Thus, 'In order to determine how effectively a business is being managed, information is needed about how it uses its assets to generate profits' (Messenger and Shaw 1993: 172) with profitability vital to the financial health of a firm. Ratios are used when assessing the financial performance of an organization because they allow comparisons to be made with other businesses in the same sector. They can be more useful than analysis of absolute numbers; for example, comparing the net profit of one airline with another that has greater ticket revenue.

The Singapore International Airlines (SIA) accounts shown in Tables 11.1–11.4 relate to both

Table 11.1 **Audited results for SIA, year ending 31 March 1999**

	THE GROUP			THE COMPANY		
	1998–99 S$m	1997–98 S$m	Change %	1998–99 S$m	1997–98 S$m	Change %
Revenue	7 795.9	7 723.9	+ 0.9	7 075.2	6 968.9	+ 1.5
Expenditure	(6 941.5)	(6 725.2)	+ 3.2	(6 526.4)	(6 214.4)	+ 5.0
OPERATING PROFIT	854.4	998.7	– 14.4	548.8	754.5	– 27.3
Surplus on sale of aircraft, spares and spare engines	211.3	157.1	+ 34.5	191.6	150.1	+ 27.6
Dividends from unquoted subsidiaries and associated companies, gross	–	–	–	129.7	127.7	+ 1.6
Share of profits of joint venture companies	13.9	7.1	+ 95.8	–	–	–
Share of profits of associated companies	23.1	8.9	+ 159.6	–	–	–
PROFIT BEFORE EXCEPTIONAL ITEM	1 102.7	1 171.8	– 5.9	870.1	1 032.3	– 15.7
Exceptional item – surplus on liquidation of Abacus Distribution Systems	14.1	–	–	12.2	–	–
PROFIT BEFORE TAXATION	1 116.8	1 171.8	– 4.7	882.3	1 032.3	– 14.5
Provision for taxation	(80.3)	(130.9)	– 38.7	(68.6)	(112.8)	– 39.2
PROFIT AFTER TAXATION	1 036.5	1 040.9	– 0.4	813.7	919.5	– 11.5
Minority interests	(3.3)	(2.3)	+ 43.5	–	–	–
PROFIT AFTER TAX AND MINORITY INTERESTS	1 033.2	1 038.6	– 0.5	813.7	919.5	– 11.5
Extraordinary item – expenses related to SilkAir flight MI185 19 December 1997	–	(3.9)	–	–	–	–
PROFIT ATTRIBUTABLE TO SHAREHOLDERS	1 033.2	1 034.7	– 0.1	813.7	919.5	– 11.5

Table 11.2 **Notes to the SIA accounts**

	THE GROUP			THE COMPANY		
	1998–99 S$m	1997–98 S$m	Change %	1998–99 S$m	1997–98 S$m	Change %
NOTES:						
(a) Operating profit is arrived at after accounting for:						
Depreciation of fixed assets	1 172.5	1 063.9	+ 10.2	1 082.3	973.5	+ 11.2
Interest income	128.8	97.9	+ 31.6	119.2	97.2	+ 22.6
Finance charges	29.5	28.2	+ 4.6	29.1	27.6	+ 5.4
Gain on sale of investments	75.1	14.2	+ 428.9	–	–	–
Dividend income	7.4	9.6	– 22.9	3.4	3.5	2.9
Foreign exchange gain	75.9	81.3	– 6.6	60.1	55.8	+ 7.7
(b) Revenue:						
First half year	3 765.5	3 904.4	– 3.6	3 431.6	3 518.6	– 2.5
Second half year	4 030.4	3 819.5	+ 5.5	3 643.6	3 450.3	+ 5.6
	7 795.9	7 723.9	+ 0.9	7 075.2	6 968.9	+ 1.5
(c) Profit after taxation						
First half year	470.2	617.1	– 23.8	399.5	543.8	– 26.5
Second half year	566.3	423.8	+ 33.6	414.2	375.7	+ 10.2
	1 036.5	1 040.9	– 0.4	813.7	919.5	– 11.5

	THE GROUP		
	1998–99	1997–98	Change %
(d) Profit after taxation as a percentage of revenue (%)	13.3	13.5	– 0.2
(e) Profit after taxation and minority interests as a percentage of issued capital and reserves at the end of the year (%)	8.5	9.1	– 0.6
(f) Earnings per share (cents)	80.6	81.0	– 0.5
(g) Net tangible assets per share ($)	9.50	8.87	+ 7.1

Table 11.3 **SIA segment information**

(a) Analysis by business activity

	Revenue		Profit before finance charges and tax	
	1998–99 S$m	1997–98 S$m	1998–99 S$m	1997–98 S$m
Airline operations	7 163.3	7 070.9	791.9	935.5
Airport terminal services	293.3	304.8	135.5	116.4
Engineering services and others	339.3	348.2	218.9	148.1
Group	7 795.9	7 723.9	1 146.3	1 200.0

(b) Analysis of revenue from SIA airline operations by routes

	1998–99 S$m	1997–98 S$m
North and South East Asia	2 209.0	2 370.9
Americas	1 625.3	1 571.7
Europe	1 554.2	1 512.5
South West Pacific	908.6	796.0
West Asia and Africa	709.8	662.5
System-wide route revenue	7 006.9	6 913.6
Non-scheduled services and incidental revenue	217.6	223.2
Sub-total	7 224.5	7 136.8
Inter-company transactions	(61.2)	(65.9)
Total	7 163.3	7 070.9

Table 11.4 **Audited balance sheets for Singapore Airlines Group at 31 March 1999**

(All figures are Singapore dollars)	The Group		The Company	
	1999 S$m	1998 S$m	1999 S$m	1998 S$m
Share capital	1 282.6	1 282.6	1 282.6	1 282.6
Distributable reserves	8 652.4	7 844.0	7 469.1	6 896.0
Non-distributable reserves				
Share premium	447.2	447.2	447.2	447.2
Capital	6.3	6.3	–	–
Special non-dist. reserve	1 800.0	1 800.0	1 800.0	1 800.0
Shareholders' funds	12 188.5	11 380.1	10 998.9	10 425.8
Minority interests	18.3	14.1		
Deferred income	578.2	177.1	386.1	177.1
Deferred taxation	447.2	441.5	365.8	365.8
Long-term liabilities	565.6	523.3	559.9	516.0
	13 797.8	12 536.1	12 310.7	11 484.7
Represented by:				
Fixed assets	11 666.8	11 398.0	10 580.9	10 451.7
Subsidiaries	–	–	679.5	772.6
Associated companies	223.0	102.8	11.1	11.1
Joint venture companies	152.8	125.5	97.4	97.4
Long-term investments	943.7	936.5	883.3	876.8
Current assets	4 212.3	3 144.5	3 032.2	2 004.9
Less: current liabilities	(3 400.8)	(3 171.2)	(2 973.7)	(2 729.8)
	1 797.8	12 536.1	12 310.7	11 484.7

(Source: SIA)

SIA Group borrowings

	Loans – unsecured		Lease commitments – secured	
	31.3.1999 S$m	30.9.1998 S$m	31.3.1999 S$m	30.9.1998 S$m
Repayable within one year	29.3	24.0		
Repayable after one year	5.7	7.1	559.9	557.3
	35.0	31.1	559.9	557.3

In January 2001 UK £1 = S$2.4 approximately

the company (the airline) and the group's activities; the latter includes Singapore Airport Terminal Services, SIA Engineering Group, Silk Air and a tour operation – in other words, it is *vertically integrated.* According to Page (1999: 165), Silk Air was established in 1992 and operates routes to Malaysia, Thailand, Vietnam, Cambodia, Indonesia and the Philippines; 'the route network reflects the decision of the Indonesian government to allow Singapore carriers to fly on a range of routes acknowledged as secondary gateways for business and leisure travel'.

Published company results are usually accompanied by quite detailed comments; in the case of Singapore Airlines, they are as follows:

1 The Company's operating profit for the financial year 1998–99 was $549 million, a decrease of $206 million (–27.3 per cent) from 1997–98, reflecting the economic downturn in Asia. Revenue rose $106 million (+1.5 per cent) to $7,075 million, and expenditure increased by $312 million (+5 per cent) to $6,526 million. Capacity grew 7.7 per cent, while traffic increased at a lower rate of 7.3 per cent. Consequently, the overall load factor slipped 0.3 per cent to 68.8 per cent. The passenger seat factor was up 2.0 percentage points to 72.5 per cent, but cargo load factor declined 2.5 percentage points to 66.4 per cent. Overall yield decreased 5.2 per cent, unit cost fell 2.7 per cent, and the breakeven load factor deteriorated 1.7 percentage points to 66.9 per cent.
2 The Company's profit before tax was $882 million, down $150 million (–14.5 per cent), after accounting for a surplus of $192 million from the sale and leaseback of four B747–400 passenger aircraft, the outright sale of one A310–200 passenger aircraft and the sale of spares and spare engines. Profit after tax decreased by a smaller amount of $106 million (–11.5 per cent) to $814 million as provision for taxation dropped $44 million (–39.2 per cent) because of lower chargeable income.
3 The operating profit of the subsidiaries rose $83 million (+38.6 per cent) to $298 million. This was mainly attributable to higher profits from Singapore Airport Terminal Services Group, SIA Engineering Group, Auspice and SIA Properties, partially offset by an operating loss incurred by SilkAir. The profit after tax of the subsidiaries increased by a higher amount of $113 million (+64.6 per cent) to $289 million, after accounting for a surplus of $26 million from the sale of one A310–200 and B737–300 aircraft by SilkAir.

The use of ratios allows specific trends to be monitored over time; the following examples relate performance ratios to the published Singapore Airlines accounts. The 'liquidity' of any company is important since it demonstrates the solvency of the business; in other words, how easily expenses can be met with cash payments. One of the ratios that measures liquidity is the current or working capital ratio which is expressed as:

$$\frac{\text{Group current assets}}{\text{Group current liabilities}}$$

$$\frac{\text{S\$m } 4{,}212.3}{\text{S\$m } 3{,}400.8}$$

This provides a ratio of 1.23:1 indicating that the company's liabilities are covered.

The fixed assets to current assets ratio is important because 'generally it is the current assets which earn profits for the firm. The higher the ratio of current assets to fixed assets, the more profitable the firm should be' (Messenger and Shaw 1993: 186).

$$\frac{\text{Group fixed assets}}{\text{Group current assets}}$$

1999 (S$m) 1998 (S$m)

$$\frac{11{,}666.8}{4{,}212.3} = 2.8:1 \qquad \frac{11{,}398.0}{3{,}144.5} = 3.6:1$$

s

The profitability of the business can be assessed using the following ratios, usually expressed as a percentage:

$$\frac{\text{Group profit before tax}}{\text{Group total revenue}}$$

1998–99 (S$m) 1997–98 (S$m)

$$\frac{1{,}116.8}{7{,}795.9} \times 100 = 14.3\% \qquad \frac{1{,}171.8}{7{,}723.9} \times 100 = 15.2\%$$

The capital structure of a business can be assessed by use of the gearing ratio which shows the extent of debt compared to equity or share capital, expressed as:

$$\frac{\text{Debt}}{\text{Equity}}$$

The Group

1999 S$m

$$\frac{35}{12{,}188.5} = 0.0028$$

1998 S$m

$$\frac{31.1}{11{,}380.1} = 0.0027$$

Ratio analysis is a useful tool but it can only give some indication of future trends and must be considered in the general economic climate which was severe in South-east Asia in the late 1990s although recent evidence from the Asian Development Bank has indicated that the situation is in fact changing (see Chapter 17 for more detail).

Multinational enterprises

With increasing globalization of tourism enterprises (see Chapter 6), many have become 'multinational'; that is, they undertake commercial activity outside their home country – the terms multinational corporations (MNC) and transnationals are used interchangeably. In some tourist destinations, especially developing countries, 'the power and size of transnational corporations has an enormous impact ... (because) their investment remains seductive. Initially, development may bring jobs and increased prosperity but long-term stability is not guaranteed' (Curtin and Busby 1999: 138). Destination choice changes with consumer fashion and the country may have experienced relatively little benefit once 'leakages' are accounted for. Financing such companies assumes a greater international dimension where their activities are able to attract not only government inducements and sweeteners in the case of large resort developments in less developed countries, but are very attractive to large finance companies which are assured of significant financial returns. This is illustrated by Tribe (1995: 234) who refers to the French government providing 'a comprehensive infrastructure package including new roads and rail connections ... (and) a loan at preferential interest rates' in order to entice Disney to locate their attraction in the country. Apart from the estimate that the development would lead to 18,000 construction and 12,000 operational jobs, the attraction was predicted to earn US$700 million in foreign currency each year. Therefore, large multinational enterprises are powerful agents in the tourism development process, especially from the financial perspective.

In central and eastern Europe, the newly democratic countries 'have recognized that linkages between the service sector and other sectors of the economy, including manufacturing and agriculture, are desirable and that transnational corporations operating in tourism can play a vital role in the creation of employment, output growth and development' (Go and Pine 1995: 12).

The key attraction for businesses to operate in more than one country is the ability to declare profits in nations with lower tax rates, i.e. to operate what is known as 'transfer pricing'. Bull (1991) illustrates this argument in Table 11.5.

Table 11.5 illustrates a multinational tour operator based in country X, where the corporation tax rate is 45 per cent and operating an airline registered in country Y which allows it to pay tax on stated profits at 15 per cent. The tourist accommodation and other services are provided in country Z which has a tax rate of 20 per cent. All figures are converted to sterling (£) to permit comparisons to be made; at a cost of £1,000 per holiday, the tax liability would be £25.50 if the actual costs were reported in each country. However, with operations across more than one boundary, the organization can state profits in the 'tax-minimizing' nations such that total tax paid is £20.00. On top of this benefit, is the advantage of foreign exchange scheduling and 'options' open to large companies with respect to the financial 'futures' market; for a detailed discussion of exchange rates see (Tribe 1995: 220–24).

Sources of finance

The Singapore Airlines accounts shown above illustrate how a business can be financed through the issue of shares and bank loans. Shareholders usually expect to receive a percentage of the annual profits and this is taken in the form of a 'dividend'; at the same time, they believe the value of their shares will improve. From the company perspective, raising finance through the issue of more shares is attractive since it is relatively low risk, i.e. if the company does not make a profit, they will not issue a dividend whereas a bank loan must be 'serviced' regardless of

Table 11.5 **Multinational tour operator 'transfer pricing'**

Country	Tax rate	'True' cost price A	Contribution to selling price B	'True' net profit B – A	'True' tax liability
X	45%	150	180	30	13.50
Y	15%	300	340	40	6.00
Z	20%	450	480	30	6.00
		900	1 000		25.50

Alternative scenario

Country	Transfer price (stated costs) C	Stated profit B – C	Tax paid
X	170	10	4.50
Y	290	50	7.50
Z	440	40	8.00
			20.00

(Source: Adapted from Bull 1991)

profits. Retained profits are another source of financing new developments.

An alternative is for a company to raise finance by selling debentures; these are loans with a fixed rate of interest over a specified period of time. In November 1998, the large vertically integrated tour operator Airtours launched a £250 million 'convertible' bond through finance company Merrill Lynch; interest was to be paid at between 5.25 and 5.75 per cent until January 2004 'when it converts into ordinary shares at a 20–25% premium over Airtours' share price on the date the bond was issued' (Osborne 1998).

The principal ratio used to evaluate financial returns to investors is the return on capital Employed (ROCE), expressed as:

$$\frac{\text{Profit (before interest to debt holders)}}{\text{Capital employed}} \times 100$$

In some countries, government assistance for particular types of tourism development is available; as a result of the 1969 Development of Tourism Act, in Britain, many hotels were constructed or improved under the Hotel Development Incentive Scheme. This 'assisted the building of more than 1,300 new hotels and extensions in England, providing more than 50,000 new bedrooms, plus many other amenities and facilities, in the period from April 1968 to March 1973' (English Tourist Board 1976: 1). Approximately £43 million was provided in grants and £4 million in loans. The government provided this financial assistance because there was an urgent need to improve and increase the amount of serviced accommodation; the principal imperfection was that the English, Scottish and Wales Tourist Boards 'had absolutely no discretion as to where new hotels should be sited. The Scheme took no account of such factors as balance of distribution and differing rates of expected tourism growth, nor the management ability of applicants' (English Tourist Board 1976: 2). The 1969 Act also provided Section 4 grant aid, so-called because it appeared in section 4 of Part 1 of the Act; this finance has stimulated a wide range of developments in Britain although it is no longer available in England. The Wales Tourist Board approved finance for projects ranging from serviced accommodation to visitor attractions in 1998–99, and from £10,000 to £300,000 in value (Wales Tourist Board 1999: 29).

Investment

To remain competitive, businesses need to invest either in the replacement of fixed assets, the addition of more assets or a combination of both. In making these decisions, companies will assess such capital investment programmes using methods such as 'payback' period, net present value (NPV) and internal rate of return (IRR). 'Payback' shows how quickly an investment will have covered its cost through the cash flow it generates. In Table 11.6, an airline is considering whether to purchase two small jets or one large one.

The large aircraft will have covered its cost by the end of year 4 whereas acquisition costs for the two smaller jets will have been met before the end of the fourth year. Two aircraft may provide the flexibility a 'low-cost' carrier requires although individual passenger capacity is less. The drawback with this method is that it does not include cash flow beyond the payback period despite the asset having a residual value. Messenger and Shaw (1993: 212) state that 'a project may be chosen in preference to another just because it has a quick payback time while another with a slower time may in fact have a longer life with greater cash flows'.

Table 11.6 **Payback example**

Year		Large aircraft £ (million)	2 × small passenger jets £ (million)
	Capital expenditure	−38	−29
1	cash flow	+7	+5
2	cash flow	+9	+7
3	cash flow	+10	+11
4	cash flow	+12	+12

A further example of looking beyond the short term comes from Sir Richard Branson who refers to keeping the 'big picture' in mind even during recessionary times; in 1992, Virgin Atlantic was attempting to finance the installation of seat-back video screens in all its aircraft and needed $10 million to do this. The company had not been able to raise the money and, in desperation, Branson rang the chief executive of Boeing, Phil Conduit, to ask if Virgin 'bought ten new Boeing 747–400s' they would get 'individual seat-back videos in economy class. Phil was amazed that anyone was thinking of buying planes during that recession, and he readily agreed'. Branson asked the same question of Airbus and they agreed; Virgin found it easier to raise $4 billion credit to purchase 18 new jets than to get $10 million for the video screens. Not only did Virgin Atlantic get a new fleet but it was 'at the cheapest price we've ever been able to acquire planes before or since' (Branson 1998: 434).

Go and Pine (1995), however, believe net present value (NPV) and internal rate of return (IRR) to be the most commonly used measures of investment. NPV makes the assumption that money received now has a higher value than money received next month or next year, i.e. the sooner it is received, the sooner it can be invested in alternative projects. Messenger and Shaw (1993: 217) consider the main advantage to be 'that it considers the time value of money, so that the value of money received in the future can be compared with present sums'.

Supranational investment

A number of institutions exist at supranational level, i.e. beyond the boundaries of one nation and some have a significant effect on the international tourism industry. Two examples will be reviewed here: the World Bank and the European Union (EU).

EU funds

The Eden Project case study in Chapter 8 illustrated how new tourist developments can be financed through a combination of private and public sector investment. Businesses in areas of Europe that have been designated for EU assistance, as in Table 11.7, can apply for grant aid from the EU although it is usually on a 'matched funding' basis, i.e. the applicant will be supported pound for pound, or euro for euro. The county of Cornwall, where the Eden Project is located, has recently been redesignated: from a 5b area to objective 1 status.

The impact of EU funding is not well researched and neither is there a 'commonly agreed method to measure it' according to Bull (1999: 149). Research on the island of Bornholm, in the Baltic sea, by Bull (1999: 157) showed that 'for many of the small businesses, the EU support was crucial because it opened the channels to commercial capital'; this was at a time when access to loans was 'extremely difficult ... the approval of support from the EU was conceived of as a credibility stamp for the project, which made it easier to obtain additional capital from other sources'.

The World Bank Group

In 1944, representatives from a number of nations met at Bretton Woods in New Hampshire to discuss the reconstruction that would be necessary after the war; the World Bank and the International Monetary Fund (IMF) were the result of this summit. The World Bank Group comprises the International Bank for Reconstruction and Development (IBRD), the International Finance Corporation (IFC), the International Development Agency (IDA), the International Centre for Settlement of Investment Disputes (ICSID) and the Multilateral Investment Guarantee Agency (MIGA).

Pryce (1998: 81) identifies the global distribution of IFC investments in tourism (shown in Table 11.8) and gives examples such as:

> a beach hotel resembling a traditional Swahili village on Galu beach, south of Mombasa, Kenya and the Sinalei Reef Resort in Samoa ... (the) IFC offers the flexibility of a merchant bank with the resources of a development bank capable of taking a long-term view.

Table 11.7 **Priority objectives for European Structural Funds**

Objective 1	Promoting the development and structural adjustment of regions whose development is lagging behind
Objective 2	Converting the regions or parts of regions seriously affected by industrial decline
Objective 3	Combating long-term unemployment and facilitating the integration into working life of young people and of persons exposed to exclusion from the labour market, promotion of equal employment opportunities for men and women
Objective 4	Facilitating the adaptation of workers to industrial changes and to changes in production systems
Objective 5a	Promoting rural development by speeding up the adjustment of agricultural structures in the framework of the reform of the common agricultural policy
Objective 5b	Promoting rural development by facilitating the development and structural adjustment of rural areas
Objective 6	Promoting the development and structural adjustment of regions with an extremely low population density

(Source: European Commission 1996, cited in Bull 1999)

Table 11.8 **Global distribution of IFC investments in tourism, as at August 1998**

	Investment (US $ million)	Number of projects
Africa	97.0	41
Asia	99.0	16
Europe	78.0	9
Latin America and Caribbean	90.0	10
Central Asia, Middle East and North Africa	83.0	10
Total	447.0	86

(Source: International Finance Corporation cited in Pryce 1998)

The 'not for profit' sector

The 'not for profit' or voluntary sector, as it is frequently termed, has different objectives to the commercial world. This does not mean that operational practices are inefficient; in fact, the reverse can be true. In Britain, the largest organization in this sector to affect tourism is the National Trust, a registered charity, which was established in 1895 and, as can be seen from Table 11.9, is now the custodian of many assets. The Trust has to balance the needs of visitors with the requirements of conservation for future generations and relies on a variety of financial sources as shown in Table 11.10 and summarized in Exhibit 11.1.

Conclusion

The ability to raise finance is clearly very important in tourism development; entrepreneurs with a proven track record will find access to capital much more straightforward than individuals with just a business idea. All too often in the analysis of tourism growth and development, the 'hidden' role of finance is neglected, since major infrastructure projects such as large attractions and accommodation units require substantial investment and funding to make the projects reach fruition. One of the difficulties which certain sectors of the tourism sector face is the payback period over which finance and investment are expected to make a return. Where the private sector has been unable to finance large projects, there is growing evidence in many countries that the public sector will assist private sector projects such as tourist attractions which can be seen to have a wider community benefit beyond usage by tourists, to justify public sector assistance. This also reflects the integral role which tourism can play in certain communities where financing tourism projects creates local employment. This chapter has also indicated that financing arrangements can frequently be a matter of putting together a combination of bank loans, public sector support and, perhaps, venture capital funds. In making investment decisions, bankers and investors will use a range of accounting ratios to compare the 'target' business with others. It is important to note that other factors, such as the composition of the senior management team, will also be considered by investors. As the National Trust data show, organizations in the 'not for profit' sector can be responsible for a wide range of tourism and heritage assets and yet still manage them on slender financial resources.

Exhibit 11.1 **The National Trust**

The National Trust was founded in 1895 by three leading Victorian philanthropists (Octavia Hill, Robert Hunter and Hardwicke Rawnsley) who were concerned about the growing impact of industrialization and economic and urban development on the natural environment. They were particularly concerned about the impact on the English countryside and coastline, as coastal resorts developed (see Chapter 2). Over 100 years later, the National Trust is a major agency concerned with the preservation and conservation of England and Wales, built and natural heritage and the scope of their activities is shown in Table 11.9. What Table 11.9 shows is that they are now charged with a diversity of activities and in recent years have developed a more commercialized approach to the maintenance and financing of the properties and activities they are involved in. Of 263 sites listed as open in Table 11.9, some are open at a charge. In 1996/97, a total of 11,624,587 visits were paid to these properties (11.2 million in 1998).

Table 11.9 **Possessions of the National Trust**

National Trust properties open in 1998	
Historic houses	164
Castles	19
Gardens	160
Mills/industrial archaeology	47
Churches/chapels	49
Prehistoric/Roman sites	9
Landscape parks	73

What Tables 11.9 and 11.10 also show is that the National Trust is a major land owner and has significant interests in the British coastline. In terms of employment, the National Trust is not a major employer given its scale of activities but it relies upon volunteers for the bulk of its workforce and employs seasonal staff to cope with the peak demand from tourism and recreational visitors.

Table 11.10 **National Trust: key statistics**

Total land area protected by the Trust = 272,659 hectares
Total miles of coast protected by the Trust = 565
Number of listed buildings owned by the Trust = 2,792

People

Total number of members (at Oct. 1997) = 2,558,563

Total number of full-time staff = 2,537

Total number of part-time staff = 605

Total number of seasonal staff = 3,625

Total number of volunteers = 35,179
– total hours worked = 2 million

(Source: extracts from the National Trust's *Annual Report to Members 1998/9*)

Table 11.11 **National Trust: summary statement of financial activities**

Income

	1998/99 £m	1997/98 £m
Membership	55.7	51.6
Legacies	33.3	30.7
Investment income	25.2	24.3
Rents	20.9	19.2
Grants and contributions	13.0	15.2
Enterprises	11.4	11.6
Appeals and gifts	10.2	7.3
Admission fees	8.6	8.7
Sales of leases	2.7	4.4
Other property income	1.4	1.8
Total	182.4	174.8

Expenditure		
Routine maintenance/running costs	85.4*	81.6
Capital projects	37.9*	34.0
Membership, publicity and education	16.0	15.1
Acquisitions	8.9*	6.9
Charity administration	1.9	1.7
Income generation	1.7	1.5
Total expenditure	151.8	140.8
General fund operating surplus	15.0	12.8
Other resources for future conservation	15.6	21.2
Total	182.4	174.8

(*routine maintenance/running costs; capital projects; acquisitions)

Property expenditure

	£m
Conservation and advisory	4.7
Support services and costs	5.4
Acquisitions	8.9
Houses and cottages	10.7
Gardens	12.0
Property management	17.9
Coast and countryside	35.9
Historic buildings and collections	36.7
Total	132.2

(Source: extracts from the National Trust's *Annual Report to Members 1998/9*)

The Trust's Report for 1998/99 discusses the many issues which have exercised the minds of both salaried and elected individuals, from deer hunting to the Snowdon Appeal. When reviewing the financial statement in Table 11.11, the following point should be considered:

> In recent years the taxation policies of successive Governments have been damaging for charities in general and for the Trust in particular. The burden of irrecoverable VAT (Value Added Tax) is great, and the abolition of Advance Corporation Tax means that the dividend income received by the Trust and its pension fund is sharply reduced, while the steady lowering of the basic rate of income tax reduces the benefit to the Trust of covenanted subscriptions and donations. The Government is well aware of our concerns, but clearly does not propose to do anything to reverse the trend. Instead, its view is that charitable giving should increase to fill the gap. (Chairman's Statement, the National Trust's Annual Member's Report 1998/99)

Despite this situation, the Trust has benefited from the loyalty of its membership; for example, legacies increased from £30.7 million in 1997/98 to £33.3 million in 1998/9. A further $2.6 million came from the Royal Oak Foundation, an affiliated organization in the United States. The Chairman of the Finance Committee also notes the 'vigour of our staff' and that 'National Trust Enterprises turned in a solid performance': this is the trading arm and covenants all profits to the charity, contributing £11.4 million in the last year.

Even with acquisitions during the year under review such as the former council house home of Sir Paul McCartney, one of the Beatles, in Liverpool and other property, the Trust achieved an operating surplus of £15 million.

Discussion questions

1. List the positive and negative criticisms of using ratios to measure the performance of a business.
2. Outline how multinational companies have affected international tourism development.
3. Describe how the operation of a 'not for profit' organization differs from one in the private sector.

References

Branson, R. (1998) *Losing my Virginity – The Autobiography*, London: Virgin Publishing.

Bull, A. (1991) *The Economics of Travel and Tourism*, Melbourne: Pitman.

Bull, B. (1999) 'Encouraging tourism development through the EU structural funds: a case study of the implementation of EU programmes on Bornholm', *International Journal of Tourism Research*, **1** (3): 149–65.

Curtin, S. and Busby, G. (1999) 'Sustainable destination development: the tour operator perspective', *International Journal of Tourism Research*, **1** (2): 135–47.

English Tourist Board (1976) *The Hotel Development Incentives Scheme in England*, London: English Tourist Board.

Go, F. and Pine, R. (1995) *Globalization Strategy in the Hotel Industry*, London: Routledge.

Messenger, S. and Shaw, H. (1993) *Financial Management for the Hospitality, Tourism and Leisure Industries*, Basingstoke: Macmillan.

The National Trust (1999) *Annual Report to Members 1998/9*, London: The National Trust.

Internet resources

By going to the weblink at www.thomsonlearning.co.uk students can access the following study on the Thomson Learning website. The study by J. Deegan and D. Dineen (1997) *Tourism Policy and Performance* examines the performance of the Irish tourism industry in the period from 1981 until the mid-1990s and utilizes some of the concepts discussed to monitor the performance of tourism enterprises and the wider performance measures for entire countries.

Osborne, A. (1998) 'Airtours seeks £250m from bond issue', *Daily Telegraph*, 25 November.

Page, S.J. (1999) *Transport and Tourism*, Harlow: Addison Wesley Longman.

Pryce, A. (1998) 'The World Bank Group and tourism', *Travel and Tourism Analyst*, **5**: 75–90.

Tribe, J. (1995) *The Economics of Leisure and Tourism: Environments, Markets and Impacts*, Oxford: Butterworth-Heinemann.

Wales Tourist Board (1999) *Annual Report 1998/99*, Cardiff: Wales Tourist Board.

Further reading

BDO Stoy Hayward Travel Group (1998) *The Travel Industry – An Industry Accounting and Auditing Guide*, London: Accountancy Books.

Owen, G. (1994) *Accounting for Hospitality, Tourism and Leisure*, London: Pitman.

Useful web addresses

The easyJet annual accounts are available at www.easyjet.com

12 Tourism and entrepreneurship

Learning outcomes

After studying this chapter, you should be able to:

- Understand the range of characteristics common to entrepreneurs.
- Analyse the factors affecting entrepreneurs.
- Appreciate the wide variety of successful tourism entrepreneurs.

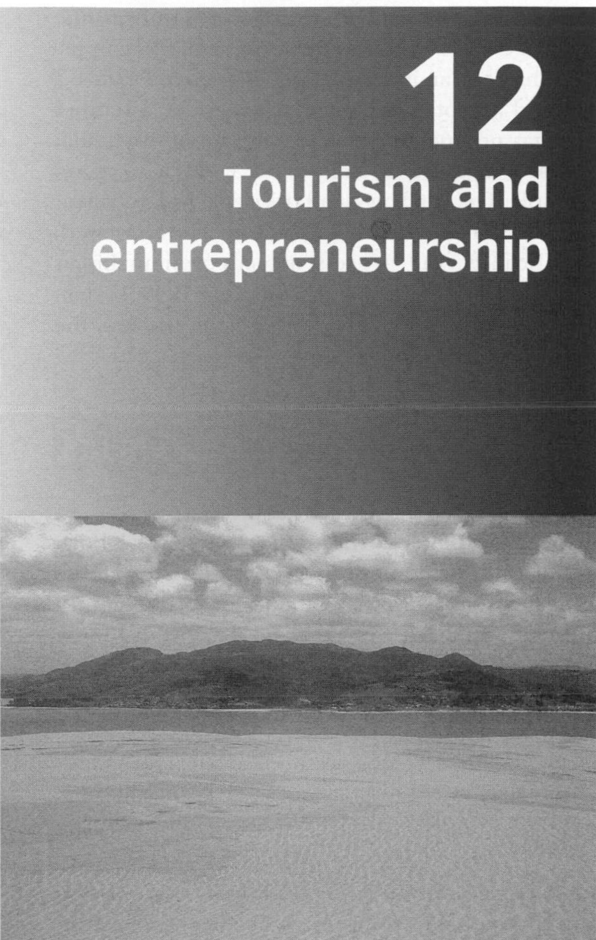

Overview

The travel and tourism industry has given rise to a diverse range of entrepreneurs in the 150 or so years since Thomas Cook's first excursion. However, there is 'relatively little appreciation of the specific operating characteristics of tourism firms, and especially of tourism entrepreneurship' (Shaw and Williams 1990: 67). This chapter reviews some definitions and characteristics of entrepreneurs, together with the environment in which they operate.

Introduction

According to Drucker (1985) there is no explanation 'as to why entrepreneurship emerged as it did in the late nineteenth century and as it seems to be doing again today ... The changes are likely to lie in changes in values, perception, and attitude, changes in demographics, in institutions ... perhaps changes in education as well' (Drucker 1985: 12). Besides a lack of explanation for entrepreneurship, there is little in the way of economic theory for the entrepreneur. Casson (1982: 9) considers that the subject has become the domain of 'sociologists, psychologists and political scientists'; in his view, this is because of the assumption that we all have 'free access' to the information needed for decision-making which, therefore, becomes 'the mechanical application of mathematical rules for optimization ... trivializes decision-making, and makes it impossible to analyse the role of entrepreneurs in taking decisions of a particular kind'. Medlik (1996: 94) argues that an entrepreneur is 'a person who undertakes an enterprise, makes decisions on and controls its conduct, and bears the risk'. In contrast, Youell (1996: 79), similarly, emphasizes that it is 'an individual who is prepared to take a risk and accept a challenge or undertake a venture that has no guarantee of success'; he observes that Richard Branson is frequently cited as a good example. The challenge and risk elements are evident when many tourism businesses are reviewed. Significantly, the process of entrepreneurship is 'more holistic and dynamic' (Morrison 1998: 1) than any one perspective can explain: none the less, the focal point is the individual.

Characteristics of entrepreneurs

A common belief is that entrepreneurs are born rather than made and, indeed, some personalities appear to have an innate ability; for example, with publicity, Richard Branson and the Virgin brand. Casson (1982: 6) comments that:

> many of the qualities with which the heroic stereotype is imbued are simply a reflection of contemporary cultural attitudes ... the stereotype is useful as an articulation of the view that there is a correlation between various personal characteristics and entrepreneurial activity.

With consideration, there can be no doubt that entrepreneurship comprises a number of elements. McMullan and Long (1990) consider these to be a combination of creativity and/or innovation, uncertainty and/or risk-taking, and managerial and/or business capabilities. Taking personal characteristics further, Stallinbrass (1980), Brown (1987) and Shaw and Williams (1994: 133) recognize that entrepreneurs at the owner-manager level may well have 'non-economic motives for entering the business'. These motives comprise a need for independence, the need to achieve (Hisrich and Peters 1992), job satisfaction – or self-actualization, and 'environmental factors' (Shaw and Williams 1990: 77).

Not surprisingly perhaps, there are also differences in motivation between males and females. The 'overwhelming majority' of women in Goffee and Scase's (1985: 62) survey who had started their own businesses were 'university graduates who had been employed in a variety of middle-management positions ... (whose) career prospects were limited because of the existence of various gender-related prejudices'. Of particular interest is the observation that many of these female entrepreneurs 'organize their businesses on the basis of trust ... employees are committed to the employer's goals' and will accept lower wages because of greater individual autonomy and job satisfaction; the 'payoff' for the entrepreneur is that a 'high trust organizational culture, then, has important economic advantages' (Goffee and Scase 1985: 68).

According to Brown and Scase (1994: 158), the appeal of entrepreneurship for graduates lies in 'possibilities for obtaining a greater degree of personal independence whereby their life chances will not be controlled by the arbitrary and discretionary judgements of others'. Drucker (1985) considers that longer years in education played a part in the emergence of the entrepreneurial economy in the United States although there are plenty of examples of individuals who did not pursue their studies beyond school, notably Richard Branson in the travel business. Ultimately, 'personal qualities which are rewarded through entrepreneurship are imagination and foresight, and skill in organizing and delegating work' (Casson 1982: 347).

The political/economic environment

Not surprisingly, larger tourism economies 'have a wider range of entrepreneurial opportunities' (Shaw and Williams 1994: 121); deregulation and 'liberalization' in western countries and Australia over the last decade have provided some of these opportunities. The advent of the 1979 Conservative government in Britain led to sweeping changes to many national policies: 'rolling back the frontiers of the state' created opportunities for both established and budding entrepreneurs. In the United States, deregulation of civil aviation in 1978, immediately spawned a range of low-cost carriers (for example, People's Express) – few of which survive today; deregulation of the coach transport business came in 1982 and led to the creation of many small-scale businesses with only Greyhound surviving out of the two large operators. The pace of change in European aviation was more slow than in the United States with policy being 'liberalized' from the mid-1980s onward; as a result, relatively few new airlines were established in the early years – Virgin's Maastricht service being one of these. In recent years, Greek-born entrepreneur Stelios Haji-Ioannou has developed the direct-sell, low-cost carrier easyJet, with the distribution benefits of new technology being recognized through a small discount for bookings made via the internet.

British deregulation of the passenger coach business, created by the 1980 Transport Act, allowed brother and sister Brian Souter and Ann Gloag to develop national bus routes, with their company Stagecoach. This was followed by the opportunity to bid for railway interests with the privatization of British Rail; Stagecoach acquired the South West Trains franchise. Music and aviation entrepreneur Richard Branson has expanded his travel interests by acquiring the 'cross-country' and West Coast Inter-City franchises, thereby creating Virgin Rail – having already benefited from the 'liberalization' of flights within the European Union. In 1998, Stagecoach acquired 49 per cent of the Virgin Rail Group and Virgin increased its stake from 41 to 51 per cent (Branson 1998).

The socio-cultural environment

Looking outside Europe, Drucker (1985: 1), in commenting on the United States, notes 'a profound shift from a "managerial" to an "entrepreneurial" economy'. This has been further enhanced by social innovation; just as the commercial bank and civil service resulted from the Industrial Revolution: 'the present age of entrepreneurship will be important for its social innovations – and especially for innovations in politics, government, education, and economics – as for any new technology or material product' (Drucker 1989: 247). Entrepreneurship is an integral part of North American culture and is, indeed, 'taught in school from kindergarten through to the twelfth grade, it has been integrated into college and university curricula, and is ... promoted through ... government Small Business Development Centers in every state' (Welsch 1998: 59). Entrepreneurs on that continent have the status of 'modern hero'.

However, in societies which show a marked respect for 'seniority' and authority the environment is unlikely to be conducive to the creation of large numbers of entrepreneurs. Dondo and Ngumo (1998: 18) consider the education, especially in primary schools, received by Kenyans is not only very conformist but that 'natural curiosity is suppressed'. When coupled with respect for 'rank', they believe the cultural environment is a poor base for entrepreneurship.

Innovation

It was only in the middle of the twentieth century that innovation as a key feature of entrepreneurship became established (Schumpeter 1952). Hisrich and Peters (1992: 8) observe that innovation 'is one of the most difficult tasks for the entrepreneur. It takes not only the ability to create and conceptualize but also the ability to understand all the forces at work in the environment'.

Schumpeter identified five types of innovation:

- Introduction of a new good – or an improvement in the quality of an existing good.
- Introduction of a new method of production.
- The opening of a new market.
- Conquest of a new source of supply of raw materials or half-manufactured good.
- The creation of a new type of industrial organization.

Some of these types can be observed by reviewing Branson's Virgin Atlantic airline: quality has been raised across the board through competition, true sleeper beds have been introduced, new markets have been opened to Tokyo (1991) and Hong Kong (1994) with the new Airbus A340–300, Washington, DC and Johannesburg (1996) and St Lucia (1999) to name a few.

Public sector entrepreneurship

Within the public sector, there are examples of both solo and group entrepreneurs; for example, Maria Glot, Eddie Fenn and Ian Page at Bradford City Council in the early 1980s – putting an industrial city on the tourist map. Davidson and Maitland (1997: 177) note that in the public sector in Britain, there was 'an element of hegemonic change ... in the face of evidence that the Thatcher values of enterprise and initiative were actually taken up by local government staff. In many cases, there was a change in attitude from regulation to entrepreneurship'.

The demise of traditional manufacturing in the early 1980s prompted Bradford Metropolitan Council to set aside funds for the development of tourism to the area. Textiles and engineering had dominated up until the 1970s but by the 1980s, the city's image was one of bleak de-industrialization. Themed packages, such as 'The Flavours of Asia' and ones based on the Brontë Sisters, were developed: 2,000 were sold in 1981/82, rising to 25,000 over the following two years (Buckley and Witt 1985), confirming that there can be entrepreneurship in a public service institution although it is likely to be 'far more difficult to innovate than even the most bureaucratic company' (Drucker 1985: 163). Davidson and Maitland (1997: 176) argue that 'a new approach to planning is emerging which seeks to combine private sector requirements with a greater sense of public purpose: entrepreneurial planning'.

Characteristics of small and medium-sized enterprises

Successful entrepreneurship does not necessarily result in businesses with a multi-million turnover. Globally, there are thousands of flourishing small and medium-sized tourism enterprises (SMTE) although it should be recognized that a small enterprise owner is not automatically an entrepreneur. Table 12.1 illustrates the wide range of categories.

The following section features some of these categories of entrepreneur.

Travel and tourism entrepreneurs

Brian Souter and Ann Gloag, representing rail and coach operation, and Richard Branson, with an airline and rail perspective, have already been mentioned. When it comes to tour operating, there are few barriers to entry into the business: the single greatest, in Britain, is probably the Civil Aviation Authority's ATOL (Air Travel Organizer's Licence) financial requirement. In the United States, Sheldon (1995: 405) cites the growth from 588 tour operating firms in 1978 to 1,001 by 1985 although only 34 per cent of those operating in 1978 were still in business seven years later; she notes that 'the situation is similar in European countries and seems to be characteristic of the industry'. Instability is largely a result of the easy entry and exit from this sector of tourism. When reviewing tour operation, Yale's (1995: 24) comments are particularly apposite: 'starting a new tour operating company can be seen as a creative business requiring imagination and strong nerves, so it has tended to attract entrepreneurial characters with strong personalities, most of them men'. The British tour operating industry is strewn with well-

Table 12.1 **Organizational structures and entrepreneurial characteristics**

Category	Entrepreneurial characteristics
Self-employed	Use of family labour, little market stability, low levels of capital investment, tendency towards weakly developed management skills
Small employer	Use of family and non-family labour; less economically marginalized but shares other characteristics of self-employed group
Owner-controllers	Use of non-family labour, higher levels of capital investment, often formal system of management control but no separation of ownership and control
Owner-directors	Separation of ownership and management functions, highest levels of capital investment

(Source: Goffee and Scase 1983, modified by Shaw and Williams 1994)

known names and their former brands: Harry Goodman and Intasun, Freddie Laker – whose Skytrain Holidays evolved out of the airline – and Vic Fatah, founder of SunMed and managing director of Inspirations to name but three. However, a large number of contemporary entrepreneurs are simply emulating names from the past such as Vladimir Raitz who, many would argue, first established the mass market for package holidays, by air charter, in 1950. This section presents vignettes of a range of travel and tourism entrepreneurs: some have a national profile and others a local one but all display entrepreneurial characteristics.

Erna Low – and Erna Low Consultants

There are so few female entrepreneurs in the tourism industry, at least in Britain, that Erna Low stands out like a beacon; she first began organizing winter sports holidays in 1932. As a Viennese graduate, teaching German in London, the tours were a means of getting to see her family in Vienna. The *Morning Post* advertisement in January 1932 proclaimed 'Viennese under-graduette (*sic*) taking party to Austria, fortnight £15' – for this, clients received rail travel, 10 days' full board at what was then the only hostelry in Solden, ski hire, instruction and German lessons. Lift passes were not included because there were none.

During World War II, Erna worked for the BBC monitoring German broadcasts and, unable to travel, created the house party concept. A middle-class clientele were attracted to family parties in Sussex, teenage parties in Cornwall and Christmas parties in Surrey; the cost for the last: £9 for 11 days. Allegedly, at least 20 marriages resulted from these. When foreign travel did resume, the British government imposed a £50 foreign exchange ceiling on money taken out of the country. This led to creative holiday packaging whereby the more that could be paid for in sterling, the more spending money was available in the resort. Erna Low offered two weeks in a first-class hotel in Murren, Switzerland, for 38 guineas – leaving £17 spending money.

Another innovation from this time was her introduction of a disco carriage on the weekly snow train and, for those who flew, the advice to wear ski boots and gear in order to save on the baggage allowance. The house parties continued and led in February 1953, to another first: the chalet party. In the 1950s, Erna Low started to offer other destinations – Majorca, the Spanish coast, Corsica, the Adriatic and Algarve. By 1972, with a turnover of £1.5 million and a staff of 60, she sold out – three years later, when the business was in difficulties, she bought her name back and started again. That company was sold in 1979 and she formed Erna Low Consultants to represent the resorts of La Plagne, Flaine and Les Arcs, recruiting recently graduated Joanna Yellowlees-Bound at the same time. One facet of many successful entrepreneurs is the ability to rely on trusted staff, Joanna's judgement of information technology was accepted and the office computerized – she is now one of two directors besides Erna.

A review of Erna Low's career shows not only the importance of innovation but the need to build an appropriate image – when applying for her job, Joanna (like a lot of people) thought Erna Low was an institution, not a real person. The business today comes within the small employer category although Erna has also been through the owner-controller and owner-director stages.

Stelios Haji-Ioannou and the easyGroup

Born in Athens, in 1967, Stelios obtained an Economics degree from the London School of Economics in 1987 and a Master's in Shipping Trade and Finance, from City University, the following year. Joining his father's Troodos shipping company, Stelios became the founding chairman of the Cyprus Marine Environment Protection Association in 1992; this group of Cyprus-based business people pursue a common interest in sustainable development.

Stelios' first venture, Stelmar Tankers, was formed in 1992, involving his older brother and younger sister as shareholders. Three years later, easyJet was launched as a low-cost carrier, flying out of Luton. In 1998, a holding company called easyGroup was formed in order to build on recognition of the 'easy' brand. The first of these new ventures was easyEverything – more than cyber-cafés, these internet access outlets contain between 400 and 600 terminals offering cheap 'surfing'; the first began trading in June 1999 and more are planned across

Europe. In spring 2000, easyRentaCar was launched, taking on the might of the established companies Avis, Hertz, National and Europcar, with the unique idea of only one model of car and very low hire cost. An easyBank is also in the offing.

Despite running a modern fleet, easyJet will acquire 15 more aircraft when funds are raised through a 25 per cent flotation on the Stock Exchange. This will also lead to share ownership by staff. Stelios says that what motivates him is 'succeeding in using new technology particularly the internet to bring down the price of goods and services to consumers'. There is no doubt that Stelios has moved from the category of owner-controller to owner-director. EasyJet's website address is: http://www.easyjet.com.

Tim Smit – the Lost Gardens of Heligan and the Eden Project

Whilst not quite a household name yet, Tim Smit's profile was raised by the two Channel 4 television series in the UK documenting the restoration of the gardens at Heligan, near Mevagissey in Cornwall. Not only did the series win a best documentary award but they are the biggest selling in the history of this television channel; the accompanying text won Illustrated Book of the Year 1997. The Gardens also won Garden of the Year 1996 and 1999. The Lost Gardens of Heligan are the result of Tim Smit building a talented team around him, since 1990, in order to restore the completely overgrown grounds. This estate had been one of the Tremayne family homes for centuries and had fallen into decline largely as a result of the Great War (1914–18) when only some of the gardeners who had been called up returned. The restoration caught the 'public's romantic imagination', as Tim puts it, because he views the social background as equally important as the plants, some of which are exceedingly rare.

Before considering Tim's next venture, it is valuable to look at his background. After reading for an Anthropology and Archaeology degree at Durham University, he worked as Assistant County Archaeologist (for Durham) between 1976–77. He is the first to admit that because the salary was so low, he also played in a rock band which had been established whilst at university. In 1977, he left the job – and has never worked for anybody else since – in order to pursue a 'rock-and-roll' career. Unfortunately, this coincided with the 'punk' boom and he spent some time unemployed. This led to him approaching Abbey Road studios with the offer of using their 'dead time' to record in return for payment if he was successful. The session musicians were recruited the same way and, luckily, he secured a deal. As Tim, puts it he 'was able to pay all the risk takers something which gave me credibility'. A series of hits produced wealth and he realized that material possessions were no substitute for low self-esteem; he comments, 'I have never been in thrall of money, except that it buys you freedom'. By the end of the 1980s, Tim and his family had decided to move to Cornwall where he would construct a studio and compose film music. Shortly after, a chance conversation was to lead to the restoration of Heligan, now a major West Country attraction with more than 200,000 visitors a year. There is no doubt that Tim has successfully marketed the concept of 'The Lost Gardens' and expanded the visitor profile from being quite a narrow one of 'tweeds' and the older person to 'romance' and lifestyle choice. Heligan as a 'brand' is being developed into a 'product manufacturing outlet to supply quality grocers and restaurants'. Marketing now occurs at local, national and international levels.

A challenge on the same scale as, or greater than, Heligan's restoration started in 1994 with the Eden Project, discussed in detail in Chapter 8. Tim Smit's ventures demonstrate the importance of a good management team and, especially in the early years at Heligan, the value of voluntary labour. Many individuals would have been daunted by the sheer scale of the task ahead and, therefore, one of the characteristics must be commitment to goals, coupled with a creative streak in marketing. Tim Smit has progressed from the joint owner-controller phase to owner-director as the number of employees has increased. To quote Tim, 'the real driver is an ideal to create successfully working communities at both Heligan and Eden. This creates a highly motivated staff and in turn leads to a sense of "tribe" where everyone works for each other'. To gain a true picture of the scale of restoration undertaken, Tim's book (Smit 1997) is recommended. The excellent website is found at: www.heligan.com.

Prue Leith, OBE

At the age of 20, Prue Leith founded Leith's Good Food Limited and ran the business, as managing director, for the next 35 years; besides corporate hospitality catering, she won contracts for the Queen Elizabeth II Conference Centre and the Edinburgh International Conference Centre. In 1969, she established Leith's Restaurant and later, in 1975, Leith's School of Food and Wine. Her expertise on all matters culinary has been brought to the public's attention through published articles in the *Daily Mail, Sunday Express, Guardian* and *Mirror* – besides 12 books. She has also presented television series on three British channels.

Besides finding the time to raise two children, Prue has been a non-executive director on nine companies, ranging from British Transport Hotels and British Rail in the early 1980s, to Whitbread, Halifax plc and venture capital firm Triven in the late 1990s. A former Businesswoman of the Year (1990), Prue has remarked that 'you either make lots and lots of money or you lose a packet' in the restaurant business and that, working on a 20-year cycle, 'probably 50 per cent occupancy is where you should break even. We used to break even on 54 per cent when I ran the business'.

Nonetheless, Nicholas (1999: 14) observes that although Prue Leith 'has certainly worn the T-shirt and eaten the stew of entrepreneurialism ... she declines to describe herself as an entrepreneur'. Prue states 'I think my talent in business is stickability. I am immensely dogged, and go on and on and on, trying to get it right'. This author would argue that many entrepreneurs exhibit just this characteristic of attention to quality and detail. She is another example of the enterprising individual who progresses from the owner-controller stage to that of owner-director.

Before launching Leith's in 1960, Prue had studied at Cape Town University and the Sorbonne in Paris; this emphasis on education is something she has returned to in the 1990s. The appointments are too numerous to review here; a few examples illustrate the theme – Chairman of the RSA, Governor of Ashridge Management College, council member of the National Council for Vocational Qualifications, the Oxford Museum of Modern Art, and committee member of the National Training Task Force. During her time as chairman of the RSA (Royal Society of Arts, Manufactures and Commerce), she clearly felt strongly about the links between entrepreneurialism and education; she is on record as stating that 'there are a lot of good think tanks around, but the RSA is a think and do tank'. One project close to her heart is Focus on Food; she believes that, as part of the strategy to make students more aware of food, schools should become 'community learning centres – not just for children, but for all ages and open 24 hours a day'.

Prue's latest project is what has been referred to as a 'theme park dedicated to good eating'; she is the driving force behind the National Centre for the Culinary Arts, based on a 28-acre derelict Georgian mental hospital in Stafford. It, usefully, has the backing of Delia Smith, Gary Rhodes and Jane Asher, all high-profile culinary presenters. The Centre expects to attract half a million visitors a year – but why the choice of Stafford? According to Prue, the town 'does not have a single first-class Michelin-starred restaurant and it could do with some bucking up. Also, it is easy to reach from almost everywhere'. Apparently, the croissant rides, jam pits for children and European Union wine lake proposals are non-starters. Prue has replica historical kitchens, croft-food yard, kid's cookery school, culinary museum and rare domestic animal breed more in mind.

Roger Thompson, OBE, and Guide Friday

Visitors to a number of Britain's cities will subconsciously notice double-decker buses in a subtle yet distinctive green and cream livery. These belong to Guide Friday, the company founded by Roger Thompson in 1974; his first driver-guiding service was launched the year before and targeted at London hotels and American travel agents – but it was called *Girl Friday*. Apparently, the company name was changed 'to alleviate excessive demands on the girl driver guides.' Roger Thompson moved to Stratford-upon-Avon in 1975 and developed 'The Stratford Go Round'; this tour pioneered open-top buses and, innovatively, permitted visitors to get on and off at points on the route. Not only were the five Shakespearean properties linked this way, Roger emphasized the social history – as at Heligan, this element helps to bring the attraction to life. Expansion began in 1988, after the Stratford operation had been firmly established, with tours available in Cambridge and, shortly after, Oxford, Edinburgh, Bath and York. This level of development necessitated six British branch offices and a further one has recently opened in Dublin. At the beginning of the twenty-first century, Guide Friday is the largest city sightseeing tour company in the world, running over 120 buses, in 35 destinations, employing over 750 staff and carrying more than 1.5 million visitors a year. Outside the UK, tours in Seville and Berlin are now well established; a new branch has just opened in Paris using new open-top buses in a special French livery. Further destinations are planned.

The Guide Friday tourism product makes a valuable contribution to visitor management in historic cities by linking major attractions in a continuous circuit thereby reducing the number of cars and noise pollution. The company has also pioneered the conversion of diesel engines to LPG (liquefied petroleum gas) which results in 70 per cent cleaner emissions; this service is now provided to other bus operators. Guide Friday has also diversified by establishing a conference division which provides corporate hospitality, ground handling, private tours and an educational package called the Shakespearean Experience.

Apart from a spell in the police force, in Cornwall, Roger Thompson spent his working life in tourism, running his own hotel before moving to London. He died unexpectedly, in November 1996, at the early age of 55; his wife continues in the 'family firm' as Public Relations Director. Looking back on Roger's achievements, a number of points can be made. First, with Guide Friday, he was committed to setting a high standard of customer care and quality of product; not only has this been achieved, it is reflected by the awards of the British Tourist Authority's 'Come To Britain' trophy and the English Tourist Board's 'England for Excellence' award – in two separate years. Second, a concern for environmental transport led to the introduction of LPG-powered buses. In the wider world of tourism, he was founder member of the Association of Driver Guide Operators, Vice President of the Heart of England Tourist Board, founder of Shakespeare Country Association of Tourist Attractions, founder member of BITOA (British Incoming Tour Operators Association), initiated the first Blue Badge Guide course for the Heart of England, and was for many years a director of the annual Stratford-upon-Avon Festival. Roger Thompson is yet another example of the type of entrepreneur committed to 'growing' their own business at the same time as raising standards across the industry. The business appears to engender loyalty amongst its employees as many came to work at the Stratford head office before the 1988 expansion. Roger Thompson was very much an owner-controller (Shaw and Williams 1994). The Guide Friday website is found at: http://www.guidefriday.com.

Martin Woods, Tourism and Marketing Manager, South Somerset District Council

South Somerset District Council, through Martin Woods' activities, has become a leader in the field of rural destination marketing. His award-winning and practical approach to sustainable tourism has made the work of the council a subject for national recognition culminating in an England for Excellence destination award in 1991 and another with the Parrett Trail Partnership for walking holiday promotion in 1998.

Martin Woods left a career in planning to start a tourism unit in 1987, in an area with no history of tourism promotion; with a blank sheet of paper and what he termed a 'non-obvious destination', he developed an innovative strategy that had niche marketing as its core. The strategy was based on three simple premises: attract the right people, 'spread the load' and measure the benefits. Local support for this approach of abandoning wholesale and largely unmonitorable promotion for the gradual development of a series of themes based on special interests came from the trade. This support grew as tourism in south Somerset began to take off. The 'niche approach' is now widely practised in local, regional and national destination marketing. A good example is in the area of walking; where there was only a series of unconnected footpaths, Martin Woods created a plan to develop 40 circular walks and three regional trails throughout South Somerset. Obstacles were overcome and the plan unfolded over ten years to make the district one of the best areas for walking outside the UK's National Parks. Innovative packaging and a clear sales strategy led to 40,000 sales of walk products and much national publicity. Today the Leland trail, the Parrett Trail, and the Liberty Trial remain role models for walking development and have generated numerous other examples all over the UK.

The initiatives have brought in millions of pounds to the area over the last decade and had numerous unexpected spin-offs in terms of local appreciation of the environment. They have interestingly given rise to a substitution effect where locals forsake going further afield to holiday in their own area. A measure of this was provided by a MORI survey of local residents, which found a 53 per cent awareness and use of tourism publications – giving the work of the tourism unit a clear mark of respect from the local population – critical if future plans are going to be financed and accepted. The pattern developed in walking is repeated with the niche markets and products. In 1990, Martin formed a partnership with historic houses and gardens called the Classic Gardens Partnership; the partnership work up an annual collaborative marketing campaign which involves attendance at national gardening shows, a high-profile publication and incentive schemes. As a result, there has been a rise in visits to the gardens, both National Trust and private, of 50,000 visits.

More recently he has worked to get the National Cycle Route (see Chapter 7) into South Somerset and his regional route around south Somerset has been held up as a model of good practice. Marketing techniques have also broken new ground. 'Above-the-line' advertising has been replaced by the use of direct mail. High-quality brochures conveying sensitive rural images are sent to consumer groups with a strong likelihood of coming to south Somerset. These people are given the opportunity of staying on the database of 50,000 to receive subsequent brochures Of those receiving the brochures, the majority elect to remain on the database and are repeat visitors, many coming five times or more. It is these people who form the core of the area's £50m per annum tourist trade. Martin Woods is a clear example of a public sector 'intrapreneur', working creatively within an organization.

Susan Achmatowicz and Country Lanes

In 1998, the English Tourist Board presented Susan with the England for Excellence Green Award for Tourism and Environmental Management, reflecting five years' effort with her business Country Lanes. She typifies the female graduate entrepreneur, possessing a BA in European History from Toronto University and an MBA in Marketing and Finance from Alberta. Between 1983 and 1988, Susan worked for the Bankers Trust Company in London which, by the time she left, meant responsibility for 120 staff and a £10 million operating budget. A change of direction came in 1988 when she ran Clifton Nurseries Limited as Managing Director; during this period, she produced a ten-year strategic plan for the Waddesdon Estate in Buckinghamshire and was interim manager of the much-visited manor.

Since 1992, Susan has been owner-manager of Britain's first quality bicycle touring business, combining this with consultancy for Virgin Trains, English Heritage and other organizations.

She has both created opportunities and taken advantage of contemporary developments; for example, the creation of the 6,000-mile National Cycle Network – one of the Millennium projects – has raised awareness of leisure cycling possibilities. In 1992, she became the exclusive UK agent for Backroads, America's number one active travel operator, before launching her own group bicycle tours aimed at upmarket overseas visitors the following year. As she comments, it was surprising to have the first tour (in the New Forest) booked entirely by British residents.

In 1994, Country Lanes opened a New Forest cycle hire facility near the company offices in Fordingbridge and introduced self-guided tours with flexible start dates. The 'One Day Get-Away', a joint venture with South West Trains, was launched in 1995 offering cycling from Brockenhurst. Also that year, Virgin Vacations Adventure Add-Ons were developed for airline Virgin Atlantic. The following year, transport minister John Watts opened the Country Lanes Cycle Centre at Moreton-in-Marsh rail station in the Cotswolds, opening up another touring area.

Besides a joint venture with Thames Trains, the website was launched in 1996 (www.country-lanes.co.uk). The internet has allowed Country Lanes to compete on the global stage despite being a classic example of a SMTE (small to medium-sized tourism enterprise); for example, reservation details can be submitted on-line for the bed and breakfast tours. The product range currently comprises day tours, supported group tours from April to October, and year-round self-guided itineraries.

Virgin Trains appointed Susan as a consultant in 1997 and, whilst looking at ways of improving cycle carriage on trains, the idea of converting railway carriages into cycle hire centres was developed. In 1998 there was the opening of the third rail station enterprise, in the Lake District National Park; the Cycle Centre at Windermere is a joint venture with Virgin Trains and North Western Trains. Two former Motorail carriages were donated for conversion into cycle centres for Brockenhurst and Moreton-in-Marsh railway stations; the Brockenhurst project was 'Highly Commended' in the British Airways Tourism for Tomorrow 1999 awards.

Country Lanes demonstrates two of Schumpeter's innovation types: the introduction of a new product – or improvement in the quality of an existing one – and the opening of a new market. With regard to organizational structure, the business reflects the entrepreneurial characteristics defined by the owner-controller category (Shaw and Williams 1994; Goffee and Scase 1983). (Country Lanes website address: http://dspace.dial.pipex.com/countrylanes/.)

Conclusion

This chapter has drawn on the wide range of research conducted into entrepreneurship by authors in Europe and North America. What emerges is an understanding that successful entrepreneurs are likely to possess a number of personal characteristics although no two will be alike; one individual may exhibit a high degree of innovation but wish to limit the amount of risk exposure, another will perceive the 'self-actualization' process as more important. A good track record in a previous business, as Susan Achmatowicz possesses, is undoubtedly of great help and provides a network of contacts to draw upon.

Besides these individual features, the wider economic and political environment is extremely important; in a highly regulated environment, there is little incentive for personal enterprise. For example, the deregulation of the British bus network provided a 'golden opportunity' for the founders of the Stagecoach empire. Finally, the socio-cultural environment must be considered to have a major effect. Media portrayal of entrepreneurs in the United States frequently show success as something to be admired whereas respect tends to be more grudging in western Europe.

Discussion questions

1. Why is the study of entrepreneurship important?
2. Outline the features that make a small-scale business proprietor an entrepreneur.
3. Identify the pre-conditions in the wider economy conducive to entrepreneurship.

Internet resources

By going to the weblink at www.thomsonlearning.co.uk students can access the following two studies on the Thomson Learning website. The study by A. Seaton and M. Bennett (1996) *Marketing Tourism Products: Concepts, Issues, Cases* discusses the issues associated with marketing small tourism businesses and should be read in conjunction with new studies in the field such as the major report by R. Thomas *et al.* (2000) *The National Survey of Small Tourism and Hospitality Firms: 20000 Skills Demand and Training Practices*, Centre for the Study of Small Tourism and Hospitality Firms, Leeds Metropolitan University, Leeds.

The second study by D. Fennell and D. Weaver (1997) 'Rural tourism in Canada: the Saskatachewan vacation farm operator as entrepreneur' in S.J. Page and D. Getz (eds) (1997) *The Business of Rural Tourism: International Perspectives*, examines a detailed case study of a tourism enterprise and its evolution, development and problems in developing the rural tourism market which pinpoints many of the problems highlighted in tourism business startups.

4. Discuss the statement 'many of the qualities with which the heroic stereotype is imbued are simply a reflection of contemporary cultural attitudes' (Casson 1982: 6).

References

Branson, R. (1998) *Losing my Virginity – The Autobiography*, London: Virgin Publishing.

Brown, B. (1987) 'Recent tourism research in S.E. Dorset', in G. Shaw and A. Williams (eds) *Tourism and Development: Overviews and Case Studies of the UK and the SW Region*, Working Paper No. 4, Department of Geography, University of Exeter.

Brown, P. and Scase, R. (1994) *Higher Education and Corporate Realities – Class, Culture and the Decline of Graduate Careers*, London: UCL Press.

Buckley, P. and Witt, S. (1985) 'Tourism in difficult areas, case studies of Bradford, Bristol, Glasgow and Hamm', *Tourism Management*, **6** (3): 205–13.

Casson, M.C. (1982) *The Entrepreneur: An Economic Theory*, Oxford: Martin Robertson.

Davidson, R. and Maitland, R. (1997) *Tourism Destinations*, London: Hodder & Stoughton.

Dondo, A. and Ngumo, M. (1998) 'Africa: Kenya', in A. Morrison (ed.) *Entrepreneurship: An International Perspective*, Oxford: Butterworth-Heinemann, 15–26.

Drucker, P.F. (1985) *Innovation and Entrepreneurship*, London: Heinemann.

Drucker, P.F. (1989) *The New Realities*, London: Heinemann.

Goffee, R. and Scase, R. (1985) *Women in Charge: The Experiences of Female Entrepreneur*, London: Allen and Unwin.

Hisrich, R.D. and Peters, M.P. (1992) *Entrepreneurship – Starting, Developing and Managing a New Enterprise*, second edition, Homewood, Illinois: Irwin.

McMullan, W. and Long, W.A. (1990) *Developing New Ventures: The Entrepreneurial Option*, New York: Harcourt Brace Jovanovitch.

Medlik, S. (1996) *Dictionary of Travel, Tourism and Hospitality*, second edition, Oxford: Butterworth-Heinemann.

Morrison, A. (ed.) (1998) *Entrepreneurship – An International Perspective*, Oxford: Butterworth-Heinemann.

Nicholas, R. (1999) 'What on earth is Prue Leith up to now?', *Real Business*, February: 13–14.

Schumpeter, J. (1952) *Can Capitalism Survive?* New York: Harper and Rowe.

Shaw, G. and Williams, A.M. (1990) 'Tourism, economic development and the role of entrepreneurial activity', in C.P. Cooper (ed.) *Progress in Tourism, Recreation and Hospitality Management*, Volume 2, Chichester: John Wiley: 67–81.

Shaw, G. and Williams, A.M. (1994) *Critical Issues in Tourism: A Geographical Perspective*, Oxford: Blackwell.

Sheldon, P.J. (1995) 'Tour operators', in S. Witt and L. Moutinho (eds) *Tourism Marketing and Management Handbook*, Hemel Hempstead: Prentice Hall: 402–10.

Smit, T. (1997) *The Lost Gardens of Heligan*, London: Victor Gollancz, in association with Channel 4 Books.

Stalinbrass, C. (1980) 'Seaside resorts and the hotel accommodation industry', *Progress in Planning*, **13**: 103–74.

Welsch, H. (1998) 'America: North', in A. Morrison (ed.) *Entrepreneurship: An International Perspective*, Oxford: Butterworth-Heinemann, 58–75.

Yale, P. (1995) *The Business of Tour Operations*, Harlow: Longman.

Youell, R. (1996) *The Complete A–Z Leisure, Travel and Tourism Handbook*, London: Hodder & Stoughton.

Further reading

Page, S.J., Forer, P. and Lawton, G.R. (1999) 'Small business development and tourism: *terra incognita*?' *Tourism Management*, **20**: 435–59.

13 Tourism and information technology

Learning outcomes

This chapter examines the interface between tourism and information technology. It introduces the concept of information technology and its impact on the tourism sector. After reading this chapter, you should be able to:

- Understand the scope of information technology and its impact on the tourism sector.
- Distinguish between a computer reservation system and a global distribution system.
- Understand the scope of the Internet and the role of travel services it provides.
- Recognize what a destination management system is.

Overview

This chapter examines the significance of information technology in the development of tourism enterprises. It outlines the role of information technology as a tool which is vital to tourism operations. The evolution of information technology in tourism is discussed and the rise of global distribution systems is reviewed. The significance of the internet and World Wide Web as communication technologies that have altered the distribution channels in tourism to allow direct selling are critically examined and the prospects for tourism retailing are discussed.

Introduction

The speed and pace of change in tourism during the 1990s and new millennium has been assisted from a business and consumer's perspective by the development and implementation of information technology (IT) defined by Poon (1993) as 'the collective term given to the most recent developments in the mode (electronic) and the mechanisms (computers and communications technologies) use for the acquisition, processing, analysis, storage, retrieval, dissemination and application of information'. This means that the use of a range of electronic, computer-based and communications-based technologies are increasingly being used to aid the operation and execution of business processes in tourism. One of the main tasks undertaken is the processing and facilitating of the flow of information within and between organizations and to and from the consumer. This involves the use of a range of information technologies which comprise three basic elements: software, hardware and people who operate the IT systems (ITSs). According to Cooper *et al.* (1998: 424) these ITSs commonly involve the use of 'computers, videotext and teletext, telephones/faxes, management information systems (MISs), modems, multimedia kiosks, computer networks, the Internet, satellites and wireless communication systems'.

The major impact of ITSs has been in relation to the impact on business operations initially, by cutting down the costs of operation and providing more interactive capabilities and in being able to tailor products and operations more flexible to meet the needs of customers. For example, Sheldon (1997) pointed out that each airline booking generates 25 transactions that need processing in an integrated booking system. This poses many challenges for tourism enterprises and organizations as we move towards a knowledge-based economy where information and the ability to harness and access it is a key to maintaining a competitive edge. In extreme cases this can require business re-engineering to implement technology so that organizations can achieve certain strategic benefits, namely 'establishing entry barriers; affecting switching costs; differentiating products/services; limiting access to distribution channels; ensuring competitive pricing; decreasing supply costs and easing supply; increasing cost efficiency; using information as a product in itself; and building closer relationships with customers' (Buhalis 1998: 410). In other words, in some situations, IT can offer new management opportunities and challenges. Buhalis (1998: 410) identifies four ways in which IT can be used strategically by businesses:

- To gain a competitive edge.
- To improve business performance and productivity.
- To facilitate new ways of managing and organizing business activities.
- To develop new businesses.

This chapter provides an overview of the principal areas where tourism and IT interact and a range of examples. There is a growing literature on this expanding area of tourism research and the following publications by Sheldon (1997), Inkpen (1998) O'Connor (1999) are very worthwhile for further reading since they deal with many of the technical issues and up-to-date developments. One of the easiest ways to begin any examination of IT in tourism is to consider the distribution channels in tourism and how the tourism industry deliver their products and services to the consumer. Figure 13.1 shows that the consumer normally purchases the 'tourism product' in one of four ways: through a travel agent, via a tour operator, through a regional tourism organization (RTOs) or directly using IT to purchase the product(s). In the case of RTOs (see Chapter 14), it is notable that in a climate of declining state financial resources for RTOs in New Zealand, more innovative RTOs such as Tourism Auckland are acting as an intermediary and raising funds through commissions on the sale of travel products. At each point of sale, the exchange of information is vital and for it to flow quickly, accurately and directly between the customer, intermediaries and the suppliers involved in Figure 13.1, IT is vital. Although IT is not a solution for poor business performance for individual enterprises or tourism organizations, the use of IT does raise a number of fundamental challenges for the tourism sector. These are a long-term vision for the strategic importance of IT and the introduction and maintenance of the most appropriate technology for business processes and on-going training and staff development (see Chapter 10). IT also has another vital role to play given the nature of the tourism product – it is perishable and cannot be stored or resold at a later stage (i.e. it is useful in selling and filling capacity or trying to match supply with demand which is the ultimate aim of managing tourism). In the tour operator sector, this is reflected in the sale of 'last-minute holidays' at a substantial discount to fill capacity. IT also enables retailers to provide up-to-date representations and descriptions of the products they are selling through the use of IT. In this respect, IT can assist in co-operation within the tourism industry through fast and accurate communication and may offer some of the potential tools to assist in global strategies.

Figure 13.1 **The distribution channels in tourism**

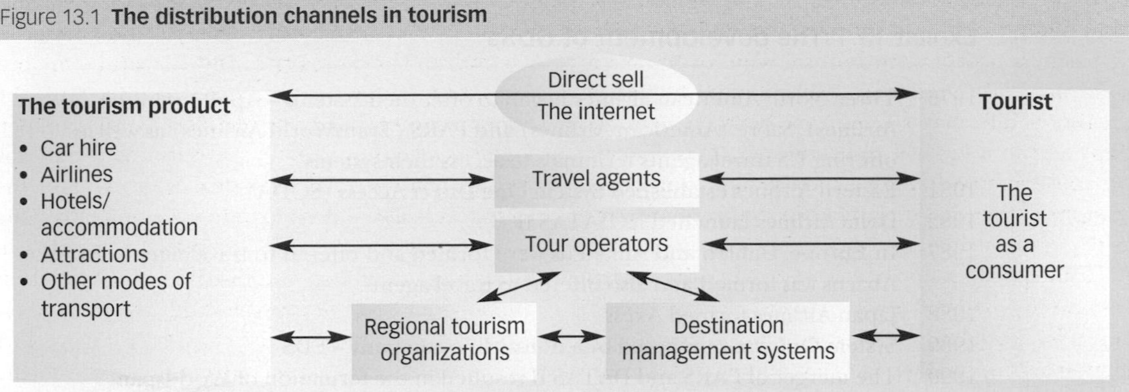

One of the most profound changes which have occurred in tourism through the impact of IT is the ability of the tourism industry to respond to the changing requirements of consumers seeking high quality and value for money. IT has offered many opportunities for the tourism industry to find new ways of meeting this demand, where the rapid expansion of the more sophisticated or 'new tourist' (Poon 1993) challenged the industry to address the demands for smaller market segments. This is reflected in the greater degree of interactivity which IT is offering the consumer, particularly in an age of accurate information and detail on the products and experiences being sold to consumers. This is heralding what marketers are calling the 'one-to-one' marketing approach, where using customer intelligence through the use of loyalty schemes and integration of the customers demands (e.g. automated checkout) and improved service provision are designed to enhance levels of customer satisfaction. This has also been extended through the use of the internet as a communication medium. In effect, IT has really revolutionized the marketing, distribution, operational functions of tourism in both the private and public sector (see Chapter 14).

To understand the impact and significance of IT on specific aspects of the tourism industry, especially the different sectors such as the airlines, hotels and retailers, it is useful to outline the major IT developments in the 1980s and 1990s and their implications for tourism in the new millennium.

From computer reservation systems to global distribution systems in tourism

According to Sheldon (1997) the current technology used in the tourism industry dates to the 1950s and the development of the early computer reservation systems (CRSs) pioneered by the airline industry. These CRSs grew rapidly in the 1970s and 1980s and in a typical CRS, one would find:

- A central site housing the computer systems driving the CRS.
- The network hardware at the central site and computer staff required to maintain it.
- A series of front-end communication processors to process information and on-line storage devices at the central site.

This is complemented by satellite communications to remote communications concentrators in key cities that relay data from the earth station. These are then relayed to reservation terminals and airports, giving rapid communication. The major changes in the 1990s was the move from CRSs which contained largely airline information for the proprietary airline, to systems containing data for multiple airlines. Sheldon (1997) examines the shift from CRSs to global distribution systems (GDSs) and Exhibit 13.1 traces the development of GDSs.

Exhibit 13.1 **The development of GDSs**

1976	Three North American airlines began to offer their systems – Apollo (United Airlines), Sabre (American Airlines) and PARS (TransWorld Airlines) as well as offering US travel agents terminals to access their systems
1981	Eastern Airlines established System One Direct Access (SODA)
1982	Delta Airlines launched its DATAS II
1987	In Europe, Galileo and Amadeus were formed and offered to travel agents. In Asia, Abacus was formed and also offered to travel agents
1988	Japan Airlines formed Axess
1989	System One was purchased by a non-airline company – EDS
1990	The merger of PARS and DATAS II resulted in the formation of Worldspan In Japan, All Nippon Airways and Abacus formed Infini
1993	Galileo and Apollo were merged to establish Galileo International
1994	System One merged with Amadeus

(Source: Page 1999: 187, modified from Sheldon 1997: 24)

The value of GDSs in the USA according to Sheldon (1997) was enormous and the main booking mechanism for travel, since a CRS will only show one airlines schedule whereas a GDS can show multiple carriers including flight schedules, passenger information, fare quotes and rules for travel and ticketing details. This has also been accompanied by the airlines move towards the internet. Yet IT is not just confined to the traditional distribution channels as Figure 13.2 shows. More recently, IT has been used in baggage and cargo handling systems (see Figure 13.2) and cabin automation and in-flight entertainment (see Page 1999 on the leading-edge technology used by Singapore Airlines), safety systems on tourist transport and gate management and control at airports. What Figure 13.2 shows is how the management of luggage loading/unloading and the passenger flows are managed through the use of IT so that all elements in the system interconnect and the flow of passengers and luggage are managed to optimize the throughput. Despite computer tracking systems for luggage, many American airlines are now experiencing high levels of luggage loss. A report in *USA Today*, 5 September (2000) reported that United lost 7 in 1,000 of all passengers' luggage, exceeded only by America West, which is a very high rate of loss given the technology available to track luggage. Denver International Airport (Goetz and Szyliowicz 1997) opened five years late due to the problems with its automated baggage system. Similarly, the UK's air traffic control project at Swanwick found 15,000 errors in the computer software and is expected to be £100 million over budget. Therefore, one should not over-estimate the problems of implementing new IT and the cost overruns which can be incurred in new projects with a large IT component. The cost of investment is also illustrated with Singapore Airlines Abacus GDS in Asia which has 12,500 terminals in 5,000 travel agencies. In fact commentators have argued that the introduction of GDSs is one of the single most important mechanisms for the globalization of the tourism industry. According to French (1998) the major tourism generating markets of North America, Europe and Asia–Pacific are fast approaching saturation with most travel agencies possessing reservation systems provided directly by or linked to one of the four leading GDSs (i.e. Amadeus, Galileo, Sabre and Worldspan). The market is saturated in that revenue growth in GDSs and profits are likely to stagnate. This is partly a function of the challenge posed by the internet. For example, the internet has allowed new intermediaries to enter the tourism market and Expedia, a virtual on-line travel agent is turning over business of $1 million a day, equivalent to two tickets every minute. Therefore, given the scale of such changes induced by IT and the role of the internet in generating tourism business, attention now turns to the internet.

Figure 13.2 **Luggage loading and unloading in the airport system**

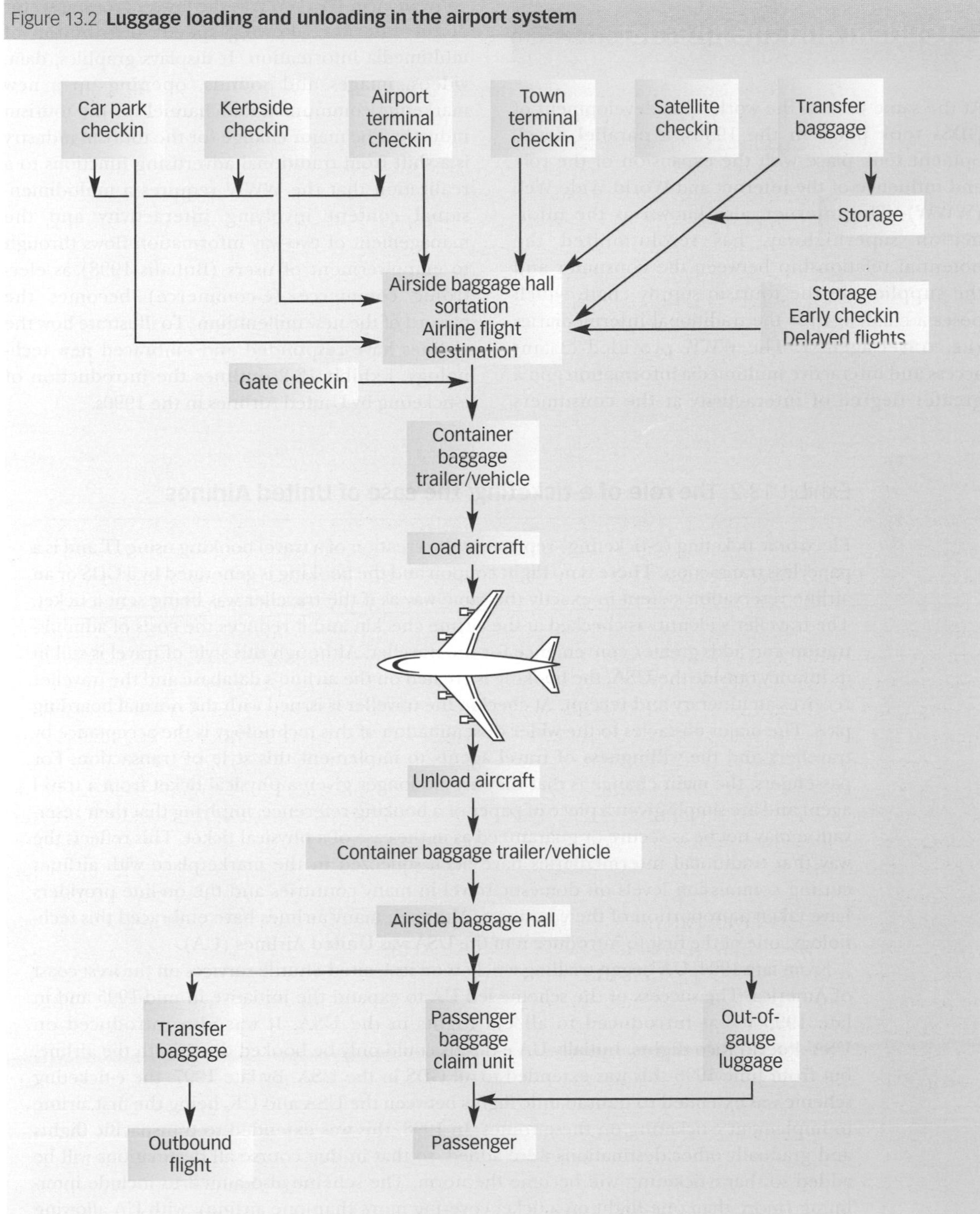

(Source: Page 1999)

Tourism and the internet

At the same time as the world-wide development of GDSs took place in the 1990s, a parallel development took place with the expansion of the role and influence of the internet and World Wide Web (WWW). The internet, also known as the information superhighway, has revolutionized the potential relationship between the consumer and the suppliers in the tourism supply chain which poses a challenge for the traditional intermediaries (i.e. travel agents). The WWW provided instant access and interactive multimedia information and a greater degree of interactivity at the consumers convenience. The WWW is the fastest growing sector of the internet, allowing speedy distribution of multimedia information. It displays graphics, data, videos, images and sounds, opening up a new marketing communication channel for the tourism industry. The major change for the tourism industry is a shift from traditional advertising functions to a realization that the WWW requires a multidimensional content involving interactivity and the management of two-way information flows through to empowerment of users (Buhalis 1998) as electronic commerce (e-commerce) becomes the byword of the new millennium. To illustrate how the airlines have responded and embraced new technology, Exhibit 13.2 outlines the introduction of e-ticketing by United Airlines in the 1990s.

Exhibit 13.2 **The role of e-ticketing: the case of United Airlines**

Electronic ticketing (e-ticketing) represents the creation of a travel booking using IT and is a paperless transaction. There is no flight coupon and the booking is generated by a GDS or an airline reservation system in exactly the same way as if the traveller was being sent a ticket. The traveller's identity is checked at the airline checkin and it reduces the costs of administration and adds greater convenience for the traveller. Although this style of travel is still in its infancy outside the USA, the booking is created on the airline's database and the traveller receives an itinerary and receipt. At checkin the traveller is issued with the normal boarding pass. The major obstacles to the wider dissemination of this technology is the acceptance by travellers and the willingness of travel agents to implement this style of transaction. For passengers, the main change is that they are no longer given a physical ticket from a travel agent and are simply given a piece of paper or a booking reference, implying that their reservation may not be as secure or guaranteed as in the case of a physical ticket. This reflects the way that traditional intermediaries have been squeezed in the marketplace with airlines cutting commission levels on domestic travel in many countries and the on-line providers have taken a proportion of their business. Although many airlines have embraced this technology, one of the first to introduce it in the USA was United Airlines (UA).

From late 1994, UA began trialling e-tickets on its United Shuttle services on the west coast of America. The success of the scheme led UA to expand the initiative in mid-1995 and in late 1995 it was introduced to all UA flights in the USA. It was also introduced on USA–Puerto Rico flights. Initially UA e-tickets could only be booked direct with the airline, but from June 1996 this was extended to all GDS in the USA. By late 1997, the e-ticketing scheme was extended to transatlantic flights between the USA and UK, being the first airline to implement e-ticketing on these routes. In 1998, this was extended to transpacific flights and gradually other destinations were added, so that in due course all destinations will be added so that e-ticketing will become the norm. The scheme also aimed to include interlining (more than one flight on a ticket covering more than one airline), with UA allowing up to 16 flights on one single ticket made through a GDS. The main problem for the airlines with interlining is receiving payment through the USA's Bank Settlement Plan and Airlines

Reporting Corporation. The growth in e-ticketing is reflected in UA's 72 per cent growth in the number of flight coupons issued between September 1997 and September 1998. Despite these innovations, the experience of many travellers is that the e-ticket presents many problems for the airlines at the checkin stage, especially where the ticket is issued outside the host airline's main country of operation. Instead of speeding up travel it can in some cases act as a hindrance to travel – a feature acknowledged by United Shuttle checkin staff.

According to Smith and Jenner (1998), the internet is still in its infancy with forecasts that almost every individual under 55 in the developed world will have access to the internet by the year 2010. Travel purchases are forecast to become a significant element in customer expenditure on-line. In the USA, consumers are signing up to the internet at the rate of one million a month. The top internet WWW pages are now visited 10 million times a month and in 1997 some 3 trillion email messages were sent over the internet. This is a significant development for the introduction of any new technology. The internet is dominated by North America although the rate of growth in Europe and Asia is beginning to show substantial progress. Users are encouraged to use sites by the specific internet browser they use (i.e. the software they use to find and select pages of information) complemented by hypertext links (electronic cross-referencing tools which move the user from one web page to another). According to the World Tourism Organization (WTO) (1999), in 1997 only 37 per cent of travel industry websites had on-line booking facilities while this had risen to 76 per cent in 1998. One of the key drivers was the success of other companies. The WTO (1999) indicated that the value of travel sales world-wide on the WWW has risen from US$2.23 billion in 1998 to US$4.1 billion in 1999 and is predicted to rise to US$16.60 billion in 2003. By 2003, Jupiter Communications (cited in WTO 1999) expect the profile of travel sales to be: 59 per cent airline bookings; 25 per cent hotel bookings; 12 per cent car rentals and 4 per cent cruises/tours.

According to Smith and Jenner (1998: 72) 'The top five web sites have a monthly audience of around 10 million individuals (each of whom may access the site several times a month)'. The typical internet users are according to Smith and Jenner (1998: 69) 'mature, in work, well-educated and high spending'. Surveys of the use of the internet, whilst only indicative of use, suggest that over a third of users are aged 22–30, with almost 20 per cent aged 30–40. According to the WTO (1999) NPD Research found that 70 per cent of users of the internet had visited a travel page. This equated to 5.4 million US adults making a travel reservation on the WWW in 1997 which had risen to 6.7 million adults in 1998. In addition, 33.8 million US adults in 1998 used the WWW for general holiday planning, illustrating the more informed tourist seeking information to maximize their use of vacation time. This is an enormous growth in use of the WWW for travel planning in the USA since only 3.1 million US adults used the internet for this purpose in 1996. In Europe, the WTO (1999) expect that the internet will generate US$1.7 billion in travel sales by 2002, which is a substantial increase on the 1997 figure of US$7.7 million in sales of travel products. For the hotel industry world-wide, this is likely to translate to a growth in on-line bookings from US$100 million in 1997 to US$3.1 billion in 2002 which could equate to 9 per cent of total revenue for hotels.

To use the internet, users must use a browser (software that allows one to search and visit sites). Then to search for information on the web, one has to use a 'search engine' or 'directory', the most popular being Netscape and Yahoo! Other popular search engines include Excite, AltaVista and the Microsoft Corporation. Examining the role of travel and tourism and products on the internet is an almost impossible task because there is no easy way of identifying what constitutes a travel page. For this reason, the following exercise will help to familiarize you with some of the ideas and arguments put forward so far on the growing interactivity which the internet offers travellers. Examine the student exercise overleaf.

With the continued growth of the Internet, it is not surprising to find other sectors of the travel and tourism industry seeking to adopt and harness its powerful impact in a marketing and sales role which is why attention now turns to the concept of destination management systems.

Student exercise

Travel sites on the World Wide Web

Using an internet connection, search the following site: http://www.yahoo.com

Once you are into the Yahoo! home page, search using the following term: 'travel'.

How many categories of travel can you observe?
How many sites are there?

Now search for the following company and examine their home page: http://www.travelocity.com

What does this site allow you to do? How many categories of travel products and activities do they allow you examine?
Does it replace the need for visiting a travel agent?

Lastly, search for the following site: http://www.lonelyplanet.com

What is the Lonely Planet site?
Look at their health site: What does the site contain? How useful would it be for travellers going to destinations with significant health risks?

Destination Management Systems

There is a growing recognition in the public sector (see Chapter 14) that to develop and enhance the tourist experience in a destination, the public organizations responsible for tourism also need to develop a presence on the WWW. This is reflected in the development of Destination Management Systems (DMSs) which are used to co-ordinate, develop and facilitate the production and delivery of the destination's tourism product. The initiative is usually taken by regional tourism organizations (RTOs) (see Chapter 14) and may be very helpful for small and medium-sized tourism enterprises to promote and sell their products. As a form of tourism marketing, DMSs in their most advanced state allow the reservations, promotion and distribution of tourism to take place. However, in their crudest form, DMSs are a storage mechanism with information on tourism suppliers, visitor attractions and other activities in the destination region. Figure 13.3 illustrates a typical configuration of a DMS which illustrates the economies of scale which can be achieved by amalgamating a wide range of data sources and material in one place so that it only has to be maintained in one location. As the WTO (1999) argue, the economies achieved by using IT are the creation and maintenance of one website which is only equivalent to the printing and distribution of a glossy brochure to large audience. Much of this has evolved from the work of RTOs with background information on the region and data on individual products. Many RTOs make this information available through tourist information centres (see Connell and Reynolds 1999 for an up-to-date review of this issue in the UK). Although the original function of many RTOs was not to sell products or to compete with tour operators, many recognize that simply distributing information on its own is not effective. A natural development for many RTOs has been the development of DMSs which allow customers to book products in the destination (pre-trip or after arrival). Not only does this bring extra revenue in commissions for RTOs (as noted at the outset of the chapter) but it also allows one port of call for all services where a wide range of small tourism businesses are involved.

According to the WTO (1999), DMS have been implemented on a piecemeal basis in the late 1980s and early 1990s and they summarize in Table 13.1 the

Figure 13.3 **A typical Destination Management System**

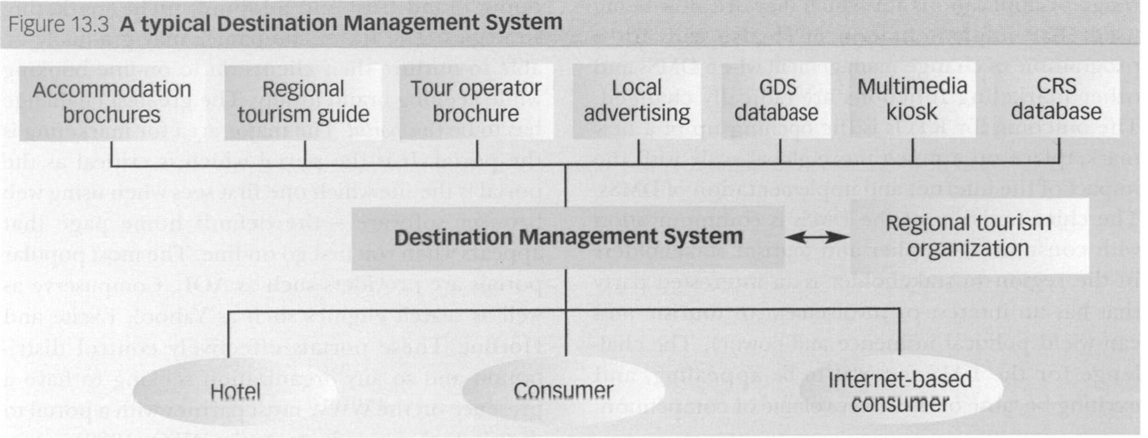

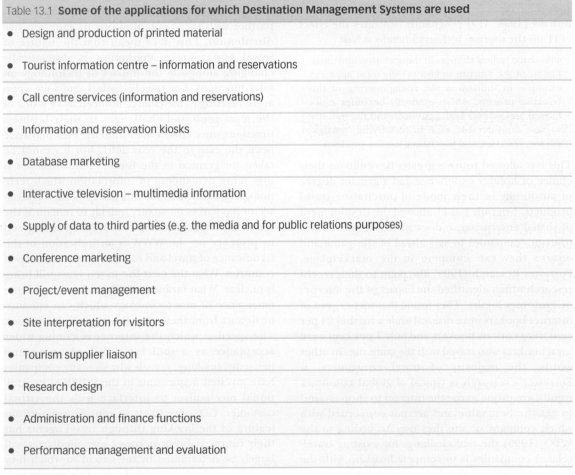

Table 13.1 **Some of the applications for which Destination Management Systems are used**
• Design and production of printed material
• Tourist information centre – information and reservations
• Call centre services (information and reservations)
• Information and reservation kiosks
• Database marketing
• Interactive television – multimedia information
• Supply of data to third parties (e.g. the media and for public relations purposes)
• Conference marketing
• Project/event management
• Site interpretation for visitors
• Tourism supplier liaison
• Research design
• Administration and finance functions
• Performance management and evaluation

(Source: Modified from WTO 1999)

range of applications for which they are now being used. The implementation of IT also calls for a programme of change management when DMSs and other marketing functions are radically changed. The outcome for RTOs is the opening up of a new marketplace on a much more global scale with the impact of the internet and implementation of DMSs. The chief function of the DMSs is communication with consumers, supplier and tourism stakeholders in the region (a stakeholder is an interested party that has an interest or involvement in tourism and can wield political influence and power). The challenge for the DMS is for it to be appealing, and exciting because of the sheer volume of competition.

Conclusion

Buhalis (1998: 419) poignantly illustrates the effect of IT on the tourism industry whereby it has:

> stimulated radical changes in the operation and distribution of the tourism industry ... the most apparent example in tourism is the re-engineering of the booking process, which gradually becomes rationalised and enables both consumers and the industry to save considerable time in identifying, amalgamating, reserving and purchasing tourism products.

This has allowed tourists greater flexibility in their choice of holiday experience and a greater degree of autonomy in their mode of purchasing travel products. Not only has IT allowed the development of virtual enterprises, it does add more pressure to tourism companies to stay ahead of the game and ensure they can compete in the marketplace. Forrester Research (1999) also point to their recent research which identified the impact of the internet on customer loyalty. They found that 69 per cent of internet bookers were disloyal while a further 24 per cent were curious bookers and only 7 per cent were loyal bookers who stayed with the same site. In other words, the majority of travel consumers, if Forrester's research is typical of global consumer trends, are prone to use the internet to shop around to get the best value and are not concerned with which company or site they use. According to the WTO (1999) the real challenge for existing travel-related companies is to compete head on with the new intermediaries that have entered the market by building relationships and alliances, as well as developing brand trust and adopting niche marketing strategies. The travel companies may gradually be able to nurture their clients on to on-line booking while keeping brand loyalty. The greatest challenge has to be the *portal*. The major area for marketing is the portal. It is the portal which is critical as the portal is the site which one first sees when using web browser software – the default home page that appears when you first go on-line. The most popular portals are providers such as AOL, Compuserve as well as search engines such as Yahoo!, Excite and HotBot. These portals effectively control distribution and so any organization seeking to have a presence on the WWW must partner with a portal to distribute their products. As the WTO (1999) argue, currently portals view travel companies as providing information of interest to its users. With portals like Yahoo! reporting 50 million page views per day, it is going to be essential for tourism organizations to partner with these organizations to gain effective distribution. This does mean that the nature of travel and tourism marketing is dramatically changing alongside the impact of technology on sales functions. For travel retailers and tour operators, reacting to the change induced by IT is one of the most profound challenges to their business functions since their establishment. This may have been the case in the year 2001, but it cannot be taken for granted in the future. The consumer is now more demanding of information which technology can provide fast and cheaply. The tourism sector has had to move very quickly to remain at the forefront of discretionary consumer spending and its presence on the WWW is an indication of the significance of travel and tourism in most developed countries. What the next five to ten years will bring is unclear. What businesses will need to watch is the emergence of new technology which can enhance or detract from their core functions as businesses. The speed at which the internet is gaining wider acceptance as a tool for travel planning and belatedly, booking, reveals why so many companies have invested major sums in the WWW as its additional mechanism to interface with the virtual customer. GDSs are likely to remain a significant feature of the booking through travel agents but their future viability as travel intermediaries will largely be determined by the extent to which they can offer their clients added value to compete with their virtual counterparts.

Discussion questions

1. Why is IT essential for tourism business? What functions does it allow businesses to undertake more efficiently?
2. What is the role of the World Wide Web in on-line bookings for travellers? How will it affect the tourism industry providers such as travel agents?
3. How is IT used in a management context in large tourism-related environments such as airports?
4. How are destinations using IT to enhance the visitation and attractiveness of their localities' attributes?

References

Ashford, H., Stanton, H. and Moore, C. (1991) *Airport Operations,* London: Pitman.

Buhalis, D. (1998) 'Strategic use of information technologies in the tourism industry', *Tourism Management,* **19** (5): 409–23.

Connell, J. and Reynolds, P. (1999) 'The implications of technological developments on tourist information centres', *Tourism Management,* **20** (4): 501–10.

Cooper, C., Fletcher, J., Gilbert, D., Wanhill, S. and Shepherd, R. (1998) *Tourism: Principles and Practice,* Harlow: Longman.

Forrester Research (1999) *Travel Bookers Aren't Loyal,* Cambridge, MA: Forrester Research.

French, T. (1998) 'The future of global distribution systems', *Travel and Tourism Analyst,* **3**: 1–17.

Goetz, A. and Szyliowicz, J. (1997) 'Revisiting transportation planning and decision making theory: the case of Denver International Airport', *Transportation Research A,* **31** (4): 263–80.

Inkpen, G. (1998) *Information Technology for Travel and Tourism,* second edition, Harlow: Longman.

O' Connor, P. (1999) *Electronic Information Distribution in Tourism and Hospitality,* Wallingford: CAB Publishing.

Page, S.J. (1999) *Transport and Tourism,* Harlow: Addison Wesley Longman.

Poon, A. (1993) *Tourism, Technology and Competitive Strategies,* Wallingford: CAB International.

Sheldon, P. (1997) *Tourism Information Technology,* Wallingford: CAB Publishing.

Smith, C. and Jenner, P. (1998) 'Tourism and the Internet', *Travel and Tourism Analyst,* **1**: 62–81.

Wen, H.J. (2000) 'Internet' in *The IEBM Handbook of Information Technology in Business* (2000) edited by M. Zeleny, London: Thomson Learning, pp. 126–133.

World Tourism Organization (1999) *Marketing Tourism Destinations Online: Strategies for the Information Age,* Madrid: World Tourism Organization.

Further reading

Buhalis, D., Tjoa, A. and Jafari, J. (eds) (1998) *Information and Communication Technologies in Tourism,* New York: Springer Verlag.

O' Connor, P. (1999) *Electronic Information Distribution in Tourism and Hospitality,* Wallingford: CAB Publishing.

Sheldon, P. (1997) *Tourism Information Technology,* Wallingford: CAB Publishing.

World Tourism Organization (1995) *Global Distribution Systems in the Tourism Industry,* Madrid: World Tourism Organization.

Useful web addresses

On-line travel booking sites

www.expedia.co.uk
www.Deckchair.com
www.ebookers.com
www.airtickets.co.uk
www.easyjet.com

Internet resources

By going to the weblink at www.thomsonlearning.co.uk students can access the following two studies on the Thomson Learning website. The studies are derived from the *International Encyclopedia of Information Technology in Business* and the first by J. Seitz (2000) examines the role of the World Wide Web for businesses which is of interest for tourism enterprises.

The second study by H.J. Wen (2000) on the internet is also of great significance for tourism businesses given the growth of e-business and commerce based on the internet as a means of communicating directly with customers.

www.go-fly.co.uk
www.britishairways.com

On-line travel agents

www.Bargainholidays.com
www.teletext.com
www.Lastminute.com
www.eBAy.com (for USA)
www.ebay.co.uk (for the UK)
www.qxl.co.uk
www.Thomascook.co.uk
www.americanexpress.com

Train booking in the UK

www.virgintrains.com
www.thetrainline.com

Accommodation sites

www.LeisureHunt.com
www.hilton.com
www.hyatt.com
www.HotelBook.com
www.Hotels.com
www.Vacationspot.com

Car rental

www.hertz.com
www.ukcarandvanrental.co.uk
www.dollar.com

Coach travel in the UK

www.nationalexpress.co.uk

Global distribution systems

www.sabre.com
www.galileo.com
www.pegsinc.com

For a comprehensive listing of the world's airline websites see Page (1999) with many of the world's airports also listed.

Tourism industry use of the internet

www.canberra.edu.au/uc/internet-study

See the above website for a summary of an Australian study of internet usage in the Australian Capital Territory (ACT), Canberra.

14 The role of the public sector in tourism

Learning outcomes

This chapter examines the way in which the public sector assists and directs the development of the tourism sector. After reading the chapter, you should be able to understand:

- Why the public sector intervenes in the tourism sector.
- How and why policies towards tourism are developed and implemented.
- How a developing tourism destination such as China used the policy process to change the direction and philosophy underpinning the tourism sector and its development after 1978.
- What the role of an national tourism organization is and its organizational structure.
- The role of other public sector agencies in the tourism sector.

Overview

This chapter discusses the role of the government in the facilitation and development of tourism. The role of government as an agency which acts as a guide to facilitate and manage the role of the private sector in tourism is examined. The activities of national and regional tourism organizations are discussed and the co-ordination and liaison role which many such organizations undertake is reviewed. The marketing function undertaken by such organizations is also examined.

Introduction

Within most countries, when one talks of the tourism sector, the immediate thoughts turn to the private sector, with its motivation being profit driven, characterized by entrepreneurs (see Chapter 12) who invest in business opportunities. This gives rise to a wide range of organizations in the tourism sector and outside the tourism sector which meet the needs of tourists for a profit usually working in a free market economy. Yet as Pearce (1989) illustrates, in tourism:

> Provision of services and facilities characteristically involves a wide range of agents of development. Some of these will be involved indirectly and primarily with meeting the needs of tourists, a role that has fallen predominantly to the private sector in most countries. Other agents will facilitate, control or limit development ... through the provision of basic infrastructure, planning or regulation. Such activities have commonly been the responsibility of the public sector with the government at various levels being charged

> with looking after the public's interest and providing goods and services whose cost cannot be attributed directly to groups or individuals (Pearce 1989: 32).

This quotation from Pearce summarizes the basic issues which this chapter will examine: Why are the public sector involved in tourism? How are they involved and how is this manifest in different organizations charged with managing tourism from a public sector perspective? The development of tourism in specific countries is a function of the individual government's predisposition towards this type of economic activity. In the case of outbound tourism, governments may curb the desire for mobility and travel by limiting the opportunities for travel through currency restrictions, as with the case of South Korea in the 1980s, while still encouraging inbound travel. Similarly, in the USSR under the former communist rule, the opportunities for domestic tourism were controlled by limiting the supply of holiday infrastructure. However, such examples are not the norm because most governments seek to maximize the domestic population's opportunities for mobility and travel by the provision of various modes of transport to facilitate the efficient movement of goods and people at a national level. In fact, the development of transport to facilitate inbound tourism is often motivated by government's desire to increase earnings from tourist receipts. To achieve the government's objectives to facilitate tourist travel, policies are formulated to guide the organization, management and development of tourism which is where the public sector has an important role to play. The tourism policies developed by national governments are influenced by their changing attitudes, outlook and political ideology.

The public sector's involvement in tourism

The public sector do not normally have an involvement in tourism to directly profit from interaction with tourists. The following reasons characterize the public sector interest in tourism:

- To improve the balance of payments in a country, region or locality.
- To aid regional or local economic development.
- To help diversify the economy.
- To increase income levels in a country, region or specific locality.
- To increase state revenues from taxation.
- To generate new employment opportunities.
- To achieve political goals in relation to promoting a country's political acceptability as a place to visit.
- To promote the development process through tourism, especially in less developed countries.

This will normally involve a policy of intervention whereby political objectives are achieved and the key term here is *policy*.

Tourism policy

The term 'policy' is frequently used to denote the direction and objectives an organization wishes to pursue over a set period of time. According to Turner (1997), the policy process is a function of three inter-related issues:

- the intentions of political and other key actors
- the way in which decisions and non-decisions are made
- the implications of these decisions.

The policy-making process is a continuous one and Figure 14.1 outlines a simplified model of the policy process which is applicable to the way tourism issues are considered by government bodies. In a tourism context, Hall and Jenkins (1995) examine the issue of policy-making. To illustrate the significance of tourism policy and how governments use and influence it, the example of China is examined as a practical example, then the lessons and principles associated with tourism policy and the agencies involved in its formulation and implementation are considered.

Tourism policy and development in China

Tourism in China has undergone pronounced changes since the country opened its doors to the west and tourism in 1978. Visitor arrivals in 1978 were 1.8 million and expanded to 17.8 million in 1985 and almost doubled in the next six years, reaching 33.3 million in 1991. By 1996, visitor

Figure 14.1 **The policy-making process**

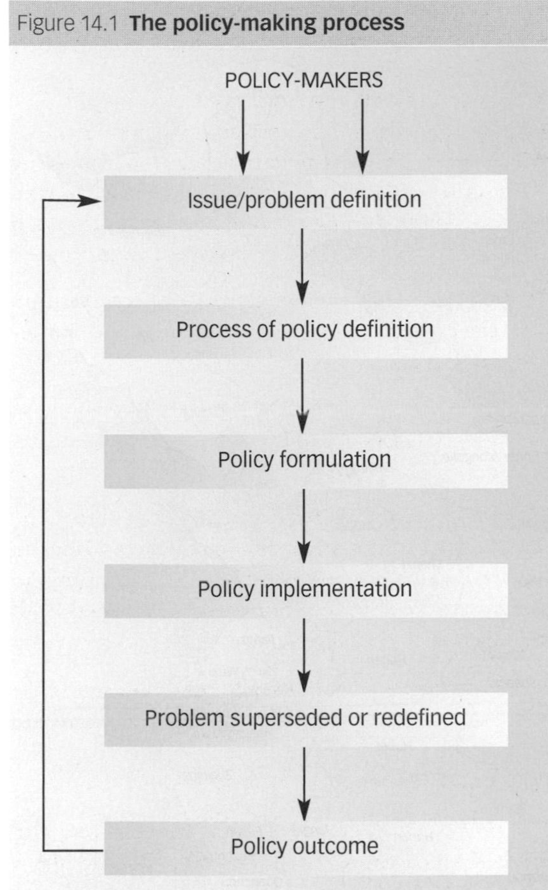

arrivals reached 51.1 million and in 1997, they reached 57.5 million. This is impressive growth and Zhang *et al.* (1999) examine how policy developments have contributed to and characterized tourism development during this period. Prior to 1978, tourism was merely used as a political tool by the state to expand China's socialist influence through the guests and visitors it invited to visit. Therefore, tourism was totally politicized. Zhang (1995) argued that the years 1978–1985 were characterized as politics plus economics, following the economic reform in China. In this period, a failure of government intervention meant that a number of problems occurred:

- demand exceeded supply in terms of facilities and services (e.g. in aviation, hotels and travel agencies)
- pricing of tourism products was rudimentary moving from a non-market system
- the management of tourism was ineffective, with no incentives for quality service among employees and standards fell below international standards
- foreign investment was permitted in hotels to assist in improving the quality and supply, and by 1985, with 45 hotels with such investment
- a need to decentralize the management of the tourism industry to stimulate development
- a lack of education and training facilities, leading to managers being trained overseas.

Tourism receipts increased from US$262.9 million in 1978 to US$1.25 billion in 1985 but the pace of change was too fast and the period has been described by Zhang *et al.* (1999) as 'disorder tourism', where inadequate state co-ordination, control and planning meant that the supply of hotel accommodation outstripped the capacity of the aviation sector. While hotel occupancy in some of the top regions performed well with adequate infrastructure (e.g. Beijing, Shanghai and Guandong) other areas had low occupancy rates (e.g. Shaanxi and Guangxi). The influx of 1.8 million tourists after 1978 also caused carrying capacity problems.

1986–1991

In 1985, China's Seventh Five Year National Plan (the main instrument for centralized state economic and social planning in a state command economy) identified tourism as a comprehensive development activity which could yield foreign exchange earnings with the shift from politics and economic to economics and politics in relation to tourism policy and development. To address the 'disorder period', the China National Tourism Administration (CNTA) developed a National Tourism plan 1986–2000. Among the major goals were to enter the ranks of the top tourist receiving countries while improving quality standards while focusing on 21 tourist cities including Beijing, Xi'an, Guangzhou, Shanghai and Guilin for the period up to 1990 (see Figure 14.2). Some of the policy changes and developments for the tourism industry prompted by the state included:

- greater co-ordination of tourism, with the establishment of the National Tourism Commission in 1988 with an initial focus on civil aviation followed by hotels and travel agencies
- restoration of tourist attractions in the top 14 tourist cities, such as the Forbidden City (as embodied in the famous film *The Last Emperor*)

Figure 14.2 **Tourist cities in China up to 1991**

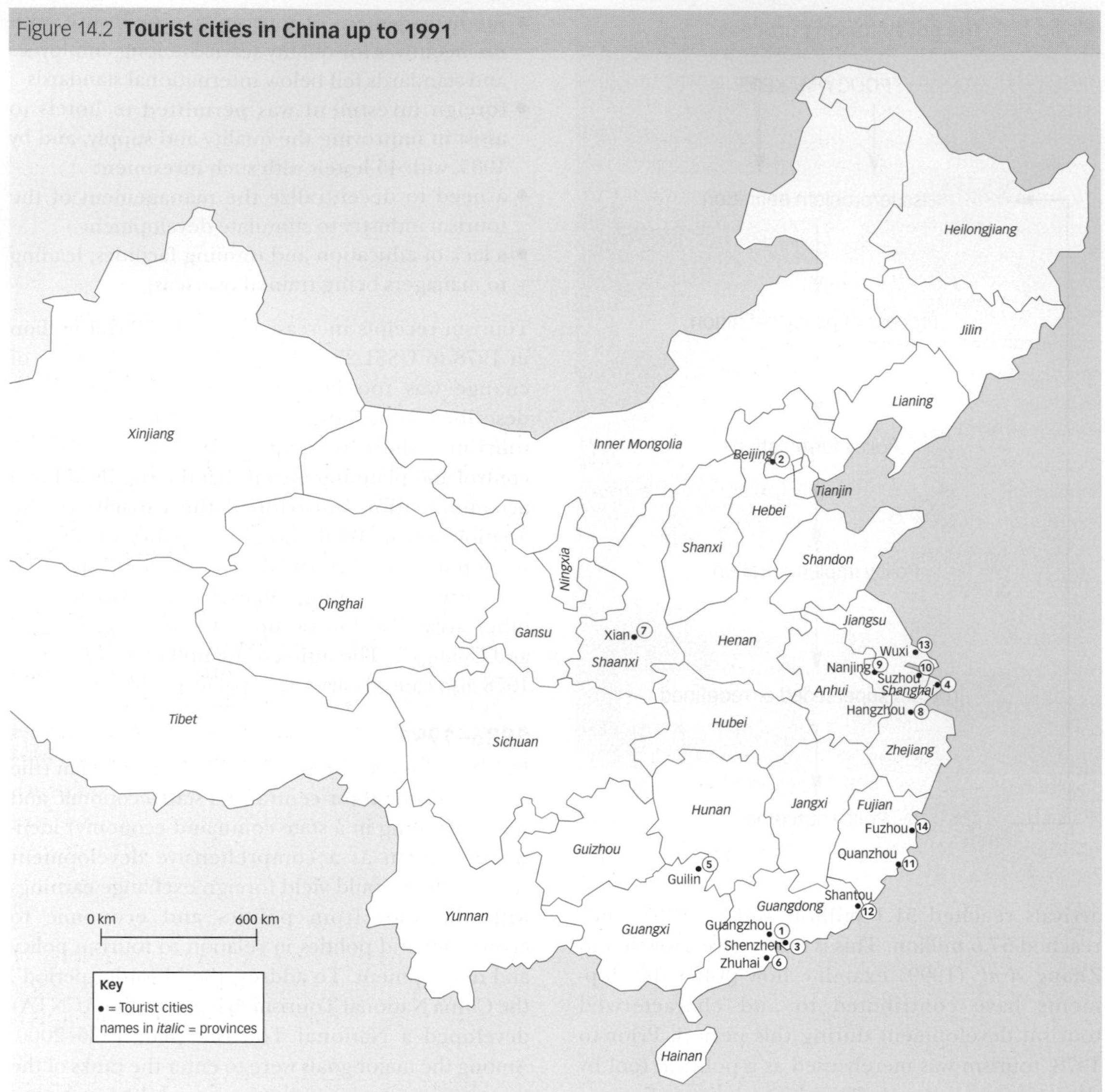

- reform in the aviation sector, with reform in the Civil Aviation Authority of China with the aim of transforming the airlines and airports into independent corporations
- improved education and training, with regional tourism bureaux governing tourism education for their region
- greater regulation of the tourism sector by the CNTA
- the promotion of international tourism, with CNTA's budget for overseas marketing increased from US$1.4 million in 1986 to US$3.2 in 1991 following the decline of tourist arrivals and the impact of the Tiananmen Square incident.

By 1991, tourism in China comprised 2,130 hotels, 1,561 travel agencies and employed 708,000 staff directly with approximately five times that indirectly.

1992 to the present

In 1992, Deng Xiao-Ping introduced the policy of China developing a 'market economy under socialism' which meant that tourism would become more geared to the market system. One consequence was the promotion of outbound travel to Chinese nationals and in attracting more international arrivals. This led to new rules for Chinese nationals travelling overseas, allowing them to join China Travel Services to nearby countries like Thailand, Singapore and Malaysia and greater outbound travel. Foreign aviation investors were also permitted as joint venture airlines and investment in commercial airports. After 1992, a number of purpose-built resorts were constructed for the international market, with attractive incentives for overseas investors. The pricing of tourism products were also decentralized to tourism corporations and by 1994, all tourism enterprises were operating in a market economy. With a market system, the CNTA introduced a Tour Guide Registration system in 1995 to improve the competence and delivery of tour guiding, with guides required to be registered with CNTA based upon a qualifying examination. The move aimed to make tour guides self-employed rather than state employees and subject to market forces, where complaints could lead to registration being revoked. Measures to improve the market were also introduced for the travel agent sector with a bond system established where agencies had to deposit a sum with CNTA in case of customer complaints or agency bankruptcy.

In the aviation field, competition has been very significant with not all airlines operating at a profit. To move to a market system, CNTA has undertaken tourism promotion, with its budget increased from US$ 3.2 million in 1991 to US$6.4 million in 1993, developing a number of themed promotions including 'Theme Years', 'Major Markets', 'Niche Markets' and 'Visit China 1997' year. To assist with promotion, China joined the Pacific Asia Travel Association (PATA) in 1993. Visitor arrivals increased in the 1990s and goals to achieve revenue targets from international tourism were achieved with the tourism industry growing accordingly. By 1995, China's tourism industry comprised 3,720 hotels, 3,826 travel agencies, 34 airlines and directly employed 1 million staff and approximately 5 million indirectly.

So what does this example tell us about tourism policy and development?

- China to all intents and purposes was a developing country in terms of tourism in 1978, with a limited private sector able to develop tourism.
- The government had played a major role as an operator of tourism infrastructure and plant up to 1978.
- Post-1978, the role of the state expanded to become one of regulator, stimulator of investment, a promoter of tourism opportunities, a co-ordinator of tourism activities among government departments and promoted the establishment of education and training initiatives.
- As a planner, with a National Tourism Plan, the state has set the direction of tourism policy and development with a shift from politics to economics in the philosophy underpinning tourism development.
- In a developing country, tourism may need to be pump-primed and a lead taken by the state to promote development.
- Control of the direction and development of tourism is essential as the 'disorder tourism' phase in China suggests.
- The state needs to foster overseas investment where internal resources are limited. The investment climate is essential to gain internationally recognized and quality development.
- In the policy arena, the power base, key actors (e.g. Deng Xiao-Ping), institutional arrangements and interest groups provide a powerful influence on tourism policy-making and policy measures can gradually change the direction and nature of tourism development as the Chinese example shows.

The China study provides a range of examples of tourism policy-making and for that reason, attention now turns to the public policy framework for tourism

The public policy framework for tourism

At a global scale, there are a number of agencies who have an influential impact upon tourism. The most significant agency is the World Tourism Organization (WTO) which assists its members to maximize the benefits of tourism, market identification, assisting in 'tourism planning as an executing agency of the United Nations Development Programme (UNDP), providing statistical information, advising on the harmonization of policies and practices, sponsoring education and training, and identifying funding sources' (Cooper *et al.* (1998: 226). The WTO is based in Madrid and has a very useful web site (http://www.world-tourism.org) which provides regular newsletters and press releases as well as a statistics database (for subscribers) and a list of the reports it produces. At an international level, a number of associated organizations also undertake activities which impact upon tourism, including transport industry bodies such as the International Air Transport Association (IATA), the International Civil Aviation Organisation (ICAO) and interest groups such as the Air Transport Action Group (ATAG) (see Page 1999 for more detail on the range of material they produce). The Organisation for Economic Cooperation and Development (OECD) also has an involvement in tourism, producing publications for its member countries. These bodies have a co-ordinating and influencing role on governments and at a regional level, bodies such as PATA exercise considerable influence over tourism organization and policy. The more complex level of organization in the transnational framework which the European Union presents (EU) presents a policy for producing a transnational policy framework (see Downes 1999 for more detail) with so many interest groups and organizations to consider.

According to Cooper *et al.* (1998: 227) the EU's role in tourism is one of simplifying, harmonizing and reducing restrictions on trade, which in this case is travel. The main thrust of the EUs tourism activities are directed towards improving the quality of tourism services, encouraging the development of inbound tourism from outside the EU as well as improving the business environment for tourism enterprises and ensuring a sustainable environment for tourism. Given the diversity of tourism products and experiences within member states, the EU effectively leaves tourism policy to the member states. However, the EUs main action occurs in relation to the gathering of tourism statistics, improvements to transport infrastructure that impacts upon tourism (see Page 1999) and the easing of frontier formalities and image promotion with the European Travel Commission (a non-profit making body with 21 member countries). The impact of EU grants on tourism has been extensively researched and a number of good studies exist (e.g. Pearce 1992 and Bull 1999). The reason for the EU's intervention in tourism, according to Cooper *et al.* (1998) can be summarized as follows:

- developing tourism as a common good that collectively benefits many businesses, with the NTO acting as a broker between suppliers and potential visitors
- infant industry development as part of regional policy (including peripheral areas), where commercial viability requires public sector support through the provision of essential infrastructure and financial incentives
- improving the tourism product, via the implementation of measures such as training programmes for tourism workers (Cooper *et al.* 1998: 227).

However, it is the government agencies which exercise the greatest level of influence over tourism activities within a country as Figure 14.3 shows.

National tourism organizations

One of the most useful sources to consult on tourism organizations is Pearce (1992) which examines a wide range of country examples of tourism organizations, especially NTOS. There are wide variations in the administrative frameworks developed within countries to manage and promote tourism. The NTO is usually a state-funded or hybrid organization which is state and private sector funded and often located within a ministry of tourism (see Figure 14.4 for the structure of the NTOs in the UK). The NTO may be inside or outside the ministry of tourism, depending on whether the state wants a government or semi-government agency to direct tourism. It normally has a board of directors, a constitution enacted by law and a degree of independence from the political system. The funding of the NTO is often agreed by the ministry by a purchasing or direct funding agreement, usually annually. In some countries, the NTO is termed a convention and visitor bureau, where revenue is raised from a range of sources (such as the private sector and sometimes through taxes). The 1990s have seen many changes to NTOs, particularly to their funding as states have sought to encourage the private sector to contribute more to the running of NTOs with some countries using tourist taxes as a means of funding the NTO. The structure of the Singapore Tourism Board (STB) is illustrated in Figure 14.5, highlighting the wide range of responsi-

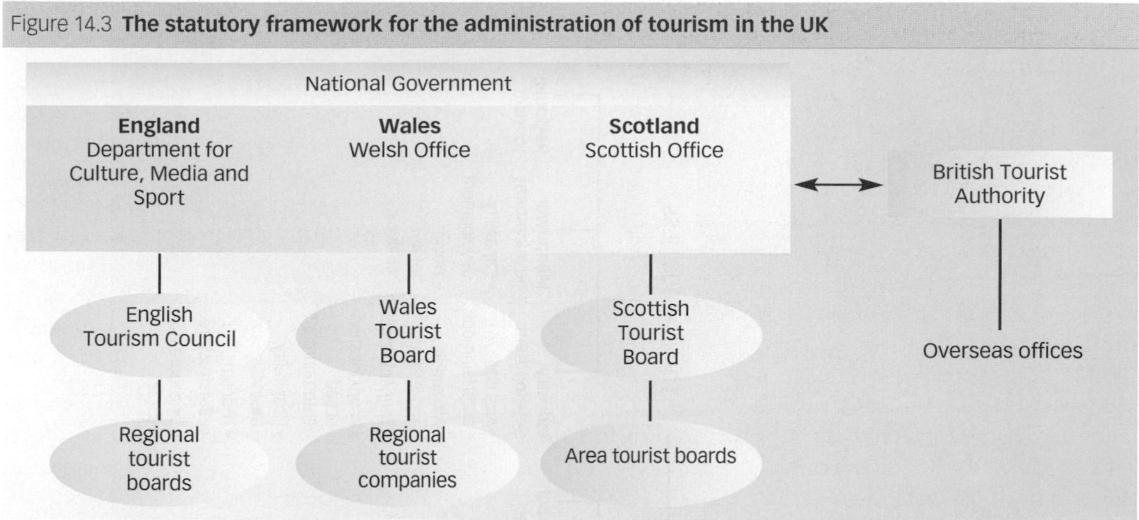

Figure 14.3 **The statutory framework for the administration of tourism in the UK**

Figure 14.4 **The structure of national tourism organizations in the UK**

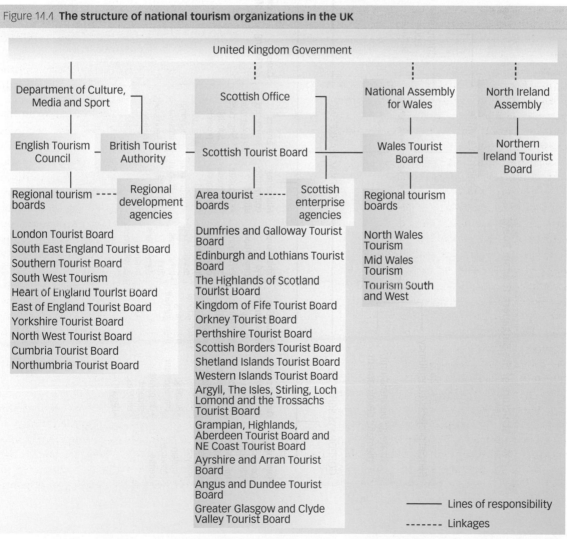

United Kingdom Government

Department of Culture, Media and Sport

English Tourism Council

British Tourist Authority

Regional tourism boards

Regional development agencies

London Tourist Board
South East England Tourist Board
Southern Tourist Board
South West Tourism
Heart of England Tourist Board
East of England Tourist Board
Yorkshire Tourist Board
North West Tourist Board
Cumbria Tourist Board
Northumbria Tourist Board

Scottish Office

Scottish Tourist Board

Area tourist boards

Scottish enterprise agencies

Dumfries and Galloway Tourist Board
Edinburgh and Lothians Tourist Board
The Highlands of Scotland Tourist Board
Kingdom of Fife Tourist Board
Orkney Tourist Board
Perthshire Tourist Board
Scottish Borders Tourist Board
Shetland Islands Tourist Board
Western Islands Tourist Board
Argyll, The Isles, Stirling, Loch Lomond and the Trossachs Tourist Board
Grampian, Highlands, Aberdeen Tourist Board and NE Coast Tourist Board
Ayrshire and Arran Tourist Board
Angus and Dundee Tourist Board
Greater Glasgow and Clyde Valley Tourist Board

National Assembly for Wales

Wales Tourist Board

Regional tourism boards

North Wales Tourism
Mid Wales Tourism
Tourism South and West

North Ireland Assembly

Northern Ireland Tourist Board

——— Lines of responsibility

------- Linkages

Figure 14.5 **Structure of the Singapore Tourism Board**

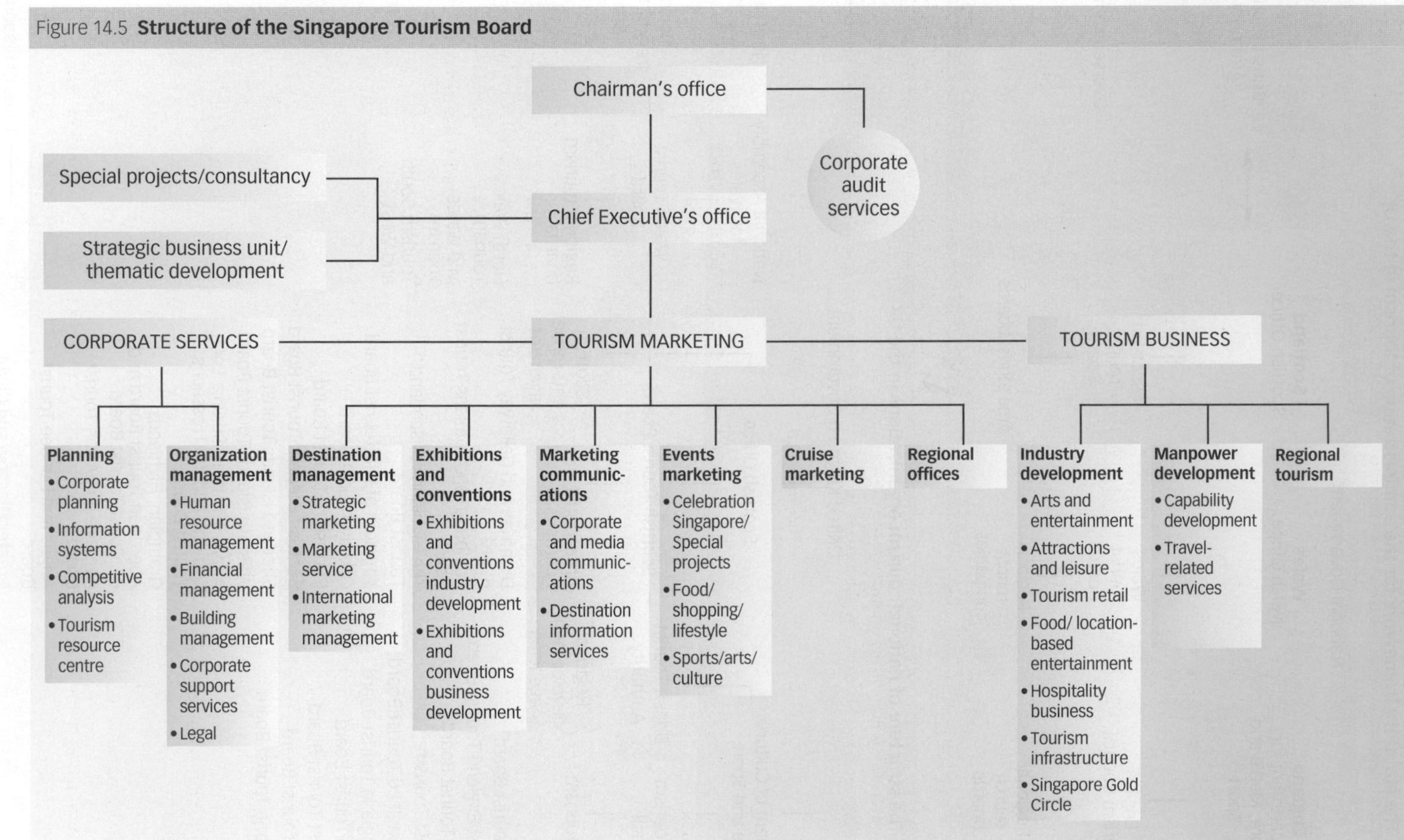

bilities NTOs undertake. The STB is one of the larger NTOs in an international context funded by the state and established in 1964 to promote Singapore as a tourist destination. As Figure 14.5 shows, there are three main divisions (excluding the two offices attached directly to the Chief Executive's office). The three main divisions within the STB are:

- *Corporate services,* comprising planning and management functions.
- *Tourism marketing,* comprising destination marketing, exhibition and convention marketing, marketing communications, events marketing, cruise marketing and the 12 regional offices operated by the STB overseas to market Singapore to inbound markets.
- *Tourism business,* comprising industry development, manpower development and regional tourism issues such as market development.

In 1996, the STB launched its Tourism 21: Vision of a Tourism Capital (see Exhibit 14.1) which was a public–private sector initiative for developing tourism in Singapore in the new millennium so Singapore would become a regional tourism capital in South-east Asia (see Hall and Page 2000 for more detail).

Clearly, the NTO performs a wide range of roles but its main functions can largely be categorized into:

- development (including research and tourism plans)
- information provision
- pricing
- controlling access to key tourist sites
- marketing.

It is this last function – marketing – to which attention now turns.

Marketing tourism and the NTO

Oppermann and Chon (1997) highlight a key factor associated with the growth of tourism in less

Exhibit 14.1 The Singapore Tourism Board's vision for tourism and Tourism 21

The STB's vision for tourism in Singapore is based on the following principles:

- To evolve Singapore into a tourism capital.
- To establish Singapore as a world-class destination, tourism hub and business centre.
- The Vision of Singapore as a tourism capital embodies an exciting and memorable destination; a regional hub for travellers and tourism investors; and a centre of excellence in tourism business expertise, ideas and networks. It is a vision of a vibrant and progressive city-state, yet filled with Asian warmth and hospitality; a place where East and West meet, and the old and new co-exist in harmony; a gateway for travellers and business professionals to make their voyage into the region and beyond.

(Source: Modified from STB (http://www.stb.com.sg/corporate/index/htm))

In terms of Tourism 21, the STB will be realized through six strategic thrusts:

- redefining tourism
- reformulating the product
- developing tourism as an industry
- configuring new tourism space
- partnering for success
- championing tourism.

This is designed as a new blueprint for Singapore's tourism industry in the new millennium.

developed countries (LDCs) which is the aggressive marketing by NTOs, the ability of the countries to finance tourism infrastructure development and rapid economic growth. There is a growing literature on the role of NTOs in the development and promotion of tourism in destination areas (World Tourism Organization 1996) and a recent World Tourism Organization report (World Tourism Organization 1997) highlighted the budgets which these organizations used for promotional purposes and attention now turns to the marketing of tourism in South-east Asia by NTOs to illustrate the diversity of activities they undertake. Exhibit 14.2 provides some insights into these activities.

Exhibit 14.2 **The marketing of South-east and south Asian tourism by national tourism organizations**

Michael Hall and Stephen Page

The recent reports by the World Tourism Organization (1996, 1997), are the first comprehensive synthesis of the marketing of the region and the activities of the NTOs as well as the revenue expended on different activities. While the World Tourism Organization (1996) are not able to provide detailed data for every destination, due to the reliance upon NTOs responding to a questionnaire survey, the material analysed does at least provide an indication of how the region fares in a global context and the types of activities which NTOS undertake in each country which responded. At a global scale, the World Tourism Organization regional breakdown of total budgets expended upon tourism show that Europe remains the largest spender on marketing tourism with a total of US$ 1,004 million spent followed by East Asia Pacific with US$559 million, the Americas with $432 million, Africa with $130 million, South Asia with $56 million and the Middle East with US$25 million. Thus a total expenditure for those countries responding of US$2,207 million was spent on tourism marketing and promotion in 1995. The methods of funding the NTOS in Asia are outlined in Table 14.1 which highlights the dominant role of central government in supporting marketing and promotion and the limited role of the private sector (excluding Bangladesh, Hong Kong and China and to lesser degree in the case of the Philippines and Maldives).

Table 14.2 outlines the manner in which the NTOs spend their budgets on tourism marketing and promotional activities in Asia where advertising and promotion consume the majority of the budgets, usually in excess of 75 per cent of the total funding for each NTO. Table 14.3 shows that, within a global context, a number of the Asian destinations (e.g. Singapore, Thailand, Korea, Hong Kong) are competing aggressively for the international visitor market through the amount of money spent on promotional activities. This is further developed in Table 14.4 where the expenditure in local currencies for the period 1991–1995 indicates the significant sums spent by South-east Asian destinations. It is also interesting to observe which types of target markets the various Asian destinations are seeking to develop (Table 14.5). As Table 14.5 shows, most destinations are seeking the high-spending long-haul and medium-haul outbound markets from the USA, Japan as well as intra-regional travel from within Asia–Pacific (Hall 1997). Although the prioritization of markets and the precise mix of inbound tourists varies according to destinations, there is a clear focus on a core range of source markets which are a function of historical ties, growing outbound markets and the location and attraction of each destination. What is also clear from the analysis of NTOs by the World Tourism Organisation (1996) is that the governments of some destinations (e.g. Singapore and Thailand) are now major players in terms of the budgets and promotional activities funded to develop tourism (see Singh and Chon 1996 for a detailed analysis of the situation in Singapore). This, of course, does not include the marketing and promotion undertaken by other tourism businesses (e.g. airlines) which is complementary to the work of the NTOs and certainly significant in the image formulation and direct contribution to the development of inbound tourism. In the case of Singapore, Raguraman (1997) discusses the impact of airline development to nation-building although few studies have examined the co-operative marketing undertaken between NTOs and airlines in pursuit of similar goals – to increase visitor arrivals. Oppermann and Chon (1997: 131) argue that 'historically, the principal marketing role of NTOs has been seen in the fairly narrow promotional terms of creating and communicating overall appealing destination images and messages to the target market'.

It is evident from the World Tourism Organization (1996) data that this narrow role is also changing with a growing interest in private–public sector partnerships to market the region reflected in the Tourism Authority of Thailand's collaboration with airlines, hotels and tour operators – 'The World Our Guest' campaign. This sought to invite 11,000 travel intermediaries (e.g. travel agents and tourists) in response to the adverse publicity associated with the spread of AIDS, the Gulf War and political unrest in 1992. There have been few critiques of the role of national tourism promotion, although perhaps the most candid and meaningful is that by Leong (1997) focused on Singapore. Leong (1997) examines the historical development of tourism promotion by the Singapore Tourist Promotion Board since 1964 and notes that:

> Before political independence in 1965, Singapore was like any other Southeast Asian city, an apparent haphazard maze of diverse land uses … Beginning in the late 1960s, urban and industrial development progressively bulldozed such landscapes and living traditions … Two mass campaigns instituted at this time were Keep Singapore Clean and Towards a Green Garden City – self-conscious efforts of the new nation-state to construct and transform a new environment for tourism and urban development. (Leong 1997: 78)

Even so images promoting tourism in Singapore use the multicultural traditions of the country, ethnic traditions, unique and exotic images associated with festivals, eating and cultural performances. Thus the multicultural traditions replace the absence of scenic landscape and heritage attractions, as a living form of tourism organized around the theme of ethnicity. By commodifying ethnicity, with the Chinese, Malay, Indian and other ethnic groups, a particular form of food tourism has been developed and promoted in the absence of other conventional products based upon the historical and indigenous people.

Yet one should not also underestimate the role of other tourism promotion agencies and initiatives in the region. For example, in recent years ASEAN nations have undertaken joint promotion, marketing and research activities such as Visit ASEAN Year in 1992 (Hall 1997). Such initiatives have had value not only in promoting the image of the region externally but also encouraging greater intra-ASEAN travel. In addition to the activities of government promotional initiatives, the private sector is also playing an increasingly important role. For example, the private sector Indonesian Tourism Promotion Board launched a five-year campaign in 1994 to encourage inbound tourism from Japan, Taiwan, Singapore, Germany and Australia with an initial budget in 1994 of US$14 (Wall and Nuriyanti 1997). However, what has assisted in the rapid development of Indonesia's inbound tourism is the ability of Indonesia's Tourist Development Corporations to provide and develop infrastructure in peripheral locations and in the main destinations (Hall 1997). This co-ordinated approach together with the provision of capacity on airlines to facilitate the growth in arrivals.

In contrast, Raguraman (1998) examines the situation in India where a key factor associated with the slow growth in international arrivals is the lack of access by air. Although tourism is a central component of the national planning process in India, Raguraman (1998) highlights the emphasis needed for improving marketing and promotion for overseas tourism: better co-ordination with operators, improved tourism information services and co-ordination of the national tourism development with the activities of the various states in India. In 1994–1995, the DOT allocated 60 per cent of its budget to marketing and publicity (US$20.7 million), of which US$17.2 million was for overseas promotion. Nevertheless, Raguraman (1998) argues that this is relatively small for a country the size of India, when compared to Malaysia and Singapore where the expenditure on promotion is almost double. This also has to set against a growing competitive market for South-east Asian tourism. Even so, it is clear that the NTOs in South and South-east Asia, that a substantial element of the promotional budget have designated for overseas promotion (which also includes intra-regional markets) to build the image of the destination.

Table 14.1 **The funding of national tourism organizations in Asia in 1995**

Country	Funding of NTOs' total budget Percentage of total budget					Funding of promotional budget Percentage of promotional budget derived from	
	Central government	Local authorities	Taxes	Contribution of private sector	Other	Public funds	Non-public funds
Bangladesh (1)	–	–	15.00	–	85.00	–	–
China	100.00	–	–	–	–	–	50.00
Hong Kong (2)	–	–	90.00	10.00	–	95.00	5.00
India (2)	100.00	–	–	–	–	–	–
Indonesia (2)	100.00	–	–	–	–	–	–
Korea Republic of	–	–	–	–	100.00	100.00	–
Malaysia	100.00	0	0	0	0	100.00	–
Maldives	100.00	–	–	–	–	–	4.76
Myanmar (4)	100.00	–	–	–	–	–	–
Nepal (4)	100.00	–	–	–	–	–	–
Pakistan	100.00	–	–	–	–	–	–
Philippines	–	25.00	1.00	4.00	70.00	99.00	1.00
Singapore (4)	–	–	–	–	100.00	100.00	–
Sri Lanka	100.00	–	–	–	–	100.00	0
Taiwan (Prov of China) (3)	100.00	–	–	–	–	–	–
Thailand (5)	100.00	–	–	–	–	100.00	–

(1) Provisional
(2) Fiscal year: April 94–March 95
(3) Fiscal year: July 94–June 95
(4) Fiscal year: April–March
(5) Fiscal year: October–September

(Source: World Tourism Organisation 1996)

Table 14.2 **National tourism organization budgets in Asia: allocation of funds by activity, 1991–95**

Country	Activity	% of budget				
		1991	1992	1993	1994	1995
China	Advertising	–	–	23.55	30.41	32.42
	Public relations and press	–	–	7.95	11.41	5.95
	Promotional activities	–	–	24.07	43.49	40.74
	Public information					
	Research activities	–	–	6.26	3.59	20.90
	Other	–	–	38.17	11.11	–
	TOTAL	–	–	100.00	100.00	100.00
Hong Kong (1)	Advertising	60.50	56.05	60.03	60.79	48.18
	Public relations and press	9.63	8.89	8.72	7.11	7.32
	Promotional activities	27.32	30.85	27.13	21.64	32.88
	Public information	–			–	–
	Research activities	1.23	1.82	1.61	1.23	2.47
	Other	1.32	2.38	2.50	9.22	9.15
	TOTAL	100.00	100.00	100.00	100.00	100.00
Macau	Advertising	48.95	32.98	38.60	29.08	47.35
	Public relations and press	1.50	3.35	3.84	4.03	3.01
	Promotional activities and public information	49.55	63.66	57.56	66.89	48.79
	Research activities	–	–		–	0.85
	Other	–	–	–	–	–
	TOTAL	100.00	100.00	100.00	100.00	100.00
South Korea	Advertising	43.82	50.51	54.79	51.07	57.28
	Public relations and press	1.30	2.60	1.77	0.94	1.66
	Promotional activities	52.41	43.01	38.62	42.78	39.30
	Public information	–	–		–	–
	Research activities	0.22	0.19	0.13	0.12	0.24
	Other	2.16	3.69	4.68	5.09	1.53
	TOTAL	100.00	100.00	100.00	100.00	100.00
Indonesia (1)	Advertising	22.35	22.24	20.84	20.83	17.58
	Public relations and press	–	–	–	–	–
	Promotional activities	77.65	77.76	79.16	79.17	82.42
	Public information	–	–	–	–	–
	Research activities	–	–	–	–	–
	Other	–	–	–	–	–
	TOTAL	100.00	100.00	100.00	100.00	100.00

Table 14.2 ***contd.***

Country	Activity	% of budget 1991	1992	1993	1994	1995
Malaysia	Advertising	43.42	37.13	–	–	–
	Public relations and press	12.14	7.68	–	–	–
	Promotional activties	27.98	36.71	–	–	–
	Public information	14.22	15.19	–	–	–
	Research activities	2.25	3.29	–	–	–
	Other					
	TOTAL	100.00	100.00	–	–	–
Philippines	Advertising	32.73	22.20	29.41	30.29	24.74
	Public relations and press	–	–	–	–	–
	Promotional activities	56.24	70.82	63.04	62.50	68.18
	Public information	–	–	–	–	–
	Research activities	–	–	–	–	–
	Other	11.03	6.98	7.55	7.21	7.08
	TOTAL	100.00	100.00	100.00	100.00	100.00
Singapore (2)	Advertising	46.04	44.74	47.33	44.85	–
	Public relations and press	6.72	8.84	8.52	7.44	–
	Promotional activities	46.41	44.97	43.09	46.64	–
	Public information	0.05	0.36	0.28	0.11	–
	Research activities	0.78	1.08	0.78	0.96	–
	Other					
	TOTAL	100.00	100.00	100.00	100.00	–
Thailand (3)	Advertising	43.76	43.79	46.84	68.92	58.81
	Public relations and press	12.23	13.51	21.66	11.73	12.66
	Promotional activities	35.09	33.74	24.12	15.73	24.53
	Public information	–	–	–	–	–
	Research activities	7.18	6.97	6.34	3.03	3.02
	Other	1.75	1.99	1.04	0.58	0.98
	TOTAL	100.00	100.00	100.00	100.00	100.00
Bangladesh (4)	Advertising	82.72	93.90	92.59	32.89	51.35
	Public relations and press					
	Promotional activities	17.28	6.10	7.41	67.11	48.65
	Public information	–	–	–	–	–
	Research activities	–	–	–	–	–
	Other	–	–	–	–	–
	TOTAL	100.00	100.00	100.00	100.00	100.00
India (5)	Advertising	60.09	60.09	60.66	60.09	60.10
	Public relations and press	–	–	–	–	–
	Promotional activities	29.04	29.05	29.32	29.05	29.09
	Public information	6.58	6.57	6.63	6.56	6.56
	Research activities	0.54	–	–	–	–
	Other	3.74	4.30	3.39	4.29	4.25
	TOTAL	100.00	100.00	100.00	100.00	100.00

Maldives	Advertising	6.34	7.51	8.22	7.51	7.55
	Public relations and press	7.66	6.30	6.99	5.58	5.64
	Promotional activities	68.22	70.11	68.23	71.66	69.11
	Public information	14.67	11.55	13.55	12.61	14.18
	Research activities	3.12	4.53	3.01	2.63	3.52
	Other					
	TOTAL	100.00	100.00	100.00	100.00	100.0
Nepal (7)	Advertising		57.86	48.15	29.00	25.36
	Public relations and press		1.26	1.59		2.61
	Promotional activities		30.82	33.86	51.14	18.44
	Public information		1.89		5.25	
	Research activities		7.55	8.47	7.53	2.70
	Other		0.63	7.94	7.08	2.70
						(6) 48.20
	TOTAL		100.00	100.00	100.00	100.00
Sri Lanka	Advertising			0.24	1.22	1.14
	Public relations and press			7.20	4.26	3.31
	Promotional activities			86.10	85.14	83.35
	Public information			6.22	7.80	10.03
	Research activities			0.24	0.49	0.68
	Other				1.10	1.48
	TOTAL			100.00	100.00	100.00

(1) Fiscal years: April 91–March 92 to April 95–March 96
(2) Fiscal year: April–March
(3) Fiscal year: October–September
(4) Fiscal years: July 90–June 91 to July 94–June 95
(5) European market only
(6) This amount is allocated to a tourism promotional fund which is spent on specific promotional activities rather than regular ones
(7) Fiscal year: 16 July–15 July

(Source: World Tourism Organization 1996)

Table 14.3 **Promotional budgets of the top 40 national tourism organizations in 1994 and 1995**

Rank 1995	Country	1994	US $ 000s 1995	% change 1994–95
1	Australia (1)	75 811	87 949	16.01
2	United Kingdom (2)	77 885	78 710	1.06
3	Spain	77 457	78 647	1.54
4	France	62 729	72 928	16.26
5	Singapore (3)	49 695	53 595	7.85

Table 14.3 ***contd.***

Rank 1995	Country	US $ 000s 1994	1995	% change 1994–95
6	Thailand (4)	42 907	51 198	19.33
7	Netherlands	43 800	49 700	13.47
8	Austria (5)	45 694	47 254	3.41
9	Ireland	41 830	37 811 (6)	–9.61
10	Portugal	34 904	37 271	6.78
11	Israel	25 000	33 300	33.20
12	Switzerland	27 613	32 233	16.73
13	New Zealand (7)	29 718	31 597	6.32
14	Canada (2) (8)	11 743	31 504	168.28
15	Puerto Rico	20 117	30 807	53.14
16	Korea, Republic of	30 486	30 308	–0.58
17	Hawaii (USA) (7)	20 861	28 686	37.51
18	Hong Kong (2)	24 940	28 637	14.82
19	Morocco	21 588	24 541	13.68
20	South Africa (3)	27 758	23 809	–14.23
21	Mexico	55 087	22 574	–59.02
22	Egypt	21 000	21 000	0.00
23	Cyprus (9)	18 561	20 790	12.01
24	Turkey	18 804	20 520	9.12
25	Germany	17 375	20 151	15.98
26	India (2)	19 127	18 648	–2.50
27	Finland	18 000	17 777	–1.24

28	Bermuda (2)	16 871	16 565	–1.81
29	Tunisia	15 124	16 423	8.59
30	USA (10)	14 000	15 000	7.14
31	Croatia	13 241	14 498	9.49
32	Italy	9 412	14 198	50.85
33	Aruba	13 455	12 876	–4.30
34	Philippines	9 898	7 080	–28.47
35	Poland	4 641	6 709	44,56
36	French Polynesia	5 853	6 629	13.26
37	Hungary	6 450	6 612	2.51
38	Costa Rica	7 168	6 450	–10.02
39	Curaçao	5 913	5 671	–4.09
40	Macau	2 657	5 083	91.31

(1) Fiscal years: July 93–June 94; July 94–June 95
(2) Fiscal years: April 94–March 95: April 95–March 96
(3) Fiscal year: April–March
(4) Fiscal year: October–September
(5) Including domestic tourism
(6) Data for 1995 is provisional
(7) Fiscal year: July–June
(8) Excludes partnership funding from state/territorial authorities and the private sector for 1994/95
(9) Promotional budget does not include fixed costs of the central administration
(10) Estimation excluding Hawaii

(Source: World Tourism Organization 1996)

Table 14.4 **Promotional budgets of Asian national tourism organizations, 1991–1995**

	Unit of currency	1991	1992	1993	1994	1995
North-east Asia						
China (1)	Yuan renminbi	16 890	24 190	36 800	37 055	42 922
Hong Kong (2)	Dollar (HK$)	129 897	145 867	148 911	194 527	223 372
Korea, Republic of	Won (W)	14 104 736	16 582 326	21 363 191	24 388 974	24 246 468
Macau	(MOP)	13 302	15 269	21 054	21 255	40 666
Taiwan (Prov. of China) (3)	New Taiwan dollar	9 500	20 379	14 027	10 281	9 421
South-east Asia						
Indonesia (2)	Rupiah (Rp)	5 250 661	6 018 288	6 662 126	8 750 960	9 345 897
Malaysia	Ringgit ($M)	61 078	65 000	–	–	–
Philippines	Peso (P)	58 300	194 910	202 420	256 020	183 130
Singapore (4)	Dollar ($S)	60 788	60 021	67 793	72 604	74 818
Thailand (5)	Baht (B)	410 764	496 066	607 774	1 072 664	1 279 957

(1) Excluding staff costs
(2) Fiscal years: April 91–March 92 to April 95–March 96
(3) Fiscal years: July 90–June 91 to July 94–June 95
(4) Fiscal year: April–March

(Source: World Tourism Organization 1996)

Table 14.5 **The top ten target markets for Asian destinations in 1995**

Country	Target markets 1	2	3	4	5	6	7	8	9	10
China	United States	Japan	Singapore	United Kingdom	France	Germany	Australia	Spain	Israel	
India (1)	Germany	France	Italy	Spain	Netherlands	Switzerland	Sweden & Scandinavia			
Indonesia	Japan	United Kingdom	Singapore	United States	Germany	Australia	Taiwan	Malaysia	Netherlands	France
South Korea (2)	Japan	United States	Taiwan	Germany	United Kingdom	Australia	Hong Kong	Canada	Singapore	France
Malaysia	Japan	United States	United Kingdom	Australia	Germany	Hong Kong	Taiwan	Singapore	France	Thailand
Philippines	Asia/ Pacific	Europe	United States							
Singapore (3)	Japan	United States	United Kingdom	Australia/ New Zealand	France/Italy/ Spain	Hong Kong Taiwan	Germany	Asia (5)	South Korea	Switzerland
Sri Lanka	Germany	France	United Kingdom	Japan	Scandinavia	Benelux	Italy	Switzerland	Austria	Spain
Taiwan	Japan	Europe	North America	Asia (4)	Australia/ New Zealand					
Thailand	Japan	United States	Taiwan	Germany	England	Malaysia	Hong Kong	South Korea	Singapore	Australia

(1) European market
(2) Data refers to 1993
(3) Data refers to 1994
(4) Excluding Japan
(5) Excluding Japan, Australia, New Zealand, South Korea, Hong Kong and Taiwan

(Source: World Tourism Organization 1996)

What the case study in Exhibit 14.2 illustrates is the diversity of experiences and the extent to which the NTOs pursue specific goals and can be very aggressive in tourism promotion when significant marketing budgets are allocated. However, other bodies within countries also complement the role of the NTOs, namely the regional tourism organizations and the local authority bodies.

Other agencies involved in tourism in the public sector

Below the NTO in most countries, there is often a complex web of organizations which complement the work of the NTO at the regional and local level, as is the case in the UK where a range of statutory tourism boards operate in the regions. While their activities are often a scaled-down version of the NTOs' work at a regional level, they often implement national policy and pursue integrated activities with the NTO providing guidance in a top-down approach. Pearce (1992) examines the activities of the RTOs in different countries and discusses their varied roles. Page and Hall (1999) observe that in New Zealand the majority of RTOs are funded directly or indirectly by local taxpayers with further funds being made available through either a membership base and/or co-operative marketing activities. The RTOs are primarily domestic marketing organizations although some of the larger RTOs (e.g. Auckland, Rotorua, Christchurch, Queenstown) also seek to attract the international holiday visitor, while other RTOs in major centres such as Wellington, Dunedin and Taupo also seek to attract the international MICE [Meetings Incentives Conferences and Events] visitor.

However, one of the growing areas of activity in the 1980s and 1990s has been a growth in the interest and response of the public sector at the local level, often at the city or locality level where tourism has become a major issue to manage. Page and Thorn (1997) examine the situation in New Zealand where the Resource Management Act and its principles of sustainable planning combined with a market-led approach to tourism policy and planning placed the emphasis on the public sector in the regions and localities to plan and manage tourism growth. An interesting insight is provided by Page and Hall (1999) who point to the 1997 Inquiry by the Parliamentary Commissioner for the Environment on the *Management of the Environmental Effects Associated with the Tourism Sector* highlighted the potential for negative environmental and socio-cultural impacts of tourism development, particularly with respect to Maori. The Inquiry concluded that the environmental qualities underpinning tourism are at risk in some areas and noted that visitor pressure on some 'icon' attractions (e.g. Waitomo Caves and Milford Sound) cannot be sustained in the medium term without attention being given to reducing adverse visitor effects. In the light of the new NZTB [New Zealand Tourism Board] tourism marketing campaign for New Zealand it is also notable that the Inquiry concluded that the marketing activities of NZTB may have outstripped the capacity of the tourism sector to manage the environmental consequences of tourism growth.

This is interesting as it questions the market-driven approach of the NZTB by another government agency while Page and Thorn (1997) illustrated that the role of local and regional councils in New Zealand highlighted that many localities were unprepared for the impact of tourism, given the forecasts presented later in Chapter 27. As a consequence, there is a greater role for the public sector as Dredge and Moore (1992: 20) mooted where:

> increased tourism growth will result in greater challenges for the integration of tourism and town planning. These challenges will be brought about by the need for the development of attractions, transport, support services and infrastructure to cater for increased visitor numbers, and the implications this will have for land use planning ... Planners have a responsibility to meet challenges offered by the growth in tourism and to understand how their activities affect tourism.

The outcome of this statement is reflected in cities such as Cambridge in the UK pursuing an active policy towards visitor management in the 1980s as a city that receives over 3.3 million visitors a year with a population of 100,000 in a small historic city.

The role of the local authority: the example of visitor management in Cambridge, UK

Cambridge ranks among one of the UKs most historic cities and tourism is estimated to yield in excess of £180 million a year and supports over 5,000 jobs. The physical and social impacts of tourism in Cambridge (see Chapters 18 and 19 for a discussion of impacts) led to Cambridge City Council (CCC) setting out the following objectives for tourism in 1992 in the Deposit Draft Cambridge Local Plan:

- To conserve the local life, beauty and character of Cambridge.
- To ensure a satisfying and enjoyable experience for visitors.
- To achieve the above objectives by management and selective development without general promotion.

The areas for action in a visitor management programme designed to manage tourism in the city to mitigate some of the impacts included:

- Moving the balance of the visitor mix from day to long-stay visitors.
- Managing the impact of English language courses in the summer season.
- Improving information to encourage visitors to disperse throughout the city.
- Managing coaches and public transport (see Human 1994 for more detail).

Conclusion

This chapter has examined the role of the public sector in the management and organization of tourism emphasizing the role of different agencies and bodies in this process. The formulation and implementation of tourism policies is not a static unchanging process as the example of China shows. In this respect, tourism is highly politicized even though theoretically NTOs are beyond the realms of political influence. In practice, they are often vehicles of national political ambitions by countries seeking to harness the economic and political benefits of a buoyant tourism industry. One of the key objectives of the NTO is to assist in the development of supply and promote the growth and management of demand to meet supply. Through the policy, the NTO and government departments may use a range of instruments and other government measures such as land use planning and control measures, building regulations, measures to regulate and direct the market as well as investment incentives, which were illustrated in the example of China. The state can also play a major role in non-tourism areas such as the provision of transport infrastructure (see Page 1999) and this area is not always planned with tourism interests in mind, though in countries with an increasingly private sector demand-driven focus, the needs of the tourism sector are more carefully programmed into new developments such as airports and new infrastructure projects. There is also growing evidence of the NTOs seeking private sector finance through partnerships with industry to develop areas of their work for the tourism industry. Voluntary tourism bodies at the local and these are assuming a greater role. Without a strong public sector role in tourism, the wider public good of the tourism sector and society is not easily reconciled with the needs of the private sector for profit and development. The public sector acts as an anchor and counterbalance to the private sector, although it needs to work in harmony with the private sector rather than in opposition for a viable and successful industry.

Internet resources

By going to the weblink at www.thomsonlearning.co.uk students can access the following two studies on the Thomson Learning website. The first is from the study by R. McLennan and R. Smith (1998) *Tourism in Scotland* and examines the public policy framework for tourism in Scotland up until the late 1990s. Although such frameworks are constantly evolving, this study does highlight many of the wider public policy issues associated with the development of tourism in a specific country. This should be read in conjunction with the second study which offers a more systematic review of tourism and public policy.

The second study by C.M. Hall and J. Jenkins (1995) *Tourism and Public Policy* is now a classic study in this field and the section here provides an excellent overview of how to study tourism public policy and its wider significance for tourism studies and decision-making.

Discussion questions

1. Why does the public sector involve itself in tourism?
2. What is the role of a national tourism organization?
3. How do tourism organizations interact with the private sector?
4. Why are some governments scaling down the role of the public sector in tourism in favour of a greater role for the private sector?

References

Bull, B. (1999) 'Encouraging tourism development through the EU structural funds: a case study of the implementation of EU programmes on Bornholm', *International Journal of Tourism Research*, **1**: 149–65.

Cooper, C., Fletcher, J., Gilbert, D., Shepherd, R. and Wanhill, S. (1998) *Tourism: Principles and Practices*, Harlow: Longman.

Downes, J. (1999) 'European Union progress on a common tourism sector policy', *Travel and Tourism Analyst*, **1**: 74–87.

Dredge, D. and Moore, S. (1992) 'A methodology for the integration of tourism in town planning', *Journal of Tourism Studies*, **3** (1): 8–21.

Hall, C.M. (1997) *Tourism in the Pacific Rim*, Melbourne: Longman Cheshire.

Hall, C.M. and Jenkins, J. (1995) *Tourism and Public Policy*, London: Routledge.

Hall, C.M. and Page, S.J. (eds) (2000) *Tourism in South and South East Asia: Issues and Cases*, Oxford: Butterworth-Heinemann.

Human, B. (1994) 'Visitor management in the public planning policy context: a case study of Cambridge', *Journal of Sustainable Tourism*, **2** (4): 221–30.

Leong, L. (1997) 'Commodifying ethnicity: state and ethnic tourism in Singapore' in M. Picard and R. Wood (eds) *Tourism, Ethnicity and the State in Asian and Pacific Societies*, Honolulu: Hawaii University Press: 71–98.

Oppermann, M. and Chon, K. (1997) *Tourism in Developing Countries*, London: Thomson Learning.

Page, S.J. (1999) *Transport and Tourism*, London: Addison Wesley Longman.

Page, S.J. and Hall, C.M. (1999) 'New Zealand', *International Tourism Report*, **4**: 47–76.

Page, S.J. and Thorn, K. (1997) 'Towards sustainable tourism planning in New Zealand: public sector planning responses', *Journal of Sustainable Tourism*, **5** (1): 59–77.

Pearce, D.G. (1989) *Tourist Development*, Harlow: Longman.

Pearce. D.G. (1992) *Tourist Organisations*, Harlow: Longman.

Raguraman, K. (1997) 'Airlines as instruments for nation building and national identity: a case study of Malaysia and Singapore, *Journal of Transport Geography*, **5** (4): 236–56.

Raguraman, K. (1998) 'Troubled passage to India', *Tourism Management*, **19** (6): 533–44.

Singh, A. and Chon, K. (1996) 'Marketing Singapore as an international destination', *Journal of Vacation Marketing*, **2** (3): 239–57.

Turner, J. (1997) 'The policy process', in B. Axford, G. Browning, R. Huggins, B. Rosamond and J. Turner, *Politics: An Introduction*, London: Routledge: 409–39.

Wall, G. and Nuriyanti, W. (1997) 'Marketing challenges and opportunities facing Indonesian tourism', *Journal of Travel and Tourism Marketing*, **6** (1): 69–84.

World Tourism Organization (1996) *Budgets of National Tourism Administrations: A Special Report*, Madrid: World Tourism Organization.

World Tourism Organization (1997) *Budgets and Marketing Plans of National Tourism Administrations*, Madrid: World Tourism Organization.

Zhang, G. (1995) 'China's tourism since 1978: policies, experiences and lessons learned', in A. Lew and L. Yu (eds) *Tourism In China: Geographic, Political and Economic Perspectives*, Boulder, Co.: Westview Press.

Zhang, H., King, C. and Ap, J. (1999) 'An analysis of tourism policy in modern China', *Tourism Management*, **20** (4): 471–86.

Further reading

Hall, C.M. and Jenkins, J. (1995) *Tourism and Public Policy*, London: Routledge.

Pearce, D.G. (1992) *Tourist Organisations*, Harlow: Longman.

Useful web addresses

A range of useful web resources is available which outline the destination attributes of different tourist destinations in addition to those sponsored by destination organizations such as national, regional and local tourism organizations. They include:

The CNN site:

http://www.cnn.com/travel/city.guides/index/html#profile

This site is useful since it contains a great deal of destination-specific data on individual destinations for the business and non-business traveller that can be searched by location.

The Yahoo! site

http://www.yahoo.com

which has a Yahoo! Travel section that can be searched by destination with information on:

- essentials
- facts at a glance
- history and culture for the destination
- activities and events at the destination
- attractions
- off the beaten track advice and tips
- transport advice
- further reading.

The *Lonely Planet Guide site* which is aimed at independent traveller and certainly one of the most authoritative sources of information for the traveller.

http://www.lonelyplanet.com

also has destination guides which can be searched by destination and they contain a good range of information that is independent and impartial and destination specific and complements the very good series of books which they also publish.

Section 4
Marketing tourism

The last chapter introduced the role of the public sector and the impact of national tourism organizations and other similar bodies which often promote and market destinations. This section of the book focuses on the issue of what marketing is in relation to tourism. Chapter 15 examines the many concepts and issues associated with tourism marketing, extending our understanding of the tools and techniques used by marketers in a tourism context. This is followed by a focus on how marketing is used in one particular context – the marketing and management of tourist destinations. An understanding of marketing and its concepts is fundamental to ascertaining how businesses and organizations involved with tourism communicate their message to consumers.

15 Marketing tourism: concepts and issues

Learning outcomes

After reading this chapter and answering the questions, you should be able to:

- Understand some of the main terms associated with marketing.
- Recognize the consequences of marketing in the tourism industry and be aware of its distinguishing features.
- Realize the importance of understanding the customers' needs, market segmentation and the linkages with aspects of tourist demand and motivation.
- Explain the role and nature of marketing plans, describing some of the main analytical techniques.

Overview

Tourism marketing is a fascinating subject, at the core of the tourism industry. As the nature of the tourism industry rapidly changes, so too does the nature of tourism marketing, at international, national, regional, destination and the firm level. Core marketing concepts and issues are fairly universal and constant, but the tourism marketing reflects some of the special characteristics of this industry. This chapter introduces a range of concepts and issues related to tourism marketing. There are numerous excellent texts dedicated in their entirety to this subject (most of which are referred to here), thus what is presented is, of necessity, an introduction. Nevertheless, marketing texts agree that a central theme of marketing relates to responding to the needs and wants of customers and this is reflected in the following sections.

Introduction

The concept of marketing first came about in the 1950s, from which time there has been some debate as to what exactly marketing consists of. Within the tourism literature (Cooper *et al.* 1998; Middleton 1995; Vellas and Becherel 1999) there seems to be a general acceptance of the definition provided by the UK Chartered Institute of Marketing (1984) that marketing is 'the management process responsible for identifying, anticipating and satisfying customer requirements profitably'.

In most organizations the marketing function is central to the structure of the firm. However, behind the marketing function is what is termed a 'marketing concept', a philosophy which helps to guide the firm's marketing activities. In general terms there are five identifiable marketing concepts that can influence any area of a firm's activities. These are shown in Exhibit 15.1.

In practice, different organizations define and apply their marketing activities in a way that is most relevant to their product or service. The tourism industry is regarded as a 'service' industry. In the context of the marketing needs of tourism services, there are several distinguishing attributes that differ from the marketing needs of a specific product. These characteristics are reflected in Exhibit 15.2.

Exhibit 15.2 shows us that the tourism product can be more accurately thought of as a combination of several different services. While some of the basic principles of marketing apply to all products, there are clearly some special considerations to make in investigating the tourism industry. Having said this, there are some further characteristics of marketing to ensure, in the case of tourism, that the firm is successful. These include:

- a customer orientation
- a focus on the firm's external environment
- accurate marketing research information, particularly in relation to customers and competitors
- products that meet tourists' needs
- differentiation, i.e. that the tourism firm's products are different in some way from the competition
- the manipulation of the various marketing opportunities in such a way to create customer satisfaction.

It is against this background that marketing managers in tourism firms need to operate. In most tourism firms the marketing function is at the heart of the firm's organizational strategy. Here, the most crucial question the marketing manager must ask herself is 'why should my customers buy my products, rather than those of my competitors' (Holloway and Robinson 1995: 23). The remainder of this chapter will introduce some of the relevant concepts and issues associated with answering this question.

Exhibit 15.1 **The marketing concept**

The product concept
An approach that assumes that customers are mainly interested in the quality, performance or features of the product. Thus marketing activities focus on product development and improvement.

The production concept
An approach which believes that customers are, generally, price sensitive. Here the aim will be to make products efficiently and distribute them widely enough to raise volume and drive down costs.

The selling concept
Assumes that customers need to be persuaded to buy enough of the firm's products. Here a greater emphasis will be placed on advertising and promotion.

The marketing concept
Has as its basis the importance of understanding customer needs and aiming to fulfil them more effectively than the competition. There is a more obvious link with marketing research and is likely to adopt a balance of the other concepts.

The societal concept
Here a concern for society is expressed, rather than simply satisfying customers and generating profits. Marketing approaches aim to encompass the interests of society as well as the customers concerned.

(Source: Adapted from Peattie 1992)

Exhibit 15.2 **Characteristics of tourism services**

Intangibility

Tourism as a service is essentially intangible. It is not possible to test out the tourism service before it is purchased. Opinions and attitudes may be sought beforehand, or a repeat purchase may rely upon previous holiday experiences, but ultimately the purchase of tourism products is the purchase of a service, i.e. something intangible.

Inseparability

In this sense the production of the service (say the holiday) and the consumption of it (by tourists) occurs at the same time. It is clear that the tourist needs to be present to consume the service, i.e. the two are inseparable. In fact, the tourist's use of the service is crucial to its overall success. Their participation and enjoyment of the holiday (the tourism service) is central.

Heterogeneity

In tourism, as in other services, it is often difficult to achieve standardization in the output of services. No two holidays are alike. Hotel rooms in the same establishment may differ, the weather changes or holidays may be designed for individual customers. Most accommodation providers would aim to have a 'standard' room, where customers can expect a 'norm'. However, it is often the case that tourism services do differ and hence heterogeneity is a feature of tourism.

Perishability

Tourism services cannot be stocked or held over. Hotel rooms or aircraft seats left vacant on one night or flight cannot be kept for future use. If they are not used when available, they are lost forever. Thus service products are said to be perishable.

Inelasticity of supply

Tourism products are inelastic in that often they cannot be easily adapted. If demand suddenly falls, this is unlikely to have a significant effect on the price. Tourism products are dependent on existing structures (hotels, transport and facilities) at destinations.

Elasticity of demand

While it is more difficult to quickly adapt tourism products, demand is very elastic. Sudden events, such as fuel price rises, terrorist acts, exchange rate changes can quickly influence demand. Moreover, certain destinations can quickly become less fashionable.

Complementarity

When a holiday is purchased, often it is not just a single service, but several sub-products that complement each other. Failure in one if these areas (e.g. airport delays) can seriously affect the overall experience.

High fixed costs

The cost of developing tourism products, such as a holiday, involves high fixed costs (hotels, aircraft and trains). Such investment is not a guarantee of future profits.

Labour intensity

Tourism is a labour-intensive industry and the tourist experience is greatly influenced by the skill of the staff they come into contact with.

(Source: Adapted from Baker 1993; Cannon 1992; Vellas and Becherel 1999)

The marketing mix

It is clearly important for marketers to have a thorough understanding of the tourism products a firm has to offer. However, long-term success calls for a clear understanding of how potential tourists respond to a number of variables when deciding what to purchase. Marketers need to recognize that it is the mix of these variables that will go a long way to determine the extent to which the firm satisfies the needs of the market. These variables are referred to as the marketing mix. Individually, they include the product, the price, physical distribution, intermediary or channel of distribution and promotion. This has been simplified to the four Ps of product, price, place and promotion. It is the contribution of these variables, which constitutes the total product and provides the basic opportunity for satisfying customer needs. The marketing mix is illustrated in Figure 15.1.

It can be seen from Figure 15.1 that different types of marketing decisions/marketing mixes will need to be made for different types of tourists. A tourism product aimed at retired people is unlikely to be advertised in a magazine for young people, for instance. Thus, as Vellas and Becherel (1999: 98) state 'different markets require different marketing mixes at different times in their life cycle'.

Figure 15.1 **The marketing mix**

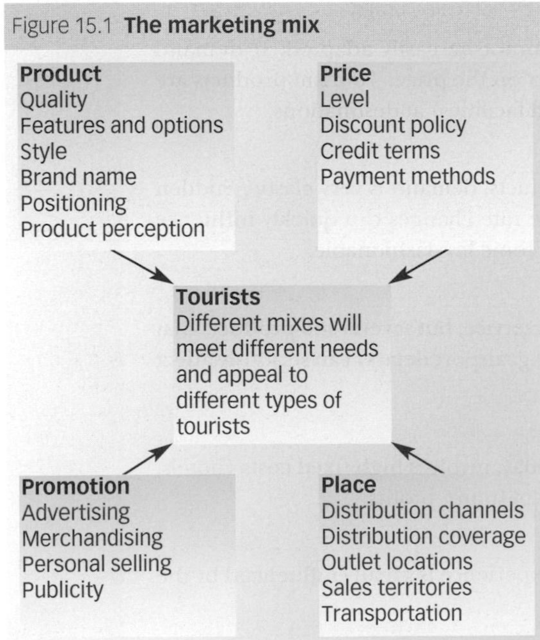

(Source: Developed from Cannon 1992; Holloway and Robinson 1995)

Within the tourism literature there is some debate as to whether the four Ps are comprehensive enough to reflect the nature of marketing decisions in the tourism industry. Cooper *et al.* (1998) call for more research, but believe that the four Ps offer a suitable framework. Vellas and Becherel (1999) refer to an additional three Ps being necessary, in the case of service providers. These are:

- *People.* In the tourism industry, people, i.e. staff are important particularly in terms of their skills of customer care, how friendly they are and their appearance.
- *Physical evidence.* Within accommodation, for example, considerations of the furnishings, décor, environment, ambience, layout, cleanliness and noise level are all important.
- *Process.* Here aspects such as how efficiently procedures work, for example, service time, waiting time, customer forms and documents all need to be evaluated.

However the marketing mix is defined, it is necessary that marketing mix decisions are aimed at the right target market and are consistent with the marketing concept of the particular tourism firm. Exhibit 15.3 reveals how the marketing mix should be targeted for a particular market, in this case outbound tourism from China. However, whatever the scenario for the tourism firm it is clear that knowing the customer and meeting their expectations is the only way to succeed. The next section will investigate this more thoroughly.

Knowing the customer

Marketers in the tourism industry, as marketers elsewhere, need to know all aspects of the buying behaviour of the customers within the firms target markets. In Chapter 4, we addressed the question 'Why do people go on holiday?' while the tourism marketer must understand this, he/she must also understand why some people choose to go to Ibiza while others choose Iceland. Moreover, why do some choose to travel independently, when others prefer

Exhibit 15.3 The marketing implications of Chinese cultural values

Mok and DeFranco (1999) note that China has one fifth of the world's population and the greatest number of potential customers in any country of the world. It is also predicted that China's outbound tourism market will grow significantly because travel restrictions have been relaxed and disposable income levels of a growing middle class are increasing. Based on a detailed review of literature a conceptual framework is proposed of dominant Chinese cultural values. Within this framework are developed a series of hypotheses, which are aimed at informing marketers and forming the basis for marketing mix decisions and further research:

- Chinese tourists are more likely to engage in shopping activities during their trips.
- Chinese consumers are more likely to be influenced by opinion leaders than are westerners.
- Chinese consumers are more responsive to relationship marketing techniques.
- Chinese consumers are more likely to be brand conscious than westerners.
- Tourism services consumption decisions for individuals in China are likely to be the result of group decisions.
- Chinese consumers are less responsive to advertising which is openly critical of competitors.
- Chinese consumers are more sensitive to products or services which concern numbers (e.g. certain numbers (8) are associated with luck or getting rich, while other numbers (4) have negative associations).

As China's economy grows, the demand for consumer products and services will also grow. However, if tourism firms wish to enter this market, understanding the Chinese cultural values and how the Chinese shape their preferences and expectations is a necessary first step. From this, the implications for a successful marketing mix will become clear.

(Source: Developed from Mok and DeFranco 1999)

to travel as a group? In fact, the questions tourism marketers need to answer in respect of tourist buying behaviour can be broken down further:

- Who are the customers/tourists?
- What types of tourism products do they buy?
- Who do they travel with (alone, couple, family)?
- Which suppliers do they use?
- What are the needs they aim to satisfy?
- Where/how do they buy their tourism products?
- When do they buy them (last minute, in advance)?
- How long do they go on holiday for?
- How often do they travel?
- How much are they prepared to pay?
- How do they decide which tourism products to buy?
- What influences their travel decisions?
- How do previous holidays affect future plans?

The answers to these questions will clearly help the marketer to decide how best to market their products. For most tourism firms it is unlikely that their range of products will appeal equally to all types of potential tourist. Rather, the products are aimed, primarily at particular types oft tourist (e.g. young adults, who are singles, travelling with friends, without children). Such groups represent the 'target market'. Vellas and Becherel (1999: 59) refer to three options for targeting markets.

Undifferentiated marketing

Where the firm tries to sell as much as possible and their products have to the broadest appeal. This would be a characteristic of mass market tour operators.

Airtours plc for example of Airtours and Cresta holidays (among others) under the UK Leisure Group division of the parent company (www.airtours.com).

Differentiated marketing

Here the firm perhaps aims at particular target markets and designs separate products and marketing programmes for each market. The costs to the firm of this are larger, but total sales may be greater. For example JMC offer a Summersun brochure for summer holidays to various destinations in one brochure, their target markets are also differentiated in terms of 'Essentials' (sun, sea and sand holidays for under £99), Wintersun holidays, Airfares only, All Inclusive holidays, Familyworld and Select (for top of the range holidays) (www.jmc.com).

Concentrated marketing

In this approach the firm concentrates on a specific target market. Rather than aim at all tourists, the firm chooses a very specific market and aims to capture a large share of this particular market. Guerba, for example, is a long-established specialist tour operator concentrating on trekking and adventure holidays to destinations such as the Himalayas, Africa and Central America (www.guerba.com).

While a strategy to approach a target market is necessary, it is also important to understand that different tourists buy their holidays in different ways. Some people buy a holiday after careful study of travel brochures and guides, press reviews, discussions with their friends and colleagues and after a careful comparison of competing products. Others, who purchase the same holiday, may do so on impulse, after happening to see it advertised. For the purchase of most products, there is a buying process, as shown in Figure 15.2.

Figure 15.2 has some similar attributes to Figure 4.1 regarding the holiday decision-making process. Here, it can be seen that the experience of the holiday feeds back into future buying decisions. As mentioned, some may take time with each stage and consider alternatives carefully, while others pass rapidly through to the actual purchase.

Figure 15.2 **The buying process**

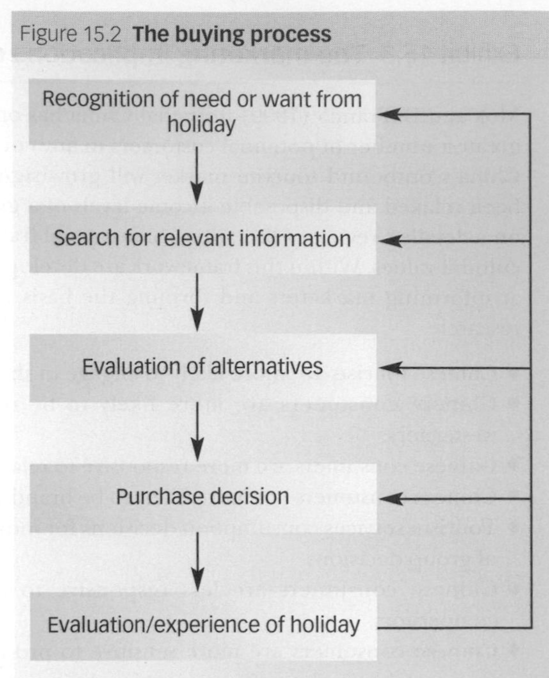

At each stage in the buying process there are implications for the tourism marketer. Of particular importance is how potential tourists search for relevant information on which to base their decisions. This is of special relevance in the tourism industry where attracting new visitors to a destination or new customers to a tourism service is always necessary. Here, marketers need to communicate their products to new customers, but to do this they need to know where the potential customer searches for that information. Exhibit 15.4 describes a study in this context.

Exhibit 15.4 shows that, among other aspects, new visitors vary considerably in their approaches to buying tourist products. Thus, it can be concluded that buying behaviour is a complex process. While it may be possible to identify some common characteristics, a wide or 'shotgun' approach to communicating to customers may be wasteful as it fails to recognize who the customer is and how they behave. Tourism products and services have to be targeted, not only to target markets, but often to specific types of consumer. This approach, known as market segmentation, is discussed in the next section.

Exhibit 15.4 **Buyer behaviour: strategies to reach the first-time visitor**

Vogt *et al.* (1998) outline a study investigating how tourists search for and use information about a chosen destination they have not visited before. Self-selected samples were questioned about their information searches regarding travel to a series of destinations in the US Midwest. The results found that the following information sources/places (in rank order) were most likely to be used:

1 Own travel files (and past experience)
2 Highway Welcome Centers (tourist information)
3 Family and friends
4 Local libraries
5 Bookshops
6 Magazine articles/advertisements
7 Newspaper articles/advertisements
8 Television
9 Radio

However, against this there were significant differences between those who were 'well travelled' versus those who considered themselves to be 'inexperienced' travellers. The former group was more likely to rely heavily on their prior experiences, whereas inexperienced travellers were more likely to respond to magazine and newspapers, then possibly to seek more information from bookshops and libraries. Other factors influencing peoples' information searches included how familiar they were with the destination, the length of time allowed for planning a trip and intention to travel. The study concluded by arguing that strategies by marketers for communicating to first-time and repeat visitors should be separate marketing exercises. First-time visitors were likely to be attracted by special events at the destination or by accommodation deals featured in magazines and newspapers.

(Source: Adapted from Vogt *et al.* 1998)

Market segmentation in tourism

In Chapter 4 we identified different types of tourists and classified them into groups, on the basis of their motivations to travel. This came after discussion of factors influencing tourist motivations. In this context, market segmentation is the 'process whereby producers organise their knowledge of customer groups and select for particular attention those whose needs and wants are best able to supply with their products' (Middleton 1995: 65). Target markets can be segmented in many ways. For instance, in Chapter 4 factors influencing motivation were used as a basis and in Chapter 3 factors affecting tourism demand were noted. Such variables could be used to start segmenting potential customers in this context too. These could be considered under several headings of consumer characteristics:

- *Geographic* – region, climate, urban, rural.
- *Demographic* – age, sex, ethnicity, social class.
- *Personal and psychological* – education level, lifestyle, values, beliefs, attitudes.
- *Sociocultural* – family influences, peer group influences, cultural norms, status.
- *Economic* – economic climate, employment security, political stability.
- *Buying behaviour* – previous experience, purchasing preferences, attitudes to adverts.

Marketing research can help to classify into segments customer groups on the basis of how important these variables are in determining buyer characteristics. By understanding customers, marketers can develop strategies to better the firm's position in the marketplace. In addition, segmentation can be used to determine the response of different segments to a marketing strategy. Overall though, as Vellas and Becherel (1999: 60) state market segmentation can improve the 'competitive position and better serve the needs of customers'. Achieving advantage over the competition introduces a new dimension in marketing which we will turn to next.

Competition

Identifying a market and the presentation of a distinctive service to a market segment are only the first stages of effectively developing a market. Having developed the tourism product, the firm must hold onto it. This involves competitor analysis. Kotler (1988) argues that firms need to know the following about their competitors:

- Who they are.
- What their strategies are.
- What their objectives are.
- What their strengths and weaknesses are.
- How they react.

Some firms develop approaches to their target markets that seem to assume they and their customers exist in a vacuum. This approach enables rivals to learn from their mistakes, exploit their weaknesses and enter the market. In fact, doing this is referred to as 'poisoned apple marketing' (Cannon 1992). As a form of product development, by allowing the competition to be the first with a particular type of tourism product, the competitor takes the biggest risks. However, where lead times are long or the competitor has recognized the risks and overcome them, they may have gained a considerable advantage.

Most firms do not like the uncertainties and risks of competition. Many would prefer to monopolize the market and have the largest share. In 1998, the small number of large tour operators in the UK prompted an investigation by the UK government through its agency, the Monopolies and Mergers Commission. Nevertheless, by increasing its share of the market, firms can minimize its harsh effects. In Chapter 6 we saw that in order to reduce competition firms can either combine with their rivals (integration in its various forms) or else they can agree to co-operate with each other. In terms of integration, this can be through merger (firms agree to amalgamate) or by takeover (one firm acquires sufficient shares in another to have a controlling interest, with or without consent). It can be seen, therefore, that within this type of business environment a regular feature of tourism marketers should be the review of the competition. As we shall see in the next section, this should range widely to include external threats to the firm as well as the immediate rivals.

Planning for the future

Like any other organization, firms in the tourism industry aim to survive, make a profit and, in many cases, grow. To do this requires that the firm have a strategic marketing plan in place which is flexible and a regular feature of managerial activity. Thus, typical questions that need to be addressed to inform planning for the future include:

- What is the core business and what are the firm's overall objectives?
- What is the current position in the marketplace?
- What are the firm's marketing objectives?
- What is the nature of the environment in which the firm operates and how will this change in the future?
- What strategies are there to achieve marketing objectives?
- What tactics are there to achieve the strategies?
- Is there a sufficient budget for this activity?

Generally speaking, a variety of techniques need to be applied to address such questions. Previous sections have introduced the need for customer and competitor analysis, in planning for the future two particular questions are pertinent: where are we now, and where do we want to go? In determining this, PEST and SWOT analyses are helpful.

PEST analysis

PEST analysis is an acronym for 'Political, Economic, Socio-cultural and Technological', and refers to the external environment within which the firm operates. To inform future plans, this method provides a framework to help investigate the various factors that will affect the firm. While some of these are beyond the control of the individual firm, an awareness of them is important.

Political

What is the political environment of the destination area? Are there visa restrictions; are there political stability or government elections? What is the government's attitude to tourism?

Economic

What are the economic positions of both generating and destination areas? What affect will exchange rates, inflation, credit charges, value of investments, labour costs, unemployment, have on the firm?

Socio-cultural

What are the attitudes of the host community to tourism? What are the attitudes of tourists in the target market? What effect will new fashions and preferences have? What is the role of the family?

Technology

What are the technological advances relevant to the firm? What effects will new forms of promotion, distribution, ticketing and the internet have?

PEST analysis is particularly important in the tourism industry; as we have seen the industry is so vulnerable to rapid change. Exhibit 15.5 shows how political stability is a prerequisite for tourism. A firms response to the ever changing market involves all departments in an organization. While PEST provides an awareness of the external environment, SWOT analysis is one of the main tools used to develop business strategies.

SWOT analysis

SWOT is an acronym for 'Strengths, Weaknesses, Opportunities and Threats'. This technique provides a framework which enables an organization to assess their position within a market in relation to the competition. Information gathered in a marketing audit can assess the company's internal strengths and weaknesses and the external opportunities and threats that it faces. SWOT analysis is not limited to the context of marketing; it can be applied to the whole company, to destinations or tourism products. Some of the common factors are now considered.

Strengths and weaknesses – internal

Products, people, the organization, financial position.

Opportunities and threats – external

Competition, nature of the market, new technology, economic position, legal framework, political situation.

These and other methods of planning for the future are valuable techniques for the tourism marketer. However, as shown in Chapter 2, tourism can be particularly susceptible to sudden changes and events. This phenomenon poses particular problems for tourism marketers. Exhibit 15.5 illustrates this in the context of war and how marketers are planning to cope.

Approaches to marketing planning

Marketing plans are central to a firm's strategy. According to Edgell *et al.* (1999: 113) 'the key is to have a well-thought-out marketing plan'. Specifically for tourism, Edgell *et al.* (1999) suggest a six-stage framework to help marketers analyse the marketplace and develop a strategic marketing plan. While such plans will obviously differ, in accordance with the particular tourism product, these stages represent a useful structure.

Needs analysis

Here the first step is to articulate the general objectives of the organization. This might include increasing the number of customers, the services they purchase and their repeat custom.

Research and analysis

Detailed analysis in all respects is an important second stage. Such methods may include SWOT and other

Exhibit 15.5 **Marketing in the Republic of Croatia**

The Republic of Croatia declared its independence from the former Yugoslavia in 1990. Prior to this, tourism in the region was making in excess of US$ 2 billion, with two thirds coming from inbound tourism. Due to the war, the situation in 1991–1992 radically changed:

- Some 22 per cent of the natural areas and 37 per cent of areas with cultural or historical significance were either occupied (to 1993) or destroyed.
- The number of accommodation facilities was reduced by one third.
- Direct war damage on hotels and the renovation of other buildings necessary (after being used by displaced persons) was estimated at 3 billion Austrian Schillings (approximately US$ 215 million).
- Total tourist revenue was estimated to have fallen by 68 per cent.
- The loss of bed nights for the accommodation sector for the period 1990–1995 was estimated as 71 per cent for inbound tourism and 43 per cent for internal tourism.
- The total loss of income in all aspects as a result of the war for Croatia was estimated as being a minimum of US$10 billion.

To rebuild the tourism industry after such a devastating effect was, nevertheless, a priority. To do this the Croatian government instigated the Main Tourist Plan of Croatia. Strategic marketing at the national level was complemented by regional and local level marketing plans. Central to the plan was a SWOT analysis of tourism in Croatia. This found the accommodation sector to be a particular weakness, while low prices were a strength. To rebuild the tourism industry the strengths of good scenery, climate and the hospitality of the people represents a marketing 'opportunity'. It is hoped that by 'following the market' and learning from competitors (e.g. Turkey) Croatia will, once again, be able to create an appropriate tourism identity.

(Source: Adapted from Meler and Ruzic 1999)

types of examination of the marketing function within the organization. Externally PEST analysis is useful and other forms of competitor analysis. Customer research is also important, to include market segmentation and target market identification.

Creative infusion

Edgell *et al.* (1999) suggest that after reviewing the results of the research a stage of creativity, of finding ideas to distinguish the firm's marketing plan from its competitors should be undertaken.

Strategic positioning

To this point the firm's position in terms of its current and future customer needs, competitive advantage and competitor's position, together with a creative component has helped to shape the strategic position. This also refers to how the firm perceives its customers against its competitors' perceptions.

Marketing plan development

Each market segment should have a separate marketing plan to capture new and repeat custom. Such plans have SMART goals (specific, measurable, achievable, relevant and time bound). The accomplishment of goals is achieved through an identification of critical success factors (tasks that are vital to overall success). A definition of the marketing mix is also important to include aspects of pricing and promotion strategies.

Training, implementation, evaluation and adjustment

Training all who might be involved with the tourism product or service (including other organizations) is essential. Following this, once implemented, continual evaluation and adjustment of plans are needed.

Conclusion

Harris and Katz (1996; 26) state that tourism marketing 'is not an easy task ... it is more than just advertising; it requires a co-ordinated, phased plan involving dozens of specialised tasks'. This chapter has introduced the marketing role in tourism and stressed the importance of knowing the customer and competitors. Further, of crucial importance to the tourism marketer is being able to plan for the future by carefully designed, flexible marketing plans. As changes in tourism, involving technology and lifestyle preferences, constantly evolve, marketers who are able to adapt their strategies and marketing methods accordingly are more likely to achieve success.

Discussion questions

1. Identify a firm in the tourism industry. From the information you have, how would you describe its marketing mix?
2. Critically analyse the marketing implications of the fact that many markets for a range of tourism and leisure products are experiencing static growth, volatile consumer demand and intense competition.
3. Critically evaluate the role and importance of the following in contemporary tourism and marketing:
   - the World Wide Web
   - brand management
   - sponsorship.
4. Discuss the contention that the battle for customers in tomorrow's tourism industry will be fought not over price but over hearts and minds.

References

Baker, M.J. (ed.) (1993) *Chartered Institute of Marketing: The Marketing Book*, second edition, Oxford: Butterworth-Heinemann.

Cannon, T. (1992) *Basic Marketing*, third edition, London: Cassell.

Chartered Institute of Marketing (1984) in L. Lumsden (1997) *Tourism Marketing*, London: Thomson Learning.

Cooper, C., Gilbert, D., Fletcher, J., Wanhill, S. and Shepherd, R. (1998) *Tourism: Principles and Practice*, second edition, London: Longman.

Edgell, D.L., Ruf, K.M. and Agarwal, A. (1999) 'Strategic marketing planning for the tourism industry', *Journal of Travel and Tourism Marketing*, **8** (3): 111–20.

Harris, G. and Katz, K. (1996) *Promoting International Tourism*, Los Angeles: The American Group.

Holloway, J.C. and Robinson, C. (1995) *Marketing for Tourism*, Harlow: Longman.

Kotler, P. (1988) *Marketing Management: Analysis, Planning, Implementation and Control*, sixth edition, New Jersey: Prentice Hall.

Meler, M. and Ruzic, D. (1999) 'Marketing identity of the tourist product of the Republic of Croatia', *Tourism Management*, **20** (4): 635–43.

Middleton, V.T.C. (1995) *Marketing in Travel and Tourism*, Oxford: Butterworth-Heinemann.

Internet resources

By going to the weblink at www.thomsonlearning.co.uk students can access the following two studies on the Thomson Learning website. The first study is by A. Seaton and M. Bennett (1996) *Marketing Tourism Products: Concepts, Issues, Cases* and examines the marketing concept as it applies to tourism. It examines the peculiarities of tourism as a service and product and how it differs from other services.

The second study by R. Wright (1999) *Marketing: Origins, Concepts and Environment* is a useful complement to the first study since it is an overview of the marketing concept, the way it evolved, issues of definition and the way it has emerged as a powerful tool for businesses.

Mok, C. and DeFranco, A.L. (1999) 'Chinese cultural values: their implications for travel and tourism marketing', *Journal of Travel and Tourism Marketing*, **8** (2): 99–114.
Peattie, K. (1992) *Green Marketing*, London: Longman.
Vellas, F. and Becherel, L. (eds.) (1999) *The International Marketing of Travel and Tourism: A Strategic Approach*, London: Macmillan.
Vogt, C.A., Stewart, S.I. and Fesenmaier, D.R. (1998) 'Communication strategies to reach first-time visitors', *Journal of Travel and Tourism Marketing*, **7** (2): 69–89.

Further reading

Holloway, J.C. and Robinson, C. (1995) *Marketing for Tourism*, Harlow: Longman.
Lumsden, L. (1997) *Tourism Marketing*, London: Thomson Learning.
Middleton, V.T.C. (1995) *Marketing in Travel and Tourism*, Oxford: Butterworth-Heinemann.
Vellas, F. and Becherel, L. (eds.) (1999) *The International Marketing of Travel and Tourism: A Strategic Approach*, London: Macmillan.

Useful web addresses

www.airtours.com
www.jmc.com
www.guerba.com

16 Marketing tourism: destination management

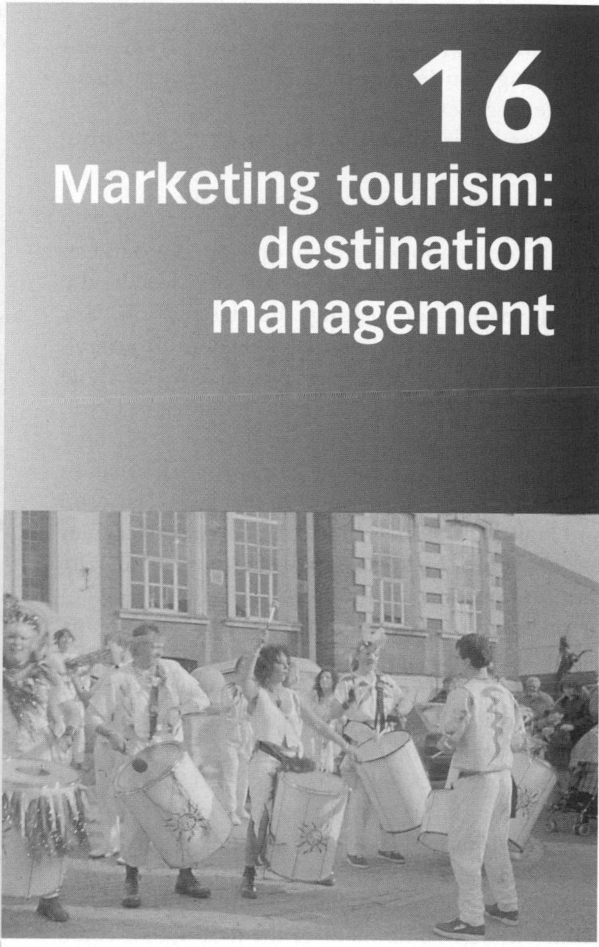

Learning outcomes

After reading this chapter, and answering the questions, you should be able to:

- Understand the main components of destinations and the influences on tourist flows to them.
- Recognize some of the particular 'pull' factors associated with the final decision to select a destination.
- Be aware of aspects of marketing tourist destinations including marketing planning, segmentation, imagery and promotion.
- Understand the need for development policies at tourist destinations.

Overview

Although the term 'destination' has several meanings, in our context it can be thought of as the target area that tourists will visit. As such, several dimensions are important in the successful management of destinations. This chapter will, first, investigate what destinations are and how they are used. Second, discussion will focus on particular aspects of destination selection before an examination of destination marketing and policy formulation.

Introduction

Tourist destinations are a core component of most tourists' holiday experiences, whether they visit a coastal resort as part of a mass package holiday through to urban destinations where visitors seek a city break or experience to a rural or wilderness experience with the isolation and tranquillity without the numbers of people present in urban and coastal resorts. In essence, a destination is a place in which visitors spend time as part of their tourist trip and is usually the place they stay in although it can be just one part of a broader itinerary where a wide range of destinations are visited as part of a coach or cruise ship holiday. Within any tourist destination, it is possible to discern a number of elements that coalesce to make it a place to visit and stay for tourists. In this respect, a destination comprises a number of core components. Some authors (e.g. Cooper *et al.* 1998: 103) refer to these components as the '4As':

- Attractions
- Amenities (e.g. accommodation, food and beverage outlets, entertainment, retailing and other services)
- Access (e.g. transport networks and infrastructure)
- Ancillary services (e.g. local organizations).

Popular destinations are often developed around an attraction (Swarbrooke 1999), and may well be the initial reason for visiting the destination. For example, a tourist destination might develop around a natural, built or cultural attraction, such as Table Mountain in South Africa or the Pyramids in Egypt. As for amenities, access and ancillary services, these can either make it possible to visit the destination and enhance the experience of that visit (Davidson and Maitland 1997). 'These component services may be provided by different organisations in the different sectors of the industry (private and public) or on some occasions be delivered by one organisation as an integrated package' (Rogers and Slinn 1993: 5). In the last case, examples such as Center Parcs and Sandals Beach Resorts in Europe, and the international French chain Club Med provide 'all-inclusive packages' (see Chapters 2 and 9). With this type of holiday it may be easier for the tourism organization to better control the standard of quality. However, in other destinations, where there is less uniformity of quality across the destination a failure in one component of the destination could detract from what might otherwise have been a very satisfactory holiday experience.

The careful management of tourist destinations is crucial if tourism is to be maintained at acceptable levels. We have seen in previous chapters how volatile the industry is (e.g. Chapter 2) and susceptible to rapid change. One dimension of this is changes in consumer tastes. As tourists become increasingly more experienced and sophisticated in their tastes, their expectations from tourist destinations have increased. Another dimension is that if development at a destination is not managed in a controlled way it may be possible that aspects of the destination (e.g. natural beauty) are lost. As Davidson and Maitland (1997: 95) state 'one reason tourism needs to be managed is that the market response to increasing demands for tourism activities often leads to unacceptable adverse impacts: to the environment; to the local economy; or to the host population'. To combat this Mathieson and Wall (1982: 111) argue that:

> long term strategies provide control and responsibility to prevent the destination exceeding capacity and the inevitable decline in visitation that follows. It is possible to devise appropriate strategies for destinations at each stage of their life cycle such that the destination formula is constantly reviewed and adjusted in order to achieve sustainable tourism, as well as meeting customer demands.

Tourism destinations are made up of different groups, sometimes referred to as stakeholders. Exhibit 16.1 shows how an attempt was made to recognize the needs of different groups who were affected by a tourism development strategy. In most case these stakeholders include:

- *The host community*. This refers to local people who live and work in the area where tourism development takes place.
- *The tourism industry*. In many cases the industry is behind the actual development and aims to achieve a good return on its investments.
- *The public sector*. As shown in Exhibit 16.1, the public sector often has an important management role. Often tourism is seen as an opportunity to provide employment, increase income and prompt development at a variety of scales.
- *Tourists*. Though not generally involved in new destinations, in developing existing destinations, tourists are looking for a pleasant holiday and a good level of service at the destination.
- *Other groups*. In individual destinations there may be concerns from other persons or groups, such as pressure groups and local chambers of commerce.

There are examples of good practice evident in many areas and clearly good destination management is not only achieving environmental or socio-cultural objectives but economic ones too. One example, the coastal region of South Sinai, Egypt is cited by Shackley (1999). South Sinai is among the fastest growing resort areas and located in a fragile desert environment. Consequently, some particularly sensitive areas have been protected and ideas put forward for an aerial tramway between a village and the top of Mount Sinai. Other measures proposed include the development of a visitor centre and specified walking and camel trails. Inevitably a place such as Mount Sinai with its cultural and religious significance is bound to attract

Exhibit 16.1 **Resort development strategy in Mexico**

In the 1960s, Mexico adopted a national-scale approach for developing new beach resorts. This came about after a realization that, while Mexico had a long tourism tradition, there was a greater potential for tourism development. Added to this, Mexico had no long-term policies, tourism objectives, funding and marketing mechanisms, nor any criteria for tourism planning and development.

To address these issues, the Bank of Mexico conducted a detailed examination of the tourism resources available. Five potential tourist resorts were identified: Cancun (on the Caribbean coast); Ixtapa (between Mexico City and Acapulco); Los Cabos and Loreto (both on the Pacific coast in the southern part of the peninsula of Baja California); Bahas de Hautulco (on the Pacific coast in the state of Oxaca). The locations of these sites are shown in Figure 16.1.

The criteria for their selection included considerations of:

- land ownership
- climatic conditions
- environmental impact
- soil type
- transportation access
- telecommunications
- closeness to population centres
- the socio-economic levels of the local population
- the host community's experience of and attitudes to tourism.

In addition, the five locations had good beaches, scenic surroundings, climatic desirability and the availability of land for development. The Mexican government established a tourism fund and set up an agency called INFRATUR (a Spanish acronym for the National Fund for Tourism Infrastructure). INFRATUR set about developing two resorts in the early 1970s. This involved identifying land use zones for hotels, residential, commercial, public facilities and conservation areas. Transportation networks and an airport were also developed. Following the initial success of these areas, the government upgraded the Department of Tourism to cabinet secretariat level and developed a new agency (FONATUR) to replace INFRATUR. Important precedents now were to gain private investment for tourism development activities and to continue to development in the remaining resorts. By the late 1980s this had been achieved and FONATUR estimated that the five resorts now accounted for a quarter of all tourists visiting Mexico.

In this case the resort development strategy was based on identifying problems, establishing objectives and formulating policies, followed by a strategy for developing tourist destinations. For the 1960s the idea of planned and integrated resorts was quite innovative. The government of the day had recognized that well-planned resorts were less likely to generate negative environmental and socio-cultural impacts, while providing a better tourist experience. Local populations benefited in terms of employment opportunities and in setting up smaller scale tourism services. Overall, therefore, this strategy greatly assisted Mexico in realizing its tourism potential

(Source: Inskeep 1994)

Figure 16.1 **Location of selected resorts in Mexico**

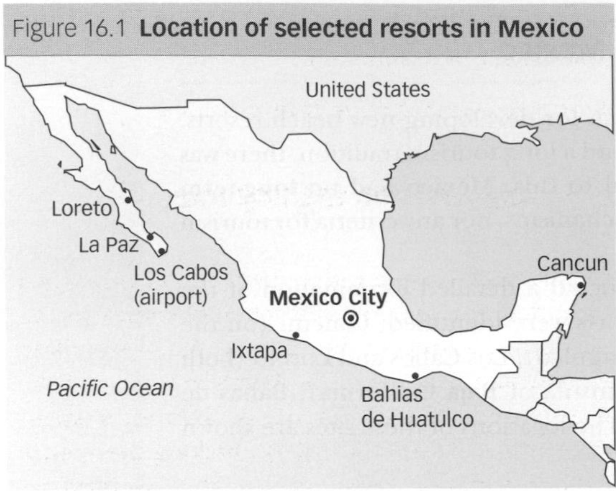

numerous visitors, but these measures will hopefully divert pressure away from its current concentration on sensitive areas and have the added benefits of educating visitors and using the indigenous population in the workforce.

Patterns of destination use and influences on tourist flows

According to Rogers and Slinn (1995: 120): 'Tourist demand fluctuates on an hourly, daily, weekly and seasonal basis, but the service has to be delivered when demanded.' For most tourism products there is a seasonal cycle of peak demand in the 'high' season offset by far reduced levels of demand in the 'low' season. This pattern of use can have major implications for the management of destinations. During the high season resources at some destinations can become so overstretched that the visitor experience suffers due to congestion, overcrowding and shortages in supply. Similarly in the low season demand may be such that facilities are closed down for long periods of the year. Clearly these issues have an impact on tourist flows and the host population. Where there are high peaks and troughs in demand over the season there is often over-booking, high prices and overcrowding, all of which are unsatisfactory for the tourist and industry alike. If tourists do not receive a satisfactory experience then the likelihood of return is lessened and ultimately the destination loses its reputation. The responses to lessen the worst effects of seasonality vary, related to the individual circumstances of each destination. Some attempt to shift demand to the shoulder months (mid-way between low and high season) by price setting may assist in this. Recent research by Commons and Page (2001) indicated that the tourism industry may be reluctant to reduce prices even in the shoulder season to stimulate demand even when tourists see this as a major factor which would promote visitation and spending in the destination region.

The extent to which destination management can influence tourist flows and patterns of use is limited in some senses. As previously mentioned there are numerous extrinsic factors beyond the control of the industry that can drastically impede or create tourist demand. Some destinations where the attractions are particularly strong may face great difficulty in stemming excessive demand. In Venice and in the Yellowstone National Park, visitor numbers are restricted at peak times and essentially the destination is 'closed' to more tourists. Such measures enable visitors to have a satisfactory experience and the limited numbers help to ensure that the destination does not become too degraded. The level of marketing is another means by which the patterns of use can be influenced. To limit numbers a destination may effectively be 'de-marketed', i.e. little information produced and limited promotion. While this may be useful at some destinations, others with an international reputation or where well-known festivals or sporting events are being hosted, may mean that these methods may not be particularly effective. As mentioned in Chapter 4, differentiated marketing efforts aimed at particular market segments may be a useful strategy. Knowing the customer is essential so that a destination is successful in positioning itself to meet and exceed the needs of a particular market segment. This, of course, can work conversely when the needs are not known or understood. Holloway (1994) for instance, notes that the construction of airports on the smaller Greek islands led to increased tourist flows, but a reduction in the number of high-spending wealthier tourists who preferred the relative isolation of the islands when they had previously only been served by a ferry service.

Other methods of influencing tourist flows to a destination and its patterns of use include variations in price and direct intervention by local authorities. Within the tourism industry there are many influences on pricing, all of which have implications for the management of destinations. In some locations the price of tourism products may be high where the market is price inelastic and such customers are willing to pay high prices to retain the notion of 'exclusivity' (for example at the luxury resorts of Malibu and Monaco). Alternatively, local authorities may use legislation to restrict tourist numbers or limit development. Examples include visa restrictions and a ban on the use of private cars. Such measures may be used to stem the number of tourists or as an attempt to attract certain types of tourist (high spending) or divert tourists to other destinations where there is spare capacity.

It can be seen, therefore, that careful and sympathetic management at the tourist destination can be used to influence tourist flows and patterns of use. This may well be easier when there are fewer 'components' of a destination, but successful marketing and pricing strategies can attract tourists out of season and encourage the sustainable use of a destination.

Selecting a destination

In Chapter 4 (Tourist motivation) we saw that to understand what makes an individual select a particular holiday destination required the examination of various 'push' and 'pull' factors. This explanation showed how motivation 'pushes' people into making a decision to travel to satisfy a need and then how they are 'pulled' or attracted to a destination. It was argued that these push and pull factors help us to understand why people want to travel and the destinations they choose to visit.

In selecting a destination it was noted that a range of personal and family influences (age, life-cycle, gender) and social and situational influences (work, income, social class) were both constraints and opportunities for individuals in their tourism decision-making. While these and other aspects such as money and time are pertinent in destination selection, there are other aspects, which are of particular relevance in the final selection of a tourism destination. These include:

- family decision-making roles
- satisfaction with destination services
- personal recommendation
- tourist use of destinations.

These aspects will be briefly investigated.

Family decision-making roles

Morgan (1996) suggests that the family often act as a single decision-making unit when it comes to the selection of a tourism destination. When travelling together all members of the family are users of the tourism product. The presence of children is particularly influential (Bruni 1990) affecting the nature of the destination selection, activities undertaken whilst there and the distance travelled. For other types of family unit, Fodness (1992) found that young couples often equally share in the gathering of information about potential destinations. However, these roles change through the family life-cycle. Zalaton (1998) noted differences in husband and wife roles in destination selection. While the former may have more influence in financial aspects, the latter was particularly important in gathering information and the actual selection of the destination.

Satisfaction with destination services

Laws (1995) notes how labour intensive the tourism industry is and in terms of the contact tourists are likely to have with those working in the industry. Many of these are associated with workers based at or associated with the destination. For instance, before travel to the destination has begun contact may have been made with travel agents of the national tourism organization. In the journey to the destination airline and airport staff, customs officials may have been met. During their stay contact with workers associated with the accommodation, catering, entertainment or at attractions is also likely to have taken place. The important issue here is that the nature and quality of the contact/association with those at or in some way related to the destination will feed into current or future decisions on destination selection. The extent to which people are satisfied with services at the destination is, therefore, crucial for repeat custom.

Plate 16.1 A Brazilian-style band playing in Exeter to promote a new arts and crafts venue
Such features are an important element of the ambience and image of a destination and can affect the tourist's feelings about a visit.

phenomenon in most destination areas'. The realization that the uncontrolled growth of tourism in many destinations has, in fact, destroyed the very resource on which it was founded (Pearce 1991). This suggests that destination policy formulation will be the key to a more sustainable approach to tourism development. The use of the destination life-cycle (see Chapter 2) is worthwhile as an organizing framework for destination development. The aim here would be to encourage collaborative policy-making across the industry and enable the development of management strategies to achieve sustainable levels of tourism.

A central problem, though, is that both tourism development and tourist activity have varying positive and negative impacts on tourist destinations and on the different stakeholders who are involved. Nevertheless, the economic, social and environmental impacts of tourism are often concentrated in destination areas and it is therefore vital that sound destination policy formulation takes place. Laws (1995) argues for such policies to adopt an holistic view to anticipate and control the industry's effects and establish a range of inputs necessary for the better development of the destination.

When setting out on destination policy formulation, the context of any regional or national tourism plans should be considered in the hope that a more integrated tourism system will result (Gunn 1993; Inskeep 1994). Policy formulation provides the framework to allow a destination to develop and cope with change. Often a useful starting point is to examine the history of a destination's development to see how previous conflicts arose and were reconciled. By understanding how a destination has reached its present stage in development, policies can be better informed to achieve the desired future.

The example of Mallorca is often quoted, where a policy of u-turn on the largest Balearic Island indicated a specific reaction by Spanish tourism authorities to the problems of mass tourism (Davidson 1992; Laws 1995; Morgan 1996). By the late 1980s a variety of problems were faced by the once popular tourist destination. These included an aged tourism infrastructure, environmental deterioration, low-yielding businesses, a reliance on German and UK markets, and a lack of local marketing control all at a time when consumers were demanding greater levels of quality. As a result the Spanish authorities developed policies to improve the quality, widen the customer base and implement controls for development. In one sense, the need for such policies could have been anticipated earlier, with Mallorca clearly having reached the stagnation/decline stage in its life-cycle. A realization of this might have pre-empted certain policy decisions and highlighted the need for a more sustainable approach. If one accepts the underlying assumptions behind the destination life-cycle then it is fair to assume that destinations face an inevitable decline and may be the cause of their own destruction. This comes about through uncontrolled growth and lack of planning in relation to resource use. If successful destination development policies are in place which can anticipate change then destination life-cycles can be extended.

While historical knowledge is helpful, fundamental to the development of a destination is a detailed knowledge of the nature of resources that are available (Laws 1995). An audit of such resources may highlight certain opportunities and assist the planning/policy formulation processes. An audit of resources used in conjunction with other research techniques is valuable to gain a full picture of the possible impacts on the destination by the tourism industry. It is fair to say that the auditing of resources at destinations should be an on-going process so that problems can be identified at an early stage.

Another dimension of the destination policy formulation process is the consideration of the various stakeholders and external influences that will impinge upon the decision-making process. Given the wide variety of people involved, disagreements are inevitable. Laws (1995: 39) notes that parties can be 'poles apart', with some arguing for 'further development, others opposing it, perhaps even arguing for a reduction of current levels of tourism activity'. Clearly if destination policies are to be successful all of those involved with the destination need to be involved with the formulation of policies at various stages (Gunn 1993; Inskeep 1994; Murphy 1985). There are examples of successful collaborative policy-making and Inskeep (1994) notes that crucial in this is the involvement of local residents. Thus, the life-cycle model can provide a benchmark for reviewing management decisions and suggest actions for community involvement. It is clear that the development of tourist destination policies are at one level of tourism policy formulation if they feed into an integrated regional or national policy. The background and nature of the destination is constantly changing and this suggests that policies need to be dynamic too.

Conclusion

This chapter has shown that destinations are made up of four principal components: attractions; amenities; access; and ancillary services. The management of destinations across all of these components is necessary if overall quality is to be maintained and this is probably achieved at destinations where these are integrated in some way (e.g. all-inclusive resorts). Management of destinations is also necessary to ensure that adverse impacts do not ruin the very resources which may 'pull' tourists to visit in the first place. The use of tourist destinations is an important dimension as there are seasonal patterns that vary as the destination progresses through its life-cycle. Affecting tourist use of destinations are a variety of external factors which managers need to be aware of. These include knowing the customer, which influences marketing and pricing decisions. Marketing destinations is, in itself, a vital aspect for the success or failure of a destination. Understanding how tourists select a destination is clearly important, as are the more specific aspects of destination image, promotion and segmentation within the marketing planning process. Using such information within destination policy formulation is also integral to success. There is a constant process of change in tourism destinations as they pass through various stages of the destination life-cycle and within any region or country, destinations will be at various stages of development. Destinations compete with each other for both the domestic and international visitors to ensure their viability, and the growth of greater co-operative marketing efforts among destinations adjacent to each other can assist in a wider regional marketing of regions with a cluster of destinations and attractions and these types of collaborative efforts are beginning to affect the way destinations within defined regions are now beginning to see the benefits of collaboration rather than wasteful competitive marketing.

Discussion questions

1. Identify and describe the main components of a selected destination.
2. Suggest the main 'pull' factors for a selected destination.
3. How important are personal recommendations in the final decision to select a destination?
4. Why are destination development policies important?

References

Ashworth, G. and Goodall, B. (eds) (1988) *Marketing in the Tourism Industry: The Promotion of Destination Regions*, Beckenham: Croom Helm.

Briggs, S. (1997) *Successful Tourism Marketing*, London: Kogan Page.

Brunt, P.R. (1990) 'Tourism trip decision-making at the sub-regional level', unpublished PhD thesis, Bournemouth, Bournemouth University.

Commons, J. and Page, S.J. (2001) 'Seasonality and tourism: the case of Northland, New Zealand', in T. Baum (ed.) *Tourism and Seasonality*, Oxford: Pergamon.

Cooper, C., Gilbert, D., Fletcher, J., Wanhill, S. and Shepherd, R. (1998) *Tourism: Principles and Practice*, second edition, London: Longman.

Davidson, R. (1992) *Tourism in Europe*, London: Pitman.

Davidson, R. and Maitland, R. (1997) *Tourism Destinations*, Bath: Hodder & Stoughton.

Fodness, D. (1992) 'The impact of the family life-cycle on the vacation decision making process', *Journal of Travel Research*, **31** (2): 8–13.

Gunn, L.A. (1993) *Tourism Planning: Basics, Concepts, Cases*, third edition, New York: Taylor & Francis.

Holloway, J. (1994) *The Business of Tourism*, fourth edition, London: Pitman.

Holloway, J.C. and Robinson, C. (1995) *Marketing for Tourism*, third edition, Harlow: Longman.

Inskeep, E. (1994) *National and Regional Tourism Planning: Methodologies and Case Studies*, London: Routledge.

Jenkins, O.H. (1999) 'Understanding and measuring tourist destination images', *International Journal of Tourism Research*, **1** (2): 1–15.

Laws, E. (1995) *Tourist Destination Management*, London: Routledge.

Mathieson, A. and Wall, G. (1982) *Tourism: Economic, Physical and Social Impacts*, Harlow: Longman.

Morgan, M. (1996) *Marketing for Leisure and Tourism*, Hemel Hempstead: Prentice Hall.

Murphy, P.E. (1985) *Tourism: A Community Approach*, London: Methuen.

Pearce, P.L. (1991) 'Analysing tourist attractions', *Journal of Tourism Studies*, **2** (1): 46–55.

Pearce, P. (1993) 'The fundamentals of tourist motivation', in D.G. Pearce and R. Butler (eds) *Tourism Research: Critiques and Challenges*, London: Routledge.

Priestly, G.K., Edwards, J.A., and Coccossis, H. (1996) *Sustainable Tourism? European Experiences*, Wallingford: CAB International.

Rogers, H. and Slinn, J. (1993) *Tourism: Management of Facilities*, London: Pitman.

Shackley, M. (1999) 'Tourism development and environmental protection in southern Sinai', *Tourism Management*, **20** (4): 540–49.

Swarbrooke, J. (1999) *The Development and Management of Visitor Attractions*, Oxford: Butterworth-Heinemann.

Zalaton, A. (1998) 'Wives' involvement in the tourism decision process', *Annals of Tourism Research*, **25** (4): 890–903.

Further reading

Inskeep, E. (1994) *National and Regional Tourism Planning: Methodologies and Case Studies*, London: Routledge.

Jenkins, O.H. (1999) 'Understanding and measuring tourist destination images', *International Journal of Tourism Research*, **1** (2): 1–15.

Pearce, P.L. (1991) 'Analysing tourist attractions'. *Journal of Tourism Studies*, **2** (1): 46–55.

Swarbrooke, J. (1999) *The Development and Management of Visitor Attractions*, Oxford: Butterworth-Heinemann.

Internet resources

By going to the weblink at www.thomsonlearning.co.uk students can access the following two studies on the Thomson Learning website. The two studies are derived from E. Laws (1995) *Tourist Destination Management* and the first examines many of the issues associated with the marketing of tourist destinations. The second discusses the policy issues associated with destination development and should be read in conjunction with Chapter 14 of this book and the two studies on the Thomson weblink.

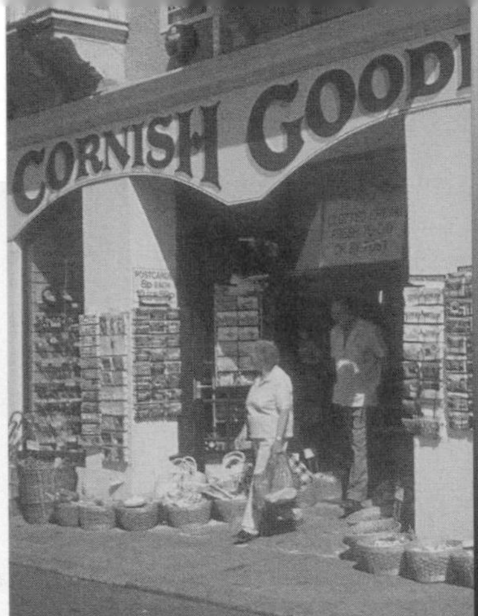

Section 5

The impact of tourist activity

In this section of the book, the impacts associated with tourists' activities and effects are considered as a way of understanding some of the costs and benefits of tourism. Impacts are a major element of tourist activity and their scope, effect and duration on the host society are complex and vary in terms of their intensity and effect according to the specific location and nature of the impacts. In Chapter 17, the most frequently cited impact used by governments and private sector enterprises to justify tourism activity – economic impacts – are reviewed. The chapter examines not only the nature of economics as a framework for understanding economic impacts but also critically examines both the costs and benefits of tourism as an economic activity that can generate employment and foreign currency while contributing to the balance of payments at a national level. Chapter 18 which discusses the nature of social and cultural impacts that are inevitably associated with tourism development. The chapter evaluates the problems of gauging the extent to which tourism-induced changes to societies and the cultural values are a direct result of tourist activity. The chapter considers many of the concepts and frameworks developed by anthropologists and sociologists to examine this specialized area of study. This is followed by a review of the third area of impact – that resulting from tourism activity on the environment. The environment is viewed as a finite resource which is also directly affected by tourism development and examples of impacts and measures to ameliorate these impacts are discussed. The tourism impacts associated with the environment have also generated a wide range of opinions and views on how to accommodate tourism and the environment, given their symbiotic relationship. Therefore, the next chapter (Chapter 20) considers the challenge of sustainability, which reviews the evolution of the debate on the extent to which tourism can be a sustainable development option. This is both a controversial and was one of the most widely researched areas of tourism in the 1990s, although the lack of agreement and measures to implement sustainable tourism are discussed and evaluated in this chapter.

17 Economic impacts

Learning outcomes

After studying this chapter, you should be able to:

- Explain what is meant by the terms economics, supply and demand.
- Define the positive and negative economic impacts of tourism.
- Outline methods for measuring tourism's economic impacts.

Overview

Among the most significant reasons cited by government and private sector tourism businesses for developing tourism is the associated economic gain. Tourism is cited as an industry that can assist in generating foreign exchange and can improve the economy and employment prospects of countries, regions and cities. While the economic advantages of tourism are certainly clear, many negative aspects are apparent. To understand the nature of the economic impacts of tourism, it is important to have an understanding of economics and some of the basic concepts related to its study so that one can understand the economic impacts generated by tourism.

Introduction

The economic aspects of tourism have been widely studied and early research on tourism impacts tended to focus on the positive economic gains rather than negative aspects relating to the environment and society. The justification for tourism development generally focuses on the potential for positive economic impacts and tourism has flourished across the world because of their perceived benefit. The global economic importance of tourism is illustrated by the World Travel and Tourism Council (WTTC).

Tourism generates:

- 11 per cent of gross domestic product
- 200 million jobs

- 8 per cent of total employment
- 5.5m new jobs per year until 2010 (WTTC 2000)

although there are concerns about the use of such measures due to the problems of validating such estimates of global tourism activity.

According to Mathieson and Wall (1982), the magnitude of the economic impacts of tourism is influenced by five factors:

- the type of tourism facility and attraction for tourists
- the volume and level of tourist spending
- the level of economic development in the region
- the extent to which tourist spending is maintained and recirculated in the region
- the extent of seasonality in the region.

These factors determine whether economic impacts are positive or negative.

Tourism gives rise to different benefits and costs and the nature and scope of economic impacts tend to depend on geography and socio-economic structures. There are distinctions between developed and less developed countries and core and peripheral areas within a country. For this reason, establishing the economic impact for specific countries is a difficult exercise. To derive a greater understanding of tourism and the economic impacts it generates, attention now turns to the nature of economics.

What is economics?

Like many social science subjects, there is little agreement on how to define an area of study such as economics. However, according to Craven (1990: 3) 'economics is concerned with the economy or economic system [and] the problem of allocating resources is a central theme of economics, because most resources are scarce'. Therefore Craven (1990 : 4) argues that: 'Economics is the study of methods of allocating scarce resources and distributing the product of those resources, and the study of the consequences of these methods of allocation and distribution.'

What is meant by scarcity and resources?

The term scarcity is used to illustrate the fact that most resources in society are finite and decisions have to be made on the best way to use and sustain these resources. Economists define resources in terms of:

- natural resources (e.g. the land)
- labour (e.g. human resources and entrepreneurship)
- capital (e.g. man-made aids to assist in producing goods)

and collectively these resources constitute *the factors of production* which are used to produce commodities. These commodities can be divided into:

- goods (e.g. tangible products, such as an aircraft or a hotel room)
- services (e.g. intangible items, such as services of a tour guide)

and the total output of all commodities in a country over a period of time, normally a year, is known as the *national product*. The creation of products and services is termed *production* and the use of these goods and services is called *consumption*. Since, in any society, the production of goods and services can only satisfy a small fraction of consumers' needs, choices have to be made on the allocation of resources to determine which goods and services to produce (Lipsey 1989). The way in which goods and services are divided among people has been examined by economists in terms of the distribution of income and the degree of equality and efficiency in their distribution. Many of these issues are dealt with under the heading of 'microeconomics', which Craven defines as:

> the study of individual decisions and the interactions of these decisions [including] ... consumers' decisions on what to buy, firms' decisions on what to produce and the interactions of these decisions, which determine whether people can buy what they would like, whether firms can sell all that they produce and the profits firms make by providing and selling.
> (Craven 1990: 4)

Therefore, microeconomics is concerned with certain issues, namely:

- the firm
- the consumer
- production and selling
- the demand for goods
- the supply of goods.

Economists also examine a broader range of economic issues in terms of *macroeconomics* which is concerned with:

the entire economy and interactions within it, including the population, income, total unemployment, the average rate of price increases (the inflation rate), the extent of companies' capacities to produce goods and the total amount of money in use in the country (Craven 1990: 5).

Therefore, macroeconomics is mainly concerned with:

- how the national economy operates
- employment and unemployment
- inflation
- national production and consumption
- the money supply in a country.

Within micro- and macroeconomics, tourism economists examine different aspects of the tourism system which is based on the analysis of the concepts of demand and supply.

Demand

Within economics, the concern with the allocation of resources to satisfy individuals' desire to travel means that transport economists examine the demand for different modes of travel and the competition between such modes in relation to price, speed, convenience and reliability. Economists attempt to understand what affects people's tourism behaviour and the significance of tourism in a destination.

Tourism economists have examined the demand for travel and tourist products, recognizing the significance of demand as a driving force in the economy. This stimulates entrepreneurial activity to produce the goods and services to satisfy the demand (Bull 1995). More specifically, tourism economists examine the *effective demand* for goods or services which is the aggregate or overall demand over a period of time. Since income has an important effect on tourism demand, economists measure the impact using a term known as the *elasticity of demand*. As Bull (1995) has shown, it is measured using a ratio calculated thus:

$$\text{Elasticity of demand} = \frac{\text{percentage change in tourism demand}}{\text{percentage change in disposable income}}$$

in relation to two equal time periods. The significance of this concept is that the demand for goods to fulfil basic needs (e.g. food, water and shelter) is relatively unchanging or *inelastic* while the demand for luxury items, such as holiday and pleasure travel, is variable or *elastic*, being subject to fluctuations in demand due to factors such as income or price. Thus, *elasticity* is used to express the extent to which tourists are sensitive to changes in price and service. For example, primary demand is usually more elastic than derived demand. The different elements which comprise the tourism product (e.g. transport, accommodation and attractions) are complementary and it is difficult to separate out one individual item as exerting a dominant effect on price since each is inter-related in terms of what is purchased and consumed.

To assess the impact of price on the demand for tourism, economists examine the *price–elasticity of demand*, where an inverse relationship exists between demand and price (Bull 1995). For example, it is generally accepted that the greater the price, the less demand there will be for a tourism product due to the limited amount of the population's disposable income which is available to purchase the product is calculated thus:

$$\text{Price elasticity} = \frac{\text{percentage change in quantity of tourism product demanded}}{\text{percentage change in tourism product price}}$$

The concept of *cross-elasticity* needs to be considered as destinations tend to be considered substitutes when they are in a similar area or offer a similar product. Waggle and Fish (1999) examined Hong Kong, China and Taiwan to see if the tourism markets are complementary or competitive. Research indicated that Hong Kong and China are competitive destinations whereas a different outcome was noted in the case of Hong Kong and Taiwan. This has ramifications for marketing policies and the effects of currency fluctuations, unrest and other external factors. Other contributory factors which influence the demand for tourism include the impact of tourist taxation, the amount of holiday entitlement available to potential tourists as well as the effects of weather, climate and cultural preferences for holidaymaking which are expressed in terms of seasonality. These factors also need to be viewed in the context of the economics of each specific part of the tourism product.

Supply

Economists are also interested in the *supply* of a commodity (e.g. hotel rooms) which is often seen as a function of its price and the price of alternative goods. Price is often influenced by the cost of the factors of production.

Bull (1991) suggests that the principle questions which economists are interested in from the supply side are:

- What to produce.
- How to produce it.
- When, where and how to produce it.

Supply may be viewed from two perspectives: first, that increasing demand requires an increase in facilities and infrastructure to cope with added pressure – this centres on the concept of extending capacity; second, that tourism may be stimulated by the provision of more facilities – this is creation and/or anticipation of demand. Borooah (1999) suggests that, for hotels, it is those who are already constrained by capacity who are responsible for most room increases. Borooah undertook an econometric[1] analysis of the supply of hotel rooms in Queeensland, Australia and found that the sector is strongly responsive to increase in earnings per occupied room but less influenced by increases in room occupancy rate or by changes in the interest rate. For commercial operators, the main objective in supply terms is to maximize profitability from the available capacity, which is usually expressed in terms of the *load factor* – as discussed in Exhibit 17.1.

The economic characteristics of the tourism industry

There are numerous debates within the tourism literature on the extent to which tourism is a business, an industry, a service or just a phenomenon. The World Travel and Tourism Council (WTTC) examines the extent to which tourism can be defined as an industry and the ways in which the tourism economy can be defined (http://www.wtc.org).

The *travel and tourism industry* describes the direct effect of travel demand and relates to services such as accommodation, catering, entertainment, transport and attractions. WTTC portray this as the tip of the iceberg. The *travel and tourism economy* refers to the wider effects of flow-through of travel demand across the economy. This includes the *travel and tourism industry* but also those businesses which support it, such as printers, publishers, wholesalers, utilities, administration, computing and security firms.

One of the main justifications for tourism development is the potential for economic benefits. Tourism is often encouraged to draw in much needed foreign exchange, generate employment and improve economic and social prospects in a destination area.

There are a number of characteristics of tourism which distinguish it from other industries, goods and services. These are as follows:

- *Tourism is an invisible export industry* – there is no tangible product and consumers tend to make a purchase without seeing the product first.
- *Tourists require supporting goods and services* – expansion of existing infrastructure and services may be required or new ones created.
- *Tourism is a fragmented product* – it consists of a number of elements, such as transport, accommodation as well as landscape and cultural resources.
- *Tourism is a highly price and income elastic product.*
- *Tourism is a perishable product* – if a hotel room is not booked one night, then it is lost.
- *Tourism is subject to unpredictable external influences,* such as currency, politics, tourist motivation and taste.

(Source: Holloway and Robinson 1995; Mathieson and Wall 1982)

Murphy (1985) states that the only constant in tourism is change. It is an industry dependent on a complexity of external factors. At a general level, the demand for tourism is governed by three economic cycles.

Short-term economic cycles

This type of economic cycle defines periods of dramatic change. Short-term cycles tend to be highly

Exhibit 17.1 Load factor calculation

The load factor calculation is a ratio of average load to peak load that relates to efficiency of usage. This can be calculated for a range of tourist services, such as accommodation, transport and attractions. Transport companies can maximize passenger revenue by minimizing costs and pricing their product or service at a competitive rate. Certain travel markets are very price sensitive, which means that consumers may be easily persuaded to switch to another operator or mode of transport if the price rises beyond a critical level (the demand for youth accommodation is a good example of a price-sensitive market). Despite price sensitivity, airlines and other modes of transport distinguish between scheduled routes which operate a regular timetabled service and charge higher fares and charter services operated on behalf of tour operators to carry holidaymakers who have purchased a transport-only component or package holiday from the tour operator. The price differential for scheduled and charter passengers is reflected in the passenger load factor which the scheduled airline needs to reach to achieve a profit on each departure. Scheduled routes charge a higher tariff but operate on a lower load factor compared to charter flights where a lower unit cost is charged but a higher load factor (often 90 per cent) is needed to yield a profit. Seasonality in the demand for tourism services may affect the load factor and peak usage at popular times means that transport operators use premium pricing to manage the supply and maximize profit to offset losses in times of limited demand. Therefore, load factor measures the impact of peaking. It can assist in the identification of the relative efficiency of sectors within the tourism industry. Knowing this may help in drawing up appropriate strategies to raise efficiency levels, such as promotions, special breaks and discounts. Load factor is calculated by using the following formula:

$$\frac{\text{Average load} \times 100}{\text{Peak load}}$$

The example below of hotel occupancy rates in the city of Exeter and the seaside area of Torbay in Devon, UK illustrates how the load factor calculation may be worked out.

Percentage hotel occupancy by Month 1993–94 – the city of Exeter

Nov	Dec	Jan	Feb	Mar	Apr	May	Jun	Jul	Aug	Sep	Oct
34	28	36	44	40	47	46	42	57	61	55	37

Mean average occupancy = 44%

Load ratio factor = $\frac{44}{61} \times 100 = 72\%$. This indicates the percentage efficiency is 72%.

Percentage hotel occupancy by month 1993–94 – Torbay

Nov	Dec	Jan	Feb	Mar	Apr	May	Jun	Jul	Aug	Sep	Oct
23	17	10	20	26	35	42	59	66	76	58	37

Mean average occupancy = 39%

Load ratio factor = $\frac{39}{76} \times 100 = 51\%$. This indicates the percentage efficiency is 51%.

Table 17.2 **Asian economic development: percentage rates of GDP growth, 1995–1999**

Country	1995	1996	1997	1998	1999
Hong Kong	3.9	4.5	5	–5.1	2.9
South Korea	8.9	6.8	5	–6.7	10.7
Singapore	8.4	7.5	8	1.5	5.4
Taiwan	6.4	6.1	6.7	4.6	5.7
China	10.5	9.6	8.8	7.8	7.1
Indonesia	8.2	7.8	4.7	–13.2	0.2
Malaysia	9.8	10	7.5	–7.5	5.4
Philippines	4.7	5.8	5.2	–0.5	3.2
Thailand	8.9	5.9	–1.8	–10.4	4.1
Vietnam	9.5	9.3	8.2	4.4	4.4
Bangladesh	4.4	5	5.4	5.2	4.4
India	7.6	7.5	5	1.2	3.3
Pakistan	5.1	5	1.2	3.3	3.9
Average GDP growth rate for Asia	8.3	7.5	6	2.3	6.2

(Source: Asian Development Bank 2000, Asian Development Outlook)

Orams (1999) examined the economic value of whale watching to the economy of the South Pacific island of Vava'u in Tonga and highlights the significance of one major tourist activity for the local economy (see Table 17.3). From this, Orams notes that whales are worth about $750,000 in revenue to the community of Vava'u each year.

Aguilo and Juaneda (2000) state that tourist expenditure is a key variable in the economic analysis of the costs and benefits of tourism. Their study of tourist spending characteristics in the Balearics denotes that by establishing expenditure profiles, the tourism product may be better understood in relation to profitability. Aguilo and Juaneda (2000: 635) argue how valuable it is to know more about tourist spending and observe that 'There is a certain type of clientele whose spending power is limited and it doubtful whether catering to this group is profitable. In contrast, other types reflect levels of spending comparable to traditional "quality tourism".'

Mules (1998) examined the economic contribution of tourists by identifying three components: numbers of tourists, length of stay and average expenditure. Mules's study of tourism spending in Australia examines how tourism expenditure changes over time. The results have implications for government policy aimed at achieving higher GDP through tourism. The study showed that for Australian tourism, real expenditure over time from

Table 17.3 **The economic value of whale watching in Vava'u, the Kingdom of Tonga**

Calculation of economic benefit of whale watching in Vava'u

	Direct expenditure of visitors on whale watching[1]	Other expenditure of whale tourists[2]	Whale watch operators expenditure in Vava'u[3]	Whale watch business employees expenditure in Vava'u[4]	TOTAL
Estimated totals for all permitted whale watch operators	\$78 000–\$116 000	\$570 000	\$47 000	\$44 000	\$739 000–\$777 000

Notes:
1. Direct expenditure includes items such as boat fares, food, camera film and souvenirs. This was given as a range.
2. Other expenditure includes accommodation, transport, other food and souvenirs, other attractions.
3. Whale watch operators expenditure includes wages, fuel, boat maintenance, supplies and administrative costs.
4. Estimate of the proportion of wage bill spent in the local community.

(Source: Orams 1999)

1985 to 1995 was dependent on growth in tourist volume, in particular the narrow market segment of the mass Asian market.

Employment

There are three types of employment which may be generated by tourism:

- *Direct* — jobs created as a result of visitor expenditure and directly supporting tourism activity, e.g. hotels.
- *Indirect* – jobs created within the tourism supply sector but not as a direct result of tourism activity.
- *Induced* – jobs created as a result of tourism expenditure as local residents spend money earned from tourism.

Several factors influence tourism-related employment patterns. Type of tourist activity has an effect on employment as some forms of tourism are more labour intensive than others. Farm tourism, particularly farm accommodation, does not necessarily create new employment whereas resort development will create a variety of new jobs. Employment opportunities for host communities may also be questioned as the benefits of tourism employment may not always be widely felt by local people. Employment of local people will be based on the local skill base. In most cases, there will be few managerial posts in local tourism development but many jobs requiring minimal skill – low paid and little reward. Managerial grade jobs may be advertised across a wide geographic area to attract well-qualified and experienced candidates. Employment benefits may often be disguised as tourism jobs may attract people from other sectors or people not normally part of the economic workforce. This includes those who take second jobs, holiday work or those who generate extra revenue from an existing business (such as farm tourism).

Economic benefits may be induced from tourism spending which directly benefits the tourism environment. While it is accepted that spending to a greater or lesser extent assists in local economic development, more refined ways of ensuring a flow of money to specific development projects is a more innovative approach. Much discussion about introduction of tourist taxes exists but there is little consensus as to the desirability of such a policy. One of the ways this is currently being evaluated is the visitor payback concept which is outlined in Exhibit 17.2.

Exhibit 17.2 **Visitor payback schemes**

The term 'visitor payback' is defined by the Tourism Company (1998: 3) as 'the process of visitors choosing to give money (or other help) to assist the conservation or management of places they visit.' Rather than a compulsory facet, such as a tourist tax, this works on a voluntary basis. From January 1996 to June 1997 a project, run by the Tourism Company (UK-based consultancy) with funding from the EU, set out to monitor the operational aspects and effectiveness of five practical initiatives in visitor payback. Most visitor payback schemes are established to raise funds for conservation work. Examples of this include the Tarka Project in Devon, UK, a sustainable rural tourism initiative established in 1989, incorporated the following visitor payback methods:

- a 5% levy on merchandise sold by members of the Tarka Country Tourism Association
- voluntary levies on accommodation and visitor services – for example, one hotel applied a 25p per person per night voluntary levy and most tourists were content to pay
- donation boxes
- a 'Friends of Tarka' membership scheme.

Visitors are more likely to donate money if they know where their gift is being used. In the example of the Tarka Project (a region promoted on the strength of connections with Henry Williamson's novel *Tarka the Otter* – so, an existing wildlife/conservation ethos may underlie visitor motivation), visitors were informed that the conservation fund would be used for work such as pond clearing, rights of way upkeep, habitat restoration and monitoring of otter populations in the area.

Visitor payback methods include:

- donation
- sponsorship
- membership
- supplements
- merchandising
- voluntary charges
- participation.

The amount of money raised will depend on:

- the number of visitors
- the level of visitor appreciation of the environment
- the willingness of tourism operators to be involved
- the type of payback method in operation.

Amounts can be quite substantial, however, if the mix of these factors is right. Visitors to the Yosemite National Park (one of the most popular recreation areas in USA) donate an annual sum of US$1 million for example to the high-profile Yosemite Fund, through merchandising, individual and corporate donations, legacies and a 'Friends' scheme. Funds are used directly for habitat restoration, trail maintenance, visitor management, cultural/historic conservation and research.

As tourism continues to grow, many destinations do not have budgets and resources to cope with environmental damage and the costs associated with tourist development. In many places, there are no entrance fees and public sector finance is often unable to meet the demands for conservation and restoration work. Tourist taxes on businesses often do not directly benefit those managing tourism. Bearing this in mind, visitor payback schemes give an opportunity of generating revenue which can be used to fund projects in the local area.

Economic costs

Inflation

Tourism development often creates inflationary effects on local economies, relating to land, property and goods. The increased demand for land increases the price. While this is beneficial to those selling land, there is a negative side-effect on the local population, particularly those who are not involved in tourism. Local people are then forced into competition for land and housing with tourism development interests. This problem is commonplace in developed countries, especially in picturesque rural and coastal settlements which are attractive to tourists but continue to exist as working communities. The coast of Cornwall in the UK is a good example of this, where fishing villages such as Polperro have become popular for the purchase of second homes. The increased demand for cottages has pushed up the average price to the extent where it is very difficult for local residents, especially young people, to get onto the property ladder by purchasing their own home.

Opportunity costs

Opportunity costs relate to the time, effort and money of developing tourism at the expense of other activities or areas of investment. If a government invests in tourism, then the money spent is unavailable for other uses. This may be detrimental to the well-being of local communities. Tourism investment can, of course, benefit local people through improved infrastructure, services and employment potential. This necessitates a cost-benefit approach to the analysis of tourism impacts.

Dependency

Heavy reliance on a single industry in any region or country is a risky strategy in the long term. Dependency on tourism is a much criticized policy, particularly for less developed countries and peripheral regions in the developed world. Some less developed countries rely on tourists from a small number of generating countries. Changes in these markets are not controllable and decreases in demand for tourism will have huge effects on the receiving country. The concentration index is used to identify the level of dependency on one or more generating countries and is calculated as follows:

$$\frac{\text{Tourist arrivals from primary markets}}{\text{All tourist arrivals}} \times 100$$

It is more favourable for a destination to attract a broad base of tourists so if there is a downturn in one particular market, then the consequences are not so damaging.

Seasonality

Seasonality is one of the major disadvantages in tourism and can cause negative economic effects on a destination. Although the high season may bring the opportunity to generate significant revenue from tourism, the economic gain must be sufficient to allow an income which will support individuals and the economy throughout the year. A high incidence of seasonality generally means that employees have jobs for only part of the year. It also means that the investment made in the tourism business is idle for part of the year. So, profits have to be made in a shorter time period than in most industries and spread across the year may not seem as lucrative as imagined. Some hotels, attractions and other tourism-related enterprises close down entirely in the off-peak season. Others, depending on location and climate, attempt market diversification, promotion and incentives to retain more even business. This is also discussed in Exhibit 17.1.

Some countries have little control over seasonality issues due to climatic conditions; for example, tourists prefer to avoid the monsoon season in South Asia.

Leakage

In many cases, foreign exchange generated by tourism activity may not benefit the economy of the destination. Foreign investors in the shape of multinational corporations (MNCs) which control accommodation, travel and tour organization receive substantial proportions of tourist spending. Leakage may occur through:

- repatriation of profits generated from foreign capital investment
- vertical integration
- not sourcing services and goods locally
- payment for holidays made in generating country.

Bull (1995) notes that large, well-developed destinations demonstrate the lowest leakage rates as they contain supply industries which can compete with foreign imports and therefore retain more money within the local or regional economy. In less developed countries, there is a higher propensity to import due to a lack of supporting industries (see Chapter 24). In this case, the multiplier effect cannot develop to its full potential as most of the tourist revenue filters out of the destination. Martin de Holan and Phillips (1997) state that leakage as high as 75 per cent occurs in Cuba for four reasons:

- lack of industries producing goods and services to support tourism
- inadequate distribution systems
- enormity of firm inefficiency in the local economy
- presence of international hotels.

Income and employment

While promoters of tourism promise jobs and improved income to host communities, in many cases there is a negative aspect to this. Many jobs in tourism are renowned for being menial, low paid and seasonal. Better paid, managerial posts may not be available to local people. The income generated by tourism activity may not benefit the poorest in a society. First, it may leak out of the destination to a foreign investor and; second, it may only filter to those who have direct interest in a tourism business or those who exist within a certain type of economy. Oppermann and Chon (1997) question whether tourism is a useful tool in securing regional economic development in developing countries and state that this remains to be thoroughly investigated. Martin de Holan and Phillips (1997) question Cuba's strategy of low-cost high-volume tourism. This is explored in Exhibit 17.4.

Measuring the economic impacts of tourism

Hall and Page (1999: 121) note that 'considerable debate has arisen over methodological problems in the economic analysis [of tourism]'. These debates focus on three areas:

- economic multipliers and cost-benefit analyses
- evaluation of opportunity costs
- the role of tourism in economic development.

There are significant problems in trying to obtain accurate measures of the economic impacts of tourism. However, several measures can be used to give an overview of the effect of tourism. Multipliers are used extensively to examine the effect of revenue generation from tourism.

The tourism multiplier

A multiplier is a statistical expression of how much income or employment (depending on whether one is referring to income or employment multipliers) is generated buy a certain amount of tourist spending. The multiplier concept (see Archer 1977, 1982) is based on the premise that tourist expenditure will inject additional cash flow into the regional economy and increase regional income. The size of the multiplier is based on the proportion of additional income spent within the region. Table 17.4 shows the multiplier rates for a selection of less developed countries.

Exhibit 17.4 **Economic aspects of tourism in Cuba**

Tourism in Cuba suffered greatly as a result of the revolution in 1959, with numbers dropping from 350,000 in 1958 to a negligible number in 1962. Following political changes and the collapse of the Soviet Union, tourism expansion was identified as a mechanism for economic development. Tourism has been presented as the most successful sector of the Cuban economy and has been depicted as a 'model industry' because of its ability to generate foreign currency and investment. Government objectives for tourism are to:

1 Increase tourism revenue and profitability
2 Increase tourist arrivals year on year.

The strategy taken by the government is that of 'price leadership'— low price, low cost, high volume. For this to work effectively, costs must be lower than the price charged. In this respect, attempting to increase tourist volume has identified economies of scale. However, there are problems in trying to increase tourist numbers.

- *The problems of inelastic demand.* There is a high substitution elasticity, which means that aggressive marketing by one Caribbean country will affect the tourist volume to another. A price war could cripple the tourism industry in Cuba.
- *A limitation in infrastructure constrains tourism growth.* An increase in visitors will require improvements in supply of tourism facilities. The government cannot afford to undertake this work.
- *A high level of external competition from other Caribbean countries.* However, low brand loyalty and increasing standards of quality means that the tourism industry has to continually improve if tourist volumes are to be retained. There is a low level of internal competition as government policy has stifled privatization.
- *Cuba is unable to tap into the American market* like other Caribbean countries because there is an embargo in place which prevents American citizens visiting the country.
- *There is high leakage* so economic benefits are not fully appreciated and impossible to be a true low-cost producer. Repatriation of profits takes place due to a large number of international hotels and managers.
- *A lack of management skill* exists in Cuba, limited by communist-style production. Management has to be sourced from overseas. While, Cubans will gain the necessary skills in time, the gap in the meantime will increase the costs of tourism to the country.

Cuba is in danger of developing a tourism industry with declining returns which does not benefit the economy or people of the country. Martin de Holan and Phillips (1997:791) question whether Cuba can make low-cost/high-volume tourism work. 'Increasing the number of tourists ... will increase costs due to infrastructure and internal supply limitations resulting in an increasing leakage curve and a decrease in the hard currency contribution of the tourism sector despite increasing revenues.'

(Source: Martin de Holan and Phillips 1997)

Table 17.4 **The multiplier effect in a selection of less developed countries**

Country	Income multiplier
Turkey	1.96
Egypt	1.23
Jamaica	1.23
Bermuda	1.09
Singapore	0.94–0.98
Seychelles	0.88
Bahamas	0.79
Tonga	0.42
Kiribati	0.37
Niue	0.35

(Source: Oppermann and Chon 1997: 115)

The income is received by other businesses which also spend within the region and so on. The income multiplier is the ratio of income to the tourist spending that generated it. There are three types of spending:

- *Direct spending* – this is the money spent by tourists on the services they need on holiday, such as accommodation, food, shops, attractions.
- *Indirect or generated spending* – this represents the expenditure of tourism businesses on goods and services.
- *Induced or additional spending* – this is expenditure by the resident community spending of income earned directly or indirectly from direct spending (tourist expenditure).

The multiplier does not show how income generation through tourism affects each sector of the local economy. To do this, another method is utilized called the input–output model (IO). This shows the flow of current transactions through a given economy for a given time period. Various types of businesses are grouped together into industrial sectors and arranged in a matrix. The total value of all sales made by each sector is calculated. This is a slightly more satisfactory method. Studies that demonstrate the IO model in operation include Archer (1995) – a study of the impact of international tourism on the economy of Bermuda; Archer and Fletcher's (1995) study of the Seychelles; Leones, Colby and Crandall's (1998) study of ecotourists in Arizona and; Lee and Kwon's (1995) research on the economy of South Korea. A study by La Lopa, Chen and Nelson (1998) shows the use of multiplier and input–output methods to assess the economic impact of the 1996 Oldsmobile Classic (golfing tournament) on the Greater Lansing area of Michigan, USA. The total spending by those who attended the event was $1,811,055. The input–output analysis showed a 76 per cent capture rate,[2] giving a total of $1,376,401.46. The multiplier generated a figure of 2.39, indicating a significant economic effect. This means that for every $1 spent by a visitor to the tournament, the total economic impact was $2.39.

Alternative measures

Zhou *et al.* (1997) report on a relatively new technique to examine the impact of tourism – computable general equilibrium (CGE). Other techniques used to evaluate economic values include contingent valuation (Lee, Lee and Han 1998; Lindberg and Johnson 1997) and the use of a social accounting matrix (SAM) (see Wagner 1997). Walpole and Goodwin (2000) provide an alternative method of researching the economic impact of tourism, stating that macroeconomic techniques (such as input–output analysis) are inappropriate for use at local levels due to lack of existing data. Walpole and Goodwin's study of the effects of ecotourism in the Komodo National Park of Indonesia set out to examine employment, distribution effects and tourism-induced change rather than regional economic impact. Techniques used included estimations from survey-based data and use of secondary data sources, referred to as 'local economic inquiry' (Walpole and Goodwin 2000: 565). This may be the only feasible approach to assessment if there is a lack of data for the area.

Conclusion

Tourism is a major global industry that provides huge opportunity for economic growth, foreign exchange earnings as well as employment and income generation for both the macro- and micro-economy. It has been seen that tourism results in a range of economic impacts, both positive and negative, depending on the location and socio-economic foundation of a destination. Future challenges for the industry include:

- reducing leakage of tourism revenue from desination economy
- ensuring wider and more equal distribution of economic benefits
- developing strategies to ensure appropriate return on investment
- balancing the needs of commercial operators with socio-economic stability in destination areas.

For any government seeking to develop tourism, greater attention to these aspects will assist the tourism industry in striving towards a more sustainable future. All too often, a critical awareness of the true economic costs of tourism to host communities and regions are obscured or glossed over in attempts to develop employment in declining regions or cities as well as in the less developed world. Yet for tourism to reach its full potential, developing a tourism product and visitor industry based on the ability of the local economy and environment to support tourism-related growth needs careful planning and management and in this respect, the economic aspects of tourism cannot be seen in isolation from the wider economic growth and development of countries, regions and places since they need to be carefully integrated into the economic structures and existing social and cultural structures. In this respect, development planning in less developed countries needs to adopt a broader evaluation of tourism so that the expected benefits are balanced with the costs and impacts to the area being developed.

Discussion questions

1. Explain the effect of leakage on tourism destination.
2. What is the tourism multiplier and how does it work?
3. Discuss the positive and negative economic impacts of tourism.
4. Explain the meanings of macroeconomics and microeconomics. Discuss how these concepts relate to the tourism industry.

Notes

1. Econometric refers to mathematical analysis.
2. Capture rate indicates the amount of spending retained in the local economy.

Internet resources

By going to the weblink at www.thomsonlearning.co.uk students can access the following two studies on the Thomson Learning website. The first by P. Cullen (1997) *Economics for Hospitality Management* offers a number of useful insights into the structural changes in the accommodation, food and drink sectors which service tourist needs.

The second study by R. McLennan and R. Smith (1998) *Tourism in Scotland* examines the issues associated with attempting to assess the economic impact of tourism in one geographical region which in this case is Scotland. This should be read in conjunction with other web resources on the economic impact of tourism such as the recently published Economic Impact of the America's Cup Regatta: Auckland 1999–2000, which can be accessed at www.otsp.govt.nz/Tourismframe.htm and by selecting the America's Cup icon which outlines the economic impact of a sporting event on a large city's tourism economy.

References

Aguilo, E. and Juaneda, C. (2000) 'Tourist expenditure for mass tourism markets', *Annals of Tourism Research,* **27** (3): 621–37.

Archer, B. (1977) *Tourism Multipliers: The State of the Art,* occasional papers in economics No. 11, Bangor: University of Wales Press.

Archer, B. (1982) 'The value of multipliers and their policy implications', *Tourism Management,* **3** (2): 236–41.

Archer, B. (1995) 'The impact of international tourism on the economy of Bermuda', *Journal of Travel Research,* **34** (2): 27–30.

Archer, B. and Fletcher, J. (1995) 'The economic impact of tourism in the Seychelles', *Annals of Tourism Research,* **23**: 32–47.

Asian Development Bank (2000) *Asian Development Outlook,* Manila: Asian Development Bank.

Borooah, V.K. (1999) 'The supply of hotel rooms in Queensland, Australia', *Annals of Tourism Research,* **26** (4): 985–1003.

Bull, A. (1995) *The Economics of Travel and Tourism,* second edition, Melbourne: Longman.

Butler, R. (1980) 'The concept of the tourist area life cycle of evolution: implications for management of resources', *Canadian Geographer,* **14** (5): 5–12.

CNN (2000) 'Whale watching surfaces as big business', www.cnn.com/2000/nature/08/23/whale.watching.cnn/ (accessed 14/9/2000)

Craven, J. (1990) *Introduction to Economics,* second edition, Oxford: Blackwell.

Hall, C.M. and Page, S.J. (1999) *The Geography of Tourism and Recreation: Environment, Place and Space,* London: Routledge.

Holloway, J.C. and Robinson, C. (1995) *Marketing for Tourism,* Harlow: Longman.

Hoyt, E. (2000) *Whale Watching 2000: Worldwide Tourism, Numbers, Expenditures and Expanding Socioeconomic Benefits,* Crowborough: International Fund for Animal Welfare.

la Lopa, J.M., Chen, K. and Nelson, K. (1998) 'Economic impact of the 1996 Oldsmobile Classic Golf Tournament in the Greater Lansing area', *Journal of Vacation Marketing,* **4** (2): 175–85.

Lee, C. and Kwon, K. (1995) 'Importance of secondary impact of foreign tourism receipts on the South Korean economy', *Journal of Travel Research,* **34** (2): 50–54.

Lee, C., Lee, J. and Han, S. (1998) 'Measuring the economic value of ecotourism resources: the case of South Korea', *Journal of Travel Research,* **36**: 40–47.

Leones, J., Colby, B. and Crandall, K. (1998) 'Tracking expenditures of the elusive nature tourists of south-eastern Arizona', *Journal of Travel Research,* **36**: 56–64.

Lindberg, K. and Johnson, R.L. (1997) 'The economic values of tourism's social impacts', *Annals of Tourism Research,* **24** (1): 90–116.

Lipsey, R.G. (1989) *An Introduction to Positive Economics,* seventh edition, London: Weidenfeld & Nicolson.

Martin de Holan, P. and Phillips, N. (1997) 'Sun, sand, and hard currency. Tourism in Cuba', *Annals of Tourism Research,* **24** (4): 777–95.

Mathieson, A. and Wall, G. (1982) *Tourism. Economic, Social and Physical Impacts,* Harlow: Longman.

Mules, T. (1998) 'Decomposition of Australian tourist expenditure', *Tourism Management,* **19** (3): 267–71.

Murphy, P. (1985) *Tourism. A Community Approach,* London: Routledge.

Oppermann, M. and Chon, K. (1997) *Tourism in Developing Countries,* London: Thomson Learning.

Orams, M. (1999) *The Economic Benefits of Whale Watching in Vava'u, the Kingdom of Tonga,* Centre for Tourism Research, Massey University at Albany, Auckland, New Zealand.

Smeral, E. (1998) 'Economic aspects of casino gambling in Austria', *Journal of Travel Research,* **36**: 33–39.

Swarbrooke, J. (1999) *Sustainable Tourism Management,* Wallingford: CAB International.

Szivas, E. and Riley, M. (1999) 'Tourism employment during economic transition', *Annals of Tourism Research,* **26** (1): 747–71.

The Tourism Company (1998) *Visitor Payback. Encouraging Tourists to Give Money Voluntarily to Conserve the Places they Visit,* Ledbury: The Tourism Company.

Waggle, D. and Fish, M. (1999) 'International tourism cross-elasticity', *Annals of Tourism Research,* **26** (1): 191–94.

Wagner, J. (1997) 'Estimating the economic impacts of tourism', *Annals of Tourism Research,* **24** (3): 592–608.

Walpole, M.J. and Goodwin, H.J. (2000) 'Local economic impacts of dragon tourism in Indonesia', *Annals of Tourism Research,* **27** (3): 559–76.

World Travel and Tourism Council (2000) The WTTC/WEFA Satellite Accounting Programme, http://www.wttc.org

Zhou, D., Yanagida, J.F., Ujjayant, C. and Leung, P. (1997) 'Estimating economic impacts from tourism', *Annals of Tourism Research,* **24** (1): 76–89.

Further reading

Bull, A. (1995) *The Economics of Travel and Tourism,* second edition, Melbourne: Longman.

Martin de Holan, P. and Phillips, N. (1997) 'Sun, sand, and hard currency. Tourism in Cuba', *Annals of Tourism Research,* **24** (4): 777–95.

Oppermann, M. and Chon, K. (1997) *Tourism in Developing Countries,* London: Thomson Learning.

Useful web addresses

See the *World Travel and Tourism Council*'s website on economic aspects of tourism

http://www.wttc.org

See the *World Tourism Organization*'s website for economic data on tourism

http://www.world-tourism.org

See Hoyt (2000), which examines the economic impact of whale watching as a growing activity within the ecotourism and adventure tourism sector and *International Fund for Animal Welfare*

http://www.ifaw.org

Learning outcomes

After studying this chapter, you should be able to:

- Define the social and cultural impacts of tourism.
- Explain the factor which affect the extent of social and cultural impacts.
- Understand a range of current issues illustrating social and cultural impacts.

18 Social and cultural impacts

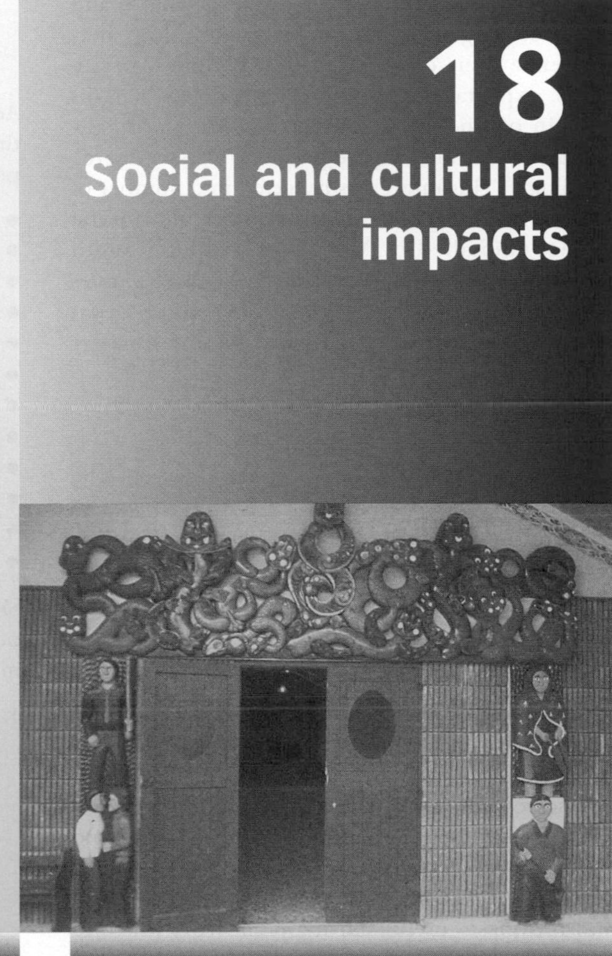

Overview

For many nations, tourism is seen as an easy way of generating income, particularly foreign exchange (see Chapter 17). In some cases, little capital expenditure is required by the host society as external investment is available. The economic spin-offs are viewed as the most important aspect of tourism development. As the economic impacts of tourism are more readily measurable, other types of impact tend to remain more hidden; in particular, the social and cultural effects. However, insidious social and cultural change may incur more significant costs than economic benefits in the long term. This chapter explores the nature of these social and cultural impacts.

Introduction

The history of tourism indicates that tourism is a social event. Resort development and sightseeing came about partly through fashions and social responses to the natural and built environment. In fact tourism is a global phenomenon which is essentially taste driven, with regions coming in and out of fashion and often the topic of social conversation. This is often embodied in the concept of which places are 'in vogue' and 'must see' destinations. This is reflected in the example of Ireland in the late 1990s: a global Celtic revival, based on Irish culture where heritage has had a profound effect on promoting the country as a tourist destination. In this respect, tourism is about people and how people as tourists interact with other locations and peoples, engaging in experiences that may influence their own or the host community attitudes, expectations, opinions and lifestyles. This domain of study with tourism studies is normally identified with anthropology[1] and to a lesser degree sociology.[2] This interest is reflected in a number of seminal studies in tourism and its social and cultural impact embodied by MacCannell (1976), Smith (1977) and De Kadt (1979). Each of these studies confirms what Murphy (1985: 117) argued that tourism is a 'socio-cultural event for the traveller and the host'.[3]

The nature of socio-cultural impacts

Socio-cultural impacts relate to changes in societal value systems, individual behaviour, social relationships, lifestyles, modes of expression and community structures. The focus of socio-cultural impacts tends to be on the host community, i.e. the people who reside in tourist destinations, rather than the tourist generating region. Mathieson and Wall (1982) state that socio-cultural impacts are 'about the effects on the people of host communities, of their direct and indirect associations with tourists'. Lea (1988) outlines the dimensions of tourist–host encounters and provides a useful starting point from which to define social and cultural aspects. This is illustrated in Figure 18.1.

Elements of culture

According to Mathieson and Wall (1982:), culture is the 'conditioning elements of behaviour and the products of that behaviour', consisting of 12 elements:

- handicrafts
- language
- traditions
- gastronomy
- art and music
- history
- local work
- architecture
- religion
- educational system
- dress
- leisure activities.

Sharpley (1994) states that from a social and cultural perspective, the rapid expansion of tourism is important in two respects:

1 Development of tourism as a vehicle for economic modernization and diversification almost invariably leads to changes and developments in the structure of society. This may be positive or negative. In the positive sense, there may be society-wide improvements in income, employment opportunities, education, local infrastructure and services. On the negative side, there may be a threat posed to traditional social values, the creation of factions of society who may take advantages of others and adaptation or weakening of cultural values.

Figure 18.1 **The dimensions of tourist–host encounters**

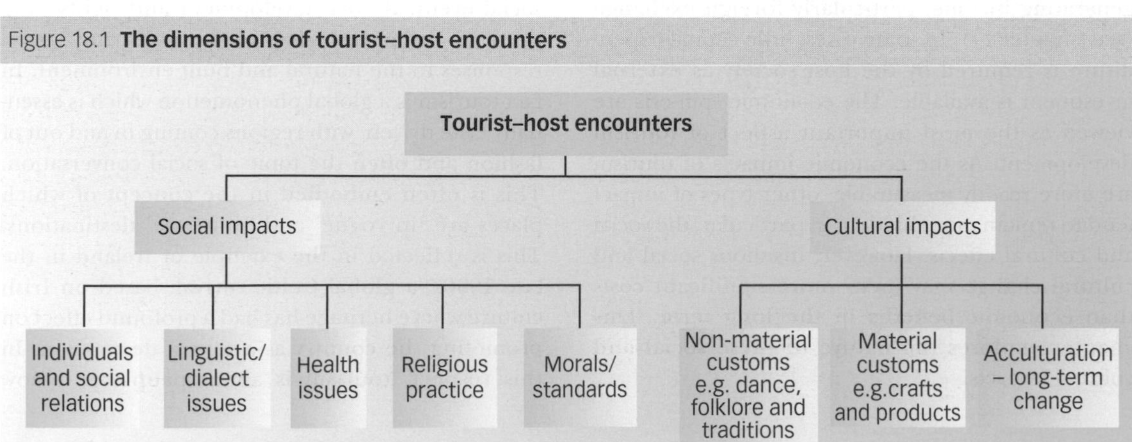

(Source: Modified from Shaw and Williams 1994: 87)

2 All tourists, to a lesser or greater extent, inevitably take on holiday their own beliefs, values and behavioural modes, what may be termed 'cultural baggage'. Cohen (1972) states that people tend to travel in an 'environmental bubble' (see Murphy 1985: 6). Therefore, the scope for mixing of cultures is great.

This gives rise to two ideas about the socio-cultural effect of tourism. First, that the interaction between host and guest could dilute or destroy traditional cultures. This reflects the literature which considers tourism primarily as a threat to culture and peoples. Second, that the interaction between host and guest could create new opportunities for peace and greater understanding. This alternative perspective acknowledges the benefits that tourism can have in allowing exchange of cultures in promoting greater awareness on both sides. There is evidence to prove both of these aspects are correct and a consensus is by no means easy to generate.

While it is possible to generalize about socio-cultural impacts, it is more problematic to define the extent to which they have occurred. The study of the impact on society and culture is complicated by the nature of more general social and cultural change. The forces of change are many and varied, tourism being just one factor. Other aspects which must be acknowledged include the role of advertising and media, the effect of multinational corporations, the aspirations of government, education and immigrants. Given the complexity of influencing factors, it is hard to extrapolate tourism as one example of potential socio-cultural impact. It might be argued that if cultures are continually changing, what is wrong with change as a result of tourism? Leaving this debate to one side, the main assumption about socio-cultural impacts is that if the tourist generating country has a 'stronger' economy and culture than the receiving country, then the socio-cultural impact is likely to be higher than if the other way around. The greater the difference, the greater the impact. Thus for example, the socio-cultural effect of British holidaymakers to France is less than that of a developing country such as Vietnam.

Factors influencing socio-cultural impacts

Having explored the general context, it is now apposite to consider the range of factors which influence the nature and extent of socio-cultural impacts. Sharpley (1994) outlines four factors which shape the effects.

Types and numbers of tourists

The traditional view is that low numbers of tourists, particularly independent travellers, result in a low impact, therefore a high tourist volume results in a high impact. In other words, those who integrate with local services and people have less impact than those who rely on externally provided mass tourism facilities. The independent traveller may have more effect on an isolated community not exposed to outside influence compared with a large, established resort. Therefore, it might be argued that mass tourism in self-contained resorts e.g. Club Méditerranée, may have less impact. This is a much debated point (see e.g. Wheeller 1993).

Importance of the tourism industry

The primary purpose of tourism as an industry is economic growth and/or diversification of the local economy. The impacts of tourism are likely to be less in a mixed economy than on an economy reliant on tourism. Pattullo (1996) outlines examples from the Caribbean Islands where, traditionally, reliance on single industries leads to social and economic problems.

Size and development of the tourism industry

A large number of tourists in a small community will tend to have a large impact. Larger communities may remain less affected. In relation to the tourism life-cycle model, there are more likely to be impacts in the developmental stage as facilities grow and changes take place. Many areas in the UK now want smaller numbers of higher spending tourists and some countries are following this particular mode of development, e.g Seychelles. Established resorts are likely to experience less change than newly emerging destinations.

Pace of tourism development

Some destinations have witnessed rapid growth which has been relatively uncontrolled. Social impacts are likely to be higher in these areas. Local communities need to adapt gradually to the needs and benefits of change and tourists.

Other related aspects which need to be considered include the nature of the host–guest encounter, the nature of the destination and cultural similarities. Williams (1998) comments that cultural similarity or dissimilarity is one of the major factors in shaping socio-cultural impacts. Impacts tend to be greater where the host and guest relationship is both culturally and geographically far apart. This is represented in Figure 18.2.

Thus, where the tourist and the host are culturally similar, as in the case of western Europeans or Americans/Canadians, then the socio-cultural impacts will be limited. Williams (1998) notes that even for the rapidly expanding markets of South-east Asia, over 75 per cent of international visitors originate from within the region (i.e. these are intra-regional travellers). In a part of the world where impacts might be expected to be significant, a large proportion of visitors will share sufficient socio-cultural background resulting in fewer impacts than might be anticipated.

The nature of the host–guest relationship and community attitudes to tourism generally depend on:

- type of contact between host and guest
- importance of the tourism industry to the community
- community tolerance threshold. (De Kadt 1979)

Contact between host and guest may arise in three scenarios:

- tourist purchase of goods and services from local people (shops, hotels)
- tourist and local resident use of same facilities (beaches, shops, bars)
- purposeful meeting to exchange ideas and information.

The demonstration effect

De Kadt (1979) defines the demonstration effect as 'changes in attitudes, values or behaviour which can result from merely observing tourists'. This may be advantageous or disadvantageous to the host community. It is said that observing other peoples may encourage hosts, particularly in developing countries, to adapt or work for things they lack; in other words, it may assist development. More commonly, it is detrimental, causing discontent and resentment (Mathieson and Wall 1982) because the degree of wealth and freedom of behaviour displayed by the tourist imposes an impossible goal. Local people may turn to illegal means to obtain the level of wealth they desire, thus crime rates may increase as a result of tourism in a destination. The demonstration effect has the greatest influence on young people and may create generation gaps and class differences, between those who desire change and those who wish to retain traditional ways of life. The young and especially the educated tend to migrate. Norberg-Hodge (1992) observes the effect of a sudden influx of western tourists in Ladakh, Nepal, on young men and states

Figure 18.2 **The host–guest relationship**

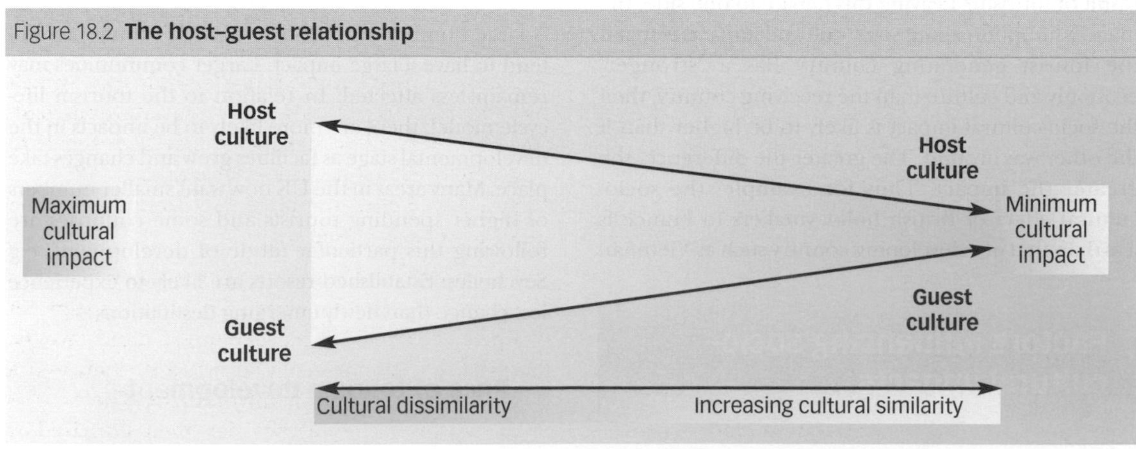

(Source: Modified from Williams 1998)

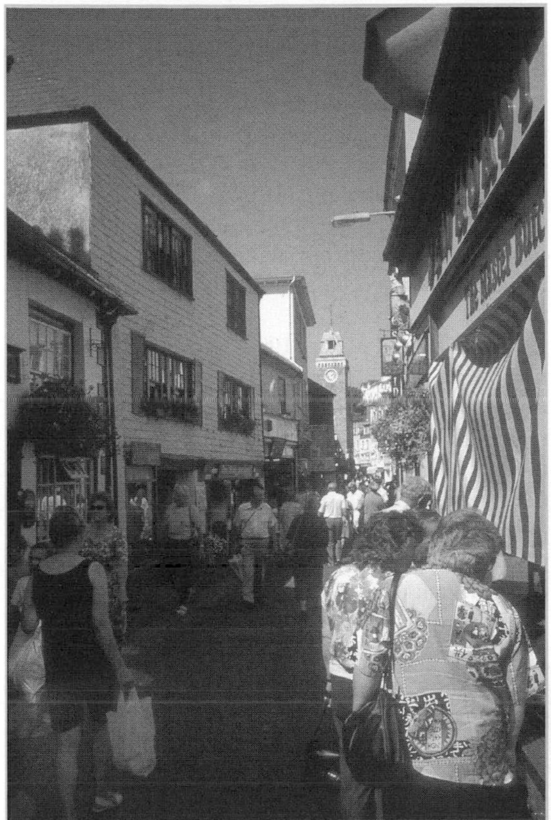

Plate 18.1 Looe, Cornwall, UK
Tourists and residents often use the same services, as in this street scene.

that feelings of inferiority have resulted. 'They rush after the symbols of modernity: sunglasses, Walkmans, and blue jeans several sizes too small – not because they find those jeans more attractive or comfortable, but because they are symbols of modern life' (Norberg-Hodge 1992: 98). An increase in aggression was also noted. The young people want the material side of modern life but cannot see so readily the negative aspects of it – such as stress, unemployment, environmental degradation, disenfranchisement. This type of change may be a disruptive force to traditional kinship over time.

Acculturations

Many impacts of tourism appear relatively quickly while others tend to manifest themselves more gradually. Cultural change falls into this last category and over time, more long-term cultural change may result from tourism. External influences and the evolution of society results in change, regardless of the existence of tourism. Enhanced networks of communication, technology and the emergence of the global market are all part of this process. However, the role of tourism needs to be understood to ensure that culture is not unnecessarily damaged. The infiltration of western culture into less developed countries is viewed as problematic as different views, attitudes, behaviour patterns, aspirations and expenditure patterns may not be easily adapted from one culture to another. In addition, unique and interesting ways of life may be pushed aside for western ideals which are not necessarily appropriate for the future of global society. Sharpley (1994) notes the example of tourism in Nepal, now becoming a mainstream tourist destination (250,000 visitors in 1994 and only 14 per cent go on treks). A visible westernization of Kathmandu is occurring as a result of tourism. This type of change is sometimes referred to as 'coca-colonization'.[4] Ritzer (1996) has considered this in terms of the effects of globalization in the fast-food industry as 'McDonaldization' – the wider implications of this are worthy of consideration as this relates to acculturation through tourism.

International tourism is thought to influence sociocultural change through the process of acculturation. The theory of acculturation rests on the notion that contact between cultures results in sharing and adoption of one another's values and attitudes. A major concern is that when a culturally weak society comes into contact with a culturally strong one, the process will be more one-way, that is the values and attitudes of the strong nation are transferred to the weak nation. Thus, acculturation is more pronounced in less developed countries, particularly those which have had less contact with western society in the past. Tourism induced acculturation may be difficult to disentangle from wider cultural change.

Two arguments dominate the literature on the cultural impacts of tourism:

1 Tourism results in the transformation of cultural events into commercialized products or spectacles which are devoid of all meaning. Culture may be trivialized by tourism in an attempt to make it a product to be consumed by tourists. The process of cultural commodification is much criticized by authors such as Urry (1990).

2 Tourism results in preservation and revitalization of traditional cultural practices by providing financial support and engendering community pride. This is seen as contributing positively to the goals of sustainable tourism.

Furze *et al.* (1996) state that the development of consciousness assists in defending indigenous societies against the might of multinational companies, developers and governments and cite the example of Australian Aboriginal communities. Pedregal (cited in Bossevain 1996) talks about the idea of self-consciousness in the southern Spanish coastal community of Zahara de los Atunes in response to tourist arrivals. The summer season is said to drive the locals crazy and they feel hostile towards the presence of tourists or 'others'. The end result is that local people close themselves off from tourists and continue their own cultural pastimes but away from the eyes of tourists. Host communities may be subject to what is termed 'zooification' if tourists are curious about local people and their way of life. This refers to tribal people being turned into sights to be viewed by the tourist. This is particularly marked for tribal people. Tribal people may put on special events for visitors such as a demonstration of dancing or traditional customs. The danger is that these events may lose their cultural significance if performed at inappropriate times and reasons. The Padaung women of Thailand have become victims of this.

Mowforth and Munt (1998) provide further illustration. At the Busman Camp of the Kalahari in Botswana, the indigenous people take off their western style T-shirts and begin to dance when tourists arrive. The Tuareg tribe in Algeria cover their tents with plastic sheets for better weather-proofing but when tourists visit, they replace them with animal hides in the traditional style. The Kuna tribe in Panama rehearse their tribal dance before

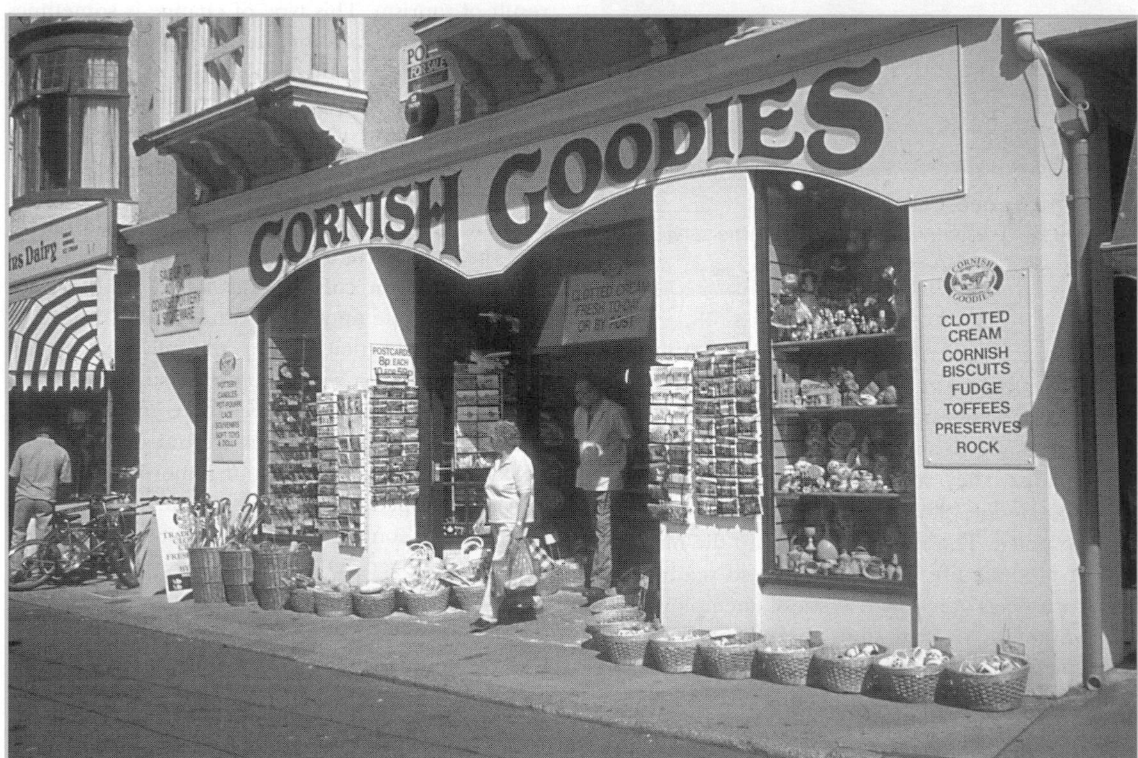

Plate 18.2 Retail outlet, Cornwall
The theme of this retail outlet might be questioned in terms of cultural commodification. Should the tourist view of Cornwall be as a place which just produces clotted cream and fudge or should tourists be more aware of the social and economic realities of the area?

the arrival of the tourist cruise ship. From the tourist perspective this raises questions of authenticity and objectification of culture from the host perspective. Mathieson and Wall (1982) outline the developed world interest in the material culture of Aboriginals (see also Simons 2000). The ancient sand paintings of desert tribes have been adapted to the use of acrylics and canvas for the export market. This cheapens and degrades the traditional artwork because the aesthetic qualities are deemed to be more important than true meanings and function. Cohen (1979) constructed a framework to illustrate tourist settings in relation to authenticity (see Figure 18.3).

The socio-cultural effects of tourism

Language

As a social vehicle of communication, language is a key indicator of acculturation. Tourism can lead to language change in three ways:

- Economic changes through the hiring of immigrant or expatriate labour. Seasonal workers and second home owners may exacerbate this. In some areas, there may be a diminishing trend of local dialects due to migration patterns, e.g. Isle of Skye, Scotland.
- Demonstration effect where the local community aspires to achieving the status of the visitor.
- Direct social contact and the need to converse to make commercial transactions. Sometimes, the host is obliged to learn the main incoming tourist language in order to deal with their requirements and to ease the transition to a foreign destination.

Religion

In some tourist regions, religion has become a commodity. Religious buildings and events are spectacles to view. Many religious sites attract large numbers of visitors, who may or may not possess the beliefs of that particular religion. Some of the most well-visited sites have religious connections, such as cathedrals, abbeys and spiritual centres, such as Mecca, Bethlehem and Lourdes. Increasing conflict exists between local worshippers, devout visitors and sightseers. Traditional ceremonies, rites and practices are not always recognized by the tourist, who may view such events in a frivolous and direspectful way. It has been known for tourists to be spectators at burials and weddings and even to participate a feature embodied in the following statement from Tourism Concern (1994): 'Guests looking for something more novel than a typical Anglican service can enjoy a traditional Thai wedding, complete with a blessing by Buddhist monks, chanting and drum parades. Thai wedding gowns can be hired for the

Figure 18.3 **Tourist perception of a scene**

Nature of scene	Real	Staged
Real	AUTHENTIC e.g. visit to a living, working town. The function of the settlement is unchanged by the tourist presence and the host community continues to go about their daily business. Visitors integrate into the scene	DENIAL OF AUTHENTICITY (STAGING SUSPICION) e.g. costumed hosts in Thai villages, where traditional apparel is worn regardless of tourist presence. Visitors may think locals are dressing up especially
STAGED	STAGED AUTHENTICITY (COVERT TOURIST SPACE) e.g. tribal dancing for visitors, where the tourists believe that they are witnessing a culturally important event but the host community have set it up deliberately as entertainment	CONTRIVED (OVERT TOURIST SPACE) e.g. tourist village, heritage centre. The visitor is fully aware that the attraction is not authentic and visits knowingly

(Source: Modified from Cohen 1979)

Plate 18.3 Rope-making demonstration
This demonstration of rope-making 1860s' style is part of an overt tourist space. While the demonstrator is wearing historic costume and displaying skills from a bygone age, visitors are fully aware of the degree of authenticity.

occasion.' This trivializes the cultural significance of the event because it is being offered as a 'novel' product to tourists. In Bhutan, tourists are not permitted to visit certain monasteries, in a bid to prevent tourism from disrupting religious life. In many countries, particularly Islamic ones, tourist clothing can cause offence. For example, in the Gambia with its predominantly Muslim population, female tourists who wear tight clothes, shorts or a short skirt and men wearing short-sleeved shirts are viewed as indecent. In the Maldives, where the population is Islamic, no topless bathing is allowed. In Zanzibar, Islamic beliefs are offended by improper tourist clothing and behaviour. These are just a few examples. Philp and Mercer (1999) discuss the extent to which Buddhism has become commodified in contemporary Burma in an attempt by the military junta to legitimate its authority. The promotion of tourism has relied on strong images of Buddhist traditions and cultural heritage. There has been concern about authenticity issues as well as substantive effects on indigenous peoples in the creation of a strategic tourist product.

Health

Health issues associated with travel are a growing area of interest but scant attention has been paid to the relationship with social and cultural impacts, with the exception of sex tourism (Clift and Carter 2000). The initial study by Clift and Page (1996) provided a good overview of health issues in relation to international tourism and the different dimensions of tourist health and how behaviour issues affect the interaction tourists have with hosts. There is increasing concern about the spread of disease through tourism at a variety of levels from minor diseases to the spread of HIV and AIDS through sex tourism. Standards of health care may improve in tourism destinations as better facilities are introduced to cope with increased seasonal populations although evidence from many destinations is that health services are often stretched in peak seasons and serious issues lead to tourist repatriation where medical insurance exists. In some destinations, a cultural difference in safety standards can create unknown levels of risk for tourists who engage in outdoor adventure activities and the negative publicity associated with accidents and misadventure can rebound on the local and national tourism industry. In terms of the positive impact of tourism on developing countries and healthcare, it is apparent that some tour operators donate funds to healthcare projects. Kuoni, for example, support a community health project in Thailand, in conjunction with the charity PLAN International UK. The project is focused on the construction of a community health centre, establishing a mobile health clinic and providing nutrition advice and training in healthcare to local people. Kuoni customers are given the opportunity to contribute and are invited to visit the project by arrangement.

Crime

Tourism and crime is a new emerging area of study within tourism but there is no universal agreement on whether tourism development leads to increased crime in a locality. Tourists are vulnerable because they are in unfamiliar surroundings, may be carrying expensive consumer items with them, such as cameras or camcorders, may be carrying cash and credit cards as well as passports which are a valuable commodity in the black market. Tourists may engage in crime and illicit activities such as violent/drunken behaviour (the lager louts of the Costas in Spain), drug smuggling and sex tourism (see Oppermann 1999). As an example of the last, in the 1990s, a Sunmed 'Go Places' brochure for the Pattaya resort in Thailand said this: 'Five or so paces outside your accommodation and you will have received more lewd invites than you could imagine.' Bangkok and Manila have gained reputations for the high incidence of prostitution and sex tourism. The European city destination of Amsterdam contains a well-known red light district which is a cultural icon in itself and focus for tourist activity. Certain areas of the world have a reputation for posing threats to tourist well-being, such as Jamaica and Florida. In the late 1980 and early 1990s, several high-profile cases of tourist attacks in Florida provoked fear. Studies of Florida in the early 1970s showed that the incidence of crime rose during the main tourist season. However, it is apparent that out of all the reported cases of crime in Florida, only a small minority are aimed at tourists. The effect of media reporting may be at fault in this instance.

Host perceptions of impacts

There is substantial literature on the host perception of tourism impacts (Brunt and Courtney 1999; Faulkner and Tideswell 1997; Hernandez and Cohen 1996; Korca 1996). Variables which contribute to host perception of tourism can be categorized as:

- extrinsic
- intrinsic.

Extrinsic factors relate to factors which affect the community at a broader level, such as pace of tourism development, type of tourism, cultural differences between host and guest and tourist–host ratio. Intrinsic factors relate more specifically to the people, such as demographic structure, employment in the tourism industry, proximity of residence to tourism areas. Hall and Page (1999: 127) comment that many studies of the social impacts of tourism have been undertaken in less developed countries. While this research is important, there must be caution in applying research findings from one culture to another. In fact, a study by Page and Lawton (1996), which examined the impact of tourism on the host community in Devonport, Auckland, New Zealand, found that residents would be prepared to accept a growth in tourist numbers if the growth was appropriately managed, despite initial concerns by local politicians that tourism growth should be halted.

Frameworks for measuring socio-cultural impacts

Ways of assessing the extent of social impacts have emerged over the last 30 years in an attempt to provide some evidence of the effects of tourism on host communities.

Doxey's Irridex (irritation index) (Figure 18.4) was developed following research in Barbados, the West Indies and Ontario and remains as one of the most widely cited frameworks for thinking about host responses to tourism. The model supposes that impacts of tourism on the host community may be translated into degrees of resident irritation. It is based on four stages of response which increase through time in sequence. The initial stage – euphoria – arises at the outset of tourism and describes the scenario where a small number of travellers arrive in a location. There is little tourist infrastructure so visitors use local accommodation and services. Hence, there is a high degree of informal contact between host and guest and high economic benefits as local people benefit directly from tourism activity. Tourists are welcomed and the host population feels euphoric. As time progresses and tourism development begins, the host population may start to take tourism for granted (apathy). This may reflect an increasingly formal type of contact between host and guest as more services are

Figure 18.4 **Doxey's Irridex**

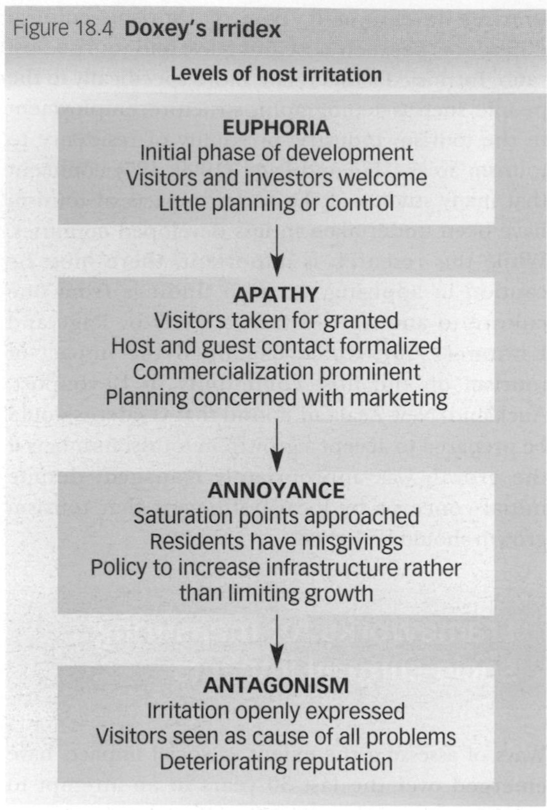
Levels of host irritation
EUPHORIA
Initial phase of development
Visitors and investors welcome
Little planning or control
APATHY
Visitors taken for granted
Host and guest contact formalized
Commercialization prominent
Planning concerned with marketing
ANNOYANCE
Saturation points approached
Residents have misgivings
Policy to increase infrastructure rather than limiting growth
ANTAGONISM
Irritation openly expressed
Visitors seen as cause of all problems
Deteriorating reputation

(Source: Modified from Doxey 1975)

developed, foreign investors begin to take control of the industry and local people begin to get used to servile roles. The annoyance stage generally reflects the stage when a destination reaches saturation point, where tourism has become a dominant force in the environment and adaptations are necessary to cope with the numbers of tourists. The final stage of the Irridex – antagonism – is an extreme point where the host population blames tourism for all the negative aspects of life in the area.

Teo's (1994) study of the socio-cultural impacts in Singapore, illustrates the negative effects of lack of contact between the host and guest. The average length of stay at three days implies minimal contact and no opportunity to engage. Tourists tend to remain in enclaves or 'ghettos'. Teo's attempt to measure the host response to tourism using Doxey's Irridex showed that:

- 75 per cent welcomed tourists for economic purposes
- 75 per cent thought that locals received poorer levels of service than tourists
- 99 per cent thought that tourists were overcharged
- 78 per cent rarely communicated with tourists – if they did, it was to give directions.

The results of a survey of residents indicated that the appropriate measure using the Irridex was apathy. Mason and Cheyne (2000) conducted research in the Pohangina Valley, a rural area of North Island, New Zealand. Using a questionnaire approach, it was deemed that the residents had not yet reached the euphoria stage. Ap and Crompton (1998) have developed a tourism impact scale which has yielded valid and reliable data on resident perceptions of impacts and is more reliable than the widely cited study by Doxey and other research which has imitated the same conceptual framework. This is because Ap and Crompton (1993) recognize that host communities are not homogenous. Those published studies still using unidirectional and redundant models such as Doxey have still not grasped the major progress made in the analysis of social and cultural impacts in tourism research. Krippendorf (1987) defines four categories of local person: those who are in continuous and direct contact with tourist; those who own tourism businesses but have little contact with tourists; those who are in direct and frquent contact with tourists but only gain part of their income from tourism; and those who have little or no contact with tourists. Each category is likely to have a different view of tourism and its impacts.

Wider issues relating to social and cultural impacts of tourism

It is also important to recognize some of the wider ramifications of tourism development where economic objectives have been placed before community concerns. One of the most significant debates over recent years has centred on the displacement of local communities to make way for tourism. Tourism has also caused governments to act in ways which contravene the rights of local people. This has been a primary issue for indigenous peoples as they enter into tourism as both spectacle and manager.

Plate 18.4 A guided tour, Bath, UK
This group of tourists in Bath is touring the city with a guide. This may help reduce the impact of visitors on the resident population and aid interpretation and understanding of the locality.

Displacement

In recent years, various instances of local people being moved away from their place of residence to make way for tourism development have been recorded. This is termed displacement. Land is taken for various reasons, such as the construction of hotels, tourist infrastructure, golf courses and reserves. Tourism Concern, the non-government organization that works to protect communities, ran a campaign 'Our Holidays, Their Homes' to highlight the issue that when we travel, we are more often than not going to a place where people live and work. Displacement illustrates the nature of the power relationships between the forces of tourism development, government and local communities. It is usually the local people who lose out (Mowforth and Munt 1998).

The Universal Declaration of Human Rights (1948) which states the basic standards that must underpin contemporary global society is clearly contravened by some examples of tourism development, illustrated in Table 18.1.

Tourism and local communities – planning and management issues

Much work has been undertaken to identify ways in which the impact of tourism on local communities might be lessened. In conjunction with this, attempts to involve the local community in the tourism development and management process should be noted. If one of the objectives of tourism development is to benefit the host population, some consideration must

Exhibit 18.1 **Examples of displacement**

- In Guatemala, 300 families were evicted in June 1996 from land they claimed belonged to the state. Police burned down their homes to create the land needed for a Spanish businessman's plan for a tourist complex.
- The Masai tribe in Kenya have been subject to the vagaries of government wishes since the end of World War II to be moved away from certain areas of land for conservation reasons. It was thought that pastoral agriculture was to blame for the degradation of the environment. Tribes were moved to other areas and reserves created for tourism. Wildlife numbers have not increased as a result.
- One of the most famous cases of displacement occurred in Burma in the mid-1990s, when 1996 was declared 'Visit Myanmar Year' by the military government. Communities were forced to relocate their homes and clear up shabby buildings to make way for hotels. Worse than this was the claim that over two million people were forced into labour camps to build the necessary tourism infrastructure (roads, railways, hotels and other facilities) if Burma was to become a favoured destination.
- In October 1992 and for some time after, the radical Islamic group *El-Gamaat el Islamiya* campaigned against tourism in Egypt, stating that mass tourism offends Islam. Thirty western tourists were injured and five died after shootings and bombings. The main issue centred around tourist's lack of respect for the values of the host community – for example, Islamic women dress in a style which covers their bodies from head to toe and alcohol is not consumed. The actions cut tourism industry revenue by one third.
- At Kuah, Malaysia in 1989, 29 shop owners living close to a jetty were forced to move and their shops and homes were demolished. This was because the Tourism Development Committee considered the building to be an eyesore. As part of a later Tourist Development Beautification Project, a new tourist shop and restaurant were constructed on the site.
- About 300 native Hawaiians were evicted from Makua Beach, Honolulu by the Hawaiian government in 1996 to release the land for development into a beach park.

be given to the host perspective on impacts and local community carrying capacity values should be part of tourism planning. This is important in all host communities but is a more sensitive issue in relation to tourism which affects indigenous and tribal peoples.

Indigenous tourism

According to Butler and Hinch (1996), indigenous tourism relates to a form of tourism that is directed by indigenous peoples or where indigenous culture is the tourist attraction. Table 18.2 illustrates the theoretical nature of tourism as it relates to indigenous culture. This illustrates the link between the notions of culture and control.

Altman and Finlayson (1993) outline some of the previous research on Aboriginal tourism which has tended to find that Aboriginal people are reluctant to participate directly in tourism activity because they feel that involvement with non-Aborigines is intrusive and negative. Socio-cultural considerations are put before economic ones as Aborigines do not feel it important to participate in the formal labour market. Aboriginal people tend to be directly involved in the manufacture and sale of artefacts and so based in the cultural tourism sphere. However, there are many examples of successful ventures where there is: a high degree of Aboriginal control; appropriate enterprise scale; accommodation of social and cultural factors; and an element of consumer and industry education.

Table 18.1 **Contravention of human rights associated with tourism development**

Human right	Examples of where contravened by tourism
The right to freedom of movement	Local people restricted from using some tourist beaches in the Caribbean, e.g. Grenada
	In Kenya, tribal families not permitted to graze cattle in the Keilado Ghana sanctuary any longer
The right to land, water and natural resources	In Goa, local people suffer from water shortages while tourists in luxury hotels have fresh, piped supplies
The right to health and well-being	In Thailand, the health of residents living next to golf courses has been affected by toxins in water supplies from chemical grass treatments
The right to respect and dignity	In Hawaii, much of the hotel development has taken place on sacred and culturally significant sites In St. Lucia, an all-inclusive resort development was built on the sacred site of the first inhabitants of the island
The right of the child to protection	Sex tourism in Sri Lanka has resulted in some children working as prostitutes

(Source: Based on a speech by Cecil Rajendra, Malaysia, Tourism Concern 1992, Pattullo 1996)

Involving the community in tourism planning

Involving local communities in managing tourism is one of the precepts of sustainable tourism development. In addition, as Ap and Crompton (1998: 120) state, 'for tourism to thrive in an area it needs support from the area's residents'. The rationale for involving the host community in tourism decision-making includes allowing those who will be involved with or affected by tourism to have their say in how it should be developed. Another reason is that local people often have knowledge of their home environment which can assist in planning tourism development. The overall aim of community involvement is to reduce the conflict between tourism and the host community (Swarbrooke 1999). Methods of

Table 18.2 **Indigenous culture, control and tourism**

Theme/control	Low degree of control	High degree of control
Indigenous theme present	Culture dispossessed (e.g. Padaung women, Burma)	Culture controlled (e.g. Masai, Kenya and Tanzania)
Indigenous theme absent	Non-indigenous tourism (e.g. all-inclusive resort)	Diversified indigenous (e.g. Quichua Indians, Equador)

(Source: Modified from Butler and Hinch 1996)

Plate 18.5 Tamatea marea, Motohi, Northland, New Zealand
This cultural icon, an entrance to a Maori marea (meeting house) illustrates the importance of preserving the heritage of the indigenous people of a nation. This can assume great significance to the visitor experience if managed in a sensitive way.

community involvement are varied but may include consultation with the host community about tourism plans and proposals or allowing some input to policies. The host community with the assistance of a supporting organization may promote codes of conduct for incoming tourists (see Exhibit 18.2). In some instances, local people have been the progenitors of tourism projects. The Quicha indians in Equador are a good example, as is the Big Apple project in Herefordshire, UK. While some social and cultural change is inevitable, it seems more appropriate for local communities to control the rate of change through tourism. The fast pace of change in North Sulawesi has meant that it has been difficult for the host community to contribute and adapt to the development of tourism. Tour operators have taken control of the industry and policies have not been imposed to ensure appropriate forms of development which benefit local people (see Ross and Wall 1999).

Conclusion

Tourism results in a range of social and cultural impacts of varying magnitude. Several factors influence the extent of social and cultural impacts. It must be acknowledged that while tourism may have economic benefits which are generally easy to assess, it is likely that there will be some impact on the host community in both the short and long term. Discussion of social and cultural impacts often emphasize the negative aspects but it must be remembered that there are positive elements too. It is difficult to make accurate assessments of the extent to which tourism causes social and cultural change because it is just one force of change which operates. This type of change is also less tangible and occurs gradually. Despite this, it is certainly clear that those who control tourism activity must

Plate 18.6 Indigenous craft workshop, western Canada
This workshop creates carvings and totemic symbols, open to visitors in western Canada. The interplay between the tourist as onlooker and the indigenous craftsman is evident in this picture. Indigenous control of this venture ensures culture remains in the hands of those to whom it belongs.

Exhibit 18.2 **Gambia Tourism Concern and host community involvement**

Gambia Tourism Concern has recently published 'Tips for tourists' in the latest issue of their magazine *Concern*. This has been generated by the host community in an attempt to ensure less conflict between the social and cultural values of host and guest. Beach boys, also known as 'bumsters' sell the magazine to tourists on the beach. The hope is that tourists will consider these guidelines while on holiday in the Gambia. The guidelines are reproduced below in summary version – the full guidelines contain tips on each aspect but are too long to reproduce here.

Tips for tourists

As a tourist are you intimidated or at a loss, not knowing how to behave, react or deal with the unfamiliarity around you? If so, please don't see yourself as a fish out of water. Read these tips and develop an idea on how to take things in your stride. Don't believe them to be commandments of DOs and DON'Ts but just rough points to ensure that you gain the most from your holiday and the opportunity to learn while respecting local traditions and culture.

1 Dress codes
2 Photographing without permission
3 Racist or anti-social remarks or attitudes
4 Off-hand responses to salutations
5 Being judgmental
6 Giving false impressions
7 Reneging on promises
8 Refusal to associate
9 Open alcoholism.

take some responsibility for the cost to host communities. It is also apparent that in some cases tourism has been developed at the expense of the host community, where economic gain has been placed as a higher priority than the well-being and integrity of the local people. There are signs that more innovative ways of managing host–guest conflict are emerging but there is still a great deal of concern about the long-term implications of an ever growing global tourism industry.

Discussion questions

1. Discuss whether tourism results in communication or corruption of culture.
2. Explain why local community involvement in tourism development and management can reduce socio-cultural impacts.
3. Discuss the factors which seem to influence the extent of socio-cultural impacts in relation to tourism.
4. Why do the socio-cultural impacts of tourism appear to be more pronounced in developing countries?

Notes

1. Anthropology is the study of how human societies work.
2. Sociology is the study of people in society.
3. It is sometimes difficult to separate social and cultural elements and so the term 'socio-cultural' tends to be used frequently in tourism literature.
4. This refers to the Coca-Cola drink, a product of the United States of America, that has gained world-wide popularity. It has become a symbol of westernization.

References

Altman, J. and Finlayson, J. (1993) 'Aborigines, tourism and sustainable development', *Journal of Tourism Studies,* **4** (1): 38–50.

Ap, J. and Crompton, J.L. (1993) 'Residents' strategies for responding to tourism impacts', *Journal of Travel Research,* **22** (1): 47–49.

Ap, J. and Crompton, J.L. (1998) 'Developing and testing a Tourism Impact Scale', *Journal of Travel Research,* **37**: 120–30.

Bossevain, J. (ed) (1996) *Coping with Tourists. European Reactions to Mass Tourism,* Oxford: Berghahn.

Brunt, P. and Courtney, P. (1999) 'Host perception of the socio-cultural impacts of tourism', *Annals of Tourism Research,* **26** (3): 493–515.

Butler, R. and Hinch, T. (eds) (1996) *Tourism and Indigenous People,* London: Routledge.

Clift, S. and Carter, S. (eds) (2000) *Tourism and Sex,* London: Continuum.

Clift, S. and Page, S.J. (eds) (1996) *Health and the International Tourist,* London: Routledge.

Cohen, E. (1972) 'Rethinking the sociology of tourism', *Annals of Tourism Research,* **6** (1): 18–35.

De Kadt, E. (1979) *Tourism – Passport to Development,* New York: Oxford University Press.

Doxey, G.V. (1975) 'A causation theory of visitor–resident irritants, methodology and research inferences', Conference Proceedings: Sixth Annual Conference of Travel Research Association, San Diego: 195–98.

Faulkner, B. and Tideswell, C. (1997) 'A framework for monitoring community impacts of tourism', *Journal of Sustainable Tourism,* **5** (1): 3–28.

Furze, B., De Lacy, T. and Birckhead, J. (1996) *Culture, Conservation, and Biodiversity: The Social Dimension of Linking Local Level Development and Conservation Through Protected Areas,* Chichester: John Wiley.

Hall, C.M. and Page, S.J. (1999) *The Geography of Tourism and Recreation: Environment, Place and Space,* London: Routledge.

Internet resources

By going to the weblink at www.thomsonlearning.co.uk students can access the following two studies on the Thomson Learning website. They are both derived from the study by R. Butler and T. Hinch (eds) *Tourism and Indigenous Peoples.* The first study is an overview of the existing state of knowledge and studies published on this growing area of interest among tourism researchers and anthropologists.

The second study is a focus on the case of New Zealand and the impact of tourism on the indigenous population – the Maori of New Zealand – which highlights the concerns of developing tourism in a bicultural society.

Hall, C.M. and Page, S.J. (eds) (1996) *Tourism in the Pacific: Issues and Cases,* London: Thomson Learning.

Hernandez, S. and Cohen, J. (1996) 'Residents' attitudes towards an instant resort enclave', *Annals of Tourism Research,* **23** (4): 755–79.

Korca, P. (1996) 'Resident attitudes towards tourism impacts', *Annals of Tourism Research,* **23** (3): 695–97.

Krippendorf, J. (1987) *The Holidaymakers: Understanding the Impact of Leisure and Travel,* Oxford: Butterworth-Heinemann.

Lea, J. (1988) *Tourism and Development in the Third World,* London: Routledge.

MacCannell, D. (1976) *The Tourist: A New Theory of the Leisure Class,* London: Macmillan.

Mason, P. and Cheyne, J. (2000) 'Residents' attitudes to proposed tourism development', *Annals of Tourism Research,* **27** (2): 391–411.

Mathieson, G. and Wall, A. (1982) *Tourism: Economic, Social and Environmental Impacts,* Harlow: Longman.

Mowforth, M. and Munt, I. (1998) *Tourism and Sustainability. New Tourism in the Third World,* London: Routledge.

Murphy, P. (1985) *Tourism: A Community Approach,* London: Routledge.

Norberg-Hodge, H. (1992) *Ancient Futures. Learning from Ladakh,* London: Rider.

Oppermann, M. (1999) 'Sex tourism', *Annals of Tourism Research,* **26** (2): 251–66.

Page, S.J. and Lawton, G. (1996) 'The impact of urban tourism on destination communities: implications for community-based tourism in Auckland', in J. Jenkins, G. Kearsley and C.M. Hall (eds) *Tourism Planning and Policy in Australia and New Zealand,* Melbourne: Irwin: 209–26.

Pattullo, P. (1996) *Last Resorts. The Cost of Tourism in the Caribbean,* London: Cassell.

Philp, J. and Mercer, D. (1999) 'Commodification of Buddhism in contemporary Burma', *Annals of Tourism Research,* **26** (1): 21–54.

Ritzer, G. (1996) *The McDonaldization of Society,* Thousand Oaks: Pine Forge Press.

Ross, S. and Wall, G. (1999) 'Ecotourism: towards congruence between theory and practice', *Tourism Management,* **20** (1): 123–32.

Shaw, G. and Williams, A.M. (1994) *Critical Issues in Tourism: A Geographical Perspective,* Oxford: Blackwell.

Sharpley, R. (1994) *Tourists, Tourism and Society,* Huntingdon: Elm.

Simons, M.S. (2000) 'Aboriginal heritage art and moral rights', *Annals of Tourism Research,* **27** (2): 412–31.

Smith, V. (ed.) (1977) *Hosts and Guests: An Anthropology of Tourism,* Philadelphia: University of Pennsylvania Press.

Swarbrooke, J. (1999) *Sustainable Tourism Management,* Wallingford: CAB International.

Teo, P. (1994) 'Assessing socio-cultural impacts: the case of Singapore', *Tourism Management,* **15** (2): 126–36.

Tourism Concern (1992) 'The universal declaration of human rights and tourism', Information Sheet, London: Tourist Concern.

Tourism Concern (1994) 'Juxtapositions', *In Focus,* **11**: 8.

Urry, J. (1990) *The Tourist Gaze,* London: Sage.

Wheeller, B. (1993) 'Sustaining the ego', *Journal of Sustainable Tourism,* **1** (2): 121–29.

Williams, S. (1998) *Tourism Geography,* London: Routledge.

Further reading

Brunt, P. and Courtney, P. (1999) 'Host perception of the socio-cultural impacts of tourism', *Annals of Tourism Research,* **26** (3): 493–515.

Butler, R. and Hinch, T. (eds) (1996) *Tourism and Indigenous People,* London: Routledge.

Simons, M.S. (2000) 'Aboriginal heritage art and moral rights', *Annals of Tourism Research,* **27** (2): 412–31.

19 Environmental impacts

Learning outcomes

After studying this chapter, you should be able to:

- Understand the importance of the environment as a tourism resource.
- Recognize the positive and negative impacts of tourism on the natural environment.
- Identify a range of examples of environmental impact.

Overview

One of the phrases most frequently used by tour operators and tourism marketers to describe a destination is 'unspoilt'. For many tourists, the desire to escape to a seemingly untouched environment is strong and tourism generally takes place in the world's most attractive environments. Since the onset of mass travel, concern has developed about the desirability of tourism. In many locations, tourism development has taken place with little regard for the natural environment. While it is recognized that tourism is an important contributor to the economy, there is a growing body of knowledge that recognizes the importance of managing and protecting the environment. This chapter outlines the major environmental impacts of tourism.

Introduction

Tourism development in many places has led to a deterioration in environmental quality. The growth of tourism has prompted debate about environmental consequences and the desirability of further development. In the 1960s, the effects of mass tourism and increasing awareness of the human impact on the environment led to a general realisation that nature is not an inexhaustible resource which was embodied in the seminal study by Young (1973). This was a notable turning point in the analysis of tourism's impact on the natural and built environment, questioning the validity of uncontrolled growth. More recent studies in this vein are Krippendorf (1987) and Wood and House (1991). These studies are symptomatic of the fact that total international tourist numbers have risen rapidly not only at a global scale but also the regional distribution has changed away from a European focus to a more widespread pattern, covering less developed countries and new, exotic and extreme locations. For some destinations, the environmental effects of tourism have led to direct threats to the industry, as the success in attracting tourists leads to negative impacts on the attractiveness of the environment. Environmental damage as a result of tourism is difficult to gauge for a number of reasons, as outlined by Mathieson and Wall (1982). The main problem is that of disentangling the effects of tourism from the effects of human existence. Coupled with the complex and fragmented nature of tourism provision, the problem is further compounded. Nevertheless, Edington and Edington (1986: 2) point out that 'a proper understanding of biological, or more specifically, ecological factors can significantly reduce the scale of environmental damage associated with recreational and tourist development'.

The relationship between tourism and the environment is complex but may be viewed from three perspectives. This demonstrates the holistic approach to the term environment, which includes the natural and socio-cultural interface. The three perspectives are:

1 tourist–environment interactions
2 tourist–host interactions
3 host–environment interactions.

When these relationships break down, problems inevitably ensue. While the term environment may be used to denote an all-encompassing view of both the natural and social worlds, for the purposes of this chapter, concentration is focused on the natural or physical environment which is defined by Mieczkowski (1995: 8) as the 'combination of non-living, i.e. abiotic, physical components, with biological resources, or the biosphere, including flora and fauna'. Tourism and the environment are closely linked – without an attractive environment, tourism cannot succeed and in some cases, without tourism, environmental conservation is at risk. In other words, a symbiotic relationship exists between tourism and the environment: each is dependent upon the other for maintaining a balance so that if the environment deteriorates, it will directly impact upon tourism. Mathieson and Wall (1982: 97) argue that: 'In the absence of an attractive environment, there would be little tourism. Ranging from the basic attractions of sun, sea and sand to the undoubted appeal of historic sites and structures, the environment is the foundation of the tourist industry.' Farrell and Runyan (1991: 26) also suggest that 'natural resources, the ecosystem, regional ecology ... contribute to all tourist locations', emphasizing the need to recognize environmental impacts. These issues, among others, will be explored in this chapter.

The nature and scope of the environmental impacts of tourism

To facilitate the study of environmental impacts of tourism, it is advisable to break 'tourism' into its component parts. While there is some overlap between these categories, this provides a satisfactory basis for analysis. Broadly, tourism comprises:

1 travel
2 tourism destination development
3 tourism-associated activities.

Travel

Much concern has been expressed about increasing levels of transport on roads and in the air in industrialized nations and the consequent wider effects on the environment and human health (see Page 1999 for more detail and a case study of British Airways Environmental Strategy). Awareness of pollution emanating from various transport modes as well as direct effects on landscape and amenity values has escalated as transport infrastructure is further developed. The study of transport is one aspect of tourism which highlights the conflict between the environment and the industry. On the one hand, enabling travel is an essential criterion for tourism; roads, cars, aircraft and airports are all needed to permit the easy passage of tourists from home to destination and back again. Conversely, the negative effects result in pollution of the natural environment and damage to the quality of landscapes. Balance is required between these two aspects but this is not readily achievable. While aspects of travel such as road, rail and shipping are well known, the impact of air travel is less well established due to the more recent emergence of scientific findings. With this in mind, the focus of this section is concerned with the impacts of air travel.

Air travel

World-wide, over 1 billion people (one fifth of the world's population) now travel by air. The damage caused to the environment starts before the aircraft even takes off. Airports require substantial tracts of land in order to operate safely and efficiently. The scale of destruction linked with building an airport is significant – for example, Frankfurt's third runway resulted in the felling of half a million trees. London Heathrow Airport's plan for a fifth terminal resulted in the longest planning inquiry in British history. Most airports started life as small airfields on the edge of urban areas where noise was acceptable and access easily gained. As urban areas and airports have expanded, noise has become a significant problem. Heathrow, which has 200,000 landings per year, is alleged to be one of the worst airports in the world for disturbance to the local population. In 1960, 5 million passengers flew from the airport and by 1993, this had increased to 45 million. With the opening of the fifth terminal, this figure is likely to increase to 80 million. Half of these journeys are for leisure purposes. Local residents have formed groups to oppose noise levels caused by aircraft and now compose an umbrella organization called the Federation of Heathrow Anti-Noise Groups. Concorde is the worst offender – although there are only a small number of these, they are extremely noisy. Thirty countries have restricted its use. Annex 16 of the Convention on International Civil Aviation contains guidelines on aspects of aircraft noise and new jet aircraft must meet regulations at the manufacturing stage. Older aircraft not meeting these regulations are being phased out or redeployed to the less developed world where less stringent noise standards exist. Many airports charge a levy on noisy aircraft and regulate the volume of aircraft of certain noise categories that may land over a given time ('the noise budget'), especially at night. London Heathrow, Gatwick and Stansted airports operate a noise budget for all night flights.

Significant research and development work is now taking place in relation to the environmental impact of air travel. Aircraft account for 13 per cent of total transport fuel consumption. Most people tend to think about noise and siting of airports but one of the most crucial areas is pollution. The world fleet currently consumes about 180 million tonnes of aviation fuel per year. This will grow despite more fuel-efficient engines. Jet kerosene is currently the only significant fuel used. Like all fuels, on combustion kerosene produces:

- carbon dioxide (CO_2)
- water (H_2O)
- carbon monoxide (CO)
- hydrocarbons (HCs)
- nitrogen oxides (NO_x)
- sulphur dioxide (SO_2).

Emission standards for unburned hydrocarbons, CO_2 and NO_x are laid down for new aircraft by the International Civil Aviation Organisation but these only apply to takeoff and landing. The key factor in the environmental effect of air travel is altitude. Although aircraft are responsible for only a small amount of hazardous pollutants, emissions have a greater impact because of the highly sensitive regions where they are emitted – particularly in the upper atmosphere. Nitrogen oxides (1–1.5 million tonnes per year) in the lower atmosphere (35–39,000 feet) lead to ozone formation at ground level, urban smog and contributes to global warming. In the upper atmosphere, nitrogen oxide destroys high level ozone and may negate the effect of the Montreal Protocol on CFC phase-out in relation to consumable products. Water in the upper atmosphere is of concern because water vapour freezes into clouds which reflect heat back to earth, reacting with nitrogen oxides to destroy ozone. Carbon monoxide causes low level ozone formation. Some 500–600 million tonnes of carbon dioxide are emitted from the world civil aviation fleet (about the same amount as from all sources of greenhouse gases in the UK) (Aviation Environment Federation 1996) which contributes to the greenhouse effect. The overall assessment of the environmental effects of air travel is complicated by the newness of the subject (and unproven associations) and the complexity of atmospheric chemistry. A lack of consensus remains over the precise impact of aircraft and scientific research is continuing and is attracting the attention which car pollution did in the 1970s and 1980s.

Tourism destination development

Tourism destinations comprise a wide diversity of environments, from purpose-built resorts to remote natural areas. In general it is possible to identify broad categories of impact that may affect all destinations to a greater or lesser extent as outlined by Wood and House (1991): inappropriate development; loss of habitat; extinction of species; pollution; and loss of spirit. According to the European Environment Agency (1998), tourism creates significant contributions to the following environmental problems:

- waste
- reducing levels of biodiversity
- pollution of inland waters
- pollution of marine and coastal zones.

In a European context, the environments which tend to be most directly affected by tourism are coastal and alpine areas. The Mediterranean Sea is commonly cited as the world's dirtiest sea (see Croall 1995). The Mediterranean Action Plan set up in 1995 intends to take measures to prevent, abate and combat pollution of the Mediterranean Sea but information on progress is not readily available. Table 19.1 illustrates a range of environmental

Table 19.1 **Summary of environmental impacts in specific habitats**

Habitats influenced	Effect of tourism development
Marine waters	Pollution from sewage outfall Sea dumping of waste Oil pollution from tourist boats Litter and threat to marine creatures
Coastal habitats	Habitat loss and fragmentation Deterioration in ecological diversity Destabilization of sand dunes Erosion of coastal landscape
Inland waters	Sewage pollution Eutrophication Oil pollution from boats and barges Disturbance from watercraft of bird communities
Upland heaths, mires and tundra	Erosion Habitat loss and fragmentation Disturbance to nesting birds
Agricultural land	Loss of area for production Conflict between adjacent agricultural uses and tourism
Semi-natural grasslands	Loss of open landscape Habitat loss
Heathlands, scrub and rocky area	Habitat loss and fragmentation
Forests	Habitat loss and fragmentation Disturbance from recreational activities

(Source: After European Environment Agency 1998)

impacts in relation to specific habitats. A habitat is defined as 'the place in which a species of animal or plant lives, providing a particular set of environmental conditions' (Cordrey 1996).

There are two types of environmental impacts which occur in destination development:

- those affecting the integrity and composition of the natural environment
- those affecting the tourist experience of the environment.

In essence, these two categories overlap but need to be viewed from different perspectives. For example, the effects of trampling on vegetation induce direct environmental change whereas overcrowding affects tourist enjoyment but has a different overall impact on the natural environment. It is also interesting to consider the question of responsibility for tourism impacts. Kavallinis and Pizam (1994) found in a study of the perception of tourism impacts on the Greek island of Mykonos that tourists were more critical of impacts than the host community. Tourists considered residents and entrepreneurs to have greater responsibility for producing negative environmental impacts. Residents believed that they were to blame for much of the environmental impact. It is not always appropriate to say that 'tourists' damage the environment – there is in reality a complexity of interactions, decision-making, economic imperatives and responsibilities which affect the outcome.

The following sections outline the major environmental impacts of tourism in destinations.

Inappropriate development

Tourism development whether it takes place on the micro- or macro-scale may be classed as inappropriate where it fails to be sensitive to the natural environment. Large tracts of the Mediterranean coastal strip are now covered by urban sprawl to cater for the mass tourism market. Waugh wrote as early as 1930: 'There is no track quite so soundly beaten as the Mediterranean seaboard.' Theroux (1996: 34) describes the Spanish coast as 'utterly blighted'. The effect of tourism is expressed vividly by Theroux (1996: 35) thus: 'I felt intensely that the Spanish coast, especially here on the Costa del Sol, had undergone a powerful colonisation, of a modern kind ... It had robbed the shore of its natural features, displaced headlands and gullies and harbours with futile badly-made structures.' This type of development occurs as a result of short-term planning in environmental terms. Resort developments, while contained on specific sites, are normally built on greenfield sites in undeveloped areas, often with no planning control. A chain reaction of tourism related development often follows. Most visitors need services while on holiday or a day out and this creates pressure for development to meet visitor needs and expectations. Problems occur if facilities are not constructed in harmony with the local environment. Static caravan sites scattered around the coasts of Britain which often cause negative landscape effects pre-date planning controls. Instances of over-development include Lake Tahoe (California–Nevada border) which has been subject to intense commercial development and a consequent deterioration in scenic quality (Iverson *et al.* 1993). The Waikiki area of Honolulu (see Plate 19.1) has also been subject to high-density tourism development with skyscraper hotels obscuring views of the coast. Newly developing resorts in island countries are also displaying signs of unplanned development, such as Pattaya, in Thailand which is considered to be over-developed (Mieczkowski 1995) (see Plates 19.1 and 19.2).

In some cases, inappropriate development has been removed, for example the poorly built hotels of Calvia, Mallorca, which were demolished in the late 1990s to make way for environmental enhancements. In England, the National Trust has been active in turning the tide of inappropriate developments. At Kynance Cove, Cornwall, the Trust demolished unsightly café and shop buildings. The buildings also contributed to site erosion as visitors would follow a particular route past them. The Trust re-routed the paths, restoring the damaged ground surface and controlling the movement of visitors to reduce the physical impact of visitors to the site. A similar approach was taken at the Giants Causeway in County Antrim, Northern Ireland. The National Trust in England and Wales also has a policy of removing unsightly caravan sites from coastal land acquired through its Enterprise Neptune campaign. However, this has been seen to cause conflict with the local community in some cases, where local business is dependent on visitors who stay on such sites.

Plate 19.1 Waikiki Beach, Honolulu, Hawaii
At Waikiki Beach in Honolulu hotels have been constructed adjacent to the beach.

Plate 19.2 White Rocks Holiday Complex, Malta
Does this development blend in with the local environment?

Loss of natural habitat and effects on wildlife

Development of facilities and subsequent tourist use may result in rapid or more gradual effects on habitats. In Nepal, deforestation resulting in the felling of thousands of trees for building tourist lodges and provision of fuel for hot water, heating and cooking has resulted in a dramatic depletion of the country's forest cover. Croall (1995) states that one trekker consumes 5–10 times more wood than a Nepali in a day and that a single lodge may consume one hectare of virgin forest per year for running facilities. The development of lodges and trails can result in impacts on natural resources. Trampling, for example, through walking or horse riding causes disturbance to vegetation and soil. Reduced ground vegetation cover or loss of tree seedlings through trampling causes soil to become exposed and therefore vulnerable to both erosion and compaction. Trail widening and muddiness may result. Composition of flora leading to elimination of species is also likely.

There is much research on the effects of tourism on wildlife and nature conservation. The rapid growth of nature-based tourism has resulted in the exposure of vulnerable environments and species to pressure from visitors. As a result of habitat effects and as a direct result of tourism activity, wildlife can be disturbed. There is a debate about whether tourism and nature conservation can co-exist in mutual benefit and it is possible to identify a number of examples of instances where tourism has incurred costs and benefits. One example is the Golden Toad, known to exist only in the Monteverde Cloud Rain Forest in Costa Rica, which is on the verge of extinction. The orange-coloured toad, depicted on postcards and on entrance signs to one of the most popular lodges in the area, has declined in numbers at the same time as ecotourism has evolved in the area. It is possible that an alien organism brought in by ecotourists may have caused a plague (Honey 1999).

Another species more directly affected by tourism activity is the Loggerhead Turtle. Prunier, *et al.* (1993) provide evidence for this, having studied the turtles on the Greek island of Zakynthos, one of the most important nesting areas in the Mediterranean. Nesting takes place in the peak tourist season between June and August and of the hatchlings, only one or two in every thousand will reach adulthood. Concern was expressed in 1979 about this 'endangered species'. The development of tourism threatens the turtle in six ways:

1 Loss of beach nesting areas – developers and tourist encroach on the habitat and tree planting to provide shade for tourists may cause a barrier to successful nesting.
2 Nestings females and young turtles disoriented by artifical illumination – the turtle is phototactic and moves towards a light source. The usual movement is towards the reflection of the sun on the sea but lights from beach-front developments attract the turtles inland where they dehydrate or become road casualties.
3 Noise – turtles are confused by loud noises.
4 Traffic – on the beach, traffic causes sand compaction, creates an imbalance of gases absorbed by the eggs and may activate hatchlings at the wrong time.
5 Pollution – litter and tar may be consumed and cause choking and death.
6 Activities in water – turtles become entangled in fishing lines, drown in nets and are injured in collision with water craft.

At a site in Turkey, a healthy population of 1,400 turtles was recorded in 1977. This had dropped to 800 by 1987 and research indicates this was a result of tourism development. Difficulties arise in attempts to conserve the species as it is impossible to replenish colonies with members from another – each population is genetically isolated. This means that preventative measures on-site are needed to ensure the survival of the species. Initiatives which have been taken include the introduction of legislation regulating water craft, the establishment of a National Marine Park, a tourist and tour operator awareness campaign, banning of evening charter flights and demolition of illegal buildings which interfere with nesting turtles.

The Galapagos Islands, 600 miles of the coast of Ecuador, are considered to be one of the foremost locations for wildlife tourism. Organized ecotourism started in the late 1960s with visitor numbers of about 6,000. In 1996, these visitor numbers were up to 62,000. The environment of the Galapagos is the main attraction – sea lions, marine iguanas, giant tortoises, penguins and an array of unusual reptiles, birds, plants, insects and fish. Strict rules on tourist activity apply. Visitors must follow guides, stay on paths, not take food, not litter, and must wash off before going to another island. Despite this, red and blue-footed boobies have been observed to change their nesting locations and display behaviour in relation to tourist use of trails. Iguanas wait for tourists to feed them bananas.

Wildlife viewing is increasing in popularity and forms one of the major activities associated with ecotourism. The impacts of this are trampling of vegetation by foot and vehicular traffic and disruption of wildlife behaviour. In the Amboseli National Park, Kenya, cheetahs have learned to avoid tourists and delay their activities according to tourist presence. Feeding and harassment of wildlife causes unnatural behaviour changes which may result in spatial and temporal displacement leading to lower quality food sources, inferior cover and increased competition. Longer term changes may lead to the alteration of the structure and size of the population and local extinction (Marion and Farrell 1998). Whale watching has become one of the boom sectors in ecotourism. Exhibit 19.1 explores this in more detail.

Pollution

Water quality and sewage treatment are often neglected following tourism development, sometimes due to lack of planning controls and other times due to lack of finance to back schemes. In the Mediterranean, horror stories of raw sewage being pumped straight out to sea have been prolific. This results in a number of different impacts. Increased nutrients in the water rob the water of oxygen causing eutrophication in lakes and subsequent death to aquatic life. Plagues of jellyfish feed on the increased nutrients and float ashore, causing problems for sea-bathing tourists. Water-borne diseases such as diarrhoea and typhoid can also occur. There has been a move towards limitation of problems and preventive measures have been installed in many locations. Tighter regulations, new technology and improved waste water management systems and innovations such as ultra-violet treatment systems are important environmental measures for resorts.

According to the Marine Conservation Society (MCS), plastic debris is the greatest hazard to marine creatures. Sea creatures can become entangled in items such as plastic loops used to hold drinks cans together or can swallow plastic bags. More than 90 per cent of gannet nests on the Welsh island of Grassholm contain plastic litter. A survey undertaken in September 1999 covering over 170 beaches in the UK (Beachwatch '99), to link in with the International Coastal Clean-up occurring in more than 75 countries, discovered that much of the beach rubbish is left by tourists. Some 39 per cent of the litter found came from tourism and this figure is rising while other categories such as fishing and shipping are decreasing, according to regular survey data. The survey identified an average of 1,913 pieces of litter per km of beach, with the total haul weighing 11.6 tonnes.

Loss of spirit

Much less of a tangible effect but still crucial is the impact of tourism on the ambience of a location. A loss of atmosphere might be individually perceived but it may also have wider implications for tourism. The spirit of a place might be the main attraction and once that spirit is diminished, then tourists may no longer desire to visit. That is over and beyond the ramifications for the integrity of the environment and the host community. Changes in character may be incremental so the loss of spirit may occur gradually or may take place more rapidly, in the instance of resort development.

Overcrowding and traffic congestion

When the volume of tourists exceeds the capacity of an environment, then overcrowding occurs. Geographical and temporal considerations are required when assessing overcrowding because in general it affects certain parts of a site and/or certain times of the day or year. Overcrowding is a problem for two reasons as it:

- poses an increased risk of environmental damage through erosion
- restricts visitor appreciation of the destination.

Traffic, particularly the private car, attracts much attention as an area of research. In the UK, concern is directed at both rural and urban tourism. While tourist traffic is not generally the major cause of congestion, at certain times of the year and in particular regions and destinations, it adds significantly to the pressures of general road use.

A large proportion of rural tourists visit the countryside by car and the biggest increase in car use is predicted for rural areas. For towns and cities,

Exhibit 19.1 **Whale and dolphin watching**

According to Hoyt (2000), 9 million tourists engaged in this activity and spent £655 million, dramatically rising from 5.4 million tourists and £311 million in 1994. Whale watching has seen significant growth over the last ten years and is enjoyed in a variety of international locations, from the poles to the equator. While there are no international regulations, many countries have introduced strict regulations to protect the creatures, such as limiting noise and speed of boats, number of boats, distance allowed from creatures and swimming. Some are calling a halt to activities. In New Zealand and the Azores, concern has been expressed about the amount of human contact between the creatures and swimmers, which is thought to cause stress. At Kaikoura, South Island, New Zealand, there is a moratorium on the setting up of new tourist business related to whale watching and existing businesses have agreed to a voluntary code of practice to allow the whales sufficient rest time. The Whale and Dolphin Conservation Society is currently campaigning for an international ban on swimming with all marine creatures. Boats also cause problems by following the creatures too closely. Contact with the creatures can lead to changes in behaviour such as more leaping and disturbance to habits, such as the need to rest during the day and hunt at night. More research is required to prove that human contact does cause stress problems but until then, the precautionary principle should be adhered to.

Whale watching has been proven to be beneficial to conservation when its economic potential exceeds that of hunting. Orams (1999) showed that in Tonga, the economic value of the whale watching industry is about $T1 million ($NZ1.2 million) per year. A Humpback Whale in Tongan waters is calculated to be worth $T30,000 a year or $T1.6 million in tourism dollars during its lifetime. This outweighs any commercial value that could be gained from killing the whales (see Chapter 19 for a more detailed analysis of this). Hector's Dolphins are a rare species found only in New Zealand. Research into disturbance through tourism affecting Hector's Dolphins in Porpoise Bay reports that the dolphins, when boats and swimmers were absent, spent most daylight hours in the southern end of the bay close to the surf zone and a small reef system. This 'prime habitat' was also popular with swimmers, although the current levels of boat or swimming activities were not found to displace the Hector's Dolphins. Reactions to swimmers were classified as weak and non-significant, perhaps (the researchers speculated) because the dolphins could easily avoid them. Reactions to dolphin-watching boats were stronger, with dolphins tending to approach the boats during the early part of an encounter but then becoming less interested. By 70 minutes into an encounter, the dolphins were either actively avoiding the boat or equivocal towards it. The dolphins were also significantly more tightly bunched when a boat was present in the bay and this might indicate stress. The scientists concluded that whilst the present level of disturbance was not affecting the dolphins heavily, an increase in tourism in Porpoise Bay would be cause for concern (Bejder *et al.* 1999).

The town of Puerto Madryn, Patagonia is close to one of the world's best marine reserves, the Valdes Peninsula. While fishing is still an important employer, ecotourism, especially whale watching, is increasingly popular in the area. In 1972, seven people came to view Southern Right Whales but in 1998, 90,000 tourists were recorded. In a bid to protect Grey Whales during the mating season and reproductive cycle, whale watching will be limited in the state of Low Southern California, Mexico. According to an agreement signed between the Secretariat of Environment, Natural Resources and Fishery (Semarnap) and the State Bureau of Tourism (CET), the number of tourists will be limited and only 102 crafts will be allowed to enter the lagoons where Grey Whales mate in January and April. The imperative is the need to comply with regulations on species conservation. To put this into context, during the previous whale watching season, more than 20,000 Mexican and foreign tourists arrived in the State, which meant an additional income of more than US$60 million.

(Sources: Bejder *et al.* 1999; Marine Conservation Society 1999; Orams 1999; Whale and Dolphin Conservation Society 1999)

Plate 19.3 Whale watching, South Pacific
Whale watching is now a major eco-tourism activity in the South Pacific, where mammals, such as this Humpback Whale on its migration path, can be observed. (Source: Mark Orams)

Plate 19.4 Hooker Glacier, Mount Cook National Park, New Zealand
Wilderness areas such as the Hooker Glacier in the Mount Cook National Park are under pressure from international visitors who displace other visitors seeking true wilderness experiences. This poses a challenge for visitor management techniques in the natural environment.

Plate 19.5 Traffic congestion
Traffic congestion in tourist areas causes a deterioration in resident quality of life and local air quality as well as spoiling visitor experiences.

growing congestion from commuter and tourist traffic is leading to restrictions being imposed on use of roads at certain times. Road traffic can damage the built environment through pollution and vibration as well as negatively affecting tranquillity and atmosphere. Car parks are required to contain traffic volume at destinations but in some locations inappropriate parking causes damage to verges and vegetation, such as off-road parking on moorlands. The increasing popularity of off-road driving damages vegetation, causes erosion and adds to localized pollution. At the extreme end of the spectrum, in some of the National Parks of the UK and the USA, road closures have been necessary to stem the untenable flow of traffic (e.g. Yellowstone and the Peak District).

In a survey undertaken of National Park superintendents in the USA, air quality problems were perceived to be a significant effect of tourism – mainly from exhaust fumes from tourist vehicles (Wang and Miko 1997). Koenen *et al.* (1995) calculated that about 19 per cent of carbon monoxide air pollution is caused by tourism in Las Vegas. Congestion often results in new journey patterns where people travel to different places to avoid queues and/or where they know they are able to park. This spreads the problem to a wider area (Countryside Commission 1992).

Wear and tear

Physical damage to the environment is often more marked in the countryside but is also an issue for urban areas. Sensitive locations, such as peat moorlands and sand dunes are prone to serious damage by a range of users, such as horse riders, mountain bikers, walkers and off-road vehicles.

Riverbanks are subject to the wash from pleasure boats, a problem suffered in the Norfolk Broads, UK, where the problem is exacerbated by the weakening of reeds by fertilizer run-off. Other problems of wear and tear include litter. On Dartmoor, UK, up to 250 trailer loads of litter collected every year

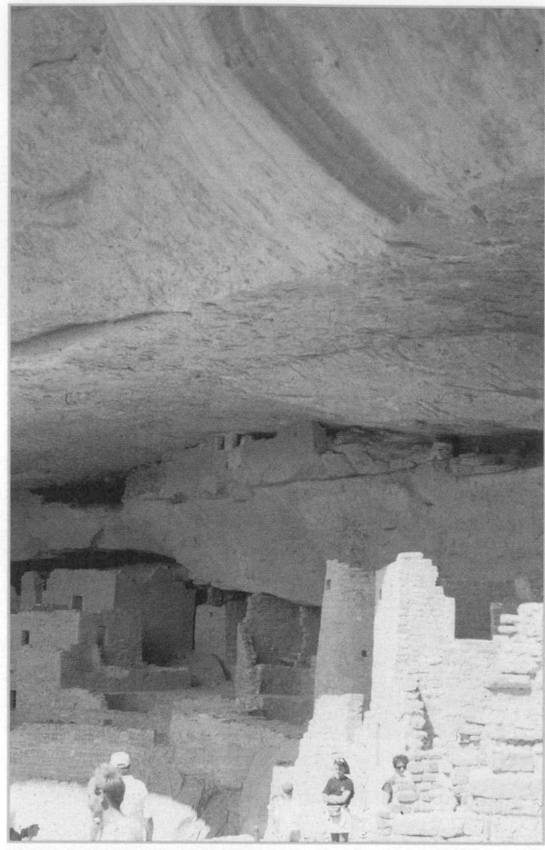

Plate 19.6 White Cliffs World Heritage Site, Mesa Verde National Park, USA

from one small area. In Rome, coins thrown by tourists into the Trevi Fountain are chipping the marble. The English Tourist Board and Employment Department Group (1991) report that Westminster Abbey's three million annual visitors cause damage to the physical fabric of the interior. The thirteenth-century Cosmati Pavement in front of the high altar is literally being worn away. Pieces of statuary are stolen and the increased exposure to humidity, light and dust from the volume of visitors is a threat to artwork, materials and ornamentation. The famous caves at Lascaux in the Dordogne, southern France, containing 17,000-year-old Quaternary cave paintings provide an example of where action was needed to eliminate the effect of tourism on the integrity of the resource base. Perspiration and breath from the large numbers of tourists to the caves altered the micro-climate, leading to an increase in carbon dioxide, temperature and humidity. In addition, artificial lights used to illuminate the interior gave favourable conditions for the growth of mosses, algae and bacteria. These began to have a damaging effect on the quality of the paintings. The caves were closed to visitors in 1963 and are now only open to scholars by arrangement. They must go through a disinfectant chamber before entry, must not speak once inside and are allowed a maximum of 20 minutes in the caves. A replica, named 'Lascaux Two' was constructed in 1983 to enable 2,000 tourists per day to experience something of the paintings (Edington and Edington 1986; Mieczkwowski 1995).

Activities

In relation to the impact of tourism activities, it is worth drawing out a few selected examples to indicate to what extent popular holiday activities can affect the natural environment.

Skiing/alpine tourism

Mountain ecosystems are generally quite fragile but many are prone to intensive use, through skiing, trekking and other mountain/snow sports. Skiing is seen by many as a damaging activity because it requires associated developments, such as lodges, resorts, roads and ski slopes and causes severe erosion and deforestation (Hudson 1999). A great deal of damage is caused in the initial construction and development stages (Todd and Williams 1996). In some resorts, lack of snowfall and tourist demand for the snow experience means that snow cannons have been employed. These require large amounts of water to produce sufficient snow to form a satisfactory slope for skiing and according to May (1995) lead to a shorter growing season, reduced river currents which affect fish populations and destruction of forest cover causing soil erosion.

Ecotourism

While the premise of ecotourism is to assist in conservation and well-being of local communities, it is often the case that ecotourism-based activities lead to deterioration in environmental quality.

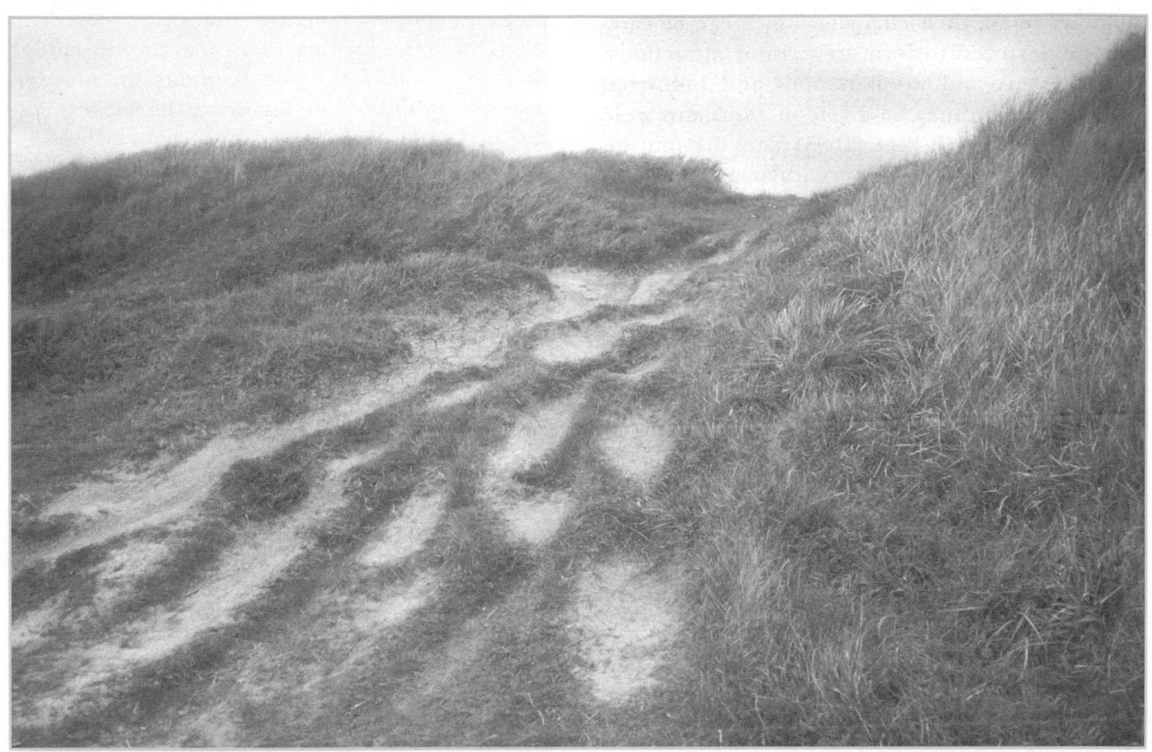

Plate 19.7 Surface erosion
Damage to surface vegetation caused by intense use by visitors on foot.

Swarbrooke (1999: 320), for example, argues that 'today's ecotourism package can easily become tomorrow's mass market tourism product'. Early ecotourism destinations such as Kenya, the Galapagos Islands and Thailand have already suffered extensive impacts as a result of increased numbers of ecotourists (Boyd and Butler 1996). Cater (1993) cites the example of Belize, where development has involved the clearance of mangrove swampland, drainage and infilling using topsoil literally shaved off the wetland savannah a few miles inland. Thus, two distinctive ecosystems have been destroyed. Well-documented cases of lack of planning, improper management and negative impacts indicate that a desire for short-term benefits has in some cases resulted in inappropriate forms of development (Wight 1993), and increasingly ecotourism is being associated with the wider greening of tourism products by the tourism industry globally.

Positive environmental impacts of tourism

The damaging aspects of tourism are significant and receive deserved attention. However, it is essential to recognise that positive impacts may be gained from tourism activity. Doswell (1997) notes that tourism can focus attention on significant environmental issues and stimulate initiatives to conserve and enhance the environment. The main areas to examine are threefold.

Conservation of redundant and/or historic buildings for alternative uses

Tourism can provide the impetus for converting disused buildings into foci for tourism activity. Many buildings retain their character which can be carefully modernized to form new visitor attractions. Examples are old woollen mills and industrial premises, which may be given an alternative role through tourism use. Page (1995) states that tourism can potentially reinforce vernacular architectural forms. Tourism may provide the financial means to restore and/or maintain historic buildings in an appropriate way. This may also provide the basis for future development in tourism with planning approvals likely to be more easily obtained for building conversion or brownfield sites rather than new, greenfield locations. If existing buildings can be used in creative yet sensitive ways, tourism can prove to be a beneficial force of redevelopment. Use of derelict land for development of urban parks or country parks is widespread in industrialized nations. Despoiled land, such as the old open-cast coal mines of Northumberland, has been restored to both agricultural and recreational uses.

Enhancement of local environments

If tourism is viewed as an important source of income, it is likely that local government will seek to retain and increase visitor numbers by improving the general amenity value of the local environment. This is relevant to a range of environments, including rural, coastal and urban areas. For many historic cities, improvements may consist of landscaping which reflects the heritage character of the townscape which simultaneously assists the visitor experience. However, it might be said that such enhancements detract from the original form. The Center Parcs development in Sherwood Forest, UK, resulted in the planting of 500,000 trees, the seeding of native grasses and wild flower species, heathland re-creation and management and an overall increase in ecological diversity. While developments of this type tend to be criticized for their scale and siting in natural areas, in most cases, the environmental management which accompanies development improves the environment which might have been subject to previous intensive use, such as forestry plantation. Heathland fauna, such as the Nightjar and Grass Wave Moth are reappearing. Creation of waterways has attracted 12 species of dragonfly and damselfly (sufficient numbers to meet English Nature's criteria for selection as a Site of Special Scientific Interest). The first recorded sighting in Nottinghamshire of an Emperor Dragonfly was in Sherwood Forest.

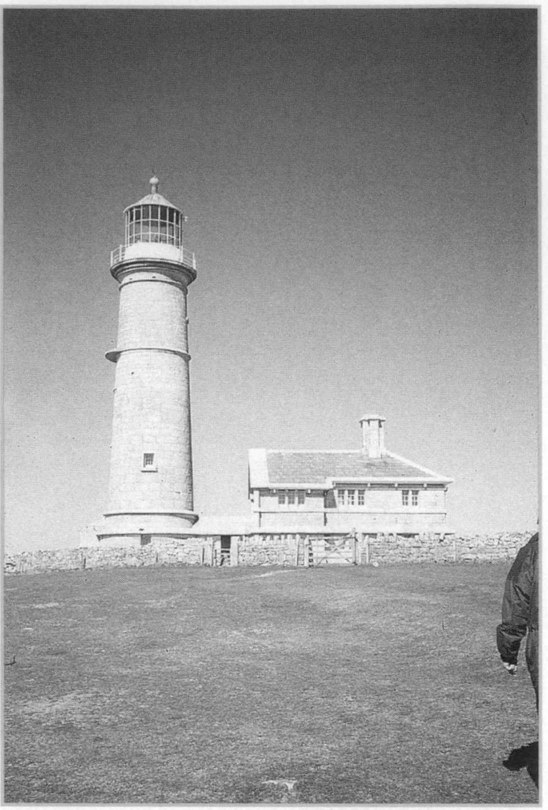

Plate 19.8 Lighthouse on Lundy Island, Bristol Channel, UK
This old lighthouse has been restored and maintained for use by visitors. The old lighthouse keeper's house in the right of the picture is let by the Landmark Trust, a specialist building conservation body in the UK, as self-catering accommodation. This illustrates the potential use for abandoned buildings in a tourism context.

Protection of wildlife

It has been seen in various locations world-wide that tourism discourages poaching because it places economic value on wildlife and protection of natural resources. In many less developed countries, tourism acts as a force of conservation as it offers an alternative economic use. National Parks, such as Amoseli in Kenya and Etosha in Namibia, are viewed as tools of conservation and economic development. Tourist spending generates local employment, demand for local goods and crafts and helps to justify protection of natural resources. Doswell (1997) comments that tourism draws attention to issues relating to biodiversity, endangered species and the human impact on the environment. However, Sindiga and Kanunah (1999) state that in some of the Kenyan National Parks, tourist carrying capacities have been exceeded and animals are harassed by tourist vehicles, disrupting their usual habits and behaviour. Appropriate environmental policy and management is required to ensure protection of the environment and a satisfactory visitor experience. The existence of tourism in Antarctica (see Hall and Johnston 1995) has installed safeguards against degradation of wildlife and habitat. Visitors wishing to see a pristine environment means that there is a public eye watching over the area, inhibiting mining and commercial exploitation. 'Environmentally-sound travel to Antarctica will continue to be an essential element in creating public support for protective legislation and in guarding against attempts to exploit the mineral wealth and rich wildlife of this continent' (IAATO 1991).

Conclusion

Many environmental impacts resulting from tourism have been acknowledged. In some cases, programmes of work have been established to reduce these effects and a pledge towards developing more responsible forms of tourism has been made. In other instances, effects are less well known and/or accepted by those who seek to gain maximum economic benefits, regardless of the environmental costs. It is likely that the future will involve closer examination of environmental impacts. Research is at a relatively early stage of development and there is still much work to be undertaken to establish clear knowledge of cause–effect, systems and interactions. Wider uptake of auditing procedures and improvements in corporate environmental management through legislation and consumer demand will invoke a higher degree of environmental consciousness in tourism-based enterprises. These aspects are more fully discussed in Chapter 20 'The challenge of sustainability'.

Discussion questions

1. Why might it be argued that the ultimate success of tourism relies on an understanding of the environmental impacts?
2. Argue the case that tourism and the environment are mutually beneficial.
3. Which impacts are more serious – those which directly affect the physical environment or those which directly affect tourist enjoyment?
4. To what extent is the tourist responsible for environmental impacts of tourism?

References

Aviation Environment Federation (1996) *Aviation and the Environment*, Hounslow: British Airways.

Bejder, L. Dawson, S.M. and Harraway, J.A. (1999) 'Responses by Hector's Dolphins to boats and swimmers in Porpoise Bay, New Zealand', *Marine Mammal Science*, **15** (3): 738–50.

Boyd, S. and Butler, R. (1996) 'Managing ecotourism: an opportunity spectrum approach', *Tourism Management* **17** (8): 557–66.

Cater, E. (1993) 'Ecotourism in the third world: problems for sustainable tourism development', *Tourism Management*, **14** (2): 85–90.

Internet resources

By going to the weblink at www.thomsonlearning.co.uk students can access the following study on the Thomson Learning website. The study is by C.M. Hall from C.M. Hall and S.J. Page (eds) (1996) *Tourism in the Pacific: Issues and Cases* on 'The environmental impact of tourism in the Pacific' which develops a number of interesting insights and findings related to the way in which tourism impacts upon Pacific Islands which are fragile environments easily affected by tourists and tourist development.

Cordrey, L. (ed.) *The Biodiversity of the South West. An Audit of the South West Biological Resource,* RSPB and County Wildlife Trusts and South West Regional Planning Conference.

Countryside Commission (1992) *Trends in Transport and the Countryside,* Cheltenham: Countryside Commission.

Croall, J. (1995) *Preserve or Destroy. Tourism and the Environment,* London: Calouste Gulbenkian Foundation.

Doswell, R. (1997) *How Effective Management Makes a Difference,* Oxford: Butterworth-Heinemann.

Edington, J.M. and Edington, M.A. (1986) *Ecology, Recreation and Tourism,* Cambridge: Cambridge University Press.

English Tourist Board and Employment Department Group (1991) *Tourism and the Environment. Maintaining the Balance,* London: English Tourist Board.

European Environment Agency (1998) *Europe's Environment: the Second Assessment,* Luxembourg: OOPEC.

Farrell, B.H. and Runyan, D. (1991) 'Ecology and tourism', *Annals of Tourism Research,* **18** (1): 26–40.

Hall, C.M. and Johnston, M.E. (eds) (1995) *Polar Tourism,* Chichester: John Wiley and Sons.

Holden, A. and Kealy, H. (1996) 'A profile of UK outbound "environmentally friendly" tour operators', *Tourism Management,* **17** (1): 60–64.

Honey, M. (1999) *Ecotourism and Sustainable Development. Who Owns Paradise?,* Washington: Island Press.

Hoyt, E. (2000) *Whale Watching 2000: Worldwide Tourism Numbers, Expenditures, and Expanding Socioeconomic Benefits,* Crowborough: International Fund for Animal Welfare, UK.

Hudson, S. (1999) *Snow Business: A Study of the International Ski Industry,* London: Continuum.

International Association of Antarctica Tour Operators (IAATO) (1991) *Antarctica Visitor Guidelines. Press Release,* Kent: IAATO.

Iverson, W.D., Sheppard, S.R.J. and Strain, R.A. (1993) 'Managing regional scenic quality in the Lake Tahoe Basin', *Landscape Journal,* **12** (1): 23–29.

Kavallinis, I. and Pizam, A. (1994) 'The environmental impacts of tourism – whose responsibility is it anyway? the case study of Mykonos', *Journal of Travel Research,* **23** (2): 26–32.

Koenen, J.P., Chon, K-S. and Christianson, D.J. (1995) 'Effects of tourism growth on air quality: the case of Las Vegas', *Journal of Sustainable Tourism,* **3** (3): 135–42.

Krippendorf, J. (1987) *The Holidaymakers: Understanding the Impact of Leisure and Travel,* Oxford: Butterworth-Heinemann.

Marine Conservation Society (1999) Beachwatch '99, http://www.mcsuk.mcmail.com

Marion, J.L. and Farrell, T.A. (1998) 'Managing ecotourism visitation in protected areas', in K. Lindberg, M. Epler Wood, and D. Engeldrum, *Ecotourism. A Guide for Planners and Managers. Volume 2,* North Bennington: The Ecotourism Society: 155–82.

Mathieson, A. and Wall, G. (1982) *Tourism. Economic, Physical and Social Impacts,* Harlow: Longman.

May, V. (1995) 'Environmental implications of the 1992 Winter Olympic Games', *Tourism Management,* **16** (4): 269–75.

Mieczkowski, Z. (1995) *Environmental Issues of Tourism and Recreation,* Lanham: University Press of America.

Orams, M. (1999) *The Economic Benefits of Whale Watching in Vava'u, the Kingdom of Tonga,* Centre for Tourism Research, Auckland: Massey University at Albany.

Page, S.J. (1995) *Urban Tourism,* London: Routledge.

Page, S.J. (1999) *Transport and Tourism,* Harlow: Addison Wesley Longman.

Prunier, E., Sweeney, A. and Geen, A. (1993) 'Tourism and the environment: the case of Zakynthos', *Tourism Management,* **14** (2): 137–41.

Sindinga, I. and Kanunah, M. (1999) 'Unplanned tourism development in Sub-Saharan Africa with special reference to Kenya', *Journal of Tourism Studies,* **10** (1): 25–39.

Swarbrooke, J. (1999) *Sustainable Tourism Management,* Wallingford: CABI.

Theroux, P. (1996) *The Pillars of Hercules,* London: Penguin.

Todd, S.E. and Williams, P.W. (1996) 'From white to green: a proposed environmental management system framework for ski areas', *Journal of Sustainable Tourism,* **4** (3): 147–73.

Wang, C-Y. and Miko, P.S. (1997) 'Environmental impacts of tourism on U.S. National Parks', *Journal of Travel Research,* **35** (4): 31–36.

Whale and Dolphin Conservation Society (1999) Press Archive. http://www.wdcs.org.uk

Wight, P. (1993) 'Sustainable ecotourism: balancing economic, environmental and social goals within an ethical framework', *Journal of Tourism Studies,* **4** (2): 54–66.

Wood, S. and House, K. (1991) *The Good Tourist,* London: Mandarin.

Young, G. (1973) *Tourism: Blessing or Blight?,* Harmondsworth: Penguin.

Further reading

Olsthoorn, X. (2001) 'Carbon dioxide emission from international aviation: 1950–2050', *Journal of Air Transport Management,* **7** (2): 87–93.

Shackley, M. (1998) 'Stingray city' – managing the impact of underwater tourism in the Cayman Islands', *Journal of Sustainable Tourism,* **6** (4): 328–38.

Tyler, D. and Dangerfield, J.M. (1999) 'Ecosystem tourism: a resource-based philosophy for ecotourism', *Journal of Sustainable Tourism,* **7** (2): 146–58.

Useful web addresses

Marine Conservation Society
www.mcsuk.mcmail.com

Whale and Dolphin Conservation Society
www.wdcs.com

20 The challenge of sustainability

Learning outcomes

After studying this chapter, you should be able to:

- Define the meaning of sustainable tourism.
- Outline the principles and a range of sustainable practice in global tourism.
- State the difficulties of achieving sustainable tourism.

Overview

One of the most important aspects of tourism management in the twenty-first century will be devising ways of improving environmental performance. Tourism managers and decision-makers need to be fully conversant in the need to minimize impacts on host communities and the natural environment but at the same time ensuring the existence of a viable tourism industry and maximum local benefits. This poses an enormous challenge. This chapter explores the underlying principles of the argument for sustainable tourism and outlines how some tourism organizations are introducing new practices to improve environmental performance.

Introduction

As the impacts of tourism become apparent, concern about the quality of the environment and the future of the tourism industry begin to emerge. Increasingly, wide recognition of the negative effects of tourism development and activity (see Chapter 19) has led to a focus on alternative forms of tourism and improved environmental practice. The principle which underlies this focus is sustainable development; translated into tourism terms this becomes *sustainable tourism*. A large amount of literature exists on the topic of sustainable tourism, in the academic arena (e.g. Bramwell *et al.* 1996; Hall and Lew 1998; Swarbrooke 1999; plus a journal dedicated to the topic, the *Journal of Sustainable Tourism*). Consumer-oriented publications also reflect concerns (Elkington and Hailes 1992; Wood and House 1991). Coverage in the media is also increasingly apparent, for example on television travel shows (the British Airways Tourism for Tomorrow Awards are televised on the ITV travel programme *Wish You Were Here* in the UK). According to Prosser (1994: 19), sustainable tourism 'seeks to sustain the quantity, quality and productivity of both human and natural resource systems over time, while respecting and accommodating the dynamics of such systems'. This is based on the idea of optimizing returns while protecting the resource base. Prior to exploring the concept and practice of sustainable tourism, it is necessary to gain some understanding of the context in which the concept of sustainability developed. This is best accomplished by considering the development of environmental thinking.

The rise of environmental concern

It is a commonly held view that the 'green' movement is a recent invention. However, the roots of concern about the human impact on the environment can be traced back to ancient civilizations. Ancient Greek literature reveals the philosophy of the earth being viewed as a living goddess. In Roman times, written evidence exists of concerns about land degradation and soil erosion through intensive use and even the effect on human health from using lead cooking vessels. Through the sixteenth and seventeenth centuries, the dominant view of the environment in Europe was centred around man's mastery of nature – that man could conquer the environment and use its resources for human progress. This tends to be viewed as the imperial or anthropocentric perspective on the environment and it has dominated human thinking to the present day. Conversely, the scientific study of nature around the late 1700s onwards gave rise to the notion of the inter-relationships of the natural world and a valuing of flora and fauna – the arcadian or ecocentric perspective. This is illustrated in Figure 20.1.

Many commentators began to realize the negative implications of growth (in industry and population) and challenged the notion of this dominant world view. One of the early critics was Thomas Malthus, who stated that human population growth was increasing at a rate which would outstrip food production. The rapid social and economic changes of the nineteenth century brought about a need for resource management and preservation, best exemplified by the emergence of wilderness preservation societies and early proponents of the National Parks movement in North America. Ecology as an academic discipline became recognized from 1850 and gave rise to a new era in environmental thinking which built on the foundations of the arcadians.

Figure 20.1 **A simplified illustration of environmental thinking**

Ecocentrism ←	→ Anthropocentrism
Natural environment is the core concern. Quality of the environment more important than human progress	*Humans are a dominant force. Mastery of the natural environment for maximum human gain*

The early part of the twentieth century demonstrated a preponderance of groups dedicated to preserving and conserving habitats, species, built heritage and access to open areas. However, the environment became high profile in a social and political sense in the 1960s. Policies for economic growth during the post-World War II period worked on the premise that the more goods the industrial system produced, the more satisfied consumers would be (the greatest happiness for the greatest number of people or 'maximum utility'. The age of consumerism and the industrial processes that gave rise to it did not recognize any environmental responsibilities and production continued while environmental pollution began to increase. Tourism, while not an industrial process, may be seen to be part of this production process, as it requires resources and produces pollution in a number of different forms. From the 1960s, the conventions of economic growth began to be questioned and this, along with several high-profile environmental catastrophes (such as the *Torrey Canyon* oil disaster in 1967), sparked off the beginning of the contemporary environmental movement. Many environmental groups, such as Friends of the Earth, also originate from this period.

The development of the sustainability concept

Early proponents of a new approach to the economy and the environment came in the form of authors (from economists such as J.K. Galbraith to biologists such as Rachel Carson) and pressure groups (concerned with micro and macro issues). Concern focused on both environmental and societal issues. Discussion at international government levels were also apparent. The 1962 United Nations conference promoted the idea of a balance between social and economic development and from then on instigated several long-term sub-groups to examine areas of concern (e.g. the Research Institute for Social Development, Environment Programme). Representatives from the governments and non-government organizations of 119 countries met in 1972 at Stockholm (United Nations Conference on the Human Environment) in an attempt to consider environmental problems. The conclusion reached by the conference was that development and the environment could exist together in mutual benefit but gave no indication as to how this might be achieved.

The International Union for the Conservation of Nature and Natural Resources (IUCN) published the World Conservation Strategy which promoted sustainable development in 1980. In 1984, the United Nations General Assembly appointed a Commission headed by the Norwegian Prime Minister Gro Harlem Brundtland. The Commission, entitled the World Commission on Environment and Development, was charged with exploring environmental and development philosophies and putting forward proposals for change and action. The resulting publication *Our Common Future* set out critical objectives for the future of economic growth and the environment and stated that some painful decisions would have to be made by governments. Sustainable development was defined in the document as development that meets the needs of the present without compromising the needs of those of future generations.

Defining sustainability and sustainable tourism

The most widely accepted definition of sustainable development is that cited in *Our Common Future*:

> Development that meets the needs of the present without compromising the needs of future generations. (World Commission on Environment and Development 1987: 8.)

While this provides a relatively neat summary, the meaning and application of the concept is more problematic. Sustainable development allows for economic development but within the parameters of resource conservation. Sustainability as a concept may be viewed from opposites: at one extreme is economic sustainability where what is being sustained is the economy at whatever cost; diametrically opposed to this is ecological sustainability, where the natural environment takes priority over any economic development.

In addition to defining sustainability, there is a need to consider degrees of sustainability. Turner *et al.* (1994) produced a spectrum of sustainable development, defining positions ranging from 'very weak' sustainability to 'very strong' sustainability, as illustrated in Figure 20.2.

The deep ecologist, Arne Naess pointed out the distinction between 'shallow' and 'deep' ecology (Devall and Sessions 1985). This has become widely accepted and is even reflected in the tourism literature in reference to tourism by Acott *et al.* (1998), who outline the characteristics of deep and shallow forms of ecotourism and emphasize the relationship between tourism and wider debates about sustainability and the environment. In other words, sustainability and sustainable tourism do not represent an absolute standard.

The challenge of sustainability in tourism

Recognition of the damaging effects of tourism has led to a focus on encouraging 'alternative tourism'. Alternative tourism raises the question 'alternative to what?' Most commentators agree that this refers to an alternative to mass tourism. If viewed in this way, then sustainable tourism becomes a niche market. In reality, this is what seems to have occurred. A variety of niche markets with an alternative theme have emerged and terms such as ecotourism, green tourism, sustainable tourism, nature tourism, soft tourism and adventure tourism to name but a few have become part of international and domestic tourism markets. Growth in

Figure 20.2 **Degrees of sustainability**

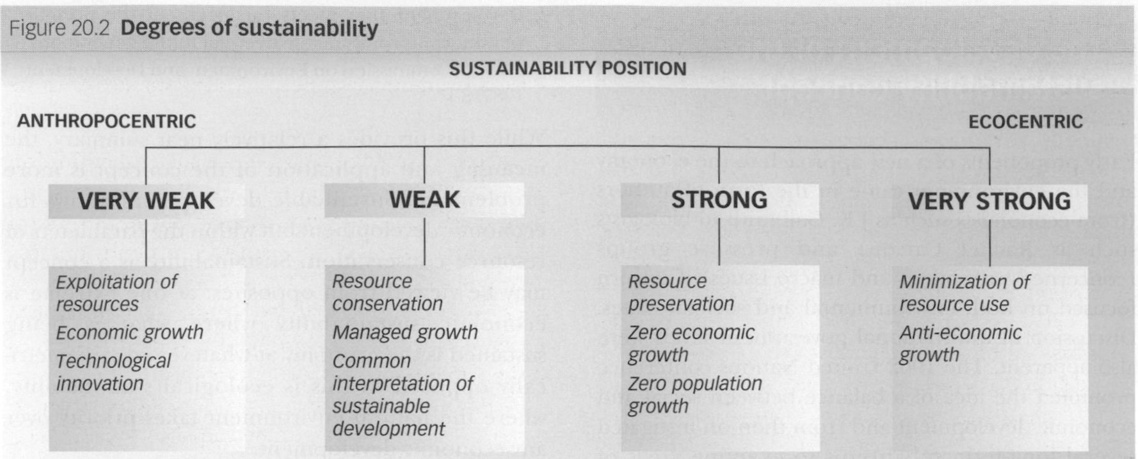

(Source: Adapted from Turner, Pearce and Bateman 1994)

these areas has been particularly marked since the beginning of the 1990s. To some extent, this pattern of product growth is contrary to the ideals of sustainable development. The reason for this is that the diversity of tourism products and environments has increased (as alternative tourism favours less exploited areas, environmentally sensitive or rural areas and culturally different regions which are prone to negative impacts if improperly managed) while mass tourism destinations continue to exist within the traditional management framework. The conclusion to this argument is that sustainable tourism should be viewed more as an ethos than a product or niche market. The ideals of sustainability need to infiltrate the entire tourism system if environments and people are to be protected from the negative forces of change. There are signs that this is beginning to happen. Attention to environmental management (a more practical and achievable perspective of tackling the problems from a business perspective) is becoming more widespread. Large companies, such as tour operators, hotel chains and airlines are starting to demonstrate an awareness of the consequences of tourism development and activity. There is some criticism that this type of reaction is merely 'lip-service' but it is at least a step in the right direction. In addition, one cannot imagine any kind of tourism activity being developed without in some way, reducing the quantity and/or quality of natural resources somewhere. Some of these aspects will be discussed throughout the chapter.

What is sustainable tourism?

The word 'green' connotes many ideas and contradictions. What is 'green' to one individual or society may not be to another. Deep green environmentalists argue that truly environmentally aware individuals would spurn holidays altogether. Krippendorf (1987) states that if people can be persuaded to stay at home, they may be encouraged to improve their own environment rather than escape from it and damage another elsewhere. Krippendorf (1987) argues for greater 'humanism' in life, of which tourism is just one small component. The idea of humanism seeks to reverse trends of consumerism and encourage greater satisfaction in non-consumptive forms of activity. However, what has happened in reality is that people expect more and more. Instead of finding satisfaction in a two-week full-board holiday in Torquay, the travel market has encouraged more sophisticated travellers who wish to see more unusual environments. So, the reality is very complex. If home and work are more satisfying, does this remove the need to escape? Probably not. Tourism has become part of modern life and the way forward is to not try to stop tourism but to explore alternative ways of developing and operating. A response to the recognition of the impacts of tourism has led to the development of an alternative approach generally known as 'sustainable tourism'.

Initially, sustainable tourism was considered to be most relevant in the countryside, where the relationship between the visitor and the natural environment is most obvious (see Chapter 22). This led to a concentration on what was generally termed 'green tourism' – the green emphasizing use and conservation of natural resources. In UK, the first major event where 'green tourism' was at the fore was the 1990 'Shades of Green – Working Towards Green Tourism in the Countryside' conference held in Leeds. Sponsored by the Countryside Commission, English Tourist Board and Rural Development Commission, the objective was to encourage good practice in rural tourism – good practice defined as tourism that respects the environment and community. In this respect, 'green tourism' is nothing new. Walking, cycling, staying in small scale accommodation, eating local food, using public transport, observing wildlife – these activities, encouraged by marketers of green tourism, are acutely traditional. What is new is the marketing, promotion and packaging behind it. Throughout the 1990s, the green term has generally fallen away and a more overarching term – sustainable tourism – has become more prominent.

Defining sustainable tourism

Sustainable tourism is a nebulous concept and to some extent has become moulded to fit the needs of conservationists, governments, communities and developers. Thus, there is no universally accepted definition. The main remit of sustainable tourism is to strike a balance between *the host* (local community), *the guest* (visitors) and *the environment*. This three-way relationship is at the core of sustainable tourism principles and requires careful consideration to maximize positive benefits and minimize negative effects. It is clear that sustainable tourism does not imply a 'no-growth' policy, but it does recognize that limits to growth exist and that environments must be managed in a long-term way. Clarke (1997) suggests four ways in which sustainability in tourism can be viewed:

- as polar opposites – sustainable and mass tourism are at opposite ends of the spectrum
- as a continuum – where shades of sustainability and mass tourism are recognized
- as movement – where positive action can make mass tourism more sustainable
- as convergence – where all tourism strives to be sustainable.

Swarbrooke (1999: 13) provides a useful definition of sustainable tourism: 'tourism which is economically viable but does not destroy the resources on which the future of tourism will depend, notably the physical environment and the social fabric of the host community', observing the need to achieve a balance in the tourists' use of tourist resources and environments they visit and consume.

In both academic and practitioner circles, there has been an emphasis on sustainable tourism as a major focus of attention – illustrated by the amount of published work and the plethora of applied initiatives globally. There is much debate as to the meaning of sustainable tourism but two strands seem to summarize the main contention. McKercher (1993) identifies these as:

1 development centred
2 ecologically centred.

Development-centred ideas consider sustainable tourism as a way of sustaining the tourism industry, where *ecologically centred ideas* concentrate on placing priority on the environment and biodiversity over economic gain. These terms are mutually exclusive so the debate is polarized. If these lines are pursued then no consensus can be achieved. Therefore, one of the challenges of sustainability is to move towards a clear, workable definition with which all stakeholders are reasonably satisfied. Further to this, the concept of sustainable tourism appears to be composed of two elements. The first is *acting in an environmentally conscious way*. This relates to integration of environmental practices into everyday processes and operations, such as: recycling; using products which cause less harm to the environment – such as biodegradable washing powders, ozone-friendly cleaning sprays; conserving energy; minimizing waste through purchasing package-free goods or composting and recycling; using locally produced organic produce; reducing the need to travel. These are practical kinds of activities that individuals and businesses can participate in. The second way of looking at *sustainable tourism as an underpinning philosophy*. Sustainable tourism constitutes a way of thinking about the environment where tourism takes place, respecting the landscape, wildlife, people, existing infrastructure and cultural heritage of a tourism destination. The latter is a more holistic, philosophical perspective that underlies the first element.

The rationale for sustainable tourism

Tourism which is sustainable should:

- Stimulate awareness of tourism impacts.
- Be well planned, with a strategy identifying limits of acceptable change/carrying capacities.
- Generate direct and indirect local employment.
- Support viability of local enterprises.
- Provide income which is retained in the local area as much as possible.
- Support diversification in local and regional economies.
- Encourage local community involvement.
- Support existing infrastructure and provide justification for retention and improvement of local services.
- Respect the integrity of the local environment, culture, people, infrastructure and character of an area.
- Promote local pride.
- Assist in conservation works in the natural and built environment.
- Be carefully monitored with strategies for minimizing negative impacts in place.

Sustainable tourism in practice

The evidence for the existence of sustainable tourism lies in case studies and examples of good practice which exists globally. It is clear that sustainable tourism can be interpreted in a variety of ways, from

Plate 20.1 Coverack, Lizard Peninsula, Cornwall, UK
Small-scale bed and breakfast enterprises operated by local people are an identifiable part of sustainable tourism. Economic benefits help to maintain a diverse economic base in a community and closer contact between visitor and host enables more direct benefits to be sought.

Plate 20.2 A fish market
Enterprises such as this fish market may be a visitor attraction in its own right. Visitors spending money in such local enterprises also assist the local economy.

small-scale community ventures to environmental/ technical management in hotels. Interestingly, it has been the large corporations with multinational interests that have responded most quickly to pressure than smaller, locally based tourism ventures. Many of these initiatives are well documented and what follows is a number of notable examples:

- 1990 – Consort Hotels adopted the message 'Conservation in Comfort' which was translated to a number of selected hotels. An example of how this translated to practice is an example of a package – the 'Go Green Weekend' which included talks by local naturalists, nature walks, a nature interpretation room and fresh wholefood produce on the menu. The general aim was to fill surplus capacity in the off season and create a new niche market.
- 1991 – Inter-Continental Hotels Group put together an environmental reference manual giving guidelines and instructions to staff on environmental management. The aim of this manual was to increase staff awareness of environmental concerns and encourage a more pro-active approach. Hotel Inter-Continental in Nairobi, Kenya is one good example of a large hotel which has incorporated improved environmental management into its operations management, a summary of which is incorporated in Table 20.1.
- 1992 – The International Hotels Environment Initiative produced a revised manual *Environmental Management for Hotels: the Industry Guide to Best Practice.* This included a voluntary code of conduct and useful reference material on how to upgrade procedures and systems, such as waste management, energy consumption, noise, congestion, purchasing and training. A second edition was published in 1996 (see IHEI 1996).
- Canadian Pacific Hotels launched *The Green Partnership Guide* which identifies environmental improvements and how they might lead to reduced operating costs.

There have been a significant number of what might be termed 'area' projects based on sustainable

Table 20.1 **Environmental management at the Hotel Inter-Continental, Nairobi**

Environmental issue	How addressed	Benefits
Energy	**Reusing the condenser from the discarded liquid chillers to install a flash steam heat-exchange unit**	By saving on the cost of a new heat exchanger (US$40,000) and using the heat exchanger recovered from the water chillers, the only cost incurred was US$2,000 for installation and modifications. Fuel consumption has been reduced by 24,000 gallons (90,909 litres), which amounts to US$34,000 per annum. Carbon dioxide and sulphur dioxide emissions have also been reduced. The boiler now operates at 50% capacity and uses less energy
Emissions	**Replacement of CFC 12 liquid chillers** Like most traditional refrigeration and freezers, the Inter-Continental Nairobi's liquid chillers were operating on R12 which contains chloroflorocarbons (CFCs) – an ozone-depleting substance. These chillers have now been replaced with more ozone-friendly R-134a (HFC-134a) chillers. The cost of this replacement was US$200,000	Less pollution
Energy	**Twin-speed motors in the air conditioning cooling towers** When cooling demand falls and the water temperature is low, the motor operates at a lower speed	As the motors frequently operate a lower speed, approximately 8000 kwh of energy are saved per month. This equates to a reduction of US$8,400 in energy costs per annum. The noise level of the towers has been reduced by 60%
Visitor communication	**'The Green Plant' newsletter** Carries information on general environmental issues as well as on the hotel's environment programme	Communication of environmental objectives to the consumer
Environmental information booklets	The booklets were developed to improve hoteliers' understanding of environmental issues and provide practical suggestions on simple, low-cost measures to improve environmental performance. They were disseminated to over 50 small and medium-sized hotels and to other Inter-Continental Hotels in Kenya and Africa in place of a traditional Christmas card	The response has been very positive. Several hotels, including eight Inter-Continental hotels in Africa have now implemented environmental management programmes

(Source: *Environmental Good Practice in Hotels* from the International Hotel and Restaurant Association Environmental Award published by the International Hotel and Restaurant Association and UNEP 1996)

tourism development. Some have achieved success, others less so. These can generally be classed as follows:

- *Regional rural projects.* These cover a large area of mainly rural regions, such as the Alto Minho region of Portugal and the Mid-Wales Festival of the Countryside (see Chapter 23) and tend to focus on regional economic development with a tourism focus. Usually run in partnership between public sector bodies.
- *District-wide projects.* Usually run by a single authority (often in partnership) and covering a specific, generally politically defined area, such as Project Explore in South-east Cornwall, National Park Authority projects such as Kruger (see Middleton and Hawkins 1998).
- *Local community initiatives.* Originated and run by local people as a 'bottom-up' approach, rather than a 'top-down' approach. Good examples of these are beginning to emerge in the international arena. Rathlin Island off the coast of Northern Ireland; Capirona in Equador where a community of Quichua Indian families have developed ecotourism as a means of economic development.
- *Urban/single-site visitor management.* Includes town centre management schemes set up to restore part of a historic city incorporating tourism objectives, environmental management in seaside resorts (e.g. Malaga City – see Barke and Newton 1995). This also includes management of particular locations, such as a honeypot site or visitor attraction, e.g. Niagara Falls, Ayers Rock (Uluru) and Pompeii. Single-site sustainable tourism incorporates visitor attractions based on the sustainability theme, such as the Eden Project, the Earth Centre and Earth Balance in the UK.

Plate 20.3 Promenade enhancement scheme
This promenade enhancement scheme has been designed and constructed with local materials, allowing greater harmonization with the local environment.

Plate 20.4 Sustainable tourism
Sustainable tourism may be embodied within attractions. This example is Earth Balance, a small-scale initiative set up in a declining industrial area in the north-east of England. The concept is to demonstrate that the area can seek a new, sustainable future.

Tools for sustainability

One of the great drawbacks of sustainability is the difficulty in finding ways to put it into practice. To ease this, processes and practices have been developed. The concept of 'best practice' environmental management is now widely accepted as a means of achieving total quality management in all industries and is of direct relevance to tourism. Evaluation processes have existed since the 1970s in the manufacturing industries and have developed from business organization theory and global management perspectives.

Corporate environmental management

From the late 1980s, environmental management procedures have become part of the tourism industry, assisted by the Rio Summit in 1992. A survey of tour operators and environmental awareness in 1991 found that most businesses had not seriously addressed environmental issues and that the recession meant that they were not even on the agenda. Most tended to follow the strategy of 'see it now before it's gone' (Elkington and Hailes 1992). Several studies in the 1990s attempted to track the behaviour of tour operators as research and awareness of tourism impacts became more widespread in the consumer market (Carey *et al.* 1997; Curtin and Busby 1999; Holden and Kealy 1996). Research demonstrates that it tends to be the smaller, independent and more specialist tour operators who display greater environmental awareness and participate in more ethical and sustainable practice (Fennell and Malloy 1999). McKercher (1993: 11) states that 'in a free market system, such a diverse and highly unregulated industry as tourism will likely continue to defy most efforts to limit its expansion' which is a worrying indictement of the tourism industry and sustainability. In the UK, the British Standards Institute have developed a standard procedure and kitemarking system for corporate environmental management. This is known as BS 7750 (known internationally as ISO 14000/140001). The procedure entails an annual independent assessment of company environmental practice.

Environmental impact assessment (EIA)

An environmental impact assessment is a projective assessment of the adverse and beneficial impacts of a specific development used in the planning control system. The assessment covers the period from initial planning to post-development. It is an in-depth, co-ordinated assessment of the environmental ramifications of development, which covers not only impacts but the quality of environmental management systems (Middleton and Hawkins 1998). This information assists decision-makers in evaluating the consequences of a development and thus deciding whether an application should be approved or made conditional on implementing environmental management procedures. For tourism purposes, developments such as marinas, ski resorts, holiday villages (such as Center Parcs) and other large-scale resort developments would require an EIA. As Ding and Pigram (1995) note, if the process is effective and meets the correct objectives, then it is a very useful technique. However, there are three main issues upon which one can criticize the effectiveness of EIA:

- Global implementation is patchy. While most developed nations have adopted legislation on EIAs, many less developed countries have not done so. The USA was at the forefront of EIA in the 1970s, while the European Union adopted legislation in 1985. In Australia as in many other countries, proposed tourism developments are subject to EIA before planning approval is given.
- While it is a mandatory requirement for large-scale development, smaller developments are not generally subject to the same process. Therefore, environmental damage is still likely to occur over the long term through the operation of smaller enterprises.
- EIA is only applicable to new developments, not existing operations which cause environmental damage.

In addition, there are secondary issues to consider. The developer is generally assigned to collect data on the proposals so the accuracy may be questioned. Second, as Buckley (1991: 233) comments, EIA 'operates at the scale of the individual project'. In other words, the process fails to recognize effects on an interactive and cumulative level, not integrating environmental, social and economic factors very effectively (Mowforth and Munt 1998). For example, the issue of over-development in the area may not be acknowledged. There are also concerns about the lack of a feedback loop for ensuring effective monitoring.

Environmental auditing

One of the most innovative projects emanating from attempts to look at the environmental performance of existing tourism businesses is the idea of environmental auditing. Auditing is different to EIA because it evaluates existing business practice rather than potential problems. Ding and Pigram (1995) state this is a relatively new idea and not yet well developed in Australia. In UK, the Green Audit Kit has been developed as an auditing tool. The kit comprises a loose-leaf binder containing six sections on aspects of environmental management. These are energy, transport, purchasing, waste, health and local environment. It is designed as a 'do-it-yourself' environmental audit manual (Dingle 1995). The kit was first trialled as part of the South Devon Green Tourism Initiative which ran from 1992–1994 and later adopted by the Countryside Agency for wide use across England. This type of environmental evaluation is voluntary.

The deficiencies in EIA procedure can be resolved to some extent by applying the two processes together, that is EIA prior to development, then auditing following development. Auditing can provide the feedback required to assess impact prediction.

Environmental policies and statements

Many companies have developed statements about their environmental performance, policies and practices. These range in length from a sentence or two (e.g. most tour operators), a page in a brochure (e.g. Kuoni 'Caring for our World') to a full booklet (e.g. Center Parcs) and even an annual report (e.g. British Airways). In many cases, very little of substance is conveyed but some organizations provide detailed information about how environmental and community work is contributed to or how impacts are assessed and monitored. The essential aspect is to ensure that policies are put into action, otherwise they are useless.

Agenda 21

Despite the commendable attempts by the United Nations to raise awareness and stimulate action on social and environmental issues world-wide, there was very little evidence of action. A process of change began after the 1992 United Nations Earth Summit in Rio de Janeiro where commitments to action were made by governments across the globe. One of the key outcomes of this conference was Agenda 21 – an international action plan or 'blueprint' for sustainable development. Signed by 182 heads of state, Agenda 21 commits national governments to considering the environment and development across a number of different activities and is now being implemented in countries across the world. About two thirds of the Agenda 21 action plan requires implementation at local levels and local authorities and communities are working together to achieve this objective.

Exhibit 20.1 **British Airways environmental department**

British Airways, based at Heathrow Airport, UK, is the world's largest international passenger airline. The company recognizes the significance of environmental issues and takes an active role in attempting to minimize impacts and create opportunities for conservation and communities. The Environment Branch of British Airways advises, supports, monitors and measures environmental performance.

Environmental policy

The corporate goal of British Airways is to be a 'good neighbour, concerned for the community and the environment' (1999a: 6). Policy objectives include:

- to develop awareness and understanding of the interactions between the airline's operations and the environment
- to maintain a healthy working environment for all employees
- to consider and respect the environment and to seek to protect the environment in the course of its activities.

British Airways has produced an environmental strategy as a way of achieving these broad objectives. Policy is then translated into practice which is measured through target setting.

Environmental impacts and environmental management

Tackling environmental issues is achieved through a dedicated section within British Airways – the Environment Branch. An Annual Environmental Report is produced, which charts current practice, progress and sets targets for improved environmental performance. Through reviews and consultation, five environmental issues have been highlighted as significant in the operation of British Airways: noise, emissions, waste, congestion and tourism. For each of these areas of impact, targets have been set to reduce negative effects. To cite an example, in the emissions category, recent objectives to reduce emissions included:

- to produce an inventory of CO_2 emissions from world-wide ground energy by April 2000
- to achieve 30 per cent improvement in fuel efficiency by 2010 compared to 1990.

Achievements are also monitored, for example, a 9.5 per cent reduction in total ground energy consumption was recorded 1998–1999. It is clear that British Airways is committed to pursuing a more responsible approach in its operations.

Tourism for Tomorrow Awards

Since 1992, British Airways has run an award scheme to encourage more responsible forms of tourism. The awards are directed at tour operators, hotels and other organizations associated with tourism. The concept centres around an annual selection of examples of best practice in sustainable tourism, judged by a panel of experts. Previous winners have included the Hanauma Bay Nature Reserve Management Plan, Hawaii, Pacific Eco Beach resort, Broome in Western Australia and the Sea-to-Sea (C2C) Cycle Route, UK. The winners of the awards, which are divided into categories (global, long haul, Americas, Europe, United Kingdom, Pacific, southern plus other special categories), are widely publicized, including a feature on a UK-based holiday television programme.

Conservation programme

Travel assistance is offered to individuals involved in conservation projects through British Airways Assisting Conservation (BAAC). Set up in 1984, the initiative aims to offer free or low-cost flights to assist those running conservation schemes across the world with project costs. About 250 tickets per year are allocated. Projects which have benefited include the International Gorilla Conservation Programme, Seahorse Conservation in Vietnam and the Philippines and organizations such as the Royal Geographical Society and the Smithsonian Institution.

In addition:

- British Airways donates money to conservation schemes directly. In 1998, £200,000 was donated globally from a scheme where for every traveller with the British Airways Holidays, £1 is donated to conservation charity.
- British Airways Holidays produce 'Eco Notes' which provide travellers with information on the environmental aspects of their destination.

(Sources: British Airways 1999a, 1999b, 1998)

Plate 20.5 Groningen, the Netherlands
Agenda 21 seeks to encourage a more sustainable approach to all aspects of life. Use of alternative modes of transport, such as the bicycle, is likely to increase in the future.

Agenda 21 affects most areas of global activity, including tourism. Tourism has been recognized in some local action plans, for example Devon County Council in the UK and Calvia in Majorca (see Chapter 23) – both of which are important regions for tourism activity. In addition, defined elements of tourism activity, such as transport, food, accommodation, waste management and entrepreneurialism are an integral part of local Agenda 21 plans. Various methods of assessing the potential and actual impact of tourism have been generated, mostly to assist in planning procedures and in improving environmental performance. The idea of Agenda 21 has been adapted more specifically to the tourism industry by the World Travel and Tourism Council, the World Tourism Organization and the Earth Council (the last is the body established to translate Agenda 21 principles into practice). Agenda 21 for the Travel and Tourism Industry (1996) recommends actions for tourism-specific organizations in the public and private sector to adopt sustainable principles. Grant (1996) provides a useful overview of this.

Visitor management

At the core of sustainable tourism lies good practice in visitor management. Visitor management is an approach which aims to protect the environment while providing for visitor enjoyment, a theme which is also discussed in Chapter 26. There are different methods for different types of location which work on both macro- (i.e. a nation, region or area) and a micro- (settlement or site) level. Strategic decisions about visitor management must be made in relation to carrying capacity. Visitor management covers a broad spectrum of strategies and tools but generally, there are three main areas – as demonstrated in Figure 20.3.

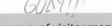

Figure 20.3 **Summary of visitor management strategies**

CONTROL VOLUME
(e.g. limit numbers, encourage alternative visit timing and locations)

MODIFY BEHAVIOUR
(e.g. codes of conduct, signposting)

ADAPT RESOURCE
(e.g. harden footpath surface, construct purpose-built facilities)

(Source: Modified from Employment Department Group and English Tourist Board 1991)

Visitor management may also be divided into two forms (Grant 1994):

1. *Hard measures* – aligned with physical and financial restrictions on access. Examples are road closures, parking fees, entrance charges, fencing, zoning and restrictions on vehicle size.
2. *Soft measures* – associated with encouraging desired behaviour rather than restricting undesirable activities. Examples are marketing and promotional material, signs, interpretation, information provision and guided walks.

The two forms are not mutually exclusive. The hard measures are somewhat easier to apply with immediate results but may not solve the problem alone. A combination of hard and soft initiatives are considered appropriate in most cases as the following three measures show.

- *Spatial distribution as a visitor management strategy* aims to spread economic benefits of visitor activity geographically, extend recreational opportunities and experiences and reduce pressure on stressed

Plate 20.6 A Kauri tree
This historic tree is hundreds of years old and plays a major role in Maori culture and is under pressure from visitors to Northland, New Zealand. Boardwalks have had to be constructed and wire fences put up to prevent damage from visitors.

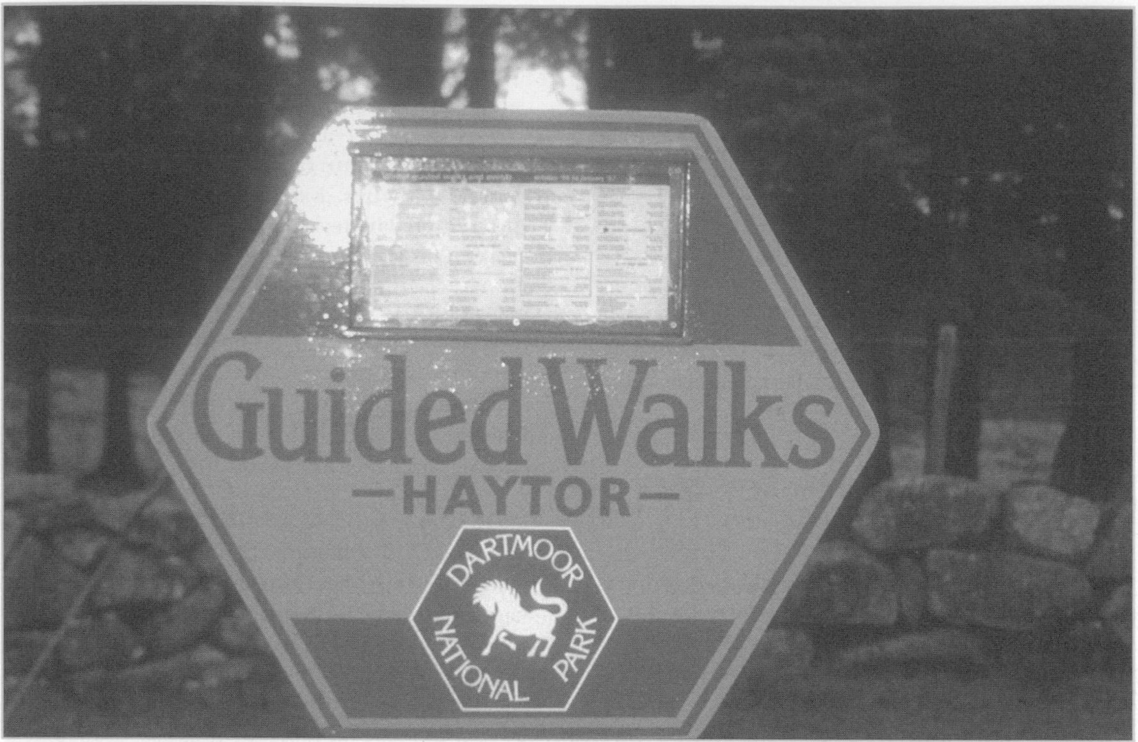

Plate 20.7 Guided walks

Guided walks are a popular form of visitor management. On Dartmoor, the National Park Authority operates a large variety of walks which aim to introduce aspects of history, ecology, landscape and archaeology in an enjoyable way. Visitors who lack confidence or who may be in danger of inadvertently damaging the environment can benefit from this.

environments. This may be achieved through a number of tools:

- information packs, outlining attractions and accommodation in the wider area
- marketing of less well-known areas
- ticketing strategies (e.g. joint ticketing, discounts, high charges)
- visitor assistants
- interpretation (e.g. trails, information, routing, tours)
- transport links.

In addition to protecting environmental resources, sometimes it is necessary to prevent conflict between recreational users of an area. Zoning is a method of managing conflicting activities by spatial separation. Commonly found on reservoirs and lakes where sailing, water skiing, angling and conservation purposes might conflict. The Peak District National Park is zoned into five recreational areas, indicating levels of intensity of use, from wild areas through to areas of highest intensity recreational use. Lundy Island, England's only Marine Nature Reserve, is managed partly through a system of zoning designed to meet the needs of marine conservation and recreation.

- *Temporal distribution aspects* address how visits might be spread throughout the year rather than just at peak times. Tools of temporal distribution are:
  - timed ticketing
  - promotion of out-of-season packages
  - special events
  - all-year facilities.

In addition, *demarketing* is an active policy of not marketing a location is another option for areas where visitor capacity has been reached or attempts are being made to limit promotion of a more fragile environment.

Plate 20.8 A visitor centre, Looe, Cornwall, UK
This picture shows an example of interpretation located within a visitor centre. The aim of this interpretation is to encourage visitors to gain an understanding of the area surrounding the popular seaside resort of Looe in Cornwall, including wildlife, walks, history and local literary figures.

- *Ways of altering visitor behaviour* are also an important part of visitor management. One method employed quite extensively is use of codes of conduct. The aim of a code of conduct is to change tourist's behaviour and attitude. Mowforth and Mason (1995) provide a useful overview of codes of conduct. Friends of Conservation have produced guidelines aimed at tourists to assist in maintaining a balance between enjoyment and conservation. Entitled the *Traveller's Code*, it covers issues of accommodation, culture, dress, food and drink, out and about, shopping, transport, adventure and booking.

Carrying capacity and the limits of acceptable change

Much of the discussion about managing environmental and tourist resources considers the concept of carrying capacity. There are four main types of carrying capacity as illustrated in Figure 20.4.

The notion of carrying capacity, while quite acceptable in theory, is criticized for its inherent difficulty in application. Swarbrooke (1999) provides a critique of the carrying capacity idea:

- some types of capacity are subjective
- measuring techniques are crude, not taking into account:
  - type of destination and nature of environment/community;
  - type of tourism and tourists.
- carrying capacity does not address the complexity of the issue of acceptable/unacceptable situations. It is too simplistic to say that a few extra people make a difference
- measurements of carrying capacity do take account of the costs of reducing capacity into account, such as jobs and income.

A more recent approach to this subject is the limits of acceptable change (LAC) which incorporates a more holistic approach. Limits are set according to

Figure 20.4 **Types of carrying capacity**

PHYSICAL
A measure of the number of tourists that may be accommodated on a site

PERCEPTUAL
A measure of the number of people that may be accommodated on a site before the visitor experience is damaged

ECONOMIC
A measure of the number of people that may be welcomed to a location before the economy of the area is adversely affected

ECOLOGICAL
A measure of the number of people that may be accommodated on a site before damage occurs to the environment

Exhibit 20.2 **Alcúdia's plan of highest quality**

Alcúdia is a small peninsula on the north-eastern coast of Mallorca and is one of the most visited parts of the island. It offers natural beauty, varied scenery, history and a range of tourist facilities. Mass tourism has developed over the last 20 years:

- Pol-lèntia is an outstanding archaeological site, with evidence of Roman settlement. The site has been interpreted for visitors and a self-guided trail leaflet is available.
- S'albufera de Mallorca is the largest and most important wetland area in the Balearics and its first protected area (declared a National Park in 1988). The site is characterized by its ecological richness, including plants, fish, invertebrates, fungi, mammals and, most significantly, birds.
- Promotion of cycling through a booklet freely available to tourists giving ten cycling routes which give opportunities to explore off the beaten track.
- Promotion of Alcúdia as an 'Ecotouristic Community' through a leaflet outlining the major plant and animal species to be found and the location of nature reserves.
- Attendance at the World Travel Market in London to promote the area's attraction and the ideals of sustainable tourism.

Sisman (1994: 60) suggests that 'environmentalism should be much more integrated into society as a whole, not an adjunct to it'. The implications of this is that sustainable tourism should be a philosophy that infiltrates the whole of the tourism industry rather than being a niche market or minority view. To be successful, Sisman advocates 'a working partnership that blends good environmental practice and profitable business for mutual long-term advantages'. (Sisman 1994: 59). A plethora of environmental guidelines and charters has been prepared by environmental groups for the tourism industry to implement. Sisman believes these have failed because such groups lack an understanding of business. No doubt, environmental groups would counter this with the view that business does not understand the environment. This is at the core of the problem of achieving sustainability. Redclift (1987: 36) cites the importance of integrating the sustainable development concept into international structures, otherwise there is a danger that it will become 'yet another discarded development concept'.

Conclusion

Despite confusion over meanings of sustainable tourism, it is clear that protection of the resources which tourism depends on is central to sustainable development (Hall and Lew 1998). Sustainability has been described by Middleton (1998) as 'a simple idea with global appeal but a massively complex process'. It is vital to recognize this complexity and not to be fooled into thinking that sustainable tourism can be achieved by devising a policy statement or undertaking one aspect of environmental management. In reality, sustainable tourism is somewhat of an oxymoron – while appropriate management is achievable at the site level, it cannot be overall purely because of the need for travel. The best that the tourism industry as a whole can do is move towards better environmental practice. May (1991) provides six steps which can be taken to move closer to the goal of sustainability:

- better understanding of the value of environments
- more complete information about environments, local values and susceptibility to outside influences
- greater attention to the regional effects of development
- use of environmental economics in relation to assessing development
- improved measurements of environmental factors for use in environmental accounting
- developments should be designed with long-term environmental quality in mind.

These issues provide a continuing challenge for the development and management of tourism in the stwenty-first century.

Discussion questions

1. Why is ecotourism not necessarily a form of sustainable tourism?
2. To what extent are multinational corporations in tourism displaying green credentials?
3. Explain the meaning of sustainability in a tourism context and suggest why this might conflict with other perceptions of sustainability.
4. Why is sustainable tourism so difficult to achieve?

References

Acott, T. La Trobe, H. and Howard, S. (1998) 'An evaluation of deep ecotourism and shallow ecotourism', *Journal of Sustainable Tourism*, **6** (3): 238–53.

Barke, M. and Newton, M. (1995) 'Promoting sustainable tourism in an urban context: recent developments in Malaga City, Andalucia', *Journal of Sustainable Tourism*, **3** (3): 115–33.

Bramwell, B., Henry, I., Jackson, G., Prat, A.G., Richards, G. and van der Straaten, J. (eds) (1996) *Sustainable Tourism Management: Principles and Practice*, Tilburg: Tilburg University Press.

British Airways (1998) *Assisting Conservation*, Harmondsworth: British Airways.

British Airways (1999a) *British Airways Annual Environmental Report 1999*, Harmondsworth: British Airways.

British Airways (1999b) *Tourism for Tomorrow Awards*, Harmondsworth: British Airways.

Buckley, R. (1991) *Perspectives in Environmental Management*, New York: Springer Verlag.

Carey, S., Gountas, Y. and Gilbert, D. (1997) 'Tour operators and destination sustainability', *Tourism Management*, **18** (7): 425–31.

Clarke, J. (1997) 'A framework of approaches to sustainable tourism', *Journal of Sustainable Tourism*, **5**: 224–33.

Curtin, S. and Busby, G. (1999) 'Sustainable destination development: the tour operator perspective', *International Journal of Tourism Research*, **1** (2): 135–47.

Devall, B. and Sessions, G. (1985) *Deep Ecology. Living as if Nature Mattered*, Utah: Gibbs Smith.

Ding, P. and Pigram, J. (1995) 'Environmental audits: an emerging concept in sustainable development', *Journal of Tourism Studies*, **6** (2): 2–10.

Dingle, P. (1995) 'Practical green business', *Insights*, C35–45, London: English Tourist Board.

Dymond, S. (1997) 'Indicators of sustainable tourism in New Zealand: a local government perspective', *Journal of Sustainable Tourism*, **15** (4): 279–93.

Elkington, J. and Hailes, J. (1992) *Holidays That Don't Cost The Earth*, London: Gollancz.

Employment Department Group and English Tourist Board (1991) *Tourism and the Environment. Maintaining the Balance*, London: English Tourist Board.

Fennell, D. and Malloy, D. (1999) 'Measuring the ethical nature of tour operators', *Annals of Tourism Research*, **26** (1): 928–43.

Grant, M. (1994) 'Visitor management', *Insights* A41–46, London: English Tourist Board.

Grant, M. (1996) 'Tourism, sustainability and Agenda 21', *Insights*, A85–90, London: English Tourist Board.

Hall, C.M. and Lew, A. (eds) (1998) *Sustainable Tourism. A Geographical Perspective*, Harlow: Addison Wesley Longman.

Holden, A. and Kealy, H. (1996) 'A profile of UK oubound "environmentally friendly" tour operators', *Tourism Management*, **17** (1): 60–64.

Honey, M. (1999) *Ecotourism and Sustainable Development: Who Owns Paradise?*, Washington: Island Press.

International Hotels Environment Initiative (IHEI) (1996) *Environmental Management for Hotels: The Industry Guide to Best Practice*, second edition, Oxford: Butterworth-Heinemann.

Krippendorf, J. (1987) *The Holidaymakers Understanding the Impact of Leisure and Travel*, Oxford: Butterworth-Heinemann.

Lane, B. (1994) 'Sustainable rural tourism strategies: a tool for development and conservation', *Journal of Sustainable Tourism*, **2** (1&2): 102–11.

May, V. (1991) 'Tourism, environment and development. values, sustainability and stewardship', *Tourism Management*, **12** (2): 112–18.

Internet resources

By going to the weblink at www.thomsonlearning.co.uk students can access the following study on the Thomson Learning website. The study is by L. Lumsdon (1997) *Tourism Marketing* and examines the issue of sustainable tourism in a marketing context which has a number of synergies with other chapters in this book, particularly Chapters 17 and 18.

McKercher, B. (1993) 'Can tourism survive sustainability?', *Tourism Management,* **14**: 131–36.

Middleton, V.T.C. (1998) 'A marketing approach to the sustainability issue', Conference Presentation at University of Westminster, 8 December 1998.

Middleton, V.T.C. and Hawkins, R. (1998) *Sustainable Tourism. A Marketing Approach,* Oxford: Butterworth-Heinemann.

Mowforth, M. and Mason, P. (1995) *Codes of Conduct in Tourism,* Occasional Papers in Geography, No.1, Department of Geographical Sciences, University of Plymouth.

Mowforth, M. and Munt, I. (1998), *Tourism and Sustainability. New Tourism in the Third World,* London: Routledge.

Muller, H. (1994) 'The thorny path to sustainable tourism development', *Journal of Sustainable Tourism,* **2** (3): 131–36.

Prosser, R. (1994) 'Societal change and growth in international tourism', in E. Cater and G. Lowman (eds) *Ecotourism: A Sustainable Option?,* Chichester: Wiley: 19–37.

Redclift, M. (1987) *Sustainable Development. Exploring the Contradictions,* London: Routledge.

Ritchie, J.R.B. (1998) 'Managing the human presence in ecologically sensitive tourism destinations: insights from the Banff-Bow Valley Study', *Journal of Sustainable Tourism,* **6** (4): 293–313.

Ritchie, J.R.B. (1999) 'Policy formulation at the tourism/environment interface: insights and recommendations from the Banff-Bow Valley Study', *Journal of Travel Research,* **38**: 100–10.

Sisman, D. (1994) 'Tourism: environmental relevance', in E. Cater and G. Lowman (eds) *Ecotourism: A Sustainable Option?,* Chichester: Wiley: 57–68.

Swarbrooke, J. (1999) *Sustainable Tourism Management,* Wallingford: CAB International.

Turner, R.K., Pearce, D. and Bateman, I. (1994) *Environmental Economics: An Elementary Introduction,* New York: Harvester Wheatsheaf.

Wheeller, B. (1991) 'Tourism's troubled times. Responsible tourism is not the answer', *Tourism Management,* **12**: 91–96.

Wood, K. and House, S. (1991) *The Good Tourist,* London: Mandarin.

World Commission on Environment and Development (1987) *Our Common Future,* Oxford: Oxford University Press.

Further reading

Middleton, V. and Hawkins, R. (1998) *Sustainable Tourism. A Marketing Approach,* Oxford: Butterworth-Heinemann.

Mowforth, M. and Munt, I. (1998) *Tourism and Sustainability. New Tourism in the Third World,* London: Routledge.

Swarbrooke, J. (1999) *Sustainable Tourism Management,* Wallingford: CAB International.

Useful web addresses

Econett
www.wttc.org

Cooperative Research Centre for Sustainable Tourism
www.crctourism.com.au

Section 6

Trends and themes in the use of tourist resources

In the last section of the book the impact of tourism was reviewed and attention now turns to a number of different forms of tourism which have impacts on the environment. This section reviews the main tourism environments which attract tourist activity and discusses the nature of tourism in each context as well as the principal issues associated with each particular form of tourism. In Chapter 21, the significance of urban tourism is discussed as a context for many forms of tourist visit and the problems of accurately analysing this form of tourism is discussed. The impact of urban tourism on city environments and the interactions it has with the city economy are reviewed together with the nature of tourist activities in city environments. This is followed in Chapter 22 with a contrasting example of rural tourism. The problems of defining what comprises a rural environment for tourism is a major focus of this chapter and the impacts and effects of this form of tourism on the rural environment are also examined. This is followed in Chapter 23 with a review of the stereotypical tourism environment – the coastal environment and resort tourism. Chapter 23 discusses both the evolution of the coast as a context for tourism activity and its predisposition as a location for resort development which is the concentration of facilities to service tourist needs. Lastly, Chapter 24 reviews the impact of tourism activity in the less developed world which has become a popular destination in recent years for tourist trips due to the exotic appeal and relatively low costs now offered to western tourists through package travel. In each chapter, the nature of the form of tourism is discussed and where possible, examples illustrating the impacts of tourism activity highlighted in the previous section of the book are outlined to show how the impacts occur in specific tourism environments.

Learning outcomes

After reading this chapter you should be able to:

- Appreciate the significance of cities as tourism destinations.
- Consider the ways in which urban areas fulfil a wide range of tourist needs.
- Develop an understanding of the complexity of towns and cities in the analysis of tourist resources.

21 Urban tourism

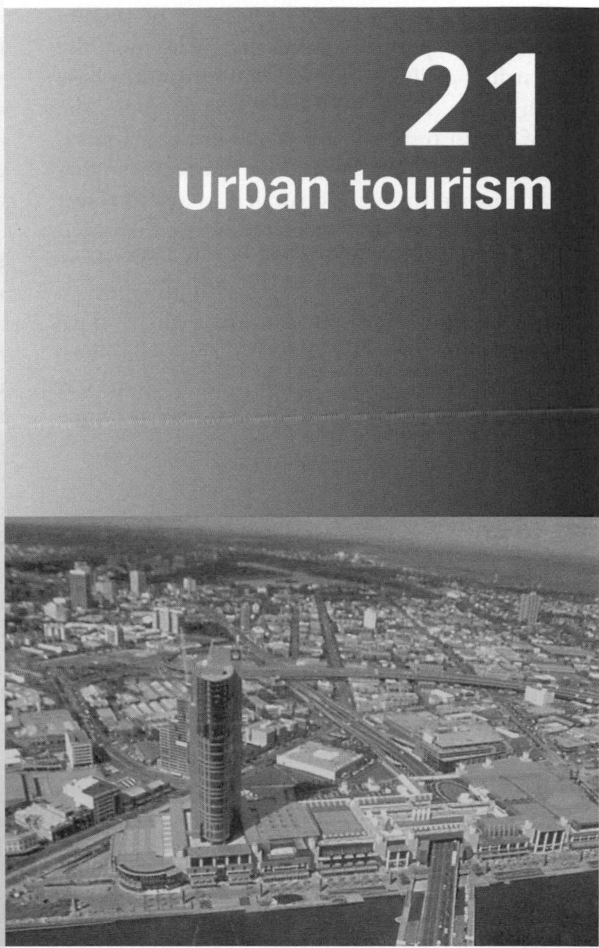

Overview

This chapter commences with a review of the concept of tourism resources as a phenomenon which the tourist uses as a consumer during their activities in different locations. The ways of classifying resources are briefly reviewed and the chapter then moves on to examine the growing importance of urban tourism as an environment for tourism. The chapter discusses the concept of urban tourism and its limited development as a concept, and the ways in which researchers have approached urban tourism. The importance of urban environments and their ability to absorb large numbers of visitors and the prospects for impacts are reviewed. The chapter also considers issues related to the visitor experience for urban tourism. The discussion also outlines the issues associated with the ways in which tourists learn about the urban tourism environment and the issues which impact on the experience of urban tourism.

Introduction

With the development and growth of tourist destinations, a consistent theme in recent research over the last 20 years is the concept of tourist resources which are consumed at specific points in time by tourists in different environments. As Chapter 2 outlined, tourism and resort development is not a new concept in the United Kingdom and in Europe as well as in other parts of the world. But in recent years, many of the current environments which have emerged or been developed as tourism destinations have become concerned with the issue of sustainability (see Chapter 20), which has at its roots the safeguarding of the future use of the resource base in each locale. In the following four chapters, the issue of tourist resources in specific environments is examined in a variety of different contexts ranging from the urban through to rural, coastal and resort environments to the less developed world. To understand the synergies and themes which unify these chapters it is interesting to begin by highlighting a number of fundamental concepts which have evolved in both the tourism and recreational literature in the last 25 years that have influenced the way we look at, analyse and understand tourist resource environments.

Concepts and themes in the analysis of tourist resources

In some respects, the overlap between recreation and tourism is evident when one begins to try and explain how concepts have been devised to understand how tourists use certain resources (see Hall and Page 1999 for a discussion of the recreation-tourism continuum). In 1960 Clawson *et al.* (1960) examined ways of classifying outdoor recreation and resources based on the principle of distance and zones of influence in terms of whether the resource base had a national, regional, sub-regional, intermediate or local zone of influence. This research is shown in Table 21.1 which helps explain the 'pull' of the resource and they identified a simple model of use where three zones existed:

- a 0–16 km zone, many resource needs for recreation can be met in terms of golf, urban parks and the urban fringe
- a 16–32 km zone, the range of activities in greater, though particular types of resource tend to dominate activity patterns (e.g. horse riding, hiking and field sports)
- a 32 km or greater, sports and physical pursuits with specific resource requirements (e.g. orienteering, canoeing, skiing and rock climbing) exist.

What Clawson *et al.* (1960) highlight is that while the majority of recreational activities are undertaken near to home, it is the more distant resources within countries and outside countries (i.e. overseas) that are the focus of the tourist. With increased mobility, resources have become much more accessible to those tourists able to afford the cost of travel, although in terms of domestic tourism, Clawson *et al.*'s (1960) classification to a large degree is still a good analysis of the difference between recreational and tourist resource users.

For tourists, the principle inherent in this research was that visitors would use different resources depending upon their accessibility, appeal and attraction base. This has led to research which describes the features and attractions of specific resource environments. For example, inventories of the attractions and accommodation in resorts are frequently undertaken by tourist agencies and the differences are noted in relation to the status and quality of destinations to identify the strengths, weaknesses, opportunities and threats (SWOT analysis) (see Chapter 16). Much of the research on the tourist and recreationalist use of resources has been undertaken by geographers (Hall and Page 1999) and they use specific concepts and approaches to model and classify the users of specific resources as will be shown in the case of urban tourism below.

Why is urban tourism important as an environment for tourism activity?

Urbanization is a major force contributing to the development of towns and cities, where people live, work and shop (see Johnston *et al.* 1994 for a definition of the term urbanization). Towns and cities function as places where the population concentrates in a defined area and economic activities locate in the same area or nearby, to provide the opportunity for the production and consumption of goods and services in capitalist societies. Consequently, towns and cities provide the context for a diverse range of social, cultural and economic activities which the population engage in, and where tourism, leisure and entertainment form major service activities. These environments also function as meeting places, major tourist gateways, accommodation and transportation hubs and as central places to service the needs of visitors. Most tourist trips will contain some experience of an urban area; for example,

Table 21.1 **A general classification of outdoor recreational uses and resources: implications for tourism resource use**

	TYPE OF RECREATION AREA		
Item	**User oriented**	**Resource based**	**Intermediate**
General location	Close to users; on whatever resources are available	Where outstanding resources can be found; may be distant from most users	Must not be too remote from users; on best resources available within distance limitation
Major types of activity	Games such as golf and tennis; swimming; picnicking; walks; horse riding; zoos; play by children	Major sightseeing, scientific, historical interest; hiking, mountain climbing, camping, fishing and hunting	Camping, picnicking, hiking, swimming, hunting and fishing
When major use occurs	After hours (school or work)	Vacations (i.e. tourism)	Day outings and weekends (possibly some domestic tourism)
Typical size of areas	One to a hundred or at most to a few hundred acres	Usually some thousands of acres, perhaps many thousands	A hundred to several thousand acres
Common types of agency responsibility	City, county or other local government; private	National Parks and national forests primarily; state parks in some cases; private especially for seashore and major lakes	Federal reservoirs; state parks; private

(Source: Modified from Clawson *et al.* 1960: 136)

when an urban dweller departs from a major gateway in a city, arrives at a gateway in another city-region and stays in accommodation in an urban area. Within cities, however, the line between tourism and recreation blurs to the extent that at times one is indistinguishable from the other, with tourists and recreationalists using the same facilities, resources and environments although some notable differences exist. Therefore, many tourists and recreationalists will intermingle in many urban contexts. Most tourists will experience urban tourism in some form during their holiday, visit to friends and relatives, business trip or visit for other reasons.

Urban tourism: a relevant area for study?

Ashworth's (1989) landmark study of urban tourism acknowledges that a double neglect has occurred. 'Those interested in the study of tourism have tended to neglect the urban context in which much of it is set, while those interested in urban studies have been equally neglectful of the importance of the tourist function in cities' (Ashworth 1989: 33). While more recent tourism textbooks (e.g. Shaw and

Williams 1994) have expanded upon earlier syntheses of urban tourism research in a spatial context (e.g. Pearce 1987), it still remains a comparatively unresearched area despite the growing interest in the relationship between urban regeneration and tourism (see Law 1992, 1993, 1996 for a detailed review of the relationship of tourism and urban regeneration). The problem is also reiterated in a number of subsequent studies as one explanation of the neglect of urban tourism. Despite this problem, which is more a function of perceived rather than real difficulties in understanding urban tourism phenomena, a range of studies now provide evidence of a growing body of literature on the topic (Ashworth 1989, 1992; Page 1995). As more studies are now appearing, it is still not a distinct area of tourism studies. This is because urban tourism research is quite descriptive.

According to Ashworth (1992), urban tourism has not emerged as a distinct research focus: research is focused on tourism in cities. This strange paradox can be explained by the failure by planners, commercial interest and residents to recognize tourism as one of the main economic rationale for cities. Tourism is often seen as an adjunct or necessary evil to generate additional revenue, while the main economic activities of the locality are not perceived as tourism related. Such negative views of urban tourism have meant that the public and private sector has used the temporary, seasonal and ephemeral nature of tourism to neglect serious research on this theme. Consequently, a vicious circle exists: the absence of public and private sector research makes access to research data difficult and the large-scale funding necessary to break the vicious circle, for primary data collection using social survey techniques, is rarely available. The absence of large-scale funding for urban tourism research reflects the prevailing consensus in the 1980s that such studies were unnecessary. However, with the pressure posed by tourists in many European tourist cities in the 1990s and the new millennium (e.g. Canterbury, London, York, Venice and Florence), this perception is changing now that the public and private sector are belatedly acknowledging the necessity of visitor management (see English Tourist Board/Employment Department 1991 for a discussion of this issue) as a mechanism to enhance, manage and improve the tourists' experience of towns and places to visit.

Understanding the nature and concept of urban tourism

Shaw and Williams (1994) argue that urban areas offer geographical concentration of facilities and attractions that are conveniently located to meet both visitor and resident needs alike. But the diversity and variety among urban tourist destinations has led researchers to examine the extent to which they display unique and similar features. Shaw and Williams (1994) identify three approaches:

- the diversity of urban areas means that their size, function, location and history contributes to their uniqueness
- towns and cities are multi-functional areas, meaning that they simultaneously provide various functions for different groups of users
- the tourist functions of towns and cities are rarely produced or consumed solely by tourists, given the variety of user groups in urban areas.

Ashworth (1992) conceptualizes urban tourism by identifying three approaches towards its analysis, where researchers have focused on:

- The supply of tourism facilities in urban areas, involving inventories (e.g. the spatial distribution of accommodation, entertainment complexes and tourist-related services), where urban ecological models have been used. In addition, the facility approach has been used to identify the tourism product offered by destinations.
- The demand generated by urban tourists, to examine how many people visit urban areas, why they choose to visit and their patterns of behaviour, perception and expectations in relation to their visit.
- Urban tourism policy, where the public sector (e.g. planners) and private sector agencies have undertaken or commissioned research to investigate specific issues of interest to their own interests for urban tourism.

Theoretical studies of urban tourism by Mullins (1991) and Roche (1992) offer explanations of the sudden desire of many former towns and cities with a declining industrial base which are now looking towards the service sector activities such as tourism with the potential to generate new employment opportunities. These studies examine urban tourism in post-industrial society and question the types of process now shaping the operation and development of tourism in post-industrial cities, and the implications for public sector tourism policy. These studies highlight the role of the state, especially local government, in seeking to develop service industries based on tourism consumption. For example, many local authorities in western Europe are pump-priming tourism development as a means of stimulating the urban economy, particularly where leisure and culture-based spending can be harnessed to create new employment. It is possible to identify the following types of urban tourist destination:

- capital cities
- metropolitan centres, walled historic cities and small fortress cities
- large historic cities
- inner city areas
- revitalized waterfront areas
- industrial cities
- seaside resorts and winter sport resorts
- purpose-built integrated tourist resorts
- tourist entertainment complexes
- specialized tourist service centres
- cultural/art cities (after Page 1995: 17).

The visitor experience of urban tourism

There is a growing interest in tourist satisfaction and what constitutes the experiential aspects of a tourist visit to a locality (see Chapters 25 and 26). In terms of urban tourism, the innovative research by Graefe and Vaske (1987) offers a number of important insights as well as a useful framework. Graefe and Vaske (1987) acknowledge that the 'tourist experience' is a useful term to identify the experience of

Plate 21.1 Crown Casino, Melbourne, Australia
Casinos are a major source of revenue for urban environments and attract a significant visitor population. The Crown Casino in Melbourne is the largest casino in the southern hemisphere.

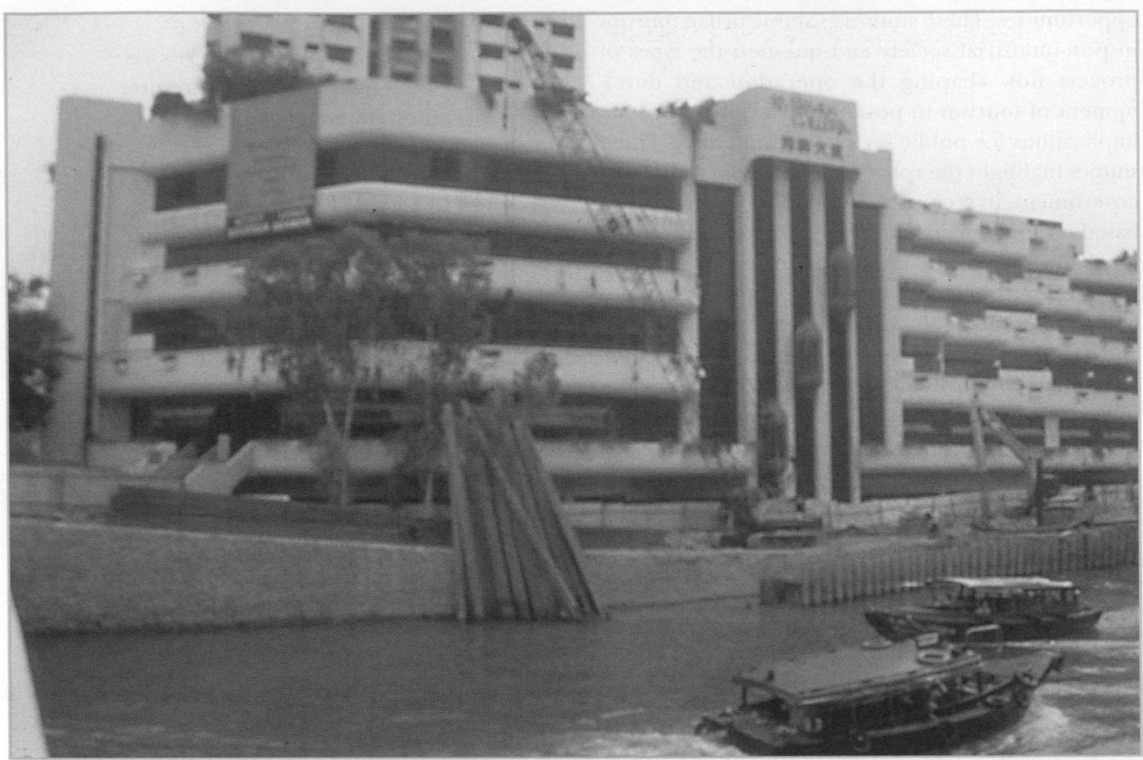

Plate 21.2 Waterfront development, Singapore
Waterfront development has also been a major beneficiary of urban tourism as this picture of Singapore suggests.

an individual which may be affected 'by individual, environmental, situational and personality-related factors as well as the degree of communication with other people. It is the outcome which researchers and the tourism industry constantly evaluate to establish if the actual experience met the tourist's expectations' (Page 1995: 24). Operationalizing such a concept may prove difficult in view of the complex array of factors which may affect the visitor experience (Figure 21.1). For example, where levels of overcrowding occurs at major tourist, this can have a negative effect on visitors who have a low tolerance threshold for overcrowding at major tourist sites. Yet other visitors may be less affected by use levels thereby illustrating the problem within tourism motivation research – predicting tourist behaviour and their responses to particular situations. In fact Graefe and Vaske (1987: 394) argue that 'the effects of increasing use levels on the recreation/tourist experience can be explained only partially as a function of use level'. Therefore, the individual tourist's ability to tolerate the behaviour of other people, level of use, the social situation and the context of the activity are all important determinants of the actual outcome. Thus, evaluating the quality of the tourist experience is a complex process which may require a careful consideration of the factors motivating a visit (i.e. how the tourists' perception of urban areas makes them predisposed to visit particular places), their actual patterns of activity and the extent to which their expectations associated with their perceptions are matched in reality (Page 1995: 25).

The market for urban tourism

Identifying the scale, volume and different markets for urban tourism remains a perennial problem for

Figure 21.1 **The tourist experience of urban tourism**

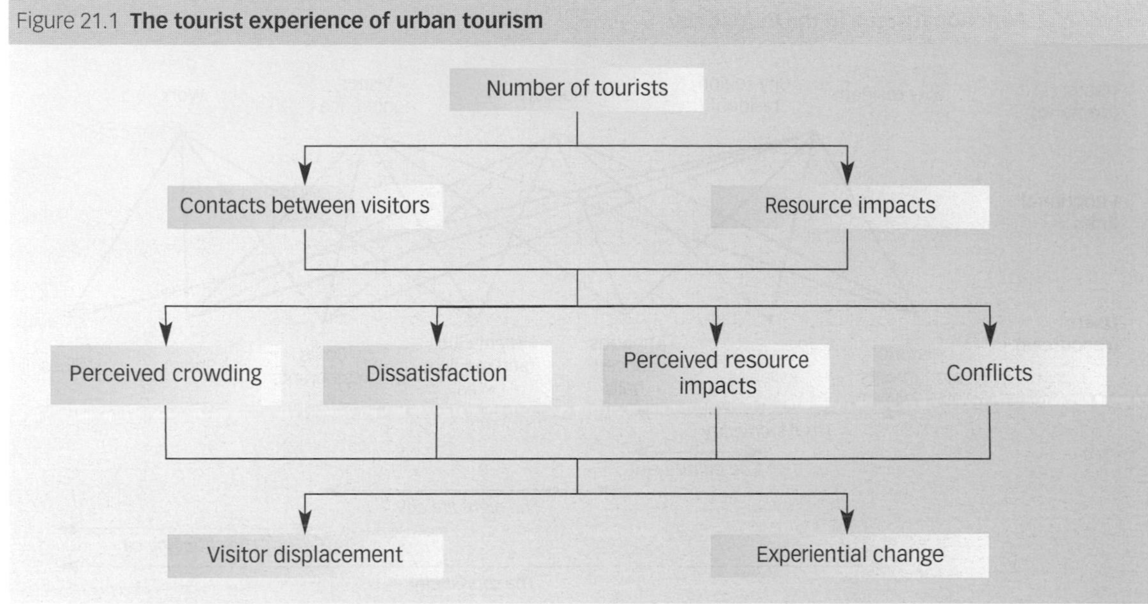

(Source: Modified from Graefe and Vaske 1987)

researchers. Urban tourism is a major economic activity in many of Europe's capital cities but identifying the tourism markets in each area is problematic. The principal international data sources on urban tourism, are the published statistics by the World Tourism Organization and the Organisation for Economic Co-operation and Development. Such data sources commonly use the domestic and international tourist use of accommodation as one measure of the scale of tourism activity. In the context or urban tourism, it requires researchers to have an understanding of spatial distribution of tourist accommodation in each country to identify the scale and distribution of tourist visits. In countries where the majority of accommodation is urban based, such statistics may provide preliminary source of data for research. Whilst this may be relevant for certain categories of tourist (e.g. business travellers and holidaymakers), those visitors staying with friends and relatives within an urban environment would not be included in the statistics. Even where statistics can be used, they only provide a preliminary assessment of scale and volume and more detailed sources are needed to assess specific markets for urban tourism. Figure 21.2 describes two methods of classifying urban tourists based on individual motives for visiting urban destinations, although Jansen-Verbeke (1986) points to the methodological problem of distinguishing between the different users of the tourist city. For example, Burtenshaw *et al.* (1991) discuss the concept of functional areas within the city, where different visitors seek certain attributes for their city visit (e.g. the historic city, the culture city, the night life city, the shopping city and the tourist city – Figure 21.2) where no one group has a monopoly over its use. Residents of the city and its hinterland, visitors and workers all use the resources within the tourist city, but some user groups identify with certain areas more than others. Thus, the tourist city is a multi-functional area which complicates attempts to identify a definitive classification of users and the areas/facilities they visit.

Ashworth and Tunbridge (1990) prefer to approach the market for urban tourism from the perspective of the consumers' motives, focusing on the purchasing intent of users, their attitudes, opinions and interests for specific urban tourism products. The most important distinction they make is between use/non-use of tourism resources, leading them to identify intentional users (who are motivated by the character of the city) and incidental users (who view the character of the city as irrelevant to their use). This twofold typology is then used by Ashworth and Tunbridge (1990) to identify four specific types of users:

Figure 21.2 **Functional areas in the tourist city**

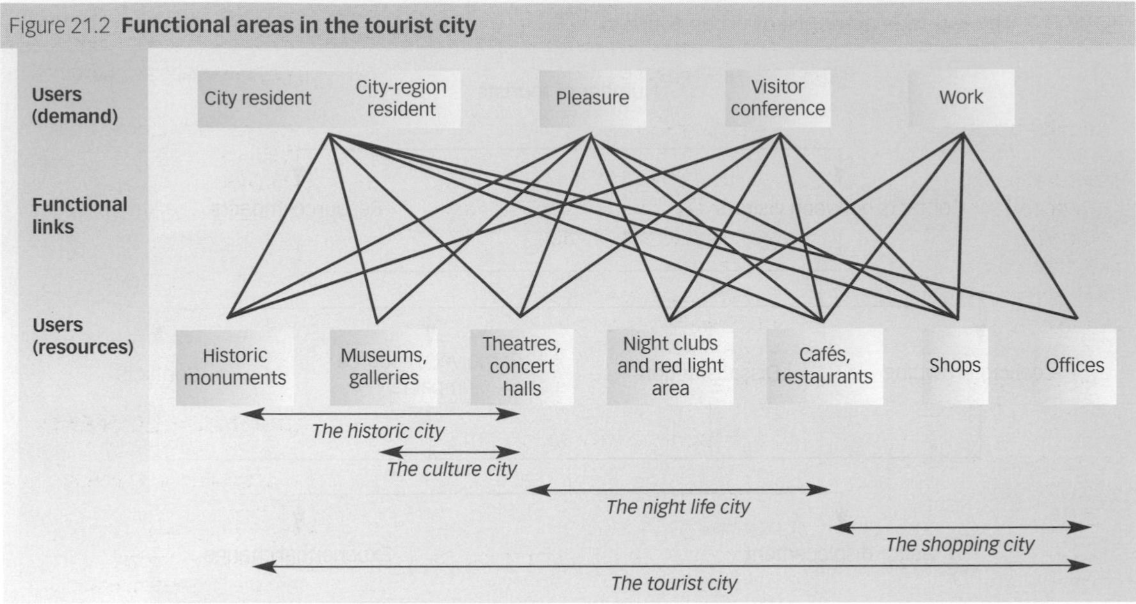

(Source: Modified from Burtenshaw *et al.* 1991)

- intentional users from outside the city-region (e.g. holidaymakers and heritage tourists)
- intentional users from inside the city-region (e.g. those using recreational and entertainment facilities – recreating residents)
- incidental users from outside the city-region (e.g. business and conference/exhibition tourists and those on family visits – non-recreating visitors)
- incidental users from inside the city-region (e.g. residents going about their daily activities – non-recreating residents).

Such an approach recognizes the significance of attitudes and the use made of the city and services rather than the geographical origin of the visitor as the starting point for analysis. This is a more sophisticated approach to understanding the tourist demand for urban areas. But it does raise a practical problem – that tourists tend to cite one main motive for visiting a city, but in any destination there are likely to be a wider range of motives beyond one principal reason to visit. It is likely that there will a variety of user groups in line with Ashworth and de Haan's (1986) examination of users of the tourist-historic city of Norwich. This multi-use nature of urban visitors advanced by Ashworth and Tunbridge (1990) was also developed in a geographical context by Getz (1993) in terms of the tourism business district where the attractions of the city, the central business functions and services provided in the city were consumed by three user groups: residents, workers and visitors, which makes it difficult to precisely identify the contribution of the tourist in supporting these services and resources.

The urban tourist experience: behavioural issues

Any assessment of urban tourist activities, patterns and perceptions of urban locations will be influenced by the supply of services, attractions and facilities in each location. In an urban context, we need to try and understand how the urban visitor consumes the services and resources produced for their visit and experience. One useful framework developed in the Netherlands by Jansen-Verbeke (1986) to accommodate the analysis of what the tourist consumes and what is produced for their visit is that of the 'leisure product' (Figure 21.3). As Figure 21.3 shows, the facilities in an urban environment can be divided into the 'primary elements', 'secondary elements' and 'additional elements'. To distinguish between user groups, Jansen-Verbeke (1986) identified 'tourists' and 'recreationalists' first and second reasons for visiting three Dutch towns

Figure 21.3 **The elements of tourism**

PRIMARY ELEMENTS		SECONDARY ELEMENTS
Activity place	**Leisure setting**	• Hotels and catering facilities • Markets • Shopping facilities
Cultural facilities • Concert halls • Cinemas • Exhibitions • Museums and art galleries • Theatres	**Physical characteristics** • Ancient monuments and statues • Ecclesiastical buildings • Harbours • Historical street pattern • Interesting buildings • Parks and green areas • Water, canals and river fronts	
Sports facilities • Indoor and outdoor		**ADDITIONAL ELEMENTS**
Amusement facilities • Bingo halls • Casinos • Festivities • Night clubs • Organized events	**Socio-cultural features** • Folklore • Friendliness • Language • Liveliness and ambience of the place • Local customs and costumes • Security	• Accessibility and parking facilities • Tourist facilities: information offices, signposts, guides, maps and leaflets

(Source: Modified from Page 1995, based on Jansen-Verbeke 1986)

(Deneter, Kampen and Zwolle). Jansen-Verbeke found that the inner city environment provides a leisure function for various visitors regardless of the prime motivation for visiting. As Jansen-Verbeke (1986: 88–89) suggests: 'On an average day, the proportion of visitors coming from beyond the city-region (tourists) is about one-third of all visitors. A distinction that needs to be made between week days, market days and Sundays.' Among the different user groups, tourists tended to stay longer, with a strong correlation with 'taking a day out', 'sightseeing' and 'visiting a museum' as the main motivation to visit. Nevertheless, leisure shopping was also a major 'pull factor' for recreationalists and tourist, though it is of greater significance for the recreationalists. Using a scaling technique, Jansen-Verbeke (1986) asked visitors to evaluate how important different elements of the leisure product were to their visit. The results indicate that there is not a great degree of difference between tourists and recreationalists rating of elements and characteristics of the city's leisure product. While recreationalists attach more importance to shopping facilities than events and museums, the historical characteristics of the environment and decorative elements combined with other elements such as markets, restaurants and the compact nature of the inner city to attract visitors. Thus, 'the conceptual approach to the system of inner-city tourism is inspired by common features of the inner-city environment, tourist's behaviour and appreciation and promotion activities' (Jansen Verbeke 1986: 97). Such findings illustrate the value of relating empirical results to a conceptual framework for the analysis of urban tourism and the necessity of replicating similar studies in other urban environments to test the validity of the framework and interpretation of urban tourists' visitor behaviour.

Tourist perception and cognition of the urban environment

How individual tourists interact and acquire information about the urban environment remains a relatively poorly researched area in tourism studies, particularly in relation to towns and cities. This area of research is traditionally seen as the forte of social psychologists with an interest in tourism, though much of the research by social psychologists has focused on motivation (e.g. Guy and Curtis 1986, on the development of perceptual maps). Reviews of the social psychology of tourism indicate that there has been a paucity of studies of tourist' behaviour and adaptation to new environments they visit. This is somewhat surprising since 'tourists are people who temporarily visit areas less familiar to them than their home area' (Walmesley and Jenkins 1992: 269). Therefore, one needs to consider a number of fundamental questions related to:

- How will the tourists get to know the areas they visit?
- How do they find their way around unfamiliar environments?
- What type of mental maps and images do they develop?

These issues are important in a tourism planning context since the facilities which tourists use and the opportunities they seek will be conditioned by their environmental awareness. This may also affect the commercial operation of attractions and facilities, since a lack of awareness of the urban environment and the attractions within it may mean tourists fail to visit them. Understanding how tourists interact with the environment to create an image of the real world has been the focus of a research in social psychology and behavioural geography (see Walmesley and Lewis 1993: 95–126). Geographers have developed a growing interest in the geographic space perception of all types of individuals (Downs 1970), without explicitly considering tourists in most instances. Behavioural geographers emphasize the need to examine how people store spatial information and 'their choice of different activities and locations within the environment' (Walmesley and Lewis 1993: 95). The process through which individuals perceive the urban environment is shown in Figure 21.4. Whilst this is a simplification, Haynes (1980) notes that no two individuals will have an identical image of the urban environment because the information they receive is subject to mental processing. This is conditioned by the information signals received through one's senses (e.g. sight, hearing, smell, taste and touch) and this part of the process is known as perception. As our senses may only comprehend a small proportion of the total information received, the human brain sorts the information and relates it to the knowledge, values and attitudes of the individual through the process of cognition (Page 1995: 222). The final outcome of the perception and cognition process is the formation of a mental image of a place. These images are an individual's own view of reality, but they are important to the individual and group when making decisions about their experience of a destination, whether to visit again and their feelings in relation to the tourist experience of place.

As Walmesley and Lewis (1993: 96) suggest:

> the distinction between perception and cognition is, however, a heuristic device rather than a fundamental dichotomy because in many senses, the latter subsumes the former and both are medicated by expense, beliefs, values, attitudes, and personality such that, in interacting with their environment, humans only see what they want to see.

Consequently, individual tourists knowledge of the environment is created in their mind as they interact with the unfamiliar environment (or familiar environment on a return visit) they are visiting.

According to Powell (1978: 17–18) an image of the environment comprises ten key features which include:

1 A spatial component accounting for an individual's location in the world.
2 A personal component relating to the individual to other people and organizations.

Figure 21.4 **How individuals perceive the tourism environment**

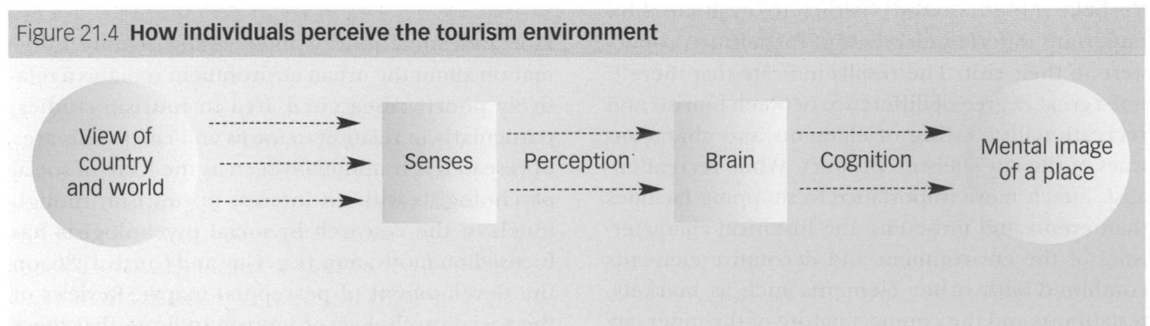

3 A temporal component concerned with the flow of time.
4 A relational component concerned with the individual's picture of the universe as a system of regularities.
5 Conscious, subconscious and unconscious elements.
6 A blend of certainty and uncertainty.
7 A mixture of reality and unreality.
8 A public and private component expressing the degree to which an image is shared.
9 A value component that orders parts of the image according to whether they are good or bad.
10 An affectional component whereby the image is imbued with feeling.

Among geographers, the spatial component to behavioural research has attracted most interest, and they derive much of their inspiration from the pioneering research by Lynch (1960). Lynch's research asked respondents in North American cities to sketch maps of their individual cities and, by simplifying the sketches, derived images of the city. Lynch developed a specific technique to measure people's urban images in which respondents drew a map of the centre of the city from memory, marking on it the streets, parks, buildings, districts and features they considered important. 'Lynch found many common elements in these mental maps that appeared to be of fundamental importance to the way people collect information about the city' (Hollis and Burgess 1978: 155). Lynch (1960) found five elements in the resulting maps after simplifying the maps. These were:

- *Paths* which are the channels along which individuals move.
- *Edges* which are barriers (e.g. rivers) or lines separating one region from another.
- *Districts* which are medium-to-large sections of the city with an identifiable character.
- *Nodes* which are the strategic points in a city which the individual can enter and which serve as foci for travel.
- *Landmarks* which are points of reference used in navigation and way finding, into which an individual cannot enter.

Pearce (1977) produced one of the pioneering studies of cognitive maps of tourists. Using data from sketch maps from first-time visitors to Oxford, England, the role of landmarks, paths and districts was examined. The conclusion drawn indicated that visitors were quick to develop cognitive maps, often by the second day of the visit. The interesting feature of the study is that there is evidence of an environmental learning process at work. Walmesley and Jenkins' (1992: 272) critique of Pearce's (1977) findings note that:

- the number of landmarks, paths and districts increased over time
- the number of landmarks identified increased over a period of 2–6 days, while recognition of the number of districts increased from 2 to 3
- the resulting sketch maps were complex with no one element dominating them.

A further study by Pearce (1981), examined how tourists came to know a route in Northern Queensland (a 340 km strip from Townsville to Cairns). The study indicated that experiential variables are a major influence upon cognitive maps. For example, drivers had a better knowledge than passengers, while age and prior use of the route were important conditioning factors. But as Walmesley and Jenkins (1992: 273) argue, 'very little concern has been shown for the cognitive maps of tourists' except for the work by Aldskogius (1977) in Sweden and Mercer (1971) in Australia.

The significance of such research for the tourist and visitor to the urban environment is that the information they collect during a visit will shape their image of the place, influencing their feelings and impressions of a place. Furthermore, this imageability of a place is closely related to the:

> legibility by which is meant the extent to which parts of the city can be recognised and interpreted by an individual as belonging to a coherent pattern. Thus a legible city would be one where the paths, edges, districts, nodes and landmarks are both clearly identifiable and clearly positioned relative to each other. (Walmesley and Lewis 1993: 98)

Although there may sometimes be confusion among individuals regarding recognition of Lynchean urban landscape elements, it does help researchers to understand how individuals perceive the environment. Even so, Walmesley and Lewis (1993) review many of the issues associated with the methodology of imagery research and raise a range of concerns about deriving generalizations from such results. Such studies do have a role to play in understanding how people view, understand and synthesize the complexity of urban landscapes into images of the environment. Nevertheless, criticisms of spatial research of individual imagery of the environment are that it uses a 'borrowed methodology, a potpourri of concepts, and liberal doses of borrowed theory' (Stea and Downs 1970: 3, cited in Walmesley and Lewis 1993). In a tourism context, Walmesley and Jenkins (1992) observed that tourism cognitive mapping may offer a number of useful insights into how tourists learn about new environments and for this reason, it is pertinent to consider how visitor behaviour may be influenced by the ability to acquire spatial knowledge and synthesize it into meaningful images of the destination to assist them in finding their way around the area or region.

Quality issues in urban tourism: the major challenge for the new millennium

The competitive nature of urban tourism is increasingly being reflected in the growth in marketing and promotion efforts by towns and cities as they compete for a share of international and domestic tourism markets. Such competition has led to tourists' demands for higher standards of service provision and improved quality in the tourist experience. But developing an appropriate definition or concept of urban tourism quality is difficult due to the intangible nature of services as products which are purchased and consumed.

In the context of urban tourism, three key issues need to be addressed. First, place marketing generates an image of a destination that may not be met in reality due to the problems of promoting places as tourist products. The image promoted through place marketing may not necessarily be matched in reality through the services and goods which the tourism industry delivers. As a result, the gap between the customer's perception of a destination and the bundle of products they consume is reflected in their actual tourist experience, which has important implications for their assessment of quality in their experience. Second, the urban tourism product is largely produced by the private sector either as a package or a series of elements which are not so easily controlled or influenced by the place marketer. Third, there are a large range of associated factors which affect a tourist's image of a destination, including less tangible elements like the environment and the ambience of the city which may shape the outcome of a tourist's experience. As a result, the customer's evaluation of the quality of the services and products provided is a function of the difference (GAP) between expected and perceived service. It is in this context that the concept of service quality is important for urban tourism. Gilbert and Joshi (1992) present an excellent review of the literature, including many of the concepts associated with the service quality. In the case of urban tourism, it is the practical management of the 'gap' between the expected and the perceived service that requires attention by urban managers and the tourism industry. In reviewing Parasuraman *et al.*'s (1985) service quality model, Gilbert and Joshi (1992: 155) identify five gaps which exist between:

- The expected service and the management's perceptions of the consumer experience (i.e. what they think the tourist wants) (Gap 1).
- The management's perception of the tourist needs and the translation of those needs into service quality specifications (Gap 2).
- The quality specifications and the actual delivery of the service (Gap 3).
- The service delivery stage and the organization/providers communication with the consumer (Gap 4).
- The consumers' perception of the service they received and experienced and their initial expectations of the service (Gap 5).

Gilbert and Joshi (1992) argue that the effective utilization of market research techniques could help to bridge some of the gaps. For:

- Gap 1 – by encouraging providers to elicit detailed information from consumers on what they require.
- Gap 2 – the management's ability to specify the service provided needs to be realistic and guided by clear quality standards.
- Gap 3 – the ability of employees to deliver the service according to the specification needs to be closely monitored and staff

training and development is essential: a service is only as good as the staff it employs.

- Gap 4 – the promises made by service providers in their marketing and promotional messages need to reflect the actual quality offered. Therefore, if a city's promotional literature promises a warm welcome, human resource managers responsible for employees in front-line establishments need to ensure that this message is conveyed to its customers.
- Gap 5 – the major gap between the perceived service and delivered service should be reduced over time through progressive improvements in the appropriate image which is marketed to visitors and the private sector's ability to deliver the expected service in an efficient and professional manner.

Such an approach to service quality can be applied to urban tourism as it emphasizes the importance of the marketing process in communicating and dealing with tourists. To obtain a better understanding of the service quality issues associated with the urban tourist's experience of urban tourism, Haywood and Muller (1988) identify a methodology for evaluating the quality of the urban tourism experience. This involves collecting data on visitors' expectations prior to and after their city visit by examining a range of variables (see Page 1995 for a fuller discussion). Such an approach may be costly to operationalize, but it does provide a better appreciation of the visitation process and they argue that cameras may also provide the day-to-day monitoring of city experiences. At a city-wide level, North America and European cities have responded to the problem of large visitor numbers and the consequences of mass tourism for the tourist experience by introducing town centre management schemes and visitor management schemes (see Page 1995 for more detail on the developments and application of such schemes).

Graefe and Vaske (1987) argue that the development of a management strategy is necessary to:

- deal with problem conditions which may impact on the tourist experience
- identify causes of such problems
- select appropriate management strategies to deal with problems (see Graefe and Vaske 1987 for more detail on operationalizing this approach to improving the tourist experience).

Conclusion

Tourism's development in urban areas is not a new phenomenon. But its recognition as a significant activity to study in its own right is only belatedly gaining the recognition it deserves within tourism studies. The reasons why tourists visit urban environments, to consume a bundle of tourism products, continues to be overlooked by the private sector which often neglects the fundamental issue – cities are multi-functional places. Despite the growing interest in urban tourism research, the failure of many large and small cities which promote tourism, to understand the reasons why people visit, the links between the various motivations and the deeper reasons why people are attracted to cities remains a fertile area for theoretically informed and methodologically sound research. Many cities are beginning to recognize the importance of monitoring visitor perceptions and satisfaction and the activity patterns and behaviour of tourists. For the public and private sector planners and managers with an interest, involvement or stake in urban tourism, the main concern continues to be the potential for harnessing the all-year round appeal of urban tourism activity, despite the often short-stay nature of such visitors. Ensuring that such stays are part of a high-quality experience, where visitor expectations are realistically met through well-researched, targeted and innovative products continue to stimulate interest among tour operators and other stakeholders in urban tourism provision.

These concerns should force cities seeking to develop an urban tourism economy to reconsider the feasibility of pursuing a strategy to revitalize the city-region through tourism-led regeneration. All too often both the private and public sectors have moved headlong into economic regeneration strategies for urban areas, seeking a tourism component as a likely backup for property and commercial redevelopment. The implication is that tourism issues are not given the serious treatment they deserve. Where the visitors' needs and spatial behaviour are poorly understood and neglected in the decision-making process, it affects the planning, development and eventual outcome of the urban tourism environment. Therefore, tourist behaviour, the tourism system and its constituent components need to be evaluated in the context of future growth in urban tourism to understand the visitor as a central component in the visitor experience. Managing the different elements of this experience in a realistic manner is requiring more attention among those towns and cities competing aggressively for visitors, using the quality experience approach as a new-found marketing tool. Future research needs to focus on the behaviour, attitudes and needs of existing and prospective urban tourists to reduce the gap between their expectations and the service delivered. But ensuring that the tourism system within cities can deliver the service and experience marketed through promotional literature in a sensitive and meaningful way is now one of the major challenges for urban tourism managers.

Discussion questions

1. Why is urban tourism important as an economic activity for cities?
2. Why do tourists seek urban tourism experiences?
3. How can tourism be used to aid economic regeneration in cities?
4. To what extent do cities provide a diverse tourism product which can cater for all types of tourists needs?

References

Aldskogius, H. (1977) 'A conceptual framework and a Swedish case study of recreational behaviour and environmental cognition', *Economic Geography*, **53**: 163–83.

Ashworth, G. (1989) 'Urban tourism: an imbalance in attention', in C.P. Cooper (ed.) *Progress in Tourism, Recreation and Hospitality Management*, Vol. 1, London: Belhaven: 33–54.

Ashworth, G.J. (1992) 'Is there an urban tourism?', *Tourism Recreation Research*, **17** (2): 3–8.

Ashworth, G.J. and de Haan, T.Z. (1986) 'Uses and users of the tourist-historic city', *Field Studies 10*, Groningen: Faculty of Spatial Sciences.

Ashworth, G.J. and Tunbridge, J.E. (1990) *The Tourist – Historic City*, London: Belhaven.

Burtenshaw, D., Bateman, M. and Ashworth, G.J. (1991) *The City in West Europe*, second edition, Chichester: Wiley.

Clawson, M., Held, R. and Stoddart, C. (1960) *Land for the Future*, Baltimore: Johns Hopkins Press.

Downs, R. (1970) 'Geographic space perception: past approaches and future prospects', *Progress in Geography*, **2**: 65–108.

English Tourist Board/Employment Department (1991) *Tourism and the Environment: Maintaining the Balance*, London: English Tourist Board.

Getz, D. (1993) 'Planning for tourism business districts', *Annals of Tourism Research*, **20**: 583–600.

Gilbert, D. and Joshi, I. (1992) 'Quality management and the tourism and hospitality industry', in C. Cooper and A. Lockwood (eds), *Progress in Tourism, Recreation and Hospitality Management*, Vol. 4. London: Belhaven: 149–68.

Graefe, A.R. and Vaske, J.J. (1987) 'A framework for managing quality in the tourist experience', *Annals of Tourism Research*, **14**: 389–404.

Guy, B.S. and Curtis, W.W. (1986), 'Consumer learning or retail environment: a tourism and travel approach', Conference paper presented at the American Academy of Marketing Conference, Cleveland University, W. Benoy Joseph (ed.) *Tourism Services Marketing: Advances in Theory and Practice*, American Academy of Marketing Conference, Cleveland University.

Internet resources

By going to the weblink at www.thomsonlearning.co.uk students can access the following study on the Thomson Learning website. This is by C.M. Law (1996) *Tourism in Major Cities* which offers an introduction to the problems of conceptualizing and researching urban tourism. This should be read in conjunction with more recent data on the European urban tourism statistics provided by the Federation of European Cities Tourist Offices (FECTO) which can be found on www.tourism-wu-wien.ac.at and is a comprehensive source of information on data on urban tourism.

Hall, C.M. and Page, S.J. (1999) *The Geography of Tourism and Recreation: Environment, Place and Space*, London: Routledge.

Haynes, R. (1980) *Geographical Images and Mental Maps*, London: Macmillan.

Haywood, K.M. and Muller, T.E. (1988) 'The urban tourist experience: evaluating satisfaction', *Hospitality Education and Research Journal*: 453–59.

Hollis, G. and Burgess, J. (1977) 'Personal London: students perceive the urban scene', *Geographical Magazine*, **50** (3): 155–61.

Jansen-Verbeke, M. (1986) 'Inner-city tourism: resources, tourists and promoters', *Annals of Tourism Research*, **13** (1): 79–100.

Johnston, R.J., Gregory, D. and Smith, D.M. (eds) (1994) *The Dictionary of Human Geography*, Oxford: Basil Blackwell.

Law, C.M. (1992) 'Urban tourism and its contribution to economic regeneration', *Urban Studies*, **29** (3/4): 599–618.

Law, C.M. (1993) *Urban Tourism: Attracting Visitors to Large Cities*, London: Mansell.

Law, C.M. (ed.) (1996) *Tourism in Major Cities*, London: Thomson Learning.

Lynch, K. (1960) *The Image of the City*, Cambridge, Mass: MIT Press.

Mercer, D. (1971) 'Discretionary travel behaviour and the urban mental map', *Australian Geographical Studies*, **9**: 133–43.

Mullins, P. (1991) 'Tourism urbanization', *International Journal of Urban and Regional Research*, **15**: 326–43.

Page, S.J. (1995) *Urban Tourism*, London: Routledge.

Parasuraman, A., Zeithmal, V. and Berry, L. (1985) 'A conceptual model of service quality and its implications for future research', *Journal of Marketing*, **49**: 41–50.

Pearce, D.G. (1987) *Tourism Today: A Geographical Analysis*, London: Longman.

Pearce, P. (1977) 'The social and environmental perceptions of overseas tourists', unpublished DPhil Dissertation, University of Oxford.

Pearce, P.L. (1981) 'Route maps: a study of travellers perceptions of a section of countryside', *Journal of Environmental Psychology*, **1**: 141–55.

Powell, J.M. (1978) *Mirrors of the New World: Images and Image – Makers in the Settlement Process*, Canberra: Australian National University Press.

Roche, M. (1992) 'Mega-events and micro-modernisation: on the sociology of the new urban tourism', *British Journal of Sociology*, **43** (4): 563–600.

Shaw, G. and Williams, A.M. (1994) *Critical Issues in Tourism: A Geographical Perspective*, Oxford: Blackwell.

Stea, R. and Downs, R. (1970) 'From the outside looking in at the inside looking out', *Environment and Behaviour*, **2**: 3–12.

Walmsley, D.J. and Jenkins, J. (1992) 'Tourism cognitive mapping of unfamiliar environments', *Annals of Tourism Research*, **19** (3): 268–86.

Walmsley, D.J. and Lewis, G.J. (1993) *People and Environment: Behavioural Approaches in Human Geography*, second edition, London: Longman.

Further reading

Ashworth, G. (1989) 'Urban tourism: an imbalance in attention', in C. Cooper (ed.) *Progress in Tourism, Recreation and Hospitality Management*, Volume 1, London: Belhaven.

Ashworth, G. and Tunbridge, J. (1990) *The Tourist-Historic City*, London: Belhaven.

Ashworth, G. and Tunbridge, J. (2000) *The Tourist-Historic City: Retrospect and Prospect of Managing the Heritage City*, Oxford: Pergamon.

Ashworth, G. and Voogd, H. (1990) *Selling the City*, London: Belhaven.

Bramwell, B. (1998) 'User satisfaction and product development in urban tourism', *Tourism Management*, **19** (1): 35–48.

Page, S.J. (1995) *Urban Tourism*, London: Routledge.

Page, S.J. and Hall, C.M. (due to be published 2002) *Managing Urban Tourism*, Harlow: Pearson Education.

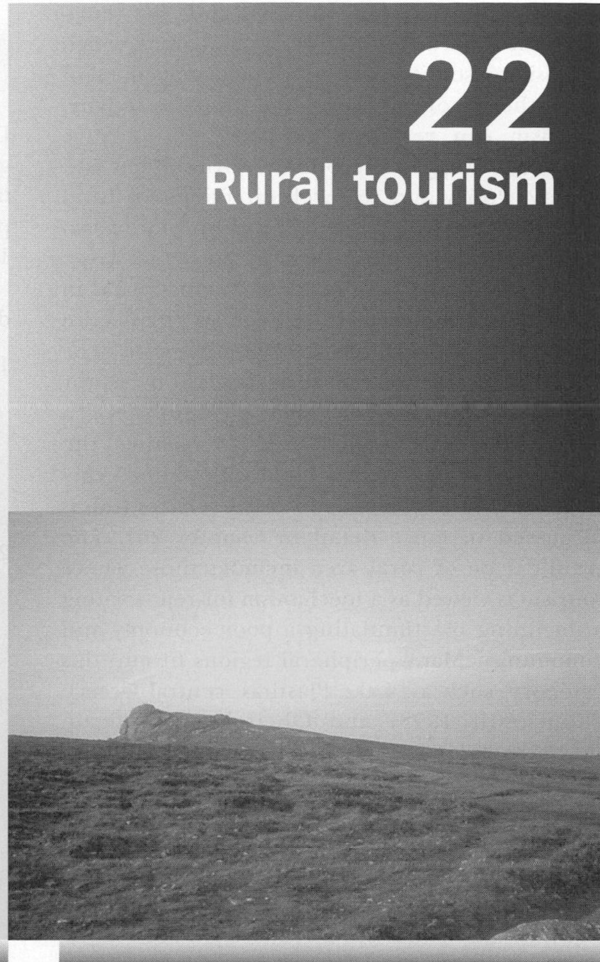

22 Rural tourism

Learning outcomes

After studying this chapter, you should be able to:

- Understand the context of rural tourism and the nature of rural areas.
- Identify the impacts of rural tourism.
- Understand the need for rural tourism management and issues for the future.

Overview

For many tourists, the countryside is an attractive choice of destination. The relationship between tourism and the environment is particularly marked in rural areas. Rural areas can be sensitive to change through tourism. Changes in the environment, effects on the social fabric and economic well-being require careful monitoring. With this in mind, recognizing the impacts and planning sensitive approaches to rural tourism is a challenge for the twenty-first century. This chapter explores the concept of rural tourism and highlights some of the issues relating to different types of tourism in the countryside setting.

Introduction

Rural areas have featured prominently in the development of tourism and leisure. In contemporary times, the countryside continues to form an important tourist destination. The appeal of the countryside as a holiday destination is complex, linked to opportunities for a variety of sports and activities, peace and quiet, space, nature and traditional ways of life. It might be argued that the countryside symbolizes a lost 'golden age'; that it contains everything that urban areas lack. Indeed, the countryside is seen as special and deserving of protection across the world, demonstrated, for example, by the designation of National Parks. The relationship between tourism and the environment is particularly close in rural areas, which necessitates sensitive planning and management of both the resource base and tourism activity. Tourism can result in positive and negative impacts on the rural economy, environment and society. Policy and research directions on rural tourism world-wide tend to focus on one of two emphases. First, many rural areas attract large numbers of tourists, for example National Parks in the USA which have seen the number of visits rise from 210 million in 1984 to 260 million in 1996. The emphasis in these areas is on visitor management. Visitor management is a management focus that aims to balance the protection of the environment with visitor experience and provision of appropriate services (this is discussed in more detail in Chapter 26). The second type of rural area includes those where tourism is viewed as a mechanism for rejuvenating a declining or stimulating a poor economy and community. Many peripheral regions fit into this category, such as: Lake Plastiras, central Greece (Koutsouris 1998) and Oberschwaben-Allgau, southern Germany (Oppermann 1997). These areas may not receive many visitors but the potential for organizing tourism services to generate more visitors and create vital income and employment is the motivating force. Keane and Quinn's landmark study (1990) recognized the significance of tourism in rural economic development and the value for local communities.

Simply defined, rural tourism is 'tourism which takes place in the countryside' (Lane 1994). This term, however, is problematic. Before we even begin to think about rural tourism as a concept, the complexity of the terms 'tourism' and 'rural' add further complications. The meaning of tourism has been dealt with already in Chapter 1 but how should we approach the definition of the term 'rural'?

The nature and scope of rurality

Defining rurality has taken much space in geographical and rural sociology texts but there is little consensus on what constitutes the phenomenon termed 'rural' (Robinson 1990; Ilbery 1997).

There are three recognizable perspectives on defining rurality:

1. *Anything non-urban.* Glyptis (1991) terms this 'land beyond the urban edge'. This is known as a negative approach to defining rurality as it implies the rural environment has few special features and transfers the onus of definition to urban commentators.
2. *Attempts to outline the elements of the countryside or the functions of rural space.* This is known as a positive perspective as the distinguishing features are identified, such as a low-density population, visual components, and forms of settlement and land use.
3. *Perception and/or user-based definitions.* Based on how individuals experience and define rurality (i.e. what people think it is). The distinction lies in the eye of the beholder. Halfacree (1995) explores the dimensions of rurality and makes the point that what one person sees in a rural area might be seen in a contrasting way by another. For example, we tend to think of the countryside as a relaxing environment, but for those who live and work there, for instance, in farming, the environment is stressful and hard work.

In 1977, Cloke published initial work on indices of rurality. Using 16 indicators, an index of rurality was constructed (see Figure 22.1).

From this work, two main types of rural areas were identified. The first is the *remote rural area,* typified by remoteness from urban areas, declining, static or modestly increasing population, an ageing popu-

Figure 22.1 **Index of rurality**

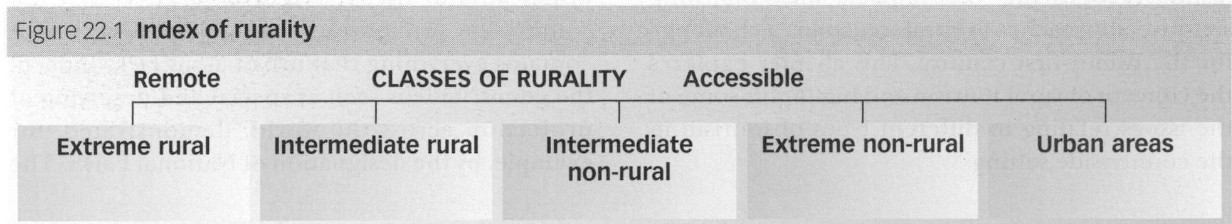

(Source: Adapted from Cloke 1977)

lation, declining employment opportunities, low female activity rates and high per capita service provision cost. The second is the *accessible rural area*, defined by relative proximity to urban areas, rapidly increasing population, high levels of commuting, youthful population structure and high levels of car ownership. A key feature of accessible rural areas is relative economic buoyancy, with lower rates of unemployment than remoter rural areas and urban areas and growth in employment opportunities.

Moving from the more geographical approach to rurality, it is worth noting alternative perspectives on the countryside. For instance, Halfacree (1993) identifies four approaches to defining rural areas:

1 *Descriptive* – which describes the countryside using empirical data and measures, such as census of population.
2 *Socio-cultural* – which draws associations between social and spatial attributes, i.e. population density affects behaviour and attitudes.
3 *Rural as a locality* – whose defining characteristics are what makes areas 'rural' – i.e. their distinctive qualities.
4 *Rural as a social representation* – how rural is perceived and relates to the social construction of the countryside by individuals and groups.

Finally, Murdoch and Marsden (1994) present an interesting framework for thinking about the contemporary countryside and the possible outcomes as a result of change:

1 *The preserved countryside* – which are accessible rural areas, characterized by anti-development and preservationist attitudes.
2 *The contested countryside* – which lies outside the main commuter zones. Farmers and developers have dominant interests and push proposals through.
3 *The paternalistic countryside* – where large estates and tenant farms dominate. Development is

Plate 22.1 Land beyond the urban edge
Is it rural?

Plate 22.2 A remote rural area
The issues, problems and opportunities in this type of area will differ significantly from the area depicted in Plate 22.1.

controlled by local landowners with a traditional and long-term view.

4 *The clientelist countryside* – which is in remote rural areas where agriculture dominates but is dependent on state subsidy. Policies are geared towards local community and employment.

The concept of the countryside can be defined in many different ways. It is multi-faceted, complex and dynamic. Halfacree (1993) states that a single, all-embracing definition of rural is not really feasible. Yet the term rural is an important distinction because behaviour and decision-making are influenced by perceptions of rurality (Halfacree 1995). It appears that there are two main ways of thinking about the definition of rurality. First, as there is no unambiguous way of defining rural areas, there is no point in trying to define it. One might ask whether definitions are significant to those who live and work in rural areas. The distinction between rural and urban is deeply rooted in planning matters; therefore the definition is crucial. With the development of policy and funding for rural development, there is an increasing need to think about the parameters of rural areas.

Conceptualizing rural tourism

While rural areas are dynamic environments and change is implicit, more radical change has been witnessed in the post-war period than any other time before, relating to social, environmental, political, economic and technological elements of the countryside. Changes in agricultural practice and policy (intensification and modernization) through time, particularly since the end of World War II, have created unemployment, falling agricultural incomes and economic marginalization of smaller farms. Jenkins *et al.* (1998: 50) term the changes in agriculture as 'industrialization' and state that in many countries and regions, farm numbers has been dramatically reduced and of those remaining, a minority contribute the majority of farm production (in both volume and value terms). With a lack of employment opportunities, out-migration to urban areas in search of work has occurred. Lower numbers of rural residents and the subsequent reduced demand for services has partly resulted in their withdrawal. A decline in rural services has been particularly marked in rural England. The Rural Development Commission (1994) illustrates the level of service provision in rural parishes (see Table 22.1). The situation is generally more marked in remoter areas.

In some areas, there has been a repopulation of the countryside. This is as a result of a reverse migration trend of urban dwellers moving to the countryside, particularly in the accessible rural areas. In some areas, tourism and recreation have spearheaded this change, as second home owners, retirees and countryside converts move to rural residences. The issue of second homes in the countryside has caused much debate, particularly in Finland and Canada, where a large majority of rural, lakeside and coastal homes are purchased for weekend and holiday use only. These part-time dwellers may exacerbate the problem of service provision, as the permanence of the community declines. Having explored the context of rural areas, it is evident that rural tourism and recreation has evolved partly due to an increase in supply of opportunities created by the need for a more diverse rural economy. This process is broadly summarized in Figure 22.2, which conceptualizes the problems of rural areas. Generally, this typifies the trans-European position but has wider applicability across the globe.

Table 22.1 **Rural services in 1994**

Rural service	% of parishes without the service
Village hall/community centre	29
Permanent shop	41
Post office	43
Primary school	52
Daily bus service	71
General practitioner	83
Bank/building society	94
Day care for elderly	92

(Source: After Rural Development Commission 1994)

It is clear that it is not an easy task to accurately define rural tourism. It is often described as a form of tourism that takes place in the countryside but this is ambiguous and on further reflection points to a broad variation of types of countryside and activities. A further complication is in trying to separate what is meant by rural tourism as opposed to countryside leisure. Curry (1994) clarifies this by expressing the components of countryside leisure in seven categories of which rural tourism is just one part. The danger of this is thinking purely about rural tourism in terms of overnight stays. It is essential to consider the activities which tourists engage in during their stay to generate a more complete analysis. Bramwell (1994) questions whether the special characteristics of rural areas shape the pattern of tourism, creating a specific form of 'rural' tourism. In addition, the commodification of rural space which has taken place in recent years intimates rural tourism has moved into a new era, away from more simple forms of farm-based tourism to a more commercial use of the countryside (Cloke 1993). Busby and Rendle (2000) examine this in relation to farm tourism and ask at what point tourism on farms becomes 'farm tourism'. Commercialization and formalization of countryside experiences is evident in the range of tourist products available in rural areas. In Malaysia, the development of what Turner *et al.* (1996) call rural awareness tourism is apparent. An 'Agro-Forestry Park' was opened in 1988 in Selangor State which is now one of Malaysia's top attractions. The initiative provides the visitor with experiences linked with agricultural development and recreational opportunities, for example an area set aside for padi cultivation, with 12 sections illustrating the range of cultivation practices used through time, can be seen from a boardwalk. There is also an

Figure 22.2 **The context of rural tourism**

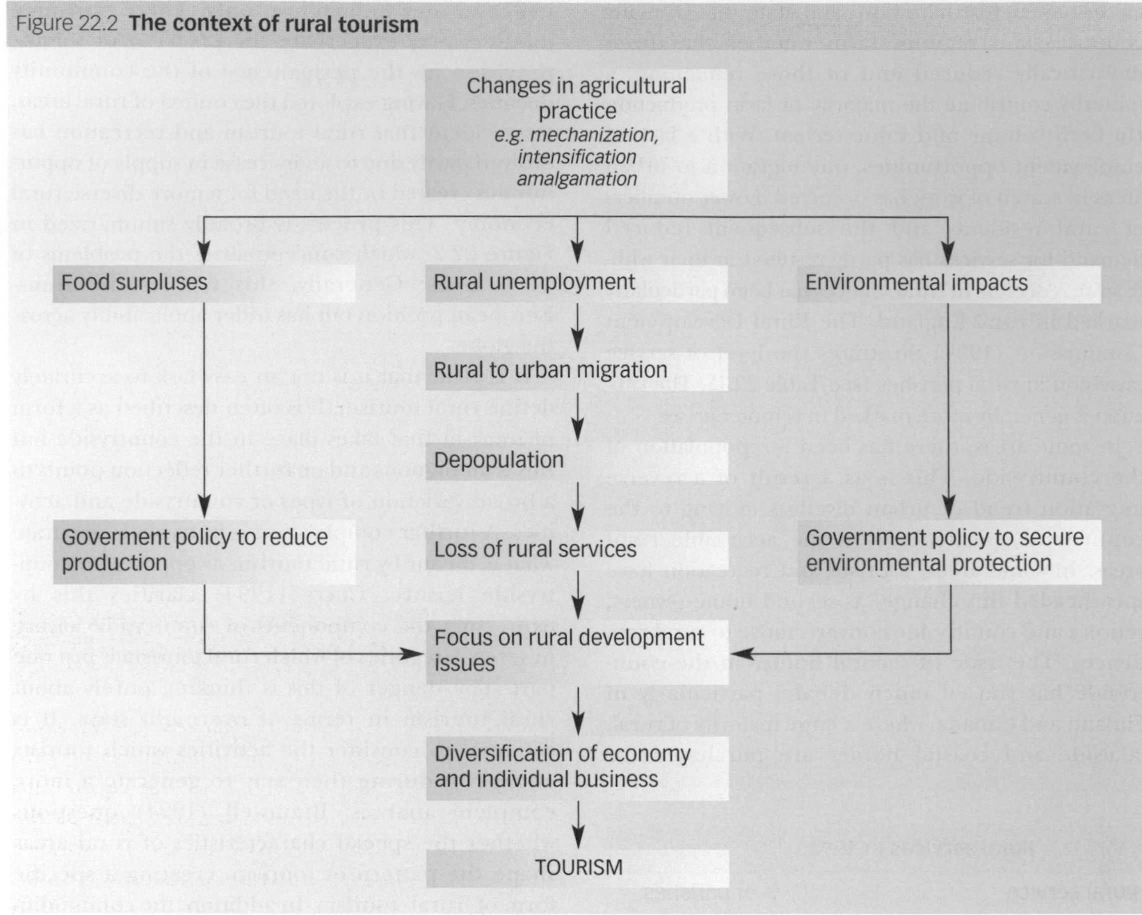

animal park, several areas specializing in horticulture, a Four Seasons Temperate house based on the climate of New Zealand, nature trails and fishing lakes. This contrasts with the form of tourism associated with wilderness areas, where the will of the individual to experience what he/she wants guides the visit. It is clear that rural tourism can vary greatly in what it purports to be. It can range from the very informal to the greatly organized product, which can represented by constructing a spectrum of rural tourism activity and experience (see Figure 22.3). So, what are the parameters of rural tourism?

Lane (1994) outlines the special features of rural tourism. These features assist in distinguishing a more specific form of rural tourism. First, it is located in rural areas. Second, it is functionally rural; that is, based on small-scale and traditional activities and enterprises, environmental aspects and heritage. Third, it is rural in scale, relating to small-scale buildings and settlements. Fourth, it relies on the traditional qualities of the countryside and develops slowly under the control of local people. Lastly, it is non-uniform; that is, it reflects the complexity of the rural environment and has several forms.

The characteristics of the rural tourism experience that create special appeal and explain why people enjoy the countryside are:

- remoteness and solitude
- peace and quiet, relaxing environment
- adventure and challenge, opportunity to pursue sport or hobby
- health and fitness concerns, fresh air
- wildlife and landscapes, interests in the environment
- experience of rural communities, culture and lifestyles

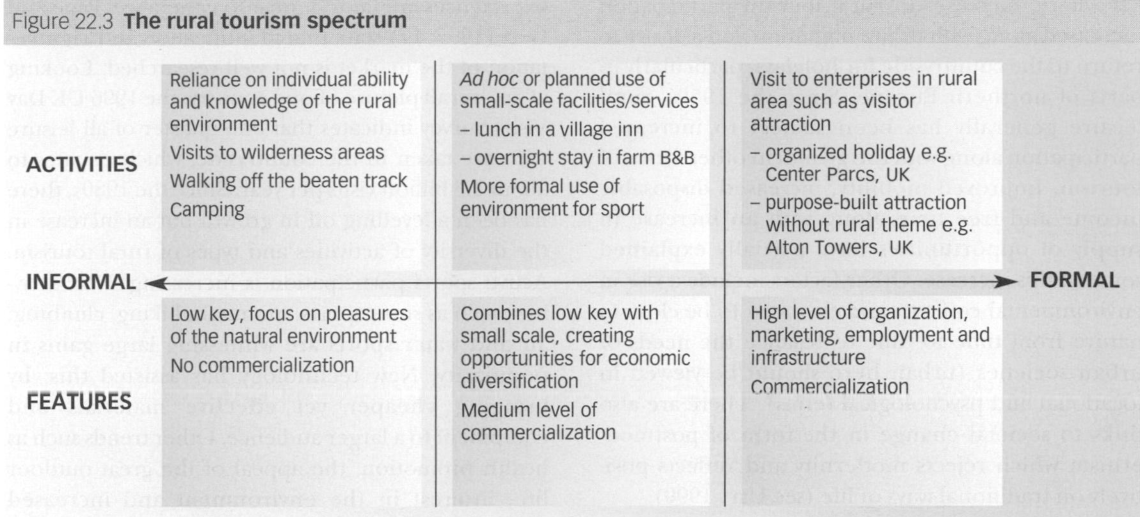

ACTIVITIES
Reliance on individual ability and knowledge of the rural environment
Visits to wilderness areas
Walking off the beaten track
Camping
Ad hoc or planned use of small-scale facilities/services
– lunch in a village inn
– overnight stay in farm B&B
More formal use of environment for sport
Visit to enterprises in rural area such as visitor attraction
– organized holiday e.g. Center Parcs, UK
– purpose-built attraction without rural theme e.g. Alton Towers, UK
INFORMAL
FORMAL
FEATURES
Low key, focus on pleasures of the natural environment
No commercialization
Combines low key with small scale, creating opportunities for economic diversification
Medium level of commercialization
High level of organization, marketing, employment and infrastructure
Commercialization

Figure 22.3 **The rural tourism spectrum**

- pleasant backcloth for being with friends and family
- a change from everyday urban life
- take part in rural activities such as conservation work
- explore historic identities, interests in heritage (Source: After Countryside Commission 1992; Page and Getz 1997)

Hall and Jenkins (1998: 28) suggest that the expansion of tourist flows in rural areas is designed to achieve one or more of the following goals:

- to sustain and create local incomes, employment and growth
- to contribute to the costs of providing economic and social infrastructure
- to encourage the development of other industrial sectors
- to contribute to local resident amenities and services
- to contribute to the conservation of environmental and cultural resources.

Sharpley and Sharpley (1997: 20) provide a neat overview of the meaning of rural tourism: 'rural tourism' may be defined both conceptually, as a state of mind and technically, according to activities, destinations and other measurable, tangible characteristics.' Overall, Sharpley and Sharpley believe rural tourism to be an economic activity which both depends on and exploits the countryside.

The growth of rural tourism

According to Sharpley and Sharpley (1997), rural tourism emerged as an identifiable activity in Europe during the latter half of the eighteenth century. Wild, mountainous regions, such as the Canadian Rockies, the Swiss Alps and the English Lake District began to attract aristocrats initially, then middle-class tourists. Thomas Cook directed the first package tour to rural Switzerland in 1863, which marked the beginning of a rapid growth in the industry in this area based on health and mountain sports. For the working classes, the countryside was viewed as a workplace until the time of industrialization and urbanization in the nineteenth century – therefore, class distinctions can be identified in the temporally uneven demand for rural tourism. Despite previous developments, it was not until the twentieth century that rural tourism became a more widely enjoyed activity when evidence demonstrates a rapid growth in demand for and supply of rural activities. Walking and cycling became increasingly popular during the inter-war years in England, especially in the Pennine Hills close to the major industrial centres of the north. Declining prosperity meant that there was a demand for inexpensive pursuits and membership of outdoor pursuit organizations, such as the Cyclists Touring Club and the Youth Hostel Association.

Elsewhere, increases in rural tourism participation increased along with urban migration and a desire to return to the countryside for holidays, particularly in parts of northern Europe. Since the 1950s, rural leisure generally has been subject to increased participation along with the growth in other forms of tourism. Improved mobility, increased disposable income and free time along with an increase in supply of opportunities have partially explained some of this increase. Other factors include a rise in environmental concern and the need to be close to nature from time to time to balance the needs of urban societies (urban here should be viewed in locational and psychological terms). There are also links to societal change in the form of postmodernism which rejects modernity and reflects positively on traditional ways of life (see Urry 1990).

In some European countries, especially in southern Europe, the traditional perspective on tourism in rural areas is that rural holidays are a cheap alternative to resort holidays. For example, rural tourism in Portugal was traditionally associated with staying on farms with the farming family. In other areas, such as Germany and Austria, rural tourism has always been linked with the more affluent. There is evidence that the traditional perspective of rural holidays as a poor relation to other forms of tourism is waning. Studies of rural tourists tend to indicate characteristics of high education and wealth among participants. In Portugal, for example, the Alto Minho region in the far west of the country is being promoted as a rural tourism destination based on sustainable principles and is attractive to educated and affluent tourists. In France, a wide range of rural tourism products are available, such as the famous gîtes and chambres d'hôte. The rural tourism product and experience has been developed and promoted on a global scale throughout the 1990s. Much of this development has become synonymous with ecotourism or specialist interest tourism that takes place in a rural environment. However, there is an inherent danger in assuming that because rural tourism relies on the countryside environment, it is somehow more environmentally friendly than resort-based tourism.

Rural tourists tend to be more affluent and better educated tourists (see Countryside Commission 1992), seeking high-quality experiences and products. However, the range of products that comprise rural tourism and the associated range of experiences are far too great to generalize. Page and Getz (1997: 17) state that identification and segmentation of the market is not well researched. Looking at an overall picture of one country, the 1996 UK Day Visits Survey indicates that one quarter of all leisure trips are taken in the countryside, which equates to about 1.3 billion visits per year. Since the 1980s, there has been a levelling off in growth but an increase in the diversity of activities and types of rural tourism. Active sports participation is increasing. New activities such as snow sports, mountain biking, climbing, air and water sports are witnessing large gains in popularity. New technology has assisted this, by bringing cheaper yet effective materials and equipment to a larger audience. Other trends such as health promotion, the appeal of the great outdoor life, interest in the environment and increased marketing of activities all partly explain this increase.

Impacts of rural tourism

The aim of tourism development in rural areas is, in general terms, to provide opportunities for economic and social development. In some areas, tourism provides the main source of income and employment, as well as providing social and environmental benefits. Inevitably, negative aspects of rural tourism development are evident also. There is a substantial literature on the impacts of tourism in rural areas (Gannon 1994; Healy 1994; PA Cambridge Economic Consultants 1987). Much of the early tourism impact research focuses on rural areas, arguably because the relationship between tourism and the environment in the countryside is more pronounced. The positive and negative impacts of rural tourism are summarized in Table 22.2.

In England, the Rural Development Commission carried out research on a sample of English rural settlements to evaluate the impact of tourism (Rural Development Commission 1996). The research found that tourism results in several benefits, the magnitude of which vary according to settlement/community characteristics and the nature and scale of tourism activity. The benefits in general are that tourism:

- Increases the range and viability of local businesses (food and non-food shops, hotels, pubs and

Table 22.2 **Summary of the positive and negative impacts of rural tourism**

Impact	Positive	Negative
Economic	Assists viability of existing tourism and non-tourism business	Encourages dependence on industry prone to uncontrollable change
	Creates new employment	Creates part-time, seasonal or low-grade employment
	Attracts inward investment	Incurs development costs and public service costs
	Encourages pluriactivity, helping to stabilize economic base	Leads to local land and house price inflation
Socio-cultural	Assists in viability of local services	Creates feeling of invasion by tourists; overcrowding and traffic
	Creates sense of pride	Increases crime
	Revitalizes local cultural traditions, events and crafts	Reduction in local services, e.g. food shops replaced by gift shops
	Leads to opportunities for social and cultural exchange	Import of new cultural ideas – challenges existing way of life
Environmental	Leads to environmental improvements in settlements	Increases wear and tear on landscape features
	Provides income for conservation of buildings and natural environment	Creates need for new developments which may not be in keeping with local area
	Fosters awareness of conservation as worthwhile activity	Increases pollution (noise, visual, air, water, litter) Affects local biodiversity

cafés, garages, indirect spending to other non-tourist businesses).

- Contributes to social and community life (encourages new businesses, provides employment, support for fund raising and community events, greater choice of recreational opportunities available to local people).
- Helps to maintain or improve services (health services, entertainment, banks, public transport).
- Brings about environmental and/or infrastructural improvements (pride generated, revenue pays for environmental improvements, larger car parks, interpretation, enhanced visual amenity).

Several negative impacts were reported. Rising house prices, traffic congestion, parking problems, disturbance and litter were the most common aspects reported. The success of rural tourism depends on maintaining a balance between the needs of a working, living community and an intrinsically valuable environment. It is with this in mind that a more sustainable approach to rural tourism has been advocated.

Sustainable rural tourism

One of the inherent dangers in thinking about rural tourism is to make it synonymous with sustainable tourism. As Clarke (1998: 130) states, 'they are not, decisively *not,* one and the same'. Lane (1994) outlines why a sustainable approach to rural tourism is required. Visitors to the countryside are increasingly mobile and are able to penetrate more remote areas than just a few years ago. Advances in modes of transport have assisted this coupled with the increasingly sophisticated marketing of new destinations. An unknown footpath can become an overused one almost overnight as a result of an editorial in special-interest publications or promotional literature. A threat from badly managed tourism is posed. Rural tourism may be managed by outsiders who have little understanding of the people, culture and heritage of that area. Undermanagement of environmental resources could lead to their ultimate degradation. Tension between conservation and rural development interests commonly exist. While realizing a need to stimulate some rural economies, reliance on tourism may lead to an unbalanced economy. A sustainable approach takes a more holistic perspective towards rural development. Page and Getz (1997) state that rurality and all of its components must be preserved and nurtured because they are, in essence, the selling point of the countryside and can be used in planning and marketing strategies. Rural tourism ideally should be included as part of an integrated rural development strategy. A sustainable approach to rural tourism should be based on a multi-faceted view of sustainability to achieve balanced development. Consideration of the needs of the community, the viability of the economy and the conservation of the environment should receive appropriate consideration. The Mid-Wales Festival of the Countryside is a good example of this type of approach.

The planning and management of rural tourism – issues

On an international scale, there are a number of different strategies adopted to manage rural tourism. To some extent, rural tourism is comparable to tourism in any area but there are some distinct features or other aspects exacerbated in rural locations which need to be recognized.

Issues in rural tourism management

- *The lack of statistical base.* It is difficult to establish volume and value of rural tourism as a specific market sector in a nation, even harder on an international scale. Many countries have different definitions of 'rural' and will therefore collect different data. Data on rural as a specific form of tourism are not easily obtainable.
- *Rural communities.* These tend to be non-uniform, for example remote versus accessible rural areas contain very different types of settlement, employment opportunities, socio-demographic characteristics. Different community structures with diverse responses to tourism exist.
- *Tourism development strategies may not benefit all rural areas.* Where there is an inadequate supply of attractions and/or accommodation, tourism cannot flourish, however good the marketing strategies to attract visitors may be. Likewise, development of tourism provision by local people may not be feasible in a depressed rural economy.
- *Tourism in rural areas is highly dependent on an attractive natural and culturally interesting environment.* This highlights the need to ensure that sustainable approaches to tourism management are adhered to. This may conflict with the desire to attract greater volumes of visitors to the countryside and requires sensitive consideration.

Providers of rural tourism – farm tourism

One of the important issues in rural tourism is that many providers are involved in tourism part time. For example, the main business of a farm is in managing land, stock, machinery and so on. Bed and breakfast may be an ancillary business which provides supplementary income. As the enterprise may not be the main thrust of a business, there may be a lack of skills in managing a tourism business. Many farmers are isolated with a lack of knowledge,

Exhibit 22.1 Mid-Wales Festival of the countryside

This programme for rural economic development was established in 1985 by the Development Board for Rural Wales in a joint venture with the then Countryside Commission for Wales (now Countryside Council for Wales) and a steering group consisting of development, tourism and conservation organizations. The philosophy of the Festival is to assist conservation, absorb recreation demand and stimulate the local economy. Thus, the approach is multi-dimensional – not solely concentrated on tourism development but on the wider implications for regional economic development (Figure 22.4). The aim of the project is to create more employment without damaging the environment The Festival runs for 6 months of the year (July–December) and is region-wide. It consists of a large number of events and activities under five main themes:

- *Nature and wildlife* – nature reserve visits, bird and mammal watching, natural history courses.
- *Working landscape* – farm visits, markets, opening of water mills, forestry exhibits.
- *Rural rides* – narrow gauge railway events, white water rafting, pony trekking, mountain biking.
- *Arts and crafts* – art, sculpture and photographic and exhibitions, open craft workshops.
- *History and tradition* – tours of castles, iron age forts, historical re-enactments.

The events are publicized through distribution of a free magazine which acts as a comprehensive guide to the Festival. Visitor numbers increased from 90,000 in 1985 to 300,000 in 1993. The Festival has resulted in the creation of 20 full-time job equivalents and has generated a £5m annual turnover in the region. In addition, the viability of many rural enterprises has been increased. Areas where there is environmental sensitivity, such as nature reserves, are managed appropriately. This may be through not marketing that particular place; by promoting low-impact use; or by carefully monitoring the effects of visitors. The Festival is a good example of a successful rural tourism initiative.

expertise and training in tourism (Busby and Rendle 2000). Organizations can give advice to farmers on how to develop and manage rural tourism businesses, such as the Ministry of Agriculture, Fisheries and Food (MAFF), the Countryside Agency, Regional Tourist Boards and local Training and Enterprise Councils in England. Many farm tourism providers belong to the Farm Holiday Bureau which assists in marketing which others choose to use other channels, such as guidebooks, adverts in tourist information centres or agencies. In France, there is a centralized system, supported by the public sector, to co-ordinate rural accommodation bookings for over 40,000 gîtes. In the 1950s, the Ministry of Agriculture initiated the gîtes scheme, giving financial assistance to farmers to restore old farm buildings to tourist accommodation. Private sector companies, such as Gîtes de France, assist in promoting accommodation and travel packages to consumers. Gîtes de France have been commended for their performance in providing an environmentally responsible product by the British Airways sponsored Tourism for Tomorrow Awards (see Chapter 20).

There appears to be much debate in the literature regarding farm tourism. It is certainly clear that many farms have diversified into providing accommodation. A survey by Evans and Ilbery (1992) indicates about 6,000 farm businesses with accommodation in England, exist mainly in the South West and uplands areas. Both large and small farms have done this contrary to the opinion that it is only small, less economically viable units which diversify into tourism. Family labour tends to be the main source of assistance in farm tourism enterprises. Successful farm tourism development

Figure 22.4 **Map of mid-Wales region**

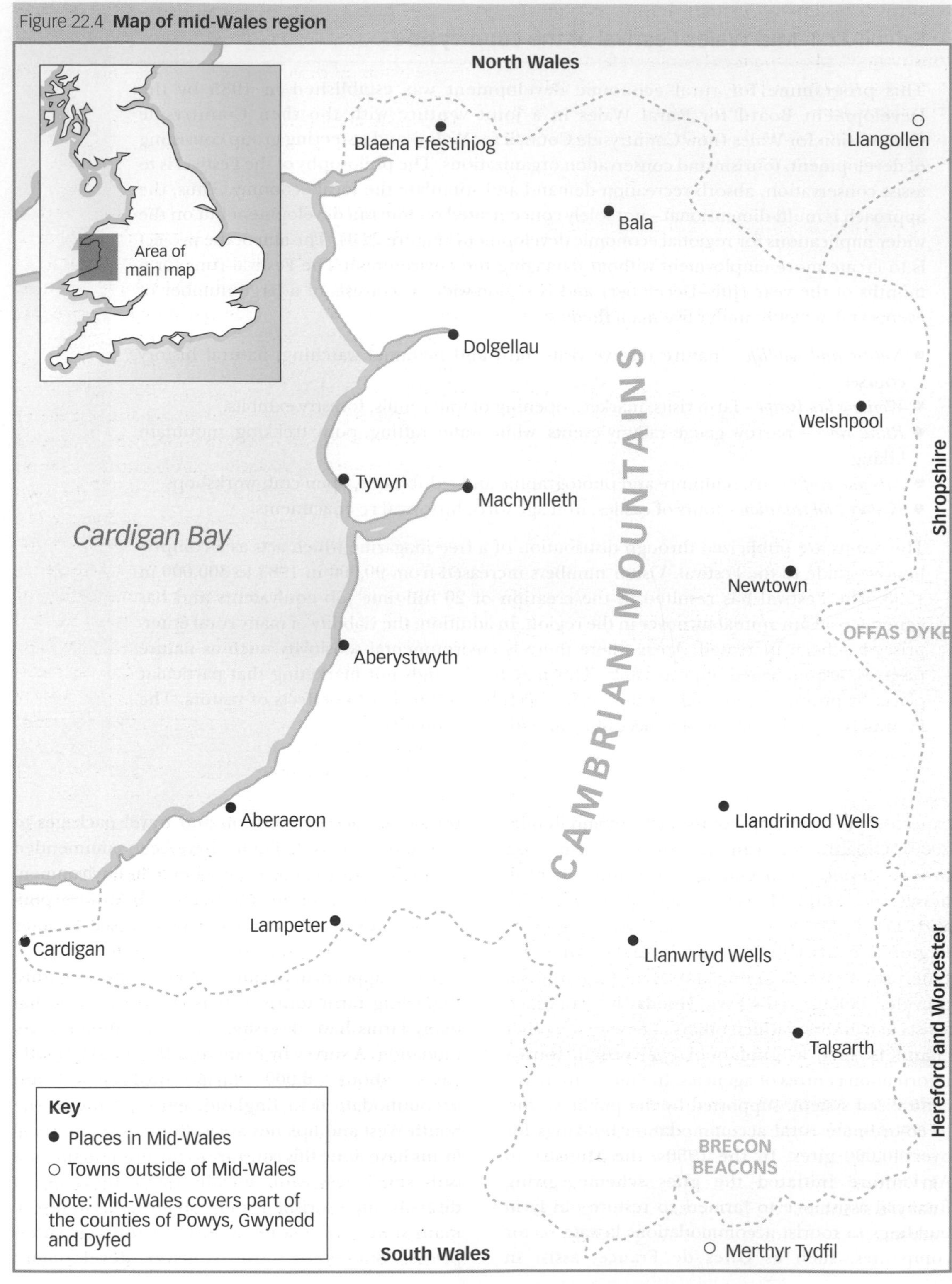

requires substantive capital input, marketing, reliance on external advice and finance. They face constraints of planning legislation and farm tourism is not necessarily a panacea in terms of solving critical problems of low farm incomes or failing businesses. Jenkins *et al.* (1998) state that the returns for small farms are limited.

Criteria for success in rural tourism

According to a study undertaken by PA Cambridge Economic Consultants (1987), rural tourism can be a significant part of local economic activity. However, total contribution depends on:

- the extent of direct and indirect benefits retained in the area
- the provision of accommodation in the area
- the existence of facilities to support tourism in the area.

Plate 22.3 Ice-cream shop, Cornwall
Farm diversification can assist in developing an existing agricultural business. This ice-cream shop in Cornwall is the result of diversification of a local dairy farm specializing in Guernsey cows. The shop attracts many visitors and is a thriving business.

In individual businesses, success in rural tourism generally depends on a combination of a number of factors. Briefly, these include: the commitment of the proprietor; the provision of additional facilities, which visitors are willing to pay a higher price for; generating visitor satisfaction and therefore recommendations and repeat visiting; ability to promote off-peak visits, thus reducing the effects of seasonality; understanding the needs and characteristics of customers and potential customers; existence of attractive natural environment and cultural/historic features of interest. Recent discussions of the suitability of branding the rural tourism product has led to various attempts to identify certain products: for example, in the UK, the Farm Holiday Bureau, a co-operative, membership-owned body consisting of over 1,000 farm accommodation providers market their own products; a similar body exists in New Zealand (the New Zealand Association of Farm Home Holidays). In south-west England a new project called Cartwheel, which aims to assist farmers in branding and marketing tourism, has recently been established – the results of which will provide evidence of whether or not this is a successful approach. The aim of branding is to help identify rural tourism destinations and communicate the benefits, such as quality (Clarke 1998).

One of the foci of rural tourism strategy in general is to encourage a higher number of overnight stays and day trips. But rural areas need significant visitor spend to support employment. Attractions are particularly well suited to drawing in visitor numbers but accommodation is needed to encourage these visitors to spend more time in that area and subsequently, more money. PA Cambridge Economic Consultants (1987: 63) state: 'The major issue for rural areas is the creation of a critical mass of tourism facilities, both accommodation and attraction projects, which can succeed in making visitors additional to the region'.

Community involvement is an important aspect of rural tourism development. Common patterns indicate that residents need to feel tangible benefits of tourism and a degree of control over development and promotion. In the absence of perceived benefits, opposition is likely to increase (Page and Getz 1997). A 'bottom-up' approach where initiatives stem from the community is likely to lead to much less antagonism from local residents as opposed to a 'top-down' approach where an outside agency imposes a particular policy of tourism development on a community. Many of the sustainable rural tourism projects around the world have been developed in a bottom-up way because there is a recognition that tourism is a way for local people to generate income and employment. For example, the Otago Peninsula Trust (Southern New Zealand) is a voluntary organization which has taken a lead in establishing many facilities which are for the benefit of both locals, the environment and visitors (Kearsley 1998). So rather than a tool of blatant commercialism, this approach recognizes the wider developmental role which tourism can play.

Management issues

Visitor management, discussed in more detail in Chapters 20 and 26, is a key part of managing tourism in rural areas. National government may provide the overall framework for tourism development, and Exhibit 22.2 illustrates tourism policy in Namibia; Table 22.3 states the framework for tourism in the rural areas of England.

At regional and local levels, more precisely defined policies for visitor management can be identified. In England, the Countryside Commission (1995) has developed a wide range of different projects aimed at achieving sustainable rural tourism utilizing various visitor management practices. Many rural tourism initiatives have arisen through organizations and groups working in collaboration, mainly public and private sector partnerships (see Exhibit 22.1). Visitor management may be aimed at encouraging certain types of desirable behaviour or limiting undesired behaviour. Demarketing, a policy of discouraging visitors, might well be part of the strategy. The Quantock Hills in Somerset, UK are not promoted by South West Tourism (the Regional Tourist Board) to help protect the area from further visits. Principles for tourism in rural areas also assist in the translation of policy to practice. The Countryside Commission, English Tourist Board and Rural Development Commission published guidelines in 1989, displayed in Table 22.3.

Exhibit 22.2 **Rural tourism in Namibia**

Namibia, a large country in South West Africa, is a country of unspoilt landscapes and significant populations of wildlife, from the Big Five to unusual insects and plantlife. The world's largest cheetah population lives here. Some 15 per cent of the country is covered by National Park designations. Since the country gained independence in 1990, tourism has been viewed as an important source of economic support. Tourism is the country's third most important industry and foreign exchange earner, after mining and fishing. Between 1993 and 1997, tourist numbers increased by 18 per cent to 500,000. Further growth is likely to see numbers rise to 770,000 by 2002. The objectives of Namibia's Development Plan are to revive and sustain national growth; create employment; reduce inequalities in income distribution; and eradicate poverty. The government is committed to developing tourism based on sustainable development which must support the objectives of the Plan. The draft Tourism Policy was published in January 1999 by the Ministry of the Environment and Tourism. The national mission statement for tourism development is:

> To develop the tourism industry in a sustainable and responsible manner to significantly contribute to the economic development of Namibia and the quality of life of all her people.

A significant amount of accommodation is available on farms as farmers seek methods of economic diversification. These enterprises are generally working farms, often extensive ranches, and offer the visitor the chance to experience life in rural Namibia. Some offer activities and excursions while others emphasize the opportunity to relax and enjoy what the local area has to offer. Guest farms are viewed as a way of generating economic benefits in harmony with the environment. However, there is some concern that tourism is less labour intensive than ranching, and that jobs are being lost as a result of tourism (Shackley 1993).

Four important principles guiding the implementation of the tourism policy

Management of the industry

The future success of Namibia's tourism sector requires appropriate marketing and management at an international level. Government intervention is needed to enhance Namibia's ability to compete in the international tourism market. The government controls about one third of accommodation in National Parks under its Wildlife Resorts initiative, for example, self-catering camps in Etosha National Park and is based on low-volume/high-spending tourists.

Local participation

The benefits of tourism will be most effectively translated at the local level if there are opportunities for local participation and equity. Local people will be encouraged to take ownership and control of tourism and its management.

Environment

The protection of biodiversity and the natural resource base is crucial: this includes environment, wildlife and culture. Natural resources must be used in a sustainable way to create employment and income.

Government's role

Government's role in tourism development should be that of a facilitator and not an operator. It should guide and facilitate the direction of tourism and provide an enabling environment for small-scale operators and the informal sector. This will lead to the achievement of sustainable and socially desirable tourism in Namibia. Recent government legislation, designed to actively encourage communities to establish conservancies, gives to communities the right to earn revenue from tourism on communal land. The Himba nomadic people living in Puros, north-west Namibia are a good example of an indigenous community which has developed a wildlife tourism initiative. While retaining their traditional herding practices, the local community has initiated game monitoring and protected wildlife from poachers, devised guidelines for appropriate tourist behaviour and started a campsite. Local people act as guides, tourists are charged a daily levy which goes directly into the local community and local crafts are sold to tourists. While, almost inevitably, some socio-cultural effects have arisen as a result of this initiative, this example demonstrates that local people can create the type of development that suits their needs without destroying the natural resource base.

(Sources: Gehrels 1997; Namibia Ministry of Environment and Tourism 1999; Shackley 1993)

Table 22.3 **Principles for tourism in the countryside**

Enjoyment	The promotion of the tourist's enjoyment of the countryside should be primarily aimed at those activities which draw on special character of the countryside itself, its beauty, culture, history and wildlife
Development	Tourism development in the countryside should assist the purposes conservation and recreation, such as bringing new life to redundant buildings, supplementing farm incomes, aid derelict land reclamation and open up new access opportunities
Design	The planning, design, siting and management of new tourism developments should be in keeping with the landscape and wherever possible should seek to enhance it
Rural economy	Investment in tourism should support the rural economy, but should seek a wider geographical spread and more off-peak visiting both to avoid congestion and damage to the resource through erosion and over-use and to spread the economic and other benefits
Conservation	Those who benefit from tourism in the countryside should contribute to the conservation and enhancement of its most valuable asset – the countryside, through political and practical support for conservation and recreation policies and programmes
Marketing	Publicity, information and marketing initiatives of the tourism industry should endeavour to deepen people's understanding of and concern for the countryside leading to fuller appreciation and enjoyment

Conclusion: the future development of rural tourism

It is clear that rural areas are an integral part of the modern tourism experience. However, rural areas need to be understood to ensure that appropriate forms of tourism are developed which assist in achieving the goals for national, regional and/or local objectives. There is an inherent responsibility to appreciate long-term effects of tourism in rural areas, recognizing both the benefits and costs related to development. The relationship between tourism and the environment is particularly strong in rural areas. There is also an imperative to understand to what extent tourism achieves the desired economic effects in rural areas and the criteria for successful business strategy need careful examination. Butler and Clark (1992) recognize that tourism is not necessarily the key to rural development, highlighting concerns about income leakage, multipliers, local labour, wages, limited number of entrepreneurs. 'The least favoured circumstance in which to promote tourism is when the rural economy is already weak, since tourism will create highly unbalanced income and employment distributions' (Butler and Clark 1992: 175). The final point must be to emphasize the need to embed tourism within a diverse rural economy to enable stable rural communities to exist.

Discussion questions

1. Explain why 'rural tourism' is a difficult term to define.
2. 'The aim of rural tourism is to aid economic development.' Discuss.
3. Discuss the reasons why tourism may have a negative impact on a rural area.
4. Suggest reasons why tourism is more successful in some rural areas than others.

Internet resources

By going to the weblink at www.thomsonlearning.co.uk students can access the following two studies on the Thomson Learning website. The first is by R. Sharpley and J. Sharpley (1997) *Rural Tourism: An Introduction* which provides an introduction to the different ways one needs to consider and understand rural tourism as a phenomenon. It outlines the problem of defining rural tourism and follows up many of the issues raised in this chapter.

The second study by R. McLennan and R. Smith (1998) *Tourism in Scotland* examines tourism and rural development in Scotland. It brings together many of the issues associated with the public sectors role in tourism as well as the implications of tourism development for rural and more remote rural areas within the Scottish context. This study exemplifies many of the common problems associated with rural tourism development.

References

Bramwell, B. (1994) 'Rural tourism and sustainable tourism', *Journal of Sustainable Tourism,* **2** (1&2): 1–6.

Busby, G. and Rendle, S. (2000) 'The transition from tourism on farms to farm tourism', *Tourism Management,* **21** (6): 635–42.

Butler, R. and Clark, G. (1992) 'Tourism in rural areas: Canada and the UK', in I. Bowler, C. Bryant and M. Nellis, (eds) *Contemporary Rural Systems in Transition. Volume 2: Economy and Society,* Wallingford: CAB International.

Butler, R., Hall, C.M. and Jenkins, J. (eds) (1998) *Tourism and Recreation in Rural Areas,* Chichester: John Wiley and Sons.

Clarke, J. (1998) 'Marketing rural tourism: problems, practice and branding in the context of sustainability', in D. Hall and L. O'Hanlon (eds) *Rural Tourism Management: Sustainable Options. Conference Proceedings 9–12 September 1998,* Ayr: SAC Auchincruive: 129–46.

Cloke, P. (1977) 'An index of rurality for England and Wales', *Regional Studies,* **2** (1): 31–46.

Cloke, P. (1993) 'The countryside as commodity: new spaces for rural leisure', in S. Glyptis (ed.) *Leisure and the Environment. Essays in Honour of J.A. Patmore,* London: Belhaven: 53–67.

Countryside Commission (1992) *Enjoying the Countryside: Policies for People,* Cheltenham: Countryside Commission.

Countryside Commission (1995) *Sustainable Rural Tourism. A Guide to Local Opportunities,* Cheltenham: Countryside Commission.

Curry, N. (1994) *Countryside Recreation: Access and Land Use Planning,* London: E&FN Spon.

Evans, N.J. and Ilbery, B.W. (1992) 'The distribution of farm-based accommodation in England and Wales', *Journal of the Royal Agricultural Society,* **153**: 67–80.

Gannon, A. (1994) 'Rural tourism as a factor in rural community economic development for economies in transition', *Journal of Sustainable Tourism,* **1** (1&2): 51–60.

Gehrels, B. (1997) 'Namibia: rhetoric or reality?', *In Focus* **23**: 15–16, London: Tourism Concern.

Glyptis, S. (1991) *Countryside Recreation,* Harlow: Longman.

Halfacree, K. (1993) 'Locality and social representation: space, discourse, and alternative definitions of the rural', *Journal of Rural Studies,* **9** (1): 23–37.

Halfacree, K. (1995) 'Talking about rurality: social representations of the rural as expressed by residents of six English parishes', *Journal of Rural Studies,* **11** (1): 1–20.

Hall, C.M. and Jenkins, J. (1998) 'The policy dimensions of rural tourism and recreation', in R. Butler, C.M. Hall and J. Jenkins (eds) (1998) *Tourism and Recreation in Rural Areas,* Chichester: John Wiley and Sons: 19–42.

Healy, R. (1994) 'The common pool problem in tourism landscapes', *Annals of Tourism Research,* **21** (3): 596–611.

Ilbery, B.W. (1997) *The Geography of Rural Change,* Harlow: Longman.

Jenkins, J., Hall, C.M. and Troughton, M. (1998) 'The restructuring of rural economies: rural tourism and recreation as a government response', in R. Butler, C.M. Hall and J. Jenkins (eds) *Tourism and Recreation in Rural Areas,* Chichester: John Wiley and Sons: 43–68.

Keane, M. and Quinn, J. (1990) *Rural Development and Rural Tourism,* Galway: SSRC, University College.

Kearsley, G. (1998) 'Rural tourism in Otago and Southland, New Zealand', in R. Butler, C.M. Hall and J. Jenkins (eds) *Tourism and Recreation in Rural Area,* Chichester: John Wiley and Sons: 81–96.

Koutsouris, A. (1998) 'The quest for a sustainable future: alternative tourism as the lever of development', in D. Hall and L. O'Hanlon (eds) *Rural Tourism Management: Sustainable Options. Conference Proceedings 9–12 September 1998,* Ayr: SAC Auchincruive: 287–308.

Lane, B. (1994) 'What is rural tourism?', *Journal of Sustainable Tourism,* **2** (1&2): 7–21.

Murdoch, J. and Marsden, T. (1994) *Reconstituting Rurality,* London: University College London Press.

Namibia Ministry of Environment (1999) Draft Tourism Policy, http://www.iwwn.com.na/namtour/namtour.html

Oppermann, M. (1997) 'Rural tourism in Germany: farm and rural tourism operators', in S.J. Page and D. Getz *The*

Business of Rural Tourism. International Perspectives, London: Thomson Learning: 108–19.

PA Cambridge Economic Consultants (1987) *A Study of Rural Tourism,* English Tourist Board and Rural Development Commission: London.

Page, S.J. and Getz, D. (eds) (1997) *The Business of Rural Tourism. International Perspectives,* London: Thomson Learning.

Robinson, G.M. (1990) *Conflict and Change in the Countryside,* London: Belhaven.

Rural Development Commission (1994) *Survey of Rural Services,* London: Rural Development Commission.

Rural Development Commission (1996) *The Impact of Tourism on Rural Settlements,* London: Rural Development Commission.

Shackley, M. (1993) 'Guest farms in Namibia: an emerging accommodation sector in Africa's hottest destination', *International Journal of Hospitality Management,* **12** (3): 253–65.

Sharpley, R. (1996) *Tourism and Leisure in the Countryside,* Huntingdon: ELM.

Sharpley, R. and Sharpley, J. (1997) *Rural Tourism. An Introduction,* London: Thomson Learning.

Turner, J.C., Davies, W.P. and Ahmad, Z. (1996) 'Challenges for sustainable rural tourism development in Malaysia', Conference Paper at Sustainable Tourism Conference, University of Central Lancashire, Newton Rigg, Penrith, April 17–19 1996.

Urry, J. (1990) *The Tourist Gaze: Leisure and Travel in Contemporary Societies,* London: Sage.

Further reading

Busby, G. and Rendle, S. (2000) 'The transition from tourism on farms to farm tourism', *Tourism Management,* **21** (6): 635–42.

Butler, R., Hall, C.M. and Jenkins, J. (eds) (1998) *Tourism and Recreation in Rural Areas,* Chichester: John Wiley and Sons.

Sharpley, R. and Sharpley, J. (1997) *Rural Tourism. An Introduction,* London: Thomson Learning.

Useful web addresses

Namibia Ministry of Environment and Tourism
http://www.iwwn.com.na/namtour/namtour.html

Learning outcomes

After studying this chapter, you should be able to:

- Understand the importance of tourism in coastal areas.
- Recognize the impacts of coastal and resort tourism.
- Identify issues relating to the development and management of tourism in coastal areas.

23 Coastal and resort tourism

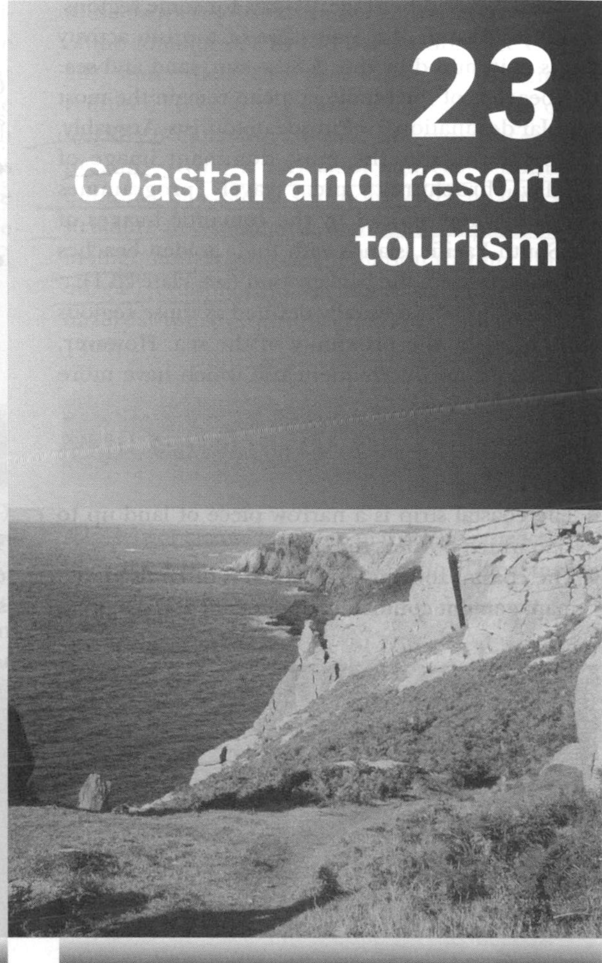

Overview

Coastal areas offer some of the most desirable resources for tourism on the globe. Sun, sand and sea (the 3 Ss) remains one of the most significant types of holiday in the world. However, new forms of coastal and marine recreation are emerging and increasing in popularity. This has broadened the coastal tourism product in recent years beyond resort holidays. While coastal tourism provides an important commercial sector of the tourism industry, tourism-related activities have been seen to cause negative environmental impacts. This chapter considers the importance of coastal areas for tourism, the nature of the coastal environment and the challenges for future management.

Introduction

The relationship between coastal areas and tourism is as old as tourism itself. Early tourists favoured seaside locations and made journeys to fashionable resorts to bathe in sea water to take advantage of its alleged curative powers. This was a major departure in the eighteenth century from a time where the sea and coast were revered as places and even feared. This is illustrated by Lenček and Bosker (1999) who state that 'the beach … historically speaking, [is] a recent phenomenon. In fact, it took hundreds of years for the seashore to be colonised as the pre-eminent site for human recreation.' The coast continues to be one of the most important environments for tourism in contemporary times building

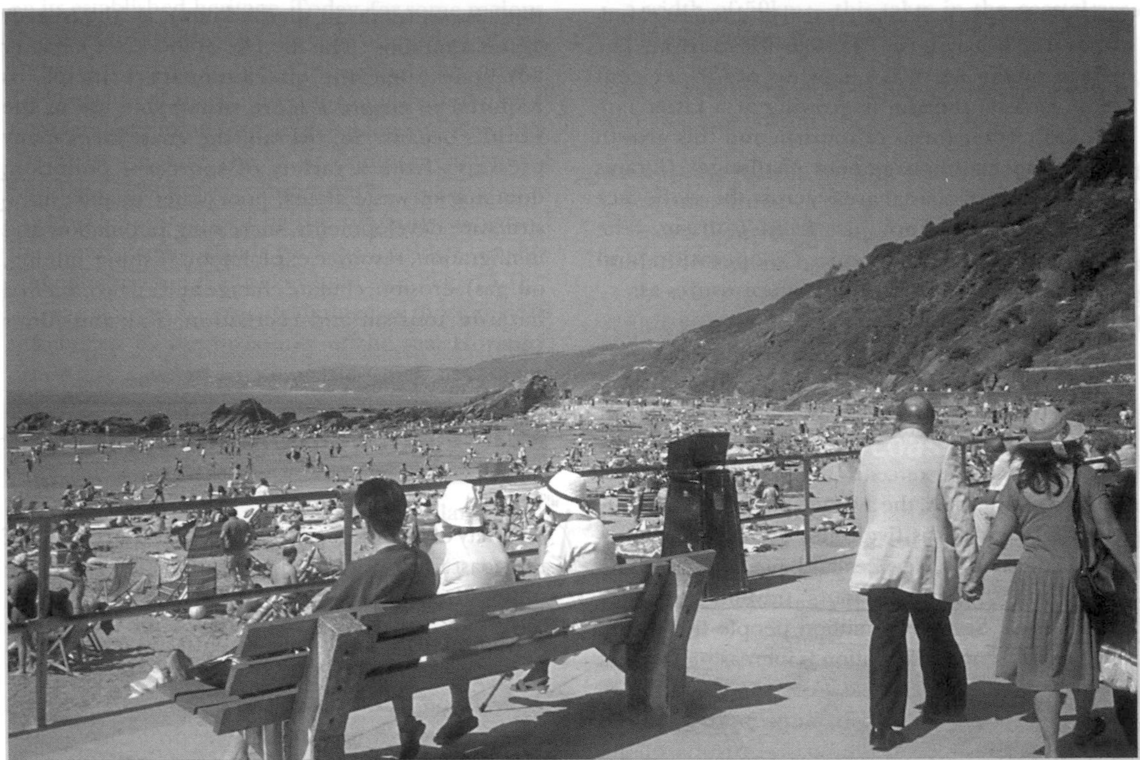

Plate 23.2 The coastal environment
The coastal environment is varied and offers many opportunities for recreation. Visitors to this location in Cornwall in England will be seeking the traditional seaside or 'bucket and spade' holiday.

made by the upper classes to old ports and small fishing villages to bathe in the sea, to drink sea water and to take in the fresh air and the sunshine, such as Scarborough and Brighton. In other parts of the world, developments took place much later. In fact, the English were considered to be quite eccentric for their tendencies to bathe in cold sea water. Doctors started the trend by writing about the curative powers of sea water. Towner (1996) notes that the most famous was Dr Richard Russell who in 1752 published his treatize entitled *Dissertation on the Use of Seawater in Diseases of the Glands.* His work led to Brighton, located on the south coast of England, becoming one of the first seaside resorts. In the eighteenth century both spas and sea-bathing places were known as 'watering places'. Ancillary facilities evolved to serve the visitors, such as libraries, theatres and rooms for cards and billiards, in addition to hotels and lodgings. The physical environment in some cases was altered, providing promenades and grassy areas for strolling and socializing.

Most of the early resorts developed in this way, some more successfully than others. Two main influencing factors should be noted:

- the proximity to London, which explains the success of resorts such as Brighton, Eastbourne and later, Margate
- the kudos attached to Royal patronage, typified by Brighton and its association with the Prince Regent and the lavish Brighton Pavilion and other more remote places such as Weymouth in Dorset and Sidmouth in Devon, both visited by George III.

Gradually, seaside visitation became more broadly participated in by other social classes. The arrival of the railway to many resorts brought the opportunity of visiting the seaside to ordinary people and released a latent demand as greater leisure time was generated through Victorian legislation like the

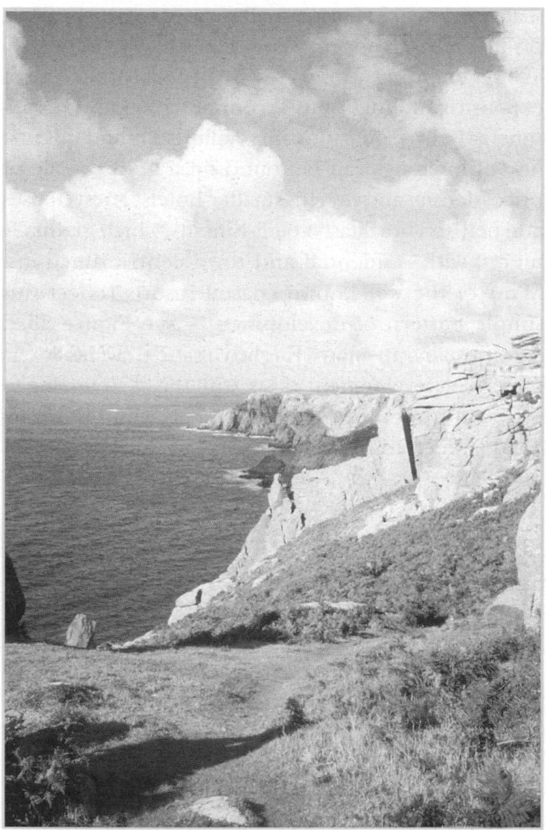

Plate 23.3 Lundy Island, UK
Visitors to this location may be seeking something quite different, perhaps ornithology, rock climbing or walking.

1872 Holiday Act. New resorts sprung up, purpose built for tourism, such as Bournemouth and Blackpool. Blackpool was popular with working-class families from nearby industrial towns. Sometimes, entire factories would close for a week in the summer and workers, having saved up all year, would go on holiday to places like Blackpool. They stayed in cheap accommodation and enjoyed shows, singing, dancing and the many attractions of the resort, such as the trams and illuminations and of course, Blackpool Tower and the Pleasure Beach. In many seaside areas in the early part of the twentieth century, holiday camps aimed at providing good value accommodation and entertainment were established by entrepreneurs such as Billy Butlin and Fred Pontin. Walton (1983) noted that in many places, working-class people, often residents at the coast, had a tradition of bathing in the sea and that it was not simply a case of one class following another.

While it might be said that the seaside resort was an English invention, they certainly did not remain the preserve of England. The warm climate of the south of France attracted visitors from the late 1700s, particularly to Nice and Cannes. Some of the French ports on the Channel coast also became fashionable, such as Dieppe, Trouville and Calais. In the early part of the nineteenth century, resorts emerged across Europe and across to the Black Sea coast of Russia. In America, small fishing villages attracted summer visitors from the late 1700s but it was not until the 1850s that coastal tourism became significant. Early mass coastal tourism was based on religious camps on the East Coast, with participants staying in tents and abiding by certain rules of behaviour. Later, large-scale commercial resorts developed. Coney Island, a tram ride from New York city, was a large resort by the 1880s with the spectacular lights of Luna Park, amusements, ballrooms and fantasy buildings. In the early 1920s, tourism started a boom in Florida, with the exotic climate and environment being the big pull.

Following World War II, the era of mass tourism began. In England, the price of foreign holidays reduced and fewer people were content with a holiday in an English seaside resort. The attraction of the '3 Ss', along with increases in disposable income, paid holiday time and a supply of affordable package holidays, led to the emergence of the beach resort as the major international tourism destination of the twentieth century. Inclusive package holidays began in the 1950s to new destinations along the coast of the Mediterranean (see Montanari and Williams 1995). Spain, in particular, became the favourite retreat for British holidaymakers and a classic study by Naylon (1967) and highlighted this trend. Similar patterns of development can be observed in other Mediterannean island destinations. The American Pacific coast became popular from the 1950s, especially with American young people, California becoming known as a surfer's paradise and bringing with it a 'beach culture'. The industry centred around Miami Beach developed further. Globally, new coastal destinations emerged on Australia's Gold Coast, the beaches of the Gambia, the all-inclusive beach front resorts of Mexico's Cancun. Coastal tourism is more popular than ever.

Coastal resort development

There are several models which have been developed to assist in the explanation of resort development. Miossec's model of tourism development (1976 cited in Pearce 1995: 15) illustrates the temporal and spatial growth of a tourist region. Smith (1992) applied this model to Pattaya in Thailand and developed a tentative beach resort model, where development is observed from no development to full resort development. Figure 23.1 illustrates the model.

Common structural features may be observed in coastal resorts as indicated by Pearce (1995). The seafront, linear in form, usually consists of the beach, a promenade, a road and a line of beach front buildings. These buildings tend to incorporate the most expensive and luxurious accommodation and restaurants as well as some tourism retailing. Behind this first line of buildings can be found on a graded scale of price, density and height, smaller hotels, guest houses and bed and breakfast establishments, which gradually merge with residential and town centre functions. Many of the well-known coastal resorts reflect this simple pattern of development – see Figure 23.2. Additionally, in many English resorts, a classic 'T' pattern of development exists, with the 'T' referring to the road from the station as it meets with the promenade, which constitutes the basic structure.

Figure 23.1 **Model of tourist resort development**

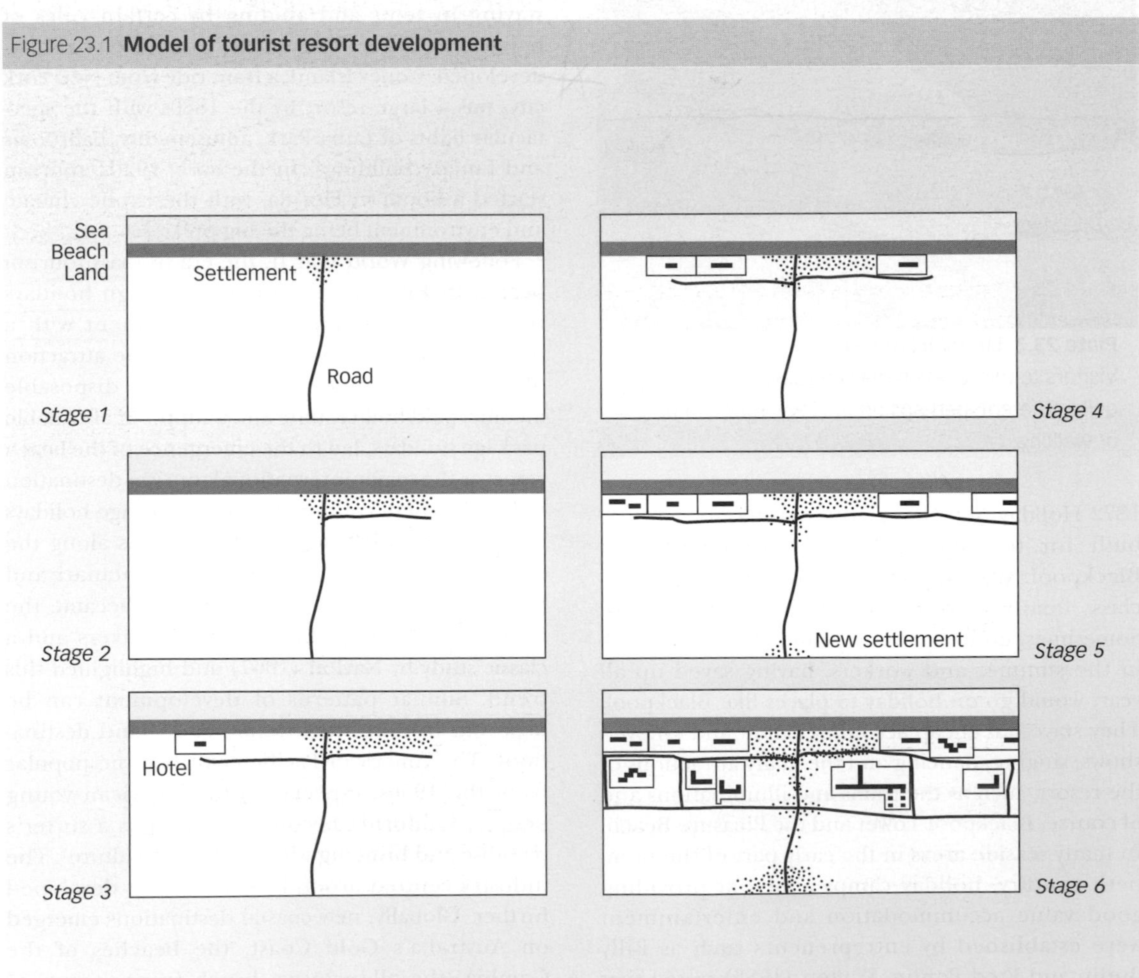

(Source: Modified from Smith 1992)

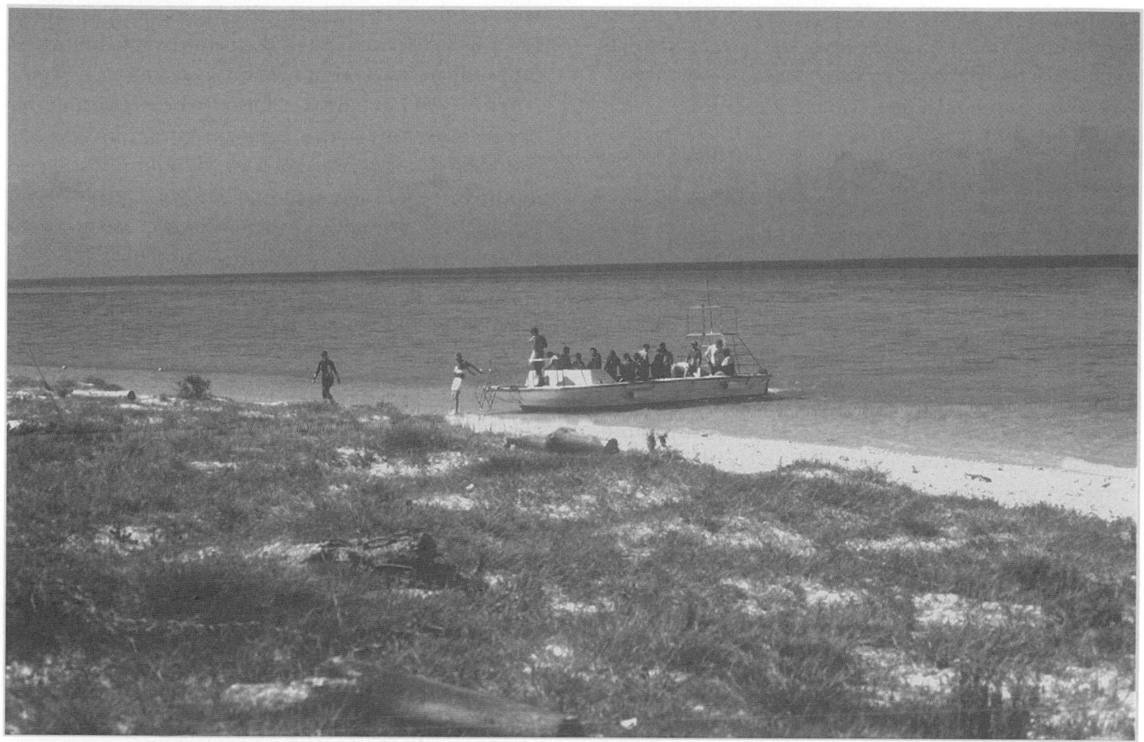

Plate 23.4 Scuba trip to the Great Barrier Reef, Queensland, Australia
(Source: Mark Orams)

Figure 23.2 **The basic morphology of the coastal resort**

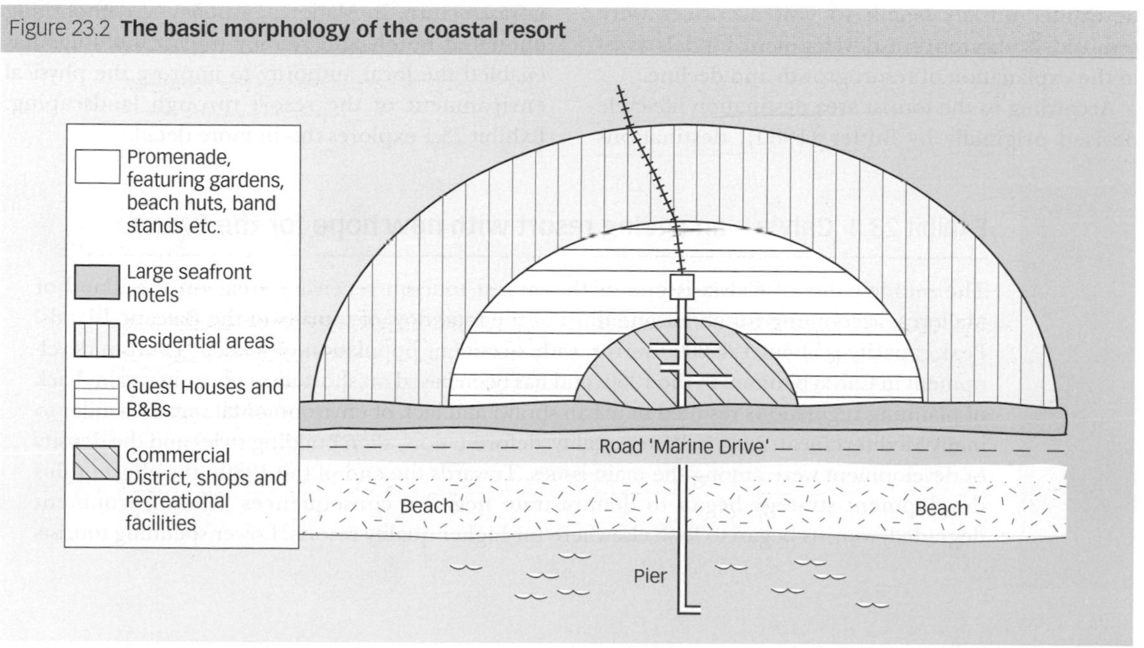

(Source: Adapted from Pearce 1995)

Swarbrooke (1999: 155) comments that it is a widely held view that the Spanish coastal resorts 'symbolize the worst aspects of coastal resort development in tourism.' The reasons for this are broadly:

- Inappropriate development, bearing little or no resemblance to local conditions, such as scale, style, materials.
- Impact on habitats and species, especially dune areas.
- Water pollution, most markedly sewage pollution of coastal waters.
- Effects on the local economy (inflation, higher land prices and in-migration of workers) and society (changes in cultural traditions, rapid changes in social composition, employment opportunities limited to lower paid work).

Torremolinos is a good example of a large-scale resort which has grown because of the rate of tourism development since the 1950s. From its origins as a small fishing village to the elite resort of the mid-part of the twentieth century to the mass market resort of today comprising over 50,000 bed spaces, Torremolinos has witnessed extensive environmental, economic and socio-cultural change. However, Torremolinos, like many other similar resorts on the Costa del Sol, Costa Brava and Costa Blanca, began to lose its tourist appeal due to the deterioration in environmental quality. Less desirable tourists began to visit as prices were reduced. Some tourism development models assist in the explanation of resort growth and decline.

According to the tourist area destination life-cycle devised originally by Butler (1980), destinations seem to follow a pattern of development. This model is similar to the concept of the product life-cycle used ostensibly in marketing and is illustrated in Chapter 2. The model has gained general acceptance and has proved to be reasonably effective in empirical trials. The model suggests that a newly emerging destination will gradually become known by tourists so initially only a small number will visit. As the destination becomes more well known, tourists will visit in larger number and tourism providers will increase their operations – the original tourists are probably less likely to want to return by this point. Eventually, the destination becomes a mass market resort with the inherent problems of environmental degradation, resulting in some tourists being motivated to find an alternative resort which is less spoiled for their next holiday. This leads to a decline in tourist numbers and affects the level of business in the resort. Strategies to rejuvenate the area may be required at this point to maintain or improve on the required numbers and types of visitors. Many English seaside resorts in the 1990s display the decline stage of the destination life-cycle. Some local authorities in an attempt to remain competitive and entice visitors to stay have launched rejuvenation strategies, for example Bridlington, Rhyl and Torbay. Many of the Mediterranean resorts have experienced this process too, such as Torremolinos as destinations were built haphazardly, without planning controls or adequate infrastructure. In Mallorca, a policy of demolishing out-dated hotels and shabby tourist buildings has enabled the local authority to improve the physical environment of the resort through landscaping. Exhibit 23.1 explores this in more detail.

Exhibit 23.1 **Calvia – an ageing resort with new hope for the future**

The municipality of Calvia is one of the largest tourism receiving areas on the island of Mallorca, accounting for about one third of the total flow of tourists to the Balearic Islands. Peak capacity is about 120,000 tourists, with a resident population of 30,000. Tourism development in Calvia boomed in the 1960s and has been based on short-term economic gain. Lack of planning regulations resulted in urban sprawl and lack of environmental regard, similar to many Mediterranean resorts. Water quality, deforestation, alien building styles and the density of development were among the main issues. Towards the end of the 1980s, the effect of this development strategy began to demonstrate negative consequences. The environment degraded, tourists began to look elsewhere for higher quality resorts. Lower spending tourists

Figure 23.3 **Map of Mallorca**

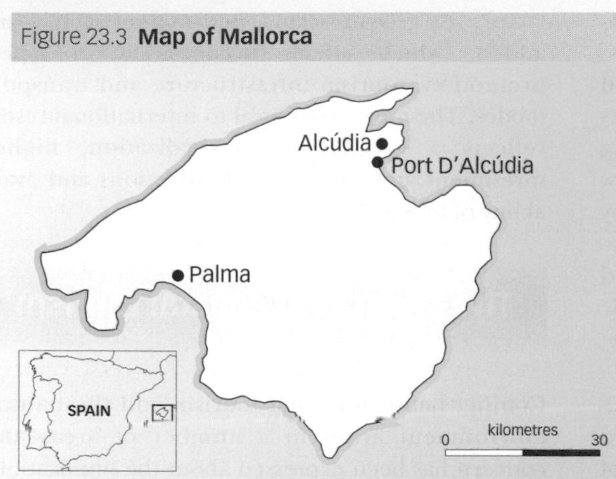

were attracted to the poor quality hotels and bars and a pattern of inappropriate behaviour based on the European 'lager lout' image set in. Calvia City Council, concerned at the problems of managing an 'ageing' tourist destination, proposed a series of policies and actions to assist the sustainable development of tourism in the resort. The strategy was published in 1995 and based on the framework of Local Agenda 21. The mission statement is:

> To develop a philosophy, strategy and programme of actions for the tourism sector based on sustainable development.

The objectives are as follows:

- To develop a possible framework for the implementation of sustainable tourism policy which could be applied to Mediterranean resorts with similar characteristics.
- To identify key subject areas applicable to resorts.
- To identify a framework for involving a wide range of bodies including residents in sustainable tourism projects in Calvia.

The long-term aim of the project is to achieve a modern coastal tourism destination offering high quality and a more appropriate bed space capacity. The underlying basis of future development will be based on the principles of sustainability with the environment and local community at the core. Already, much work has been initiated. Sea water quality is monitored on a weekly basis, obsolete hotels have been demolished reducing bed space capacity and removing ugly buildings, a proposed large-scale development has been halted. Environmental management in hotels and other buildings has been encouraged – such as waste recycling, reduced electricity, purchase of more environmentally sound products. A wide acceptance of the principles of Agenda 21 has been established through broad community consultation and participation. A significant spin-off to the Calvia initiative is the transferability of the concept of environmental management and improvement to similar resorts. Sharing good practice and integrating the principles of Agenda 21 in plans for sustainable development are seen as the way forward for the local authorities in Mediterranean resorts. Indeed, a Mediterranean Sustainable Development Agenda 21 is planned to guide areas through this process. It might be argued that such resorts have an important role to play in sustainable tourism as they provide purpose-built environments that with the correct framework can be appropriately managed to minimize negative environmental impacts.

(Source: Calvia Local Agenda 21 website)

Helber (cited in Conlin and Baum 1995) comments though that in many mature resorts, redevelopment is generally superficial – for example, new street furniture, landscaping, new façades – and that while this improves the aesthetic value, it does not tackle the underlying problem of sustaining appropriate levels of growth and attracting new markets. Often, resort development is hampered by highly fragmented land ownership, existing infrastructure and utilities, existing development and traffic congestion. In many cases, an holistic approach to resort regeneration, while desirable, remains expensive and is often impractical.

More recent attempts to understand resort developments have been made by Weaver (2000) and Prideaux (2000). Weaver states that after 20 years of debate, it is generally agreed that Butler's model typifies just one sequence of possible events in the evolution of a destination. Weaver proposes a broad context model which includes four types of tourism:

- Circumstantial Alternative Tourism (CAT)
- Deliberate Alternative Tourism (DAT)
- Sustainable Mass Tourism (SMT)
- Unsustainable Mass Tourism (UMT).

Seven possible scenarios are drawn up using the four tourism types. This is illustrated in Figure 23.4.

Butler's model fits the movement from CAT to UMT. The model can be used to categorize the status of tourism at a resort at the current time. Once this is done, it is then the responsibility of resort managers to consider all possible future scenarios. Desirable scenarios can then be pinpointed and worked towards. Weaver applies the model to Australia's Gold Coast, typified by high density urban resorts. The broad context model categorizes the Gold Coast as UMT. A desired state of SMT must be worked towards with appropriate management strategies.

Prideaux (2000) proposes another new model, termed the resort development spectrum. This model identifies five phases of growth:

- Phase 1 – Local tourism
- Phase 2 – Regional tourism
- Phase 3 – National tourism
- Phase 4 – International tourism
- Decline/stagnation/rejuvenation.

Prideaux states that development is not necessarily sequential or that growth is automatic. Another element to the model is the inclusion of market factors. As growth occurs, new market sectors are added, which affects accommodation types, promotion, tourism infrastructure and transport modes. The move from local to international resort reflects a greater professionalization, higher investment, great diversity of attractions and availability of top-quality services.

The impacts of coastal tourism

Conflict between coastal tourism and the natural environment arises in a number of areas and concern has been expressed about the implications of continued growth. Effects may be observed in a social, environmental and economic context. The main environmental issue is that the marine environment is of greater ecological diversity than land environments, with the most biologically significant areas being close to shore – such as coral reefs, estuaries and wetlands. Coral reefs, for example, are said to contain a higher biodiversity than tropical rainforests. With increasing levels of recreational use, coastal impacts are likely to remain a significant issues.

Environmental issues

Goodhead and Johnson (1995) cite some of the environmental concerns in relation to nature conservation in the marine environment. The loss of habitat is the main threat and this may arise through short and long-term disturbance. Developments such as marinas, jetties, promenades and car parks entail loss of coastal land. According to the European Environment Agency (1998), the tourism and recreation sector is expected to be a significant threat to the entire Mediterranean coastline. There is much concern about habitat destruction and disturbance of fauna. In Norway, the building of leisure cabins and the popularity of outdoor pursuits such as boating place pressures on the coastal environment. In Finland, second home lodge developments cause similar concerns and creat opportunity costs. Inter-tidal and coastal land habitats may be affected by recreational activities taking place on the beach. The effects of trampling on sand dunes is, for

Figure 23.4 **Scenarios of destination development**

	Transforms to	
CIRCUMSTANTIAL ALTERNATIVE TOURISM *Unregulated, small-scale tourism*	→	UNSUSTAINABLE MASS TOURISM *Outcome of continued, unregulated development*
CIRCUMSTANTIAL ALTERNATIVE TOURISM	→	DELIBERATE ALTERNATIVE TOURISM *Outcome of regulated and planned tourism development, small scale*
CIRCUMSTANTIAL ALTERNATIVE TOURISM	→	SUSTAINABLE MASS TOURISM *High-intensity, large-scale tourism development maintained within carrying capacity*
DELIBERATE ALTERNATIVE TOURISM *Small-scale regulated tourism*	→	SUSTAINABLE MASS TOURISM *Large-scale, regulated tourism*
DELIBERATE ALTERNATIVE TOURISM	→	UNSUSTAINABLE MASS TOURISM *Existing regulatory framework removed or not adhered to*
SUSTAINABLE MASS TOURISM	→	UNSUSTAINABLE MASS TOURISM *Carrying capacity limits not adhered to*
UNSUSTAINABLE MASS TOURISM	→	SUSTAINABLE MASS TOURISM *Reversal of environmental damage, adoption of environmental standards*

(Source: Adapted from Weaver 2000)

Plate 23.5 Oponomi, Bay of Islands, New Zealand
This relatively unspoilt beach environment illustrates the effect of low-impact tourism.

example, well documented. On the Spanish coast, the disappearance of large stretches of dune system as a result of tourism development has resulted in an unstable coastline (OECD 1993).

In some cases, environmental changes are necessary to sustain tourism. Some of the barrier islands on the eastern coast of the USA are very popular tourism destinations. Barrier islands are long, thin barriers of sand separated from the shoreline by a lagoon or marsh area. Some 2,000 miles of coast from New York to Texas contain such islands. Before World War II, 10 per cent of the barrier islands were developed – now a large proportion is covered with resorts, houses, apartments, hotels and other services. In Florida, demand for development has exceeded land available so additional island waterfront has been created by infilling marshes and building finger-like extensions into the water, such as at Boca Ciega Bay. By the early 1980s, the development rate of barrier islands took in about 6,000 acres per year. This was slowed dramatically by Congress legislation which covered small areas of undeveloped land. Erosion and coastal flooding is a severe problem in this environment, often exacerbated by groynes and sea walls in place to protect buildings but which have a longer term deleterious effect on beach stability. Erosion necessitates beach replenishment if developments are to be protected. The value of the tourism industry in most cases justifies spending. Miami Beach is a barrier island 10 miles in length (and containing $6 billion of real estate), naturally consisting of fine coral, shells and coarse grains of sand. Some $60 million was spent on replenishing the beach, making a more compact surface – better for tourists and more able to withstand coastal erosion. (Ackerman 1997).

Hall and Page (1999) discuss the effects of tourism on the coastal environment of the Pacific Islands. While similar impacts are found to elsewhere, impacts in the Pacific are more problematic because tourism is concentrated on or near ecologically and geomorphologically dynamic coastal environment. The main environmental impacts occur as a result of damage to mangroves and coral reefs. Minerbi (1992: 69) comments in the effect of resort development:

> Resorts have interfered with the hydrological cycle by changing groundwater patterns, altering stream life, and engaging in excessive groundwater extraction. Coastal reefs, lagoons, anchialine ponds, wastewater marshes, mangroves, have been destroyed by resort construction and by excessive visitations and activities with the consequent loss of marine life and destruction of ecosystems. Beach walking, snorkelling, recreational fishing, boat tours and anchoring have damaged coral reefs and grasses and have disturbed near shore aquatic life.

Effects on coral are widespread. In the Maldives, for example, an airport has been constructed on a reformed coral island; and coral is damaged by waste water from beachside hotels contaminated by chemicals found in shampoos and bathing products. As environmental impact assessments are not yet required in many less developed countries, there is less control over damaging types of development.

Wildlife issues

Effects on wildlife are notable. Shackley's (1992) study of manatee-related tourism in Florida is particularly noteworthy. Manatees are appealing to tourists because they are known to voluntarily interact with humans and are often attracted to marinas and harbours for food. Divers have been observed following and touching manatees and boat operators circling around the creatures in the water, both practices exacerbated by the docility of manatees. This occurs despite legal protection and published codes of conduct for visitors wishing to see a manatee. Shackley states that to ensure the survival of the species we would be well advised to avoid visiting them. The manatee, like other slow-moving marine mammals, is threatened by the use of personal watercraft. Many are hit each year by jet-skis which can operate in shallow waters, mangrove swamps and estuaries. Manatees are also subject to proportionately high levels of mortality from being struck by boats, particularly in areas where higher speeds are permitted. Birds are driven away by the noise of these machines thus affecting feeding and behaviour patterns. A popular pursuit which has developed recently is that of whale and dolphin watching.

Socio-economic issues

In terms of the socio-cultural impacts of coastal tourism, many of the issues cited in the earlier chapters on socio-cultural and economic impacts

Exhibit 23.2 **The impacts of coastal tourism at Dawlish Warren**

Dawlish Warren is a popular beach on the south coast of Devon, UK. It has been estimated that the site receives over 800,000 visitors per year with about 20,000 visitors a day in peak season. Dawlish Warren is also an important site for nature conservation, comprising a diverse range of habitats across 505 acres:

- sandy beach, including a sand spit
- dune system
- mudflats
- saltmarsh
- five ponds.

Rare flora and fauna can be found here including 29 nationally scarce British flowering plants (among the 600 recorded on-site) as well as being a temporary home for a large range of waders and wildfowl (about 180 species), reptiles and amphibians, mammals and insects. The site is designated as a Local Nature Reserve managed by the local authority, a Site of Special Scientific Interest (SSSI), a RAMSAR site[1] and a Special Protection Area.

Tourism was traditionally based on budget holidays and has continued to date in a similar vein. There are many holiday parks in the vicinity offering accommodation in static caravans, as well as touring and camping sites. The Warren itself has remained largely undeveloped apart from a car park, retail outlets and a funfair due to the constraints placed by the existence of the mainline railway which runs close to the site. There are no beach front hotels or promenades here. However, large numbers of visitors are attracted to the sandy beach and other attractions. Due to the ecological significance of the site, observed and potential impacts are an issue and management of the site focuses on the conflicts between conservation and recreation. The main areas for management are as follows:

- Visitor pressure on the dune system has led to a continual cycle of management, involving marram grass planting and rotational fencing to assist in stabilization.
- Some of the protective fencing erected is pulled down by visitors looking for fuel to light barbecues and bonfires on the beach.
- Erosion of the dunes occurs through wind and water processes as well as trampling feet.
- Gullies created by erosion are filled with dead scrub cut from the site and old Christmas trees following the festive period.
- Signs, local press articles and rangers encourage visitors to keep away from flocks of waders on the beach.
- Signs, gates, boardwalks need regular inspection and maintenance if required to ensure effective visitor management.
- Fire, litter, vandalism and vehicles entering the site are problems, all of which need to be kept under control.
- Dog walking has the potential to disturb bird life and some irresponsible owners allow their dogs to foul the Reserve.
- Guided walks and activities encourage greater visitor understanding of the site.
- The Reserve Visitor Centre is well used and appreciated by visitors, providing interpretation and information.

Figure 23.5 **Map of Dawlish Warren**

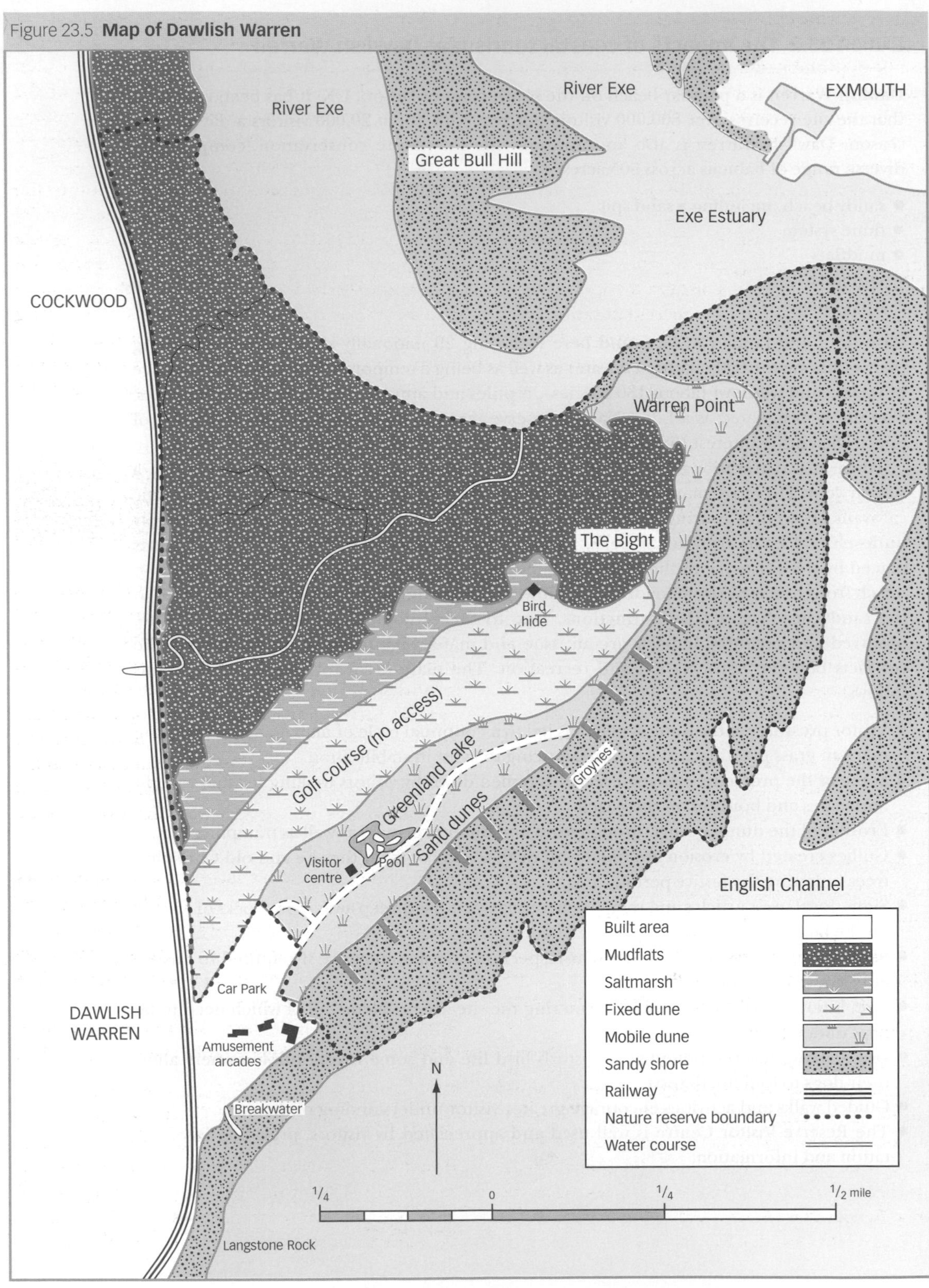

(Source: Teignbridge District Council 1990, Dawlish Warren Nature Research)

apply. A specific example of where there has been a negative effect is that local people in some areas have been prohibited from using the beaches. Some beaches in, for example, Antigua and the Gambia have become preserved for the use of exclusive beach resorts. St Thomas, an island in the Caribbean, originally contained 50 beaches but after tourism resort development, only two were left for public use (Patullo 1996). The economy in coastal areas may be stimulated by tourism, creating employment and encouraging investment. The whale-watching boom at Kaikoura on South Island, New Zealand assisted in the regeneration of a declining area, reducing unemployment and raising average household incomes with the creation of new enterprises in accommodation, catering and retailing (Orams 1998).

Protection of the coastal environment

The coast has been recognized as an environment which requires protection and sensitive management. As far back as 1972, countries such as the United States created legislation introducing the notion of coastal zone management, ideas which were soon adopted in Sweden, Australia and later more widely. This was acknowledged as a central issue at the Earth Summit in 1992 and is reflected in the Oceans Chapter of Agenda 21. Internationally, it has been agreed that coastal nations must 'commit themselves to integrated management and sustainable development of coastal areas and the marine environment'. The main objectives of coastal zone management (CZM) are to:

- Encourage sustainable use of the environment.
- Identify and resolve conflicts.
- Balance economic and environmental objectives.
- Adopt strategic planning function.

Many attempts have been made to assist in managing the impacts of tourism on coastal land and in coastal waters. Conservation in coastal areas is often approached through designations. Marine Parks and Nature Reserves have been designated on an international scale covering areas as diverse as the Great Barrier Reef, Australia to Lundy Island, off the coast of North Devon, UK.

Moves to help conserve the coastal areas of Europe have generated the idea of the European Coastal Code, first proposed by the European Union for Coastal Conservation in 1993. The aim of the code is to provide guidance to those who are responsible for coastal management as well as users to ensure ecologically sustainable development. The Code, formally adopted in 1995, is integral to the Pan-European Biological and Landscape Diversity Strategy (PEBLDS) which in turn is part of the European implementation of the Convention on Biological Diversity agreed at the Earth Summit in Rio in 1992. The Code is an attempt to bring together other codes, guidelines and action plans to form a practical set of guidelines with the aim of striking a balance between the environment and the economy.

Conclusion: the future of the coast

Herman Melville, the author of *Moby Dick,* wrote in that book: 'Strange! Nothing will content them but the extremest limit of the land', which indicates that it is highly likely that pleasure-seekers will continue to visit coastal areas in the future. The central focus of sustainable development at the coast is likely to figure prominently in the next few years. Kay and Alder (1999) state that sustainability has emerged as the dominant paradigm[2] in coastal planning and management. This raises three issues:

- The role of economic factors: local communities need to earn a living wage and businesses may prioritize financial gain over the environment.
- The role of environmental factors: the environment is the attraction in many cases, therefore it needs to be conserved.
- The role of social and cultural factors: local people should be involved in the decision-making.

What is clear is that the market for coastal tourism is increasing. The range of products on offer is expanding and has reached far beyond the traditional sun, sea and sand experience. The emergence of marine tourism poses new threats and challenges in diverse environments: whale watching in Africa, Australasia, Iceland; diving in the

24
Tourism in the less developed world

Learning outcomes

After studying this chapter, you should be able to:

- Understand the role of tourism in less developed countries.
- Recognize the impacts of tourism in less developed countries.
- Identify types of tourism which assist communities in less developed countries.

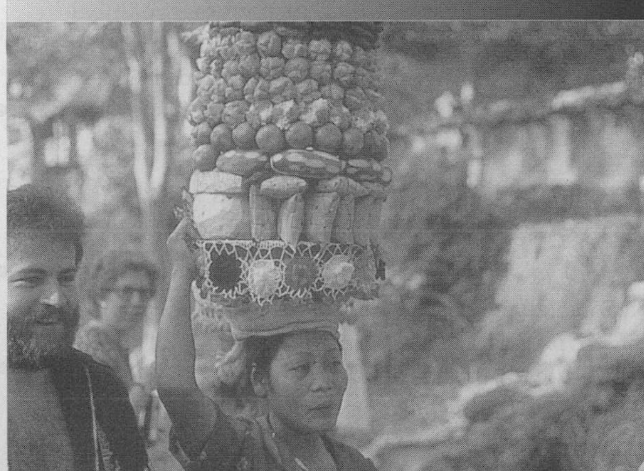

Overview

For many developing countries, tourism is a favoured choice of economic activity. The lure of generating foreign exchange from a country's natural attractions has led many nations into tourism. Some countries are now well-established providers of tourism such as Turkey, Malaysia and Mexico but other such as Bhutan and Belize are more recent entrants. While most of the world's tourism activity occurs in the developed world, some developing countries are among the world's highest volume tourist destinations.

Introduction

Tourism offers an ideal alternative economic activity to primary and secondary industries, especially if there is a lack of development choices for a less developed country. For the tourist, developing countries offer a taste of the exotic, an opportunity to encounter different cultures and to experience an unspoiled environment. While most tourism movements take place between developed countries, an exploration of global tourism arrivals over time indicates that an increasing number of people are selecting holidays in developing countries. New destinations are appearing on the world market catering for a range of tourists seeking alternative holiday experiences. Climate, culture and environment combine to form a tourism product for the 'new' tourist. Generally speaking, less developed countries are geographically located in central and South America, Africa, South Asia and the South Pacific (Hall 1992). Much concern has been expressed regarding the impact of tourism on less developed nations, with the focus on the inequality between the tourist (usually western) and the host.

The concept of development and the emergence of tourism in less developed countries

Webster (1990) defines development as the replacement of traditional values with modern ones. It is a process of change and aims to achieve improvement. Theories of modernity emerged in the 1950s and early 1960s prompted by the decline of the old colonial empires. Later, in the 1970s, thoughts turned towards a theory based on the notion of dependency, which focused on the unbalanced relationship between developed and less developed countries that has evolved in post-colonial times (see Hall and Page 2000).

Less developed countries – types and characteristics

Various labels exist to define less developed countries. Up until recently, the first, second and third world categories were used widely, but following the demise of communism across eastern Europe and the closing wealth gap between the first and second worlds, the differentiation no longer seems appropriate. The fourth world is a term used to define the least developed countries. Other definitions to consider are the east/west and north/south divides and core/periphery. These labels are used more extensively in contemporary times to distinguish development status. Table 24.1 outlines these descriptions. Mowforth and Munt (1998) explain that core relates to the focus of economic power in the global economy and that dependency theory explains how western capitalist nations have grown as a result of expropriation of resource exports from less developed countries.

Some of the characteristics of less developed countries include:

- high birth rates and population pressures
- fast rate of urbanization
- limited economic base
- high unemployment
- low literacy rates
- low levels of industrial production
- low gross national product.

There are different types of less developed countries and Swarbrooke (1999) outlines these as:

- *Least developed countries.* Incomes less than $355 per year, literacy rates of less than 20 per cent and little industrial production. There are 42 of these countries, often termed as the fourth world (Oppermann and Chon 1997).
- *Developing countries,* beyond the level of least developed but still relatively poor and non-industrialized.
- *Newly industrialized countries* (NICs). Known as 'takeoff' countries or tiger economies of South East Asia (such as Taiwan and Korea). These countries share characteristics of both less developed and developed worlds. Tend to generate outbound tourists, unlike the other types of developing countries.

It should also be noted that within each category of country, there are disparities in wealth in the

Table 24.1 **Terminology commonly used to describe development status**

Label[1]	Description	North/south	Development
First world	Westernized countries, with capitalist political and economic structures	North	Developed
Second world	Less wealthy, communist countries	North	Transitional
Third world	Poor countries	South	Less developed/developing

Note: [1]Used less extensively now, due to changes in eastern bloc countries (second world) and fall of the Iron Curtain.

population, i.e. there are some very wealthy people and many poor people.

Traditionally, development has been measured in terms of economic measures such as gross national product (GNP), economic growth rate and employment structure – measures of the economic wealth of a country. As understanding of the development process changed, it was realized that this measure was insufficient to show all aspects of development. The United Nations Development Programme uses the Human Development Index (HDI) which integrates welfare and economic aspects to produce a more holistic picture of a nation's status (see Table 24.2). Social and welfare

Table 24.2 **Selected indices used to construct a human development index for Asian and non-Asian countries**

Rank	Country	Life expectancy at birth (years) for 1995	Adult literacy rate (%) for 1995	Real GDP per capita (PPP$) for 1995	GDP index	Human development index (HDI) value for 1995
High state of human development		73.52	95.69	16 241	0.9809	0.8966
1	Canada	79.1	99	21 916	0.987	0.96
2	France	78.7	99	21 176	0.987	0.946
3	Norway	77.6	99	22 427	0.987	0.943
4	USA	76.4	99	26 977	0.992	0.943
5	Iceland	79.2	99	21 064	0.987	0.942
6	Finland	76.4	99	18 547	0.985	0.942
7	Netherlands	77.5	99	19 876	0.986	0.941
8	Japan	79.9	99	21 930	0.987	0.94
9	New Zealand	76.6	99	17 267	0.982	0.939
10	Sweden	78.4	99	19 297	0.986	0.936
25	Hong Kong, China	79	92.2	22 950	0.987	0.909
28	Singapore	77.1	91.1	22 604	0.987	0.896
30	Korea, Rep. of	71.7	98	11 594	0.972	0.894
35	Brunei Darussalam	75.1	88.2	31 165	0.995	0.889
59	Thailand	69.5	93.8	7 742	0.962	0.838
60	Malaysia	71.4	83.5	9 572	0.968	0.834

Table 24.2 **cont.**

Rank	Country	Life expectancy at birth (years) for 1995	Adult literacy rate (%) for 1995	Real GDP per capita (PPP$) for 1995	GDP index	Human development index (HDI) value for 1995
Medium state of human development		67.47	83.25	3 390	0.5297	0.6704
65	Surinam	70.9	93	4 862	0.767	0.796
66	Lebanon	69.3	92.4	4 977	0.785	0.796
67	Bulgaria	71.2	98	4 604	0.725	0.789
68	Belarus	69.3	97.9	4 398	0.692	0.783
69	Turkey	68.5	82.3	5 516	0.872	0.782
70	Saudi Arabia	70.7	63	8 516	0.964	0.778
71	Oman	70.3	59	9 383	0.967	0.771
72	Russian Federation	65.5	99	4 531	0.713	0.769
73	Ecuador	69.5	90.1	4 602	0.725	0.767
75	Korea, Dem. People's Rep. of	71.6	95	4 058	0.637	0.766
90	Sri Lanka	72.5	90.2	3 408	0.533	0.716
95	Maldives	63.3	93.2	3 540	0.554	0.683
96	Indonesia	64	83.8	3 971	0.623	0.679
98	Philippines	67.4	94.6	2 762	0.429	0.677
101	Mongolia	64.8	82.9	3 916	0.614	0.669
103	Turkmenistan	64.9	98	2 345	0.361	0.66
104	Uzbekistan	67.5	99	2 376	0.366	0.659
106	China	69.2	81.5	2 935	0.456	0.65
110	Azerbaijan	71.1	96.3	1 463	0.219	0.623

Table 24.2 **cont.**

118	Tadjikistan	66.9	99	943	0.136	0.575
122	Vietnam	66.4	93.7	1 236	0.183	0.56
Low state of human development		56.67	50.85	1 362	0.2032	0.409
131	Myanmar	58.9	83.1	1 130	0.166	0.481
132	Cameroon	55.3	63.4	2 355	0.363	0.481
133	Ghana	57	64.5	2 032	0.311	0.473
134	Lesotho	58/1	71/3	1 290	0.192	0.469
135	Equatorial Guinea	49	78.5	1 712	0.26	0.465
136	Lao People's Dem. Rep.	52.2	56.6	2 571	0.398	0.465
137	Kenya	53.8	78.1	1 438	0.215	0.463
138	Pakistan	62.8	37.8	2 209	0.34	0.453
139	India	61.6	52	1 422	0.213	0.451
140	Cambodia	52.9	65	1 110	0.163	0.422
1147	Bangladesh	56.9	38.1	1 382	0.206	0.371
152	Nepal	55.9	27.5	1 145	0.168	0.351
155	Bhutan	52	42.2	1 382	0.206	0.347
All developing countries		62.2	70.44	3 068	0.4778	0.5864
Least developed countries		51.16	49.2	1 008	0.1462	0.3439
Industrial countries		74.17	98.63	16 337	0.9811	0.9114
World		63.62	77.58	5 990	0.9482	0.7715

(Source: Modified from UNDP 1998 (http://www.undp.org/undp/hdro))

indicators include the literacy rate, infant mortality rate, life expectancy rate and calorie consumption per head (Mason 1990). The World Bank however, uses economic measures only and identifies three types of country: low income, middle income and high income. Low income, using 1992 data, is categorized as countries with a per capita income of US$675 or less. Developing countries take several paths towards development but tourism is a popular choice.

Tourism development

Agel (1993, cited in Oppermann and Chon 1997) suggests that three stages can be identified in tourism research which typify the changing perspectives on tourism development in less developed countries since the late 1950s. The first stage, from the late 1950s to 1970, was the time of great expansion and hope for future economic benefits. Tourism was considered as a tool for economic development and a generator of foreign exchange. The second stage, from 1970 to 1985, is termed by Agel as the 'disenchantment period', when the value of economic benefits was brought into question and a more critical approach to tourism development ensued. This was because many of the great hopes for tourism had not been fulfilled. The third stage covers the period from 1985 and is termed the 'differentiation period'. This distinguishing feature of this stage is the emergence of alternative forms of tourism, such as ecotourism, with an emphasis on planning for a better future.

The role of tourism in the development process is subject to many debates. Harrison (1992) comments that the justification for tourism development ultimately relies on the alleged benefits that tourism will bring. According to Hall (1992), tourism development plays the following roles in the transformation of an economy:

- A way of obtaining hard currency and improving balance of payments/indebtedness through admitting large numbers of western tourists.
- A catalyst of social change, with closer contact between the indigenous community and the tourist.
- A symbol of freedom, allowing citizens to travel freely within and outside their own country (in the case of eastern Europe).
- A mechanism for improving local infrastructure to cater for tourist need and thereby benefiting local people.
- An integral part of economic restructuring through privatization, exposure to national and international market forces and transnational corporations.
- A complement to commercial development through growth of business tourism market.

Tourism is in essence a political tool if viewed from this perspective. Governments pursue tourism development with these benefits in mind but what is often missing is a recognition of the negative impacts. In many cases, the negative impacts are less tangible than the anticipated economic effects and often receive less attention.

The nature of tourism in less developed countries

Lea (1988) comments that tourism flourishes best in those less developed countries which are most economically advanced. Oppermann and Chon (1997) state that tourism is least important in peripheral regions of developing countries while the core economic and political centres gain an above average share. Enclave and all-inclusive resorts lead to the spatial concentration of tourism and its benefits, which may be minimal anyway in the case of all-inclusive resorts. Britton's (1982) work in the South Pacific illustrates that tourism perpetuates existing inequalities in less developed countries. This is explained by four factors:

- Power and influence often controlled by foreign companies.
- Foreign tourist demands often not met by local service provision, exacerbating perceived need to build luxury facilities.
- General conditions of underdevelopment, such as structural disadvantages, influence tourism.
- Difficult for host communities to take control of tourism supply.

The outcome of this is that host nations are often unable to break out of the poverty trap and the benefits of tourism do not filter through to those in need. Governments can directly influence the direction of tourism development but often decide not to invest in tourism infrastructure. Instead, governments often give financial incentives to foreign investors to develop facilities, such as tax breaks, easing of rules on foreign labour and subsidies. Government policy tends to be centralized with little involvement of local communities. The focus tends to be on encouraging large foreign tour operators and developers to pursue tourism at the expense of indigenous operations. Traditional views on tourism can be interpreted as concentration on how much money can be generated rather than how it can be distributed to eliminate poverty in the wider population. Swarbrooke (1999) points out one of the problems with tourism in current times is the rapid growth in low-priced package holidays to less developed countries. The plight of poor countries is often ignored by tourists in search of a cheap holiday. It is one form of economic imperialism emerging in the post-colonial era as the dependency relationship with the developed world has been replicated in the tourism arena.

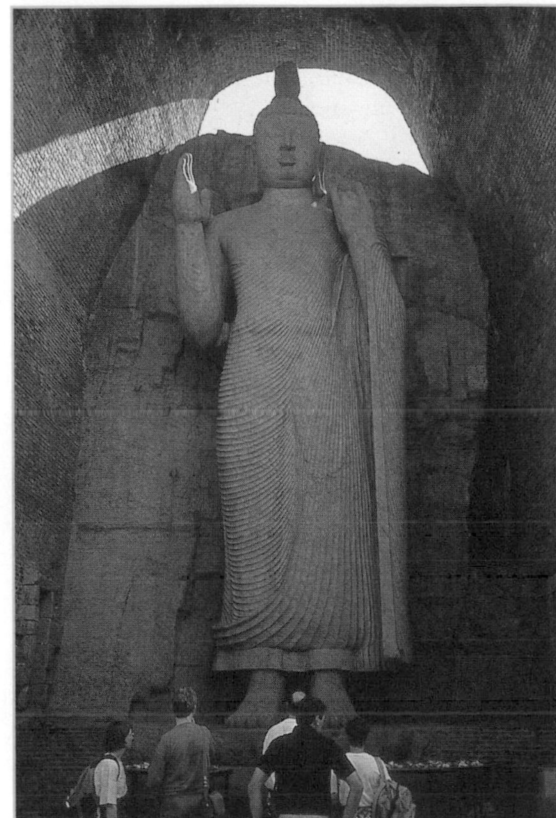

Plate 24.1 Standing Buddha, Aukana, Sri Lanka
Tourists visiting this site may have little understanding of the religious context. Does this matter?

Conceptualizing the nature of tourism in less developed countries

Mowforth and Munt (1998) provide a framework to outline the major processes which underlie the development of new forms of tourism in less developed countries. The framework consists of four elements which are outlined below:

- *Intervention and commodification.* Natural and cultural resources are transformed into products for consumption by tourists. For example, visitors to Thailand can purchase T-shirts imprinted with an image of a Padaung woman wearing brass neck rings (these neck rings damage skeletal growth but the value as a tourist attraction dictates they continue to wear them in some areas) (see Grove 1996: 98). This example links to all the points below.
- *Subservience (domination and control).* Communities and individuals in less developed countries may assume subordinate roles in order to satisfy tourists and tourism development. They may have to accept low rates of pay and menial tasks in order to take enough money home to ensure survival.
- *Fetishism.* Tourists remain unaware of life of those who serve them on holiday as commodities hide social realities. Tourists to Mynamar (formerly Burma) may not be aware of the human rights issues in the country, for example. Bradford (1996: 20) states:

> It would be easy to go to Burma and not realise what Visit Myanmar Year has cost in terms of people's lives. Looking at the smart suburbs of Rangoon, you wouldn't realise that people had been cleared out from their homes. Or seeing the moat around Mandalay fort with its glittering floating restaurant, you wouldn't imagine that it was dug out by prisoners and forced labourers.

- *Aetheticization.* Objects, feelings and experiences are turned into objects of beauty and desire. Tourists may wish to experience scenes of real poverty or dangerous situations. For example, some tours take visitors to workplaces to see local crafts being made.

Plate 24.2 Tourists observing religious temple offering ritual in Bali
The image of this temple offering represents aestheticization, where the real situation is transformed into an object of tourist desire.

Development patterns

In many developing countries, an 'uncritical faith', as Marfurt (1983) states, has led to unrestrained development and expenditure on tourism facilities. Governments often strive towards the prestige of luxury tourism developments and the associated economic statistics. Developing countries which create expansive tourism industries often create problems for their country which do not provide long-term solutions to social and economic problems. For Sri Lanka, tourism is the fourth most important foreign exchange earner. Tourist numbers reached a peak in 1982 (400,000), later falling due to civil unrest, although climbed up to 366,000 in 1997. New luxury resorts were completed in 1998 and tourism is beginning to flourish once again. Tourists are attracted by heritage, scenery and leisure facilities, particularly golf courses. Since 1994, 2000 hotel rooms have been added to the tourist capacity. The Ceylon Tourist Board is encouraging the private sector to develop new facilities, such as restaurants and visitor attractions. Ecotourism is also a feature with the famous Kandalama Hotel, in the hills 200 km from Colombo. This 160-room hotel has won the international Green Globe award for eco-management. The hotel was designed to blend in with the natural surroundings and many environmental initiatives have been put in place, for example planting trees to replace those destroyed by slash-and-burn cultivation. However, following IMF and World Bank assistance in debt restructuring, the government has provided incentives for foreign investment. Profits made by exogenous entrepreneurs may be 100 per cent repatriated, staff may be imported on tax-free salaries and local labour may be used only for menial posts. In 1992, a hotel construction project had to be abandoned due to opposition from the local people. There is a great deal of concern about child sex tourism. Thus, tourism in Sri Lanka demonstrates the type of conflict associated with adapting western development patterns to a non-western nation. However, not all developing countries follow this path of development. Others adhere to a stricter policy of protecting culture, the environment and the local economy. Exhibit 26.1 outlines one of the best examples of alternative development paths – Bhutan.

Impacts of tourism in less developed countries

While a wide-ranging discussion of the economic, socio-cultural and environmental impacts of tourism can be found in Chapter 17–19, the impacts on less developed countries warrant further attention. Some of the issues affecting less developed countries are very different and often more heightened than those affecting developed nations. The main debates focus around the wide gap between the host and

Exhibit 24.1 **Bhutan – an alternative approach to tourism development**

For centuries, the Kingdom of Bhutan, located in the Eastern Himalayas, was little touched by outside influences. The population of Bhutan (600,000) is thinly scattered across the country which covers an area of over 46,000 square kilometres. The country is mainly mountainous and borders Tibet and India.

Figure 24.1 **Map of Bhutan**

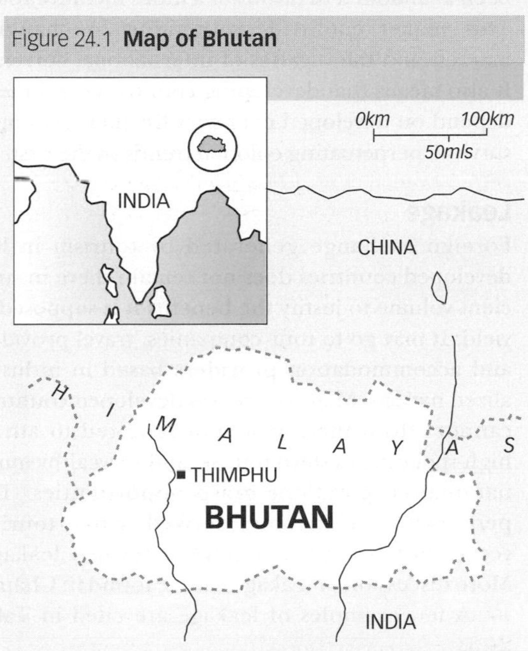

Many habitats and species make up the well-protected ecosystem, some of which are rare and endangered, such as the red panda and the snow leopard. The people of Bhutan follow a Buddhist way of life. As one of the poorest countries in Asia, there has been a move towards economic growth through tourism since 1974 when visitors were first permitted entry to the country. However, under the direction of the monarch, King Jigme Singye Wangchuck, and in tandem with the underlying cultural beliefs, Bhutan has been steered in the direction of sustainable growth rather than the 'boom and bust' or 'modernization at any cost' pattern of many other developing countries. A planned process of growth has been in place since the early 1960s For example, under Bhutanese law, the extensive forests, which have been subject to logging, will be protected to ensure that forest cover is not depleted to less than 60 per cent of the land cover (currently 72 per cent).

Tourism, now one of Bhutan's major economic sectors, has evolved in a stringently controlled way, with an emphasis on environmental and cultural protection and economic self-reliance. Tourism is recognized as a means of achieving socio-economic development but only acceptable within the confines of the conservation ethic which is deeply embedded in the Buddhist faith. The Royal Government sees the opportunity to maintain biodiversity rather than destroy it through tourism development. Contrary to popular belief, there is not a limit on annual tourist arrivals but to minimize impacts. However, a policy of attracting low-volume but high-value tourism along with a strictly enforced set of regulations (the 'tourist tariff') covering tourism management ensures effective translation of sustainable principles to practice. A brief summary of the regulations are given below:

- Visitors must travel on a pre-booked package holiday – no independent travel allowed.
- All visitors, irrespective of accommodation and choice of tour, must pay $200 per person per day, which includes accommodation, food, travel itinerary, transportation, guides.
- All bookings must be made through one of 33 companies licensed to operate in Bhutan.
- Not all areas of the country are open to access by visitors, partly to ensure that religious life can continue unimpeded and partly for safety and environmental reasons, such as heavy snow.
- All accommodation must be government approved and guides must be licensed.

guest as well as power relations. Burns and Holden (1995) summarize the problems relating to tourism in less developed countries as follows:

- development of 'islands of affluence' in a poor society
- use of scare national resources for tourist enjoyment
- the consequences of the demonstration effect (see Chapter 18)
- unreliable means of measuring the true economic benefit
- commercialization of culture and lifestyle
- beneficiaries likely to be foreign companies or already wealthy local people
- external control – tourism often in the hands of transnational corporations.

Economic perspectives

The World Bank, a major source of finance for developing countries, encouraged developing countries to invest in mass tourism as a way of generating foreign investment exchange from the late 1960s. Between 1969 and 1979, the World Bank loaned about $450 million to governments in 18 less developed countries. This included large-scale resorts in Thailand, Mexico and the Caribbean.

As far back as the early 1970s, (for example see Turner and Ash 1975; de Kadt 1979) it was recognized that tourism resulted in negative as well as positive impacts and that it could not be viewed as a panacea for less developed countries seeking economic expansion. The virtues of tourism development were originally extolled in many less developed countries based on the idea that it is a 'smokeless' industry, that uses the natural resources of a country in a non-polluting way than can provide employment, increase gross national product and improve the economy. But it soon became clear that a large proportion of tourist revenue did not remain in the host nation or benefit local communities. Employment tended to be low paid and poor quality, perpetuating the poverty experienced by many of the working population, while managerial grade jobs were given to expatriate staff.

As Lea (1988) notes, small developing economies tend towards dependence on a single primary product, for example the Windward Islands was traditionally dependent upon the banana crop. When the price for the commodity falls or the industry collapses, the economy suffers and alternative must be found. Tourism is often an activity which can be developed relatively quickly, as in the case of the Dominican Republic (Pattullo 1996). Some countries demonstrate an overdependence on tourism to the extent that traditional industries have been abandoned in favour of a more lucrative trade. This makes countries vulnerable to changing markets and the vagaries of international currency. It also means that developing countries continue to depend on developed countries for their economic survival, perpetuating colonial trends of the past.

Leakage

Foreign exchange generated by tourism in less developed countries does not remain there in sufficient volume to justify the benefits it is supposed to yield. It may go to tour companies, travel providers and accommodation providers based in industrialized nations. Many of the less developed countries cannot afford the investment required to attract high-spending western tourists and so wealthy multinational corporations grasp opportunities. The percentage of income derived from tourism returning to wealthy nations is termed leakage. More discussion of leakage can be found in Chapter 17. A few examples of leakage are cited in Table 24.3.

Some countries have demanded that multinational hotel chains should employ local workers

Table 24.3 **Examples of leakage in less developed countries**

County	Percent leakage
Aruba	40
Kenya – beach	70
safari	40
Nepal	47
Sri Lanka	30
Thailand	60

(Source: *New Internationalist* 1993: 18–19)

and purchase local produce and goods as much as possible (e.g. China) whereas others, such as in the past The Gambia, do not have the power or wealth to achieve this. The Gambian government placed a ban on all-inclusive tourist developments in 1999. The government stated that this type of holiday was not of economic benefit to the local economy, as tourists paid one price for all food, accommodation and activities before departure. This was having a deleterious effect on many local businesses which relied on international visitors. Tourists who had booked all-inclusive holidays to The Gambia in the following season with Cosmos had to either accept half-board or an alternative location (Tourism Concern 1999). All-inclusive holidays have been provocatively termed 'tourism apartheid' by Tourism Concern (1999) because they provide everything the tourist needs but deny local people the chance to benefit from tourism.

Social and cultural perspectives

The demonstration effect is clearly evident in less developing countries. Daniel (1998) reports an example of a Thai hill village where tourism has caused community conflict and is viewed by some as cultural invasion. The younger members of the community prefer the style of clothing that tourists wear and now children wear T-shirts and baseball caps in an attempt to be like the foreigners. Young people aspire to the material standards and values of tourists but are unable to achieve them. Young males have committed suicide because they could not see a way out of their lifestyle. Cultural imperialism is evident in tourists from developed countries visiting less developed countries. In Bolivia, devil-dancing attracts so many tourists and members of urban middle classes that the cost of the elaborate dancing costumes have increased beyond the reach of the indigenous dancers. The dance has transformed from its original authentic format to a stylized version that appeals to onlookers and outsiders. Sex tourism might be termed a form of leisure imperialism – or as, in the case of Thailand and the Philippines, a form of military aggression. Imperialism in gender is another issue that might be considered: it has been claimed that women in less developed countries gain less reward from tourism than men. Relationships between women from developed and less developed countries are not 'sisterly' and are based on international power structures. Traditional patterns of life and kinship are disrupted by tourism as reported by Sallah (1998) where in The Gambia, relationships between parents and children have degenerated as a result of loss of land and employment when land was taken for tourism development. Local people are often driven to begging because their means of self-support have been removed through insensitive development, lack of respect for traditional land and property rights and exogenous control of tourism businesses.

Katya Mira (1999) recounts the experience of backpacking in Mexico and the issue of beggars in Oaxaca City. As a tourist, she was constantly asked for money. On telling an old lady that she had no more money the rebuke came swiftly:

> You come all this way over here. You stay in hotels. You eat in restaurants. I live in a hut with no hot water and have no potatoes to feed my family. Look. Look at the holes in my skirt! You have no money? You don't know what 'No money' means.

This type of conflict is also illustrated in Exhibit 24.2.

Power and tourism: colonialism and neo-colonialism

Power relationships can be identified at various levels with regard to tourism. At a macro-level, the unequal nature of the relationship between developed and less developed countries is illustrated by the volume, wealth and mobility of tourists from developed countries and also the ability of developed countries to control and gain from tourism located in less developed countries. At a micro-level, unequal relationships clearly exist within less developed countries, with a powerful minority of wealthy elite with power over poor local communities. Taking the macro issue first, this may be viewed in terms of theories of underdevelopment. As western culture has become the dominant culture in the world, issues of power have been raised. The relationship between industrialized and non-industrialized nations are typified by a failure to recognize and respect differences (Hall 1992). The concept of development tends to assume that western culture is applied as a standard to others nations. Colonialism from the 1850s proved to be a valuable political instrument controlling overseas territories with the

Exhibit 24.2 **Tourism and community conflicts in the Solomon Islands**

Sofield (1996) illustrates how foreign investment in tourism in a less developed country may lead to adverse socio-cultural impacts. Using the example of the Solomon Islands in the Pacific, Sofield outlines the social conflicts that have arisen as a result of tourism development and subsequent use and takeover of resources.

Figure 24.2 **Map of Solomon Islands**

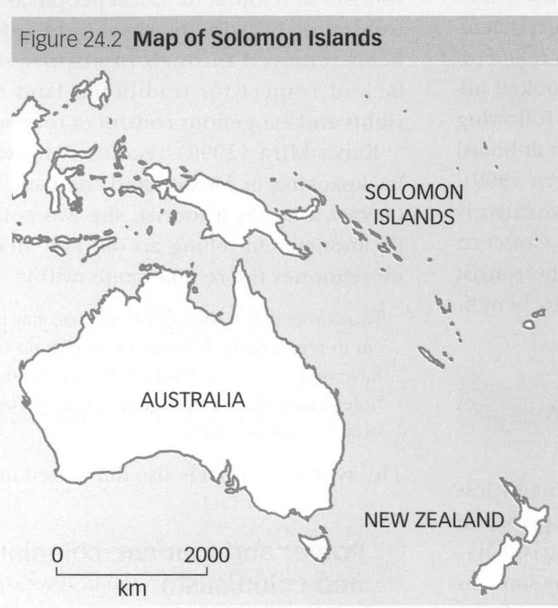

The most significant issue has been the different ideas about land ownership and the clash between traditional and modern notions. Traditional Melanesian values give rights in perpetuity to the indigenous community based on ancestral occupancy whereas modern values incorporate land as a commodity which can be bought and sold. The development in the 1980s of a four-star resort on Anuha Island, a small, uninhabited island owned under customary tenure by residents on a nearby island, caused significant problems. The major issues were:

- Desire of foreign investor to develop tourist resort provoked conflict and dissension among Solomon Islanders claiming customary ownership of the land.
- Conflict between customary owners and new owners had far reaching influences on investor confidence and security of foreign business and residents in the Solomon Islands as well as tourism to the area.
- Provoked domestic political tension, with internal disputes in the Government as well as disputes between national and local government.
- Use of the imported legal system to resolve conflict resulted in antagonism. The perception of the Solomon Islanders is that the law favours the expatriate.
- Loss of investor confidence led to lack of tourism investment and growth and declining visitor numbers from 1987 to 1992.
- Conflicts precipitated a review and renewal of tourism policies and regulations, which have improved the situation.
- Conflict between the Solomon Islands and Australia which impeded normal working relations.

The resort was dismantled and auctioned in 1992. Sofield concludes that if the local community do not support tourism development then it may not be a sustainable option.

purpose of improving the capitalist economies of the West, particularly Great Britain and France. Countries subject to colonizing powers provided cheap resources, such as labour and land. From the 1960s, a new force of colonialism began to emerge. This has been termed 'neo-colonialism' and is based on the growing power of multinational corporations. Tourism has been described as a force of neo-colonialism as it may take the form of exogenous development, controlled by overseas interests with a large proportion of income leaking overseas rather than benefiting the host nation. It might be said that tourists have superseded the armies of the colonial powers. Britton (1982) argues that Fiji is a neo-colonial economy and illustrates this with comparisons to pre-independence and a reinforcement of associated economic patterns.

Host community issues

One of the worst human rights contraventions linked with tourism in recent times is that of Myanmar. This particular example highlights the stance which tour operators may take in relation to corporate social responsibility. In 1996, the pro-democracy leader, Daw Aung San Suu Kyi, who opposes the military junta, SLORC (State Law and Order Council) called on tourists not to visit the country. This was an attempt to stop foreign exchange flowing into the country and ultimately to the government. 'Visit Myanmar Year' in 1996 was SLORC's attempt to bring in hard currency through a projected 500,000 tourists (from a base of 100,000 in 1995). From 1990, SLORC tried to attract foreign investors in hotel and tourism developments, offering ten-year tax breaks and full repatriation of profits (Mahr and Sutcliffe 1996). After the grand launch was overtaken by an uprising of 50,000 student protestors and subsequent high-profile media coverage (for example, John Pilger's TV documentary 'Inside Burma: Land of Fear'), tourists mainly stayed away. It was reported that local communities had been forcibly moved from their homes to make way for new tourism infrastructure, such as luxury hotels and new roads. Tourism Concern reported that over 2 million people were being used as forced labour to build roads, railways and other tourist facilities. Mahr and Sutcliffe (1996) report that people were forced without pay to restore the moat around Mandalay Palace. Examples of 'picturesque' ethnic peoples have been relocated to special villages where tourists can visit – an example of zooification. The long-necked women of the Padaung tribe are one of the most well-known examples. Many large corporations, such as Pepsico and Apple Computers, pulled out of the country in fear of consumer boycotts. Some tour operators decided to boycott the destination for a short time although many of the large companies continued to operate. Despite the high-profile reporting of the human rights violation and the link with tourism in Myanmar, many tour companies continue to promote the destination, highlighting the superb natural and cultural aspects but ignoring contemporary social and political issues.

On a different level, an example of where the host community has been disregarded in the planning stages of a new large-scale tourist development is the Nungwi area of Zanzibar (see Exhibit 24.3).

Environmental perspectives

As discussed in Chapter 19, tourism activity results in environmental damage. For developing countries, there are greater challenges. For many countries, tourism is just starting so there is an opportunity to manage it in a way which will lead to less negative impact. However, there are many instances where this challenge is not taken up. Less developed countries often contain areas of high biodiversity and environmental fragility; ecological disturbance can result in habitat damage and even species extinction (Doggart and Doggart 1996). Damage, for example, to the islands and coral reefs off the west coast of Thailand has led to limits on day trips (famously cited in Alex Garland's novel *The Beach*). On a positive note, tourism can be a force of positive change in less developed countries, where tourism provides a more suitable alternative land use to intensive, commercial or environmentally damaging activities, such as intensive agriculture, logging or hunting. For example, in the forests of Thailand, elephant keepers have turned to tourism since the logging ban left them unemployed in 1989. Tourism can also provide income for conservation purposes.

The Peruvian Government barred independent trekkers from the Inca Trail from 1 April 2000 in an attempt to prevent further damage to the National Park area around Machu Picchu. Access is now

Exhibit 24.3 **Resort enclave development in Zanzibar – local community issues**

Nungwi, on the northern peninsular of Zanzibar, is one among examples from around the world where the interests of corporations and foreign investment have been put before the interests and feelings of local people.

Figure 24.3 **Map of Zanzibar**

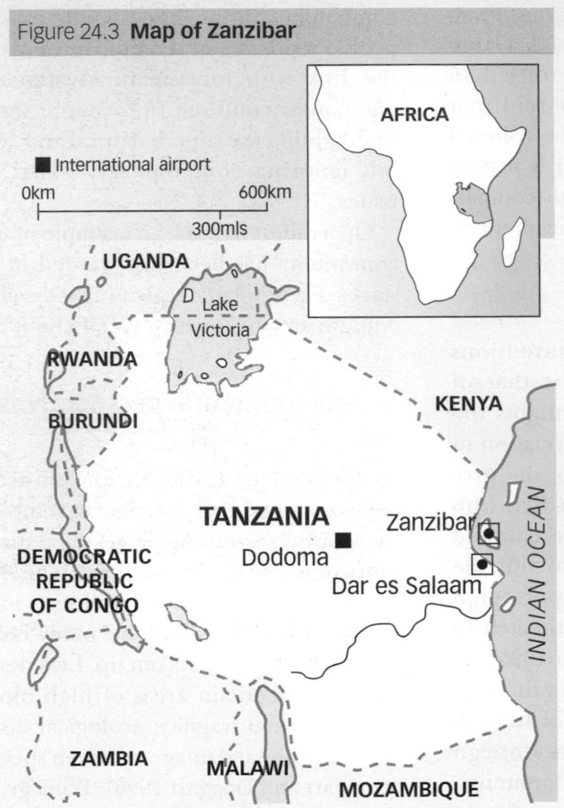

The government of Zanzibar has leased 57 square kilometres (at US$1 per year for 49 years) to the British-based East African Development Company (EADC) for a US$4 billion tourist enclave. It will be the biggest tourism development in East Africa: 14 luxury hotels, several hundred villas, three golf courses, county club, airport, swimming pools, marina and trade centre.

The main concerns are:

- There has been no consultation and local people have not been kept informed of plans.
- 20,000 people live on the peninsula. They have not been informed whether they will have to move and if so, whether they will receive compensation.
- Nungwi is a fishing and farming community, with a few small hotels and guest houses. The opportunities for a local mixed economy which would benefit the local community are likely to be lost if this development goes ahead.
- People fear the loss of fertile agricultural land and access to beaches as a result of the enclave.
- Water supply is an existing problem in the area, with a lack of supply and poor distribution.
- No social or environmental impact studies have been carried out.

At the present time, lobbying from the local community and non-government organizations has halted the development.

(Source: Modified from Tourism Concern website, www.tourismconcern.org)

restricted to those on organized treks and numbers are capped at 20,000. This is controlled by placing all tour business with 20 named operators. Prices for treks will be raised to cover higher entrance fees to the park and the increased costs of removing litter dropped by tourists. Large numbers of visitors (60,000 were recorded in 1999) have been blamed for erosion, landslides, fires and litter. From 2001 onwards, the trail is closed in January and February to aid regeneration of the environment.

One of the major growth areas of tourism that directly affect less developed countries is ecotourism. The promotion of pristine environments to the tourist poses risks to ecological integrity. Sustainable approaches to tourism development are paramount to ensure the desired benefits from tourism are achieved with a minimum risk to the environment and society (Wearing and Neil 1999). Ecotourism is an approach to tourism that aims to link nature-based tourism with social and community benefits. This form of tourism is estimated to be growing at 30 per cent compared with mainstream tourism at about 4 per cent per annum and thus poses a significant challenge.

According to Honey (1999), nearly every non-industrialized country was promoting ecotourism as part of its development strategy by the early 1990s. Ecotourism overtook primary production as the largest foreign exchange earner in some countries, e.g. bananas in Costa Rica, coffee in Kenya and textiles in India. There has been much debate about how ecotourism should operate and distinctions between nature-based tourism (which may not be at all sustainable) and ecotourism, which by definition, includes benefits to local communities and protection of the environment. Cambell (1999) illustrates the importance of community benefits and the need for appropriate planning rather than *ad hoc* development, citing a case study of Ostional, Costa Rica.

Plate 24.3 Elephant orphanage, Pinawela, Sri Lanka

Issues of equity in tourism in less developed countries

Fair trade

One of the main questions posed is how can tourism become more equitable to those in less developed receiving countries. Tourism ought to benefit the people who live in destination areas but often does not. Fair trade is an issue that has gained momentum in recent years. A range of products are now widely available for purchase which have been 'fairly traded', such as tea, coffee, chocolate and bananas. Fair trade means that the workers involved in the production of these goods have been given a fair wage and have not been subject to dangerous working conditions (for example, exposure of grape pickers to insecticides) or exploitation. Now, tourism faces a similar challenge. Organizations such as Tourism Concern and Voluntary Services Overseas (VSO) have actively campaigned to promote awareness of fair trade in tourism.

One example of where fair trade is working effectively is in St Lucia. The Sunshine Harvest Fruit and Vegetable Farmers' Co-operative consists of 66 farmers. The co-operative co-ordinates production and marketing of produce to hotels on the island. An 'adopt-a-farmer' initiative is being trialled, where hotels agree to buy produce from a specific farmer at an agreed price before planting. Smallholders are being encouraged to diversify their cropping to produce a wide range of fruit and vegetables, not just bananas. Farmers have access to favourable loan rates from local banks to help them buy seed and fertilizers. This scheme has the potential to assist in greater retention of tourism revenue on the island.

Another example is an initiative in The Gambia, instigated by local guesthouse owners and facilitated by Tourism Concern and VSO. A consortium of local entrepreneurs, development agencies, women's groups, community groups and youth groups was set up to establish a sustainable tourism product with much potential for fair trade. VSO, Gambia Tourism Concern and Tourism Concern have produced a 12-minute video shown in-flight from January 2000 on First Choice Air 2000 Gambia-bound flights. Entitled *The Gambia ... No Problem,* the video (the first of its kind) informs visitors about how to get the most out of their holiday and be sensitive to people and culture. The video is also available to watch on the internet (see the VSO website at the end of the chapter).

The integration of fair trade philosophies into tourism may be achieved in several ways but a recent attempt at co-ordination merits further attention. The International Network on Fair Trade in Tourism is outlined in Exhibit 24.4.

Exhibit 24.4 **International Network on Fair Trade in Tourism**

The aim of the International Network on Fair Trade in Tourism is to achieve more equitable tourism. It is a new initiative, based in the UK, which seeks to exchange information and experience on fair trade principles and practice, including the southern perspective. The objectives of this are to provide support to those engaged in developing fairly traded products and to develop policy in conjunction with industry, governments and trade organizations. The Network is facilitated by Tourism Concern and funded by European Commission, the Baring Foundation and the Department for International Development in the UK. The objectives of the Network are to encourage and achieve the following:

- equality in trading partnerships
- use of income to eradicate poverty through democratic decision-making
- network of fairly traded service provision across tourism operations
- community control in tourism planning and decision-making
- transparency, access to information and opportunities for training and career/business development
- ecological, social and cultural sustainability
- diversified local economies
- respect for human rights.

Fairly traded tourism products are difficult to market because of lack of funds, isolation of initiatives, small companies, lack of access to information and technology, lack of awareness of community initiatives, consumer attitude and lack of political will. Mechanisms for ensuring economic security and support for local business and community in the form of international and national trade agreements and economic supports are required for community initiatives to strive towards success. In addition, practical tools are needed to turn principles to policies and then to practice. On the positive side, increased awareness, growth in ethical consumption, awareness of sustainable development, pressure from public and non-government organizations will assist in the pursuance of these ideals. The WTO Code of Ethics (see Chapter 27 for more detail) published in 1999 is a step in the right direction but there is still much work to be done.

Community-based tourism is an expanding concept in less developed countries and provides a mechanism for ensuring as much economic benefit as possible remains in the host community. It also means that the community is able to control the direction and form of tourism. Many schemes are managed communally and profits are shared. Some communities work with tour operators or other organizations to promote their initiatives. Some communities operate 'village stays', where visitors stay with local families and engage in holiday activities such as bush walking, fishing, snorkelling and caving. There are many examples across the developing world, such as the Solomon Islands and Taquila on Lake Titicaca in Peru (see Mann 2000).

The International Porter Protection Group (IPPG) fosters the well-being of porters. Working with the trekking industry, governments, non-government organizations, the IPPG promotes safety and protection of porters and collects data on deaths, accidents and injuries. Guidelines on adequate protective clothing, medical care and financial protection in relation to rescue and medical treatment have been developed to raise awareness at grassroots level.

Community Aid Abroad Tours is a not for profit travel agency run by Oxfam Australia which supports responsible tourism in less developed countries. The principles on which tourism is organized are that:

- people, their culture and environment come first
- the inspiring community work supported by aid organizations should be part of tours

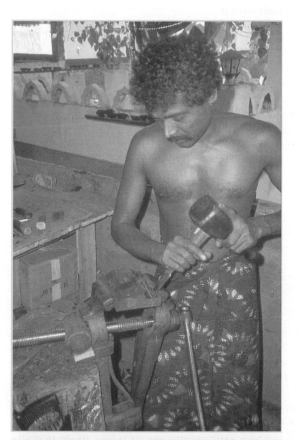

Plate 24.4 Wood carving by a local craftsman, Polonnaruwa, Sri Lanka
Tourists are able to visit this workshop and interact with the indigenous population.

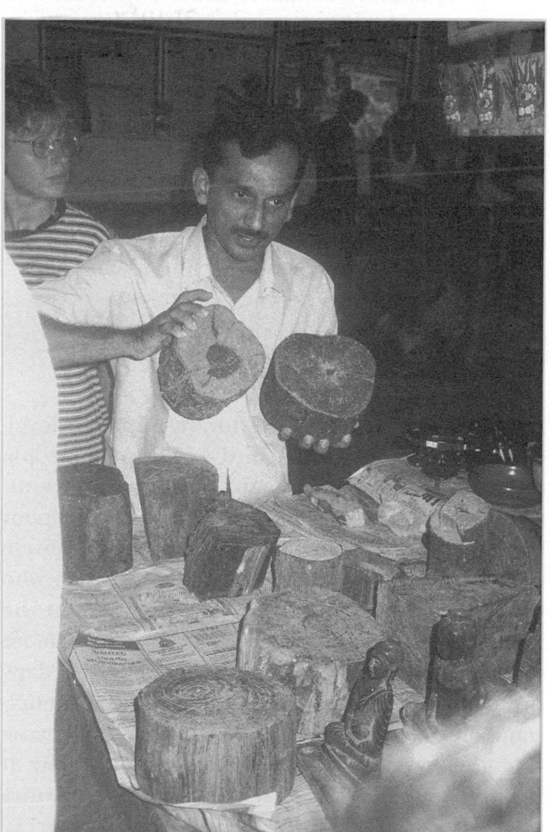

Plate 24.5 Opportunities for cultural exchange and purchase of local products, Polonnaruwa, Sri Lanka

- visitors should be introduced to host communities and their worlds, at their invitation
- the economic benefits of travel should be shared, paying fair prices for modest accommodation, local guides, restaurants, entertainment and transport; and working, where possible, with local tourism initiatives
- tours should comprise 'leisure with learning'
- money from tours helps local communities and helps to seek solutions to problems of poverty and inequity.

Tours are operated in a range of less developed countries, such as Guatemala, Laos, Madagascar, Vietnam and Aboriginal Australia. In Guatemala, tour of 15 people visit a weaving co-operative, a permaculture project and opportunities are given to talk to community members about experiences in the civil war. Mayan culture is explored with visits to a range of ancient sites.

There is still much more development work and monitoring of community-based initiatives before any conclusions can be drawn. This is still a minority aspect of tourism provision and is seen at present as a niche market, rather than a philosophy which underpins tourism management.

Conclusion

Redclift (1987) states that for sustainable development to occur in the third world, poor people must be involved in meeting their aspirations. Chambers (1986) (cited in Redclift) states that poor people are concerned with their immediate livelihoods and that it is only the enlightened rich who give priority to sustainability. This might be acceptable to a certain extent, but the reality is more complex than this simple statement suggests. Many ordinary people in less developed countries understand the nature of environment and society because traditional values on both aspects are held closer. It is government policy that often steers a country towards western ideals of development and progress.

Burns (1999) states that most societies have a desire for material wealth and social improvement; it is thus inevitable that impacts will occur and sacrifices will be made. Tourism ideas produced by consultants for government planners tend to follow either: a normative set of values, based on the traditional economic growth of western ideas or; a patronizing 'no-growth' model. Burns suggests that until community ownership is established as a proactive policy in tourism planning, then local people will continue to be poorly served by the promises of social and economic progress. Campbell (1999) emphasizes the need for some form of planning and intervention.

The Voluntary Services Overseas (VSO) campaign 'Action for WorldWise Tourism' promotes six visionary targets for the future development of tourism in less developed countries by 2015. Changes are necessary to assist countries and national economies develop as well as enabling communities to rise out of poverty. Then, the positive aspects of tourism may be felt more equitably so that:

- local businesses and people are a central part of the tourism industry
- clear government tourism strategies to retain money in the community are developed
- financial and management support is available to community tourism initiatives
- environmental standards are adopted and enforced; water, sewage and energy services extended to local communities
- tour operators offer more authentic and beneficial products to consumers through connection with community ventures
- tourists are given all opportunities to buy locally produced goods and to experience local culture.

The Department for International Development (DfiD) (1999) suggest that nature tourism is well placed to offer a viable income for local communities in developing countries. However, the problem is in ensuring that the benefits of tourism are distributed fairly. For example, DfID research shows that out of a US$300 trip for a two-night trip to Bali or Lombok to see Komodo Dragons, the National Park receives only 70 cents of this. Transparency is required to inform stakeholders where money is going.

The future of tourism in less developed countries is beset with challenges. It seems likely that the volume of tourism will continue to increase as tourists from developed countries venture further afield and those in the newly industrialized countries participate more in tourism activity. Changes need to be made if tourism is to become more sustainable across the developing world. While tourism has great appeal as a mechanism for achieving economic development, appropriate policies are needed to retain sufficient tourism revenue in the host country and fair distribution within the economy. Tourism in less developed countries raises complex issues and problems which have no easy solutions.

Discussion questions

1. Discuss the rationale for tourism as a tool for development.
2. Explain why fair trade is advocated a way ahead for tourism in less developed countries.
3. Why is tourism described as 'neo-colonialism'?
4. To what extent is the natural environment at risk from tourism development in less developed countries? Cite examples to illustrate your case.

References

Agel, P. (1993) 'Dritte-Welt-Tourismus', in G. Haedrich, C. Kaspur, K. Klemm and K. Kreilkamp (eds) *Tourismus-Management, Tourismus-Marketing und Fremdenverkehrsplanung*, Berlin: Walter sde Gruyter, 715–28.

Bradford, M. (1996) 'Postcard from Burma', *In Focus*, **19**: 20.

Britton, S. (1982) 'The political economy of tourism in the third world', *Annals of Tourism Research*, **9**: 331–58.

Burns, P. (1999) 'Paradoxes in planning. Tourism elitism or brutalism?', *Annals of Tourism Research*, **26** (2): 329–48.

Burns, P. and Holden, A. (1995) *Tourism: A New Perspective*, Hemel Hempstead: Prentice Hall.

Campbell, L. (1999) 'Ecotourism in rural developing communities', *Annals of Tourism Research*, **26** (3): 534–53.

Daniel, E. (1998) 'Spirits in the village', *Orbit*, VSO, second quarter: 8–9.

de Kadt, E. (1979) *Tourism: Passport to Development*, New York: Oxford University Press.

Department for International Development (DFID) (1999) *Changing the Nature of Tourism. Developing an Agenda for Action*, London: DfID.

Doggart, C. and Doggart, D. (1996) 'Environmental impacts of tourism in developing countries', *Travel and Tourism Analyst*, **2**: 71–86.

Grove, N. (1996) 'The many faces of Thailand', *National Geographic*, **189** (2): 82–105.

Hall, C.M. (1992) *Tourism and Politics: Policy, Power and Place*, Chichester: John Wiley and Sons.

Hall, C.M. and Page, S.J. (eds) (2000) *Tourism in South and South East Asia: Issues and Cases*, Oxford: Butterworth-Heinemann.

Harrison, D. (ed.) (1992) *Tourism in Less Developed Countries*, London: Belhaven.

Honey, M. (1999) *Ecotourism and Sustainable Development. Who Owns Paradise?*, Washington: Island Press.

Lea, J. (1988) *Tourism and Development in the Third World*, London: Routledge.

Mahr, J. and Sutcliffe, S. (1996) 'Come to Burma', *New Internationalist*, **280**: 28–30.

Mann, M. (2000) *The Community Tourism Guide*, London: Earthscan.

Marfurt, E. (1983) 'Tourism and the third world: dream or nightmare?', in L. France (ed.) (1997) *The Earthscan Reader in Sustainable Tourism*, London: Earthscan: 172–75.

Internet resources

By going to the weblink at www.thomsonlearning.co.uk students can access the following studies from the Thomson Learning website. The first is a study by M. Opperman and K. Chon (1997) *Tourism in Developing Countries*, which addresses the issue of tourism destination development and is worth reading in conjunction with the previous chapter in this book and the weblink resources. It offers a lucid insight into the problems of resort and destination development in less developed countries using a range of useful examples.

The second study is derived from C.M. Hall and S.J. Page (eds) (1996) *Tourism in the Pacific: Issues and Cases* by C.M. Hall 'The political effects of tourism in the Pacific' which develops a series of very useful insights on the political instability which is associated with a number of Pacific Island nations and the problems this poses for tourism development. It also highlights the wider problems of politics and tourism in the Pacific Island context which is worthwhile reading in conjunction with Chapter 14 in this book and the web resources since the issues are interlinked in the wider political economy of tourism development in less developed countries.

Mason, P. (1990) *Tourism,* Godalming: World Wildlife Fund.

Mira, K. (1999) 'Postcard from Mexico', *In Focus,* Tourism Concern, **33**: 20.

Mowforth, M. and Munt, I. (1998) *Tourism and Sustainability. New Tourism in the Third World,* London: Routledge.

New Internationalist (1993) 'Tourism – the facts', **245**: 19.

Oppermann, M. and Chon, K. (1997) *Tourism in Developing Countries,* London: Thomson Learning.

Pattullo, P. (1996) *Last Resorts. The Cost of Tourism in the Caribbean,* London: Cassell.

Redclift, M. (1987) *Sustainable Development: Exploring the Contradictions,* London: Methuen.

Sallah, H. (1998) 'Faulty towers', *Orbit,* VSO, second quarter: 12–13.

Shankland (1993) 'The natives are friendly', *New Internationalist,* **245**: 20–22.

Sofield, T. (1996) 'Anuha Island resort: a case study of failure', in R. Butler and T. Hinch (eds) (1996) *Tourism and Indigenous People,* London: Thomson Learning.

Swarbrooke, J. (1999) *Sustainable Tourism Management,* Wallingford: CAB International.

Tourism Concern (1999) 'Gambia bans all-inclusives', *In Focus,* Tourism Concern, **33**: 12.

Turner, L. and Ash, J. (1975) *The Golden Hordes: International Tourism and the Pleasure Periphery,* London: Constable.

UNDP (1998) *Human Development Report,* New York: United Nations.

Wearing, S. and Neil, J. (1999) *Ecotourism. Impacts, Potentials and Possibilities,* Oxford: Butterworth-Heinemann.

Webster, A. (1990) *Introduction to the Sociology of Development,* London: Macmillan.

Further reading

Hall, C.M. and Page, S.J. (eds) (2000) *Tourism in South and South East Asia: Issues and Cases,* Oxford: Butterworth-Heinemann.

Mowforth, M. and Munt, I. (1998) *Tourism and Sustainability. New Tourism in the Third World,* London: Routledge.

Oppermann, M. and Chon, K. (1997) *Tourism in Developing Countries,* London: Thomson Learning.

Useful web addresses

Bhutan
www.kingdomofbhutan.com

Tourism Concern
www.tourismconcern.org.uk

International Porter Protection Group
www.ippg.net

Community Aid Abroad
www.caa.org.au/travel

Voluntary Services Overseas (VSO)
www.vso.org.uk/gambia8.mov

Section 7 Managing tourist activities

In the last section of the book, the ensuing chapters attempt to integrate many of the issues raised in some of the previous chapters related to how the demand and supply of tourism culminates in what is termed the 'tourism experience'. Chapter 25 discusses the nature of the 'tourism experience', exploring many of the concepts and techniques used to assess how tourists rate and perceive their experience of tourism. This is a culmination of the interactions between all the chapters discussed throughout the book, where specific relationships exist that can condition and affect the way the tourist rates their holiday experience or visit to an attraction. In Chapter 26, this concept is taken a stage further highlighting how the public and private sector seek to manage this experience through specific macro techniques such as planning for tourism and micro techniques such as visitor management. This theme is then expanded in the last chapter in the book – Chapter 27 on the future of tourism, highlighting many of the management challenges facing the tourism industry and likely changes which will occur in tourism activity in the new millennium. Specific issues such as forecasting changes in tourism are discussed together with new techniques of assessing the economic contribution of tourism are reviewed. The issues facing consumers are also discussed with specific examples.

25 The tourist experience

Learning outcomes

After reading this chapter and answering the questions, you should be able to:

- Recognize that different types of tourists are likely not only to have varying needs but to exhibit different levels of satisfaction.
- Understand the means by which tourists learn where to visit at a new destination.
- Be aware of the various factors that influence holiday satisfaction.

Overview

A principal tourism planning problem in tourism is that of predicting tourists' expectations of their holidays in terms of what they require from the destination and its products. Satisfaction with the holiday experience can be very individual as it is closely related to aspects of motivation. Nevertheless, the industry needs to understand needs and expectations if products are to be successful. Understanding how tourists experience their holiday necessarily involves looking at what it means to be a tourist and aspects of how tourists learn what to do at destinations. There are also a variety of influences, some personal, others external, that affect overall levels of holiday satisfaction. This chapter examines these dimensions of the tourist experience.

Introduction: from traveller to tourist

For some, being referred to as a 'tourist' is taken in a derogatory or insulting sense. Originally, however, the terms tourist and traveller were synonymous when the word tourist first came to be used (around 1800) (Buzard, 1993). Quickly, though, the term 'tourist' gained negative connotations. Buzard (1993) shows how, through the nineteenth and twentieth centuries, the term tourist gained a negative side. By 1930 the English writer, Evelyn Waugh, wrote, 'every Englishman abroad, until proved to the contrary, likes to consider himself a traveller and not a tourist' and thereby summed up what had become a commonly held attitude (Buzard 1993: 1).

At the beginning of the twenty-first century this attitude remains prevalent. A traveller might be considered in terms of a 'business traveller', en route to a meeting and making little use of tourist resources. However, in a 'tourist-sense' (Sharpley 1994) a traveller is thought of as somebody on an extended touring holiday, such as a free independent traveller (FIT) like a backpacker on a limited budget. Here there is felt to be a sense of freedom, of adventure, of being independent and individual. Such travellers may be truly 'allocentric' to use Plog's term (see Chapter 4). In stark contrast, the term tourist is felt to reflect those 'psychocentric' people on a mass produced package holiday. The term suggests images of people who are uncultured, unknowing and naive. Buzard (1993: 1) suggests that 'the tourist is the dupe of fashion, following blindly where authentic travellers have gone with open eyes and free spirits'. Thus, while the traveller shows independence and a sense of the intrepid or daring, tourists are seen as timid and cowardly, preferring the security of the familiar. Moreover, if a modern dictionary is studied you will find several combinations associated with the word tourist. These include 'tourist-crammed', 'tourist-ridden', and 'tourist-trodden' all suggesting negative connotations. Fussell (1987: 651) refers to the form of tourism which tourists pursue as:

> not self-directed but extremely directed ... go not where you want but where the industry has decreed you shall go ... soothes you by comfort and familiarity and shields you from the shocks of novelty and oddity ... confirms your prior view of the world instead of shaking it up ... requires that you see conventional things, and see them in a conventional way.

Buzard (1993: 5) notes that the 'dichotomy (between traveller and tourist) has more to do with the society and culture that produces the tourist than it does with the encounter any given tourist or traveller may have with a foreign society and culture'. Hence, it could be argued that to consider tourists in a derogatory sense is a form of snobbery where the individual (the snob that is) regards their own 'travelling' experiences as authentic and unique, while others, 'the tourists', are full of vulgarity, repetition and ignorance. Hence, as Evelyn Waugh suggested, 'the tourist is the other fellow' (Waugh 1930).

In one sense, it could be argued that the traveller–tourist dichotomy is only an issue for those who are concerned by such things. While this may be true, it could be equally argued that the nature of this dichotomy has informed the behaviour of tourists, the types of experiences they seek and how the tourism industry has attempted to address people's needs and wants. While tourists would seem to exemplify all that is bad about tourism, Krippendorf (1987: 43) states that 'to lay all blame at their door would be as wrong as denying their responsibility'. Krippendorf and other authors note changes in the nature of tourists, which suggest that nowadays tourists are seeking new experiences which may not necessarily be associated with negative connotations.

Plate 25.1 Travellers or tourists?
This is a group visiting a temple in Bali in the 1970s when Bali was not well known as a tourist destination. Does this make this a group of travellers or tourists?

Tourists: maligned to alternative, old to new

Krippendorf (1987: 44) suggests that society has a distorted attitude to tourists. While most of us travel, tourists are a category of people who are criticized, 'whatever the tourist does, he does it wrong'. Suggesting that tourists are much maligned; Krippendorf puts forward nine types, as shown in Table 25.1.

Accepting Krippendorf's types clearly gives weight to the desire not to be classified as a tourist. However, Krippendorf's 'alternative tourist' shows characteristics that resemble features of what Poon (1993) refers to as 'new tourists'. Poon, a leading commentator on the future trends in tourism sees 'new' tourism as being flexible, segmented, customized and diagonally integrated. This is in contrast to 'old' tourism that was mass produced, rigid, standardized and packaged. These distinctions are shown in Table 25.2.

Krippendorf (1987: 30) argues that alternative tourists 'try to avoid the beaten track ... establish more contact with the local population ... and do without the tourist infrastructure'. This would begin to suggest a level of social responsibility not associated with his other categories. However, given that alternative tourists 'pave the way for mass tourism' (Krippendorf 1987: 42) they could be argued as not representing fully Poon's concept of new tourists. Here, other authors refer to the adherence to the principles of 'responsible' tourism (Mowforth and Munt 1988), such as 'limited growth' (Butler and Pearce 1995) and 'environmentally sound development' (Cooper *et al.* 1998) and could be linked to the tourism industry's concern with green issues and sustainability to nurture this emerging tourist type.

Krippendorf's much maligned tourist categories show many similarities to Poon's, old tourists in the way that such tourists embrace mass tourism and are somewhat irresponsible. The alternative tourist, however, is suggestive of new tourism, in the desire to explore, while being more aware of how they have a social, environmental and cultural impact. It can be

Table 25.1 **The much maligned tourist types**

Type	Characteristics
Ridiculous	Camera dangling before his belly, funny clothes, pale skin, fat
Naive	Inexperienced in travelling, no language skills, can't find way round, easily duped
Organized	Dependent on group and guide, follows like a sheep, feels well only with other tourists
Ugly	Behaves as if whole world belongs to him and does all the things forbidden at home
Uncultured	Lazing on beach, doesn't care about place or people, watches TV, eats same food as at home
Rich	Spends lavishly, puts wealth on show, enjoys being waited on
Exploiting	Spends holiday at the cost of other people and cultures, takes advantage of poverty of others
Polluting	Flattens everything in their way, pollutes air, tramples flowers, leaves behind dirty lakes, sea, rivers, beaches
Alternative	Different from others, explores untouched areas, paves the way for mass tourists

(Source: Developed from Krippendorf 1987: 41–42)

Table 25.2 **Poon's (1993) old and new tourists**

Old tourists	New tourists
Search for the sun	Experience something new
Follow the masses	Want to be in charge
Here today, gone tomorrow	See and enjoy but not destroy
Show that you have been	Just for the fun of it
Having	Being
Superiority	Understanding
Like attractions	Like sport and nature
Reactions	Adventurous
Eat in hotel dining room	Try out local fare
Homogenous	Hybrid

(Source: Poon 1993)

Plate 25.2 What type of tourist would stay here? This is a view from a bathroom of the Kandalama Hotel deep in the Sri Lankan jungle. Western comforts in a natural environment.

argued, therefore, that the different types of tourists have very different types of experiences at their tourist destinations. Added to this, their behaviour also varies in terms of the way in which they interact with the host population and make use of resources. Two dimensions are pertinent here: tourist learning behaviour and the effects of the holiday experience.

Tourist learning behaviour

First-time visitors to a new destination are often viewed as being destination naive (Snepenger *et al.* 1990). An information search is necessary, as it serves as a means to gain knowledge of where to visit and what to do while on holiday. However, the manner in which tourists search, the amount and sources of information they seek in order to satisfy their needs are influenced by their different tourist characteristics themselves. Destinations themselves have many different means by which information is distributed to tourists, both direct and indirect. Thus, the tourist's experience of the destination can be shown to be influenced by the way in which they learn about the destination, a process that is influenced by tourist characteristics (see Figure 25.1).

Figure 25.1, the tourist information search strategy at a new destination, illustrates two principal driving forces affecting tourist learning behaviour. These, 'contingencies' and 'tourist characteristics' influence three distinct strategies of information search, i.e. 'spatial' (the place of the search activity), 'temporal' (the timing of the search activity) and 'operational' (how the search is conducted) (Fodness and Murray 1998). Within the model important aspects found by other researchers are acknowledged. For instance, the nature of tourist learning behaviour has been shown to be closely linked to the effect of travel party compo-

Figure 25.1 **Tourist information search strategy**

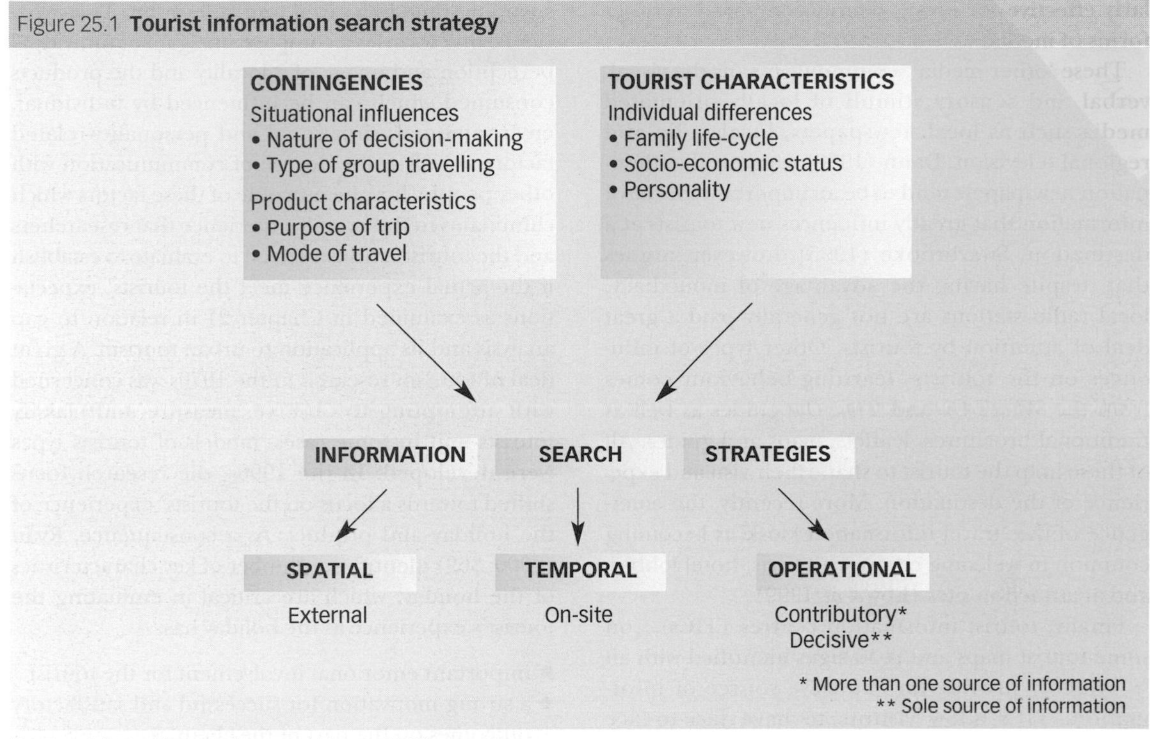

(Source: Adapted from Fodness and Murray 1998)

sition by Cooper (1981) and Snepenger *et al.* (1990). Cooper (1981) also notes how the method of transport can be an important factor influencing learning behaviour and the type of search strategy undertaken. Urry (1990) shows how both tourist experience and tourist learning behaviour are related to how the social class groups to which tourists belong are linked to particular types of behaviour. Here social classes rely on particular systems of information for their specific group. Other research has shown that people who have an educational background at a higher level search for a wider range of information (Van Raaij and Francken 1984), while younger people rely on a narrower set of sources (Andereck and Caldwell 1993).

On arrival at a new destination, where there is no prior knowledge of where to go or what to visit, tourists are likely to seek sources of information to enable them to make decisive and quick decisions of what to do 'on the spot'. Berkman and Gilson (1986) suggest that such sources may be:

1 Interpersonal – e.g. word of mouth.
2 Market-dominated sources – e.g. advertisements and promotional materials.
3 Objective sources – e.g. material provided by tourist information centres.

Word of mouth communication at the destination, such as interactions between host and tourist and among tourists themselves are rated as the most important information source influencing tourists' decisions and their experience of the destination (Murray 1991). In fact, it is commonplace at many destinations for tourists to consider themselves as 'message senders' passing on their recommendations (good and bad) to their fellow tourists (Dann 1996). Such conversations can be particularly influential.

In other circumstances tourists, unfamiliar with a destination, may rely on signing as a principle source of information for direction to local attractions (Grant *et al.* 1996). Signposts often display symbols to give indications to visitors of possible attractions on offer. Other outdoor advertising, such as posters or billboards, promote attractions and may also be powerful influences to tourists who have no prior experiences on which to rely (Mayo and Jarvis 1981). Gunn (1994), however, questions whether such outdoor advertisements are particu-

[illegible] for luring visitors compared to other [illegible]edia.

[illegible] other media', commonly means the visual, [illegible] and sensory stimuli of locally orientated [illegible]ia such as local newspapers, local radio and [illegible]gional television. Dann (1996) suggests that destination newspapers tend to be an important source of information that greatly influences new tourists at a destination. Swarbrooke (1995), however, argues that despite having the advantage of immediacy, local radio stations are not generally paid a great deal of attention by tourists. Other types of influences on the tourists' learning behaviour comes from the *What's On* and *Time Out* guides as well as traditional brochures, leaflets, maps and guides. All of these help the tourist to shape their visit and experience of the destination. More recently, the emergence of the 'travel information kiosk' is becoming common in welcome centres, airports, hotel lobbies and at attraction sites (Eby *et al.* 1999).

Finally, tourist information centres (TICs), (on some tourist maps and road signs identified with an '*i*' symbol) provide an extensive source of information. TICs allow visitors to have face-to-face contact with a tourist board representative and to have access to a wide variety of paper-based promotional literature. Alternatively, unmanned stands or tourist information points and electronic marketing units provide 24-hour information. Research by Lawton and Page (1997) based on tourist use of brochures in Auckland found that while a large proportion of brochures were discarded by tourists, their influence on tourists decision to undertake an activity or to visit a site was very influential. It also confirmed the value of *What's On* guides and the significance tourists attach to such material.

Learning about how to use a tourist destination is important in the overall tourist experience and different types of tourist exhibit varying strategies in terms of their learning behaviour. But how do you assess the extent to which tourists are satisfied with their experience of the destination?

The experience of the holiday

According to Graefe and Vaske (1987), the 'tourist experience' is the culmination of a given experience which a tourist forms when they are visiting and spending time in a given tourist location. The experience one forms is a complex amalgam of individual perception and image of a locality and the products consumed which can be influenced by individual, environmental, situational and personality-related factors as well as the degree of communication with other people. It is the outcome of these factors which culminates in the overall experience that researchers and the tourism industry need to evaluate to establish if the actual experience meet the tourists' expectations as examined in Chapter 21 in relation to gap analysis and its application to urban tourism. A great deal of tourism research in the 1970s was concerned with attempting to observe, measure and classify tourists and in some cases, models of tourists types were developed. In the 1990s, the research focus shifted towards a focus on the tourists' experience of the holiday and product. As a consequence, Ryan (2000: 369) identifies a number of key characteristics of the holiday, which are critical in evaluating the tourist's experience as the holiday has:

- important emotional involvement for the tourist
- a strong motivation for successful and satisfactory outcomes on the part of the client
- a significantly long period of interaction between the tourist on the one hand and, on the other, the place and people in the holiday destination – a period wherein the tourist can manipulate his or her surroundings to achieve the desired outcomes
- manipulative processes that are themselves part of the holiday experience and a source of satisfaction and need not require confrontation that may not be acceptable to some
- a number of holiday services, so that the tourist can select among alternatives – also while a distribution chain may be said to exist between these services, in terms of satisfaction creation, the direction of the chain may not be causal
- has a structure whereby the tourist can play several different roles – each role may have separate determinants of satisfaction and each role may have unequal contributions to total holiday satisfaction
- a temporal significance not found in many service situations – it resides in the memory as a preparation for the future and is a resource for ego-sustainment during non-holiday periods.

In other words, the 'tourist experience' is a complex combination of factors that shape the tourist's feelings and attitude towards his or her visit. Yet, as tourism motivation and consumer research suggests, it is almost impossible to predict tourist responses to individual situations, as a series of interrelated impacts may affect the tourist experience and it is a dynamic entity which in constantly subject to change. Some of the wider influences which impact upon the tourist experience are shown in Figure 25.2 as discussed in Chapter 21.

For example, high usage levels of tourism resources may lead to overcrowding and this can diminish the visitor experience. Clearly different types of tourist are influenced to varying degrees. Some people have a low tolerance threshold for an overcrowded site while others are less affected by similar conditions (Page 1995). Ultimately, an individual's ability to tolerate the behaviour of other people, levels of use, the social situation and the context of the activity are all important determinants of the tourist experience.

Clearly though, the level of satisfaction with the experience of being a tourist at a particular destination will have several consequences. The outcome will influence future holiday decisions; activities undertaken and recommendations made to others. It may well be, as Ryan (1995) suggests, that once satisfaction has been achieved some tourists cease to experiment with different holidays, in order to optimize their time and money, by repeating those experiences known to create satisfaction. Pearce (1988) suggests that the sources of satisfaction differ between more and less experienced tourists at the same location – with greater levels of satisfaction likely to be gained by the more experienced tourist.

There are many factors that contribute to tourist satisfaction, some of which are beyond the tourists' control (e.g. climate, traffic, noise and pollution) While on holiday, though, there is a strong motivation to enjoy oneself, so much so that goals for enjoyment are often set and real attempts are made to overcome any hindrances (Ryan 1997). It could be argued that it is the tourists themselves who generate satisfaction and the holiday destination/tourism industry is outside this. Certain factors, though, are clearly influential (the price and quality of facilities), but other factors are more related to the individual tourist. How tourists relax, find peaceful setting or excitement, react to scenery and tourism resources, and how they interact with others may be much more personal. Other aspects such as the weather, long journeys, overcrowding and crime levels, while potential sources of dissatisfaction, may be beyond the control of either tourist, destination or the industry.

Figure 25.2 **The tourist experience**

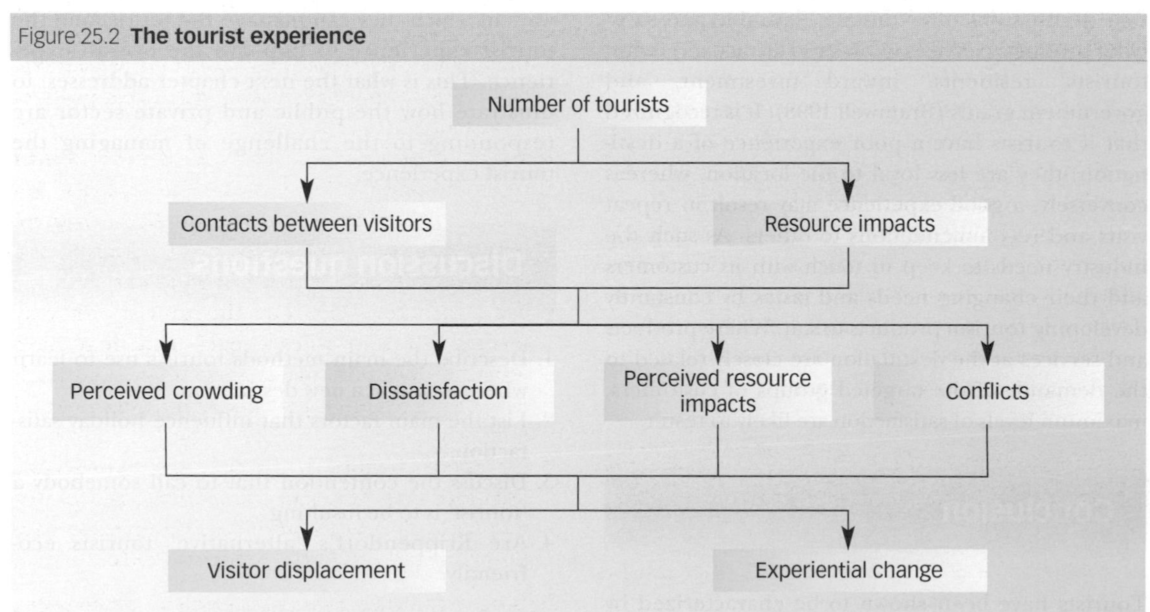

(Source: Adapted from Graefe and Vaske 1987, Page 1995)

Despite the fact that numerous extrinsic factors (e.g. satisfaction with destination services) can influence the holiday experience and therefore tourist satisfaction, the industry needs to research this area to remain in business. Tribe and Smith (1998) describe one research instrument, HOLSAT. HOLSAT is designed to increase holiday satisfaction through the use of expectations/performance analysis. Key attributes of the destination are first identified and addressed and, second, tourist's attitudes to these attributes are analysed to produce a measure of satisfaction/dissatisfaction. The attributes of the destination are categorized as:

- the physical resort and its facilities
- ambience
- restaurants, bars, shops, night life
- transfers
- heritage and culture
- accommodation.

The HOLSAT method views satisfaction as the relationship between the performance of the holiday attributes against the expectation of the performance of these attributes as declared by tourists. Dissatisfaction is considered to have been experienced when expectations exceed the actual performance.

The use of measures such as HOLSAT, among others, is illustrative of a growing interest in ensuring that destinations offer unique, desirable and satisfying products/services in order to attract and retain tourists, residents, inward investment, and government grants (Bramwell 1998). It is recognized that if tourists have a poor experience of a destination, they are less loyal to the location, whereas conversely, a good experience may result in repeat visits and recommendations to others. As such the industry needs to keep in touch with its customers and their changing needs and tastes by constantly developing tourism products to suit. Where products and services at the destination are closely related to the demands of the targeted groups of customers, maximum levels of satisfaction are likely to result.

Conclusion

Tourists have been shown to be characterized by different attributes and behaviours and can be classified in numerous ways. Evaluating the tourists' experience of a place, product and their satisfaction with service and intangible elements are a comparatively recent development within the tourism literature. Evaluating the tourist experience is a complex process which involves modelling the factors which may affect the experience and then measuring the tourists' views and attitudes, often against a scale or list of factors. This is both a time consuming and costly process and yet its value to the tourism industry should not be underestimated. The motivating factors (i.e. how the tourists' perception of what makes them choose a particular destination); their actual activities and the extent to which their expectations are matched by reality all feed into how satisfying the experience of being a tourist may be. The highly personal nature of satisfaction together with the subjectivity and changeability of human nature suggests that it is not possible for the industry to create products that will guarantee satisfaction. Nevertheless, there is a growing interest within the tourism industry on monitoring tourist satisfaction, evaluating service quality issues and understanding what people think of the product range on offer and the overall impression of a destination. Since this is a complex area but vital to the future viability and sustainability of tourism destinations, it is not surprising that many tourism destinations are concerned with ways in which they can manage the tourist and the tourist experience to improve the overall experience. This is what the next chapter addresses, to illustrate how the public and private sector are responding to the challenge of managing the tourist experience.

Discussion questions

1. Describe the main methods tourists use to learn where to visit at a new destination.
2. List the main factors that influence holiday satisfaction.
3. Discuss the contention that to call somebody a 'tourist' is to be insulting.
4. Are Krippendorf's 'alternative' tourists eco-friendly?

Internet resources

By going to the weblink at www.thomsonlearning.co.uk students can access the following study from the Thomson Learning website. The study is by M. Shackley (1997) *Wildlife Tourism* and examines the vital area of visitor management as part of the visitor's experience of wildlife tourism.

References

Andereck, K. and Caldwell, L. (1993) 'The influence of tourists' characteristics on ratings of information sources for an attraction', *Journal of Travel and Tourism Marketing*, **2**: 171–89.

Berkman, H.W. and Gilson, C. (1986) *Consumer Behaviour: Concepts and Strategies*, third edition, Boston: Kent Publishing Co.

Bramwell, B. (1998) 'User satisfaction and product development in urban tourism', *Tourism Management*, **19** (1): 35–47.

Butler, R. and Pearce, D. (eds) (1995) *Change in Tourism: People, Places, Processes*. London: Routledge.

Buzard, J. (1993) *The Beaten Track: European Tourism, Literature, and the Ways to 'Culture' 1800–1918*. Oxford: Clarendon Press.

Cooper, C. (1981) 'Spatial and temporal patterns of tourist behaviour', *Regional Studies*, **15** (5): 359–71.

Cooper, C., Fletcher, J., Gilbert, D., Shepherd, R. and Wanhill, S. (1998) *Tourism: Principles and Practice*, second edition. Harlow: Longman.

Dann, G. (1996) *The Language of Tourism: A Socio-Linguistic Perspective*, Oxford: CAB International.

Eby, D.W., Molnar, L.J. and Cai, L.A. (1999) 'Content preferences for in-vehicle tourist information systems: an emerging information source', *Journal of Hospitality and Leisure Marketing*, **6** (3): 41–57.

Fodness, D. and Murray, B. (1998) 'A typology of tourist information search strategies, *Journal of Travel Research*, **37** (2): 108–19.

Fussell, P. (ed.) (1987) *The Norton Book of Travel*, New York: Norton.

Graefe, A. and Vaske, J. (1987) 'A framework for managing quality in the tourist experience', *Annals of Tourism Research*, **14**: 389–404.

Grant, M., Human, B. and Le Pelley, B. (1996) 'The role of road and pedestrian signs in visitor management', *Insights*, September: A61–65.

Gunn, C.A. (1994) *Tourism Planning: Basics, Concepts, Cases*, third edition, London: Taylor Francis.

Krippendorf, J. (1987) *The Holidaymakers: Understanding the Impact of Leisure and Travel*, Oxford: Butterworth-Heinemann.

Lawton, G. and Page, S.J. (1997) 'Analysing the promotion, product and visitor expectations of urban tourism: Auckland, New Zealand as a case study', *Journal of Travel and Tourism Marketing*, **6** (3/4): 123–42.

Mayo E.J. and Jarvis, L.P. (1981) *The Psychology of Leisure Travel*, Boston: CBI Publishing.

Mowforth, M. and Munt, I. (1998) *Tourism and Sustainability: New Tourism in the Third World*, London: Routledge.

Murray, K.B. (1991) 'A test of services marketing theory: consumer information acquisition activities', *Journal of Marketing*, **55**: 10–25.

Page, S.J. (1995) *Urban Tourism*, London: Routledge.

Pearce, P.L. (1988) *The Ulysses Factor: Evaluating Visitors in Tourist Settings*, New York: Springer Verlag.

Poon, A. (1993) *Tourism, Technology and Competitive Strategies*, Oxford: CAB International.

Ryan, C. (ed.) (1995) *Researching Tourist Satisfaction: Issues, Concepts, Problems*, London: Routledge.

Ryan, C. (1997) *The Tourist Experience: A New Introduction*, London: Cassell.

Ryan, C. (2000) 'Marketing and service quality – wider perspectives', in C. Ryan and S.J. Page (eds) *Tourism Management: Towards the New Millennium*, Oxford: Pergamon: 369–76.

Sharpley, R. (1994) *Tourism, Tourists and Society*, Huntingdon: Elm Publishing.

Snepenger, D., Meged, K., Snelling, M. and Worrall, K. (1990) 'Information search strategies by destination – naïve tourists', *Journal of Travel Research*, **29** (1): 13–16.

Swarbrooke, J. (1995) *The Development and Management of Visitor Attractions*, Oxford: Butterworth-Heinemann.

Tribe, J. and Smith, T. (1998) 'From SERQUAL to HOLSAT: holiday satisfaction in Varadero, Cuba', *Tourism Management*, **19** (1): 25–34.

Urry, J. (1990) *The Tourist Gaze: Leisure and Travel in Contemporary Societies*, London: Sage.

Van Raaij, W.F. and Francken, D.A. (1984) 'Vacation decision, alternatives and satisfactions', *Annals of Tourism Research*, **11** (2): 101–12.

Waugh, E. (1930) *A Mediterranean Journal*, London: Duckworth.

Further reading

Fodness, D. and Murray, B. (1998) 'A typology of tourist information search strategies', *Journal of Travel Research*, **37** (2): 108–19.

Krippendorf, J. (1987) *The Holidaymakers: Understanding the Impact of Leisure and Travel,* Oxford: Butterworth-Heinemann.

Poon, A. (1993) *Tourism, Technology and Competitive Strategies,* Oxford: CAB International.

Ryan, C. (ed.) (1997) *The Tourist Experience: A New Introduction,* London: Cassell.

26 Managing the tourist experience

Learning outcomes

After reading this chapter and answering the questions, you should be able to:

- Understand why managing the tourist experience is important, but is complex in nature.
- Recognize the different roles of tourism and other agencies in respect of tourism planning and the nature of the tourism planning process.
- Be able to describe some of the common tools for managing tourists in different locations and realize why such measures are necessary.
- Acknowledge the need for service quality in tourism service providers as a means for the better management of the tourist experience.

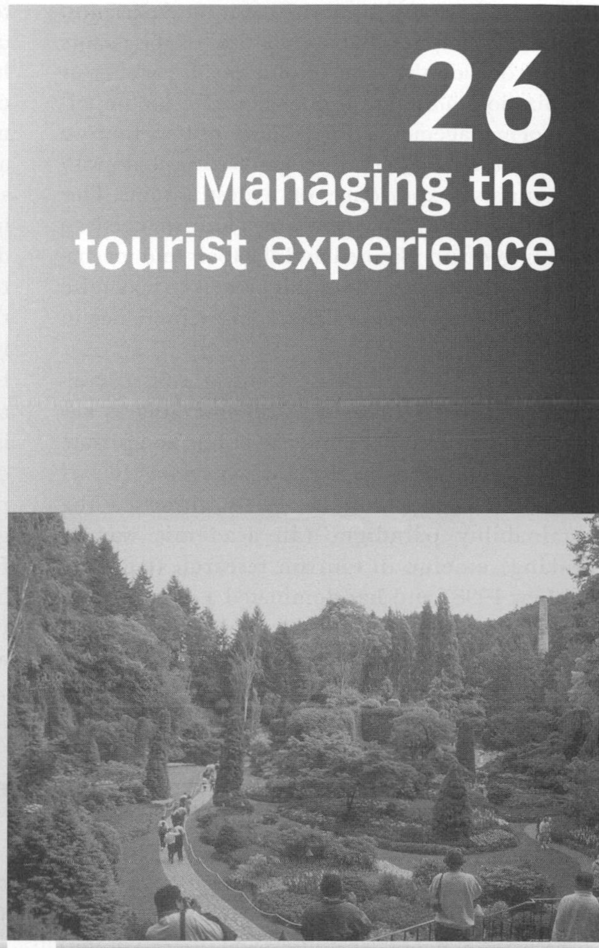

Overview

If uncontrolled, tourism development can ruin the attractiveness of a destination and, ultimately, its success. Thus, achieving an appropriate balance of development and control is necessary if destinations are to be sustainable in economic as well as in environmental and cultural terms. This suggests that sympathetic tourism planning and the careful management of visitors will be important considerations. This chapter addresses issues of tourism planning and visitor management in the context of aiming to provide a successful tourist experience and flourishing destination.

Introduction

As Chapter 25 has shown, the tourist is becoming more sophisticated in their tastes and expectations of the types of tourism products and experiences they are seeking. Within the growing tourism literature, there is a recognition that evaluating the tourist's experience is a complex activity (Ryan 1997), since it is highly subjective and based on perception and cognitive views of the environment and the products tourists consume (see Exhibit 26.1). Exhibit 26.1 shows that there are a number of general factors which can be applied to any tourism environment which functions as a destination and it highlights the diversity of attitudes and feelings that are important in assessing the extent to which a tourist was satisfied with a specific aspect of their experience and how subjective factors can affect their overall assessment of their visit or experience. Exhibit 26.1 implies that a great deal of the factors are also outside the control of a specific agency or organization, although it does illustrate the importance of management and planning tools to improve and monitor the effect of certain factors to do with the tourists' experience of a destination. This chapter examines the way in which tourism needs to be managed and planned and the tools and mechanisms developed to assist in this process to maximize the positive enjoyment of the tourist experience in specific settings.

As Chapter 20 indicated, tourism and sustainability (Aronssen 2000) are also emerging as key themes for both tourists and the public and private sector organizations in the tourism sector. In fact one could argue that the 1990s witnessed the sustainability paradigm (an academic way of thinking) emerge in tourism research (e.g. Hall and Lew 1998) and has dominated a great deal of what has been published in books and journal articles. Alongside the sustainability focus in tourism studies, within the private sector service quality issues and competing for tourist spending has assumed an important role. This illustrates one of the eternal challenges for the tourism sector – managing demand and supply issues to try and achieve a balance. One specific factor which affects supply and demand is seasonality which often impacts upon attempts to balance supply and demand. At the same time, there is a delicate balancing act between issues of sustainability and the over-development of the tourism resource base in pursuit of short-term profits and economic benefits. This can effectively mean that 'the goose that lays the golden egg is killed'. What this implies is that the economic benefits which tourism brings can be destroyed by over-development if an appropriate balance is not sought. It is against this background that management measures are essential for tourism destinations to achieve the correct balance between development and sustainability so that some of the worse excesses of tourism are avoided.

Exhibit 26.1 **Factors to consider in evaluating the tourist's experience of an urban destination**

- The weather conditions at the time of the visit.
- The standard and quality of accommodation available.
- The cleanliness and upkeep of the city.
- The city's aesthetic value (i.e. its setting and beauty).
- The tourist's personal safety from crime.
- Health and safety considerations, particularly the adequacy and availability of emergency medical care.
- The accessibility of attractions and points of interest in the city.
- The extent to which residents welcome visitors in a warm and hospitable manner.
- The ability of employees to converse in different foreign languages.
- The range of cultural and artistic amenities.
- The ambience of the city environment as a place to walk around.
- The level of crowding and congestion within the urban environment.
- The range of night life and entertainment available.
- The range of restaurants and eating establishments in the city and the extent to which a culinary theme or experience is developed.
- The pleasurability of tourist shopping.
- The price levels of goods and services in the city.
- The level of helpfulness among local people when tourists seek advice.

(Source: Modified from Haywood and Muller 1988)

Plate 26.1 Tour groups, Wellington, New Zealand
Tour groups in urban settings such as this one in Wellington are often a focal point for visitor management.

The management and planning of the tourist experience

Within the wider management literature, planning is normally one task which is subsumed under the heading of management. Although there are many divergent views on what constitutes management, McLennan *et al.* (1987) describe the principal activities in management as:

- *Planning*, so that goals are set out and the means of achieving the goals are recognized.
- *Organizing*, whereby the work functions are broken down into a series of tasks and linked to some form of structure. These tasks then have to be assigned to individuals.
- *Leading*, which is the method of motivating and influencing staff so that they perform their tasks effectively. This is essential if organizational goals are to be achieved.
- *Controlling*, which is the method by which information is gathered about what has to be done.

These four tasks are common in most forms of management and are important for tourism destinations in co-ordinating the private and public sector interests (i.e. the stakeholders which include the residents) in relation to the tourist experience. This is where a managing agency with a view of the 'tourist experience' can be important in ensuring that some of the potential interactions evident in Figure 26.1 are managed in relation to urban tourism. Although Figure 26.1 simplifies the reality of the tourist experience, it acknowledges that it is important that the management and planning of the tourist experience is delegated to the public sector at a macro-level (i.e. the destination level). Yet there are also examples of the private sector taking the lead when the public sector is not effective. With the growing integration in the supply of holiday products (see Chapter 5), large companies such as Thomson Holidays monitor and

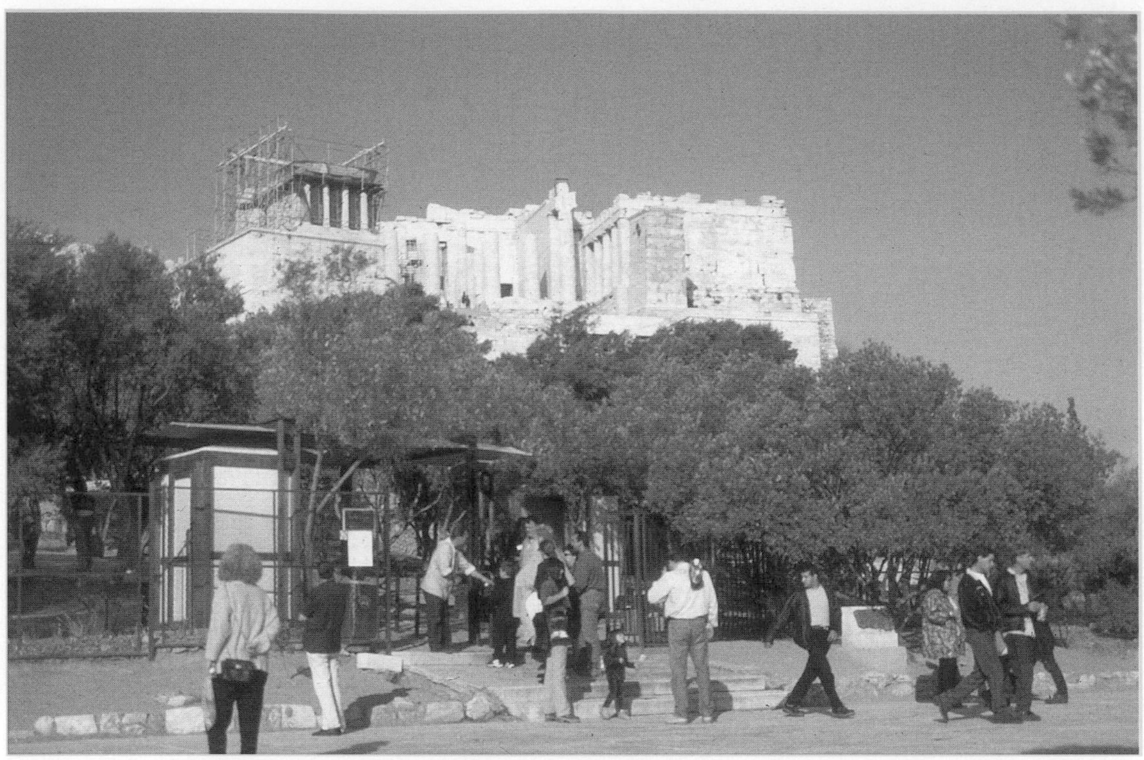

Plate 26.2 The Acropolis, Greece
The use of heritage resources such as the Acropolis in Greece pose many management problems for tourism organizations.

evaluate the quality issues and experiential aspects of tourism (see Page 1994 for more detail on the Thomson Holidays Customer Feedback Questionnaire and its use as a management tool) to make continuous improvements and immediate changes where significant events such as health problems occur (see Clift and Page 1996). Exhibit 26.1 also indicates that there are a number of stakeholders in any given destination which can impact upon the tourism industry ranging from the different businesses producing the supply of services and goods, the tourist (i.e. demand) and the residents who also impact upon the environment and experience of urban tourism. Achieving a balance between each of their needs and the viable development of the local tourism industry is a challenge. Therefore, Exhibit 26.1 shows that managing the tourist experience is a complex task and there are good reasons why the public sector is normally charged with this activity in most destinations. There are two reasons for this: first, the public sector is charged with statutory tasks that are normally in the wider public good and designed to consider the sustainability of the resource base; second, in theory, these bodies should be able to take an holistic perspective which assesses both the wider issues for a destination. This is a strategic perspective which has a five- to ten-year time frame to consider the consequences of continued tourist development. Therefore, it is important to distinguish between the management roles of NTOs, RTOS and local tourism agencies and the specific management responsibilities and planning obligations which public sector agencies such as local government perform (Howie 2000). In this respect, it is useful to consider what is meant by planning and who performs it and what it comprises in a tourism context.

Figure 26.1 **Managing the tourist experience**

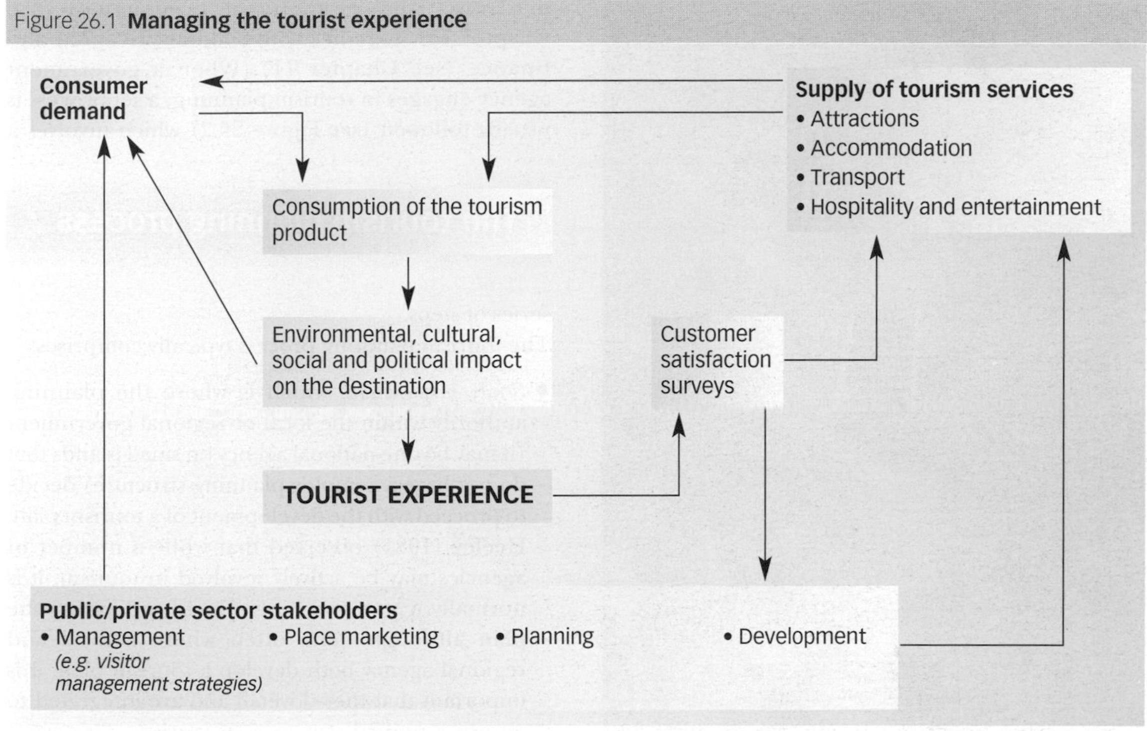

(Source: Based on Page 1995)

Planning: what is it and does it exist in tourism?

According to Chadwick (1971: 24) 'planning is a process, a process of human thought and action based upon that thought – in point of fact for the future – nothing more or less than this is planning, which is a general human activity'. What this means is that change and the need to accommodate change in the future requires a process whereby a set of decisions are prepared for future action. Hall (1999: 10) argues that:

> Demands for tourism planning and government intervention in the development process are typically a response to the unwanted effects of tourism development at the local level. The rapid pace of tourism growth and development, the nature of tourism itself and the corresponding absence of single agency responsibility for tourism related development has often meant that public sector responses to the impacts of tourism on destinations has often been ad hoc, rather than predetermined strategies oriented towards development objectives.

Planning is therefore a process which aims to anticipate, regulate and monitor change so as to contribute to the wider sustainability of the destination and thereby enhance the tourist experience of the destination or place. What Hall (1999) and other commentators recognize is that while tourism planning has followed trends in urban and regional planning, tourism is not always seen as a core focus of the planning process.

Getz (1987) observed that there are four traditions to tourism planning: boosterism, an economic-industry approach, a physical-spatial approach and a community-oriented approach while Hall (1999) has recognized that a fifth approach now exists – sustainable tourism planning, which is 'a concern for the long-term future of resources, the effects of economic development on the environment, and its ability to meet present and future needs' (Page and Thorn 1997: 60). As Page and Thorn (1997: 61) suggest: 'In most countries, tourism planning exists as a component of public sector planning, and its evolution as a specialist activity has been well documented (Gunn 1988; Inskeep 1991).' As a component of public sector planning, tourism

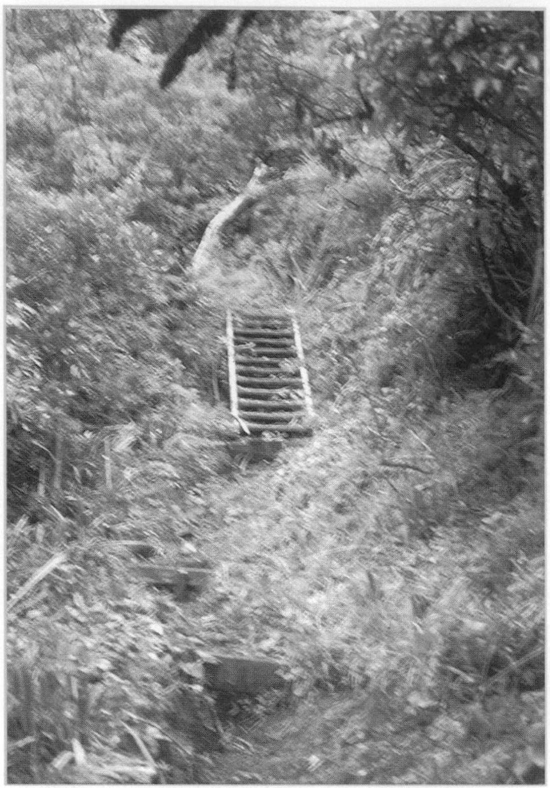

Plate 26.3 Trail management in Taranaki National Park, New Zealand
Natural environments also pose problems for visitor management, as this picture of trail management in Taranaki National Park shows.

planning (where it exists as a discrete activity or is subsumed within wider economic planning processes), aims to optimize the balance of private sector interests which are profit driven and a position where the public sector contributes to managing the growth without being directly involved in tourism development, as this rarely achieves optimal economic benefits.

According to Inskeep (1994: 6), the effective management of tourism requires certain 'organizational elements'. The most important of these in a planning context are organizational structures, which include government agencies and private sector interests groups as well as the involvement of local and regional government bodies to plan for tourism activity as well as tourism-related legislation and regulations. One also has to have appropriate marketing and promotional programmes (see Chapter 15), together with sources of capital and finance (see Chapter 11). When a government agency engages in tourism planning, a set process is usually followed (see Figure 26.2) which involves a

The tourism planning process

series of steps.

The tourism planning process typically comprises:

- *Study preparation*, which is where the planning authority within the local or regional government (it may be one national agency on small islands that do not have a complex planning structure) decide to proceed with the development of a tourism plan. Heeley (1981) observed that while a number of agencies may be actively involved in tourism, it is normally a statutory body which undertakes the plan although quite often where a local and regional agency both develop a tourism plan, it is important that they dovetail and are integrated to ensure a unified structure to tourism. This was a problem in London in the 1990s, when the 33

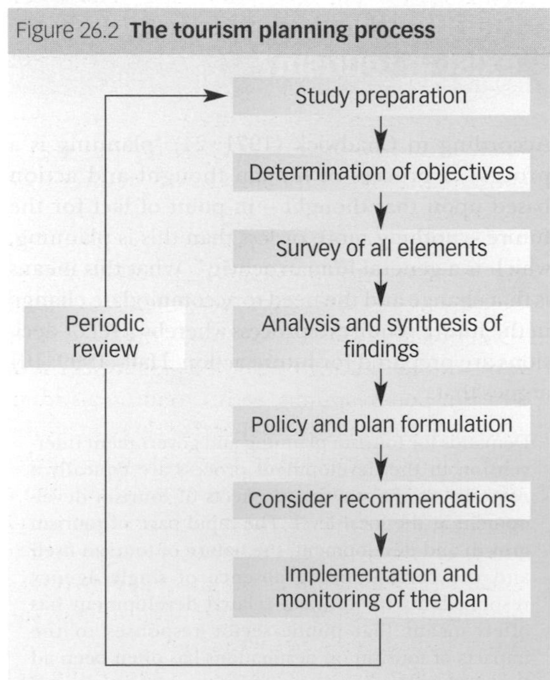

(Source: Page 1995)

London boroughs each had unified development plans but pursued different approaches to tourism (i.e. some councils promoted tourism development while others positively discouraged it despite the efforts of the London Tourist Board which sought to co-ordinate their activities in tourism).

- *Determination of objectives* is where the main purpose of the plan is identified (i.e. is it pursuing a sustainable strategy to development? Is it being undertaken in response to a crisis such as saturation tourism to identify managerial measures to reduce the social, cultural and environmental impacts?).
- *Survey of all elements* is where an inventory of all the existing tourism resources and facilities are surveyed together with the state of development, as illustrated in Figure 26.3. This will require the collection of data on the supply and demand for tourism, the structure of the local tourism economy, investment and finance available for future development. It will also involve identifying the range of other private and public sector interests in tourism within the destination or locality.
- *Analysis and synthesis of findings* is where the information and data collected in the previous stage are analysed and incorporated as data when formulating the plan. As Cooper *et al.* (1998) argue, four principal techniques are frequently used here: asset evaluation, market analysis, development planning and impact analysis (especially economic impact analysis such as input: output analysis, multiplier analysis and tourism forecasting).
- *Policy and plan formulation* is where the data gathered in the previous stage are used to establish the various options or development scenarios available for tourism. This frequently involves the drafting of a development plan with tourism policy options, with certain goals identified. Acernaza (1985) argues that there are three main elements evident in most tourism policies that are germane to the tourist experience: visitor satisfaction, environmental protection and ensuring adequate rewards exist for developers and investors. By developing a range of policy options at this stage of the planning process, the future direction can be considered.
- *Consideration of recommendations* is where the full tourism plan is then prepared and forwarded to the planning committee of the public agency responsible for the process. A period of public consultation is normally undertaken in most western industrialized countries. The draft plan is then available for public consultation so that both the general public and tourism interests can read and comment on it. A number of public hearings may also be provided to gauge the strength of local feeling towards the plan. Once this procedure is completed, the plan will then be approved by the planning authority and the final plan is then produced.
- *The implementation and monitoring of the tourism plan* is when the plan is put into action which is normally seen as an on-going process by the planning team. In some instances, legislation may be required to control certain aspects of development (e.g. the height of buildings and developments) which will need to be implemented as part of the plan. The political complexity of implementing the plan should not be underestimated (see Hall and Jenkins 1995 for more detail). Often, the political complexion of the elected representatives on the statutory planning authority may change and cause the priorities to change although if an action plan is produced alongside the plan, then it will allow for some degree of choice in what is implemented and actioned in a set period of time. At the same time as the plan is implemented, it will also need to be monitored. This is an on-going process where the planning agency assess if the objectives of the plan are being met. The operational time frame for a tourism plan is normally five years, after which time it is reviewed.
- *The periodic review* refers to the process of reporting back on the progress once the plan has runs its course and been implemented. Some of the reasons for the failure of the plan to achieve its stated objectives may relate to a change of political complexion amongst the elected members of the planning authority (e.g. where an anti-tourism lobby dominates the local authority when the plan was commissioned by a pro-tourism council); a failure to achieve a degree of consensus between the private and public sector on how to address 'bottlenecks' in the supply of services and facilities for tourists; inadequate transport and infrastructure provision; and public opposition to tourism from a misunderstanding of residents' attitudes.

Figure 26.3 **The elements of a tourism plan**

(Source: Modified from Inskeep 1991; Page 1995)

Yet as Page and Thorn (1997) show in relation to the development of sustainable tourism planning in New Zealand, while some local authorities may have plans for tourism, an absence of regional or a national plan for tourism to spread and distribute the benefits of tourism highlights the need for integration of planning between the three levels at which it commonly occurs: the national (i.e. the country level), regional (the county or state level in the USA) and local level (i.e. the specific city, district or locality). Even within cities with a multitude of planning organizations and different city councils, such as Auckland in New Zealand, achieving some degree of consensus on managing the tourist experience is necessary given the significance of tourism to the wider regional economy. However, often parochialism and vested interests and a certain degree of tunnel vision means that destinations fail to adopt a strategic perspective with a vision of the future shape and form which tourism will assume in a city-region context. This is often a failure at management level where leadership skills are required to adopt a vision of how tourism should develop over the next five years which cannot be embodied in paper plans. What planners are belatedly realizing in the context of tourism is that destinations require more than simple notions of land use planning which has remained a permanent feature of urban and regional planning where local and global processes of tourism development are recognized. Yet in the real world, *planning for tourism* is a more apt description of the way tourism is treated by the public sector, since it is frequently incorporated in wider planning considerations which influence tourism development. Ultimately, the public sector needs to recognize that: 'Tourism, like any other industry, has problems which stem from market failures and imperfections and from subsequent government responses' (Hall 1999: 18) but it is often hard to monitor the impacts of tourism because of the structural and service characteristics of the tourism sector. Nevertheless, in the new millennium, any destination which is not planning for its tourism sector will not be systematically evaluating its market position and future for a growing global economic activity which has consequences (i.e. impacts for its resident population and local economy). Whatever form of management or planning which is developed for tourism in a given locality must take a strategic view to identifying and developing a range of tourism resources and environment(s). This strategic vision will need to satisfy the long-term provision of tourist experiences that are compatible with the locality, environment and

Plate 26.4 Buchart Gardens, British Columbia
Gardens are a significant resource used by local residents and tourists alike.

resources available to planners and managers of the tourism.

Managing the tourist experience: tools and techniques

Previous sections have shown that there are numerous factors that are relevant to the tourist experience. As such, the effective management of this experience requires an integrated approach to the delivery of a range of inter-related initiatives (Grant *et al.* 1996a). The UK government defines visitor management as an on-going process to reconcile the potentially competing needs of the visitor, the place and the host community (Department of Environment and English Tourist Board 1991). These aspects are reflected in Figure 26.4.

Where such aspects are fully considered and implemented within an integrated plan, this can have the collective effect of minimizing the negative impacts of visitor activity and enhancing the tourist experience (Grant 1994). One dimension of visitor management is town centre management schemes. In general terms these usually involve a comprehensive plan combining the public authority, private sector and voluntary organization interests. The aim is usually to improve facilities, the environment and visitor convenience and safety within the town centre (see Page and Hardyman 1996 for a review of the UK). Naturally, town centre management is strongly affected by the impact of tourist since town centres are often the focus for services and facilities used by visitors. As a result, Davidson and Maitland (1997) and Human (1995) suggest that many of the concerns of town centre and visitor management overlap and complement each other. Here, rather than trying to distinguish when visitor management

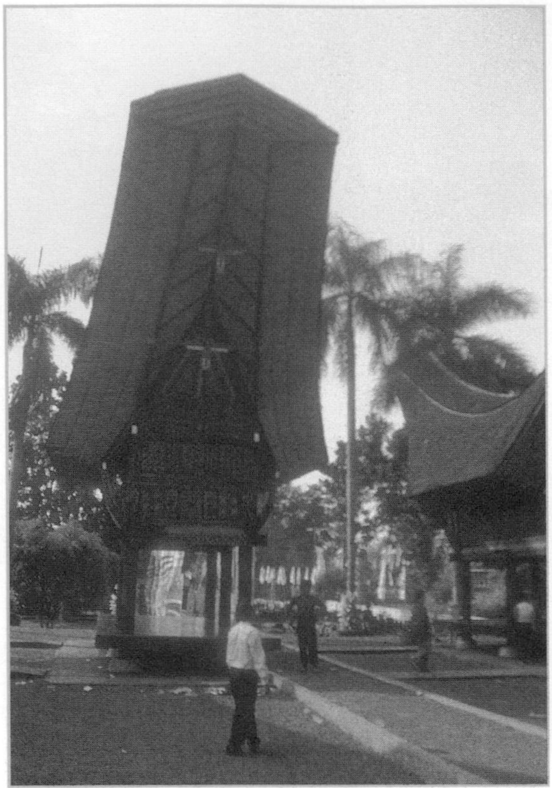

Plate 26.5 Taman Mini theme park, Jakarta, Indonesia
Man-made environments such as Taman Mini theme park may offer an artificial form of reality which can be managed and planned for tourism.

Figure 26.4 **The nature of visitor management**

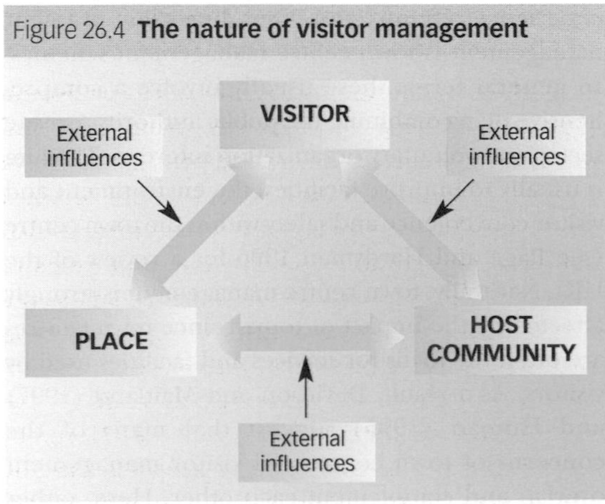

(Source: Adapted from DoE/ETB 1991)

becomes a town centre or destination management scheme, we will investigate how managing the tourist can be undertaken effectively in a general sense.

The type of measures carried out in the context of managing the tourist experience can be sub-divided into 'hard' and 'soft'. Hard measures include those that place extensive or permanent restrictions on visitor activity and relate to physical or financial measures such as closing sites to allow for restoration or the introduction of entrance fees. Grant (1994) argues that such measures may have limited value in certain locations or else cause other problems. For instance restrictions on the number of tourists may decrease the attractiveness of a destination to certain visitors or run contrary to the visitors' right to enjoy the benefits of the natural or built environment. Alternatively, soft measures, such as improved marketing, interpretation, planning and visitor co-ordination tend to be more acceptable, especially to the tourism industry. It should not be assumed that hard and soft measures are mutually exclusive. Glasson (1994) and Grant (1994) note how a combination of measures may be employed. The reason why such a course of action needs to be employed will now be discussed.

Vehicle and pedestrian management

Small historic towns and cities are often severely restricted in their ability to absorb crowds and traffic (Curtis 1998). Hence, traffic and pedestrian congestion may need to be regulated. In the case of excessive traffic, pedestrianization schemes may be implemented to discourage city centre parking through car park pricing, restricting in-town parking to disabled people and the provision of park and ride facilities (Curtis 1998; Glasson 1994; Page 1995). Moreover, improvements in public transport may also facilitate access and lessen the effects of traffic congestion (e.g. danger to pedestrians, impaired visual appeal and noise). Another aspect is the consideration of footpaths. By providing alternative access routes to the centre and well-designed signage, for example, one may not only reduce conflict between tourists and residents, but reduce congestion and ensure that visitors reach their destination quickly and safely (Grant 1994). Other ways that can reduce overcrowding in this context include guided tours, timed ticketing, queuing systems and colour-coded walks. Such measures effectively reduce the size of crowds thereby lowering the risks of fire, accidents and theft.

Providing for groups

In popular destinations there are likely to be a large number of coach arrivals. Where narrow streets exist in historic cities, coaches can cause serious problems of congestion. Hence, to control such effects, dedicated coach parks with facilities for drivers and tourists need to be provided. Where this extends to a requirement for pre-booking, it is possible for the destination to prepare for the group's arrival and ensure a quality welcome at a less congested time (Grant *et al.* 1996b). In addition, in some locations, such as Stratford-upon-Avon, town centre staff positioned at coach parks during peak times assist to combine a visitor welcome with visitor management (Hicks 1995). Such measures give benefits to the visitor. A personalized welcome can create a positive first impression and by having staff on hand to provide information and orientation on arrival, specific and immediate visitor requirements can be met.

Product development

Getz (1993) suggests that although retailing is a major activity in town centres, other activities such as entertainment, leisure facilities and hospitality services also contribute to a town's attractiveness and viability as a destination. Improvements to existing facilities and the introduction of a broader range of leisure facilities and activities will benefit residents, while providing more choice, possibly leading to a wider dispersal of tourists. As tourist destinations, particularly in urban areas, become more developed visitor management issues such as safety become more important. Hence, the introduction of closed circuit television cameras, improved street lighting, more public toilets and staff to deal with complaints of increased litter, graffiti, vandalism, unauthorized street traders and beggars may need to be put in place. Clearly where such issues are effectively tackled, this can improve the overall image of the location and ensure residents and tourists' safety (Grant *et al.* 1996).

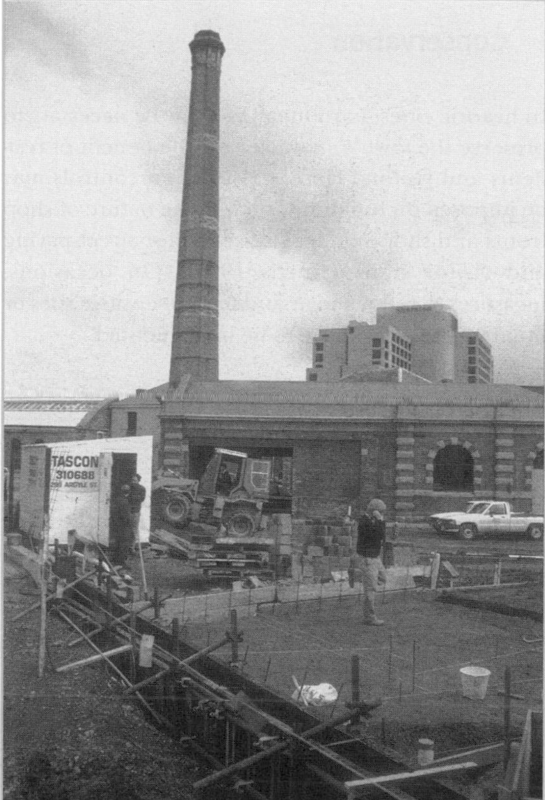

Plate 26.6 Gasworks Project, Hobart, Tasmania
Heritage projects have seen a revival in the 1980s and 1990s when tourism was seen as a major driver.

Marketing – promotional activity and information

According to the English Historic Towns Forum (1994) marketing through the promotion and provision of accurate information plays a vital role in visitor management. This is because, prior to a visit and during the visit itself, the information provided makes an impression upon visitors and helps to shape their perceptions and attitudes as well as the nature of the actual visit. Introducing packages to encourage short breaks rather than day visits and off-peak promotions are measures to manage the numbers of visitors at any one time. Here, by extending the season and getting people to stay, the visitor may be provided with a value-for-money package that also serves the local industry as well.

Conservation

In historic cities, hard measures may be necessary to preserve the town's character for the benefit of residents and visitors. Here, strict design controls may be imposed on buildings, such as the nature of shop fronts and shop signage, as well as for street paving and visitor signs (Curtis 1998). On occasions, measures to reduce wear and tear to sensitive sites or buildings may also have to be implemented.

The host community

Any visitor management scheme needs to assist local people and businesses to develop a positive attitude towards tourists. Hence, opportunities for the local community to voice their concerns and problems are vital. Most commentators advocate the involvement of local people (i.e. local government officers, retailers, tourism businesses, interest groups and citizens) in the preparation and implementation of visitor management schemes (see for example, Prentice 1993). Where such views are accommodated the schemes are more likely to have been deemed successful. Examples of visitor management schemes in different locations are shown in Exhibits 26.2 and 26.3.

Visitor management schemes, whether they are in town centres or other locations, are necessary to effectively manage the tourist experience. To create a positive experience for the visitor, while protecting the needs of the local community and the place, a combination of measures is likely to be necessary. Consultation with and an active involvement of relevant groups are essential to accommodate the needs and aspirations of all. Clearly, the success of such schemes requires a detailed knowledge of the visitor market. Without this, the marketing, interpretation and provision of facilities may not achieve their full potential. While surveys of visitor satisfaction may provide a snapshot of the extent to

Exhibit 26.2 **Easy-going Dartmoor**

Dartmoor in South Devon, UK, covers 365 square miles of outstanding natural beauty and was designated as a National Park in 1951. A right of access exists in the National Park for those on foot and horseback, but this right has been extended to those using wheelchairs. In 1999 a Countryside Access Group was formed to address a range of issues involving access to the Dartmoor area. In conjunction with the National Park authorities this group of volunteers, many disabled themselves, set about improving access throughout the area for those who were less mobile.

Their work has involved an inventory of the range of facilities available. This includes a listing of toilet facilities graded in terms of whether disabled access is available and whether they are part of the RADAR National Key Scheme (to enable disabled access to toilet facilities across the country by provision of a special key). In addition, the group has specified eight 'easy-going walks' – suitable for most people with limited mobility – and six 'more adventurous walks' – for those who want a more challenging experience. In both cases detailed maps are provided so that the visitor can be aware of what to expect in terms of gradient, surface, camber and obstacles. The group also provides details of viewpoints (where the countryside can be admired from a car), suggested driving routes and information on visitor centres.

Such an approach illustrates a management scheme designed for these particular types of visitor. As such the Dartmoor National Park Authority recognizes the needs of disabled people, those who are less mobile or those with very young children and helps to provide information and facilities for them so that their experience of Dartmoor is no less pleasurable.

(Source: Adapted from Dartmoor National Park Authority and Countryside Access Group 1999)

Exhibit 26.3 **Cape Byron Headland Reserve, Australia**

The Cape Byron Headland Reserve is located on the most easterly part of Australia, on the upper north coast of New South Wales, 800km north of Sydney. It covers 47 hectares and was originally designated as a Crown Reserve for 'Public Recreation and Preservation of Native Flora' in 1903. The area has considerable cultural and environmental significance. There is evidence of Aboriginal habitation, an early European settlement and the area has terrestrial and aquatic value. As such the area has become an important tourist destination. Some 300,000 visitors come to the area each year attracted by the scenery and the opportunity for both passive (e.g. walking) and active pursuits (e.g. hang gliding). However, as the number of visitors has increased, conflicts in terms of visitor management and the lack of sufficient financial resources became apparent. This led to the establishment of the Cape Byron Trust in 1988 with representatives from government agencies and local residents making up a management board. The trust is responsible for policies that provide strategic direction to embrace the needs of conservation, education, recreation provision and tourism management.

Through the use of a management plan, originally designed in 1989, today the Trust has adopted an attitude of 'responsible tourism' which informs all its decisions. The key features of the management strategy are:

- Unitary management (i.e. the Trust).
- On-site reserve manager.
- Broad involvement of experts drawn from local interest groups.
- Local empowerment/participation.
- Self-generated budget.
- Harmonization of management strands in the formal management plan (i.e. income–conservation–recreation).

Informing the management strategy are a number of key sustainable practices, which include:

- Employment of regular environmental audits.
- Community consultation.
- Employee education of environmental practices.
- Education of visitors regarding the principles of 'green living'.
- Interpretation to enhance the visitor understanding of the physical and cultural environment.
- Rehabilitation of degraded areas with endemic plants.
- 'Hardening' of areas to withstand increased usage without deterioration.
- Zoning of areas for specific uses.
- Issue of permits to control site/area usage.
- User charges.
- Research regarding environmental impacts stemming from tourist activities.

It can be seen that such an approach demonstrates an awareness of the need to protect and conserve the area, coupled with visitor management measures to enhance the visitor experience.

(Source: Adapted from Brown and Essex 1997)

which visitor expectations are fulfilled, this can only be a partial picture. Where monitoring is undertaken on a regular basis and includes feedback from coach operators, local attractions, shops and residents as well, a more complete picture of the effectiveness of visitor management schemes may result. This section has shown how destinations attempt to manage the tourist experience, but what of the tourism industry itself? In recent years the expression 'service quality' has entered the terminology and in the following section we shall address the extent to which service quality is a useful tool in managing the tourist experience.

Service quality: an effective tool in managing the tourist experience?

We have repeatedly seen that when the tourist has a satisfactory experience numerous benefits result. Positive word of mouth recommendations bring new custom and repeat custom. In addition, content customers may reduce the need for extra marketing expenditure and the time and costs of dealing with complaints. Thus, an obvious aim of tourism firms is to attempt to create customer loyalty, but in a competitive world, how can this be achieved? Knowing the customer is one aspect (see Chapter 15), but offering a quality service may also be an effective means of not only managing the tourist experience, but also of differentiating one tourism product from another (Powers *et al.* 1999). Levels of satisfaction though, are rather personal and subjective and are based on individuals prior experiences, perceptions and judgements (Laws 1991). Despite this, there are some common characteristics affecting tourists that represent opportunities for the tourism firm.

The tourist experience can be represented as contact with the service provider(s), other visitors, as well as with the destination itself. This could be thought of as a 'package'. This package consists of a 'core service' which relates to the principle benefits sought by the tourist. Hence, in holiday terms this would include the tour operator/accommodation provider. 'Peripheral services', such as contact with other people (e.g. customs and airport staff) when positive, can improve the overall experience considerably. As a starting point, though, the success of the tourism business must be in meeting customer expectations of the core service. Different types of customers have different expectations, and some (e.g. backpackers at youth hostels) may be more concerned with price than service quality. Nevertheless, as people become more experienced in travel, expectations rise. As Harrington and Leneham (1998: 12) state 'excellent service pays off because it creates true customer's customers who are glad they selected a firm after the service experience, customers who will use the firm again and sing the firm's praises to others'. Thus, knowing what the customer expects is the first step in delivering quality service.

An effective 'strategy' is one part of providing service quality to enhance the tourist experience. A second dimension relates to 'staff', as employee performance is also crucial. It could well be that the firm's staff could make or break the tourist experience. Positive interactions with staff can transform a negative experience and according to Van der Wagen (1994), there should be a constant focus on training personnel in interaction skills. Such programmes as 'Welcome Host' originally devised by the English Tourist Board and company schemes such as the 'Forte Commitment to Excellence' are useful to educate staff to provide quality service. The success of such programmes can be monitored through the analysis of customer comments and market research (Walker 1990).

Following 'strategies' and 'staff', a third dimension is the quality of the firm's 'systems'. Foley *et al.* (1997) argue that systems of quality control need to be created to ensure that quality service delivery is taking place. Methods of monitoring and gaining feedback on quality include 'critical incident analysis'. This involves a detailed tracing back of service failures to discover what customers found to be unsatisfactory and how this can be avoided in the future. As Chung and Hoffman (1998: 66) state 'since the customer's perception of reality is the key factor, the analysis of service failures from the customer's point of view allows managers to minimise the occurrence of service failures through adjustments in operations and human-resource procedures'. Another useful management tool in this context is suggested by Powers *et al.* (1999), that of 'zero defect'. Everybody has a level of tolerance before deciding to make a complaint. Here the goal for the firm is to identify those tolerance levels and achieve 'zero defect', i.e. no complaints. Kunst and Lemmink (1995) have shown that quality marks also offer opportunities for guiding and forming quality expectations. National and international standards such as 'BS' (British Standard) and 'ISO' (International Organisation for Standardisation) can help firms to design and implement quality management systems, the awarding of which can provide assurances to customers. Wild (1995) suggests that the introduction of such standards has led to a reduction in complaints, improved management and lessened the need for third party intervention. An important dimension in managing the tourist experience, in the context of the tourism firm, is the consideration of aspect of service quality. To achieve this firms need the three Ss, strategy, staff and systems. Firms need a strategy to better understand the expectations and satisfactions of their customers and managers need to communicate service standards to their staff and provide them with adequate training. Systems of quality may be assured through 'ISO' standards being achieved.

Conclusion

This chapter has shown that the careful management of the tourist experience is an absolutely vital but complex requirement. It touches on all that are associated with tourism in or to any location. At one level, tourism planning is necessary to ensure that tourism develops in a sustainable fashion. Often tourism planning is part of a wider planning process, where the needs of other industries as well as the local population are considered. As such, tourism planning is mainly the responsibility of public sector agencies. Here, however, there is a need for national policies to integrate with tourism policies at the regional or local level. At the destination there may also be the need to manage how tourists use the location, with others (residents) and to ensure that sensitive sites are not irreparably damaged. Overcrowding and traffic congestion are common problems which can require suitable policies, but these can be used to provide a better experience for the visitor (e.g. welcome staff). The private sector is not exempt from responsibility in this context. The success of visitor management initiatives necessarily requires the active involvement of all stakeholders. Moreover, the tourism firm needs to consider how to best manage tourist in terms of how the tourist/customer interacts with the service offered by the firm. Here, high levels of service quality are likely to lead to satisfied tourists and more custom. To be successful in this respect, firms need to have a strategy for understanding their customers, well-trained staff and an appropriate system of quality assurance.

Discussion questions

1. Why should tourism organizations be concerned with the tourist experience in destinations?
2. What factors would you consider in attempting the tourist experience in a resort area? How much of the information is likely to be in a published form already?
3. Why do tourist destinations adopt visitor management strategies? What tools do these schemes use to manage visitor flows?
4. In the natural environment, visitor pressures are difficult to manage. Why is this?

Internet resources

By going to the weblink at www.thomsonlearning.co.uk students can access the following study from the Thomson Learning website. The study is by E. Laws (1996) *Managing Packaged Tourism* and examines the issue which is central to the tourist experience – service quality and which has become the focus of so much research on assessing if tourists are satisfied with what they have experienced. This should be read in conjunction with the weblink for Chapter 4 in this book on motivation since the weblink material by C. Ryan (1995) examines the problems of measuring attitudes and satisfaction in the tourist experience.

References

Acernaza, M. (1985) 'Planificación Estratégica del Turismo: Esquesma Metológico', *Estudiios Turisticos,* **85**: 45–70.

Aronssen, L. (2000) *The Development of Sustainable Tourism,* London: Continuum.

Brown, G. and Essex, S. (1997) 'Sustainable tourism management: lessons from the edge of Australia', *Journal of Sustainable Tourism,* **5** (4): 294–305.

Chadwick, G. (1971) *A Systems View of Planning,* Oxford: Pergamon Press.

Chung, B. and Hoffman, K.D. (1998) 'Critical incidents: service failures that matter most', *Cornell Hotel and Restaurant Administration Quarterly,* June: 54–70.

Clift, S. and Page, S.J. (1996) (eds) *Health and the International Tourist,* London: Routledge.

Cooper, C.P., Fletcher, J., Gilbert, D.G. and Wanhill S. (1998) *Tourism: Principles and Practice,* Harlow: Addison Wesley Longman.

Curtis, S. (1998) 'Visitor management in small historic cities', *Travel and Tourism Analyst,* **3**: 75–89.

Dartmoor National Park Authority and Countryside Access Group (1999) *Easy-Going Dartmoor,* Princetown: Dartmoor National Park Authority.

Davidson, R. and Maitland, R. (1997) *Tourism Destinations,* London: Hodder & Stoughton.

Department for Environment/English Tourist Board (1991) *Tourism and the Environment: Maintaining the Balance,* London: English Tourist Board.

English Historic Towns Forum (1993) *Retailing in Historic Towns: Research Study 1992,* London: Donaldsons.

Foley, M., Lennon, J.J. and Maxwell, G.A. (1997) *Hospitality, Tourism and Leisure Management: Issues in Strategy and Culture,* London: Cassell.

Getz, D. (1987) 'Tourism planning and research: traditions, models and futures', Paper presented at the Australian Travel Research Workshop, Bunbury, Western Australia, 5–6 November.

Getz, D. (1993) 'Tourist shopping villages: development and planning strategies', *Tourism Management,* **14** (1): 15–26.

Glasson, J. (1994) 'Oxford: a heritage city under pressure – visitors, impacts and management responses', *Tourism Management,* **15** (2): 137–44.

Grant, M. (1994) 'Visitor management', *Insights,* **6**: A41–46.

Grant, M., Human, B. and Le Pelley, B. (1996) 'Visitor management: whose role is it anyway?' *Insights,* **7**: A159–163.

Gunn, C. (1988) *Tourism Planning,* second edition, London: Taylor and Francis.

Hall, C.M. (1999) *Tourism Planning: Policies, Processes and Relationships,* Harlow: Addison Wesley Longman.

Hall, C.M. and Jenkins, J. (1995) *Tourism and Public Policy,* London: Routledge.

Hall, C.M. and Lew, A. (eds) (1998) *The Geography of Sustainable Tourism,* Harlow: Addison Wesley Longman.

Harrington, D. and Leneham, T. (1998) *Managing Quality in Tourism,* Dublin: Oak Tree Press.

Haywood, K. and Muller, T. (1988) 'The urban tourist experience: evaluating satisfaction', *Hospitality Education and Research Journal,* 453–59.

Heeley, J. 'Planning for tourism in Britain', *Town Planning Review,* **52**: 61–79.

Hicks, M. (1995) *Stratford-upon-Avon Visitor Management Action Programme 1992–95,* Stratford: Stratford-upon-Avon District Council.

Howie, F. (2000) *Managing the Tourist Destination: A Practical Interactive Guide,* London: Contiuum.

Human, B. (1995) 'The happy host: tourism and town centre management', paper presented at the University of East Anglia, 21 September 1995.

Inskeep, E. (1991) *Tourism Planning: An Integrated and Sustainable Development Approach,* New York: Van Nostrand Reinhold.

Inskeep, E. (1994) *National and Regional Tourism Planning: Methodologies and Case Studies,* London: Routledge.

Kunst, P. and Lemmink, J. (1995) *Managing Service Quality,* London: Paul Chapman Publishing.

Laws, E. (1991) *Tourism Marketing: Service Quality and Management Perspectives,* Chichester: Wiley.

McClennan, R., Inkson, K., Dakin, S., Dewe, P. and Elkin, G. (1987) *People and Enterprises: Human Behaviour in New Zealand Organisations,* Auckland: Rinehart and Winston.

Page, S.J. (1994) *Transport for Tourism,* London: Routledge.

Page, S.J. (1995) *Urban Tourism,* London: Routledge.

Page, S.J. and Hardyman, R. (1996) 'Place marketing and town centre management: a new tool for urban revitalisation', *Cities: The International Journal of Urban Policy and Planning,* **13** (3): 153–64.

Page, S.J. and Thorn, K. (1997) 'Towards sustainable tourism planning in New Zealand: public sector planning responses', *Journal of Sustainable Tourism* **5** (1): 59–77.

Powers, T., Barrows, R. and Clayton, W. (1999) *Introduction to Management in the Hospitality Industry,* sixth edition, Chichester: Wiley.

Prentice, R. (1993) 'Community-driven tourism planning and residents' preferences', *Tourism Management,* **14** (3): 218–27.

Ryan, C. (ed.) (1997) *The Tourist Experience: A New Introduction,* London: Cassell.

Van de Wagen, L. (1994) *Building Quality Service,* Oxford: Butterworth.

Walker, D. (1990) *Customer First,* Aldershot: Gower Publishing.

Wild, R. (1995) *Production and Operations Management,* fifth edition, London: Cassell.

Further reading

Curtis, S. (1998) 'Visitor management in small historic cities', *Travel and Tourism Analyst,* **3**: 75–89.

Grant, M., Human, B. and Le Pelley, B. (1996) 'Visitor management: whose role is it anyway'?, *Insights,* **7**: A159–163.

Hall, C.M. (1999) *Tourism Planning: Policies, Processes and Relationships,* Harlow: Addison Wesley Longman.

Inskeep, E. (1994) *National and Regional Tourism Planning: Methodologies and Case Studies,* London: Routledge.

Walker, D. (1990) *Customer First,* Aldershot: Gower Publishing.

27 The future of tourism

Learning outcomes

This chapter examines a range of issues which will affect the future of tourism. After studying this chapter, you should be able to understand:

- The role and application of tourism forecasting and its importance for tourism businesses.
- The potential impact of factors affecting changes in tourism, including demographic and political factors.
- The significance of health and safety issues along with legal concerns.
- The tourism and sustainability debate.
- The skills required of tourism managers in the new millennium.

Overview

This chapter examines the issues which planners and researchers need to consider in reviewing the future development of tourism at a global scale. The chapter commences with a discussion of the area of tourism forecasting and the need for managers to understand the issues which may affect their tourism enterprises, particularly the fast changing nature of tourism trends and tastes. The chapter also reviews the factors which tourism managers and planners may need to understand in forecasting changes in tourism trends, particularly the rise of new data sources such as tourism satellite accounts and health and safety issues. The importance of the sustainability issues and skill development for tourism managers to manage the fast changing nature of tourism are also discussed.

Introduction

Tourism is not a new phenomenon in the twentieth and twenty-first centuries: it has developed through the ages but today it is undergoing profound changes and is no longer an activity or pastime for the privileged few, with the exception of consumers in less developed countries. Recognizing the nature and significance of tourism to modern day society is not the sole pursuit of the sociologist: it should be the concern of all students of tourism since tourism is not just a business: it is a phenomenon, a process, an activity, an experience. In most societies it is a popular pastime which is a major use of leisure time, where dreams, ideals and personal values are often realized. Tourism is a dominant feature of the late twentieth and early twenty-first centuries with the quest for travel, discovery, relaxation and a multitude of other reasons. At the same time, tourism is undergoing a profound series of changes and this chapter explores some of the principal changes associated with tourism in the new millennium, commencing with a discussion of the role of tourism forecasting which is helpful in considering how tourism may change over the next few years.

Forecasting changes in tourism

According to Jefferson and Lickorish (1991: 101), forecasting the demand for tourism is essential for commercial operators, 'whether in the public or private sector ... [as they] ... will seek to maximize revenue and profits in moving towards maximum efficiency in [their] use of resources'. Archer (1987) argues that:

> no manager can avoid the need for some form of forecasting: a manager must plan for the future in order to minimise the risk of failure or, more optimistically, to maximise the possibilities of success. In order to plan, he must use forecasts. Forecasts will always be made, whether by guesswork, teamwork or the use of complex models, and the accuracy of the forecasts will affect the quality of the management decision. (Archer 1987: 77)

Reliable forecasts are essential for managers and decision-makers involved in service provision to try and ensure adequate supply is available to meet demand, while ensuring over-supply does not result, since this can erode the profitability of their operation. In essence, 'forecasts of tourism demand are essential for efficient planning by airlines, shipping companies, railways, coach operators, hoteliers, tour operators' (Witt *et al.* 1991: 52). Forecasting is the process associated with an assessment of future changes in the demand for tourism. It must be

Plate 27.1 A wine tour bus outside a winery in the Yarra Valley, Victoria, Australia
Wine tours are a future growth area in tourism.

Plate 27.2 The hot springs in Rotorua, New Zealand
Traditional tourist attractions such as these hot springs continue to attract tourists seeking health experiences.

stressed that 'forecasting is not an exact science' (Jefferson and Lickorish 1991: 102), as it attempts to make estimations of future traffic potential and a range of possible scenarios, which provide an indication of the likely scale of change in demand. Consequently, forecasting is a technique used to suggest the future pattern of demand.

According to Jefferson and Lickorish (1991: 102) the principal methods of forecasting are:

- the projection by extrapolation, of historic trends [i.e. how the previous performance of demand may shape future patterns]
- extrapolation, subject to the application of [statistical analysis using] weights or variables.

In addition:

- structured group discussions among a panel of tourism transport experts may be used to assess factors determining future traffic forecasts (the 'Delphi Method').

Bull (1991) recognizes that the range of tourism forecasting techniques are determined by the methods of analysis they employ.

There are two basic types of forecasting method:

- those based on qualitative techniques, such as the Delphi Method – Archer (1987) argues that these are viewed considerably less rigorous than
- quantitative forecasting methods, using techniques developed from statistics and economic theory.

Bull (1991: 127–8) classifies the quantitative techniques forecasters use in terms of the degree of statistical and mathematical complexity based on:

- time-series analysis of trends (e.g. seasonality in travel) which involve simple statistical calculations to consider how past trends may be replicated in the future
- economic theory-based models, used in econometrics (see Witt and Martin 1992).

Plate 27.3 Estoril, Portugal
The future development of beach fronts, such as this one in Portugal, will need to consider new ways of attracting visitors in a highly competitive market.

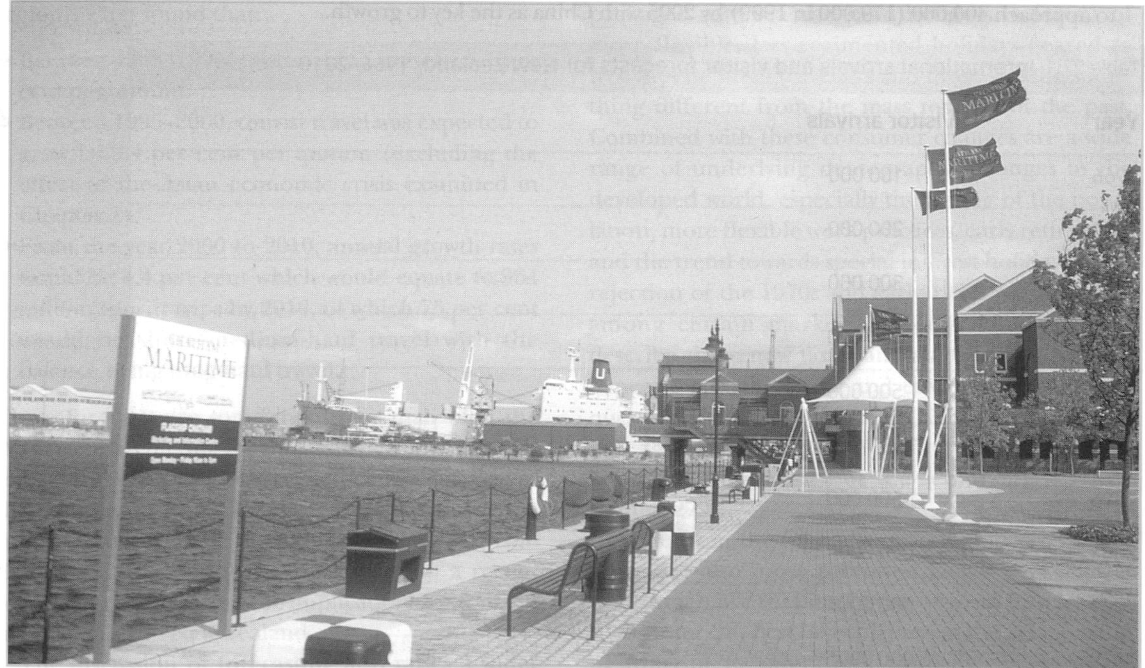

Plate 27.4 Chatham Dock waterfront development, Kent, UK
The continued redevelopment of waterfront areas highlights the continued popularity of urban tourism during the 1990s and early part of the new millennium.

Figure 27.1 **The future of tourism**

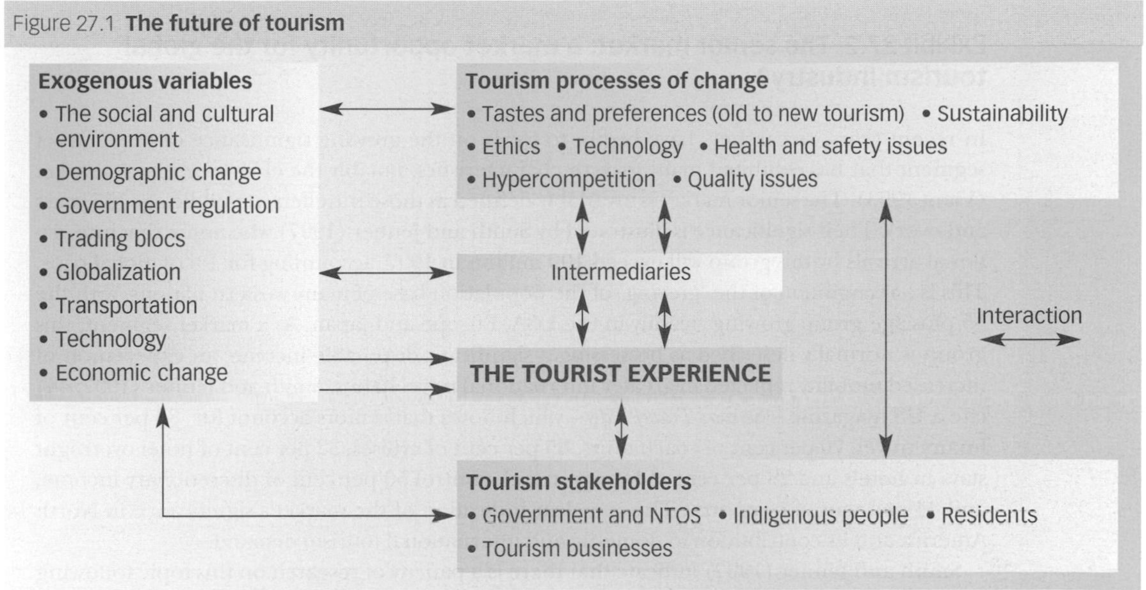

immigration can generate a demand for tourism, particularly for the purpose of visiting friends and relatives (hereafter VFR) (King 1994; King and Gamage 1994). Such studies argue that many forms of migration generate tourism flows, in particular through the geographical extension of friendship and kinship networks. The migrants themselves may travel back to their country of origin for VFR or other purposes. Moreover, the migrants to a new country may be followed by their friends and relatives who choose to visit them in their new country. These flows of tourism are very much structured by the life course of migration, with each round of migration creating a new spatial arrangement of friendship and kinship networks. The extent to which these are activated depends both on the particular characteristics of those networks, such as their intensity, reciprocity and utilization of different forms of sustaining contacts and the particularities of place. Such changes can also be related to changing lifestyles in both developed and undeveloped countries. For example, these are greater levels of prosperity among a wider range of the population and new social trends such as later marriages, couples deferring having children and the greater role of women in travel and role of the senior travellers. All of these factors directly affect patterns of tourism combined with the greater levels of discretionary spending among these groups on tourism.

Political changes

Governments directly affect the pattern of travel and can constrain and facilitate travel depending on the policies, activities and climate they promote for their citizens and visitors. In the 1990s the opening up of Eastern Europe dramatically altered the pattern of travel in Europe, especially the demand for cultural tourism in Eastern European destinations as improved infrastructure and opportunities for travel have created a host of new urban tourist destinations. No one in the early 1980s could have forecast these changes and it illustrates how rapid change can be in tourism where political forces change. Conversely, destinations emerging from political turmoil such as Vietnam, South Africa and Cambodia can also provide new opportunities for tourism. For example, in the case of Cambodia, estimates of tourism growth that increases of 35 per cent per annum in 2001–2002 could happen, based on the following factors:

- Continued growth at the Angkor Wat temple complex, one of the world's major cultural sites.
- Benefiting from regional tourism growth in adjacent destinations (e.g. Thailand and Vietnam) as the recovery in South-east Asian tourism continues in 2000 and beyond.
- Political stability in Cambodia.

Exhibit 27.2 **The senior market: a market opportunity for the global tourism industry?**

In recent years, researchers have begun to focus on the growing significance of one market segment that has exhibited many growth characteristics, notably the elderly or senior market (Viant 1993). The senior market is invariably defined as those travellers in middle age (55 years and over). Their significance is illustrated by Smith and Jenner (1997) who argue that international arrivals by this group will exceed 100 million in 1997, accounting for 1:6 of global trips. This is a recognition of the 'greying' of the population base of many western nations, with the 55 plus age group growing steadily in the USA, Europe and Japan. As a market segment, this group is normally described as possessing a significant disposable income, an expectation of increased mobility reflected in greater international travel habits. Smith and Jenner (1997: 44) cite a US magazine – *Seniors Travel Tips* – which notes that seniors account for '80 per cent of luxury travel, 70 per cent of coach tours, 65 per cent of cruises, 32 per cent of hotel overnight stays in hotels and 28 per cent of foreign travel, control 50 per cent of discretionary income, and 44 per cent of passports'. This is a clear indication of the market's significance in North America and its contribution to domestic and international tourism demand.

Smith and Jenner (1997) indicate that there is a paucity of research on this topic following a series of *ad hoc* reports by the European Travel Data Centre and Aviation and Tourism Consultancy report on the subject in 1992. WTO do not collate any comprehensive data on this market, which means researchers have to look to other sources and in some cases make estimates of demand. While Smith and Jenner (1997) debate the semantics of what is a senior traveller, they provide a useful overview of the senior population by main tourism generating countries (Table 27.2). This highlights the volume and variable proportion of the senior population in each country (see Smith and Jenner 1997 for individual profiles of the senior travel market by country). On the basis of estimates derived from their research, Smith and Jenner (1997) consider that:

- On average the senior population comprises 25 per cent of the population in most countries, with Germany, Italy, France, the UK and Spain with the largest population in this age group in the EU.
- The older people become, the less inclined they are to travel. For example, in the EU, the senior market (aged 55–59 years) made 2.4 domestic trips a year and 0.8 international trips on average. By age 75, the number of domestic trips drops to 1.3 domestic and 0.5 international trips.
- In 1993, there were an estimated 49 million senior arrivals in the EU, many of which were intra-regional and by 1996 this had risen to 60 million trips.
- The senior market is far less seasonal than other tourism markets, given its flexibility to travel in the non-peak period.
- Almost one third of senior trips made by the senior market in Europe were by air and they display a predisposition towards other land-based forms of transport (e.g. coach travel) which they perceive to be safe.

A range of specialist senior travel organizations exist which nurture such travellers (e.g. the Saga group in the UK) while outbound North American educational tours have also seen significant growth in recent years (e.g. the Elderhost group). Smith and Jenner (1997) rightly point to the future growth prospects of this market, expecting a 30 per cent growth in the EU to 83 million arrivals by the year 2000. On a global scale, they forecast a growth to 136 million arrivals in the year 2000.

Table 27.2 **Senior population aged 55 or over for main tourism generating countries, 1997**

Country	Total population ('000)	Population 55+ ('000)	Senior population (% share)
Austria	8 054	2 101	26.1
Belgium	10 204	2,725	26.7
Denmark	5 269	1 349	25.6
Finland	5 109	1 254	24.5
France	58 470	14 678	25.1
Germany	84 068	23 846	28.4
Greece	10 583	2 988	28.2
Ireland	3 556	695	19.5
Italy	57 534	16 559	28.8
Luxembourg	422	104	24.6
Netherlands	15 653	3 603	23.0
Portugal	9 868	2 535	25.7
Spain	39 244	10 257	26.1
Sweden	8 946	2 436	27.2
UK	58 610	14 971	25.5
USA	267 955	55 913	20.9
Japan	125 717	35 221	80.0
Mexico	97 563	9 043	9.3
Taiwan	21 656	3 288	15.2
Saudi Arabia	20 088	1 331	6.6

(Source: US Bureau of the Census, International Data Base, cited in Smith and Jenner 1997: 47)

- Investment in airport upgrading funded by the World Bank, Asian Development Bank and other donors) as well as complementary investment in the road and power supply (see Hall and Page 2000 for more detail).

In addition, the impact of new trading blocs such as NAFTA (the North American Free Trade Agreement) may contribute to a greater harmonization of travel regulations to ease the flow of travel in these new free trade areas. One also needs to recognize that the state is an agent of economic development in many countries where the secondary sector (e.g. traditional manufacturing activities) declined and a greater emphasis was placed on the facilitation of tourism. One of the consequences of such action is that governments need to find new tools to measure the impact and effect of tourism on the national economy and on employment generation. This is being reflected in the growing sophistication in the measurement of tourism by governments using tools such as the tourism satellite account in the 1990s. This illustrates how governments are moving towards realizing the real value of tourism to the economy and thereby promoting tourism as a national economic activity (see Exhibit 27.3).

Technological change

Virtual reality has been heralded as bringing about the major changes to tourism, by potentially replacing the pursuit of the authentic tourism experience.

Exhibit 27.3 **The tourism satellite account in New Zealand**

In June 1999, the Department of Statistics released its findings from developing a pilot tourism satellite account (TSA) using 1995 data. The TSA, developed in line with OECD and WTO guidelines, provides a wide range of economic data related to tourism by identifying the impact of tourism from the national accounts and other data sources. The findings enable one to identify a number of features including:

- The direct impact of tourism on GDP.
- Tourism expenditure as a percentage of GDP.
- Direct employment as a percentage of total employment.
- International travel expenditure as a percentage of total travel expenditure.
- Domestic personal travel expenditure as a percentage of total travel expenditure.
- Domestic business and government travel expenditure as a percentage of total travel expenditure.

Other features such as the indirect tourism value added can also be quantified. Table 27.3 summarizes the principal findings from the TSA for 1995, highlighting the NZ$4.3 bn generated by international visitors and NZ$4.8 bn derived from domestic tourism demand in New Zealand. For the year ended March 1995, total tourism expenditure in New Zealand totalled NZ$9.1 bn which highlights the substantial contribution the sector made to the national economy. Tables 27.3 and 27.3a also examine the direct value that tourism adds to GDP, which measures the direct value added by the sellers of products to tourists. Not only does this permit cross-industry comparisons that highlight the contribution other industries make to GDP, but it also illustrates the significance of the diverse range of service sector activities which contribute to tourism. As a result of the TSA, tourism employment in New Zealand is estimated to comprise 58,000 full-time equivalents (FTEs) directly employed in tourism activities and a further 60,000 FTEs indirectly engaged in tourism-related employment. The majority of the those employed in tourism work for 16,000 tourism-related small businesses complemented by major employers such as the airlines and the airports.

Table 27.3 **Direct value added resulting from tourism, 1995**

($ million)

	Characteristic tourism industries							All non-tourism industries	Total industries
	Retail trade	Accommodation, cafés and restaurants	Road passenger transport	Services allied to transport	Rail and water transport	Air transport	Amusement and recreation services		
Industry total value added	4 850	1 983	277	919	887	1 192	1 280	68 584	79 973
Industry tourism ratio	0.05	0.40	0.39	0.36	0.07	0.77	0.11	0.00	
Tourism's direct contribution to GDP	258	784	108	334	61	918	129	348	2 939
Equivalent to:									
Tourism gross output	468	1 930	196	578	113	2 422	338	576	6 621
Less tourism intermediate consumption	210	1 146	88	244	53	1 505	209	228	3 682
Total New Zealand GDP									86 577[3]
Proportion of tourism GDP to total New Zealand GDP									3.39
Components of tourism GDP									
Tourism compensation of employees	149	398	74	130	35	437	53	113	1 389
Tourism consumption of fixed capital	19	68	21	82	7	125	14	31	366
Tourism operating surplus	85	289	8	112	17	342	50	178	1 080
Tourism indirect taxes	8	29	8	9	2	13	13	27	109
Less: tourism subsidies	2	1	2	0	0	0	0	0	5

Note:
1. Totals may not add up due to rounding
2. The rail and water transport industries have been combined for confidentiality reasons.
3. Total 1995 GDP of $86,577 million differs from the total value added of all industries ($79,973 million) because it also includes GST on production, import duties and other indirect taxes.

(Source: Department of Statistics)

Table 27.3A **Tourism expenditure in New Zealand, 1995**

	$ million				
	Domestic demand				
	Business demand	**Government demand**	**Household demand**	**International visitors' demand**	**Total tourism demand**
Demand for: characteristic tourism commodities	1 060	180	1 868	2 862	5 970
Including:					
Food servicing services	72	18	258	383	731
Takings from accommodation	127	34	331	444	936
Air passenger transport	504	98	503	1 306	2 411
Amusement and recreation	16	2	221	163	402
Tourism-related commodities	24	13	324	259	619
Including:					
Retailers' margin on alcohol	0	0	8	7	15
Retailers' margin on gifts, souvenirs, books	0	0	34	89	123
Short-distance bus passenger transport	0	0	2	2	4
Hairdressing, dry cleaning, laundry services	0	0	11	8	19
Total expenditure by type of tourist	**1 084**	**193**	**2 192**	**3 121**	**6 589**
Indirect tourism demand from margin commodities	9	2	953	706	1,670
GST paid on purchases by tourists	0	0	371	478	850
Total expenditure by type of tourist	**1 093**	**195**	**3 516**	**4 305**	**9 109**

Note:
1. Not all characteristic tourism commodities or tourism-related commodities are shown.
2. Purchases of retail goods by tourists are broken up into two components. The cost to the retailer of purchasing goods is recorded as indirect demand and the retail margin (or difference between the retailer's selling price and purchase price of goods) is included in tourism-related commodities.

(Source: Department of Statistics)

While there are varied arguments about whether it will have an impact, with the increasing role of technology in the everyday lives of people, it is unlikely to remove the pursuit of 'getting away' to relax in a different environment and place. In terms of technology, one of the principal changes occurring globally is the continued growth of artificial environments for tourism and leisure activity. This is reflected in the global theme park industry which has grown to a US $11bn a year business, with an estimated 119 major theme parks spread across the world. These parks received in excess of 300 million visits in 1996, many attracting over one million visitors each a year. This is complemented by a large array of parks which attract less than a million visitors a year. The visits per capita to theme parks varies from 0.6 in the USA and Japan to 0.5 in Australia to 0.23 in Europe. These statistics illustrate the global impact of theme parks which have attracted a great deal of debate amongst researchers on the wider significance to contemporary society.

Probably one of the most incisive and current syntheses of the debates associated with the rise of theme parks in modern society is Hannigan's (1998) *Fantasy City*. Hannigan's analysis considers theme parks as one facet of the development of Fantasy City with its roots in tourism, sports, culture and entertainment which characterize the entertainment function in tourism and leisure. In theoretically informed research, Hannigan's study discusses the rise of the postmodern city. This explains the changing function of many former cities from centres of production to ones based on the tourism and leisure consumption as explained in Chapter 20. Hannigan (1998) identifies six fundamental characteristics of Fantasy City:

- A focus on themocentricity, namely that it is based on a scripted theme.
- The city is aggressively branded, reflected in the place marketing strategies and product range.
- Day and night operation is a common feature, unlike shopping malls which are largely day-time operations.
- Modularization of products, where a diverse array of components are assembled to produce a wide range of experiences.
- Solipsisticity, where the city is economically, culturally and physically detached and isolated from surrounding neighbourhoods in a City of Illusion.
- Postmodernity, where the city is constructed around the technologies of simulation, virtual reality and the thrill of the spectacle. The city draws a major source of inspiration from the Disney model, which is widely imitated. The Disney model merges the concept of the motion picture and amusement park into a fantasy world using technologies which create conditions of hyper-reality.

From the entertainment, leisure and tourism industry perspective, many powerful business interests have recognized these trends as part of the growth sector for the future. Critics of the Fantasy City concept argue that the creation of new landscapes of leisure clone reality. But city authorities have seized upon the urban regenerative effects of Fantasy City for inner cities which lost former productive functions. Even so, theme parks, which are part of the Fantasy City experience, have been criticized as the high technology playgrounds of the middle classes, of little benefit to local communities. What is clear is their role in the tourist experience, where pleasure and thrill seeking in postmodern cities is a traded commodity.

In the tourism industry, technology has revolutionized the organization, management and day-to-day running of businesses. IT has helped to reduce some of the costs of business operations. The introduction of CRSs and GDSs has assisted in the globalization of tourism business activity and the impact of the internet is all-embracing. Many of the larger tourism suppliers and major world airlines have World Wide Web sites and many now customers incentives to book on-line, with discounts to offset the commission normally paid to travel agents. The traditional sales and marketing function is evident apart from the information provision function which many travellers are now coming to expect. The use of technology in this way will certainly continue as tourism suppliers increasingly target the on-line booker, providing the flexibility of booking in your own home.

Changing business practices

What will continue to characterize the tourism industry is the pace and scale of change, with globalization and increased competition the buzz words of the new millennium. The growing trend towards increased efficiency in the tourism industry worldwide has led to the continued expansion of multinational chains providing services in many countries. The hotel industry is a good example of this. The many advantages of such concentration in the different tourism sectors are associated with economies of scale, the ability to resource promotional campaigns and a greater brand awareness using modern marketing techniques such as television, direct mailing and billboards. For these organizations, harnessing the power of the new GDSs, combined with a greater control over the distribution channel will not only improve their market share but also help to reduce seasonality problems. The problem this can cause in less developed countries is a loss of control over their tourism industry with distant decision-makers in the host country of the multinational corporation effectively determining the type of tourist and tourism they wish to promote for their hotel or operation. However, there are also more profound changes in the business environment. Page (1999) examines the concept of hyper-competition, particularly in the international airline industry.

Hyper-competition

Within the global marketplace, tourism providers are constantly striving to improve their business performance. This has to be set in the context of wider changes in the operating environment of sectors such as the airline industry which has confronted a deregulated environment, with state controls lifted to encourage competition. This has seen the role of traditional state airlines, which previously had an oligopolistic position, challenged by new entrants and competitors. D'Aveni (1998) characterized hyper-competition in this sector of the tourism industry in terms of:

- Rapid product innovation.
- Aggressive competition.
- Shorter product life-cycles.
- Businesses experimenting with meeting customers' needs.
- The rising importance of business alliances.
- The destruction of norms and rules of national oligopolies.

D'Aveni (1998) identified four processes which are contributing to the hyper-competition. These are:

- Customers require improved quality at lower prices. One area airlines have responded to is through the improvement of in-flight catering to change the perception of quality enhancements.
- Rapid technological change, enhanced through the use of IT.
- The expansion of very aggressive companies which are willing to enter markets for a number of years with a loss leader product with a view to destroying the competition so that they will harness the market in the long term.
- Government barriers towards competition are being progressively removed throughout the world, with some markets still holding back on deregulation in the aviation sector (see Table 27.4 to examine the extent to which airlines have been privatized in Asia–Pacific). Asia–Pacific is one of the last major aviation markets still to see greater competition and privatization of the state interest in aviation, although since 1995, there are examples of foreign investment, alliances and co-operation in the airline industry in Asia–Pacific to contribute to a greater liberalization in the region.

The principal changes which hyper-competition induce are related to the way the competitors enter the marketplace and how they disrupt the existing business. They do this in a number of ways:

- By redefining the product market, by shifting the benchmark on quality, by offering more at a lower price. The strategy adopted by easyJet in the UK typifies this strategy with the attempt to introduce low-cost air travel in line with other players such as Ryanair to challenge the virtual cartel on trunk route air travel of British Airways (BA), British Midland and KLM UK.
- By modifying the industry's purpose and focus by bundling and splitting industries. This can be seen in BA's response to easyJet by establishing a low-cost airline – GoEasy with a lower cost of operation from London Stansted airport.With lower landing fees and cost structures than BA's Heathrow and Gatwick operations, it has established a potential loss leader to compete head on with easyJet.
- By disrupting the supply chain by redefining the knowledge and know-how needed to deliver the product to the customer.

Table 27.4 **Airline privatization in the Asia–Pacific region, 1985–1995**

Airline	Country	Pattern of ownership			
		1985		1995	
		Private	Public	Private	Public
American Airlines	USA	X		X	
Aeromexico	Mexico		X	X	
Aero Peru	Peru		X		20%
Air Canada	Canada		X	X	
Air China	China		X		100%
Air Lanka	Sri Lanka		X		100%
Air New Zealand	New Zealand		X	X	
Air Niugini	Papua New Guinea		X		100%
Air Pacific	Fiji		X		79.6%
Air India	India		X		100%
Air Nippon Airways	Japan	X		X	
Ansett Australia	Australia	X		X	
Avianco	Colombia	X		X	
Biman Bangladesh	Bangladesh		X		100%
Canadian Air International	Canada	X		X	
Cathay Pacific Airways	Hong Kong	X		X	
China Airways	Taiwan	X		X	
Continental Airways	USA	X		X	
Delta Airlines	USA	X		X	
Garuda	Indonesia		X		100%

Table 27.4 **cont.**

Airline	Country	Pattern of ownership			
		1985		1995	
		Private	Public	Private	Public
HAL (Hawaiian)	USA	X		X	
Indian Airlines	India		X		100%
Japan Air Systems	Japan	X		X	
Japan Airlines	Japan		X	X	
Korean Air	South Korea	X		X	
Ladeco	Chile	X		X	
Lan Chile	Chile			X	X
Malaysia Airlines	Malaysia		X		30%
Merpati	Indonesia		X		30%
Mexicana	Mexico		X		35%
Northwest Airlines	USA	X		X	
Pakistan International	Pakistan		X		57.4%
Philippine Airlines	Philippines		X		33%
Qantas	Australia		X		75%
Royal Brunei	Brunei		X		100%
Saeta Air Ecuador	Ecuador	X		X	
Singapore Airlines	Singapore		X		54%
Thai International	Thailand		X		93.7%
United Airlines	USA	X		X	
Vietnam Airlines	Vietnam		X		100%

(Source: Modified from Forsyth 1997, cited in Page 1999: 76)

- By harnessing global resources from alliances and partners to compete with non-aligned business. This is very evident in the international airline industry now that the two major global alliances (the BA–Qantas One World Alliance and the Star Alliance which is a combination of Air New Zealand, Ansett Australia, United, Lufthansa, Thai Airways International, SAS, Varig and Air Canada offering services to over 700 destinations in 111 countries) have a greater degree of control over service provision.

The implications of globalization, hyper-competition and technological change for the tourism sector are that the role of the consumer is much more important especially in relation to service quality. Service quality will continue to be a major component of the future shape of tourism provision which leads on to the next major trend – health and safety issues in tourism.

Tourist health and safety issues

The term 'tourist safety' equates to concerns for the well-being, welfare and wider safety of the visitor not only while travelling from the origin area to the destination area but, particularly, the way in which their personal safety is affected by their activities. If one of the principal objectives of the tourism industry is to facilitate positive experiences, then ensuring that the tourists' well-being is assured must surely be a major objective. There is accumulating evidence that adverse experiences (e.g. accidents, injuries and health problems associated with visiting unfamiliar environments – see Figure 27.2) may pose a major problem for the tourism industry, particularly given its image as a business selling positive holiday experiences to improve one's quality of life (Clift and Page 1996). In extreme

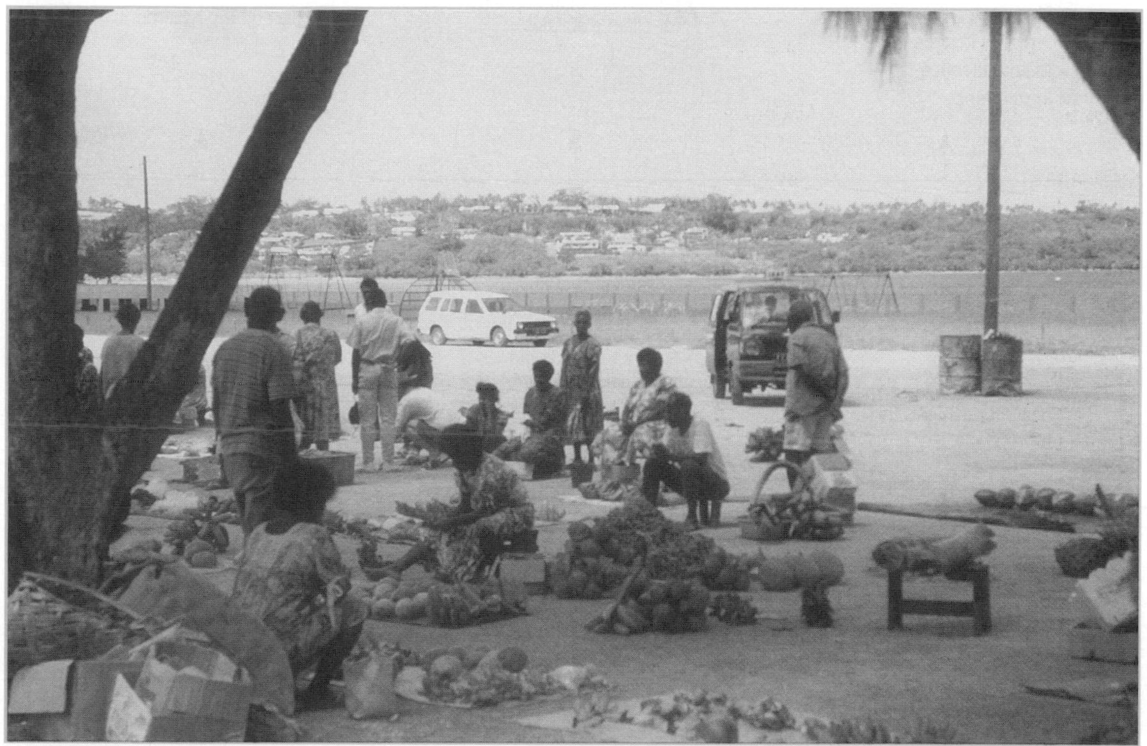

Plate 27.5 Market scene, Vanuatu

Tourists also use the facilities provided for local residents and their impact is often under-estimated.

Figure 27.2 **Risk factors for adventure tourism accidents**

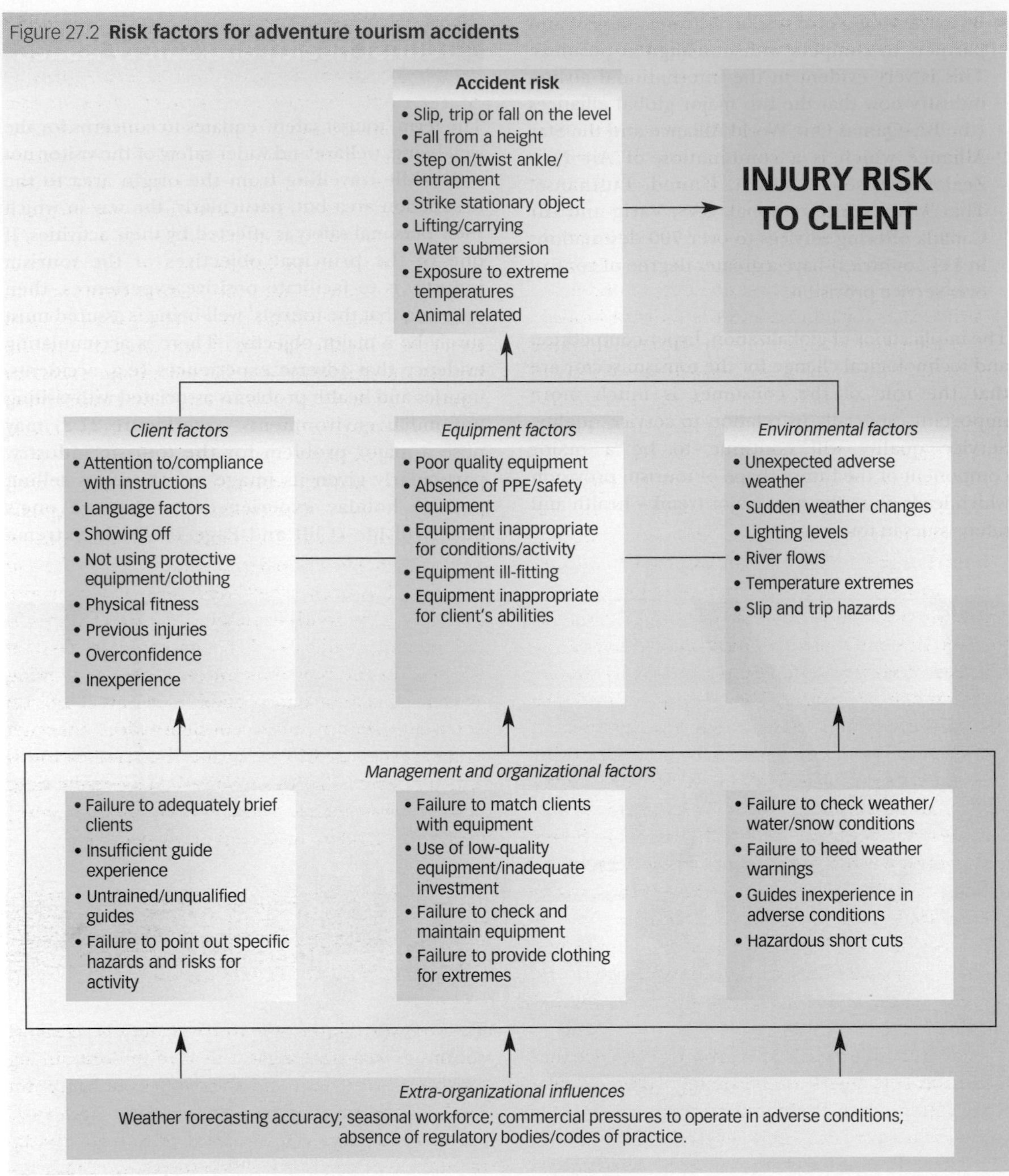

Accident risk
• Slip, trip or fall on the level
• Fall from a height
• Step on/twist ankle/ entrapment
• Strike stationary object
• Lifting/carrying
• Water submersion
• Exposure to extreme temperatures
• Animal related
INJURY RISK TO CLIENT
Client factors
• Attention to/compliance with instructions
• Language factors
• Showing off
• Not using protective equipment/clothing
• Physical fitness
• Previous injuries
• Overconfidence
• Inexperience
Equipment factors
• Poor quality equipment
• Absence of PPE/safety equipment
• Equipment inappropriate for conditions/activity
• Equipment ill-fitting
• Equipment inappropriate for client's abilities
Environmental factors
• Unexpected adverse weather
• Sudden weather changes
• Lighting levels
• River flows
• Temperature extremes
• Slip and trip hazards
Management and organizational factors
• Failure to adequately brief clients
• Insufficient guide experience
• Untrained/unqualified guides
• Failure to point out specific hazards and risks for activity
• Failure to match clients with equipment
• Use of low-quality equipment/inadequate investment
• Failure to check and maintain equipment
• Failure to provide clothing for extremes
• Failure to check weather/ water/snow conditions
• Failure to heed weather warnings
• Guides inexperience in adverse conditions
• Hazardous short cuts
Extra-organizational influences
Weather forecasting accuracy; seasonal workforce; commercial pressures to operate in adverse conditions; absence of regulatory bodies/codes of practice.

(Source: Bentley 1999)

cases, public perception of the destination may affect the volume of tourist visits, where tourists report a high incidence of health problems during their visit.

Ensuring tourist well-being is safeguarded in destinations, where tourist activities involve a high degree of risk, requires management where the excitement and challenge posed by risk behaviours are balanced with appropriate safety measures and management systems. Although a number of studies have examined the media impact and effect of crime and security issues for tourists and the tourism industry (e.g. Pizam and Mansfeld 1996), current thinking and research efforts have not grasped the concept of tourist well-being, preferring to focus on individual dimensions of safety that impact on tourists' experiences (e.g. crime, health and food safety).

Tourist accidents can have a major impact on tourism (World Tourism Organization, 1996). This is reflected in the adventure tourism industry. Within Europe, adventure tourism has been estimated to be growing at 15 per cent per annum. Adventure tourism is a rapidly expanding sector of the New Zealand tourism industry and an increasing number of visitors seek adventure activity during their stay in New Zealand. There is growing evidence that adventure and recreational injuries make a significant contribution to overseas visitor morbidity and mortality in New Zealand (Page and Meyer 1996). Moreover, some New Zealand adventure activities, notably white water rafting, scenic flights and mountain recreation, appear to present an unacceptably high risk of serious and fatal injury to clients. Table 27.5 highlights the trends in overseas visitor accident rates in New Zealand using hospital discharge records for the period 1982–1996 and illustrates some of the major causes of accidents and injuries.

Aside from injuries, there is growing evidence that tourists as consumers are becoming willing to take legal action when their tourism experience falls below minimum acceptable levels. In Europe, the EU Directive on Package Travel encourages consumers to pursue accurate representation of the product they buy and holds operators responsible. There are even legal firms now specializing in taking action against tour operators on the behalf of clients where their holiday experience was totally unacceptable, due to service breakdowns. For the tourism industry, health and safety issues are an area which will assume a greater significance as the consumer becomes more litigious.

Linked to these changes there is also a growing concern with ethical business practises in tourism which is reflected in the World Tourism Organization's (1999) development of a *Global Code of Ethics for Tourism* which is wide ranging, as Table 27.6 shows. This is a wider recognition of the understanding and complexity for tourism as an activity which has wide-ranging implications for the tourist, the tourism employee, countries and the natural environment. Linked to these concerns are the legal and moral concerns with the spread of sex tourism and the impact on children, as reflected in the excellent advocacy work of the agency End Child Prostitution and Trafficking (EPCAT). This has led the WTO and other non-government agencies such as ECPAT to establish a Child Prostitution and Tourism Watch following the Stockholm Congress against Commercial Sexual Exploitation of Children in August 1996. The campaign is supported by WTO and a website has been established (http://www.world-tourism.org/sextouri/intro.htm) to prevent, uncover, isolate and eradicate this unacceptable face of tourism. In the new millennium, there is growing evidence that these unacceptable elements of tourism are now gaining public condemnation although agencies such as ECPAT argue that eradication is difficult because highly organized paeodophile rings simply relocate their activities from country to country, preying on children in the less developed world.

Sustainability and the environment

The continued interest in tourism and sustainability continues to attract a great deal of interest among tourists, government and the tourism industry. Yet implementing strategies for sustainable tourism and monitoring their effectiveness remains a fundamental stumbling block which the tourism industry has to overcome. For example, consider the reality of countries in South Asia where rapid population growth, images of rural poverty and urbanization exist alongside the government's pursuit of tourism development to gain much needed foreign currency to assist with development objectives. Whilst existing regional surveys of the region and

Table 27.5 **Overseas visitor accidents in New Zealand using hospital discharge records, 1982–1996**

Event group	n	(%)	Adventure tourism activities*	n	(%)	(%) all cases
Motor vehicle traffic	1 604	27.4				
Motor vehicle non-traffic	59	1.0	Quad/farm bikes	18	30.5	0.3
Pedal cycle	165	2.8	*Road cycling*	95	57.6	
			Mountain biking	13	7.9	0.2
			Other/unclassified	57	34.5	
Animal related	174	3.0	*Horse (fell from)*	153	87.9	2.6
			Horse (kicked by)	18	10.3	0.3
			Bull (rodeo)	3	1.8	0.05
Watercraft related	320	5.5	White water raft	46	14.5	0.8
			Jet boat	21	6.6	0.4
			Kayak/canoe	3	1.0	0.05
			Diving	3	1.0	0.05
			Crew/fishing boat	115	36.0	
			Unspecified boat/ship	132	41.6	
Aviation related	100	1.7	*Parapenting/gliding*	27	27.0	0.5
			Skydiving	23	23.0	0.4
			Glider/unpowered	5	5.0	0.08
			Hang glider	4	4.0	0.06
			Crew/work related	4	4.0	
			Unspecified aircraft	24	24.0	
			Helicopter	13	13.0	
Falls from a height/ falls on the same level	2 027	34.6	Skiing/snowboarding	344	17.0	5.9
			Mountaineering/tramping	260	12.9	4.4
			Luge	24	1.1	0.4
			Flying fox	18	1.0	0.3
			Parapenting	9	0.4	0.2
			White water rafting	5	0.2	0.08
			Playground activity	40	2.0	
			Swimming pool/spa	27	1.3	
Struck by/strike against object or person	325	5.5	Skiing/snowboarding	20	6.2	0.3
			Mountaineering/tramping	10	3.1	0.2
			Rugby/other sports	108	33.2	
Other (non-recreational events)	1 089	18.6				
Total	**5 863**	**100**	***Total estimated adventure tourism***	**1 027**		**17.5**

Adventure tourism activities determined from content analysis of 'one-line' descriptions of accident circumstances provided in narrative fields. Adventure tourism activities shown in italics.

(Source: Bentley, Meyer, Page and Chalmers 2001)

Table 27.6 **A Global Code of Ethics for Tourism**

The World Tourism Organization developed a Code of Ethics for Tourism in conjunction with its members, following the initiative to draft a code in 1997. This is a recognition for the need to enshrine many of the principles of global action on the environment, the rights of tourists and workers considering global legislation from other bodies and outcomes such as Agenda 21. The full text of the Code can be viewed at:

http//www.world-tourism.org/pressrel/CODEOFE.htm

The basic principles inherent in the Code are:

- Tourism's contribution to mutual understanding and respect between peoples and societies
- Tourism as a vehicle for individual and collective fulfilment
- Tourism as a factor of sustainable development
- Tourism as a user of the cultural heritage of mankind and contributor to its enhancement
- Tourism as a beneficial activity for host countries and communities
- Obligations of stakeholders in tourism development
- Rights to tourism
- Liberty of tourist movements
- Rights of the workers and entrepreneurs in the tourism industry
- Implementation of the principles of the Global Code of Ethics for Tourism

(Source: World Tourism Organisation 1999)

the respective countries such as India, Pakistan and Bangladesh highlight the range of development problems facing the respective governments and the policies adopted to deal with them, urbanization is a major problem associated with each country and poses major concerns for the sustainability of tourism in these environments. For example, in 1995 the region had five of the world's top 25 largest cities: Bombay (15.1 million population); Calcutta (11.7 million population); Delhi (9.9 million population); Karachi (9.9 million population) and Dhaka (7.8 million population). Rapid urbanization is adding a new series of development problems for South Asia that also impact upon tourism. These are epitomized by Alauddin and Tisdell (1998: 192) as:

> A feature of South Asian cities is that air pollution is well in excess of health standards and domestic and industrial effluents are released to [sic] waterways with little or no treatment. Water quality is therefore very poor and a threat to human health and aquatic life. In most cases there are vast squatter settlements and these are often located in areas experiencing the most environmental problems. Therefore, the poor in cities not only have very low incomes, but also live in the worst environmental conditions, often on land that no one wants because of the environmental hazards associated with it.

No tourist can fail to observe these problems particularly as Battacharya (1995) observes in the case of Calcutta where the Hindu Survey of the Environment report found that:

> The city of Calcutta is suffering from serious environmental disorder. Collapsing sewer lines, stagnant canals, obsolete pumping stations, waterlogging, heaps of garbage, increasing noise, air and water pollution, rise in malaria and gastro-enteric diseases and shrinking wetlands are just a few of the problems plaguing the city. (Battacharya 1995: 146, cited in Alauddin and Tisdell 1998)

Not only does this highlight potential tourist health problems for visitors but also raises many moral and ethical issues for visitors when confronted with images of poverty and deprivation when their purpose of visiting may be for leisure and the consumption of pleasure. In the case of Pakistan, Mumtaz and Mitha (1996) note the link between poverty and environmental destruction where the National Conservation Strategy highlighted many of the existing problems such as loss of biodiversity and need to involve local people in any measures designed to encourage sustainable development which can reduce the degradation impacts of human activity on a fragile environment. In fact Islam (1996) found that 50 per cent of the population of Dhaka is living below the poverty line, of whom 30 per cent are in extreme poverty and the majority live in slum dwellings which house approximately three million people, where many of the basic services (e.g. water and sanitation) do not exist. In these contexts, the rhetoric and language of sustainable tourism development is almost meaningless and day-to-day life and survival of the population is juxtaposed alongside tourism activities. Therefore, these examples from South Asia highlight the need for a greater degree of realism in the tourism and sustainability debate, particularly if tourism is to be harnessed to help improve the well-being of the people affected by it.

Managing change in tourism

Managing change in a fast moving business sector such as tourism will continue to pose enormous challenges for tourism businesses in the twenty-first century. For this reason, it is useful to consider what managing tourism requires of managers and the skills and challenges they face. In a purely abstract academic context, management is concerned with the ability of individuals to conduct, control, take charge of or manipulate the world to achieve a desired outcome. In a practical business setting, management occurs in the context of a formal environment – the organization (Handy 1989). Within these organizations (albeit small tourism businesses through to multinational enterprises), people are among the elements which are managed. As a result Inkson and Dolb (1995: 6) define management as 'getting things done in organisations through other people'. In a business context, organizations exist as a complex interaction of people, goals and money to create and distribute the goods and services people and other businesses consume or require.

Tourism organizations are characterized by their ability to work towards a set of common objectives (e.g. the sale of holidays to tourists for a profit). To achieve their objectives, organizations are often organized into specialized groupings to achieve particular functions (e.g. sales, human resource management, accounts and finance) as departments. In addition, a hierarchy usually exists where the organization is horizontally divided into different levels of authority and status and a manager often occupies a position in a particular department or division at a specific point in the hierarchy. The goals of tourism managers within organizations are usually seen as profit driven, but as the following list suggests, the goals are more diverse:

- *Profitability*, which can be achieved through higher output, better service, attracting new customers and by cost minimization.
- *In the public sector*, other goals (e.g. co-ordination, liaison, raising public awareness and undertaking activities for the wider public good) dominate the agenda in organizations. Yet in many government departments in developed countries, private sector profit-driven motives and greater accountability for the spending of public funds now features high on the agenda.
- *Efficiency*, to reduce expenditure and inputs to a minimum to achieve more cost-effective outputs.
- *Effectiveness*, achieving the desired outcome and this is not necessarily a profit-driven motive.

Yet in practical terms, the main tasks of managers are based on the management process which is how to achieve these goals. Whilst management theorists differ in the emphasis they place on different aspects of the management process, there are four commonly agreed set of tasks. McLennan *et al.* (1987) describe these as:

- *Planning*, so that goals are set out and the means of achieving the goals are recognized.
- *Organizing*, whereby the work functions are broken down into a series of tasks and linked to some form of structure. These tasks then have to be assigned to individuals.
- *Leading*, which is the method of motivating and influencing staff so that they perform their tasks effectively. This is essential if organizational goals are to be achieved.
- *Controlling*, which is the method by which information is gathered about what has to be done.

Therefore, managing tourism requires a comparison of the information with the organizational goals and if necessary, taking action to correct any deviations from the overall goals. Fundamental to the management process in tourism organizations is the need for managers to make decisions. This is a constant, on-going process. To make decisions, managers often have to balance two fundamental issues. On the one hand, the ability to use technical skills within their own particular area. On the other is the need to relate to people and to use 'human skills' to interact and manage people within the organization, and clients, suppliers and other people external to the organization. Managers also need these skills to communicate effectively to motivate and lead others. There is also a third set of skills which managers need to possess. These are cognitive and conceptual skills. Cognitive skills are those which enable managers to formulate solutions to problems. In contrast, conceptual skills are those which allow them to take a broader view, often seen as 'being able to see the wood for the trees', whereby the manager can understand the organization's activities, the inter-relationships and goals to develop an appropriate strategic response (Inkson and Kolb 1995).

What is critical is the tourism manager's ability to be adaptable and flexible to change, particularly in fast moving areas such as tourism. Change is a modern-day feature of management and any manager needs to be aware of and able to respond to changes in the organizational environment. For example, general changes in society such as the decision of a new ruling political party to deregulate the economy have a bearing on the operation of organizations. More specific factors can also influence the organizational environment including:

- *Socio-cultural factors*, which include the behaviour, beliefs and norms of the population in a specific area.
- *Demographic factors*, which are related to the changing composition of the population (e.g. birth rates, mortality rates and the growing burden of dependency where the increasing number of ageing population will have to be supported by a declining number of economically active people in the workforce).
- *Economic factors*, which include the type of capitalism at work in a given country and the degree of state control of business. The economic system is also important since it may have a bearing on the level of prosperity and factors which influence the system's ability to produce, distribute and consume wealth.
- *Political and legal factors* that are the framework in which organizations must work (e.g. laws and practices).
- *Technological factors*, where advances in technology can be used to create products more efficiently. The use of information technology and its application to business practices is a case in point.
- *Competitive factors*, which illustrate that businesses operate in markets and other producers may seek to offer superior services or products at a lower price. Businesses also compete for finance, sources of labour and other resources.
- *International factors*, where businesses operate in a global environment and factors operating in other countries may impact on the local business environment.
- *Change and uncertainty* are unpredictable in free market economies and managers have to ensure that organizations can adapt while ensuring that survival and prosperity is ensured. Change may be vital for organizations to adapt and grow in new environments and the introduction of information technology is one example where initial resistance within businesses had to be overcome. Increasingly, tourism managers are having to undertake not only the role of managing, but also the dynamic role of 'change agent'. Tourism managers have to understand how systems and organizations work and function to create desirable outcomes. It is the ability to learn to manage in new situations where there are no guidelines or models to follow, which Handy (1989) views as the way people grow, especially in a managerial role.

Conclusion

This chapter has highlighted a range of issues which are relevant for the tourist and the tourism sector in the new millennium since the pace of change and development in tourism is fast. In contrast, planning and developing new areas for tourist activity are a slower process, with the provision of infrastructure such as an airport expansion taking five to ten years before the benefits are realized. This illustrates the need for tourism managers to be realistic about the ability of resorts and destinations to accommodate visitors, with a view to assessing the appropriate carrying capacity. There are no simple solutions to developing tourism in new areas and in redeveloping tourism in areas that are flagging or have lost their sparkle. Understanding global processes of tourism combined with the individual processes affecting tourism in a given area or location are no substitute for planning. Understanding the consumer is essential and monitoring their well-being and what they feel about their tourist experience remains a vital element in the tourism industry understanding its consumers. What is now being regarded as tourism is constantly expanding as new ideas and new trends develop. One of the most researched areas in the 1990s has been the boom in what is construed as ecotourism. This illustrates that the scope and extent of what we call and define as tourism is forever changing and business, entrepreneurs and planners need to adapt accordingly. The new millennium will certainly see a great deal of change in the tourism sector, especially as new transport technology is introduced and impacts upon the continued shrinking of the globe as a place to travel is enhanced by faster travel times. Above all else, anyone working and managing in the tourism industry of the new millennium will need to appreciate the need to implement new human resource policies, ensure employees are well trained and educated as well as able to cope with change. The tourism industry is an exciting sector to work in, even though some of the glamour and glitz associated with images of working on a tropical island may not always be met in reality. For anyone seeking a challenge and a career in a sector changing rapidly, the tourism industry offers a great deal of interesting and varied work. For the industry, promoting this image and creating a positive image of long-term career structures in both the tourism and hospitality sectors is vital to continue to attract high-calibre staff at all levels.

Discussion questions

1. What are the main themes in the chapter?
2. What are the main problems which the authors highlight?
3. Are health problems a significant constraint on tourist behaviour or a normal part of a tourist's expectation of an overseas trip?
4. What do you understand by the term 'tourist health'?
5. How did the plague in India affect the perception of India as a tourist destination?

Internet resources

By going to the weblink at www.thomsonlearning.co.uk students can access the following two studies on the Thomson Learning website. The first study is S. Horner and J. Swarbrooke (1996) *Marketing Tourism, Hospitality and Leisure in Europe* on the future of tourism, hospitality and leisure marketing in Europe and is useful because it provides a wide-ranging review of the factors that need to be considered in the analysis of tourism markets and marketing in the future.

The second study examines a specific issue which is assuming a growing significance in tourism research – health and safety issues and their impact on satisfaction. This study is by S. Clift and S.J. Page (eds) (1996) *Health and the International Tourist* on travel and health which highlights many of the medical issues which confront tourists in their global pursuit of travel opportunities.

References

Alauddin, M. and Tisdell, C. (1998) *The Environment and Economic Development in South Asia: An Overview Concentrating on Bangladesh*, Basingstoke: Macmillan.

Archer, B.H. (1987) 'Demand forecasting and estimation', in J.R.B. Ritchie and C.R. Goeldner (eds) *Travel, Tourism and Hospitality Research*, New York: Wiley: 77–85.

Bentley, T. (1999) 'Model of tourist operator risk factors for accidents', *Personal Communication*, Massey University, Albany, Auckland, New Zealand.

Bentley, T., Page, S.J. and Laird, I. (2000) 'Safety in New Zealand's adventure tourism industry: the client accident experience of adventure tourism operators', *Journal of Travel Medicine*, **7** (5): 239–45.

Bentley, T., Meyer, D., Page, S.J. and Chalmers, D. (2001) 'Recreational tourism injuries among visitors to New Zealand: an exploratory analysis using hospital discharge data', *Tourism Management*, **22**, **7** (5): 239–46.

Bull, A. (1991) *The Economics of Travel and Tourism*, London: Pitman.

Clift, S. and Page, S. J. (eds) (1996) *Health and the International Tourist*, London: Routledge.

D'Aveni, R. (1998) 'Hypercompetition closes in', *Financial Times*, 4 February (Global Business Section).

Edwards, A. and Graham, A. (1997) *International Tourism Forecasts to 2010*, London: Travel and Tourism Intelligence.

Forsyth, T. (1997) 'Environmental responsibility and business regulation: the case of sustainable tourism', *The Geographical Journal*, **163** (3): 270–80.

Hall, C.M. and Page, S.J. (eds) (2000) *Tourism in South and South-East Asia: Issues and Cases*, Oxford: Butterworth-Heinemann.

Hannigan, J. (1998) *Fantasy City: Pleasure and Profit in the Postmodern Metropolis*, London: Routledge.

Handy, C. (1989) *The Age of Unreason*, London: Business Books Ltd.

Inkson, K. and Kolb, D. (1995) *Management: A New Zealand Perspective*, Auckland: Longman Paul.

Islam, N. (1996) 'City study of Dhaka', in J. Stubbs and G. Clarke (eds) *Megacity Management in the AsiaPacific Region, Volume 1*, Manila: Asian Development Bank: 39–94.

Jefferson, A. and Lickorish, L. (1991) *Marketing Tourism: A Practical Guide*, Harlow: Longman.

King, B. (1994) 'What is ethnic tourism? An Australian perspective', *Tourism Management*, **15** (3): 173–76.

King, B. and Gamage, M.A. (1994) 'Measuring the value of the ethnic connection: expatriate travellers from Australia to Sri Lanka', *Journal of Travel Research*, **33** (2): 46–50.

McClennan, R., Inkson, K., Dakin, S., Dewe, P. and Elkin, G. (1987) *People and Enterprises: Human Behaviour in New Zealand Organisations*, Auckland: Rinehart and Winston.

Mumtaz, K. and Mitha, Y. (1996) *Pakistan: Tradition and Change*, Oxford: Oxfam.

Page, S.J. (1999) *Transport and Tourism*, Harlow: Addison Wesley Longman.

Page, S.J. and Meyer, D. (1996) 'Tourist accidents: an exploratory analysis', *Annals of Tourism Research*, **23** (3): 666–90.

Pizam, A. and Mansfeld, Y. (eds) (1996) *Tourism, Crime and International Security Issues*, Chichester: John Wiley and Sons.

Poon, A. (1989) 'Competitive strategies for a new tourism', in C.P. Cooper (ed.) *Progress in Tourism, Recreation and Hospitality Management Volume 4*, London: Belhaven: 91–102.

Smith, C. and Jenner, P. (1997) 'The seniors' travel market', *Travel and Tourism Analyst*, **5**: 43–62.

Viant, A. (1993) 'Enticing the elderly to travel – an exercise in Euro-management', *Tourism Management*, **14** (1): 52–60.

Witt, S.F., Brooke, M.Z. and Buckley, P.J. (1991) *The International Management of Tourism*, London: Unwin Hyman.

Witt, S.F. and Martin, C. (1992) *Modelling and Forecasting Demand in Tourism*, London: Academic Press.

World Tourism Organization (1996) *Tourist Safety and Security: Practical Measures for Destinations*, Madrid: World Tourism Organization.

World Tourism Organization (1999) *Global Code of Ethics for Tourism*, Madrid: World Tourism Organization.

Further reading

Bentley T. and Page, S.J. (2001) 'Scoping the extent of tourist accidents', *Annals of Tourism Research*, **28** (3).

Kang, S. and Page. S.J. (2000). 'Tourism, migration and emigration: travel patterns of Korean-New Zealanders in the 1990s', *Tourism Geographies*, **2** (1): 50–65.

Olsen, M. and Zhao, J. (1997) 'New management practices in the international hotel industry', *Travel and Tourism Analyst*, **1**: 53–73.

World Tourism Organization (1999) *Global Code of Ethics for Tourism*, Madrid: World Tourism Organization.

Subject index

Aboriginal tourism 286
  see also human rights; indigenous tourism
accessibility 351
accommodation 79–80, 133–50
  budget accommodation 145
  characteristics of the accommodation sector 141–2
  classifying the accommodation sector 142–5
  globalization and the accommodation sector 135–6
  non-accommodation hospitality services 147–8
  non-serviced accommodation sector 145–7
  operating performance of the global hotel industry 136–41
  and resort 144
  sector in New Zealand 139–40
  types 135
acculturations 279–81
Achmatowicz, Susan 191–2
activities 77–9, 304–5
  ecotourism 304–5
  skiing/alpine tourism 304
administration of tourism in UK 213
adventure tourism 452–3
agencies and HRM issues in tourism, international perspectives 155–8
Agenda 21 320–2, 375
  global activity 322
  protection of the coastal environment 381
aggregate tourism demand 46
air transport 107–12
  alliances and the passenger volume conundrum 110–12
  BAA 83
  environmental impacts 295
  future changes in air travel 112–13
  oligopoly in 75
  potential for cost reduction 110
  privatization in Asia-Pacific, 1985–1995 449–50
  rise of the low-cost carrier 107–10
  technological advances in 42, 98
  yield management 54, 112
airport luggage loading systems 199
Airtours 91–2
  and finance 174
Alcúdia as ecotouristic community 328
  potential for tourist interest 327
alliances and the passenger volume conundrum 110–12
allocentrics 63
altering visitor behaviour 325
alternative approach to tourism development 393
alternative measures for examining impact of tourism 270
ambience 300
American Express 86
analysis of tourist resources 334
approaches to marketing planning 241–3
  creative infusion 242
  marketing plan development 242–3
  needs analysis 241
  research and analysis 241–2
  strategic positioning 242
  training, implementation, evaluation and adjustment 243
Asian economic development 264
aspects of tourism motivation 60–7
  Dann's perspectives on tourism motivation 62–3
  factors influencing tourist motivation 64–5
  Gilbert's tourism consumer decision process 62
  Maslow's hierarchy of needs 61–2
  Plog's tourist typologies 63–4
  social class and income 66–7
  tourism and work 65–6
Association of British Travel Agents 82, 88
attraction of the coast 369
attractions 117–32
  categorizing attractions 119–20
  cathedrals and churches 123
  country parks 128
  farms 126–8
  the future for tourist attractions 130
  gardens 125–6
  historic houses and monuments 121–2
  industry-based visitor attractions 129
  leisure parks and piers 123–4
  museums and galleries 122–3
  special events 129–30
  steam railways 129
  Swarbrooke's typology of tourist attractions 118
  visitor centres 128
  wildlife attractions 124–5
  workplaces 128–9
attractions and activities 76–9
  activities 77–9
  man-made resources as attractions 77
  natural resources as attractions 76
auto-definition 63

balance of payments 262–3
  impact of tourism on 20
Bank Holidays Act 1871 35
Bhutan's alternative approach 393
Branson, Richard 175
  and risk 184
brief history of coastal tourism 369–71
British Airways 320–1
  conservation programme 321
  environmental impacts and management 321
  environmental policy 320
  investment 83
  one-time monopoly 54
  Tourism for Tomorrow Awards 310, 321
brochures 55
budget accommodation 145
business re-engineering 196
business tourism 93
business travel agents 93
Butler model of resort development 35
Butlin's 40
  all-inclusive concept 144
  domestic holiday destination 41
  see also Club Mediterranée; holiday camp
buyer behaviour 239
buying process 238

Calvia and the future of tourism 374–5
campsites
  top ten in England and Wales, 1939 and 1986 40
Cape Byron Headland Reserve 429
carrying capacity 325–6
  types of 325
cars 98–9
  flexibility 98
categorizing tourist attractions 119–20
categorizing tourist statistics 17
cathedrals and churches 123
Center Parcs 145, 147
  all-inclusive package 246
  enhancement of local environments 306
  environmental policy 320

Chadwick's classification of travellers 15
challenge of sustainability in tourism 311–12
challenges for sustainable tourism 326–8
changes in tourism 4
changing business practices and the future of tourism 447–51
  hyper-competition 448–51
characteristics of the accommodation sector 141–2
characteristics of small and medium-sized enterprises 186
characteristics of tourism services 235
China
  1986–1991 209–10
  1992 to present 210–11
  Chinese cultural values 237
  Chinese population in New Zealand 51–4
  development of tourism in 208–11
  travel patterns of Chinese New Zealanders 49–52
Chinese cultural values 237
Chinese population in New Zealand 51–4
classification of the accommodation sector 142–5
  serviced accommodation 142–5
Club Mediterranée 41
  all-inclusive concept 144, 246
  holidays world-wide 40
  mass tourism 277
  see also Butlin's; holiday camp
coach and bus transport 99
  and opening up of Eastern Europe 101
coastal resort development 372–6
  basic morphology 363
  impact at Dawlish Warren 379–80
  model 372
  pressures 369
coastal and resort tourism 367–84
  attraction of the coast 369
  brief history of coastal tourism 369–71
  and the car 99
  coastal resort development 372–6
  impacts of coastal tourism 376–81
  tourism at the coast 368–9
Cohen's categories of tourist 64
colonialism and neo-colonialism 395–7
  host community issues 397
competition 54, 240
  the Channel Tunnel 54
  perfect competition 74–5
computer reservation systems 187–99
concentrated marketing 238–9
conceptualizing rural tourism 352–5
conceptualizing tourism 11
conflicts 396
conservation 305–6, 428
consortia in the independent hotel sector 143
contestable markets 75
context of rural tourism 354
corporate environmental management 318–19
country parks 128
creative infusion 242
criteria for success in rural tourism 361–2
cruising 103–4
  growth of 104
cycling 101
  promotion of in Mallorca 328

Dann's perspectives on tourism motivation 62–3
Dartmoor National Park Authority 428
day trips 35
Days Inn 145
defining sustainability 311–14
  challenge of sustainability in tourism 311–12
defining tourism 11–12
  definitions developed by the WTO 13
  technical issues 13
definition of human resource management 154–5
Delphi method of forecasting 437
demand 259–60
demand elasticity 89, 259
demarketing 324
demographic factors affecting future trends in tourism 438–41, 457
demographic variables affecting tourism demand 49
demonstration effect 278–81
  acculturations 279–81
Department for International Development 402
dependency 267
deregulation 107
destination development policies 251–3
  scenarios 377
destination image 250–1
destination management 245–54
  destination development policies 251–3
  marketing tourist destinations 250–1
  patterns of destination use 248–9
  resort development strategy in Mexico 247
  selecting a destination 249–50
  some applications 203
  typical system 203
destination management systems 202–4
destination promotion 55, 251
determinants of tourism supply 74–6
  contestable markets 75
  monopoly 75–6
  oligopoly 75
  perfect competition 74–5
development of global distribution systems 198
development patterns of tourism in less developed countries 392
development status 386
development of sustainability concept 311
Development of Tourism Act 1969 40–1
  provision of government assistance 174–5
development of tourism in less developed countries 386–90
  tourism development 390
  types and characteristics 386–90
diaspora 53
differentiated marketing 238
dimensions of tourist-host encounters 276
Directive on Package Travel Regulations, 1993 88
disciplines contributing to study of tourism 9
disintermediation 88
Disney 65, 77
  focus for tourist activities 124
  theme parks 124
displacement 285
  examples of 286
distribution channels in tourism 197
distribution of incomes affecting tourism demand 47–8
dolphin watching 301
domestic tourism statistics 18–20
  domestic travel for pleasure 33
  how domestic tourism is measured 19
  uses of 19
domestic travel for pleasure 33
Doxey's Irridex 283–4
  definition 283

e-commerce 200
e-ticketing 200–1

Earth Summit 381
easyJet 109
network 107–9
offshoots from 81
rise of low-cost carrier 107
economic aspects of tourism in Cuba 269
economic benefits of tourism 262–7
balance of payments 262–3
employment 265–7
income 263–5
economic characteristics of the tourism industry 260–2
load factor calculation 261
long-term cycles 262
medium-term economic cycles 262
short-term economic cycles 260–2
economic costs of tourism 267–8
dependency 267
income and employment 268
inflation 267
leakage 268
opportunity cost 267
seasonality 267–8
economic impacts of tourist activity 257–74
definition of economics 258–9
demand 259–60
economic benefits 262–7
economic characteristics of the tourism industry 260–2
economic costs 267–8
measuring economic impacts 268–70
supply 260
economic perspectives of tourism in less developed countries 394–5
leakage 394–5
economics
definition of 258
definition of scarcity and resources 258–9
ecotourism 304–5
destruction of ecosystems 395
Eden Project 126–7
financing 127
Lost Gardens of Heligan and 126, 188
education and training for tourism 82
effectors of demand 62
elements of culture 276–7
elements of tourism 46, 341
Leiper's identification 10
elements of tourism demand 46
employment 265–7
and income 268
energizers of demand 62
English Channel 104
enhancement of local environments 306
entrepreneurs, characteristics of 184
and organizational structures 186
Richard Branson 184
entrepreneurship 183–94
characteristics of entrepreneurs 184
characteristics of small and medium-sized enterprises 186
innovation 185
political/economic environment 184–5
public sector entrepreneurship 185–6
socio-cultural environment 185
travel and tourism entrepreneurs 186–92
environmental auditing 319–20
environmental impact assessment 319
environmental impacts of tourist activity 293–308
positive environmental impacts of tourism 305–7
summary 296
environmental issues of coastal tourism 376–8
environmental management 312
environmental perspectives of tourism in less developed countries 397–9
environmental policies and statements 320
ethnic tourism 53
EU funding 176
priority objectives for structural funding 176
European cycle route network 102
pan-European perspective 101
European Environment Agency 376
Eurostar 55
exchange rates affecting tourism demand 48
exhibition and conference providers 93–4
incentive, conference and exhibition organizers 94
experience of the holiday 412–14
express coach services 100–1
fundamental role in domestic holidaymaking 99
National Express 100
factors affecting future tourism trends 438–41
demographic factors 438–41
factors influencing demand at tourism generating area 49–55
competition 54
government controls at destination 54–5
price 49–54
factors influencing demand from tourism generating area 46–9
demographic variables 49
distribution of incomes 47–8
government tax policies 48–9
holiday entitlements 48
personal incomes 47
value of currency/exchange rates 48
factors influencing socio-cultural impacts of tourism 277–8
importance of tourism industry 277
pace of tourism development 277–8
size and development of tourism industry 277
types and numbers of tourists 277
factors influencing tourist motivation 64–7
age 65
family life-cycle 65
gender 65
social class and income 66–7
fair trade 399–402
International Network on Fair Trade in Tourism 400
family decision-making roles 249
Fantasy City 447
farms 126–8
providers of rural tourism 358–61
fast-food sector 148
ferries 104–5
filterers of demand 62
financing tourism operations 167–82
investment 175
'not for profit' sector 177
private sector 168–73
sources of finance 173–5
supranational investment 175–7
forecasting changes in tourism 436–8
forecasting tourism growth in New Zealand 439
frameworks for measuring socio-cultural impacts 283–4
from traveller to tourist 407–8
functional areas in tourist city 340
future changes in air travel 112
future of the coast 381–2
future development of rural tourism 364
future of tourism 435–60
changing business practices 447–51
factors affecting the future shape of tourism trends 438–41
forecasting changes in tourism 436–8

managing change in tourism 456–8
political changes 441–4
sustainability and the environment 453–6
technological change 444–7
tourist health and safety issues 451–3
future for tourist attractions 130

Gambia Tourism Concern 289
gardens 125–6
Gilbert's tourism consumer decision process 62
global airline alliances 111
global amusement/theme park chains 124
Global Code of Ethics for Tourism 455
global distribution systems 197–8
development of 198
global patterns of tourism 23
globalization and the accommodation sector 135–6
Going Places 46, 89
government controls affecting tourism demand 54–5
government tax policies affecting tourism demand 48–9
growth of rural tourism 355–6

Haji-Ioannou, Stelios 187–8
health and safety issues 451–3
health 282–3
HIV and AIDS 282
risk factors for adventure tourism accidents 452
historic houses and monuments 121–2
National Trust 'top 20' 121
historical development of tourism 33–44
tourism before the twentieth century 33–5
tourism in the twentieth century 1900–1939 35–8
tourism in the twentieth century 1945–1970 38–40
tourism in the twentieth century post-1970 40–2
HIV and AIDS 282
see also health
Holiday Act, 1872 371
holiday camp 40
top ten campsites in England and Wales, 1939 and 1986 40
see also Butlin's; Club Meditérranée
holiday decision-making process 60
holiday entitlement affecting tourism demand 48
holiday, experience of 412–14
tourist experience 413
Holidays with Pay Act 1938 36
honeypots 98
host community 428
colonialism and neo-colonialism 295–7
host perceptions of socio-cultural impacts of tourism 283
host-guest relationship 278
Hotel Inter-Continental, Nairobi 316
hotel records 20
HRM issues in small tourism businesses in New Zealand 161–2
HRM issues in Wales 163
HRM problems in Latin America 157
HRM problems in Thailand 157
HRM in small tourism businesses 159–62
human development index 387–9
human resource management 153–66
agencies and HRM issues in tourism 155–8
definition of HRM 154–5
HRM issues in small tourism businesses 159–62
managing HRM issues in the new millennium 163–4
response and role of individual businesses 158–9
human rights 287
contravention of 287
hyper-competition 448–51

impact of Asian economic crisis on tourist arrivals 6
impact of tourist activity 255–330
impacts of coastal tourism 376–81
at Dawlish Warren 379–80
environmental issues 376–8
protection of the coastal environment 381
socio-economic issues 378–81
wildlife issues 378
impacts of rural tourism 356–7
impacts of tourism in less developed countries 392–9
economic perspectives 394–5
environmental perspectives 397–9
power and tourism 395–7
social and cultural perspectives 395
implications for HRM in tourism 158–9
importance of tourism industry 277
importance of urban tourism 334–5
inappropriate development 297–8
and the National Trust 297
income 263–5, 268
and employment 268
independent travel agent 90–2
index of rurality 350–1
indigenous tourism 286–7
control and tourism 287
industrial tourism 128–9
industry-based tourist attractions 129
inflation 267
information technology 195–206
computer reservation systems to global distribution systems 197–9
destination management systems 202–4
tourism and the internet 200–2
innovation 185
institutional elements in tourism supply issues 81–2
education and training for tourism 82
integrated tourism companies 86–7
Airtours 91–2
interactional segmentation 67–8
intermediary, a new category of 88
International Environmental Charter for Youth Hostels 146
International Monetary Fund 18
International Network on Fair Trade in Tourism 400
international tourism statistics 20–3
how statistics are collected 22
internet 200–1
investment 175
involving the community in tourism planning 287–8
issues of equity in tourism in less developed countries 399–402
fair trade 399–402
issues in rural tourism management 358

kitemarking 319
knowledge of customer 236–9
concentrated marketing 238–9
differentiated marketing 238
undifferentiated marketing 237–8

lack of tourism demand 46
land-based transport 98–103
car 98–9
coach and bus transport 99–100
cycling 101
express coach services 100–1
rail travel 101–3
language 281
leakage 268
examples of 394
in less developed countries 394–5
Leiper's tourism system 10
leisure parks and piers 123–4

leisure tourism 88–94
business tourism 93
business travel agents 93
exhibition and conference providers 93–4
incentive, conference and exhibition organizers 94
independent travel agent 90–2
retail multiples 89–90
tour operator 88–9
Leith, Prue 189
food museum project 148
less developed countries 385–404
colonialism and neo-colonialism 395–7
conceptualizing the nature of tourism in 391
development patterns 392
development status 386
development of tourism 386–90
equity 399–402
human development index 387–9
impacts of tourism in 392–9
location of 385
nature of tourism in 390–2
tourism in 385–404
types and characteristics 386–90
load factor calculation 261–2
local community issues 398
local events as tourist attractions 130
festival visitors, 1998 130
long-term economic cycles 262
loss of natural habitat 299–300
loss of spirit 300
Low, Erna 187

McDonaldization 135, 279
dominance of transnational corporations 148
major events as tourist attractions 129–30
attendance figures 129
man-made resources as attractions 77
resources of tourism importance 77
management of change in tourism 456–8
management and planning of the tourist experience 419–20
managing HRM issues in tourism in the new millennium 163–4
managing tourist activities 405–60
managing the tourist experience 417–34
at Cape Byron Headland 429
at Dartmoor 428
management and planning of the tourist experience 419–21
managing the tourist experience 425–30
planning, what it is in tourism 421–2
service quality 430–1
tourism planning process 422–5
managing tourist operations 151–230
market segmentation in tourism 239–40
market for urban tourism 338–40
marketing concepts and issues 233–44
marketing mix 236
marketing plan development 242
marketing planning process for destinations 250
marketing in the Republic of Croatia 242
marketing of South-east and south Asian tourism 216–25
marketing tourism 231–54
approaches to marketing planning 241–3
characteristics of tourism services 235
competition 240
knowing the customer 236–9
market segmentation in tourism 239–40
marketing concept 234
marketing mix 236
planning for the future 240–1
marketing tourism and the NTO 215–26
marketing tourist destinations 250–1
destination image 250–1
destination promotion 251
marketing planning process for destinations 250
segmentation at destinations 251
marketing the tourist experience 427
Maslow's hierarchy of needs 61–2
measurement of economic impacts of tourism 268–70
alternative measures 270
tourism multiplier 268–70
measurement of tourism 14–17
principal reasons for 14
Mediterranean Action Plan 296
medium-term economic cycles 262
Mid-Wales Festival of the countryside 359
map 360
Millennium and Copthorne Hotels 137–8
rise of the hotel chain 135
monopoly 75–6
motivation as fantasy 63
multinational enterprises and financing tourism operations 173
'transfer pricing' 174
museums and galleries 122–3
The British Museum 123
Winterthur Museum, Garden and Library 123

Namibia and rural tourism 362–3
principles guiding the implementation of tourism policy 363
National Express 100
national and international tourism data sources 18–23
data sources 18
domestic tourism statistics 18–20
international tourism statistics 20–3
National Park 428
natural resources as attractions 76
national tourism organizations 212–15
budgets in Asia 219–21
funding in Asia 218
marketing of South-east and south Asia 216–25
promotional budgets of Asian NTOs 224
promotional budgets of top 40 NTOs 221–3
structure of in UK 213
target markets for Asian destinations 225
and training 155
National Trust 121
historic houses and monuments 121–2
history 178
and inappropriate development 297
issues discussed in Report 1998/99 181
possessions 178
statement of financial activities 179–80
statistics 178–9
'top 20' properties 121
natural resources as attractions 76
National Parks 76, 428
nature and concept of urban tourism 336–7
nature and scope of environmental impacts of tourism 294–305
activities 304–5
tourism destination development 296–304
travel 294–6
nature and scope of rurality 350–2
nature of socio-cultural impacts of tourism 276–7
elements of culture 276–7
nature of tourism in less developed countries 390–2, 391

conceptualizing the nature of tourism 391
development patterns 391
needs analysis 241
New Zealand
accommodation sector 139–40
adventure tourism in 452–3
agenda for HRM 155
Chinese population in 51–4
collection of international tourism statistics 22
direct added value from tourism 445
forecasting tourism growth in 439
funding of RTOs 226
HRM issues in small tourism businesses 161–2
overseas visitor accidents 454
tourism expenditure 446
travel patterns of Chinese New Zealanders 49–52
VFR tourism 51
non-accommodation hospitality services 147–8
non-serviced accommodation sector 145–7
Norfolk Broads region 108
use by pleasure craft 106

Oasis 145, 147
oligopoly 75
operating performance of the global hotel industry 136–41
opportunity costs 267
Organisation for Economic Co-operation and Development 18, 20
data sources on urban tourism 339
involvement in tourism 212
pressures on coastal areas 369
other agencies involved in public sector tourism 226–7
role of local authority 226–7
other factors influencing tourism demand 55
other tourist facilities and services 82–3
outdoor recreational uses 335
overcrowding 300–3
overseas visitor accidents in New Zealand 454

P&O 37, 104
in association with Thomas Cook 37
merger with Stena Line 104
P&O Stena Line super-ferries 107
volume of traffic 105
pace of tourism development 277–8
package holidays 85
partnerships 81–2
alliances and the passenger volume conundrum 110–12
patterns of destination use 248–9
patterns of domestic tourism 23–4
payback 175
visitor payback schemes 266
pedestrian management 426–7
perceptions of tourism environment 343
perfect competition 74–5
personal incomes affecting tourism demand 47
personal recommendation 250
PEST analysis 240–1
planning for the future 240–1
PEST analysis 240–1
SWOT analysis 241
planning and management of rural tourism 358–64
criteria for success in rural tourism 361–2
issues in rural tourism management 358
management issues 362–4
providers of rural tourism 358–61
planning in tourism 421–2
pleasure 33
pleasure craft on inland waterways 105–7
Plog's tourist typology 63–4
political changes and the future of tourism 441–4
political/economic environment for entrepreneurship 184–5
pollution 300
Poon's old and new tourists 410
positive environmental impacts of tourism 305–7
conservation 305–6
enhancement of local environments 306
protection of wildlife 306–7
potential for cost reduction among airlines 110
Prentice's heritage attraction categories 119
price factors affecting tourism demand 49–54
principles for tourism in the countryside 364
private sector financing of tourism 168–73
multinational enterprises 173
privatization of airlines in Asia-Pacific, 1985–1995 449–60
problems associated with study of tourism 8
problems of statistical measurement of tourist populations 16
product development 427
profitability 456
promotion of destination 55
marketing the tourist experience 427
protection of coastal environment 381
Agenda 21 381
protection of wildlife 306–7
providers of rural tourism 358–61
provision for groups 427
psychocentrics 63
psychographic segmentation 67
public policy framework for tourism 211–12
public sector entrepreneurship 185–6
public sector involvement in tourism 208–11
tourism policy 208
tourism policy and development in China 208–11
public sector role 207–30
marketing tourism and the NTO 215–26
national tourism organizations 212–15
other agencies involved in public sector tourism 226–7
public policy framework for tourism 211–12
public sector involvement in tourism 208–11

quality issues in urban tourism 344–5

rail travel 101–2
effect on leisure travel 34–5
focus of travel experience 101
Railtrack 148
'tourist experience' rail journeys 104
Railtrack 148
Rapoport and Rapoport model 65
rationale for sustainable tourism 314
recreation 12
reductions in travel time 98
religion 281–2
remoteness 350
rental cars 80–1
and accommodation special packages 81
easyRentaCar 81
volume 81
research and analysis 241–2
resort and accommodation 144
resort development strategy in Mexico 247
location of selected resorts 248

resort enclave development 398
retail multiples 89–90
rise of environmental concern 310
rise of the low-cost carrier 107–10
risk factors for adventure tourists 452
role of the local authority 226–7
roles and decision-making 62
rural tourism 349–66
  conceptualizing rural tourism 352–5
  context of 354
  future development of rural tourism 364
  growth of rural tourism 355–6
  impacts of rural tourism 356–7
  index of rurality 350
  in Namibia 362–3
  nature and scope of rurality 350–2
  planning and management of rural tourism 358–64
  principles for 364
  services in 1994 353
  spectrum of 355
  summary of effects of 357
  sustainable rural tourism 358
rural tourism management issues 362–4

satisfaction with destination services 249
scarcity and resources 258–9
scope of HRM issues 154
scope of research on tourist populations 16
Scottish Tourist Board 118
sea bathing 33–4
seasonality 267–8
  effect on accommodation sector 141
segmentation at destinations 251
segmentation by purpose of travel 67
selection of destination 249–50
  family decision-making roles 249
  personal recommendation 250
  satisfaction with destination services 249
  tourist use of destinations 250
self-actualization 61
senior travel 78, 442–3
  attractive target group 65
  challenges facing market 77
  global tourism industry 442–3
  senior population for main tourism generating countries, 1997 443
service quality 430–1
serviced accommodation 142–5
short-term economic cycles 260–2
Singapore International Airlines 168–71
  leading-edge technology 198
  published company results 172–3
Singapore Tourism Board 214
  vision for tourism and Tourism 21 215
size and development of tourism industry 277
Smit, Tim 188
Smith's categories of tourist 64
social class and tourist motivation 66
  class categories 66
social and cultural impacts of tourist activity 275–92
  demonstration effect 278–81
  factors influencing socio-cultural impacts 277–8
  framework for measuring impacts 283–4
  host perceptions of impacts 283
  nature of socio-cultural impacts 276–7
  socio-cultural effects of tourism 281–3
  tourism and local communities 285–8
  wider issues relating to impacts 284–5
social and cultural perspectives of tourism in less developed countries 395
society's attitude to tourists 409–10
socio-cultural effects of tourism 281–3
  crime 283
  health 282
  language 281
  religion 281–2
  tourist perceptions 281
socio-cultural environment for entrepreneurship 185
socio-economic issues of coastal tourism 378–81
sources of finance for the tourism industry 173–5
spatial distribution 323–4
  spatial fixity 74
special events 129–30
  local events as tourist attractions 130
  major events 129–30
Stagecoach plc 100
  privatization 99
stages of resort development in Torbay 36
steam engines 129
strategic positioning 242
strategies to reach the first-time buyer 239
supply 260
supply issues 73–84
  accommodation 79–80
  attractions and activities 76–9
  determinants of tourism supply 74–6
  institutional elements 81–2
  other tourist facilities and services 82–3
  transportation 80–1
suppressed tourism demand 46
supranational investment 175–7
  EU funds 176
  The World Bank Group 176–7
sustainability 309–30
  defining sustainability and sustainable tourism 311–12
  definition of sustainable tourism 312–14
  degrees of 312
  development of the sustainability concept 311
  difficulties in achieving sustainable tourism 326–8
  rationale for sustainable tourism 314
  rise of environmental concern 310
  sustainable tourism in practice 314–17
  tools for sustainability 318–26
sustainability and the environment 453–6
sustainable rural tourism 358
sustainable tourism
  definition 312–14
sustainable tourism in practice 314–18
Swarbrooke's typology of tourist attractions 118
SWOT analysis 241, 334

technical definitions of tourism 12–14
technological change and the future of tourism 444–7
temporal distribution 324
The British Museum 122–3
themes, concepts and issues 1–32
  defining tourism 11–12
  global patterns of tourism 23
  national and international tourism data sources 18–23
  patterns of domestic tourism 23–4
  technical definitions 12–14
  tourism as academic study 6–8
  tourism as integrated study 8–10
  tourism statistics 14–17
Thomas Cook 35
  in association with P&O 37
  and call centres 90
  first excursion 97–8, 183

Thompson, Roger 189–90
Thomson Holidays 85–6
Customer Feedback Questionnaire 420
and European Commission 94
Monopolies and Mergers investigation 86
quality issues 420
tools for sustainability 318–26
Agenda 21 320–2
corporate environmental management 318–19
environmental auditing 319–20
environmental impact assessment 319
environmental policies and statements 320
visitor management 322–6
tools and techniques for managing the tourist experience 425–30
conservation 428
the host community 428–30
product development 427
promotional activity and information 427
providing for groups 427
vehicle and pedestrian management 426–7
tour operator 88–9
integrated companies and their brands 86–7
as multinational corporation 85
Tourism 21 (Singapore) 215
tourism as an area of academic study 6–8
tourism as an integrated study 8–10
tourism at the coast 368–9
tourism before the twentieth century 33–5
tourism as business 71–150
tourism 'career ladder' 61–2
tourism and community conflicts in Solomon Islands 396
Tourism Concern 285
tourism demand 45–58
elements 46, 341
factors influencing demand at tourist generating area 49–55
factors influencing demand from tourist generating area 46–9
other factors influencing tourism demand 55
tourism destination development 296–305
inappropriate development 297–8
loss of natural habitat and effects on wildlife 299–300
loss of spirit 300
overcrowding and traffic congestion 300–3
pollution 300
wear and tear 303–4
tourism development in less developed countries 390
tourism and HRM, role of individual businesses 158–9
tourism and the internet 200–2
tourism in the less developed world 385–404
concept of development and emergence of tourism 386–90
impacts of tourism in less developed countries 392–9
issues of equity 399–402
nature of tourism in less developed countries 390–2
tourism and local communities 285–8
indigenous tourism 286–7
involving the community in tourism planning 287–8
tourism multiplier 268–70
tourism and natural resources 76
tourism planning process 422–5
elements of 424
tourism policy and development in China 208–11
tourism satellite account 444
tourism as source of tax revenue 48
Tourism for Tomorrow Awards 310, 321, 359
tourism and tourism policy 208
tourism in the twentieth century, 1900–1939 35–8
tourism in the twentieth century, 1945–1970 38–40
tourism in the twentieth century post-1970 40–2
tourism and work 65–6
tourist cities in China 210
tourist experience 407–16
experience of the holiday 412–14
factors in evaluating 418
from traveller to tourist 407–8
tourist learning behaviour 410–12
tourists, maligned to alternative 409–10
'tourist experience' railway journeys 104
tourist information search strategy 411
tourist learning behaviour 410–12
information search strategy 411
tourist motivation 59–69
aspects 60–7
tourist motivation and segmentation 67–8
tourist motivation and segmentation 67–8
interactional segmentation 67–8
psychographic segmentation 67
segmentation by purpose of travel 67
tourist perception and cognition of urban environment 341–4
tourist types 409
tourist use of destinations 250
training, implementation, evaluation and adjustment of marketing planning 243
Transport Act, 1980 185
transport and tourism 97–116
air transport 107–12
land-based transport 98–103
water-based transport 103–107
transportation 80–1
integral element of tourism 80
travel 294–5
air travel 295
travel organizer 88
travel patterns of Chinese New Zealanders 49–52
travel sites on the World Wide Web 202
travel and tourism entrepreneurs 186–92
Erna Low 187
Martin Woods 190–1
Prue Leith 189
Roger Thompson 189–90
Stelios Haji-Ioannou 187–8
Susan Achmatowicz 191–2
Tim Smit 188
travel and tourism intermediaries 85–96
disintermediation 88
leisure tourism 88–94
a new category 88
types and numbers of tourists 277

UK International Passenger Survey 22–3
profile statistics 21–3
sampling errors 18
UK outbound visits 42
UK short sea ferry crossings 106
UK tourism key events, 1945–1970 38–9
understanding tourism demand 1–70
undifferentiated marketing 237–8
United Airlines 200–1
Universal Declaration of Human Rights 285
urban tourism 333–48
behavioural issues 340–1
concepts and themes in analysis of tourist resources 334

factors in evaluating tourist experience of 418
functional areas in tourist city 340
importance of urban tourism 334–5
market for urban tourism 338–40
quality issues in urban tourism 344–5
as relevant area for study 335–6
tourist perception and cognition of urban environment 341–4
understanding nature and concept of urban tourism 336–7
visitor experience of urban tourism 337–9
urban tourism as area of study 335–6
urban tourist experience 340–1
urbanization 455
US Travel Data Center 13
use of tourist resources 331–404

vehicle management 426–7
visa restrictions 55
visiting friends and relatives tourism 50, 439
visitor centres 128
visitor experience of urban tourism 337–8
visitor forecasts for New Zealand 439
visitor management 322–6
carrying capacity and limits of acceptable change 325
nature of 426
summary of visitor management strategies 323
visitor payback schemes 266
Voluntary Services Overseas 402

Wales Tourist Board 82
and finance 175
water-based transport 103–7
cruising 103–4
ferries 104–5
pleasure craft on inland waterways 105–7
wear and tear 303–4
whale watching 263–5, 301
economic value of 265
wider issues relating to socio-cultural impacts 284–5
displacement 285
wildlife attractions 124–5
protection of wildlife 306–7
wildlife issues of coastal tourism 378
Winthertur Museum, Garden and Library 123
Woods, Martin 190–1
workplaces 128–9
World Bank Group 176–7
IFC investments in tourism 177
World Tourism Organization 12
data sources on urban tourism 339
definition of tourism 12–13
Global Code of Ethics for Tourism 455
world tourism statistics 27–32
World Travel and Tourism Council 156
claim for tourism 6
global economic importance of tourism 257–8
World War I 35
aftermath of 37
World War II 36
changes in agricultural practice since 352
development of barrier islands since 378
rapid growth in tourism since 38
technological advances in aircraft performance since 98
and use of the English Channel 104
World Wide Web 88
role and influence 200
travel sites on 202

yield management 112
use by airlines 54
Youell model 65
Youth Hostel Association 145, 355
International Environmental Charter for Youth Hostels 146

Zanzibar – local community issues 398

Author index

Acernaza, M. 423
Ackerman, J. 378
Acott, T., La Trobe, H. and Howard, S. 311
Agarwal, S. 35, 36
Agel, P. 390
Aguilo, E. and Juaneda, C. 264
Alauddin, M. and Tisdell, C. 455, 456
Aldskogius, H. 343
Alford, P. 88
Altman, J. and Finlayson, J. 286
Andereck, K. and Caldwell, L. 411
Anon 55
Ap, J. and Crompton, J.L. 284, 287
Archer, B. 268, 270, 436, 437
Archer, B. and Fletcher, J. 270
Aronssen, L. 418
Ashworth, G.J. 141, 335, 336
Ashworth, G.J. and de Haan, T.Z. 340
Ashworth, G.J. and Goodall, B. 250
Ashworth, G.J. and Tunbridge, J.E. 147, 148, 339, 340
Ashworth, G.J. and Voogd, H. 81
Asian Development Bank 264
Aviation Environment Federation 295

Baker, M.J. 235
Ball, R.M. 82
Baretje, R. 21
Barke, M. and Newton, M. 317
BarOn, R.R. 12, 18, 21
Battacharya, H. 455, 456
Baum, T. 153, 154
Bejder, L., Dawson, S.M. and Harraway, J.A. 301
Bennett, M. 110
Bentley, T. 452
Bentley, T., Meyer, D., Page, S.J. and Chalmers, D. 454
Berkman, H.W. and Gilson, C. 411
Booth, A. and Francesconi, M. 158
Boroah, V.K. 260
Bossevain, J. 280
Boyd, S. and Butler, R. 305
Bradford, M. 391
Bramwell, B. 353, 414
Bramwell, B., Henry, I., Jackson, G., Prat, A.G., Richards, G. and van der Straaten, J. 309
Branson, R. 118, 175, 185
Briggs, A. 36, 37, 251
British Airways, 320, 321
British Tourist Authority 40, 42, 121
Britton, S. 390, 397
Brown, B. 184
Brown, G. and Essex, S. 429
Brown, P. and Scase, R. 184
Brunt, P. and Courtney, P. 283
Brunt, P. and Dunster, A. 77
Brunt, P., Mawby, R. and Hambly, Z. 63
Brunt, P.R. 18, 55, 60, 249, 250
Buckley, P. and Witt, S. 186
Buckley, R. 319
Buhalis, D. 190, 200, 201
Bull, A 47, 48, 54, 67, 73, 74, 80, 82, 173, 174, 176, 212, 259, 260, 268, 436, 438
Bull, P.J. and Church, A. 148, 161
Burkart, A. and Medlik, R. 4, 11, 14, 19, 33, 34, 35, 39, 49
Burns, P. 402
Burns, P. and Holden, A. 394
Burtenshaw, D., Bateman, M. and Ashworth, G.J. 339, 340
Burton, R. 37
Busby, G. 82
Busby, G., Brunt, P. and Baber, S. 82
Busby, G. and Hambly, Z. 130
Busby, G. and Rendle, S. 126, 353, 359
Butler, R. and Clark, G. 364
Butler, R. and Hinch, T. 286, 287, 290
Butler, R. and Pearce, D. 409
Butler, R.W. 35, 262, 374, 376
Buzard, J. 407, 408

Cai, L. 47
Cameron, A., Massey, C. and Tweed, D. 161
Campbell, L. 399, 402
Cannon, T. 235, 236, 240
Carey, S., Gountas, Y. and Gilbert, D. 318
Carter, S. 160
Casson, M.C. 183, 184, 193
Cater, E. 305
Chadwick, R. 11, 13, 14, 15, 18, 21, 421
Chartered Institute of Marketing 233
Chung, B. and Hoffman, K.D. 430
Civil Aviation Authority 90
Clarke, J. 313, 358, 361
Clarke, J. and Crichter, C. 37, 65
Clawson, M., Held, R. and Stoddart, C. 334, 335
Clift, S. and Carter, S. 282
Clift, S. and Page, S.J. 282, 420, 451, 458
Cloke, P.J. 350, 353
Cloke, P.J. and Park, C.C. 76
CNN 263
Cohen, R. 53, 64, 67, 277, 281
Collier, A. 5
Coltman, M. 37
Commons, J. and Page, S.J. 248
Conlin, M.V. and Baum, T. 376
Connell, J. and Reynolds, P. 81, 202
Connell, J.J. 147
Constantine, S. 35, 36
Cooke, A. 149
Cooper, C.P. 411
Cooper, C.P., Fletcher, J., Gilbert, D.G. and Wanhill, S. 5, 8, 45, 423
Cooper, C.P., Fletcher, J., Gilbert, D.G., Wanhill, S. and Shepherd, R. 46, 61, 142, 145, 165, 196, 212, 233, 236, 245, 409
Cope, R. 42
Cordrey, L. 297
Cornelius, N. 155
Countryside Commission 303, 355, 356, 362
Craven, J. 258, 359
Croall, J. 296, 299
Crouch, S. 43, 48
Cullen, P. 271
Cullingworth, J.B. and Nadin, V. 128
Curran, J., Kitchin, J., Abbott, B. and Mills, V. 161
Curry, N. 353
Curtin, S. and Busby, G. 89, 92, 173, 318
Curtis, S. 426, 428

Daniel, E. 395
Dann, G.M.S. 63, 411, 412
Dartmoor National Park Authority and Countryside Access Group 428
D'Aveni, R. 448
Davidson, R. 34, 252
Davidson, R. and Maitland, R. 185, 186, 246, 425
Davies, S. 122
De Kadt, E. 276, 278, 394
Deegan, J. and Nineen, D. 181
Deloitte Touche Tomatsu 161
Department for International Development 402
Devall, B. and Sessions, G. 311
Devon County Council Tourism Statistics 262
Ding, P. and Pigram, J. 319
Dingle, P. 319
Doggart, C. and Doggart, D. 397

Dondo, A. and Ngumo, M. 185
Dostal, A. 99, 100
Doswell, R. 305, 307
Douglas, N. and Douglas, N. 37, 43
Downes, J. 212
Downs, R. 342
Doxey, G.V. 284
Dredge, D. and Moore, S. 226
Drucker, P.F. 183, 184, 185, 186
Dymond, S. 327

Eby, D.W., Molnar, L, J, and Cai, L.A. 412
Economist 66
Edgell, D.L., Ruf, K.M. and Agarwal, A. 241, 242
Edington, J.M. and Edington, M.A. 294, 304
Edwards, A. 66
Edwards, A. and Graham, A. 438
Edwards, E. 18, 21, 66
Elkington, J. and Hailes, J. 310, 318
Employment Department Group 304
English Historic Towns Forum 427
English Tourist Board/Department of Environment 174, 175, 323, 336, 425, 426
Esichaikul, R. and Baum, T. 157
European Environment Agency 296, 369, 376
Evans, N.J. and Ilbery, B.W. 359

Farrell, B.H. and Runyan, D. 294
Faulkner, B., Oppermann, M. and Fredline, E. 117
Faulkner, B.and Tideswell, C. 283
Feng, K. 52, 53
Feng, K. and Page S. 49, 52, 53
Fennell, D. and Malloy, D. 319
Fennell, D. and Weaver, D. 192
Fockler, S. 79, 80
Fodness, D. 249
Fodness, D. and Murray, B. 410, 411
Foley, M. and Lennon, J. 121
Foley, M., Lennon, J.J. and Maxwell, G.A. 430
Forrester Research 204
Forsyth, T. 450
Foster, D. 5
Frechtling, D. 21
French, T. 109, 112, 198
FRST 439
Furze, B., De Lacy, T. and Birckhead, J. 280
Fussell, P. 408

Gannon, A. 356
Gannon, J. and Johnson, K. 146
Gartner, W.C. 48
Gehrels, B. 363
Getz, D. 79, 118, 421, 427
Gilbert, D. and Joshi, I. 344
Gilbert, D.C. 9, 62
Glasson, J. 426
Glytpis, S. 350
Go, F. and Pine, R. 135, 149, 173, 175
Goeldner, C.R., Ritchie, J.R.B. and McIntosh, R.W. 13
Goetz, A. and Szyliowicz, J. 198
Goffee, R. and Scase, R. 160, 184, 186, 192
Goldsmith, A., Nickson, D., Sloan, D. and Wood, R. 164
Goodhead, T. and Johnson, D. 376
Gordon, C. 147
Graefe, A.R. and Vaske, J.J. 337, 338, 339, 345, 412, 413
Grant, M. 322, 323, 425, 426
Grant, M., Human, B. and Le Pelley, B. 411, 425, 427
Griffith, D. and Elliot, D. 22
Grove, N. 391
Guerrier, Y. 149
Gunn, C.A. 76, 252, 253, 421
Guy, B.S. and Curtis, W.W. 341

Halfacree, K. 350, 351, 352
Hall, C.M. 5, 12, 19, 20, 216, 217, 385, 390, 395, 403, 421, 424
Hall, C.M. and Jenkins, J. 208, 227, 355, 423
Hall, C.M. and Johnston, M.E. 307
Hall, C.M. and Lew, A. 309, 328, 418
Hall, C.M. and McArthur, J. 121
Hall, C.M. and Page, S.J. 5, 6, 37, 43, 45, 47, 48, 73, 93, 114, 118, 128, 130, 135, 215, 268, 283, 307, 334, 378, 387, 403, 444
Hall, C.M., Sharples, L., Cambourne, B. and Macionis, N. 148
Handy, C. 456, 457
Hanna, M. 118, 122, 123, 124, 126, 128
Hannigan, K. 18, 447
Harrington, D. and Leneham, T. 430
Harris, G. and Katz, K. 243
Harrison, D. 390
Haynes, R. 342
Haywood, K.M. and Muller, T.E. 345, 418
Haywood, L., Kew, F. and Bramham, P. 36, 37, 65, 66
Haywood, L., Kew, F., Bramham, P. and Spink, J. 47
Healy, R. 356
Heape, R. 46
Heeley, J. 422
Hern, A. 34
Hernandez, S. and Cohen, J. 283
Hicks, M. 427
Hisrich, R.D. and Peters, M.P. 184, 185
Hodge, G. and Condon, C. 88
Holden, A. and Kealy, H. 318
Hollis, G. and Burgess, J. 343
Holloway, J.C. 33, 39, 248
Holloway, J.C. and Robinson, C. 234, 236, 251, 260
Honey, M. 299, 399
Horner, S. and Swarbrooke, J. 25, 131, 458
Horwath and Horwath 136, 138, 141, 143, 147, 148
Howie, F. 420
Hoyt, E. 263, 301
Hudson, S. 304
Human, B. 227, 425

Ilbery, B.W. 350
Inkpen, G. 196
Inkson, K. and Kolb, D. 456, 457
Inskeep, E. 74, 155, 247, 252, 253, 421, 422
International Association of Antarctica Tour Operators 307
International Hotels Environment Initiative 315
Ioannides, D. and Debbage, L.G. 47
Islam, N. 456
Iverson, W.D., Sheppard, S.R.J. and Strain, R.A. 297

Jafari, J., xviii 25
Jansen-Verbeke, M. 339, 340, 341
Jefferson, A. and Lickorish, L. 436, 437
Jenkins, J., Hall, C.M. and Troughton, M. 352, 361
Jenkins, O.H. 250
Jewell, G., Williamson, B. and Archer, K. 87
Johnston, R.J., Gregory, D. and Smith, D.D. 334

Kavallinis, I. and Pizam, A. 297
Kay, T. and Alder, XX 369, 381
Kay, T. and Jackson, G. 48
Keane, M. and Quinn, J. 350
Kearsley, G. 362
Kimes, S. 112
King, B. 50, 54, 441
King, B. and Gamage, M.A. 50, 441
Koenen, J.P., Chon, K-S. and Christianson, D.J. 303
Korca, P. 283
Kotler, P. 240

Koutsouris, A. 350
Krippendorf, J. 284, 293, 312, 408, 409, 414
Kunst, P. and Lemmink, J. 431

la Lopa, J.M., Chen, K. and Nelson, K. 270
Lane, B. 326, 350, 354, 358
Latham, J. 14, 16, 18, 19, 20, 22, 24
Lavery, P. 5, 37, 39, 42
Law, C.M. 336, 346
Laws, E. 8, 9, 56, 67, 68, 88, 95, 249, 250, 252, 253, 254, 430, 431
Lawton, G. and Page, S.J. 412
Lea, J. 276, 390, 394
Lee, C. and Kwon, K. 270
Lee, C., Lee, J. and Han, S. 270
Lee, T.R. 128
Leiper, N. 9, 12, 25
Lencek, L. and Bosker, G. 367
Leones, J., Colby, B. and Crandall, K. 270
Leong, L. 217
Lew, A. 76
Lew, A. and Wu, L. 50
Lickorish, L.J. 18
Lickorish, L.J. and Jenkins, C.L. 37, 39, 41, 42
Lindberg, K. and Johnson, R.L. 270
Lipsey, R.G. 258
Loverseed, H. 89, 92
Lumsdon, L. 66, 101, 329
Lundberg, D.E. 5
Lynch, K. 343

MacCannell, D. 276
Macdonald-Wallace, D. 88
McKercher, B. 313, 319
McLennan, R., Inkson, K., Dakin, S., Dewe, P. and Elkin, G. 419, 456
McLennan, R. and Smith, R. 227, 271, 365
McMullan, W. and Long, W.A. 184
Mahr, J. and Sutcliffe, S. 397
Mann, M. 401
Marfurt, E. 392
Marine Conservation Society 301
Marion, J.L. and Farrell, T.A. 300
Martin de Holan, P. and Phillips, N. 268, 269
Maslow, A.H. 61
Mason, P. 390
Mason, P. and Cheyne, J. 284
Mathieson, A. and Wall, G. 5, 45, 47, 48, 246, 251, 258, 260, 276, 278, 281, 294
May, V. 304, 328
Mayo, E.J. and Jarvis, L.P. 411
Medlik, S. 133, 134, 183
Meler, M. and Ruzic, D. 242
Mercer, D. 343
Messenger, S. and Shaw, H. 168, 172, 175
Middleton, V.T.C. 233, 239, 328
Middleton, V.T.C. and Hawkins, R. 317, 319
Mieczkowski, Z. 294, 297, 304
Mill, R.C. and Morrison, A.M. 5
Millar, S. 118
Minerbi, L. 378
Miossec, J. 372
Mira, K. 395
Mok, C. and DeFranco, A.L. 237
Montanari, A. and Williams, A. 371
Morgan, M. 249, 251, 252
Morrison, A. 159, 184
Mowforth, M. and Munt, I. 280, 285, 319, 325, 326, 386, 391, 409
Mules, T. 264
Muller, H. 327
Mullins, P. 336
Mumtaz, K. and Mitha, Y. 456
Murdoch, J. and Marsden, T. 351
Murphy, P.E. 5, 253, 260, 262, 276, 277
Murray, K.B. 411

Namibia Ministry of Environment and Tourism 363
National Trust 121, 179, 180, 181
Naylon, X. 371
New Internationalist 394
New Zealand Department of Statistics 140, 445, 446
New Zealand Official Yearbook 51
New Zealand Tourism Department 24
Ngoh, T. 21
Nguyen, T.H. and King, B. 54
Nicholas, R. 189
Norberg-Hodge, H. 278, 279

O'Brien, K. 93
O'Connor, P. 196
Office for National Statistics 42, 47
Oppermann, M. 283, 350
Oppermann, M. and Chon, K. 56, 215, 263, 268, 270, 386, 390, 403
Orams, M. 264, 265, 301, 302, 369, 373, 381
Organisation for Economic Co-operation and Development 369, 378
Osborne, A. 174
Ostrowski, S. 50

PA Cambridge Economic Consultants, 356, 361
Page, S.J. 20, 52, 54, 75, 76, 80, 83, 94, 98, 99, 100, 101, 102, 103, 104, 106, 107, 108, 110, 112, 113, 115, 172, 198, 212, 227, 294, 306, 336, 337, 338, 341, 342, 345, 413, 420, 421, 422, 424, 426, 448, 450
Page, S.J., Forer, P. and Lawton, G. 161
Page, S.J. and Getz, D. 159, 192, 355, 356, 358, 362
Page, S.J. and Hall, C.M. 226
Page, S.J. and Hardyman, R. 425
Page, S.J. and Lawton, G. 283
Page, S.J. and Thorn, K. 226, 421, 424
Page, S.J.and Meyer, D. 453
Parasuraman, A., Zeithmal, V. and Beryy, L. 344
Parker, S. 65
Patmore, J.A. 98
Pattullo, P. 277, 287, 381, 394
Pearce, D.G. 5, 18, 23, 24, 46, 47, 48, 207, 208, 212, 226, 251, 252, 336, 372, 373, 413
Pearce, P. 61, 343
Pearce, P. and Caltabiano, M. 61
Peattie, K. 234
Peisley, T. 104
Philp, J. and Mercer, D. 282
Pizam, A. 156, 157
Pizam, A. and Mansfeld, Y. 453
Plog, S. 63
Poon, A. 144, 195, 197, 409, 410, 438
Powell, J.M. 342
Powers, T., Barrows, R. and Clayton, W. 430
Prentice, R. 118, 119, 121, 428
Prideaux, B. 101, 376
Priestly, G.K., Edwards, J.A. and Coccossis, H. 250
Prosser, R. 310
Prunier, E., Sweeney, A. and Geen, A. 299
Pryce, A. 176, 177

Qu, H. and Zhang, H. 6

Raguraman, K. 217, 218
Rapoport, R. and Rapoport, R.N. 65
Redclift, M. 328, 402
Ringshaw, G. 92
Ritchie, B.W. 101
Ritchie, J.R.B. 14, 326
Ritzer, G. 279
Roberts, K. 65
Robinson, G.M. 350
Robinson, H. 34
Roche, M. 336
Rogers, H. and Slinn, J. 246, 248

Ross, S. and Wall, G. 288
Rossiter, J. and Chan, A. 50
Rural Development Commission, 353, 356
Russell, P. 80, 81
Ryan, C. 18, 68, 412, 413, 417, 431
Ryan, C. and Page, S.J. 8, 24

Sallah, H. 395
Sandbach, M. 48
Schumpeter, J. 185
Scottish Tourist Board 118
Seaton, A. and Bennett, M. 192, 243
Seitz, J. 205
Seristö, H. and Vepsäläinen, A. 110
Sessa, A. 74
Shackleford, P. 21
Shackley, M. 246, 363, 378, 415
Sharpley, R. 62, 276, 277, 279, 408
Sharpley, R. and Sharpley, J. 355, 365
Shaw, G. and Williams, A. 73, 160, 183, 184, 186, 190, 192, 276, 336
Sheldon, P.J. 18, 186, 196, 197, 198
Simons, M. 281
Sinclair, M.T. and Stabler, M. 47, 74, 75, 83, 94
Sindiga, I. and Kanunah, M. 307
Singh, A. and Chon, K. 216
Sisman, D. 328
Smit, T. 188
Smith, C. and Jenner, P. 129, 130, 201, 442, 443
Smith, S.L.J. 18, 148
Smith, V. 64, 276, 372
Snepenger, D., Meged, K., Snelling, M. and Worrall, K. 410, 411
Sofield, T. 396
Stabler, M.J. and Goodall, B. 148
Stallinbrass, C. 184
Statistics New Zealand 51
Stea, G. and Downs, R. 344
Stevens, T. 124, 128, 129
Swarbrooke, J. 46, 76, 77, 118, 123, 246, 287, 305, 309, 313, 325, 374, 386, 391, 412

Taylor, M. and Thrift, N. 136
Teignbridge District Council 380
Teo, P. 284
Thanopoulos, J. and Walle, A. 50
Theroux, P. 297
Thomas, R., Friel, M., Jamieson, S. and Parsons, D. 159, 192
Todd, S.E. and Williams, P.W. 304
Torrington, D. and Hall, L. 154
Tourism Company 266
Tourism Concern 281, 395, 398
Towner, J. 369, 370
Tribe, J. 46, 47, 54, 173
Tribe, J. and Smith, T. 414
Turner, J. 208
Turner, J.C., Davies, W.P. and Ahmad, Z. 353
Turner, L. and Ash, J. 394
Turner, R.K., Pearce, D. and Bateman, I. 311, 312

UNDP 389
United Nations 13, 14
Urry, J. 8, 35, 279, 356, 411
Uzzell, D.L. 118, 121
Uzzell, D.L. and Ballantyne, R. 122

Van der Wagen, L. 430
Van Raaij, W.F. and Francken, D.A. 411
Vellas, F. and Becherel, L. 233, 235, 236, 237, 240
Verginis, C. and Wood, R. 149
Viant, A. 78, 442
Vogt, C.A., Stewart, S.J. and Fesenmaier, D.R. 239

Waggle, D. and Fish, M. 259
Wagner, J. 270
Wales Tourist Board 163, 164, 175
Walker, D. 430
Wall, G. 98
Wall, G. and Nuriyanti, W. 218
Walmesley, D.J. and Jenkins, J. 342, 343, 344
Walmesley, D.J. and Lewis, G.J. 342, 344
Walpole, M.J. and Goodwin, H.J. 270
Walsh, E. 155
Walton, J. 34, 35, 369, 371
Wang, C-Y. and Miko, P.S. 303
Ward, C. and Hardy, D. 40
Warner, M., xviii
Waugh, E. 408
Wearing, S. and Neil, J. 399
Weaver, D.B. 376, 377
Webster, A. 386
Welsch, H. 185
Wen, H.J. 205
Wheeller, B. 277, 326
White, K. and Walker, M. 21
Wild, R. 431
Williams, S. 75, 278
Withyman, W. 20, 21
Witt, S.F., Brooke, M.Z. and Buckley, P.J. 436
Witt, S.F. and Martin, C. 437
Wood, S. and House, K. 293, 296, 310
World Tourism Organization 5, 13, 14, 16, 18, 19, 21, 158, 201, 202, 203, 204, 216, 218, 221, 223, 224, 225, 453, 455
Wright, R. 243

Yale, P. 124, 128, 186
Youell, R. 65, 184
Young, G. 293
Youth Hostel Association 145, 146

Zalaton, A. 249
Zhang, K. 209
Zhang, K., King, C. and Ap, J. 209
Zhou, D., Yanagida, J.F., Ujjayant, C. and Leung, P. 270
Zuzanek, J. and Mannell, R. 66

Place index

Italic page number indicate photographs (plates)

Adriatic 187
Africa 42, 104, 177, 238, 381, 385
Alcúdia 41, 327, 328
see also Mallorca
Algarve 187
Algeria 280
Americas 42, 112, 238
Amsterdam 110
Antarctica 103, 307
Antigua 381
Aruba 223, 394
Asia 3, 42, 103, 138, 177, 201, 216–25, 263, 264, 385, 449–50, 455–6
see also South-East Asia
Auckland 17, 94, *120*, 147, 226, 271, 283, 412
see also New Zealand
Australia 6, 42, 53, 79, 82, 94, 99,101, 117–18, 137, 138, 184, 217, 221, 259, 264–5, 280, 319, 321, *337*, 343, 371, *372*, 376, 381, 401, 404, 429, *436*, 447
Austria 31, 129, 187, 222, 356, 443
Azerbaijan 388
Azores 300

Bahamas 270
Bali *392*, 402, *408*
Bangladesh 216, 218, 220, 264, 455
Bath 190, *285*
Belarus 388
Belgium 55, 91, 147, 443
Belize 305, 326
Bermuda 223, 270
Bhutan 55, 282, 385, 389, 392, 393
Bicester 118
Birmingham 105, 128
Blackpool *34*, 35, 123, 124, 371
Blue Planet, Ellesmere Port 124
Bolivia 395
Borneo 382
Botswana 280
Bornholm 176
Bradford 185–6
Brighton 34, 35, 370
Bristol Airport 110
British Columbia *425*
Brunei 7, 387
Budapest 142, 145
Bulgaria 388
Buxton 97

Calais 83, 104
Calvia 374–5
see also Mallorca
Cambodia 7, 172, 389, 441
Cambridge, UK 99, 190, 226–7
Cameroon 389
Canada 31, 53, 89, 91, 102–3, 104, 118, 129,144, 145, 222, 263, *289*, 326, *326*, 353, 355, 387
Canary Islands 91
Canterbury, UK 99, *124*, 336
Caribbean 91, 112, 177, 277, 287, 369, 381, 394
Chatham *440*
Chester 99, 125
China 3, 6, 7, 31, 53, 93, 99, 104, 114, 145, 208–11, 216, 218, 219, 224, 227, 236, 237, 259, 263, 264, 388, 395
Colombia 145
Cornwall 126–7, 128, 130, 148, 176, 187, 188, 267, *279*, 297, *314*, 317, *325*, *361*, *370*
Corsica 187
Costa del Sol *see* Spain
Costa Rica 223, 299, 399
Cotswolds 191–2
Croatia 223, 242, 262
Cuba 268, 269
Curacao 223
Cyprus 187, 222
Czech Republic 31, 145

Dartmoor 303–4, *324*, 428
Dawlish Warren 379–80
Devon 35–6, 124, 127, *252*, 261–2, 266, 303–4, 319, *324*, 370, 379–80, 428
see also Dartmoor, Dawlish Warren, Exeter, Torbay, Plymouth
Disneyland 77, 124
Dover *36*, 104–5, *105*,
Dublin 129, 190

Eastern Europe 5, 48, 101, 173
Edinburgh 189
England 35, 40, 77, 81, 129, 142, 145, 174–5, 178–81, 318, 353, 355, 356, 359, 362, 369, 372, 427
see also United Kingdom
Egypt 55, 143, 222, 246, 263, 270, 286

Equador 287, 288, 317, 388
see also Galapagos Islands
Equatorial Guinea 389
Europe 6, 37, 42, 55, 81, 82, 85, 93, 101, *102*, 107, 135, 138, 143, 176, 177, 185, 187,192, 196, 201, 246, 296, 319, 345, 356, 442, 447
see also Eastern Europe, Western Europe
Exeter *252*, 261–2

Fiji 5, 37, 53, 396
Finland 22, 353, 376, 387, 443
Florence 336
Florida 91, 118, 124, 131
France 31, 37, 42, 53, 55, 118, 91, 121–2, 126, 128, 137–8, 143, 147, 221, 304, 359, 371, 387, 442, 443
French Polynesia 223

Galapagos Islands103, 299–300, 305
Gambia, The 144, 282, 289, 371, 381, 395, 400
Gatwick Airport 83, 107, 128, 295, 448
Geneva Airport 107
Germany 31, 47, 48, 91, 137–8, 147, 217, 222, 253, 263, 350, 356, 442, 443
Ghana 389
Glasgow Prestwick 83
Gloucester, UK 105
Greece 31, 50, 248, 297, 299, 350, *420*, 443
Gretna, UK 118
Guatemala 286, 402

Hawaii 37, 222, 286, 287, 297, *298*, 321
Heathrow Airport 83, 107, 113
Herefordshire 288
Himalayas 238
Hong Kong 6, 7, 31, 53, 99, 113, *114*, 143, 185, 216, 218, 219, 222, 224, 259, 264, 387
Hungary 31, 142, 145, 223

Ibiza 369
Iceland 381, 387
India 4, 101, 145, 217, 218, 220, 222, 225, 263, 264, 455
Indonesia 7, 53, 93, 112, 137, 172, 217, 218, 219, 224, 225, 264, 270, 388, *426*

Ireland 105, 129, 155, 159, 222, 443
Italy 31, 37, 48, 223, 304, 442, 443

Jamaica 270, 283
Japan 6, 48, 53, 93, 104, 113, 135, 185, 216, 217, 263, 369, 387, 442, 443, 447
Jerusalem 143

Kent 38, 104–5, 129
Kenya 176, 185, 286, 287, 300, 305, 307, 315, 316, 389, 394
Kiribati 270
Korea 216, 218, 222, 224, 386, 387, 388

Lake District 145, 147, 192, 355
Lao People's Democratic Republic 389
Laos 7, 402
Las Vegas 79–80, 130, 303
Latin America 157, 177
Lebanon 388
Liverpool Airport 107
London 83, 94, 122, *122*, 124, 126, 129–30, 137–8, 143, 304, 336, 422–3
Lundy Island 306, 324, *371*, 381
Luton Airport 107, 109, 187

Macau 6, 219, 223, 224
Madagascar 402
Malaysia 7, 53, 93, 104, 138, 172, 218, 220, 224, 225, 264, 286, 353, 385, 387
Maldives, The 216, 218, 220, 282, 378, 388
Malibu 249
Mallorca 41, 187, 252–53, 322, 327, 328, 374–5
see also Alcúdia, Calvia
Malta *134, 298*
Margate 34, 370
Mediterranean 147, 296, 297, 299, 300, 368, 371, 374–5, 376
Melanesia 37
Mexico 31, 91, 145, 222, 247–8, 301, 371, 385, 394, 395, 443
Monaco 249
Mongolia 388
Morecambe 37
Morocco 222
Myanmar 7, 218, 286, 389, 391, 397
Mykonos 297

Namibia 307, 362–3
Nepal 218, 220, 278–9, 299, 389, 394
Netherlands, The 31, *79*, 91, 99, 101, 129, 145, 147, 148, 222, *321*, 387, 443

New England 145
New Forest 191–2
New Zealand 6, *12*, 24, 42, 49–54, *78*, 82, 99, 101, *136*, 137–40, 144, 155, 159, 161–2, 164, 196, 222, 226, 262, 283, 284, 300, 453, 454, *302*, *323*, 361, 362, 369, *377*, 381, 387, *419*, *422*, 423, *437*, 439, 444–6
see also Auckland
Nice 143
Niue 270
Norfolk Broads, UK 105–7, *108*, 303
North America 6, 11, 37, 42, 104, 123, 141, 145, 185, 192, 196, 201, 343, 345, 442
Northern Europe 33, 34, 105
Northern Ireland 297, 317
Norway 376, 387
Norwich 340

Oman 388
Oxford 190, 343

Pacific Islands 5, 37, 53, 109, *146*, 176, 223, 264, 265, 270, *368*, 378, 396, 403, *451*
Pakistan 218, 264, 389, 455
Panama 280–1
Paris 55, 118, 143
Patagonia 301
Peak District 98–9
Peru 379–99, 401
Phillippines 7, 138, 145, 172
Portsmouth 251
Plymouth 124
Poland 31, 50, 223
Portugal 31, 47, 99, 135, 187, 222, 317, 356, *440*, 443
Puerto Rico 222

Rome 304
Russia 104, 208, 388

St. Lucia 185, 287, 399
Samoa 176
San Francisco *100*
Scotland 128, 143, 156, 227, 281, 365
Sellafield, UK 128
Seychelles, The 270, 277, 382
Sherwood Forest 306
Singapore 7, 53, 93, 94, 101, 113, 125, 137, 155, 214–15, 216, 217, 218, 220, 221, 224, 225, 263, 264, 270, *338*, 387
Sizewell B 128
Solomon Islands 396
Somerset 118, 190–1, 362

South Africa 104, 145, 222, 246, 441
South America 141, 385
South Australia 117–18
South Downs 128
South-East Asia 6–7, 93, 215, 216–25, 386, 441
see also Asia
South Korea 7, 53, 93, 208, 219, 225, 264, 270
South Pacific 37
Spain 31, 54, 63, *64*, 102, *103*, 135, 143, 187, 190, 221, 263, 280, 297, 317, 320, 374–5, 378, 442, 443
Sri Lanka *61*, *125*, *142*, 218, 220, 225, 287, 388, *391*, 392, 394, *399*, *401*, *410*
Stafford 189
Stansted Airport 83, 107, 109, 295
Stratford-upon-Avon 189, 190, 427
Sweden 381, 387
Switzerland 31, 37, 41, 54, 187, 222, 355

Tahiti *146*, *368*
Taiwan 6, 53, 93, 217, 218, 224, 225, 259, 264, 386, 443
Tajikistan 389
Tasmania *427*
Thailand 7, 53, 104, 157, 172, 216, 217, 218, 220, 222, 224, 225, 264, 282, 283, 287, 297, 305, 372, 387, 391, 394, 395, 397
Tokyo 185
Tonga 264, 265, 270, 301
Torbay 35–6
Torremolinos 374
Tunisia 223
Turkey 31, 222, 242, 270, 299, 385, 388
Turkmenistan 388

United Kingdom 13, 22–3, 31, 33, 34, 36, 37, 38–42, 47, 48, 53, 66, 81–2, 88–90, 97–100, 101, 103, 105–7, 118, 121, 123–30, 137–8, 144, 145, 148, 155, 158, 161, 164, 184, 186, 189, 213, 221, 240, 251, 253, 263, 277, 300, 313, 319, 321, 356, 361, 369, *440*, 442, 443
see also England, Scotland, Wales, Northern Ireland
United States of America 11, 13, 31, 53, 75, 91, 93, 99, 107, 113, 123, 124, 128, 129, 130, 135, 138, 184, 186, 191–2, 200–1, 202, 216, 223, 239, 263, 270, 297, 319, 350, 371, 378, 387, 442, 443, 447

see also New England, Yellowstone National Park, Yosemite National Park
Uruguay 145
Uzbekistan 388

Vanuatu *451*
Venice 248, 336
Vietnam 7, 172, 264, 321, 389, 441

Wales 35, 40, 77, 82, 145, 163–4, 175, 178–81, 300, 317, 358–60
Western Europe 78, 104, 337
Weymouth 34, 370

Yellowstone National Park 248, 303
York 190, 336
Yosemite National Park 266
Yugoslavia (former) 41
see also Croatia

Zakynthos 299
Zanzibar 282, 397, 398